REVIT®2024 FOR ARCHITECTURE

NO EXPERIENCE REQUIRED

THIRD EDITION

REVIT® 2024 FOR ARCHITECTURE

NO EXPERIENCE REQUIRED

THIRD EDITION

Eric Wing

SYBEX®
A Wiley Brand

To my family, Jen, Cassidy, and Jacob. Thanks for waiting patiently on the weekends, and weeknights, and on vacations as I work away.

Acknowledgments

With this volume of the book, I was given tons of time to make sure everything was in place. Although this book does not cover everything, it will be a great resource for the Autodesk exam and as a desktop reference as you work on projects. With new little tidbits peppered throughout, this book is basically brand-new, with every word and figure carefully reviewed and poured over. I feel confident we made a great book.

When I say "we" I mean that, although I am the guy who belches out words and images, and that's pretty much it, my family sacrifices most. That is because this is one of many jobs I have, so I am constantly working. It has been this way for my children's entire lives. So first and foremost, I thank my family.

Second, I'd like to thank Kimberly (Kimmy) Esquilin for perfect technical edits that actually made the words and figures make sense. Kimmy jumped into this role late and did a tremendous amount of work in a short amount of time. Her expertise was very evident, especially when it came to the more difficult portions of the book.

Last but not least is the team I worked with at Wiley. Thanks to Janet Wehner for keeping everything on schedule and helping with the images. Thank you to Pete Gaughan and Jim Minatel for allowing me to keep rolling with this book after 15 years.

About the Author

Eric Wing lives in Syracuse, New York, with his family. He is the Director of BIM Services for C&S Companies, which is a full-service engineering/architectural firm headquartered in Syracuse. Eric's degree is from Delhi University in engineering and construction. Eric is also an author for LinkedIn Learning, where he, at the time of this book's release, has 73 courses in all things BIM. Eric is also a professor at Syracuse University, where he teaches BIM at the School of Architecture as well as the School of Engineering.

About the Technical Editor

Kimberly Esquilin is a recent graduate from Syracuse University's School of Architecture. She took an introductory Revit course with author Eric Wing at SU and eventually became his undergraduate assistant. In this role, she helped students learn the fundamentals of Revit. Kimberly is currently working full-time as an architectural designer at C&S Companies in Albany, New York, and is working toward her license in architecture.

Contents at a Glance

Contents

CHAPTER 10 Stairs, Ramps, and Railings 493

CHAPTER 11 Detailing 565

INTRODUCTION

Why do you need a big, thick technical book? Well, it's true that the best way to learn is to just do it. But do you ever just *do* it and not fully *get* it? Books can serve either as the basis for learning or as supplements for your learning. No one book will teach you everything you need to know about a specific application, but you may never learn everything you need to know about an application without a book. When written appropriately, the book you purchase is there to start you off using good practices. If you have already begun, the book serves as a desktop reference. And last, a book can serve as confirmation that you're approaching an application in the correct manner.

This book about the Autodesk® Revit® tool is no exception. Although this application has proven to be easy to learn and easy to get a feel for, it's still a deep, sometimes complicated application with many procedures that require step-by-step instructions to understand fully. And to be honest, some of these features just don't work in the real world.

This book has been written by an author who is "in the trenches" using Revit every day. So, yes, you could figure out all this information on your own, but sometimes, it's nice to let someone else figure it out for you and pass that knowledge along to you in the form of a book.

Instead of lengthy paragraphs of text that ultimately lead to nontangible information, this book addresses each subject in a step-by-step approach with more than 1,000 pictures and screenshots to make sure you're on track.

Also, this book uses an actual project and relates to real-world scenarios. As you're following the step-by-step procedures in the book, you'll be encouraged to try many techniques on your own and also to embellish the procedure to fit your own needs. If you would rather stick to the instructions, this book allows you to do that as well. The book's project uses a five-story office building with a link (corridor) to a three-story multi-use building. The book's website provides the model (plus additional families) you'll need for each chapter so that you can open the book, jump to your chapter of interest, and learn something! In addition, this book is flexible enough that you can substitute your own project if you don't want to follow the book's examples.

Although it has hundreds of pages, this book doesn't waste time and space with examples of other people's triumphs but is designed for you to open to any random page and learn something.

Who Should Read This Book

Autodesk® Revit® 2024 for Architecture: No Experience Required. Does that mean that if you've used Revit, you won't find this book advanced enough? No. This book is designed for anyone who wishes to learn more about Revit Architecture. The book is also intended for architects, architectural designers, and anyone using a CAD-based platform to produce architectural-based drawings.

What You Need

Building Information Modeling (BIM) can be tough on hardware. This book recommends that you have 16 GB of RAM with a 4 GHz processor. You should also be running at least 1 GB for your graphics. If you're under these specifications (within reason), in some cases you'll be fine. Just realize, however, that when your model is loaded, your system may start slowing down.

All Revit applications are intended to run on a PC-based system. Windows 11 is recommended.

Included with the book are Revit Architecture project files that follow along with the instructions. Each chapter has one or more actual Revit models that have been completed up to the point of the instruction in that specific chapter—or even that specific section of the chapter—to allow you to jump in at any moment. Also included with the book are custom families that accompany the lessons as well as additional families and projects that you can download as a bonus. You can download the accompanying files at `www.wiley.com/go/revit2024ner`.

FREE AUTODESK SOFTWARE FOR STUDENTS AND EDUCATORS

The Autodesk Education Community is an online resource with more than five million members that enables educators and students to download—for free (see website for terms and conditions)—the same software used by professionals worldwide. You can also access additional tools and materials to help you design, visualize, and simulate ideas. Connect with other learners to stay current with the latest industry trends and get the most out of your designs. Get started today at `www.autodesk.com/joinedu`.

What Is Covered in This Book

Autodesk® Revit® 2024 for Architecture: No Experience Required covers the essentials of using the software and is organized as follows:

Chapter 1: The Autodesk Revit World

This chapter introduces you to the Revit Architecture 2024 interface and jumps right into modeling your first building.

Chapter 2: Creating a Model

This chapter begins with placing walls, doors, and windows. It's designed to point you in the right direction in terms of using reference planes and all-around best practices.

Chapter 3: Creating Views

This chapter shows you how to navigate the Revit Project Browser and create new views of the model. Also, you'll learn how to create specific views such as elevations, sections, callouts, plans, and, our favorite, 3D perspectives.

Chapter 4: Working with the Autodesk Revit Tools

In this chapter, you'll learn how to use the everyday drafting tools needed in any modeling application. You'll become familiar with such actions as trim, array, move, and copy. Although it seems remedial, this is one of the most important chapters of the book. It gets you on your way to the "Revit feel."

Chapter 5: Dimensioning and Annotating

In this chapter, you'll learn how to annotate your model. This includes adding and setting up dimensions, adding and setting up text, and using dimensions to physically adjust objects in your model.

Chapter 6: Floors

Yes! Just floors. In this chapter, you'll learn how to place a floor. You'll also learn how to add materials to a floor and how to pitch a floor to a drain.

Chapter 7: Roofs

In this chapter, we'll discuss the ins and outs of placing roofs. You'll learn how to model flat roofs, sloping roofs, pitched roofs, and roof dormers. In addition, you'll learn how to pitch roof insulation to roof drains.

Chapter 8: Structural Items

In this chapter, you'll delve into the structural module of Revit Architecture. The topics we'll cover include placing structural framing, placing structural foundations, and creating structural views.

Chapter 9: Ceilings and Interiors

This chapter focuses predominately on interior design. Placing and modifying ceilings will be covered as well as adding specific materials to portions of walls and floors. You'll also learn how to create soffits.

Chapter 10: Stairs, Ramps, and Railings

This chapter focuses on the creation of circulation items. You'll learn how to create a simple U-shaped multistory staircase to start; then you'll move on to creating a custom winding staircase. From there, you'll learn how to create a custom wood railing. You'll add ramps to the model in this chapter as well.

Chapter 11: Detailing

In this chapter, you'll learn how to draft in Revit. The procedures allow you to draft over the top of a Revit-generated section or create your own drafting view independent of the model. You'll also learn how to import CAD to use as a detail.

Chapter 12: Creating Specific Views and Match Lines

In this chapter, you'll learn how to take advantage of the multitude of views you can create and how to control the visibility graphics of those views to create plans such as furniture and dimensional plans.

Chapter 13: Creating Sheets and Printing

This chapter explores how to produce construction documents using Revit. The procedures include creating a new drawing sheet, adding views to a sheet, creating a title block and a cover sheet, and plotting these documents.

Chapter 14: Creating Rooms and Area Plans

The focus of this chapter is creating rooms and areas. The procedures lead you through the placement of rooms, and you'll learn how to set the properties of those rooms. We'll also discuss how to create room separators and how to create gross area plans. This chapter also guides you through the creation of a color-fill floor plan.

Chapter 15: Advanced Wall Topics

This chapter focuses specifically on the creation of compound walls. By using the Edit Assembly dialog, you'll learn how to add materials, split walls, and add sweeps and reveals such as parapet caps, brick ledges, and brick reveals. Creating stacked walls is also addressed.

Chapter 16: Schedules and Tags

In this chapter, you'll start bringing the BIM into your model. This chapter focuses on adding schedules and annotation tags to specific objects and materials in your model. Most importantly, in this chapter, you'll learn how your model is parameter-driven and how these parameters influence the annotations.

Chapter 17: Rendering and Presentation

In this chapter, you'll learn how to use the Revit rendering tools built into the Revit GUI. This chapter also shows you how to create walkthroughs as well as solar studies.

Chapter 18: Creating Families

With this chapter, you will get into the most valuable part of Revit: Families. We will start with what a family actually is and how they behave within your model. Then we will create a profile family and move to a more advanced door family. Look for many of these procedures on the Autodesk Revit Architecture exam.

Chapter 19: Project Management

If it is your desire to become a BIM manager or just get a great feel for how Revit manages your drawings, this is a good chapter to look at. We will start with project phasing (renovation projects), then jump to how to create a work-shared model so that several people can access the models at one time.

PRACTICE TEST ONLINE

Although this book is not an exam prep Study Guide, we've added a new online practice test for you if you are interested in preparing for the valuable Autodesk Certified Professional in Revit for Architectural Design certification exam. If you are interested in gaining this certification and furthering your career, this online practice test will help you assess your readiness for the exam, determine what sections of the book you should study more, and then increase your chances of passing it the first time! This practice test will be available by January 3, 2024. After that date go to www.wiley.com/go/sybextestprep to register and gain access to this interactive online learning environment.

Contacting the Author

As you're reading along, please feel free to contact me on LinkedIn www
.linkedin.com/in/eric-wing-9662524, and I will be glad to answer any
questions you have.

Sybex strives to keep you supplied with the latest tools and
information you need for your work. Please check the website at
www.wiley.com/go/revit2024ner, where we'll post additional content and
updates that supplement this book if the need arises.

How to Contact the Publisher

If you believe you have found a mistake in this book, please bring it to our
attention. At John Wiley & Sons, we understand how important it is to provide
our customers with accurate content, but even with our best efforts, an error
may occur.

In order to submit your possible errata, please email it to our Customer Service
Team at wileysupport@wiley.com with the subject line "Possible Book Errata
Submission."

CHAPTER 1

The Autodesk Revit World

I'm sure you've seen plenty of presentations on how wonderful and versatile this 3D Autodesk® Revit® revolution is. You may be thinking, "This all seems too complicated for what I do. Why do I need 3D anyway?"

The answer is: You don't need 3D. What do you do to get a job out—that is, after the presentation when you're awarded the project? First, you redraw the plans. Next comes the detail round-up game we have all come to love: pull the specs together and then plot. This is a simple process that works.

Well, it worked until 3D showed up. Now we have no real clue where things come from, drawings don't look very good, and getting a drawing out the door takes three times as long.

That's the perception, anyway. I've certainly seen all of the above, but I've also seen some incredibly coordinated sets of drawings with almost textbook adherence to standards and graphics. Revit can go both ways—it depends on you to make it go the right way.

One other buzzword I'm sure you've heard about is *Building Information Modeling (BIM)*. Although they say BIM is a process, not an application, I don't fully buy into that position. Right now, you're on the first page of BIM. BIM starts with Revit. If you understand Revit, you'll understand Building Information Modeling.

This chapter will dive into the Revit graphical user interface (GUI) and tackle the three topics that make Revit . . . well, Revit:

▶ The Revit interface

▶ The Project Browser

▶ File types and families

The Revit Interface

Toto, we aren't in CAD anymore!

If you just bought this book, then welcome to the Revit world. In Revit, the vast majority of the processes you encounter are in a flat 2D platform. Instead of drafting, you're placing components into a model. Yes, these components have a so-called third dimension to them, but a logical methodology drives the process. If you need to see the model in 3D, it's simply a click away. That being said, remember this: There is a big difference between 3D drafting and modeling.

With that preamble behind us, let's get on with it.

First of all, Revit has no command prompt and no crosshairs. Stop! Don't go away just yet. You'll get used to it, I promise. Unlike most CAD applications, Revit is heavily pared down, so to speak. It's this way for a reason. Revit was designed for architects and engineers. You don't need every command that an individual designing a car would need. An electrical engineer wouldn't need the functionality that an architect would require. In Revit, however, the functionality I just mentioned is available, but it's tucked away so as not to interfere with your architectural pursuits.

 N O T E   This book is designed to cut to the chase and show you how to use Revit in a step-by-step fashion without having to read through paragraph after paragraph of theory just to find the answer you're seeking. Datasets are provided on the book's accompanying website (www.wiley.com/go/revit2024ner), but you can also use your own model as you go through the book. If you don't wish to read this book cover to cover, don't! Although I recommend going from front to back, you can use the book as a desk reference by jumping to a desired topic. The datasets will be added in phases to accommodate this type of usage. Either way, get ready to learn Revit!

You'll find that, as you get comfortable with Revit, there are many, many choices and options behind each command.

Let's get started:

1. To open Revit, click the icon on your desktop (see Figure 1.1).

FIGURE 1.1   You can launch Revit from the desktop icon.

2. After you start Revit, you'll see the Recent Files window, as shown in Figure 1.2. The top row lists any projects on which you've been working; the bottom row lists any families with which you've been

working. At the top of the dialog is the Learn pulldown. This will give you access to the Autodesk Help website.

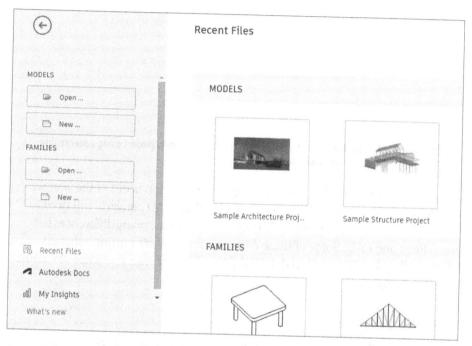

FIGURE 1.2 The Recent Files window lists any recent projects or families on which you've worked.

3. To the left of the dialog is the Models area. Click the New link.

4. The New Project dialog shown in Figure 1.3 opens. Because the new templates added to Revit 2024 won't really work for this, we'll have to find a better one.

5. Click the Browse button. This will open Windows Explorer. For Imperial users, chose Default.rte. For non-Imperial users, go up one level, and choose the appropriate folder. Select the file called DefaultMetric.rte. If you cannot find this file, please go to the book's accompanying website (www.wiley.com/go/2024revit2024ner) and download all files pertaining to the entire book—especially the files for Chapter 1.

6. Once the default architectural template is selected, make sure the button for Project is selected (not Project Template), and click OK.

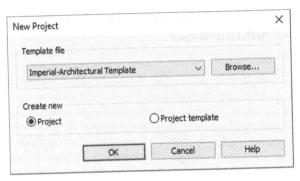

FIGURE 1.3 The New Project dialog allows you to start a new project using a preexisting template file, or you can create a new template file.

Now that the task of physically opening the application is out of the way, we can delve into Revit. Revit has a certain feel that 2D CAD converts will need to grasp. At first, if you're already a CAD user, you'll notice many differences between Revit and CAD. Some of these differences may be off-putting, whereas others will make you say, "I wish CAD did that." Either way, you'll have to adjust to a new workflow.

The Revit Workflow

This new workflow may be easy for some to adopt, whereas others will find it excruciatingly foreign. (To be honest, I found the latter to be the case at first.) Either way, it's a simple concept. You just need to slow down a bit from your CAD habits. If you're new to the entire modeling/drafting notion and you feel you're going too slowly, don't worry. You do a lot with each click of the mouse.

Executing a command in Revit is a three-step process:

1. At the top of the Revit window is the Ribbon. A series of tabs is built into the Ribbon. Each tab contains a panel. This Ribbon will be your Revit launchpad! Speaking of launchpads, click the Wall button on the Architecture tab, as shown in Figure 1.4.

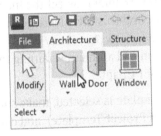

FIGURE 1.4 The Ribbon is the backbone of Revit.

2. After you click the Wall button, notice that Revit adds a tab to the Ribbon with additional choices specific to the command you're running, as shown in Figure 1.5. You may also notice that Revit places an additional Options bar below the Ribbon for more choices.

FIGURE 1.5 The Options bar allows you to have additional choices for the current command.

You'll read this throughout the book: Always remember to look at your options. With no command prompt, the Options bar will be one of your few guides.

3. After you make your choices from the Ribbon and the Options bar, you can place the object into the view window. This is the large drawing area that takes up two-thirds of the Revit interface. To place the wall, simply pick a point in the window and move your pointer in the direction that you want the wall to travel. The wall starts to form. Once you see that, you can press the Esc key twice to fully exit the command. (I just wanted to illustrate the behavior of Revit during a typical command.)

Using Revit isn't always as easy as this, but just keep this basic three-step process in mind and you'll be okay:

1. Start a command.

2. Choose an option from the temporary tab or the Options bar that appears.

3. Place the item in the view window.

Thus, on the surface Revit appears to offer a fraction of the choices and functionality that are offered by AutoCAD (or any drafting program, for that matter). This is true in a way. Revit does offer fewer choices to start a command, but the choices that Revit does offer are much more robust and powerful.

Revit keeps its functionality focused on designing and constructing buildings. Revit gets its robust performance from the dynamic capabilities of the application during the placement of the items and the functionality of the objects after you place them in the model. You know what they say: Never judge a book by its cover—unless, of course, it's the book you're reading right now.

Let's keep going with the main focus of the Revit interface: the Ribbon. You'll be leaning on the Ribbon extensively in Revit.

Using the Ribbon

You'll use the Ribbon for the majority of the commands you execute in Revit. As you can see, you have little choice but to do so. However, this is good because it narrows your attention to what is right in front of you.

When you click an icon on the Ribbon, Revit will react to that icon with a new tab, giving you the specific additional commands and options you need. Revit also keeps the existing tabs that can help you in the current command, as shown in Figure 1.6. Again, the focus is on keeping your eyes in one place.

FIGURE 1.6 The Ribbon breakdown showing the panels

In this book, I'll throw quite a few new terms at you, but you'll get familiar with them quickly. We just discussed the Ribbon, but mostly you'll be directed to choose a tab in the Ribbon and to find a panel on that tab.

To keep the example familiar, when you select the Wall button, your instructions will read: "On the Build panel of the Architecture tab, click the Wall button."

WHAT'S THAT TOOLBAR ABOVE THE RIBBON?

This toolbar is called the *Quick Access toolbar*. I'm sure you've seen a similar toolbar in other applications. It comes filled with some popular commands. If you want to add commands to this toolbar, simply right-click any icon and select Add to Quick Access Toolbar. To the left of this toolbar is the Revit Application icon. Clicking this icon gives you access to more Revit functions that will be covered later in the book. One great icon that I like to have docked on the Quick Access toolbar is the Select Objects (or Modify) icon. I like to add this icon as shown in the following graphic:

Now that you can see how the Ribbon and the tabs flow together, let's look at another feature in the Ribbon panels that allows you to reach beyond the immediate Revit interface.

The Properties Interface

When you click the Wall button, a new set of commands appears on the Ribbon. This new set of commands combines the basic Modify commands with a tab specific to your immediate process. In this case, that process is adding a wall.

You'll also notice that the Properties dialog near the left of the screen changes, as shown in Figure 1.7. The Properties dialog shows a picture of the wall you're about to place. If you click this picture, Revit displays all the walls that are available in the model. This display is called the Type Selector drop-down (see Figure 1.8).

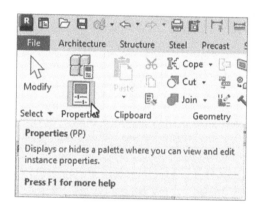

FIGURE 1.7 Click the Properties button to display the Properties dialog. Typically, the dialog is shown by default.

The objective of the next exercise is to start placing walls into the model:

1. Close Revit by clicking the close button in the upper-right corner.

2. Reopen Revit, and start a new project (Metric or Imperial).

3. On the Architecture tab, click the Wall button.

4. In the Properties dialog, select Exterior - Brick And CMU On MTL. Stud from the Type Selector. (Metric users, select Basic Wall - Exterior Brick On Mtl. Stud. This will look somewhat different throughout the book, but you get a break. It is slightly easier to work with than the Imperial wall type.)

Element Properties

There are two different sets of properties in Revit: instance properties and type properties. Instance properties are available immediately in the Properties dialog when you place or select an item. If you make a change to an element property, the only items that are affected in the model are the items you've selected.

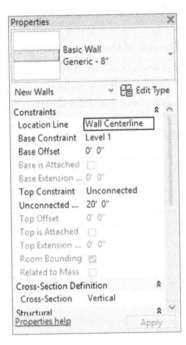

FIGURE 1.8 The Properties dialog gives you access to many variables associated with the item you're adding to the model.

The Properties Dialog

As just mentioned, the Properties dialog displays the instance properties of the item you've selected. If no item is selected, this dialog displays the properties of the current view in which you happen to be.

You also have the ability to combine the Properties dialog with the adjacent dialog, which is called the Project Browser (we'll examine the Project Browser shortly). Simply click the top of the Properties dialog, as shown in Figure 1.9, and drag it onto the Project Browser. Once you do this, you'll see a tab that contains the properties and a tab that contains the Project Browser (also shown in Figure 1.9).

Let's take a closer look at the two categories of element properties in Revit.

Instance Properties

When an element is selected or being added, the items that you can see in the Properties dialog and edit immediately are called *instance parameters*. These

You can organize these windows anyway you wish. Some people like to keep them on a separate monitor. I like to keep them exactly the way they were before we moved them around. For this book I'm moving mine back to the original position.

▶

parameters change only the object being added to the model at this time. Also, if you select an item that has already been placed in the model, the parameters you see immediately in the Instance Properties dialog change only that item you've selected. This makes sense—not all items are built equally in the real world. Figure 1.10 illustrates the instance properties of a typical wall.

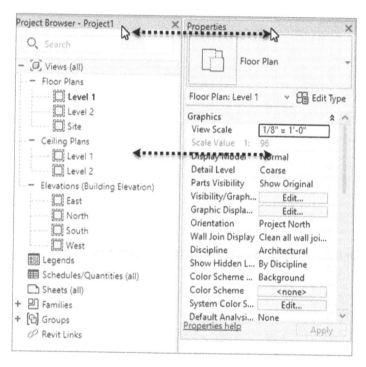

FIGURE 1.9 Dragging the Properties dialog onto the Project Browser

Type Properties

Type properties (see Figure 1.11), when edited, alter every item of that type in the entire model. To access the type properties, click the Edit Type button in the Properties dialog, as Figure 1.12 shows.

At this point, you have two choices. You can make a new wall type (leaving this specific wall unmodified) by clicking the Duplicate button at the upper right of the dialog, or you can start editing the wall's type properties, as shown in Figure 1.13.

> **WARNING** I can't stress enough that if you start modifying type properties without duplicating the type, you need to do so in a very deliberate manner.

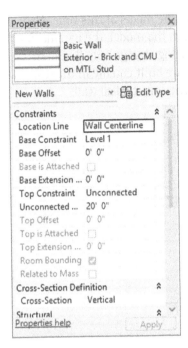

FIGURE 1.10 The instance parameters change only the currently placed item or the currently selected item.

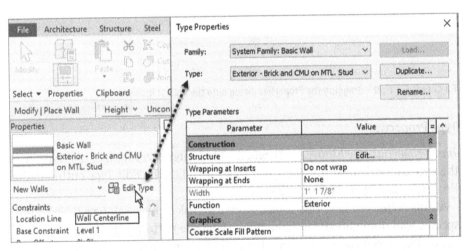

FIGURE 1.11 The type properties, when modified, alter every occurrence of this specific wall in the entire model.

Now that you've gained experience with the Type Properties dialog, it's time to go back and study the Options bar as it pertains to placing a wall:

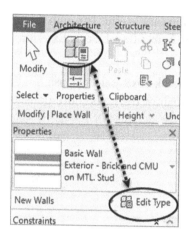

FIGURE 1.12 The Edit Type button allows you to access the type properties.

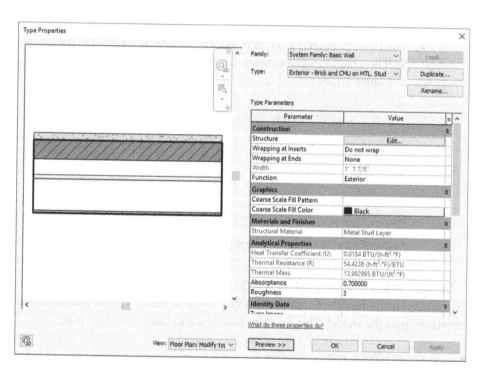

FIGURE 1.13 The type properties modify the wall system's global settings. Click the Preview button at the bottom of the dialog to see the image that is displayed.

1. Because you're only exploring the element properties, click the Cancel button to return to the model.

2. Back in the Options bar, find the Location Line menu. Through this menu, you can set the wall justification. Select Finish Face: Exterior (see Figure 1.14).

3. On the Options bar, be sure the Chain check box is selected, as Figure 1.14 shows. This will allow you to draw the walls continuously.

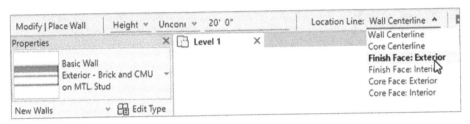

FIGURE 1.14 By selecting Finish Face: Exterior, you know the wall will be dimensioned from the outside finish.

4. The Draw panel has a series of sketch options. Because this specific wall is straight, make sure the Line button is selected, as shown in Figure 1.15.

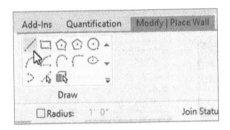

FIGURE 1.15 You can draw any shape you need.

Get used to studying the Ribbon and the Options bar—they will be your crutch as you start using Revit! Of course, at some point you need to begin placing items physically into the model. This is where the view window comes into play.

The View Window

To put it simply, the big white area where the objects go is the view window. As a result of your actions, this area will become populated with your model. Notice that the background is white—this is because the sheets you plot on are white. In Revit, what you see is what you get. . .literally. Line weights in Revit are driven by the object, not by the layer. In Revit, you aren't counting on color #5, which is blue, for example, to be a specific line width when you plot. You can immediately see the thickness that all your lines will be before you plot (see Figure 1.16). What a novel idea.

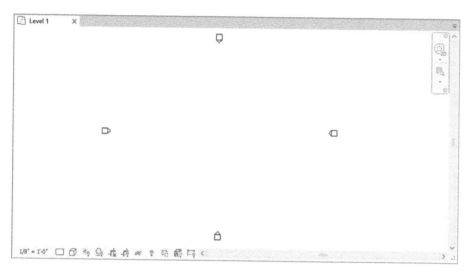

FIGURE 1.16 The view window collects the results of your actions.

To continue placing some walls in the model, keep going with the exercise. (If you haven't been following along, you can start by clicking the Wall button on the Architecture tab. In the Properties dialog, select Exterior - Brick And CMU On MTL. Stud [or Basic Wall - Exterior Brick On Mtl. Stud for metric users]. Make sure the wall is justified to the finish face exterior.) You may now proceed:

1. With the Wall command still running and the correct wall type selected, position your cursor in a location similar to the illustration in Figure 1.17. Pick a point in the view window.

2. With the first point picked, move your cursor to the left. Notice that two things happen: the wall seems to snap in a horizontal plane, and a blue dashed line locks the horizontal position. In Revit, there is no Ortho. Revit aligns the typical compass increments to 0°, 90°, 180°, 270°, and 45°.

3. Also notice the blue dimension extending from the first point to the last point. Although dimensions can't be typed over, this type of dimension is a temporary dimension for you to use as you place

items. Type **100′** (30000 mm), and press the Enter key. Notice that you didn't need to type the foot mark (′) or mm. Revit thinks in terms of feet in an imperial template or millimeters in a metric template. The wall is now 100′ (30000 mm) long (see Figure 1.17).

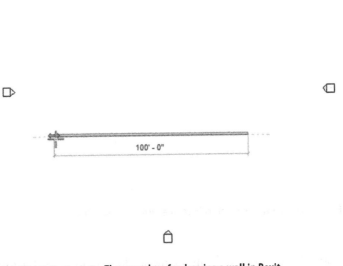

100′ - 0″

FIGURE 1.17 The procedure for drawing a wall in Revit

4. With the Wall command still running, move your cursor straight up from the endpoint of your 100′-long wall. Look at Figure 1.18.

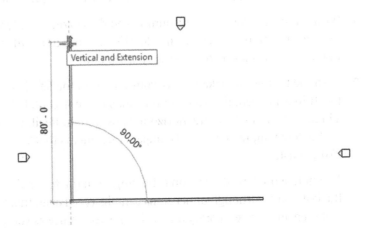

Vertical and Extension

80′ - 0

90.00°

FIGURE 1.18 How Revit works is evident in this procedure.

5. Type 80′ (24000 mm), and press Enter. You now have two walls.

6. Move your cursor to the right until you run into another blue alignment line. Notice that your temporary dimension says 100′–0″
   (30000.0). Revit understands symmetry. After you see this alignment
   line, and the temporary dimension says 100′–0″ (30000.0), pick
   this point.

7. Move your cursor straight down, type 16′ (4800 mm), and
   press Enter.

8. Move your cursor to the right, type 16′ (4800 mm), and press Enter.

9. Press the Esc key twice.

Do your walls look like Figure 1.19? If not, try it again. You need to be comfortable with this procedure (as much as possible).

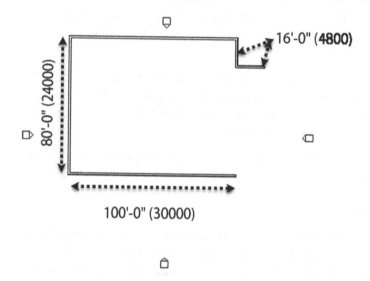

FIGURE 1.19 Working with Revit starts with the ability to work with the view window and
learn the quirks and feel of the interface.

To get used to the Revit flow, always remember these three steps:

1. Start a command.

2. Focus on your options.

3. Move to the view window, and add the elements to the model.

If you start a command and then focus immediately on the view, you'll be sitting there wondering what to do next. Don't forget to check your Options bar and the appropriate Ribbon tab.

Let's keep going and close this building by using a few familiar commands. If you've never drafted on a computer before, don't worry. These commands are simple. The easiest but most important topic is how to select an object.

Object Selection

Revit has a few similarities to AutoCAD and MicroStation. One of those similarities is the ability to perform simple object selection and to execute common modify commands. For this example, you'll mirror the two 16′–0″ (4800 mm) L-shaped walls to the bottom of the building:

1. Type **ZA** (zoom all).

2. Near the two 16′–0″ (4800 mm) L-shaped walls, pick (left-click) and hold down the left mouse button when the cursor is at a point to the right of the walls but below the top (North), 100′–0″ (30000 mm) horizontal wall.

3. As you move your mouse, you see a window start to form. Run that selection window down and to the left past the two walls. After you highlight the walls, as shown in Figure 1.20, let go of the mouse button, and you've selected the walls.

There are two ways to select an object: by using a crossing window or by using a box. Each approach plays an important role in how you select items in a model.

Crossing Windows

A *crossing window* is an object-selection method in which you select objects by placing a window that crosses through the objects. A crossing window always starts from the right and ends to the left. When you place a crossing window, it's represented by a dashed-line composition (as you saw in Figure 1.20).

Boxes

With a box object-selection method, you select only items that are 100 percent inside the window you place. This method is useful when you want to select specific items while passing through larger objects that you may not want in the selection set. A box always starts from the left and works to the right. The line type for a selection window is a continuous line (see Figure 1.21).

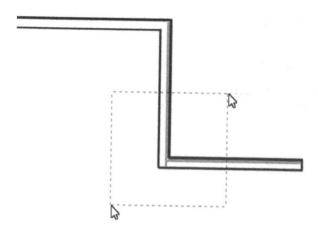

FIGURE 1.20 Using a crossing window to select two walls

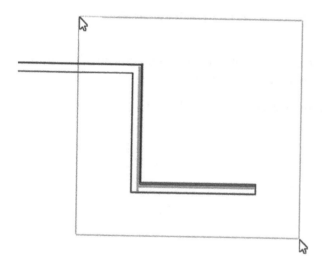

FIGURE 1.21 To select only objects that are surrounded by the window, use a box. This will leave out any item that may be partially within the box.

Now that you have experience selecting items, you can execute some basic modify commands. Let's begin with mirroring, one of the most popular modify commands.

Modifying and Mirroring

Revit allows you to either select the item first and then execute the command or start the command and then select the objects to be modified. This is true for most action items and is certainly true for every command on the Modify toolbar. Try it:

1. Make sure only the two 16'–0" (4800 mm) walls are selected.

2. When the walls are selected, the Modify | Walls tab appears. On the Modify panel, click the Mirror – Draw Axis button, as shown in Figure 1.22.

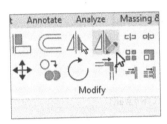

F I G U R E 1 . 2 2 **The Ribbon adds the appropriate commands.**

3. Your cursor changes to a crosshair with the mirror icon, illustrating that you're ready to draw a mirror plane.

4. Make sure the Copy check box is selected in the Options bar (see Figure 1.23).

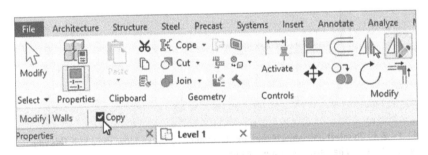

F I G U R E 1 . 2 3 **There are options you must choose for every command in Revit.**

5. Hover your cursor over the inside face of the 80'–0" (24000 mm) vertical wall until you reach the midpoint. Revit displays a triangular icon, indicating that you've found the midpoint of the wall (see Figure 1.24).

6. When the triangular midpoint snap appears, pick this point. After you pick the point where the triangle appears, you can move your cursor directly to the right of the wall. An alignment line appears, as shown

in Figure 1.25. When it does, you can pick another point along the path. When you pick the second point, the walls are mirrored and joined with the south wall (see Figure 1.26).

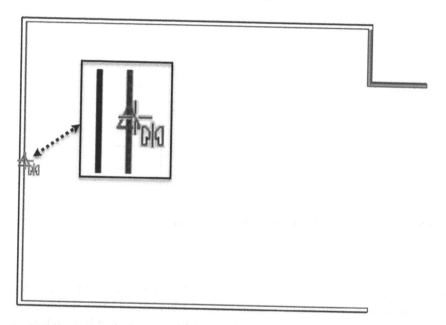

FIGURE 1.24 Revit has snaps similar to those in most CAD applications. In Revit, you'll get snaps only if you choose the Draw icon from the Options bar during a command.

Now that you have some experience mirroring items, it's time to start adding components to your model by using the items that you placed earlier. If you're having trouble following the process, retry these first few procedures. Rome wasn't built in a day. (Well, perhaps if they'd had Revit, it would have sped things up!) You want your first few walls to look like Figure 1.26.

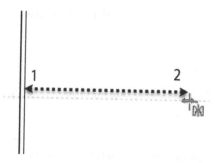

FIGURE 1.25 Mirroring these walls involves (1) picking the midpoint of the vertical wall and (2) picking a horizontal point along the plane.

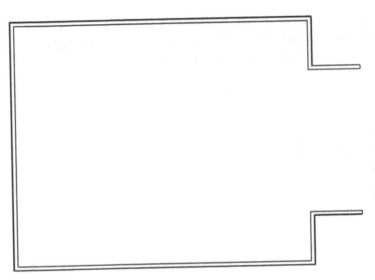

FIGURE 1.26 Your building should look like this illustration.

Building on Existing Geometry

You have some geometry with which to work, and you have some objects placed in your model. Now Revit starts to come alive. The benefits of using Building Information Modeling will become apparent quickly, as explained later in this chapter. For example, because Revit knows that walls are walls, you can add identical geometry to the model by simply selecting an item and telling Revit to create a similar item.

Suppose you want a radial wall of the same exact type as the other walls in the model. Perform the following steps:

1. Type ZA to zoom the entire screen.

2. Press the Esc key.

3. Select one of the walls in the model—it doesn't matter which one.

4. Right-click the wall.

5. Select Create Similar, as shown in Figure 1.27.

6. On the Modify | Place Wall tab, click the Start-End-Radius Arc button, as shown in Figure 1.28.

N O T E When you right-click an item, you can choose to repeat the last command. You can also select all items that are only in the current view or in the entire project.

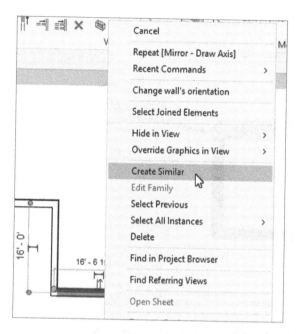

FIGURE 1.27 You can select any item in Revit and create a similar object by right-clicking and selecting Create Similar.

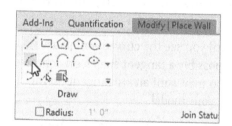

FIGURE 1.28 Just because you started the command from the view window doesn't mean you can ignore your options.

7. Again with the options? Yes. Make sure Location Line is set to Finish Face: Exterior (it should be so already).

8. With the wheel button on your mouse, zoom into the upper corner of the building and select the top endpoint of the wall, as shown in Figure 1.29. The point you're picking is the corner of the heavy lines. The topmost, thinner line represents a concrete belt course below. If you're having trouble picking the correct point, don't be afraid to zoom into the area by scrolling the mouse wheel. (Metric users do not have the concrete belt. Just pick the outside heavy line representing the brick face.)

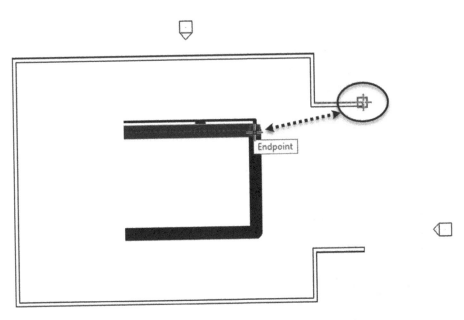

FIGURE 1.29 Select the top corner of the wall to start your new radial wall.

9. Select the opposite, outside corner of the bottom wall. Again, to be more accurate, you'll probably have to zoom into each point as you're making your picks.

10. Move your cursor to the right until you see the curved wall pause. You'll see an alignment line and possibly a tangent snap icon appear as well. Revit understands that you may want an arc tangent on the two lines you've already placed in your model.

11. When you see the tangent snap icon, choose the third point. Your walls should look like Figure 1.30.

Just because you've placed a wall in the model doesn't mean the wall looks the way you would like it to appear. In Revit, you can do a lot with view control and how objects are displayed.

View Control and Object Display

Although the earlier procedures are a nice way to add walls to a drawing, they don't reflect the detail you'll need to produce construction documents. The great thing about Revit, though, is that you've already done everything you need to do. You can now tell Revit to display the graphics the way you want to see them.

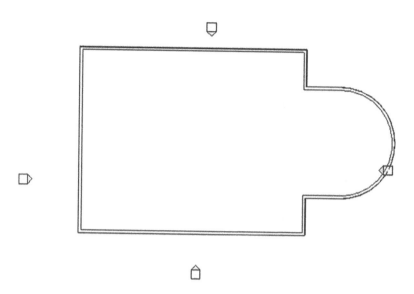

FIGURE 1.30   The completed exterior walls should look like this illustration.

The View Control Bar

At the bottom of the view window, you'll see a skinny toolbar (as shown in Figure 1.31). This is the View Control bar.

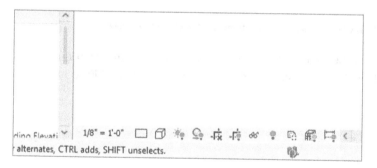

FIGURE 1.31   The View Control bar controls the graphical view of your model.

It contains the functions outlined in the following list:

Scale   The first item on the View Control bar is the Scale function. It gets small mention here, but it's a huge deal. In Revit, you change the scale of a view by selecting this menu. Change the scale here, and Revit will scale annotations and symbols accordingly (see Figure 1.32).

Custom...	Custom...
12" = 1'-0"	1 : 1
6" = 1'-0"	1 : 2
3" = 1'-0"	1 : 5
1 1/2" = 1'-0"	1 : 10
1" = 1'-0"	1 : 20
3/4" = 1'-0"	1 : 50
1/2" = 1'-0"	1 : 100
3/8" = 1'-0"	1 : 200
1/4" = 1'-0"	1 : 500
3/16" = 1'-0"	1 : 1000
1/8" = 1'-0"	1 : 2000
1" = 10'-0"	1 : 5000
3/32" = 1'-0"	
1/16" = 1'-0"	
1" = 20'-0"	
3/64" = 1'-0"	
1" = 30'-0"	
1/32" = 1'-0"	
1" = 40'-0"	
1" = 50'-0"	
1" = 60'-0"	
1/64" = 1'-0"	
1" = 80'-0"	
1" = 100'-0"	
1" = 160'-0"	
1" = 200'-0"	
1" = 300'-0"	
1" = 400'-0"	

FIGURE 1.32 The Scale menu allows you to change the scale of your view.

Detail Level   Detail Level allows you to view your model at different qualities. You have three levels to choose from: Coarse, Medium, and Fine (see Figure 1.33).

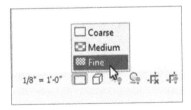

FIGURE 1.33 The Detail Level control allows you to set different view levels for the current view.

If you want more graphical information with this view, select Fine. To see how the view is adjusted using this control, follow these steps:

1. Click the Detail Level icon, and choose Fine.

2. Zoom in on a wall corner. Notice that the wall components are now showing in the view.

 TIP When you change the view control in a view, it isn't a temporary display. You're telling Revit how you want to plot this view. The view you see on the screen is the view you'll see when it comes out of the plotter.

There are other items on the View Control bar, but we'll discuss them when they become applicable to the exercises.

The View Tab

Because Revit is one big happy model, you'll quickly find that simply viewing the model is quite important. In Revit, you can take advantage of some functionality in the Navigation bar. To activate the Navigation bar, first go to the View tab and click the User Interface button. Then go to the default 3D view, which can be done by clicking the 3D view icon on the create panel, and make sure the Navigation bar is activated, as shown in Figure 1.34. (For the 3D view button, look ahead to Figure 1.39.)

FIGURE 1.34 The View tab allows you to turn on and off the Navigation bar.

One item we need to look at on the Navigation bar is the steering wheel.

The Steering Wheel

The steering wheel allows you to zoom, rewind, and pan. When you click the steering wheel icon, a larger control panel appears in the view window. To choose one of the options, you simply pick (left-click) one of the options and hold down the mouse button as you execute the maneuver.

To use the steering wheel, follow along:

1. Go back to Floor Plan Level 1, and pick the steering wheel icon from the Navigation bar.

2. When the steering wheel is in the view window (as shown in Figure 1.35), left-click and hold Zoom. You can now zoom in and out.

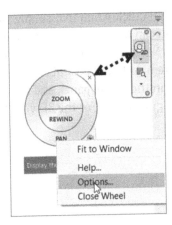

FIGURE 1.35 You can use the steering wheel to navigate through a view.

3. Click and hold Rewind in the steering wheel. You can now find an older view, as shown in Figure 1.36.

4. Do the same for Pan, which is found on the outer ring of the steering wheel. After you click and hold Pan, you can navigate to other parts of the model.

5. You can click the little dropdown arrow in the lower right corner to open the options if you want to change anything.

Although you can do all this with your wheel button, some users still prefer the icon method of panning and zooming. For those of you who prefer the icons, you'll want to use the icons for the traditional zooms as well.

FIGURE 1.36 Because Revit doesn't include zoom commands in the Undo function, you can rewind to find previous views.

When you're finished using the steering wheel, press Shift+W or right-click and choose Close Wheel.

Traditional Zooms

The next items on the Navigation bar are the good-old zoom controls. The abilities to zoom in, zoom out, and pan are all included in this function, as shown in Figure 1.37.

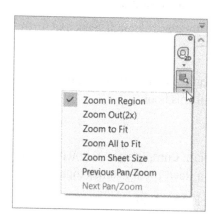

FIGURE 1.37 The standard zoom commands

Of course, if you have a mouse with a wheel, you can zoom and pan by either holding down the wheel to pan or wheeling the button to scroll in and out.

Thin Lines

Back on the View tab, you'll see an icon called Thin Lines, as shown in Figure 1.38. Let's talk about what this icon does.

In Revit, there are no layers. Line weights are controlled by the actual objects they represent. In the view window, you see these line weights. As mentioned before, what you see is what you get.

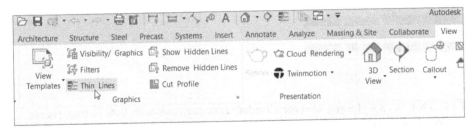

FIGURE 1.38 Clicking the Thin Lines icon lets you operate on the finer items in a model.

Sometimes, however, these line weights may be too thick for smaller-scale views. By clicking the Thin Lines icon, as shown in Figure 1.38, you can force the view to display only the thinnest lines possible and still see the objects.

To practice using the Thin Lines function, follow along:

1. Pick the Thin Lines icon.

2. Zoom in on the upper-right corner of the building.

3. Pick the Thin Lines icon again. This toggles the mode back and forth.

4. Notice that the lines are very heavy.

The line weight should concern you. As mentioned earlier, there are no layers in Revit. This subject will be covered throughout this book.

3D View

The 3D View icon brings us to a new conversation. Complete the following steps, which will move us into the discussion of how a Revit model comes together:

1. Click the 3D View icon, as shown in Figure 1.39.

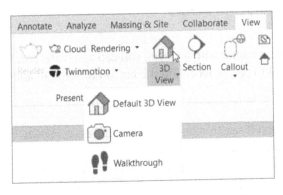

FIGURE 1.39 The 3D View icon will be used heavily.

2. On the View Control bar, click the Visual Style button and choose Realistic, as shown in Figure 1.40.

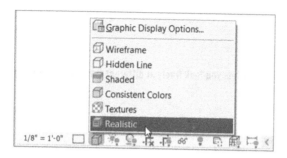

FIGURE 1.40 The Visual Style button enables you to view your model in color. This is typical for a 3D view.

3. Again on the View Control bar, select the Shadows On icon and turn on shadows, as shown in Figure 1.41.

FIGURE 1.41 Shadows create a nice effect, but at the expense of RAM.

WARNING If you turn on shadows, do so with care. This could be the single worst item in Revit in terms of performance degradation. Your model *will* slow down with shadows on.

Within the 3D view is the ViewCube. It's the cube in the upper-right corner of the view window. You can switch to different perspectives of the model by clicking the quadrants of the cube (see Figure 1.42).

TIP The best way to navigate a 3D view is to press and hold the Shift key on the keyboard. As you're holding the Shift key, press and hold the wheel on your mouse. Now move the mouse around. You'll be able to view the model dynamically.

Your model should look similar to Figure 1.43. (Metric users, you do not have the concrete belt or the concrete block coursing below the brick.)

Go back to the floor plan. Wait! How? This brings us to an important topic in Revit: the Project Browser.

FIGURE 1.42   The ViewCube lets you look freely at different sides of the building.

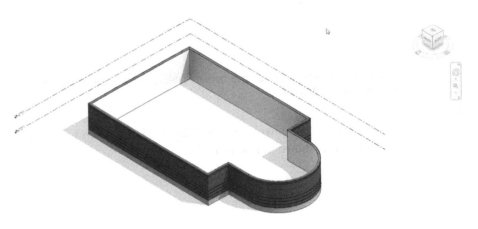

FIGURE 1.43   The model with shadows turned on

LOCK IT UP!

If you're happy with this view and you don't want to screw it up inadvertently, you can lock the orientation of the view as shown here. This is an important thing to know because, as you start creating sheets, you'll sometimes find that the 3D view you're randomly spinning around is actually on a sheet. Also, you can add text notes and dimensions to the view when it's locked. For this lesson, leave the view unlocked.

The Project Browser

Revit is the frontrunner of BIM. BIM has swept our industry for many reasons. One of the biggest reasons is that you have a fully integrated model in front of you. That is, when you need to open a different floor plan, elevation, detail, drawing sheet, or 3D view, you can find it all right there in the model.

Also, this means your workflow will change drastically. When you think about all the external references and convoluted folder structures that make up a typical job, you can start to relate to the way Revit uses the Project Browser. In Revit, you use the Project Browser instead of the folder structure you used previously in CAD.

This approach changes the playing field. The process of closing the file you're in and opening the files in which you need to do work is restructured in Revit to enable you to stay in the model. You never have to leave one file to open another. You also never need to rely on external referencing to complete a set of drawings. Revit and the Project Browser put it all in front of you.

To start using the Project Browser, follow along:

1. To the far left of the Revit interface are the combined Project Browser and Properties dialogs. At the bottom of the dialogs, you'll see two tabs, as shown in Figure 1.44. Click the Project Browser tab.

2. The Project Browser is broken down into categories. The first category is Views. The first View category is Floor Plans. In the Floor Plans category, double-click Level 1.

3. Double-click Level 2. Notice that the walls look different than in Level 1. Your display level is set to Coarse. This is because any change you make on the View Control bar is for that view only. When you went to Level 2 for the first time, the change to the display level had not yet been made.

4. In the view window, you see little icons that look like houses (see Figure 1.45). These are elevation markers. (Metric users, yours are round.) The elevation marker to the right might be in your building or overlapping one of the walls. If this is the case, you need to move it out of the way.

5. Pick a box around the elevation marker. When both the small triangle and the small box are selected, move your mouse cursor over the selected objects.

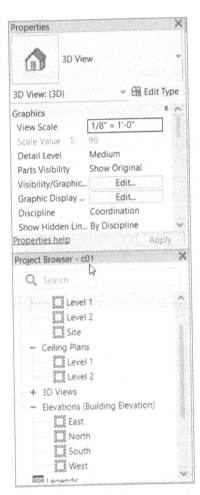

FIGURE 1.44 The Project Browser is your new BIM Windows Explorer.

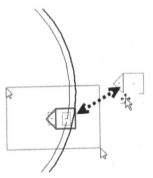

FIGURE 1.45 Symbols for elevation markers in the plan. If you need to move them, you must do so by picking a window. There are two items in an elevation marker.

6. Your cursor turns into a move icon. Pick a point on the screen, and move the elevation marker out of the way.

7. In the Project Browser, find the Elevations (Building Elevation) category. Double-click South.

8. Also in the Project Browser, notice the 3D Views category. Expand the 3D Views category, and double-click the {3D} choice. This brings you back to the 3D view you were looking at before this exercise.

Now that you can navigate through the Project Browser, adding other components to the model will be much easier. Next, you'll begin to add some windows.

 WARNING "Hey! What happened to my elevation?" You're in Revit now. Items such as elevation markers, section markers, and callouts are no longer just dumb blocks; they're linked to the actual view they're calling out. If you delete one of these markers, you'll delete the view associated with it. If you and your design team have been working on that view, then you've lost that view. Also, you must move any item deliberately and with caution. The elevation marker you moved in the previous exercise has two parts: the little triangle is the elevation, and the little box is the part of the marker that records the sheet number on which the elevation will wind up. If you don't move both items together by placing a window around them, the elevation's origin will remain in its original position. When this happens, your elevation will look like a section, and it will be hard to determine how the section occurred.

Views

By clicking all these items in the Project Browser, you're simply opening a view of the building, not another file that is stored somewhere. For some users, this can be confusing. (It was initially for me.) I like to describe it as if you are standing there with your phone taking pictures of an actual building from different perspectives. You can take as many as you want, but if you delete the pictures, the actual building obviously doesn't disappear from the earth, just those images.

When you click around and open views, they stay open. You can quickly open many views. There is a way to manage these views before they get out of hand.

In the upper-right corner of the Revit dialog, you'll see the traditional close and minimize/maximize buttons for the application. Just below them are the traditional buttons for the files that are open, as shown in Figure 1.46. Click the X to close the current view.

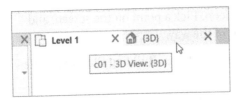

FIGURE 1.46 You can close a view by clicking the X for the view. This doesn't close Revit—or an actual file for that matter—it simply closes that view.

In this case, you have multiple views open. This situation (which is quite common) is best managed on the View tab. To use the Window menu, perform the following steps:

1. On the Windows panel of the View tab, click the Switch Windows button, as shown in Figure 1.47.

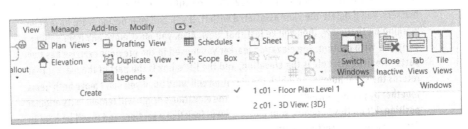

FIGURE 1.47 The Switch Windows menu lists all the current views that are open.

2. After the menu is expanded, look at the open views.

3. Go to the {3D} view by selecting it from the Windows menu and clicking the 3D icon at the top of the screen or by going to the {3D} view in the Project Browser.

4. On the Windows panel, click Close Inactive.

5. In the Project Browser, open Level 1.

6. Go to the Windows panel, and select Tile Views.

7. With the windows tiled, you can see the Level 1 floor plan along with the 3D view to the side. Select one of the walls in the Level 1 floor plan. Notice that it's now selected in the 3D view. The views you have open are mere representations of the model from that perspective. Each view of the model can have its own independent view settings.

8. Click into each view, and type **ZA**. Doing so zooms the extents of each window. This is a useful habit to get into.

You're at a safe point now to save the file. This also brings us to a logical place at which to discuss the various file types and their associations with the BIM model.

BUT I USED TO TYPE MY COMMANDS!

You can still type your commands. In the Revit menus, you may have noticed that many of the menu items have a two- or three-letter abbreviation to the right. This is the keyboard shortcut associated with the command. You can make your own shortcuts, or you can modify existing keyboard shortcuts—if you navigate to the View tab. On the Windows panel, click the User Interface button. In the drop-down menu, click the Keyboard Shortcuts button. Here you can add or modify keyboard shortcuts.

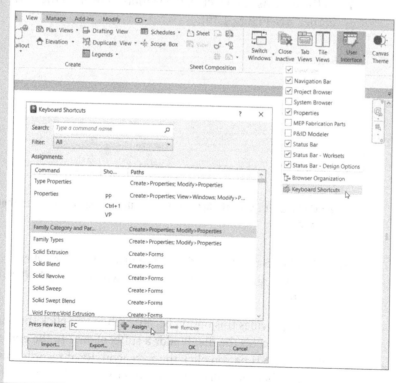

File Types and Families

Revit has a unique way of saving files and using different file types to build a BIM model. To learn how and why Revit has chosen these methods, follow along with these steps:

1. Click the Save icon (see Figure 1.48).

FIGURE 1.48   The traditional Save icon brings up the Save As dialog if the file has never been saved.

2. In the Save As dialog, click the Options button in the lower-right corner (see Figure 1.49).

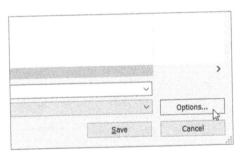

FIGURE 1.49   The Options button in the Save As dialog lets you choose how the file is saved.

3. In the File Save Options dialog is a place at the top where you can specify the number of backups, as shown in Figure 1.50. Set this value to 1.

    Revit provides this option because when you click the Save icon, Revit duplicates the file. It adds a suffix of 0001 to the end of the filename. Each time you click the Save icon, Revit records this save and adds another file called 0002, leaving the 0001 file intact. The default is to do this three times before Revit starts replacing 0001, 0002, and 0003 with the three most current files.

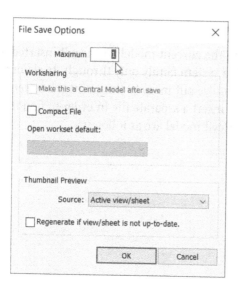

FIGURE 1.50 The options in the File Save Options dialog box let you specify the number of backups and the view for the preview.

4. In the Preview section, you can specify in which view this file will be previewed. I like to keep it as the active view. That way I can get an idea of whether the file is up to date based on the state of the view. Click OK.

5. Create a folder somewhere, and save this file into the folder. The name of the file used as an example in the book is NER.rvt. (NER stands for "No Experience Required.") Of course, you can name the file anything you wish, or you can even make your own project using the steps and examples from the book as guidelines.

Now that you have experience adding components to the model, it's time to investigate exactly what you're adding here. Each component is a member of what Revit calls a *family*.

System and Hosted Families (*.rfa*)

A Revit model is based on a compilation of items called families. There are two types of families: system families and hosted families. A *system family* can be found only in a Revit model and can't be stored in a separate location. A *hosted family* is inserted similarly to a block (or cell) and is stored in an external directory. The file extension for a hosted family is .rfa.

System Families

System families are inherent to the current model and aren't inserted in the traditional sense. You can modify a system family only through its element properties in the model. The walls you've put in up to this point are system families, for example. You didn't have to insert a separate file in order to find the wall type. The system families in a Revit model are as follows:

Walls

Floors

Roofs

Ceilings

Stairs

Ramps

Shafts

Rooms

Schedules/quantity takeoffs

Text

Dimensions

Views

System families define your model. As you can see, the list pretty much covers most building elements. There are, however, many more components not included in this list. These items, which can be loaded into your model, are called hosted families.

Hosted Families

All other families in Revit are hosted in some way by a system family, a level, or a reference plane. For example, a wall sconce is a hosted family in that, when you insert it, it's appended to a wall. Hosted families carry a file extension of .rfa. To insert a hosted family into a model, follow these steps:

1. Open the NER-01.rvt file or your own file.

2. Go to Level 1.

3. On the Architecture tab, click the Door button.

4. On the Modify | Place Door tab, click the Load Family button, as shown in Figure 1.51. This opens the Load Family dialog.

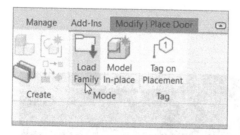

FIGURE 1.51 You can load an RFA file during the placement of a hosted family.

5. Browse to the Doors directory.

   Note that, if you're on a network, your directories may not be the same as in this book. Contact your CAD/BIM manager (or whoever loaded Revit onto your computer) to find out exactly where they may have mapped Revit.

   If you are not on a network and are not seeing any families, go to www.autodesk.com/revitcontent and select "US English Family Libraries in Imperial and Metric" to download the EXE file.

6. Notice that there is a list of doors. Open the Commercial folder, select Door-Exterior-Double_Two-Lite.rfa, and click Open. (Metric users, select M_Double-Panel 2.rfa.)

WHAT ARE ALL THESE SIZES?

Once you select the door (family) you want to use, Revit will list several door types. This allows you to simply select the one door type you want. This keeps from having to scroll through dozens of door types you won't be using in your project. Once the door is loaded, you can make as many types as you need. This is a good example of how Revit offers multiple choices with one move.

7. In this case, select all the door sizes (types) in the dialog that you see once you click the door, and click OK.

8. In the Properties dialog, click the Type Selector, as shown in Figure 1.53. Notice that in addition to bringing in the door family, you have seven different types of the door. These types are simply variations of the same door. You no longer have to explode a block and modify it to fit in your wall.

9. Select Door-Exterior-Double-Two_Lite 72″ × 80″ as shown in Figure 1.53.

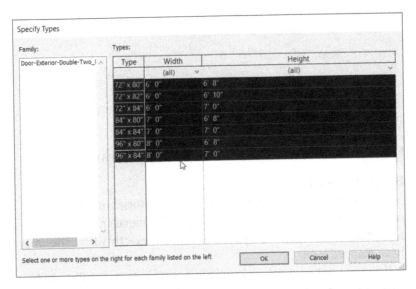

Type	Width	Height
	(all)	(all)
72" x 80"	6' 0"	6' 8"
72" x 82"	6' 0"	6' 10"
72" x 84"	6' 0"	7' 0"
84" x 80"	7' 0"	6' 8"
84" x 84"	7' 0"	7' 0"
96" x 80"	8' 0"	6' 8"
96" x 84"	8' 0"	7' 0"

Specify Types

Family:
Door-Exterior-Double-Two_L

Types:

Select one or more types on the right for each family listed on the left   OK   Cancel   Help

FIGURE 1.52 This door family has several types you can chose from.

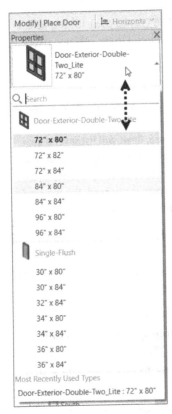

FIGURE 1.53 Each family RFA file contains multiple types associated with that family.

10. Zoom in on the upper-left corner of the building, as shown in Figure 1.54.

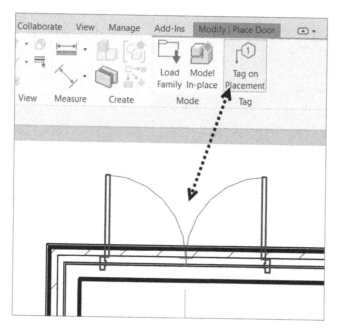

FIGURE 1.54 Inserting a hosted family (.rfa)

11. Click Tag On Placement.

12. To insert the door into the model, you must place it in the wall. (Notice that before you hover your cursor over the actual wall, Revit won't allow you to add the door to the model, as shown in Figure 1.54.) When your pointer is directly on top of the wall, you see the outline of the door. Pick a point in the wall, and the door is inserted. (We'll cover this in depth in the next chapter.)

13. Press Esc twice. Delete the door you just placed by selecting it and pressing the Delete key on your keyboard. This is just practice for the next chapter.

You'll use this method of inserting a hosted family into a model quite a bit in this book and on a daily basis when you use Revit. Note that when a family is loaded into Revit, there is no live path back to the file that was loaded. After it's added to the Revit model, it becomes part of that model. To view a list of the families in the Revit model, go to the Project Browser and look for the Families category. There you'll see a list of the families and their types, as Figure 1.55 shows.

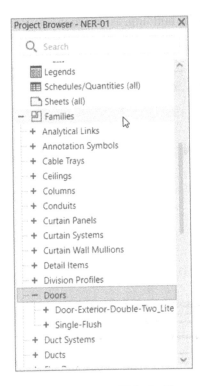

FIGURE 1.55 All the families are listed in the Project Browser.

The two main Revit file types have been addressed. Two others are also crucial to the development of a Revit model.

Using Revit Template Files (.rte)

The .rte extension pertains to a Revit template file. Your company surely has developed a template for its own standards or will do so soon. An RTE file is the default template that has all of your company's standards built into it. When you start a project, you'll use this file. To see how an RTE file is used, follow these steps:

1. Click the File tab, and select New ➤ Project.

2. In the resulting dialog, shown in Figure 1.56, click the Browse button.

3. Browsing throws you into a category with several other templates. You can now choose a different template.

4. Click Cancel twice.

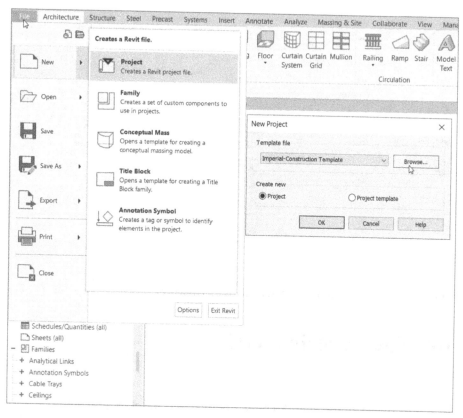

FIGURE 1.56 A new Revit model is based on an RTE template file.

Whenever you start a project, you'll use the RTE template. When you start a new family, however, you'll want to use an RFT file.

Using Revit Family Files (.*rft*)

The .rft extension is another type of template—only this one pertains to a family. It would be nice if Revit had every family fully developed to suit your needs. Alas, it doesn't. You'll have to develop your own families, starting with a family template. To see how to access a family template, perform these steps:

1. Click the File tab, and select New ➢ Family to open the browse dialog shown in Figure 1.57.

2. Browse through these templates. You'll most certainly use many of them.

3. Click the Cancel button.

FIGURE 1.57 The creation of a family starts with templates.

Are You Experienced?

Now you can...

- ✓ navigate the Revit Architecture interface and start a model
- ✓ find commands on the Ribbon and understand how this controls your options
- ✓ find where to change a keyboard shortcut to make it similar to CAD
- ✓ navigate through the Project Browser
- ✓ understand how the Revit interface is broken down into views
- ✓ tell the difference between the two different types of families and understand how to build a model using them

CHAPTER 2

Creating a Model

Now that you have a solid working knowledge of the Autodesk® Revit® interface and you understand how it differs from most other drafting applications, it's time to move on to creating the Revit model.

The first chapter had you add some exterior walls to the model, and this chapter will expand on that concept. You'll also be placing some of the components, such as doors, that were introduced in Chapter 1, "The Autodesk Revit World." Revit is only as good as the families that support the model.

To kick off the chapter, I'll focus on the accurate placement of interior and exterior walls. You also have a lot to learn about the properties of walls and how to tackle tricky areas where the walls just won't join together for you.

▶ **Placing walls**

▶ **Using reference planes**

▶ **Adding interior walls**

▶ **Editing wall joins**

▶ **Placing doors and windows**

Placing Walls

In Chapter 1, you placed some walls and then added exterior walls to the model. In this section, you'll add more walls to the model. Although adding walls to the model isn't difficult, you need to explore how to control these walls when adjacent items start moving around and corners get fussy. Also, I'll present proven methods to ensure accuracy so that I can keep you from starting down the wrong path.

Adding Exterior Walls

To continue with the perimeter of the building from Chapter 1, let's add some more exterior walls. The first few walls you added to the model were pretty basic in terms of layout. It would be nice to have only square geometry! The reality is you're going to encounter walls at different angles and dimensions to which you can't just line up other walls. To get around this, you'll add what are called *reference planes* to help lay out the building. At the end of this section, your building's perimeter will look like Figure 2.1.

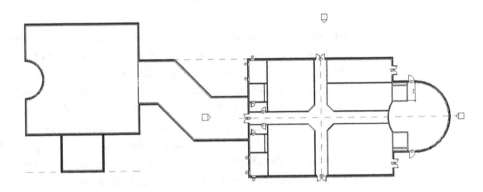

FIGURE 2.1 The footprint of your completed building

The objective of the next set of procedures is to establish some strong working points and then add walls along those guidelines. You'll also use these rules to make the necessary adjustments later in the section.

Using Reference Planes

Reference planes are construction lines that you can place in your model to establish centerlines and to use as an aid for symmetrical geometry. If you add a reference plane in one view, it will appear in another. If you add one in a plane view, you can see that same plane in an elevation. This approach is a great way to build using a common reference. Also, reference planes, by default, don't plot.

N O T E Although Revit understands the inch mark (″) and metric abbreviations such as MM, you do not need to type the unit. Revit follows the units that are set up for the model. For example, if the units are set for feet and fractional inch, all you need to type is **1 6**. So one <space> six will automatically turn into 1′-6″.

The only drawback to reference planes is that they suffer from overuse. Try to use them only as what they are: a reference. To practice using reference planes, follow these steps:

1. Open the file you created in Chapter 1. If you didn't complete that chapter, open the file NER-02.rvt in the Chapter 2 directory, which you can download from the book's website at www.wiley.com/go/revit2024ner. (You can also use your own building if you choose.)

2. Go to Floor Plan Level 1 in the Project Browser (if you aren't there already).

3. On the Work Plane panel of the Architecture tab, click the Ref Plane button (all the way to the right), as shown in Figure 2.2.

 N O T E As you move through the exercises in this book, you'll discover that the Ref Plane command is also found elsewhere in the program.

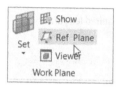

F I G U R E   2 . 2   The Ref Plane command is on the Architecture tab's Work Plane panel on the Ribbon.

4. Draw the reference plane horizontally through the center of the building, extending each end past the exterior walls. (Remember, this is a construction line. You can go long if you need to.) See Figure 2.3 for an idea of where the line should go. If you're having trouble locating the reference points for the start of the reference plane, make sure you're snapping to the midpoint of the walls. You can also type SM to snap to the midpoint of the wall.

5. Press Esc twice.

6. If the line isn't the length you want, you can stretch it. First select the line; at each end, you see blue grips. Simply pick (left-click) and hold the grip, and stretch the reference plane to the desired length, as shown in Figure 2.3.

7. Start the Ref Plane command again.

8. On the Draw panel, click the Pick Lines icon, as shown in Figure 2.4.

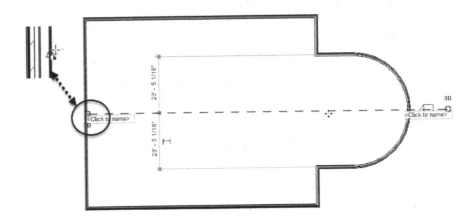

FIGURE 2.3 You can grip-edit reference planes to the required length.

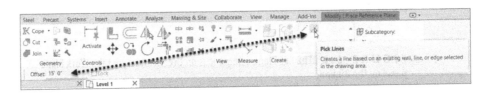

FIGURE 2.4 Offsetting a reference plane

9. Set Offset to 15′–0″ (4500 mm), as shown in Figure 2.4. (Imperial users, remember, you can type 15, and metric users type 4500.)

10. Hover your pointer above the mid-reference plane. A blue alignment line appears either above or below.

11. Move your pointer up and down. See the alignment line flip? When it flips to the top, pick the middle line. Doing so adds the line to the top.

12. With the Ref Plane command still running, hover over the middle line again. This time, offset the alignment line down. Your plan should now look like Figure 2.5.

13. Let's add one more for good measure. Zoom into the top left corner of your building.

14. Click the Ref Plane button again.

15. Simply draw a reference plane from the top corner about 50'-0" to the left as shown in Figure 2.5.

16. You should have (4) reference planes now.

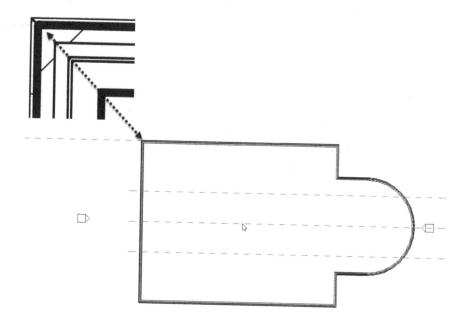

FIGURE 2.5 Reference planes are used here to aid in the placement of walls.

TIP Notice that you didn't actually use the Offset command. Revit has the offset function built into most of the commands you'll be running. You just need to remember to look at your temporary tab and your Options bar and you'll be fine.

Adding More Walls

Let's add some more walls. To do so, follow along with the next set of steps. (Before you start, here's a tip: Revit likes you to draw in a clockwise direction. That means that if you set your walls to finish face exterior and model in a clockwise direction, your wall will be in the correct orientation. If you model it counterclockwise, the wall will be inside out. To fix this, you simply hit the spacebar as you're drawing the wall, and that will flip the wall into the proper orientation.)

1. Select one of the exterior walls in the model, and right-click.

2. Select Create Similar. (You can still start the Wall command from the Architecture tab. If you do, make sure you select Basic Wall: Exterior - Brick And CMU On MTL. Stud.) Create Similar is also available on the Create panel of the Modify | Walls tab. (Metric users, select Exterior - Brick On Mtl. Stud.)

3. On the Options bar, make sure Location Line is set to Finish Face: Exterior.

4. Start drawing your new wall from the Intersection of the west wall (the one on the left) and the upper reference plane, as shown in Figure 2.6. Make sure you're using the face of the wall and not the ledge below. The enlargement in Figure 2.6 can help you. (Metric users, you do not have a ledge below.)

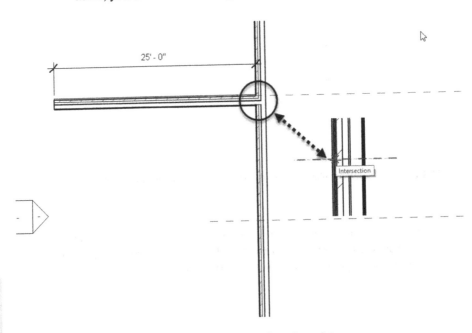

The spacebar is a handy function in Revit. When you want to flip a wall, simply pick the first point and tap the spacebar to change the orientation. ▶

FIGURE 2.6 Drawing a single wall from a defined starting point

5. If the wall is starting on the wrong side of the reference plane, tap your spacebar to flip the wall to the correct side.

6. Making sure you have a horizontal line started, type 25 (7500 mm) and press Enter.

7. Press Esc.

8. Do the same for the other side. Your plan should now look like Figure 2.7.

9. Start the Wall command again if it isn't already running. Make sure the Chain check box is selected. This will allow you to keep drawing walls continuing from the last point of the previously drawn wall.

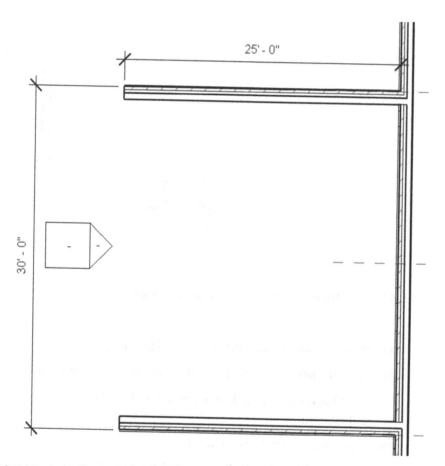

FIGURE 2.7 The two walls drawn here are 30′ (9000 mm) from outside face to outside face.

10. From the top 25′ (7500 mm) wall, pick the corner of the finish face (again, the brick face and not the ledge below). The wall may be positioned in the wrong orientation, so tap the spacebar to flip it if it is.

11. Move your cursor up and to the left at a 135° angle (Revit snaps at 45° intervals).

12. When you move your cursor far enough in this direction, Revit picks up the north finish face of the building drawn in the previous procedure. After these two alignment lines appear, pick the point on the screen, as shown in Figure 2.8.

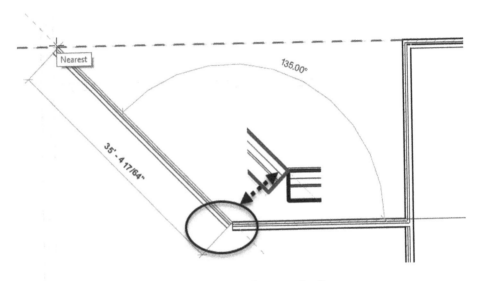

FIGURE 2.8 Allow Revit to guide you in the placement of walls.

13. Draw a horizontal wall to the left 25′ (7500 mm).

14. From the left point of that wall, draw a wall up 25′ (7500 mm).

15. From the top of that wall, draw another wall to the left 80′ (24000 mm).

16. Draw a wall down 25′ (7500 mm).

17. On the Modify | Place Wall panel, click the Start-End-Radius Arc button, as shown in Figure 2.9.

18. Because the Wall command is still running, the next point to pick is the endpoint of the arc. Before you do that, you will have to hit the spacebar to flip the wall in the correct orientation.

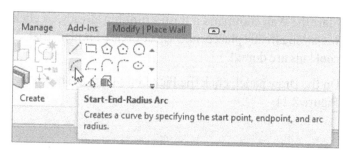

FIGURE 2.9 Draw a radial wall using the Start-End-Radius Arc method.

19. Pick a point straight down at a distance of 25'–0" (9000 mm).

20. Move your pointer to the right until Revit snaps it to the tangent radius. (You may not get a tangent snap, but Revit will hesitate when you've reached the tangency.) After this happens, pick a point.

21. On the Draw panel, click the Line button in the upper-left corner. This will allow you to draw a straight wall again.

22. Hit the spacebar if the wall is in the wrong orientation.

23. Draw a wall straight down from the end of the arc 25' (7500 mm).

24. Draw a wall to the right 80' (24000 mm).

25. Draw a wall straight up 25'–0" (7500 mm).

26. Press Esc. Your building should look like Figure 2.10.

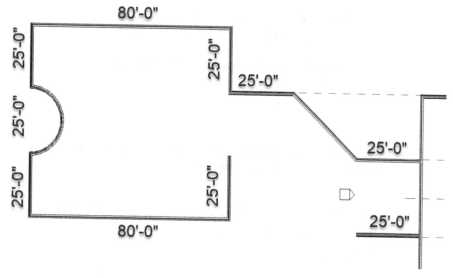

FIGURE 2.10 The building up to this point

If you're having trouble sketching the outline, remember to slow down. The next few walls will be a little tougher. You'll have to place them using the embedded offset function within the Wall command.

27. Start the Wall command if it isn't running already, or click one of the walls you already placed, and select Create Similar (that's what all the cool kids are doing).

28. On the Draw panel, click the Pick Lines icon, as shown in Figure 2.11.

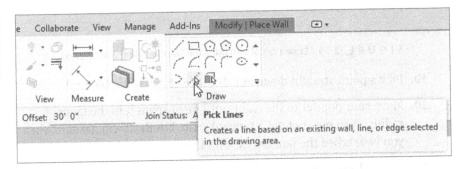

FIGURE 2.11 The Pick Lines icon lets you add a wall by using an offset from another object.

29. On the Options bar, you'll see an Offset input. Type 30 (10000 mm), and press Enter.

30. Move your cursor over the outside face of the wall, as shown in Figure 2.12. When you see the alignment line appear below the wall, pick the outside face.

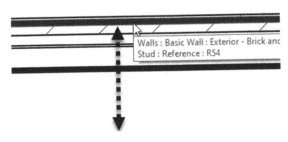

FIGURE 2.12 When you're adding a wall using the built-in offset function, it may take a few tries to get the method down.

31. Repeat the procedure for the angled wall. Make sure you offset the wall to the left (see Figure 2.13).

32. Hit Esc a few times.

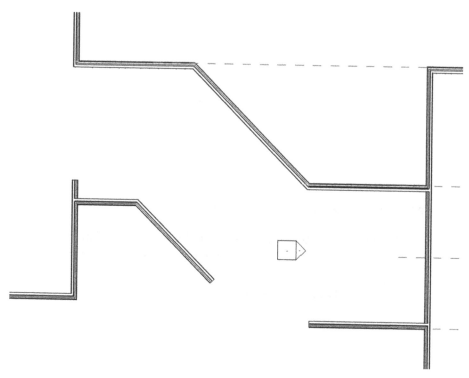

FIGURE 2.13 The walls in an incomplete state

Cleaning Up Using Trim

So, kind of a mess! It would be cool if Revit joined these walls the way you want, but that would, I'm afraid, be too much to ask. Sometimes it does, but sometimes it does not. By using the Trim command, you can clean up those overlapping corners and fill the gaps by simply selecting the walls you want joined together. There's one major thing to remember here: select the walls on the side you want to keep, not the side you want to trim away.

To get started, follow along:

1. On the Modify tab, select the Trim button on the Modify panel, as shown in Figure 2.14.

OLD-FASHIONED SHORTCUTS

Notice when you hover over the icon you see two letters in parentheses like this: (TR). This indicates you can type **TR** as a keyboard shortcut.

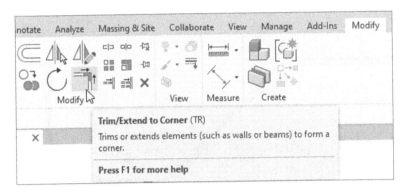

FIGURE 2.14 The Trim command is your new best friend.

2. The next step is to select the walls in the sequence and in the spots shown in Figure 2.15. The key to remember is you need to pick the object on the side you want to keep.

Your walls should look like Figure 2.16.

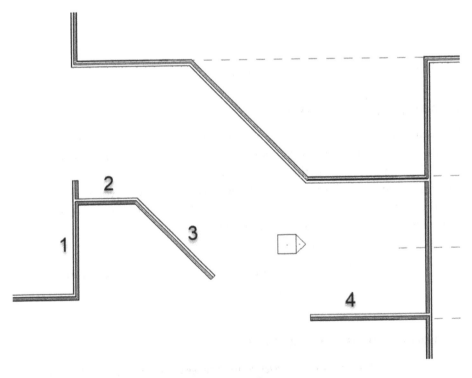

FIGURE 2.15 Using the Trim command to join the corners

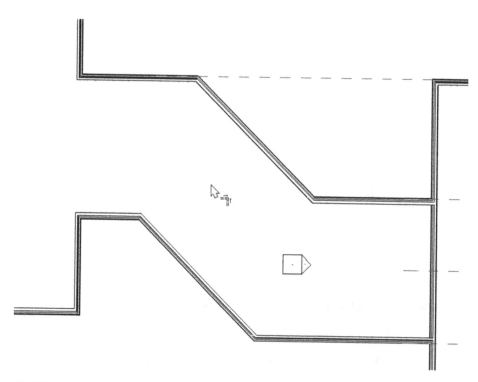

FIGURE 2.16 The walls are now clean.

3. You should add another part of the building. It's going to be a simple U-shape on the south end of the building. Start the Reference plane command (on the Architecture tab).

4. Click the Pick Lines button.

5. Set the Offset to 25′ (7500 mm).

6. Pick the outside face of the south wall as shown in Figure 2.17, and add the reference plane.

ESCAPE!

Notice in Revit that the Esc key is your go-to-person. Throughout this book, you will see me instruct you to press Esc a couple times. Always do it. With most applications, once you finish the command activities the command ends. Not so much in Revit. You can easily duplicate items by accident if you don't purposely end the command by hitting Esc a couple times.

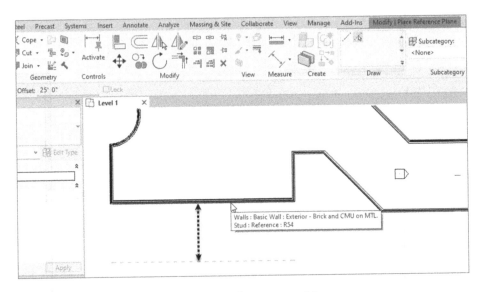

FIGURE 2.17 Adding another reference plane to our model

7. Select the south wall, right-click, and select Create Similar.

8. On the Options bar, change Offset to 15′–0″ (4500 mm).

9. Pick the midpoint on the outside face of the south wall, as shown in Figure 2.18.

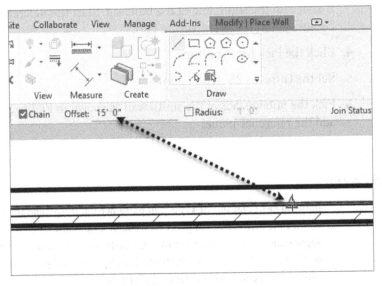

FIGURE 2.18 Adding the new walls requires picking the outside face of this wall. Make sure Offset is set to 15′–0″ (4500 mm) on the Options bar.

10. Draw the wall 25′ (7500 mm) down from the south wall by typing 25 (7500 mm) and pressing Enter.

11. After you pick the 25′ (7500 mm) distance, move your cursor up, back toward the wall, as shown in Figure 2.19, resulting in a 25′-long (7500 mm) wall.

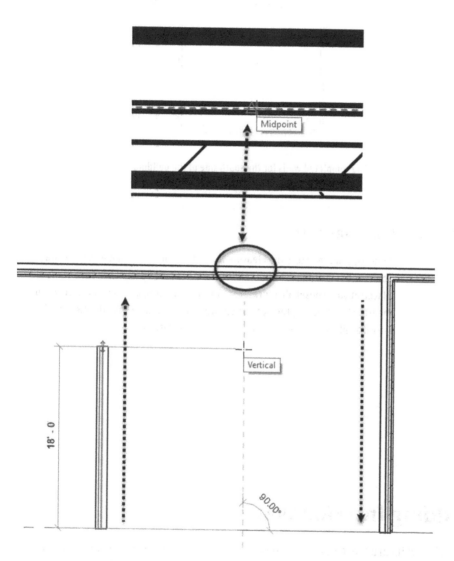

FIGURE 2.19 By using the Offset command as you draw walls, you can use one common centerline.

12. Set Offset to 0. Draw a wall across the front of the two walls, as shown in Figure 2.20. Make sure it's flipped in the right direction.

Your walls should look like Figure 2.20.

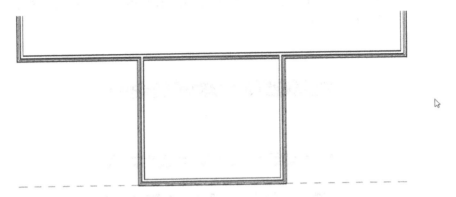

FIGURE 2.20   The completed walls for the south side of the building

---

DOES IT MEASURE UP?

In Revit, you can access the Measure function, which is the same as the Distance command in Autodesk® AutoCAD® software. To verify whether your walls are placed at your chosen distances, click the Measure icon as shown here. After you measure the distance, the Options bar will show you the result. The Measure icon is also available on the Measure panel of the Modify tab.

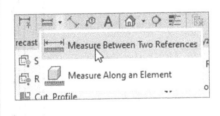

Adding Interior Walls

Interior walls are basically the same as exterior walls in terms of how they're placed in the model. This is a good thing. Luckily, you can be slightly more relaxed with the justification. Now that the building has a footprint, you can see more easily whether the walls need to be adjusted.

You'll start by laying out an elevator shaft and a stairwell, using an 8″ (200 mm) CMU wall system. Follow these steps:

1. Open or make sure you're in Floor Plan Level 1. Zoom into the northeast corner of the building, as shown in Figure 2.21.

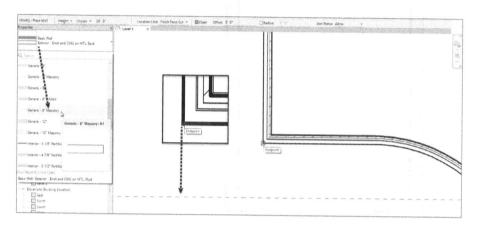

FIGURE 2.21 Start drawing the 8″ (200 mm) CMU elevator shaft in the corner indicated here. Turn on Thin Lines if you need to.

2. On the Architecture tab, click the Wall button.

3. In the Type Selector, select Generic - 8″ Masonry, as shown in Figure 2.21. (Metric users, use the Generic - 225 mm Masonry wall.)

4. For the starting point, pick the corner as shown in Figure 2.21. The wall will probably be in the wrong orientation, so if necessary, tap the spacebar to flip the wall's orientation.

5. Move your cursor downward, and type 12′ (3600 mm). The wall will be 12′ long.

6. Move your cursor to the right, and type 10′ (3000 mm).

7. Move your cursor back up the view, and pick the exterior wall.

8. Press Esc. You should have three walls that look like Figure 2.22.

At this point, you have some walls in the model. It's time to look at ensuring that these walls are accurately placed, so you need to check the dimensions.

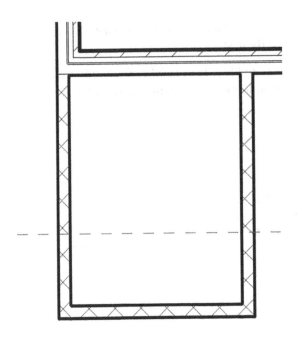

FIGURE 2.22 The elevator shaft begins to take shape.

Using Temporary Dimensions to Gain Control of Your Model

After you place items in a model, you usually need to make some adjustments. Revit does a good job with this; however, there are some rules to which you need to adhere. The goal here is to have a clear 10′–0″ (3000 mm) dimension on the inside faces of the shaft. At this point, you should assume that you don't. This is where temporary dimensions come into play. To start working with temporary dimensions, follow these steps:

1. Select the right, vertical CMU wall. A blue temporary dimension appears, as shown in Figure 2.23.

2. On the temporary dimension, you see some blue grips. If you hover your cursor over one of them, a tooltip appears, indicating that this grip represents the witness line.

3. Pick the grip to the right side of the dimension. Notice that it moves to the outside face of the wall. Pick it again, and notice that it moves to the inside face. This is exactly where you want it. Make sure the grip on the left is also on the inside face.

4. The actual increment in the dimension is blue. Select the blue dimension, type 10′ (3000 mm), and press Enter. The wall that was selected moves to accommodate the new increment, as shown in Figure 2.24.

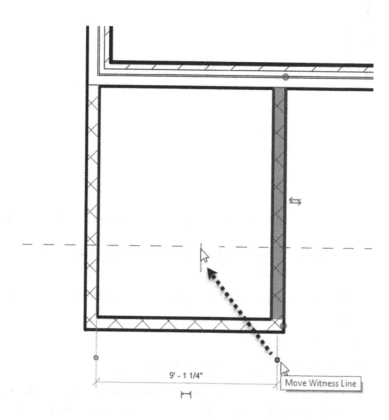

FIGURE 2.23 Temporary dimensions can be adjusted to measure from different wall faces by picking the witness-line grip.

Temporary Dimension Settings

Revit measures the default dimension for the temporary dimensions from the center of the walls—which is typically the last place from which you want to take the dimension. You can change some settings to fix this action:

1. On the Manage tab, click Additional Settings ➤ Annotations ➤ Temporary Dimensions, as shown in Figure 2.25.

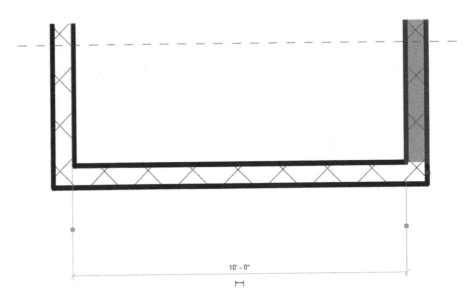

10' - 0"

FIGURE 2.24 The selected wall is the wall that will move when you type the new dimension.

2. In the Temporary Dimension Properties dialog box, select Faces in the Walls group.

3. In the Doors and Windows group, select Openings, as shown in Figure 2.26.

4. Click OK.

5. Select the south horizontal interior wall.

6. To the right of the dimension, you see a small blue icon that also looks like a dimension. If you hover your mouse over it, a tooltip appears, indicating that you can make the temporary dimension permanent, as shown in Figure 2.27. When you see this tooltip, click the icon.

7. Press Esc.

8. Select the same wall again. Notice that the permanent dimension turns blue. You know that anything that turns blue in Revit can be edited. You can change this increment any time you wish.

9. Change the dimension to 12′ (3600 mm), and click out of the dimension text. The wall moves into position, and the dimension is now an even 12′ (3600 mm).

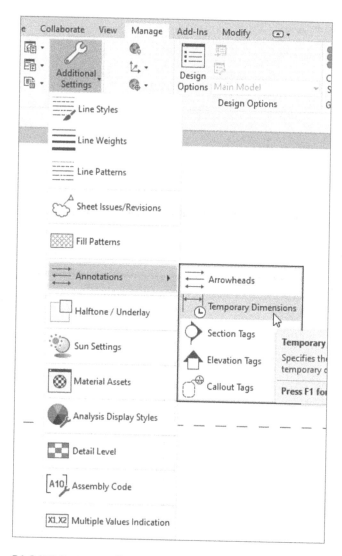

FIGURE 2.25 The Temporary Dimensions function lets you control where Revit measures the temporary dimensions.

You need one more shaft wall to create a separation between the exterior walls and the shaft, as shown in Figure 2.28. Perform these steps:

1. Select any CMU wall, and click Create Similar.

2. On the Draw panel, click the Pick Lines icon.

3. On the Options bar, type 10′ (3000 mm) in the Offset field.

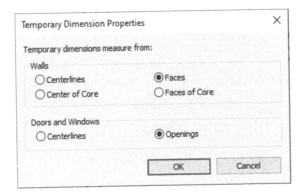

FIGURE 2.26 The most popular configuration for temporary dimensions

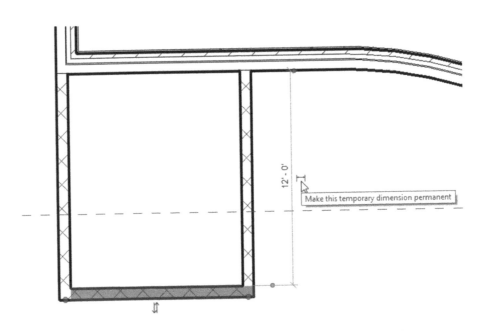

FIGURE 2.27 You can make temporary dimensions permanent.

4. On the Options bar, be sure Location Line is set to Finish Face: Interior.

5. Offset the south CMU shaft wall (from the inner line). Doing so separates the shaft from the exterior and creates a little chase.

6. Press Esc twice. Figure 2.28 shows the shaft wall. Make sure that you check your dimensions before proceeding.

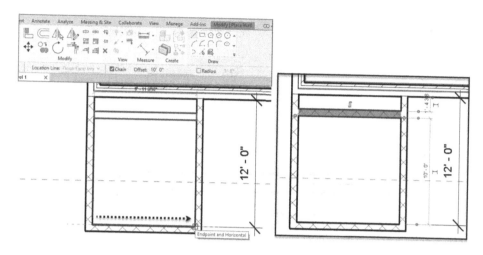

FIGURE 2.28 The shaft wall

The next task is to mirror these walls to the other side:

1. Pick a window around all the masonry walls (a window with your cursor, not an actual window).

2. On the Modify | Walls tab, click the Mirror ➤ Pick Axis button, as shown in Figure 2.29.

3. Pick the horizontal reference plane in the center of the building. Your walls are now mirrored, as shown in Figure 2.30.

4. Save the model.

You're starting to get the hang of adding different wall types—but you aren't finished yet. You still need to add quite a few interior partitions.

DID YOU SELECT TOO MUCH?

If you picked a window around all of your walls and have more items selected than you wish, you can press the Shift key on your keyboard and pick the item(s) you want to deselect. Doing so removes the item from the selection set. If the opposite happens and you want to add an item, press the Ctrl key and pick the item(s) you want to add. Your cursor will always appear with a plus or a minus sign, as shown here:

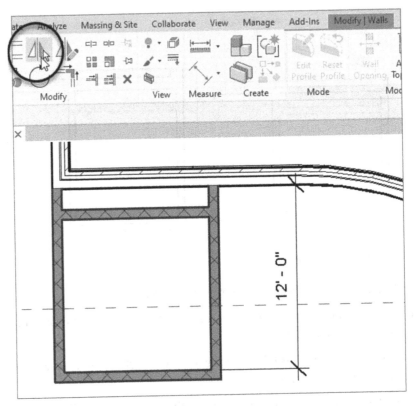

FIGURE 2.29 The Mirror ➤ Pick Axis command is activated when you have objects selected.

Placing Interior Partitions

You'll probably be placing a lot more interior walls than exterior walls. Given the dimensional nature of placing these types of walls in Revit, you don't need to bother with reference planes as often as when you place the exterior walls.

Knowing that, creating interior partitions is somewhat easier than creating the exterior variety. With the exterior type, you must place partitions carefully, and constant double-checking is crucial. With interior partitions, you can typically get the wall where you think you need it. You can then go back and make adjustments without disturbing too many adjacent items. Not that you have to do it this way—you can be accurate to begin with—but life is all about second chances!

To start adding interior partitions, you'll add the necessary lavatories and egress and then fill the spaces with offices. When completed, this stage will look like Figure 2.31.

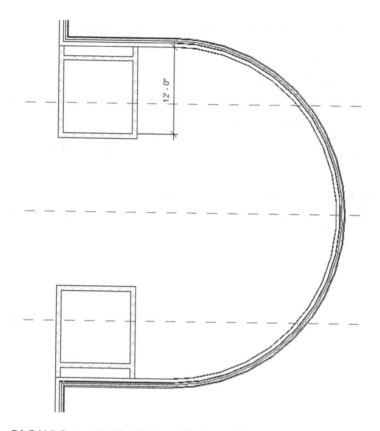

FIGURE 2.30 The elevator shaft is now mirrored.

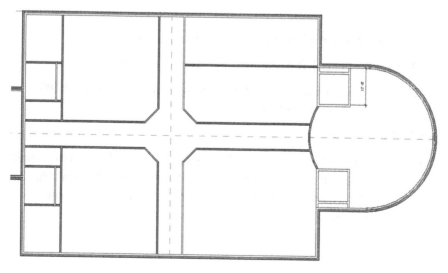

FIGURE 2.31 The east side of the building with egress and lavatories

The objective of the next procedure is to begin adding interior partitions:

1. Make sure you're on Floor Plan Level 1.

2. On the Architecture tab, click the Wall button.

3. In the Type Selector, select Interior - 6 1/8″ Partition (2-hr). Interior users select 135 mm Partition (2-hr).

4. For Height, choose Level 2 from the menu (if it isn't already the current selection).

5. For Location Line, choose Finish Face: Interior.

6. On the Draw panel, click the Start-End-Radius Arc button (upper right in Figure 2.32).

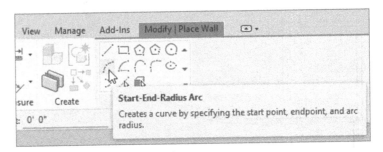

FIGURE 2.32 Choosing options should be old hat by now! The Start-End-Radius Arc button is at the middle right on the Ribbon.

7. Pick the lower-left corner of the upper CMU walls.

8. Pick the upper-left corner of the bottom CMU walls.

9. Move your cursor to the left, and specify a radius of 20′–0″ (6000 mm), as shown in Figure 2.33.

10. Press Esc twice.

11. Many times, Revit won't join the walls correctly. If this occurs, simply select the wall you just drew. At the ends, there are little blue grips. Pick and drag them into the wall you want it to join to, as shown in Figure 2.34.

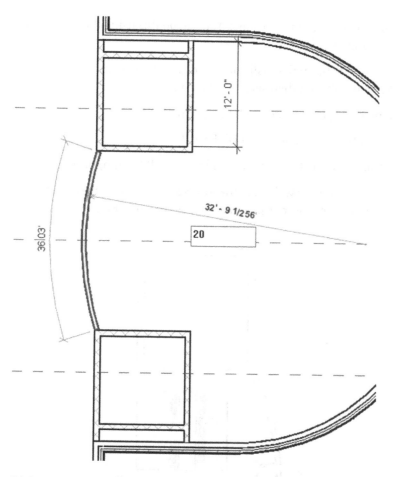

FIGURE 2.33 Drawing an arched radial wall requires a three-point method. It's similar to the Start-End-Direction command in AutoCAD.

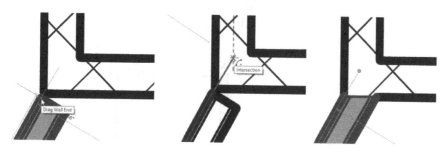

FIGURE 2.34 Editing the wall joins using grips

You now need to add some corridor walls. You can do this using the center reference plane you established earlier:

1. If you aren't still in the Wall command, select and then right-click the radial wall, and then select Create Similar.

2. On the Draw panel, click the Line button.

3. For Location Line, choose Finish Face: Interior.

4. For Offset (on the Options bar), add a 4′–0″ (1200 mm) offset.

5. To start placing the wall, pick the intersection of the center reference plane and the center of the radial wall, as shown in Figure 2.35.

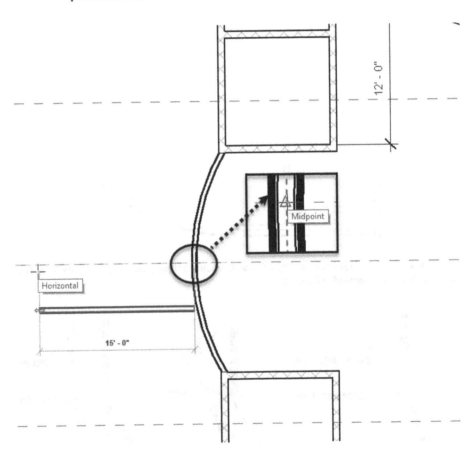

FIGURE 2.35 Drawing corridor walls using an offset can be a great time-saver.

6. Move your cursor to the left. Notice that the wall is being drawn but at an offset of 4'–0" (1200 mm) from the "line" you're drawing up the middle of the building.

7. For the second point of the wall, pick the intersection or endpoint of the vertical wall to the left.

8. Move your cursor back to the right. Notice that the other side of the wall is being drawn at a 4'–0" (1200 mm) offset. This time, it's on the opposite side of the reference line.

9. Pick the intersection of the reference plane and the radial wall as the second point, as shown in Figure 2.35.

10. If the walls don't join, drag the grips on the endpoints of the walls as we did in Figure 2.34.

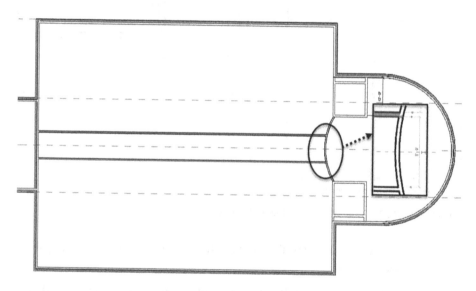

F I G U R E 2 . 3 6 Completing the main corridor. You still might have to drag the walls together to join them.

The next step is to add the lavatories. These will show up at the west end (left side) of the building. Refer to Figure 2.37 for the dimensions, and follow along:

1. Select and then right-click one of the corridor walls, and select Create Similar from the menu.

2. Look at your options, and create the lavatories shown in Figure 2.37. All of the dimensions are taken from the finish inside face.

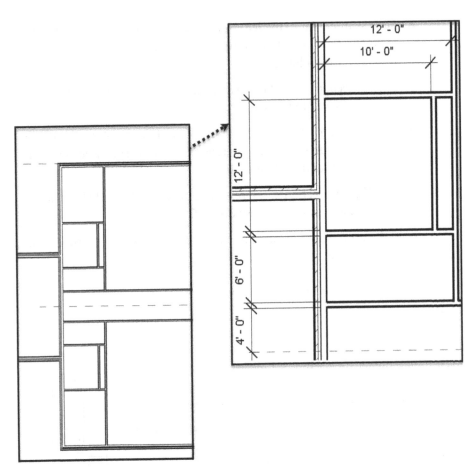

FIGURE 2.37 The lavatories at the west side of the building

Remember, if the wall is going in the wrong direction, tap the space-bar to flip it.

After you draw in the lavatory walls, mirror the walls to the other side of the building, as shown in Figure 2.38.

 WARNING Picking a grip on the end of a wall also means that you get a temporary dimension. Look at it! If it doesn't say 8′–0″ (2400 mm) to the inside face of the corridor, you have a problem. It's much better to discover these discrepancies early in the design stage than to find out that you have a dimensional issue when the drawings are going out the door. If the increment isn't 8′–0″ (2400 mm), first verify that the temporary dimension is going to the inside face. If not, pick the blue grip and move the witness line to the inside face of the walls. If the dimension is still off, move the witness line to the center reference plane. Now type 4′ (**1200** mm), and press Enter. Repeat the process for the other wall. Always check dimensions like this. The time you save could be your own!

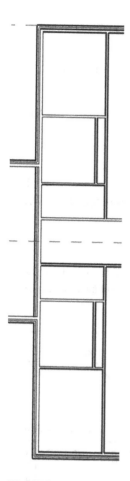

FIGURE 2.38 Both the North and South lavatories

You now need another corridor running north and south, as shown in Figure 2.39. The best way to approach this task is to add another reference plane and then add the walls in a fashion similar to the method applied to the east/west corridor. To open up the central area, you'll add 45° walls at 4′–0″ (1200 mm). Follow these steps to add the new walls:

1. Delete the top and bottom reference planes used to model the corridors. They are getting annoying.

2. On the Work Plane panel of the Architecture tab, click Ref Plane.

3. Draw a reference plane from the midpoint of the top exterior wall to the midpoint of the bottom exterior wall.

4. Click the Measure Between Two References button. Make 100 percent sure that this is the center of the building. You're going to rely heavily on this line.

5. Right-click on one of the interior partitions, and select Create Similar.

6. On the Options bar, be sure Location Line is set to Finish Face: Interior and that Offset is 4'–0" (1200 mm).

7. Pick the top intersection or endpoint of the reference plane and the exterior wall.

8. Draw the wall down to the bottom of the building.

9. Keeping the Wall command running, draw the other side of the corridor by picking the same two points along the reference plane. When you're finished, press Esc.

TIP   Are the reference planes really necessary? No, they aren't. But using them is a good, sound approach to laying out your building. These lines will be used heavily throughout the life of your project.

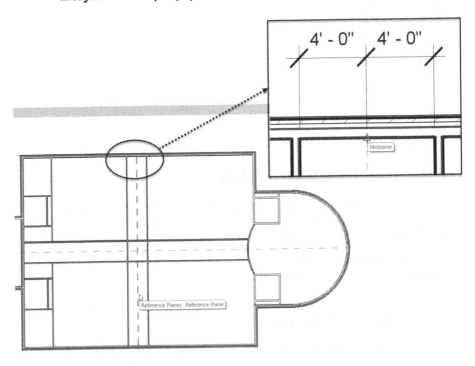

FIGURE 2.39 Using a reference plane to add two vertical corridor walls

You've created an area in the middle of the building where four walls intersect each other. In a moment, you will add 45° walls there to open the corridor at this area. See Figure 2.40 for a preview of the completed corridor intersection.

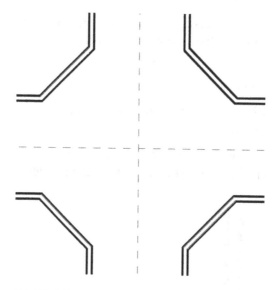

FIGURE 2.40 A preview of the corridor with the 45° walls added

1. Zoom into the intersection of the corridors.

2. On the Architecture tab, click Ref Plane on the Work Plane panel.

3. On the Draw panel, click the Pick Lines button, and change Offset to 4'–0" (1200 mm).

4. From the finish inside face of the top, horizontal corridor wall, offset the reference plane up (see Figure 2.41).

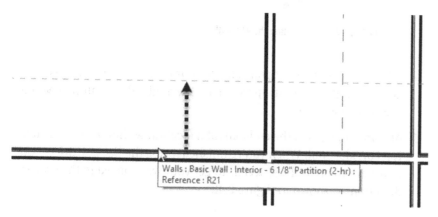

Walls : Basic Wall : Interior - 6 1/8" Partition (2-hr) :
Reference : R21

FIGURE 2.41 Adding yet another reference plane to the model. You'll delete this one.

T I P It can be tricky to get the reference plane going in the correct direction. If the reference plane is being stubborn and is still trying to offset the line down, move your cursor up a little. The reference plane will change direction.

After you establish the reference plane, you can add the new wall. It can be as simple as drawing the wall in, but there are still a few little procedures of which you should be aware:

1. Start the Wall command.

2. On the Options bar, be sure the wall's Location Line is justified from Finish Face: Exterior.

3. Pick the intersection of the reference plane and the inside finished face (right face) of the left vertical corridor wall (see Figure 2.42).

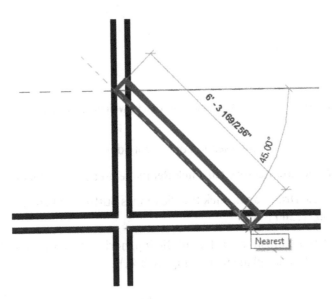

FIGURE 2.42 Adding the 45° wall

4. After you pick the start point, move your cursor to the left and down at a 45° angle. (You can approximate the angle; Revit will snap you to the correct angle.)

5. At a 45° angle, pick the endpoint at a location within the horizontal, top corridor wall. When you're finished, press the Esc key twice. You may have to press the spacebar to get your wall flipped in the proper direction, as shown in Figure 2.42.

WARNING If you proceed with assuming that these walls are a specific increment (4′ [1200 mm]) from the inside face, you may be making a big mistake. Take distances after you add walls—especially if the walls aren't 90°.

The next task is to mirror the walls. This part will be easy because you put in those reference planes:

1. Select the 45° wall.

2. Pick Mirror Pick Axis from the Modify | Walls tab.

3. Pick the vertical reference plane, and voilà! The wall is mirrored, as shown in Figure 2.43.

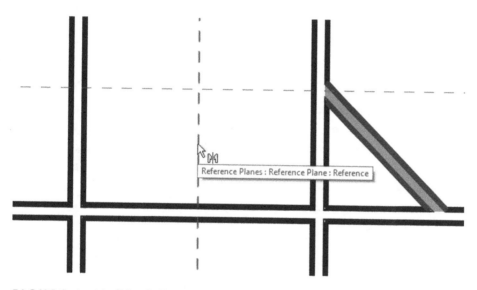

FIGURE 2.43 Using the Mirror command in conjunction with a reference plane is a good example of thinking ahead.

EYEBALLING WITH ACCURACY

You may notice that when you're using temporary dimensions, the increment always seems to snap to even increments. This is no accident. If you click the Snaps button on the Manage tab, you'll see values for Length Dimension Snap Increments and Angular Dimension Snap Increments. These values change based

(Continues)

EYEBALLING WITH ACCURACY *(Continued)*

on the zoom percentage. The closer you zoom in, the smaller the increments get. You can also add to these values by typing a semicolon and adding a new increment to the end of the list, as shown here:

Snaps   ✕

☐ Snaps Off   (SO)

Dimension Snaps

Snaps adjust as views are zoomed.
The largest value that represents less than 2mm on screen is used.

☑ Length dimension snap increments

    4'; 0' 6"; 0' 1"; 0' 0 1/4";

☑ Angular dimension snap increments

    90.00°; 45.00°; 15.00°; 5.00°; 1.00°;

Object Snaps

☑ Endpoints	(SE)	☑ Intersections	(SI)
☑ Midpoints	(SM)	☑ Centers	(SC)
☑ Nearest	(SN)	☑ Perpendicular	(SP)
☑ Work Plane Grid	(SW)	☑ Tangents	(ST)
☑ Quadrants	(SQ)	☑ Points	(SX)

[Check All]   [Check None]

☑ Snap to Remote Objects	(SR)	☑ Snap to Point Clouds	(PC)
☑ Snap to Coordination Models	(LM)		

Temporary Overrides

While using an interactive tool, keyboard shortcuts (shown in parentheses) can be used to specify a snap type for a single pick.

Object snaps	Use shortcuts listed above
Close	(SZ)
Turn Override Off	(SS)
Cycle through snaps	(TAB)
Force horizontal and vertical	(SHIFT)
Snap Mid Between 2 Points	(S2)
Force Perpendicular (Measure 3D)	(CTRL)

[Restore Defaults]

[OK]   [Cancel]   [Help]

4. Select the two 45° walls, and mirror them around the horizontal reference plane. You should now have four 45° walls, as shown in Figure 2.44.

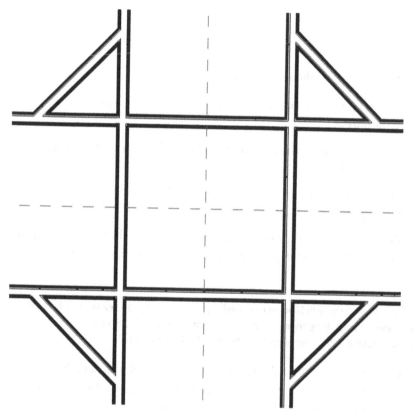

FIGURE 2.44 Stuck inside these four walls

5. Delete the temporary horizontal offset reference plane by selecting it and clicking the Delete button on the keyboard.

Now it's time for some further cleanup. Although all the modify commands will be featured in Chapter 4, "Working with the Autodesk Revit Tools," you can still use some here. You've already borrowed the Mirror command from that chapter. You might as well borrow the Split command too:

1. On the Modify panel of the Modify tab, click the Split Element button, as shown in Figure 2.45.

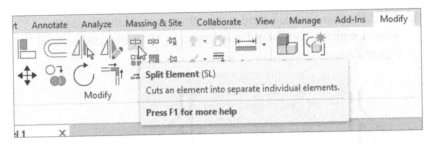

F I G U R E 2 . 4 5 Using the Split Element command

2. Always look at the Options bar! Select the Delete Inner Segment option.

3. Pick a point along the top horizontal corridor wall near the intersecting 45° wall.

4. Pick the second point along the same wall, only on the opposite side (see Figure 2.46).

5. Repeat the process for the other three walls. You should now have an open central area for your corridor, as shown in Figure 2.46.

 N O T E If the Split Element command is giving you a splitting headache rather than splitting the walls, keep trying. We'll also cover this in Chapter 4. Commands such as Split Element require a different touch than the AutoCAD Break command.

Looking back, you've accomplished quite a bit. Laying out walls and then modifying them to conform to your needs is a huge part of being successful in Revit, but you aren't finished. The next few processes will involve dealing with different types of walls that merge together. Historically, merging walls has been an issue in modeling software. Although Revit tends to clean up these areas a little better than other modeling applications, you must still cope with some sticky areas. Let's create a sticky situation!

Editing Wall Joins

A separate function in Revit deals with editing wall joins—specifically, the Edit Wall Joins command, which can come in quite handy. To get started, let's add more walls to an already busy corner of the building:

1. Zoom into the lower northeast corner of the building, as shown in Figure 2.48, and set the detail level to Fine.

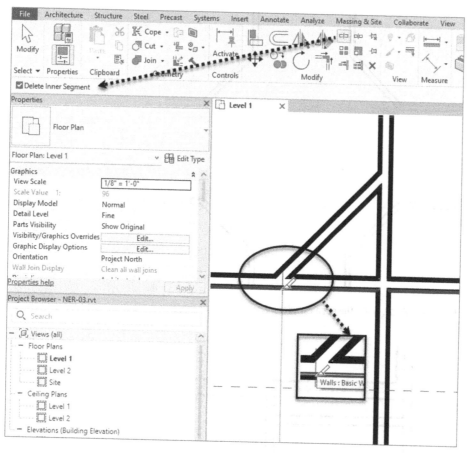

FIGURE 2.46 Split the wall at two points. If you've selected Delete Inner Segment, the result is to eliminate the wall between the two points.

2. Start the Wall command. Make sure it's the same 6 1/8" (135 mm) two-hour partition you've been using.

3. With the Chain button off and Location Line set to Finish Face: Exterior, to start the wall, pick the intersection where the CMU wall abuts the finish inside face of the exterior wall (see Figure 2.49). Again, you can turn on Thin Lines to get a better view of what you're seeing.

4. The wall may be flipped in the opposite direction from Figure 2.49. If it is, remember to press the spacebar; doing so flips it up to the proper orientation.

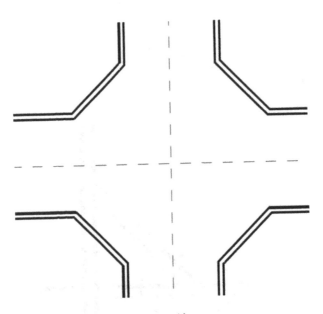

FIGURE 2.47 The open corridor

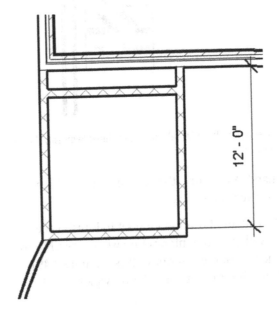

12' - 0"

FIGURE 2.48 The northeast corner

5. Pick the second point of the wall at the corridor in the middle of the building. Press Esc twice. The intersection should look like Figure 2.50.

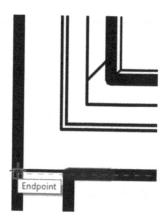

FIGURE 2.49 Adding to the mess in the corner

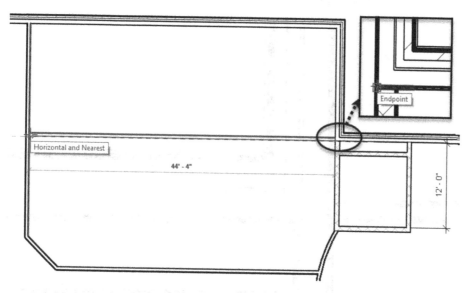

FIGURE 2.50 The wall and the resulting intersection

6. Zoom back in on the intersection. If the view doesn't resemble
   Figure 2.50 in terms of line weight, click the Thin Lines icon, as
   shown in Figure 2.51.

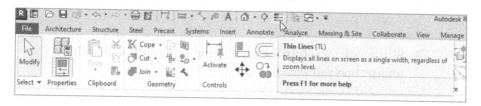

FIGURE 2.51 Click the Thin Lines icon to see how the walls are joining together.

7. On the Geometry panel of the Modify tab, click the Wall Joins button, as shown in Figure 2.52.

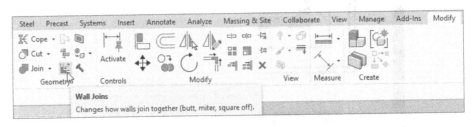

FIGURE 2.52 You'll find the Wall Joins button on the Modify tab.

8. Hover your pointer over the intersection. Revit displays a big box, as shown in Figure 2.53.

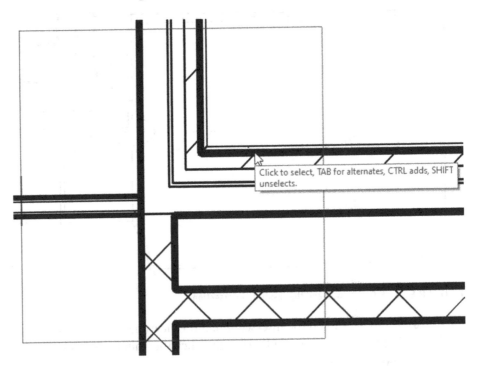

FIGURE 2.53 Choosing the intersection you wish to edit

9. Pick anywhere within the area. Doing so establishes that this is the intersection you wish to edit.

After you pick the intersection, some additional lines appear. These lines expose how Revit is actually looking at the corner.

10. On the Options bar, you now see some choices for configuring this intersection. Select the Miter option, as shown in Figure 2.54. This option is the most popular. When you are done, hit Esc a couple times.

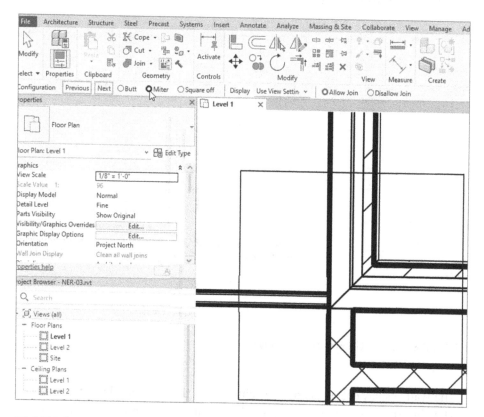

FIGURE 2.54 Adding a mitered join

Although a wall of this type would never have a 45° miter in real life, mitering the corner in Revit allows for a more uniform join between adjacent walls.

Displaying Wall Joins

Usually, in a plan view such as this no wall joins are shown. Typically, only the outside lines join, and an enlarged detail would show the specific construction methods. But in some cases, you want Revit to reveal this information. In Revit, you have two choices for the display (Figure 2.55):

Clean All Wall Joins   This option joins together the same materials in each wall, regardless of the wall type.

Clean Same Type Wall Joins   Stating the obvious, this option clean joins only within walls of the same type.

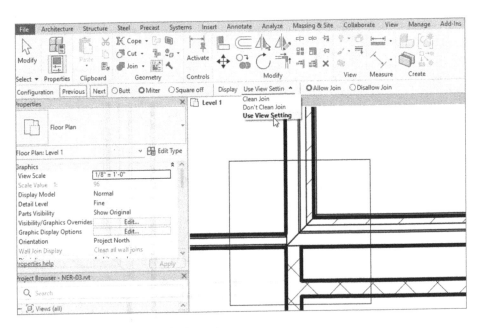

FIGURE 2.55 Choosing a display option

The Wall Display option is not selectable unless the detail level is set to Coarse. The objective of the next procedure is to identify the difference between wall join types:

1. Zoom in on the northwest corner of the east addition, as shown in Figure 2.56.

2. In the Properties dialog, change Wall Join Display to Clean Same Type Wall Joins.

3. Observe the difference between the wall joins, as shown in Figure 2.56.

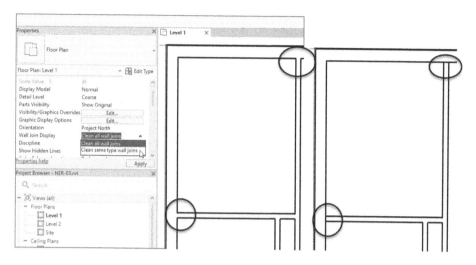

FIGURE 2.56 Choosing a Wall Join Display option in the view's properties

4. Set the wall joins back to Clean All Wall Joins.

5. Save the model.

Disallowing Wall Joins

You must deal with another important item when walls join together. In some cases, you may not want walls to join automatically even if they're the same exact wall type. To learn how to prevent this behavior, follow along:

1. Change Detail Level to Fine.

2. Select the long, horizontal 6 1/8" (156 mm) wall that comes into the corner, as shown in Figure 2.57. A blue grip appears to the right of the intersection. This represents where the wall's extents are located.

3. Hover directly over the blue grip.

4. After the blue grip highlights, right-click.

5. Select Disallow Join (see Figure 2.56).

6. When the wall is unjoined, you can pick the same blue grip and slide the wall back to where you want it to terminate (see Figure 2.58).

7. After the wall slides into place, select it (if it isn't already selected).

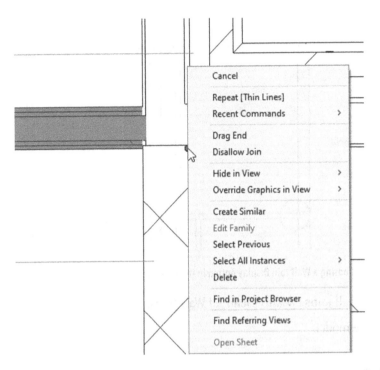

FIGURE 2.57 By right-clicking the wall's end grip, you can tell Revit to disallow that wall's join function.

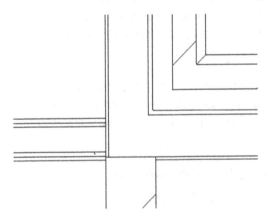

FIGURE 2.58 Slide the wall back to abut the adjacent wall.

8. Notice that there is an additional blue T-shaped icon. (If your Thin Lines is not turned on, this might be difficult to see.) Hover your cursor over this icon; click it to allow the walls to join back up, as shown in Figure 2.59.

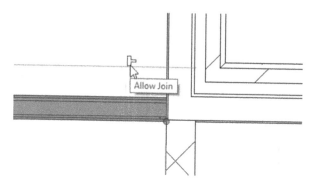

FIGURE 2.59 Allowing the walls to join back up again

As mentioned earlier, your ability to edit wall joins can determine how quickly you start either liking or disliking Revit. This book took a few extra steps in the effort of joining walls, but the experience will carry through, project after project.

We need to investigate one more area before we leave this corner: the area within the chase. Suppose you don't want to run the gypsum into this area. This is a common situation that can cause people to have fits with Revit. Let's try to avoid those fits right now!

Editing the Cut Profile

A plan view is simply a section taken 4'–0" (1200 mm) up the wall from the finish floor. In Revit, you can manually edit the profile of any wall cut in plan. This is extremely useful if, for example, you need to take sections of drywall out of specific areas without creating or adding an entirely new wall. To do this, perform the following steps:

1. Zoom in on the right side of the elevator shaft at the intersection of the exterior wall, as shown in Figure 2.60.

2. Select the east CMU wall, and right-click the blue grip on the end-point of the wall.

3. Select Disallow Join (see Figure 2.60).

4. Pick the blue grip, and drag the wall end back to the face of the wall behind the gypsum.

5. On the Graphics panel of the View tab, click the Cut Profile button, as shown in Figure 2.61.

6. Pick the finish face of the exterior wall. You're selecting the gypsum layer to be cut out of the shaft.

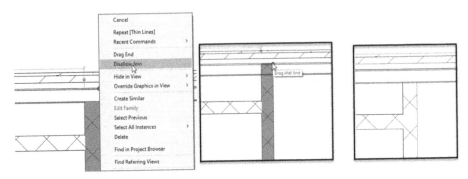

FIGURE 2.60 Pull the CMU out of the wall, disallow the join, and then drag it back into the face of the stud.

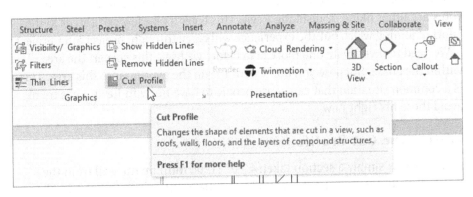

FIGURE 2.61 Click the Cut Profile button, and select the gypsum.

7. You now need to draw a very short vertical line from the inside face of the wallboard to the outside face, as shown in Figure 2.62. Press Esc.

8. When the short line is drawn in, you see a blue arrow. This arrow indicates the side of the material you wish to keep. If you pick the arrow, it flips direction. Make sure it's pointing to the right.

9. What you see here is called Sketch Mode. Because you've finished sketching the cut profile, click Finish Edit Mode, as you can see in Figure 2.63. Figure 2.64 shows the final result.

NOTE If you receive an error that says "Ends of the sketched loop don't lie on the boundary of the face being modified" when you're trying to finish the sketch, it's because you haven't drawn the line exactly from point to point. This line can't cross over, or be shy of, the material you're trying to split. If you're getting this error, select the magenta line. You'll see two familiar blue grips. Pick the grip that doesn't touch the face of the material, and drag it back.

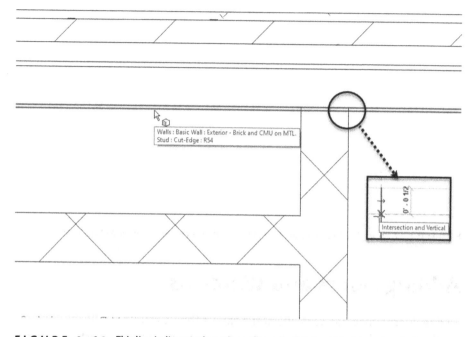

F I G U R E   2 . 6 2   This line indicates where the wallboard will be cut. The blue arrow indicates the side of the material that will remain.

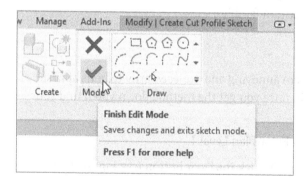

F I G U R E   2 . 6 3   Clicking Finish Edit Mode finalizes the session and completes the command.

Go through and do the same thing to the south side of the building, starting at the Edit Wall Joins section.

There are many more walls left to add, but we need to save something for Chapter 4. At this point, it sure would be nice to start adding some doors and windows to the model.

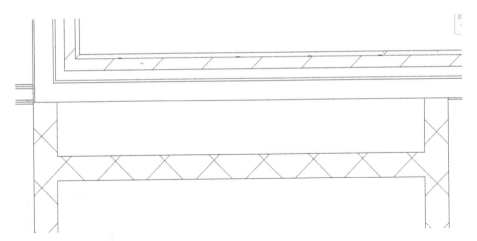

FIGURE 2.64   The finished wall with the drywall deducted from the core of the chase

Adding Doors and Windows

Adding doors and windows is one of the easiest things you'll do in Revit. Finding the correct door or window becomes a bit harder. Creating a custom door or window takes time and patience. In the following sections, you'll focus on adding these items to the model. Chapter 18, "Creating Families," will drill down into the specifics of creating custom families.

Adding Doors

Placing a door in Revit can seem annoying and unnecessarily tedious at first. But like anything else in Revit, once you get the method down you'll find your groove. Follow these steps:

1. Make sure you're in Floor Plan Level 1.

2. On the Architecture tab, click the Door button (see Figure 2.65).

3. Click the Load Family button.

4. Go to the Doors directory, then to the Commercial directory.

5. Select Door-Exterior-Single-Two_Lite.rfa.

6. Click Open, then select the 48″×84″ (1219 mm × 2134 mm) type.

7. Make sure the Tag on Placement button is highlighted, as shown in Figure 2.66.

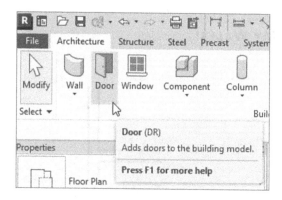

FIGURE 2.65 Adding a door

8. Move your cursor over to the south wall near the elevator shaft, as shown in Figure 2.66. Notice that if your cursor isn't within a wall, you get the NO sign. Revit won't allow you just to place a door into space; a door is considered a hosted family and needs a wall into which it must be embedded.

9. After you get your cursor positioned approximately where Figure 2.66 shows it, move your pointer up and down. Notice that the door's direction changes. This is typical behavior for a door.

10. Press the spacebar. The door swing flips direction.

11. Once the door is positioned where you want it, pick the midpoint of the wall.

12. Make the door face outward and to the left, as shown in Figure 2.66. Then pick a point in the middle of the wall. If you put it in wrong, don't worry; you can just flip it.

◄

Those shortcut overrides come in handy here! Type **SM** for Snap Mid to place the door equally between the CMU wall and the curved wall.

YIKES, LOOK AT MY WALLS!

When you place a door or any opening into a compound wall, you need to tell Revit specifically how to wrap the materials. By default, Revit will stop the brick and any other finish right at the opening. Obviously, this isn't correct. The following steps guide you through wrapping materials at an insert:

1. Select the exterior wall.

2. In the Properties dialog, click the Edit Type button, as shown here:

(Continues)

YIKES, LOOK AT MY WALLS! *(Continued)*

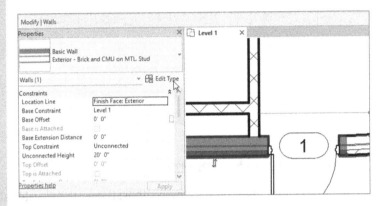

3. In the drop-down menu that specifies Wrapping At Inserts, select Exterior

4. Select Exterior for Wrapping at Ends.

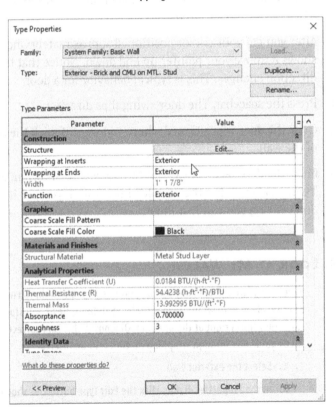

5. Click OK.

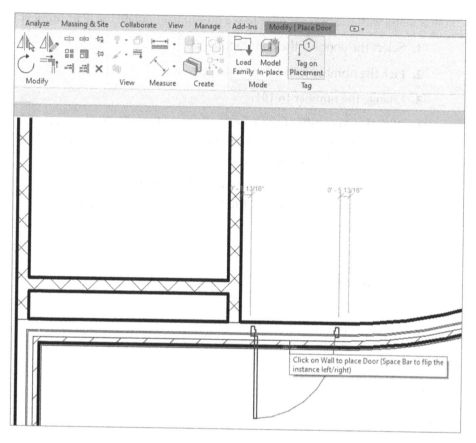

FIGURE 2.66 Placing a door always requires a host. Remember, you can press the spacebar to change the orientation and move your cursor up and down to flip the direction.

Notice that when the door is placed, a tag appears with an automatic number. This happens when Tag on Placement is activated on the Tag panel in the Modify | Place Door tab. In Revit, after you place a door, you should press Esc twice and then go right back and select the door. Doing so highlights the door and activates a few different options.

Editing Door Tags

Let's concentrate on the tag now. The number contained within the "box" is an instance parameter. That means each door in the model will contain a unique number. When you place a door, this number will be added automatically. Revit knows not to duplicate this number. As each door is placed, Revit will assign the next sequential number to the door. This number, of course, can be changed.

Follow along with the next exercise to see how to manipulate the door number:

1. Select the door (or the door tag).

2. Pick the number in the door tag.

3. Change the number to 101.

4. With the door still selected, notice that you have flip arrows as well. If the door isn't in the orientation you see in the previous figures, click these arrows to flip the door.

5. Mirror this door and its tag about the building's horizontal centerline. Notice the number for the new door is 102. See Figure 2.67.

Most items that are added to the Revit model can be selected and flipped using the same method. Also, selecting the items to be flipped and pressing the spacebar has the same effect.

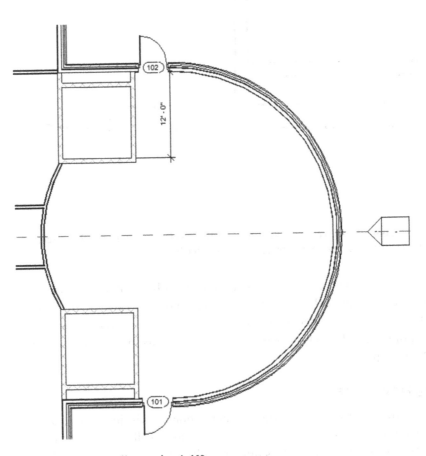

FIGURE 2.67 The new door is 102.

Loading More Families

Let's keep going. It would be nice if all the doors we needed for a project were in our model and we didn't need to keep loading them. We could do that, but I have never worked at a firm that used only a few different types of doors for every project.

1. On the Architecture tab, click the Door button.

2. On the Modify | Place Door tab, click the Load Family button, as shown in Figure 2.68.

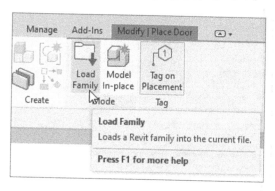

FIGURE 2.68 Click Load Family on the Mode panel.

3. Find the Doors directory, navigate to the Commercial directory, select Door-Exterior-Double.rfa (M_Door-Exterior-Double.rfa), and click Open.

4. Select 72″ × 84″ (1830 × 2134) from the Type Selector.

5. Place the double doors in the wall, as shown in Figure 2.69. Click Esc twice.

6. Mirror the door and tag you just placed using the center reference plane, the same as you did with door 101.

7. Add lavatory doors as shown in Figure 2.70, keeping all offsets 1′-0″ (300 mm) away from the walls. Use Single-Flush: 36″ × 84″ (M_Single-Flush 0915 × 2134).

8. Label the doors accordingly.

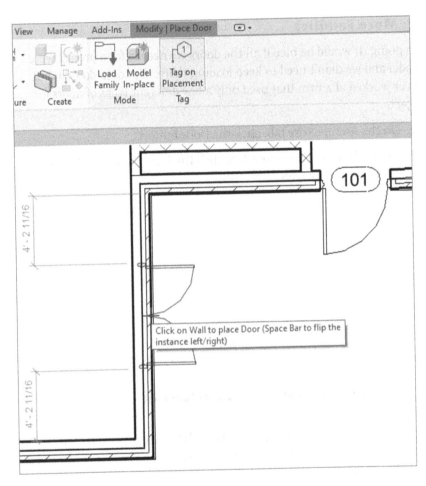

FIGURE 2.69 Placing the double doors

9. In the exterior wall that divides the east building from the corridor, add a Door-Exterior-Double72″ × 84″ door centered on the opening (metric users, use M_Double-Panel 2 1830 × 2134 mm).

10. Change the tag to read **100B**, as shown in Figure 2.70.

You need to add more doors and interior partitions, but they will be best suited for Chapter 4, "Working with the Autodesk Revit Tools," where you can be more accurate. In the meantime, let's add some simple openings.

Placing Openings in Your Walls

I like to think of openings as doors in a sense. That is, you still need to insert something into a wall to create a void. This void can contain casing as well.

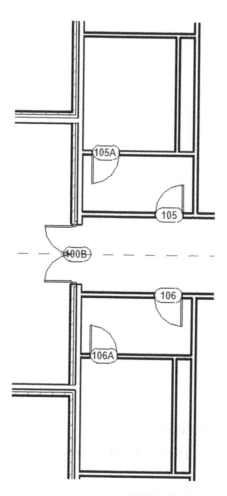

FIGURE 2.70 Adding lavatory doors. You'll have to renumber the tags.

To add an opening to the model, run through these steps:

1. On the Architecture tab, click Component, as shown in Figure 2.71.

2. On the Modify | Place Component tab, click the Load Family button.

3. Browse to the Openings directory.

4. Find the family called Passage Opening-Elliptical Arch.rfa (M_Passage Opening-Elliptical Arch.rfa), and click Open.

5. Click the Edit Type button in the Properties dialog, as shown in Figure 2.72.

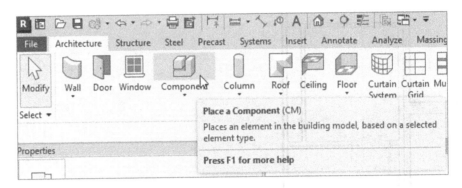

FIGURE 2.71 Clicking Component on the Architecture tab

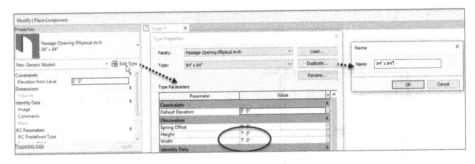

FIGURE 2.72 Adding a new type

6. Click Duplicate in the Type Properties dialog.

7. In the Name dialog, name the opening 84″ × 84″ (2100 mm × 2100 mm), and then click OK.

8. Under Dimensions, change Width to 7′–0″ (2100 mm).

9. Click OK. Then press Esc to clear the command.

10. Zoom into the area shown in Figure 2.72, and place an Interior - 6 1/8″ Partition (2-hr) wall as shown. Interior users place a 135 mm Partition (2-hr) wall as shown. This is the wall into which you'll place the opening.

11. On the Architecture tab, click Component, and place the opening into the wall as shown in Figure 2.73. If you are having trouble finding the midpoint, you can type SM to snap to the midpoint of the wall and then place the opening.

Add two more doors, and you'll be finished with this section:

1. On the Architecture tab, click Door.

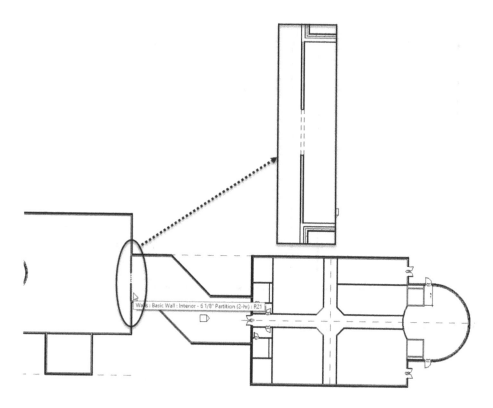

FIGURE 2.73 Two new corridor doors

2. In the Properties dialog, pick Door-Exterior-Double: 72″ × 84″ (M_Door-Exterior-Double 1830 × 2134).

3. Add the double doors to the ends of the vertical corridor, as shown in Figure 2.74.

4. Label the doors 100C and 100D.

Again, there are many more doors and partitions that you can add to the model, but that will have to wait until Chapter 4. Let's move on to add some windows.

Adding Windows

Doors, windows, openings. . .they're all the same. When you have experience adding one, the others are just as easy.

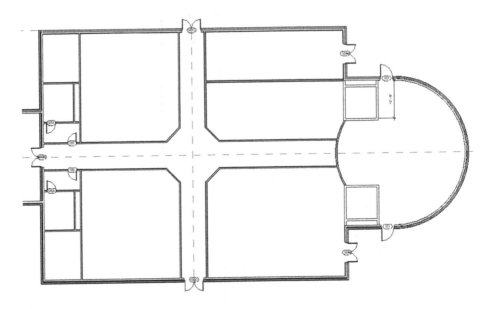

FIGURE 2.74 Two new corridor doors

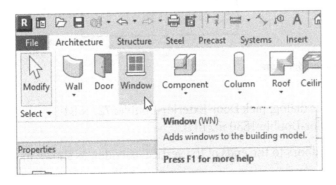

FIGURE 2.75 Adding a window is the same as adding a door.

The objective of the next procedure is to add some windows to the model:

1. On the Architecture tab, click the Window button, as shown in Figure 2.75.

2. Select the Fixed: 36″ × 72″ (M_Fixed 0915 × 1830) window from the Type Selector, and make sure the Tag On Placement button is active.

3. Add the window to the corner of the building, as shown in Figure 2.76. Be careful with the placement. If your cursor is toward the exterior of the wall, the window will be oriented correctly and the window tag will appear on the outside of the wall.

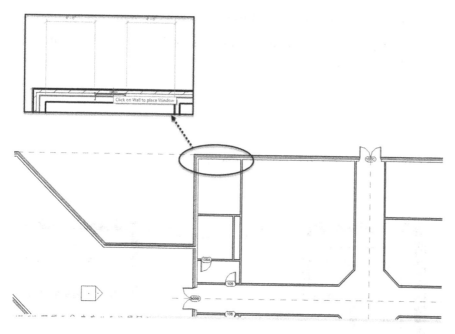

FIGURE 2.76 Depending on which side of the wall your cursor is on, you can add a window to the correct orientation.

4. Select the window and notice your temporary dimensions appear. Select the grip on the temporary dimension that is on the inside face of the exterior wall, as shown in Figure 2.77.

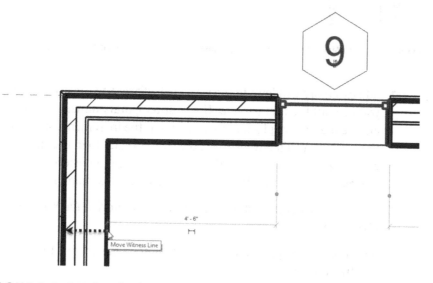

FIGURE 2.77 Dragging the grip on the temporary dimension to the outside face of the exterior wall

5. Drag the grip to the outside face of the exterior wall.

6. Change the temporary dimension to 2'-0"(51 mm), as shown in Figure 2.78.

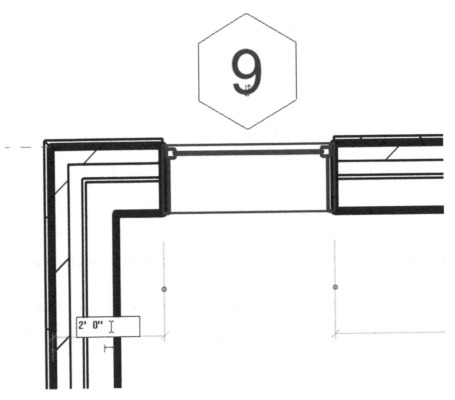

FIGURE 2.78 Make the window 2'-0" (51 mm) from the face of the exterior wall.

7. Add two more windows to the west wall adjacent to the wall in which you just put the first window. Use your temporary dimensions to ensure that you're placing the windows at the increments shown in Figure 2.79. You'll have to place the windows and then use the temporary dimensions to move them to the proper dimensions in a similar manner to placing the first door earlier in this chapter.

8. Mirror the windows and tags using the center horizontal reference plane (see Figure 2.80).

9. Select one of the placed windows. Notice the temporary dimensions and the flip arrows.

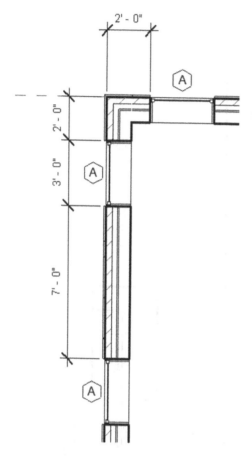

FIGURE 2.79 Placing the windows in the corner of the building and mirroring them

10. Change the tag to read **A** if it is not already. (All of the windows are type A.)

11. You get a warning stating that you're changing a type parameter. Click Yes.

Now that the windows are in place, it's time to investigate how they're built by taking a look at their properties.

Window Properties

Again, just as with doors and openings, you can check the element properties to tweak the unit even further:

1. Select one of the windows.

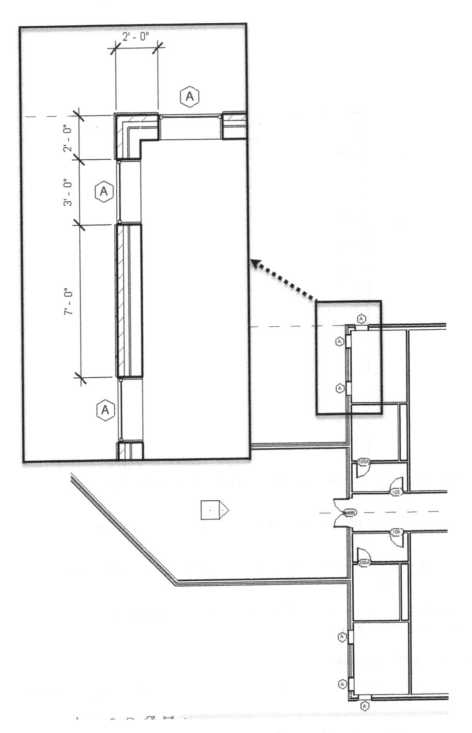

FIGURE 2.80 Changing the tag to read "A"

2. In the Properties dialog, click the Edit Type button, as shown in Figure 2.81.

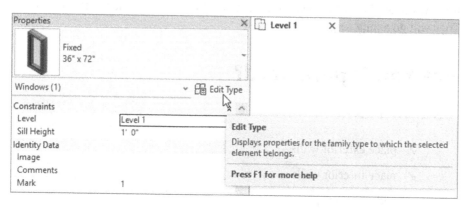

FIGURE 2.81 The Edit Type button in the Properties dialog

 TIP If you want to change an instance parameter (such as Sill Height) for every window in the model, you can. Knowing that an instance parameter applies to only one item, instead of picking just one window you can pick a window, right-click, and choose Select All Instances. From there, you can change every window's parameters in the Properties panel because you had every window selected.

3. Scroll down until you see Type Mark. Notice that this value is set to A. This is the property you changed by typing the value into the tag in the model. Window tags read the Type Mark property by default, whereas door tags read Mark, which is an instance property. In either case, Revit works both ways. If you change a tag value in the model, it changes the parameter value in the tagged object or tagged family (see Figure 2.82).

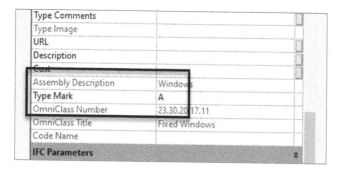

FIGURE 2.82 Changing a type parameter changes every window of that type.

Windows are among the most difficult items in Revit to use out of the box without any real customization. In Chapter 16, we'll dive into creating custom Revit windows. For now, however, remember the lessons learned in this chapter. They will go a long way.

Are You Experienced?

Now you can. . .

- ✓ place exterior walls
- ✓ place interior walls
- ✓ add reference planes
- ✓ join walls
- ✓ use the Split command
- ✓ edit a cut profile
- ✓ add doors
- ✓ add openings
- ✓ add windows

CHAPTER 3

Creating Views

One of the strongest points of the Autodesk® Revit® platform is that it is one single model. This single model, however, has to be broken down into a tangible format that allows the user to navigate through a project. Chapter 1, "The Autodesk Revit World," and Chapter 2, "Creating a Model," featured the Project Browser (which is included in this chapter as well), but what is the Project Browser managing? Well, it's simply managing views of the model. The browser also handles sheets, families, groups, and links, and it can be customized, but you'll use it to open and work with the properties of views more than anything else.

Here's an example: In the Project Browser, under Floor Plans, you'll usually see Level 1. This is a view of the model that just so happens to be a floor plan. Under Elevations (Building Elevation), you'll see East, North, South, and West elevations. These are exactly the same as the floor plans in the sense that they're just views of the model.

This chapter covers the following topics:

▶ **Creating and managing levels**

▶ **Adding sectional and elevation views**

▶ **Controlling your views for aesthetic values**

Creating Levels

This chapter focuses on the creation of views and their relationship to the model. You'll start with possibly the most important function in Revit: creating levels. The power of Revit comes with the single-model concept. By adding levels to a model, you also add floor plans. This two-way interaction is what makes Revit the BIM choice for many users.

As you wander through the floor plans in the Project Browser, you'll see Level 1 and Level 2. Not every job you'll work on will have only a Level 1 and a Level 2. Your task in this section is to create new levels that are appended to floor plans.

To follow along, open the model you've been working on, or go to www.wiley
.com/go/revit2024ner and browse to the Chapter 3 folder. Open the file called
NER-03.rvt. If you wish, you can use an actual project you're working on. You'll
just have to replace any names and specific dimensions with ones that are applicable to your project. Perform these steps:

1. In the Project Browser, double-click the South elevation. It's located
   under Elevations (Building Elevation), as shown in Figure 3.1.

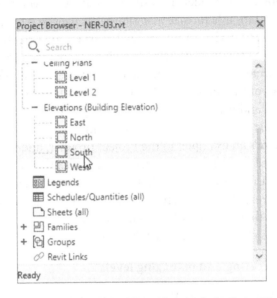

F I G U R E   3 . 1   Finding an elevation in the Project Browser

Notice that at the right side of the building there are two symbols
with a datum at the end. These are elevation markers. Unfortunately,
right now they're somewhat obscured by the exterior wall. Zoom into
this area, as shown in Figure 3.2.

T I P   As you progress through the next few steps, if you don't see what is shown in
the next two figures, try zooming in more and repeating the instructions.

2. Pick (left-click) Level 1. Note that you get several blue icons
   and a lock.

   Where the actual level line intersects the datum bubble, there is
   a hollow blue circle (grip), as shown in Figure 3.3, except that your
   view is slightly obscured by the wall. Move the bubble so that you can
   see the grip clearly.

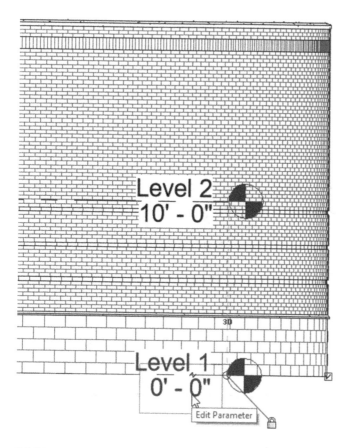

FIGURE 3.2 When dealing with levels, it's a good idea to zoom in close so you can manipulate them.

3. Left-click (pick) the grip, and hold the pick button on the mouse. You can now drag the bubble to the right.

TIP If you hover over any item in Revit and pause for a second, you'll see a tooltip. This will help you verify that you're selecting the correct item.

4. When you get to a point where the level marker is outside the building, pick a spot to place the bubble and the annotation.

5. Press Esc.

Now that the levels are physically in a position where you can work on them, you can start building on them.

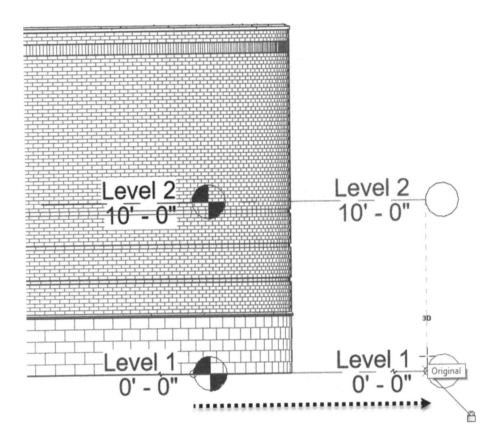

FIGURE 3.3 Picking the grip to drag the level out of the way

Adding Levels

Adding an entirely new level in Revit is quite simple. However, you need to adhere to certain procedures to ensure that you add the levels correctly.

When you use the Level feature in Revit, you should follow two procedures. The first is to look at the Options bar after you start the command. The second is to click the Modify button or press Esc when you've finished. It's easy to get confused as to how Revit wants you to proceed with adding a level, and it's also easy to create multiple levels inadvertently. Remember, in Revit you're always in a command.

To add a level, follow along:

1. Change the height of Level 2 from 10'-0" (3000 mm) to 12'-0" (3658 mm). To do this, double-click on the 10'-0" and type **12**. Then press Enter.

2. On the Datum panel of the Architecture tab, click the Level button, as shown in Figure 3.4.

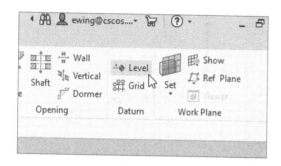

FIGURE 3.4 Adding a level from the Datum panel on the Architecture tab

3. On the Draw panel on the Modify | Place Level tab, you see that you can either draw a line or pick a line, as shown in Figure 3.5. Make sure Pick Lines is selected.

FIGURE 3.5 Choosing the options for the Level command

4. On the Options bar, make sure the Make Plan View option is selected.

5. At the end of the Options bar is the Offset field. Type 12′ (3658 mm), and press Enter. Basically the approach here is to pick Level 2 and create a new level that is offset 12′ (3658 mm) above (see Figure 3.5).

6. With the options set, hover your cursor over Level 2.
   When you come into contact with Level 2, a blue dotted line appears. If you move your cursor slightly above the Level 2 line, the blue alignment line appears above Level 2. If you inch your cursor slightly below Level 2, the blue alignment line appears below Level 2.

7. When you see the blue line appear above Level 2, pick the Level 2 line, as shown in Figure 3.6.

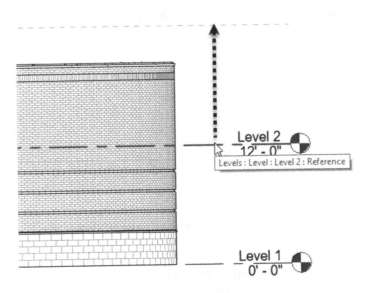

FIGURE 3.6 Waiting for the alignment to appear

TIP You may notice that speeding through the commands as you may have done in Autodesk® AutoCAD® isn't helping you at all in Revit. In Revit, you may need to slow down a bit and let Revit "do its thing." After you get the hang of the Revit behavior, you can speed up again.

You should now have a Level 3 at 24′ (7315 mm), as shown in Figure 3.7.

WARNING Just because you've created a new level, this doesn't tell Revit to shut down the command. Notice that the Options bar is still active and the Pick Lines icon still has the focus. If you start clicking around in the view area, you'll create levels. Every time you pick a point on the screen, a new level will appear. Also, Revit doesn't care if you have a level on top of another level. This situation can get ugly fast.

8. With the Level command still running, create Levels 4, 5, 6, and 7. Your elevation should now look like Figure 3.8. Also, look at your Project Browser. It shouldn't have any levels other than Levels 1 through 7 and Site. You also have new levels under the Ceiling Plans category.

9. On the Select panel of the Ribbon, click the Modify button. You've safely terminated the Level command. (You could also press the Esc key on your keyboard to end the command.)

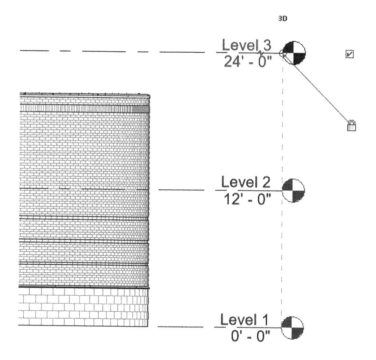

FIGURE 3.7 The completed Level 3. Remember, you're still in the Level command until you tell Revit to stop by hitting Esc.

Now that you have some experience adding levels, it's time to investigate the physical level to see how it can be manipulated and modified.

Understanding the Composition of a Level

Levels have controls that enable the user to adjust the level's appearance. As stated throughout the book, when you select a family, multiple items turn blue. The blue color indicates that these items can be modified. Also, if the level bubbles are blue, that means there is a plan with which the level is associated. If the bubble is black, then no plan is associated. When you select a level, a few additional items will appear.

To investigate further, follow along:

1. Zoom in on Level 7.

2. Select Level 7 by picking (left-clicking) either the text or the level line. This puts the focus on the level line. Notice that the text turns blue. You know that any blue item can be modified (see Figure 3.9).

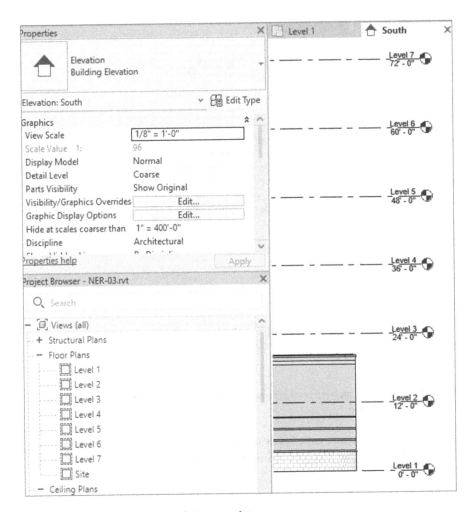

FIGURE 3.8 Levels 1 through 7 are complete.

3. Click the blue Level 7 text field. This enables you to edit the name of the level.

4. Type **PARAPET**, as shown in Figure 3.10, and press Enter.

5. Revit asks whether you want to rename any corresponding views. Click Yes (see Figure 3.11). Level 7 is now the Parapet level, as shown in Figure 3.12.

6. With the Parapet level still selected, click the 72′–0″ (21946 mm) field.

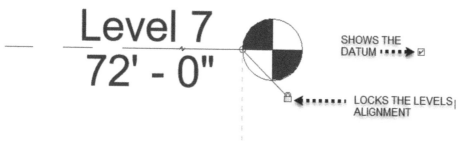

FIGURE 3.9 The selected level

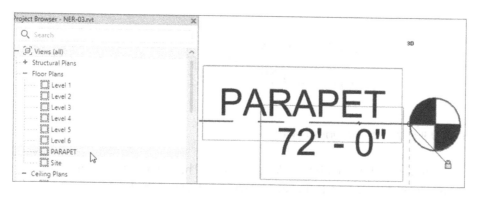

FIGURE 3.10 Renaming the level

Confirm Level Rename   ×

Would you like to rename corresponding views?

☐ Do not show me this message again   Yes   No

FIGURE 3.11 Click Yes to rename corresponding views.

7. Type 62′ (18898 mm), and press Enter. This physically drops the level to the true elevation.

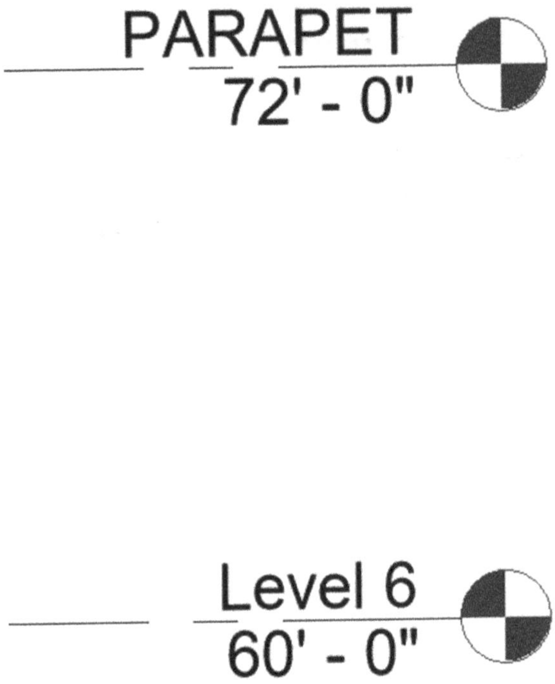

FIGURE 3.12 The renamed level

You now have two slightly overlapping levels. This can be fixed by manipulating some of the controls that appear when you select the level.

Press the Esc key a few times to clear any commands that may be active, and then follow along:

1. Select the Parapet level (if it isn't still selected from the previous exercise).

2. The blue items light up. One of them is the choice to add an elbow, as shown in Figure 3.13. Click it, and Revit bends the level.

3. Now that you've added the elbow, you need to move it. Notice the blue grip at each bend point. Pick the blue grip, as shown in Figure 3.14, and drag the Parapet level out of the level below.

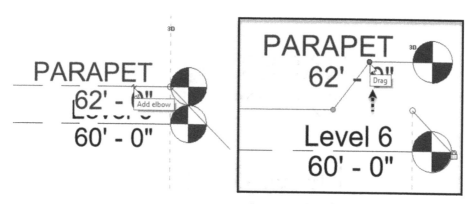

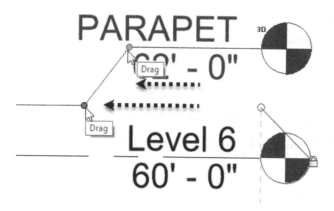

FIGURE 3.13 You can add an elbow to the elevation marker.

FIGURE 3.14 Dragging the level to a new position by using the grips provided

4. The line of the level is still in the way. The two blue grips are still available: pick and drag the horizontal line out of the way of the Parapet text, as shown in Figure 3.15.

Now that you've established the Parapet level, let's make modifications to Level 6. Luckily, the procedures are the same as when you made the modifications to the Parapet level:

1. Press Esc to clear any commands.

> Can't you just type over the dimension? In Revit, you can't have an inaccurate increment. If you type a new value to any increment, the model will change to reflect this new dimension.
> ◀

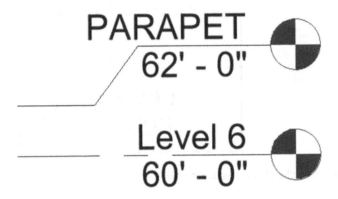

FIGURE 3.15 Making the final adjustments to the level

2. Select Level 6.

3. Pick the blue text that reads Level 6.

4. Rename it to **ROOF**.

5. Press Enter.

6. Click Yes to rename the corresponding views.

7. Press Esc. Your levels should look like Figure 3.16.

Making Other Level Adjustments

Any time we have a building with three distinct sections, levels can start to get muddled and confusing. Before we go making more levels, I'd like to slide the ends down to keep these levels from showing up in other views.

Let's do a couple simple things to pull these levels over.

1. Select the Parapet level. Notice the level is selected as well as a lock that constrains all of the levels below it.

2. Select the blue grip at the left end of the level and drag it to the right so it is about 12″ (305 mm) to the right of the wall that meets the corridor. See Figure 3.17

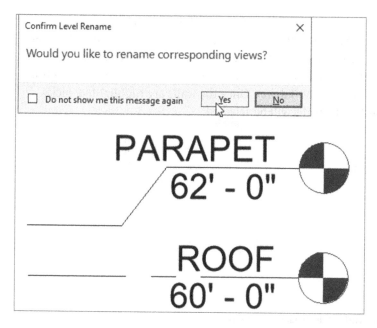

FIGURE 3.16   The Roof and Parapet levels

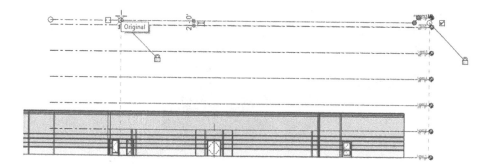

FIGURE 3.17   Dragging the levels to the right

With the two upper levels established, you can constrain some walls up to these levels. Sometimes the best way to do this is to look at the model from a 3D view:

1. Click the Default 3D View icon on the Quick Access toolbar at the top of your screen, as shown in Figure 3.18.

2. The next step is to select all the walls you want to be extended to the Parapet level. In this case, only the east building will go all the way

up to this level. Select the exterior and the elevator shaft walls, as shown in Figure 3.19. (Be sure to select all of the elevator shaft walls as well.) You must hold the Ctrl key to add to the selection. The walls turn blue when they're selected. You can also hover over one of the walls and press the Tab key. Once the walls are highlighted, pick a wall. All of the walls will be selected.

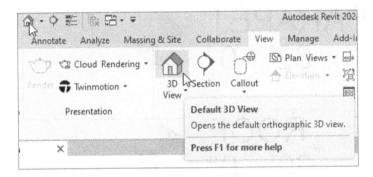

FIGURE 3.18 Clicking the Default 3D View icon

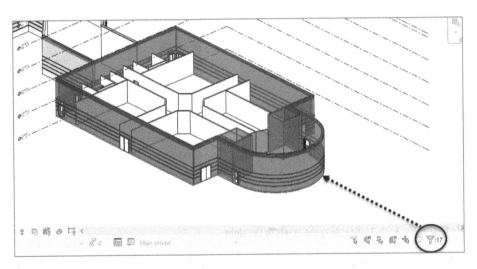

FIGURE 3.19 Selecting the walls that extend to the Parapet level

3. In the Properties dialog, under the Constraints category change Top Constraint to Up To Level: Parapet, as shown in Figure 3.20. Click Apply or move your cursor into the drawing window to set the property change. The walls should now extend to the Parapet level, as shown in Figure 3.21.

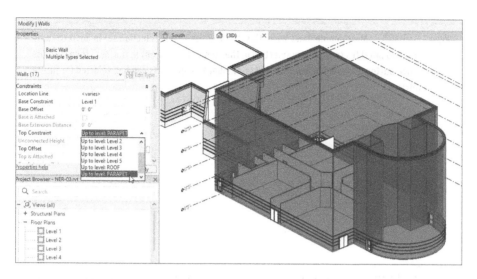

FIGURE 3.20 Setting the top constraint to Up to Level: Parapet

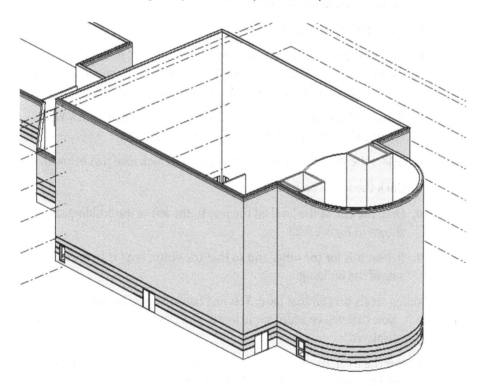

FIGURE 3.21 The walls on the east side of the building are now constrained to the Parapet level.

TIP   Most people don't know this, but you can save a selection set in Revit to come back to later! It's true. Simply select all of the elements you want in the "set," then click the Save button as shown below. This will remember the elements you had selected for future retrieval.

4. In the Project Browser, double-click the South elevation under Elevations (Building Elevation).

5. Start the Level command again.

6. Offset Level 4 up 4' (1200 mm). Remember, you're in the Level command. You must choose Pick Lines on the Draw panel. Also, you must specify an Offset value of 4'–0" (1200 mm) on the Options bar.

7. Rename the 4'–0" (1200 mm) offset level **WEST ROOF**. Click Yes to rename the corresponding views. (See Figure 3.22).

8. Select the West Roof level. Notice there is a lock icon just below it.

9. Click the lock icon to unlock it.

10. Drag the end of the level all the way to the left of the building, as shown in Figure 3.23.

11. Repeat this for the other end so that the entire level is to the west side of the building.

See? Adding levels isn't all that hard. You just need to know how Revit wants you to do it. Now that you've added some levels, you can go back and configure how they're displayed:

1. For the level, uncheck the Show Bubble check box to the *right* of the level lines by clicking the Hide Bubble check box.

2. Display the bubbles to the *left* side of the level line by selecting the Show Bubble check box. The level should now look like Figure 3.24

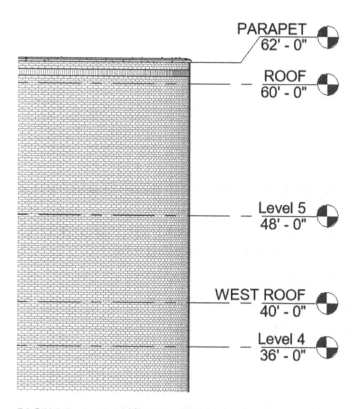

FIGURE 3.22 Adding a new level for the west side of the building

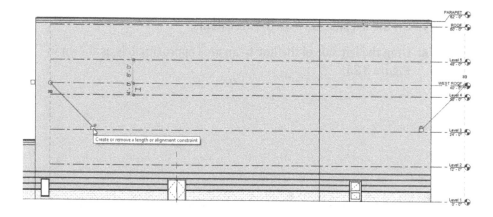

FIGURE 3.23 Unlocking the level

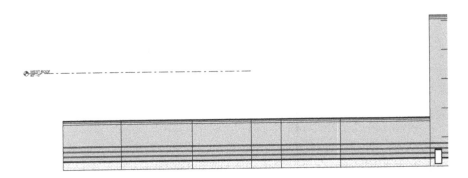

FIGURE 3.24 Using the display bubble toggles to switch the display to the appropriate side of the building

3. Add another level 2′ (600 mm) above Level 3, and call it **CORRIDOR ROOF**. Click Yes to rename the corresponding views.

4. Turn on the level information on the left side.

5. Turn off the level information on the right side.

6. Unlock both ends and drag the level to the position shown in Figure 3.25.

WARNING   On most projects, you'll have to adjust a level's display in different views. Keep in mind that if the 3D button is left on, moving the level in the current view will also move it in other views—sometimes for the better and sometimes for the worse. Switching to 2D can eliminate aggravation.

7. On the left side, turn on the 2D extents.

8. Drag the left side of the line to an area approximately as shown in Figure 3.25.

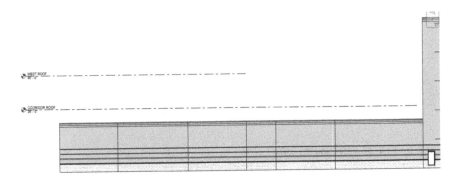

FIGURE 3.25 All the levels are in place for now.

Let's move these walls to their proper levels. Again, in this case it may be a little easier to go to a 3D view so that you can get a good perspective on the results of constraining the tops of the walls. Perform the following steps:

1. Click the Default 3D icon on the Quick Access toolbar.

2. In the 3D view, select the west side of the building, excluding the corridor and the three walls to the south, as shown in Figure 3.26. You should have seven walls selected. To check this, look in the lower-right corner of the Revit window. You see a filter icon with the number 7 next to it. (You need to press and hold the Ctrl key for multiple selections.)

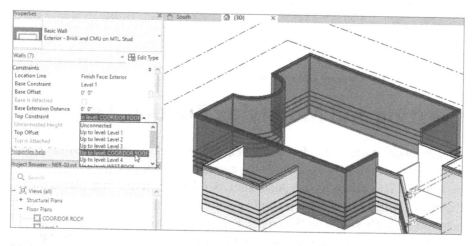

FIGURE 3.26 Selecting the west part of the building

3. In the Properties dialog, set Top Constraint to Up To Level: WEST ROOF. Click Apply or move your cursor into the view window.
   In the 3D view, your walls should grow to meet the new constraints.

4. Press Esc.

5. Select the corridor walls as well as the three south walls whose tops remain unconstrained. (You may need to rotate the view to see everything.)

6. In the Constraints category of the Properties dialog, set Top Constraint to Up To Level: CORRIDOR ROOF (see Figure 3.27).

7. Save the model.

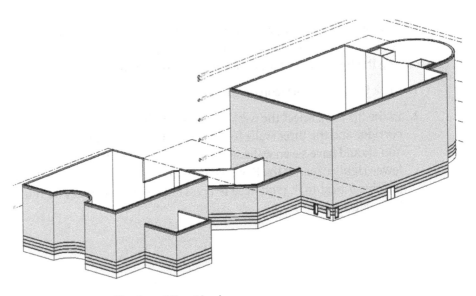

FIGURE 3.27 The three different levels

Creating and Modifying Building Sections

As your model starts to develop, you'll begin to see areas that need further attention. (Certainly, the area where the corridor hits the west building needs to be fixed.) This brings us to a good point. Sections in Revit, when placed into the model, will not only help you build a set of construction documents but also help you work physically on the model. For example, you need to fix the east wall of the west wing. However, you don't have any good views established that focus directly on this area. This is the perfect place to add a section!

Adding a Building Section

To add a section and some important wall-modify commands, follow along:

1. Go to Level 1 Floor Plan, and zoom in on the area where the corridor meets the west wing of the building.

2. On the Create panel of the View tab, select Section, as shown in Figure 3.28.

3. A section takes two picks to place into the model. You must first pick the point for the head; then you pick a point for the tail. To place the section as shown in Figure 3.29, first pick a point below the corridor and to the right of the vertical wall.

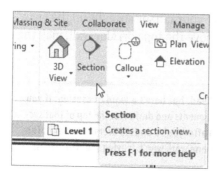

F I G U R E 3 . 2 8   The Section command is found on the Create panel of the View tab.

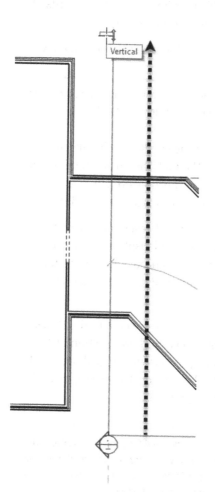

F I G U R E 3 . 2 9   Placing the section into the model

4. After you pick the first point, move your cursor straight up the view. When you're positioned directly above the top corridor wall, pick the second point (see Figure 3.29).

WARNING   I may be jumping ahead, but here's a word of caution: If you cut a section in Revit and then place detail components and draft over the top of that section, you're stuck. Don't flip or move the section after you've drafted over the top of it. The results will be bad. The walls will move, but your line work won't, leaving you with a mess.

With the section placed, a dashed line forms a box around part of the model, as shown in Figure 3.30. This forms the view extents of the section. Anything outside this box won't be shown.

5. You don't need to make an adjustment. I just wanted you to know.

NOTE   If the section isn't selected, you need to select it. You must pick the line of the section, not the bubble. When you pick the line, the section is selected.

6. With the section still selected, notice the small, blue break icon in the middle of the section (see Figure 3.31). Pick the break line (it's called the Gaps In Segments icon). The section is now broken, and you have grips controlling the ends of the break lines (see Figure 3.31).

7. At each end of the section is a blue icon that resembles a recycle symbol. This controls what the section head displays. By selecting this icon, you can choose to have a section head, a tail, or nothing. At the tail of the section, cycle through until you get a section head (see Figure 3.32).

With the section cut, it's time to open the view you've created. In the Project Browser, you now see a new category called Sections (Building Section). Click the plus icon to expand the category. In this category is a view called Section 1. When you cut the section, you added a view to the project. This view carries its own properties and can be drafted over (see Figure 3.33).

TIP   Be organized. Using BIM doesn't negate the need for basic organization. The first thing you should do when creating a section (or any new view, for that matter) is give it a name. If you don't and you leave your sections as Section 1, Section 2, Section 3, and so on, you'll find yourself wasting a lot of time looking for the right view.

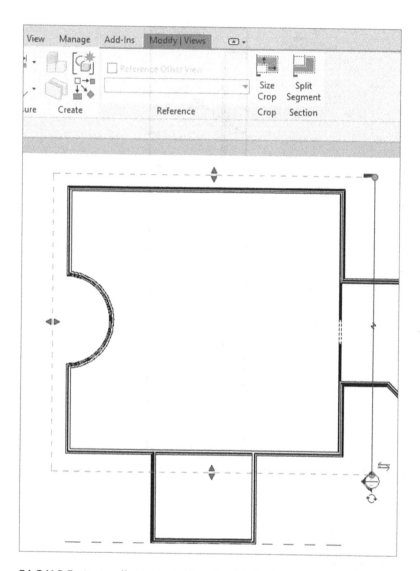

FIGURE 3.30 You can control how deep into the building you want the section to appear.

At this point, you need to name the section and open the view. You can also fix the gap in the wall while you're at it. Perform the following steps:

1. In the Project Browser, select Section 1.

2. Pause a second and click it again. This should allow you to edit the text.

3. Rename the view WEST CORRIDOR SECTION. Press Enter.

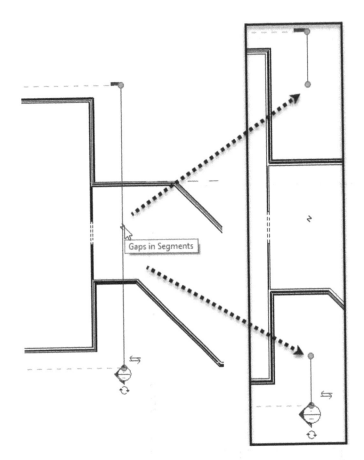

FIGURE 3.31 Adding a gap in the section. You can move your grips to be the same as the figure.

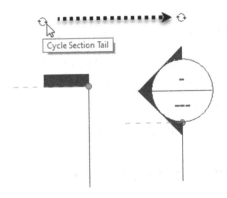

FIGURE 3.32 Cycling through the display choices

FIGURE 3.33   The Project Browser with the new section

4. Double-click the West Corridor Section in the Project Browser. Doing so opens the section. You can see the two corridor walls and the west wing beyond.

5. Notice that you can see the levels for only the west roof and the corridor roof. This is deliberate. The reason is Revit will display only levels and grids that physically pass through the extents of the section.

6. Go to the South elevation.

7. Select Level 1.

8. Unlock the left side of the level.

9. Select the grip and drag it all the way to the left so that it aligns with the other levels, as shown in Figure 3.34.

10. Go back to the West Corridor Section, and notice that Level 1 now shows up. Go back to the South elevation and do the same for Level 2.

11. In the West Corridor Section, select one of the levels and notice there is a small blue icon that says 2D. Click the blue grip and slide the levels to the right, as shown in Figure 3.35.

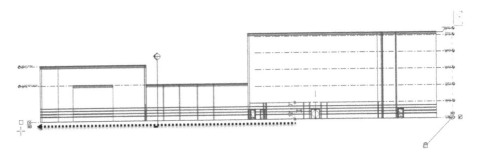

F I G U R E   3 . 3 4 Drag Level 1 to align with the west side level.

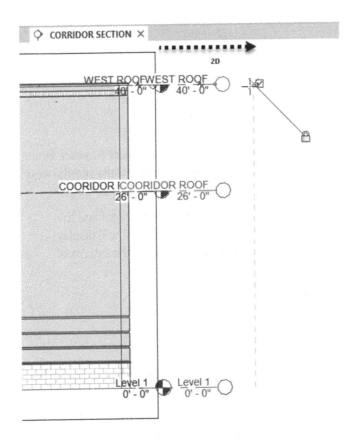

F I G U R E   3 . 3 5 Slide the level text to the right.

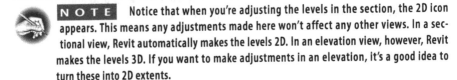

NOTE   Notice that when you're adjusting the levels in the section, the 2D icon appears. This means any adjustments made here won't affect any other views. In a sectional view, Revit automatically makes the levels 2D. In an elevation view, however, Revit makes the levels 3D. If you want to make adjustments in an elevation, it's a good idea to turn these into 2D extents.

NOTE   In Revit, you can also double-click the annotation that refers to the view you wish to open. For example, if you want to open the West Corridor Section and you're in a plan, all you have to do is double-click the section bubble, and the view will open. If you're in the section and you want to go back to a floor plan, you can double-click a datum bubble, and Revit will open that view.

Cutting a section is immensely helpful in terms of viewing the model from any perspective you want. To go even further, when you cut a section, you can also work on your model by modifying any item in the section.

Making Building Modifications in a Section

Now that you've had a good look at this side of the west wing, it's obvious that this wall needs to be repaired. In Revit, you can make a modification to a building in any view. This is good and bad. Just remember that everything you do has a downstream effect on the entire model.

The following procedure will guide you through making a modification to a wall's profile while in a section view:

1. In the Project Browser, find the West Corridor Section and open it by double-clicking the name West Corridor Section (if it isn't open already).

2. In this section, select the west (left) wall of the west wing, as shown in Figure 3.36.

3. After you select the wall, click the Edit Profile button in the Modify | Walls tab.

   You're presented with a magenta outline of the wall. This magenta outline can be modified to alter the wall's profile. On the Ribbon, Edit Profile has been added to the title of the Modify | Walls tab. This enables you to focus on the modification at hand.

> After you select a wall, you can access options to modify that wall. Edit Profile is one of those options.
>
>

4. On the Draw panel of the Modify | Walls ➤ Edit Profile tab, select the Pick Lines button, and set the offset to 2'–0" (610 mm), as shown in Figure 3.37.

5. Hover over the Corridor Roof level and offset it down 2'–0" (610 mm), as shown in Figure 3.38.

6. With the Pick Lines choice still active, change the offset to 0'.

7. Pick the edge of the wall to the right, as shown in Figure 3.39.

8. Go to the Modify tab and click the Trim button (or type TR).

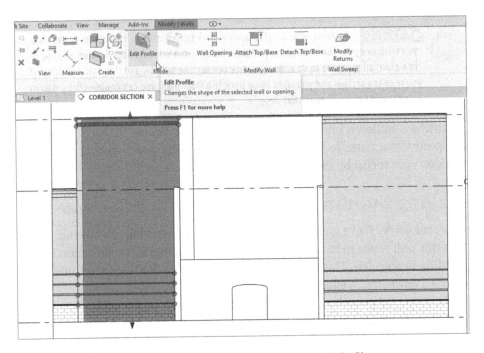

F I G U R E 3 . 3 6   Selecting the wall to be modified and clicking Edit Profile

F I G U R E 3 . 3 7   Pick Lines and offset 2'-0" (610 mm)

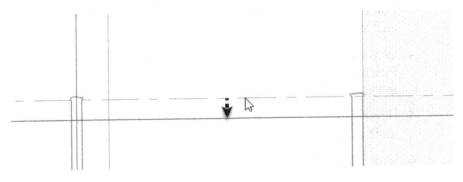

F I G U R E 3 . 3 8   Placing the offset line

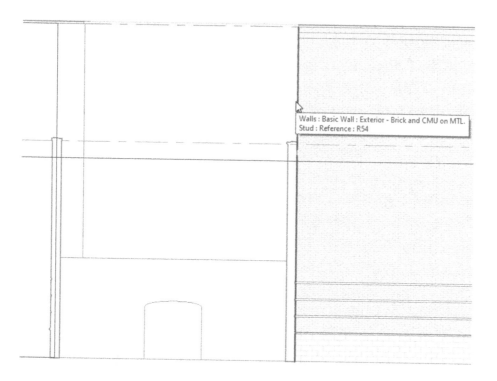

Walls : Basic Wall : Exterior - Brick and CMU on MTL.
Stud : Reference : R54

FIGURE 3.39 Select the inside edge of the wall to the right

9. Pick the spots on the lines as shown. Remember, click the lines you want to keep. See Figure 3.40.

    You now have a closed loop, as shown in Figure 3.41.

 WARNING If you don't have a perfectly closed, continuous loop with your magenta lines, Revit won't allow you to proceed to finish altering the profile of this wall. Make sure you have no gaps, overlaps, or extra line segments aside from the six lines you need to form the wall's outline.

10. On the Wall panel of the Modify | Walls ➤ Edit Profile tab, click Finish Edit Mode, as shown in Figure 3.42.

11. My wall overlapped a bit, so we have to fix it. Select the wall you just edited and click Edit Profile again.

12. Type **AL** (for Align).

13. Select the inside face of the wall to the right first.

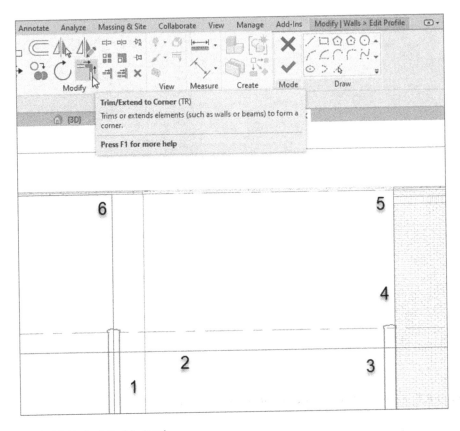

FIGURE 3.40 Trim it up!

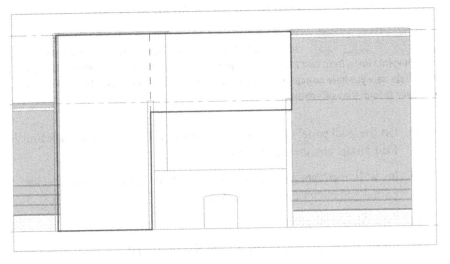

FIGURE 3.41 Closing the wall by using the trim command

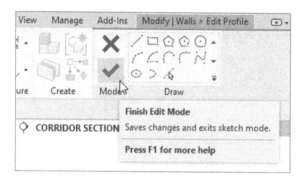

FIGURE 3.42 Clicking Finish Edit Mode

14. Select the magenta line in the wall profile as shown in Figure 3.43

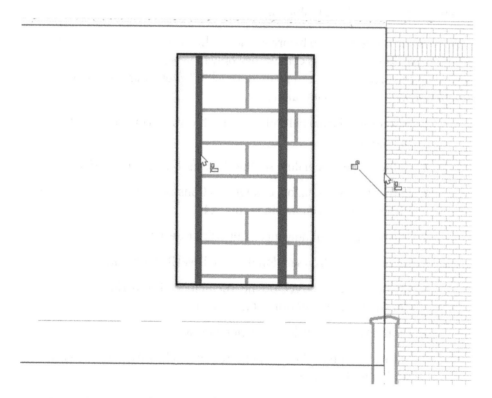

FIGURE 3.43 Sometimes it takes two tries.

15. Click the green Finish Edit Mode button. Your walls should look like figure 3.44

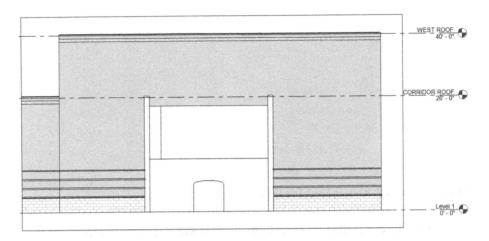

FIGURE 3.44 The finished wall profile

There is one thing left to do before you leave this section: select the two-hour fire-rated partition wall that is constrained only to Level 2. Now that you've opened up this area, the wall can go up to Level 3. To constrain the top of this wall to Corridor Parapet, follow along:

1. Select the internal (white) wall with the arched opening, as shown in Figure 3.45.

2. In the Properties dialog, set the Top Offset to –2'–0" (–610 mm).

3. In the Properties dialog, change Top Constraint to Up To Level: COR-RIDOR ROOF, as shown in Figure 3.45.

4. The partition wall now meets the brick exterior wall.

5. In the Project Browser, double-click Level 3 Floor Plan view.

6. Change the detail level to Fine. (Remember, this option is on the View Control bar at the bottom of the screen.)

7. On the View tab, click the Section button.

8. Place a section as shown in Figure 3.46. Make sure the extents are similar to the figure.

9. In the Project Browser, right-click the new section and rename it **WEST WING SOUTH WALL SECTION**. You'll use this section in Chapter 4, "Working with the Autodesk Revit Tools."

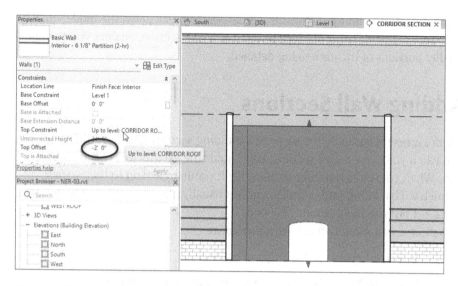

FIGURE 3.45 Choosing the properties to change a wall's constraints is becoming old hat!

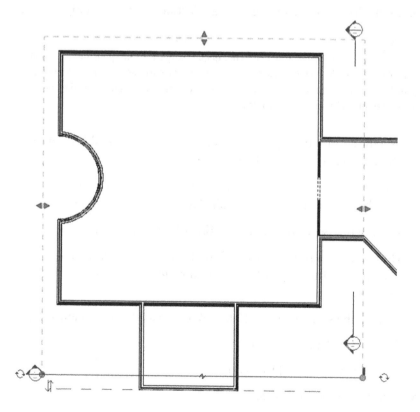

FIGURE 3.46 Adding another section to modify another wall

Adding entire building sections is a great way to break down the model quickly into large segments. Another type of section, a wall section, enables you to view smaller portions of the item being detailed.

Adding Wall Sections

A *wall section* is basically the same as a building section. The only difference is that when you place a wall section, Revit holds the extents to a much smaller area. When you add a building section, Revit wants to extend to the farthest geometry. That being said, a wall section is usually placed to show only the item being cut but not the geometry beyond.

To place a wall section, follow this procedure:

1. Go to Level 1 in the Project Browser.

2. On the View tab, pick the Section button (the same one you picked for the building section).

3. In the Properties dialog, select Wall Section, as shown in Figure 3.47.

WARNING   If you're directed to go to a specific floor plan and your view looks nothing like the one shown in the book, you need to make sure you aren't in a ceiling plan. Notice in the Project Browser that you have floor plans and ceiling plans. The two are quite different. Make sure you're in a floor plan.

4. Add the section through the corridor wall that was modified earlier in this chapter, as shown in Figure 3.48.

5. Click on the section in the Project Browser; pause and click again to edit the text. It's in a category called Sections (Wall Section).

6. Call the new section **CORRIDOR ENTRY SECTION**. Click OK.

7. Hit Esc and open the Corridor Entry Section by either double-clicking it in the Project Browser or double-clicking on the section head.

8. Change the scale to 1/2″ = 1′–0″ (1:20 mm) as shown in Figure 3.49.

9. Change the detail level to Fine.

10. Zoom in on the top of the section.

11. Select the West Roof level.

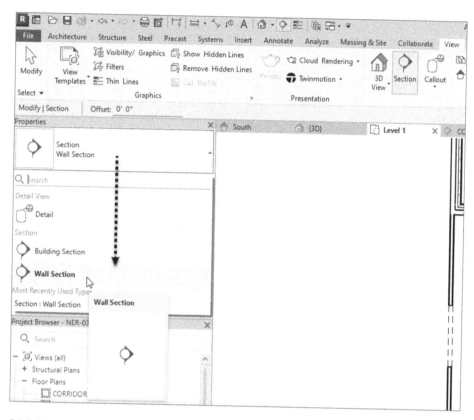

FIGURE 3.47 Changing the type of section from Building Section to Wall Section

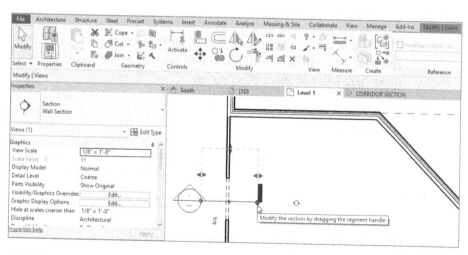

FIGURE 3.48 The wall section in the plan

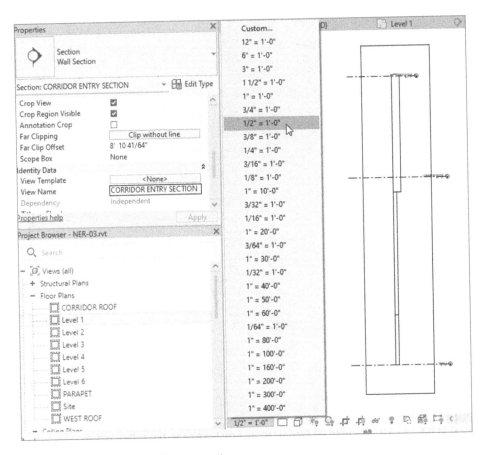

FIGURE 3.49 The corridor entry section

12. Click the small 3D piece of text that is appended to the end of the line and pick it to change it to 2D. This ensures that any adjustments you make here will not affect other views.

13. Adjust it so it looks like Figure 3.50.

14. Save the model.

You're narrowing down the types of sections you can use, and it's time to venture into a specific type of section that can enable you to create a plan-section detail.

Creating Detail Sections

There is a third type of section we need to discuss: the detail section. Revit refers to this type of section as a *detail view*, so that's how we'll start addressing it.

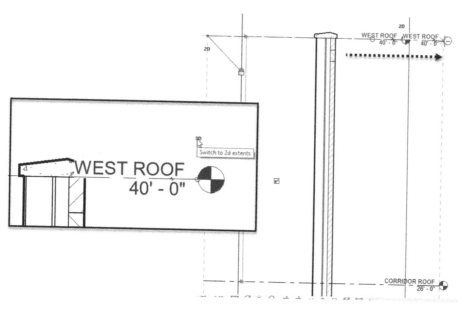

Switch to 2d extents

WEST ROOF
40' - 0"

2D
WEST ROOF   WEST ROOF
40' - 0"   40' - 0"

CORRIDOR ROOF
26' - 0"

FIGURE 3.50 Fixing the level

To add a detail section, perform the following steps:

1. Open the view called Corridor Entry Section (if you don't have it open already).

2. On the View tab, select Section (yes, the same section you've been using all along).

3. In the Properties dialog, select Detail View: Detail.

4. Place a section horizontally below the head of the opening, as shown in Figure 3.51. Make sure the section is flipped so it's looking downward.

5. In the Project Browser is a new category called Detail Views (Detail). Expand the tree, and you see your new detail. It's usually called Detail 0, depending on the number of details that have been added to the model previously.

6. Rename the detail **PLAN DETAIL AT CORRIDOR OPENING**, and press Enter.

7. Open the Plan Detail at Corridor Opening view.

8. Change the scale to 1 1/2" = 1'–0" (1:5 mm). (See Figure 3.52).

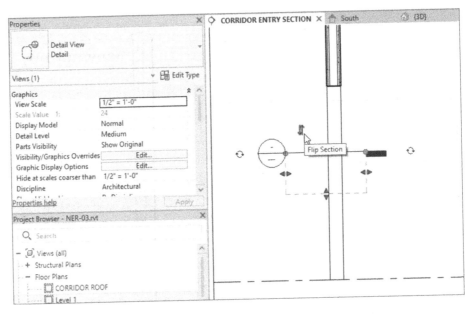

FIGURE 3.51 Creating a plan section detail

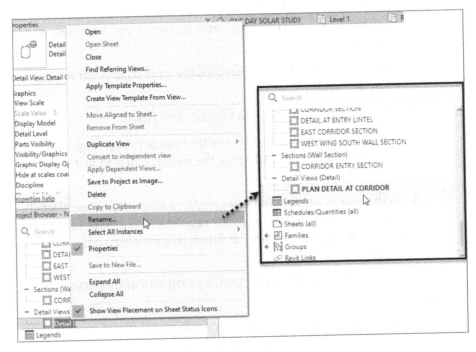

FIGURE 3.52 Viewing and naming the detail

With the detail open, you may be able to see only two dashed lines. This is because the crop region needs to be expanded, as explained in the next section.

Using Crop Regions

The border that surrounds the detail is called a *crop region*. It dictates the extents of the specific view you're in. You can adjust this crop region and use it to your advantage. To learn how to make adjustments to the crop region, follow these steps:

1. Select the crop region surrounding the detail, as shown in Figure 3.53.

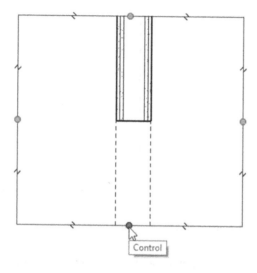

FIGURE 3.53 Stretching the crop region to view the detail

2. You see four blue dot grips, one at the midpoint of each line. Pick the top grips, and stretch the top region up until you can see the opening jamb (see Figure 3.54).

3. Repeat the process for the bottom so that you can see the entire opening.

4. With the crop region still selected, notice the break icons similar to the make-elbow icons in the level markers. Pick the break icon, as shown in Figure 3.55. Slice part of the section away, resulting in two separate cropped regions.

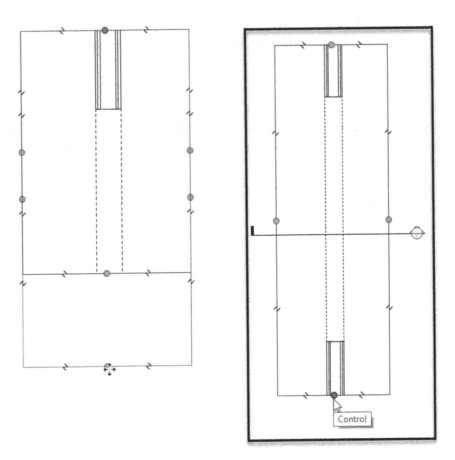

FIGURE 3.54 Keep stretching the crop region to view the detail.

5. Within the cropped regions are blue move icons. If you don't see blue icons, as shown in Figure 3.55, you need to select the crop region again.

6. Slide the sections closer together by clicking the top icon and moving the section down. See Figure 3.56. (Be careful; if you slide them too close together, you'll get a warning telling you that the two regions are being joined back to one.)

7. Save the model.

You now have nice control over how the details are shown. Let's go back and see how to make the section marker more aesthetically pleasing.

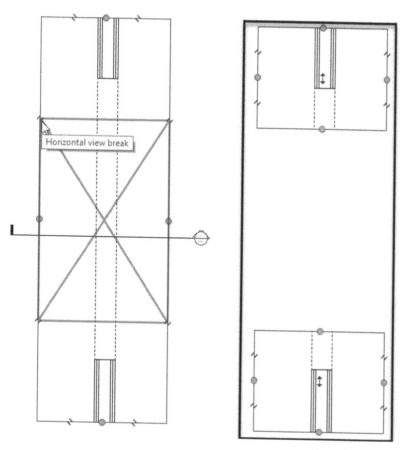

Horizontal view break

FIGURE 3.55 Splitting the section

Splitting a Section Segment

One more section item, and then you're finished! Sometimes you need to split (or *jog*) a section. You do this to show items that aren't necessarily in line with one another. You can accomplish this in Revit as follows:

1. Open the Level 1 floor plan.

2. On the View tab, click the Section button. (You can also grab a section from the Quick Access toolbar.)

3. In the Type Selector, select Building Section.

4. Pick a point above the corridor that connects to the east wing of the building for the section head, and then pick a point well below the bottom of the corridor, as shown in Figure 3.57.

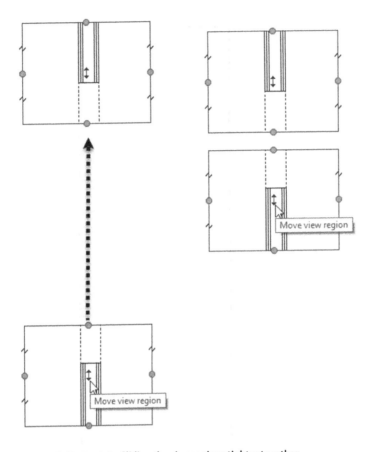

FIGURE 3.56 Sliding the view regions tighter together

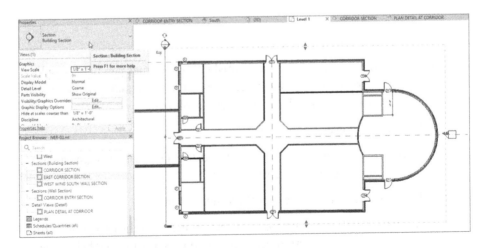

FIGURE 3.57 Adding another section to the model

5. In the Project Browser, find the section you just made and rename it **EAST CORRIDOR SECTION.**

6. Select the new section marker.

7. On the Section panel of the Modify | Views tab, click the Split Segment button.

8. Pick a point along the section line just below the centerline of the corridor, as shown in Figure 3.58.

9. Move your cursor to the right. A jog appears in the section; place the jog into the building. The section is now jogged into the building. Press Esc twice to clear the command.

Finally! You're finished with sections. Just remember that by adding a section to the model, not only are you preparing to build your construction documents, but you're also enabling access to specific elements, thus allowing you to make modifications you otherwise could not have made.

Creating Callouts

Creating an enlarged area of your model will be a task on every project you tackle. Luckily, in Revit, not only are callouts easy to add to your model, but they also directly link to the view to which they refer. This is crucial for project coordination. Another nice thing about callouts is that you can make modifications to the callout view independently of the host view from which you pull the information. The biggest change you make is the scale. Yes, your callout can be at a different scale from the main floor plan.

Here's the procedure for adding callouts:

1. In the Project Browser, under Sections (Wall Section), open the COR-RIDOR ENTRY SECTION.

2. Find the View tab on the Ribbon.

3. On the View tab, click the Callout button, as shown in Figure 3.59.

4. Pick a window around the area where the corridor firewall meets the exterior wall with the brick façade, as shown in Figure 3.60. Make sure you get at least part of the level designating CORRIDOR ROOF, as shown in Figure 3.60.

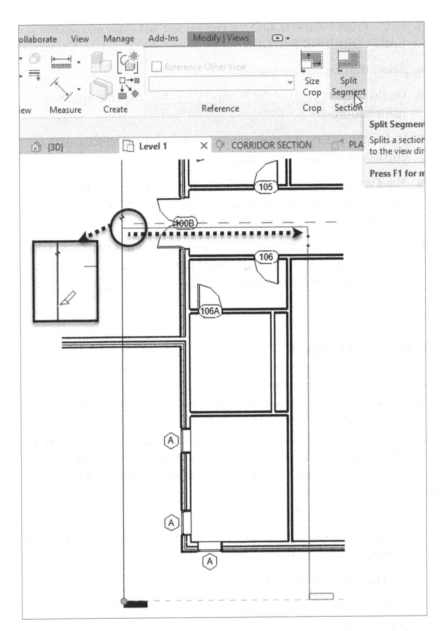

FIGURE 3.58 Jogging a section calls for splitting the segment.

5. In the Project Browser, there is a new Sections (Building Section) item. Its name is Callout Of Corridor Entry Section—Rename it to DETAIL AT ENTRY LINTEL.

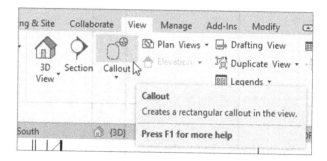

FIGURE 3.59   The Callout button is located on the View tab.

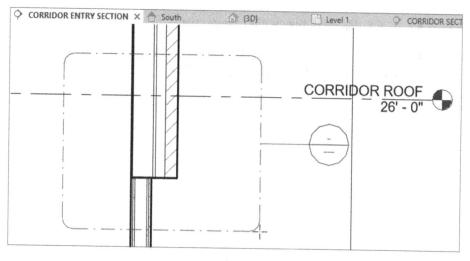

FIGURE 3.60   The callout area is directly related to the view it's calling out.

6. Select the callout you just added by picking any point along the line. A bunch of blue grips appear. These grips enable you to stretch the shape of the callout.

7. Pick the grip that connects the callout bubble to the leader coming from the callout window.

8. Drag the bubble to the location shown in Figure 3.61.

9. Pick the blue midpoint grip on the leader and create an elbow, as shown in Figure 3.61. Once completed, hit Esc a couple times.

10. In the Project Browser, find DETAIL AT ENTRY LINTEL under the Sections (Building Section) category, and open the view. (You can also double-click the callout bubble to open the view.)

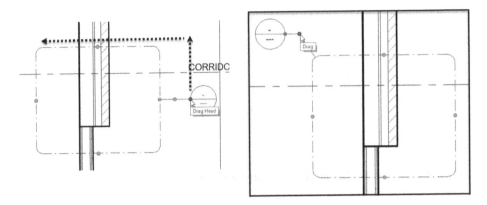

FIGURE 3.61 Adjusting callouts will be a common task.

    11. On the View control bar at the bottom of the view, change the scale to 1 1/2″ = 1′– 0″ (1:5 mm). See Figure 3.62.

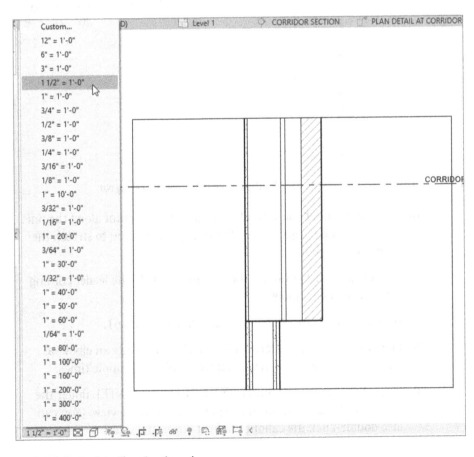

FIGURE 3.62 Changing the scale

12. Now, select the crop region that surrounds the detail, as shown in Figure 3.63.

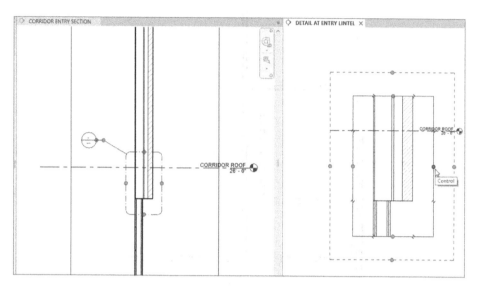

FIGURE 3.63 Modify the crop region by selecting it and stretching the grip.

After you select the crop region, you see an additional region that consists of a dotted line. This is called an *annotation region*, and it gives you a gutter in which to place text outside the area that is physically being cropped.

13. Type **WT**. This tiles the windows you have open.

The callout window is selected in the Corridor Entry Section along with the crop region in your callout. That's because the two objects are one and the same (see Figure 3.63).

14. Stretch the crop region closer to the actual wall, as shown in Figure 3.63.

15. Save the model. You'll use this detail in future chapters to get the model ready for construction documents.

Now that you've created a callout for a detail, let's go to the plan and create some callouts there. It would be nice to have some typical lavatory callouts as well as a typical elevator callout:

1. In the Project Browser, go to Floor Plan Level 1. (It may need to be maximized because you tiled the windows in the previous exercise.) Make sure it's a floor plan, not a ceiling plan.

The crop region and the callout outline are the same. If you modify one, the other changes accordingly.

2. Zoom in on the area shown in Figure 3.64.

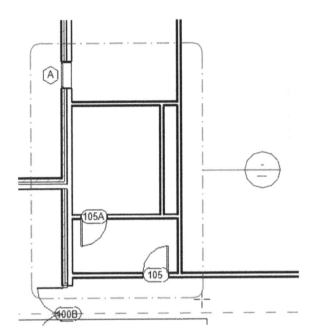

FIGURE 3.64 Creating a plan callout

3. On the View tab, select Callout.

4. Pick a window around the lavatory, as shown in Figure 3.64.

5. In the Project Browser, under the Floor Plans category, is Level 1 – Callout 1. Right-click Level 1 – Callout 1, and select Rename.

6. Rename it **TYPICAL MEN'S LAVATORY**. Now, double-click to open the view.

7. If you see remnants of the corridor section, select them, right-click, and select Hide In View, then Elements, as shown in Figure 3.65.

8. The detail level is set to Coarse. Change it to Fine. Note that the callout is placed in the Project Browser under the category where it was created; you won't see a "callouts" category.

9. Save the model.

10. Open the Level 1 floor plan.

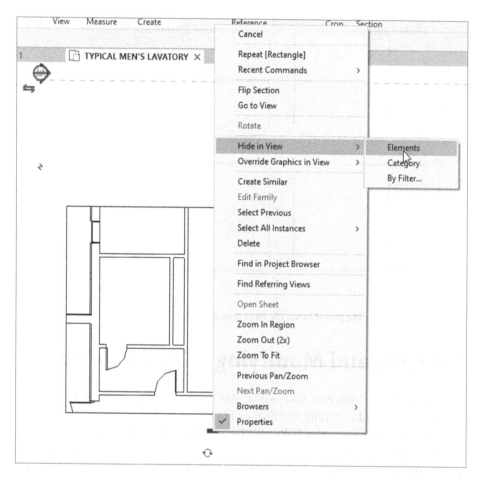

FIGURE 3.65 Hiding the section

11. Create a callout for the women's room below the corridor (directly below the men's room).

12. Name the new callout **TYPICAL WOMEN'S LAVATORY**.

13. Create one more callout around the elevator shaft in the east wing, as shown in Figure 3.66.

14. Name the new callout **TYPICAL ELEVATOR SHAFT**.

The boring views are out of the way! Let's create some perspective views of the model. Creating these views is just as easy but requires a specific procedure in which you'll take advantage of the camera function.

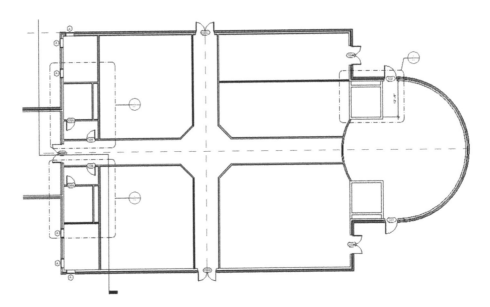

FIGURE 3.66 The plan showing the three typical callouts

Creating and Modifying a Camera View

The camera view is the view with which you'll have by far the most fun. Revit seems to lend itself naturally to this type of view.

Taking a camera view essentially tells Revit to look at a certain area from a perspective vantage point. Like a section or a callout, such a view may never see the light of day in terms of going on a drawing sheet, but camera views are perfect to see how a model is coming along from a realistic point of view.

Adding a Camera View

To create a camera view, follow these steps:

1. Go to the Level 1 floor plan.

2. On the View tab, click the drop-down arrow in the 3D View button and select Camera, as shown in Figure 3.67. (You can also access this on the Quick Access toolbar.)

3. Pick a point in the main corridor of the east wing, and move your cursor to the left—down the hallway. You want to take a perspective view as if you were standing in the intersection of the two main corridors, as shown in Figure 3.68.

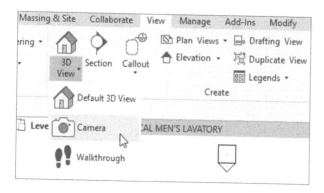

FIGURE 3.67 Adding a camera view

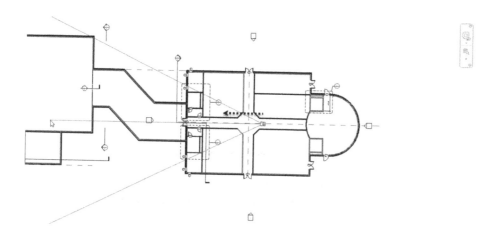

FIGURE 3.68 Placing the camera view in the main corridor

4. The second point you pick will specify how far the camera reaches into the building. Pick a point past the corridor doors, as shown in Figure 3.69.

5. Unlike when you're placing a section or a callout, Revit automatically opens the new 3D view. This doesn't mean it automatically has a useful name. In the Project Browser, you see a new view in the 3D Views category. It's called 3D View 1. Right-click 3D View 1, and name it **EAST WING CORRIDOR PERSPECTIVE.**

6. On the View Control bar located at the bottom of the view, change the Detail Level to Fine.

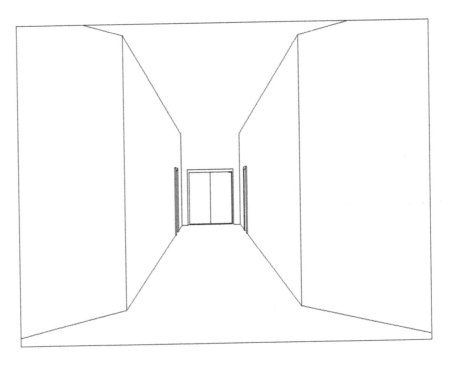

FIGURE 3.69 The perspective view down the east wing corridor

7. Next, click Visual Style, and on the flyout select Graphic Display Options at the top of the menu, as shown in Figure 3.70.

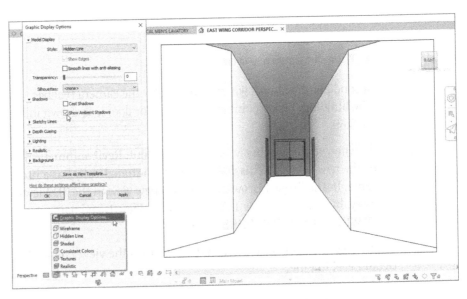

FIGURE 3.70 Setting the view control of our new perspective view

8. Click into the Shadows category and turn on Show Ambient Shadows, as shown in Figure 3.70.

When the camera is in place, you may find it difficult to modify at first. You can do quite a bit to the view, but the following section focuses on modifying the actual camera in the plan.

Modifying the Camera

After you place the camera in the model, Revit doesn't leave behind any evidence that the camera is there. If you need to make adjustments or see the location from which the view is being taken, perform the following steps:

1. Open the Level 1 floor plan.

2. In the Project Browser, right-click the East Wing Corridor Perspective view in the 3D Views category, and select Show Camera, as shown in Figure 3.71.

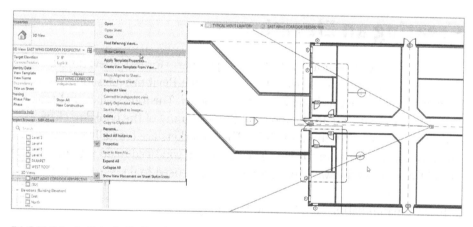

FIGURE 3.71 By finding the view in the Project Browser, you can tell Revit to show the camera in the plan.

The camera appears in the plan temporarily so you can see it. In the view, the camera icon is a triangle and a straight line. You can physically move the camera, and you can also adjust the grip on the midpoint of the triangle to swivel and to look farther into the model. Figure 3.72 shows the perspective view. You can also adjust the Perspective Mode, the Eye Elevation, and the Target Elevation settings.

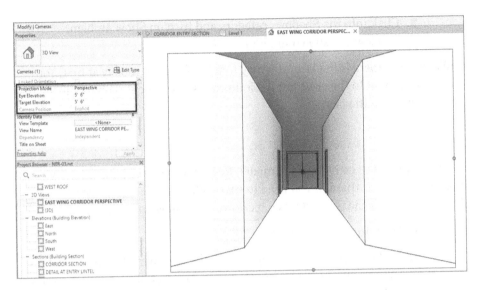

FIGURE 3.72 The perspective view settings.

Creating an Elevation

I saved the best view—or at least, the most popular—for last. Elevations are essential for any project—so essential, in fact, that Revit provides four of them before you place a single wall into the model. The four shapes that represent houses that were in the model at the beginning of the book are elevation markers, as shown in Figure 3.73. These markers are typically handy but are most certainly now in the way. The first thing you need to do is to move one of them out of the way. The second thing you need to do is to create a few new ones!

To start manipulating elevations, follow along:

1. Go to the Level 1 floor plan. In the eastern part of the corridor is an elevation. Yours may be in a slightly different location than the book's example, but it needs to be moved nonetheless (see Figure 3.73).

    You're about to move the elevation marker. To do so, however, you need to break down what an elevation marker comprises. It's actually two separate items: the square box is the elevation, and the triangle is the part of the marker that activates the view, as shown in Figure 3.74. To move this elevation marker, you must pick a window around both items and move them together. If you don't, the view will stay in its original location, leaving you wondering what is wrong with your elevation.

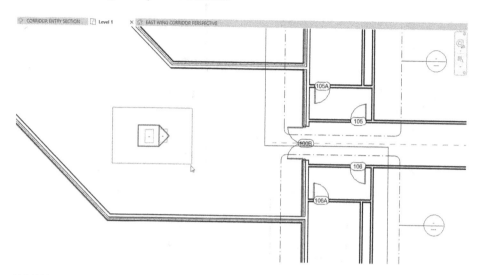

FIGURE 3.73 The elevation marker is right in the way!

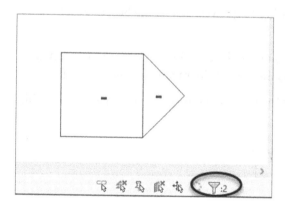

FIGURE 3.74 The elevation marker is broken down into two pieces. You need to move both together by picking a window around the entire symbol.

2. Pick a window around the elevation marker. Make sure you aren't picking any other items along with it.

3. Move your mouse over the selection. Your cursor turns into a move icon with four move arrows, as shown in Figure 3.75.

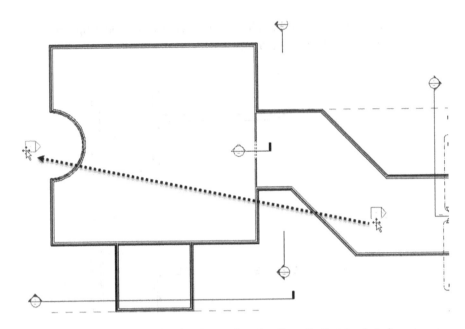

FIGURE 3.75 You can drag the elevation marker when the entire item is selected.

4. Drag the elevation marker to the west side of the building (see Figure 3.75).

Now that the elevation marker is out of the corridor, it's time to make a new one. To do so, make sure you're in the Level 1 floor plan and follow along:

1. On the View tab, click the Elevation button, as shown in Figure 3.76.

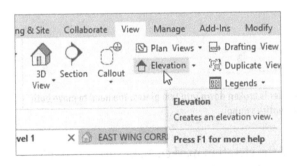

FIGURE 3.76 The Elevation button on the View tab

2. In the Type Selector, make sure Building Elevation is current.

3. Move your cursor around the perimeter of the building. Notice that the elevation marker follows the profile of the exterior walls. This is a great thing!

WARNING   When you're creating an elevation of a radial wall or nonlinear item, be sure you know the exact angle at which you're placing the elevation marker. When you're in the elevation view, you may get a false sense of the true dimensions based on the view's perspective. Draw a reference plane if you need to, and then place the elevation on that plane.

4. Pick a place for the elevation, as shown in Figure 3.77, and press Esc to terminate the command.

5. When the elevation is placed, select the triangle. You see the same extents window that you saw in the previous section. This controls how deep into the model you're viewing, and it also shows you the length of the section. Because you placed this elevation up against a wall, Revit stops the extents of the elevation at that wall.

6. Pick the top grip, and stretch the elevation past the wall, as shown in Figure 3.77.

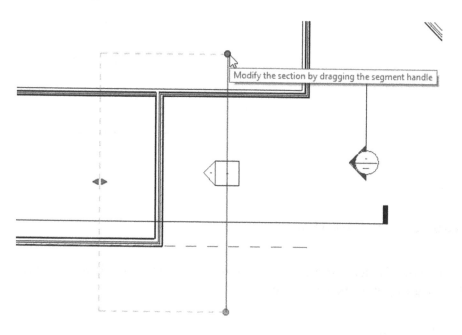

Modify the section by dragging the segment handle

FIGURE 3.77   The elevation is placed. You can select the view arrow and move the extents of the elevation into the building.

7. In the Project Browser under Elevations (Building Elevation) is a new elevation; rename it **WEST WING SOUTHEAST ELEVATION**.

8. Open the elevation.

9. On the View Control bar, change the scale to 1/4″ = 1′–0″ (1:50 mm).

10. On the View Control bar, set the detail level to Fine. (You can also set these in the Properties dialog at any time.) See Figure 3.78.

11. Save the model.

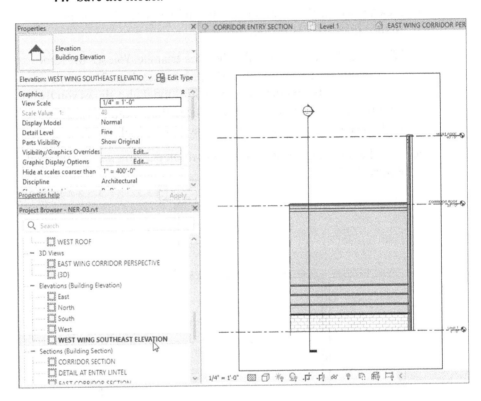

FIGURE 3.78 Elevations behave similar to sections.

You've added a new exterior elevation. You can add an interior elevation as well. It's just as easy and much more fun!

Interior Elevations

The difference between an exterior elevation and an interior elevation is the same as the difference between a building section and a wall section. Both interior and exterior elevations are executed the same way: by selecting the View tab on the Design bar. The only difference is that you can make a choice between the two in the Type Selector in the Options bar. To add an interior elevation, perform these steps:

1. Go to the Level 1 floor plan.

2. On the View tab, click the Elevation button.

3. In the Type Selector, choose Elevation: Interior Elevation, and place it in the area shown in Figure 3.79.

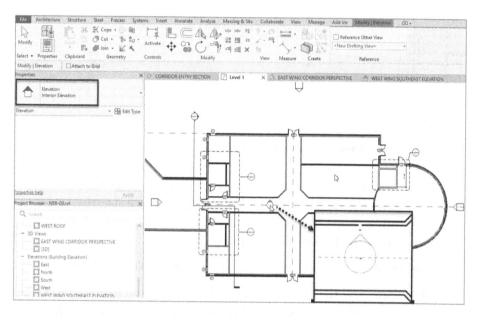

FIGURE 3.79 Adding an interior elevation and making the adjustments

4. Hover your cursor in the corridor near a point shown in the middle of Figure 3.79. Notice that when you move your cursor up, the arrow flips up. When you move your pointer down, the arrow flips down.

5. Make sure the arrow in the elevation target is pointing up, and then pick a point along the horizontal corridor, as shown at the right of Figure 3.79, to place the elevation. Once it's placed, press Esc to terminate the command.

6. Pick a window around the elevation as we did with the exterior elevation, selecting both the target and the elevation.

7. Move it to the center of the corridor as shown in Figure 3.80

8. After you move the elevation, select the arrow. Notice that the extents are outside the building. (This occurs in most cases. If it doesn't, you're good to go.) Select the elevation again and, on the left side, pick the blue grip and drag the left extent to the point shown at the left in Figure 3.80. Repeat the process for the right side as well.

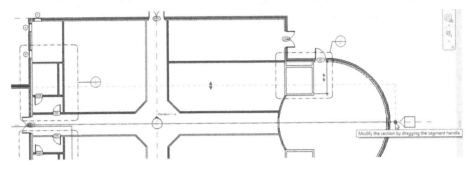

F I G U R E   3 . 8 0   Stretching the grip down to crop the view

9. In the Project Browser, there's a new elevation under the Elevations (Interior Elevation) category. Right-click the new elevation (Revit will call it Elevation 1 – a, or something similar), and call it **EAST WING CORRIDOR NORTH ELEVATION**.

10. Open the new view called East Wing Corridor North Elevation.

11. Notice that the crop region extends all the way up to the parapet. Select the crop region, and drag the top down to Level 2, as shown in Figure 3.81.

In the elevation's view, you can drag the crop region down to show only that floor. If you would rather see all of the floors, perhaps you should use a section rather than an elevation.

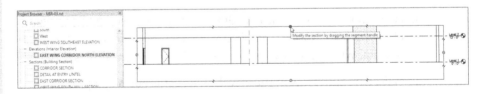

F I G U R E   3 . 8 1   Stretching the grip down to crop the view

N O T E   If you had floors already placed in the model, Revit would create the interior elevation so that it extended only to this geometry. Because you don't have floors, Revit doesn't know where to stop. If you happen to place an elevation without floors and put them in later, Revit won't make the adjustment. You'll have to adjust the interior elevation manually for the new floors.

Let's create some more elevations:

1. Go to Floor Plan Level 1. Zoom into the east wing entry area, as shown in Figure 3.82.

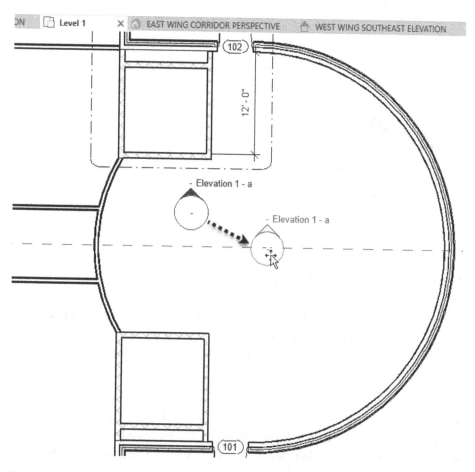

FIGURE 3.82 Add the elevation marker as shown here, and then move it to a new location.

2. On the View tab, click the Elevation button.

3. Place an elevation marker in an area similar to the one shown in Figure 3.82, and then move it to the center of the lobby.

 TIP Notice that when you're trying to place the elevation in the entry area, it seems to wander all over the place. This is because the elevation is trying to locate the radial geometry. The safest bet in this situation is to find a straight wall and aim the elevation at that wall. In this case, you should aim the elevation at the bottom of the elevator shaft. When the elevation marker is in place, you can then move it to where you need it to be.

4. With the elevation marker centered in the lobby, select the round bubble. Four blue boxes appear, as shown in Figure 3.83. These boxes let you turn on multiple views. Turn on all four views, as shown in Figure 3.83.

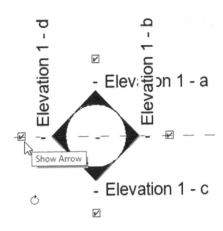

FIGURE 3.83 Turn on all four views in the lobby.

With the four elevations turned on, you have some naming to do! Up to this point, you have been going to the Project Browser to rename the elevations. Let's explore another way to rename an elevation and to view its properties as well.

Elevation Properties

With each view comes a new set of properties. For example, when you made the perspective view of the corridor, you turned on ambient shadows. Normally, in an interior elevation, you don't want to do this. Revit allows you to have separate view properties on a view-by-view basis.

To access the View Properties dialog, follow these steps:

1. On the interior elevation with the four arrows, select only the arrow facing up (north).

2. The Properties dialog provides a wealth of information about that view. You have a multitude of options as well. Find the View Name option under the Identity Data heading, and change it to **EAST WING ENTRY NORTH ELEVATION**, as shown in Figure 3.84.

3. Select the East Wing Entry North Elevation again. Notice that the view's extents are stretching past the entry atrium. Pick the blue

By changing the value in the Properties dialog, you are, in effect, changing the name in the Project Browser. Again, change something in one place, and it changes in another.

grips at the end of the elevations, and bring them into the atrium area, as shown in Figure 3.85. Also, drag the view limit up to show the radial exterior wall (see Figure 3.85).

4. Click the elevation arrow facing left (west).

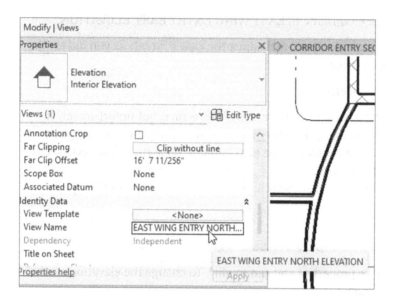

FIGURE 3.84 Changing the View Name setting to East Wing Entry North Elevation

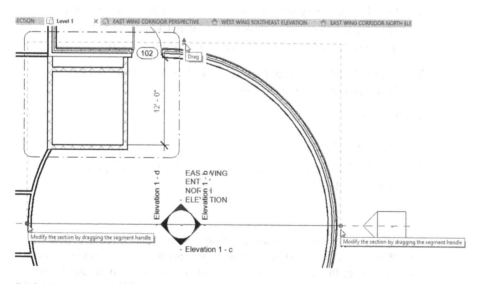

FIGURE 3.85 Making the adjustments to bring the view back into a reasonable range

5. Change View Name to **EAST WING ENTRY WEST ELEVATION**.

6. Click the arrow facing down (south).

7. Change View Name to **EAST WING ENTRY SOUTH ELEVATION**.

8. Click the arrow facing right (east).

9. Change View Name to **EAST WING ENTRY EAST ELEVATION**.

10. Select each elevation, and adjust the view's extents as you did for the north elevation.

11. Save the model.

The actual view names appear in the plan. This is nice, but unfortunately it leaves no room for anything else other than the view. Plus, no construction documents have these names right in the plan (at least, none that I have ever seen). You can turn off this feature.

Now that you can place and modify annotations, let's delve into their physical properties.

Annotation Properties

Annotations all have properties you can modify. To change the elevation symbol properties, follow along:

1. On the Manage tab, select Additional Settings ➤ Elevation Tags.

2. At the top of the Type Properties dialog, you see Family: System Family: Elevation Tag. Below that is Type. Change Type from 1/2″ (13 mm) Square to 1/2″ (13 mm) Circle (see Figure 3.86).

3. Under Graphics, change Elevation Mark to Elevation Mark Body_ Circle : Detail Number. See Figure 3.86

4. Click OK.

5. Save your work.

6. Zoom back in on the elevation markers. They should look like Figure 3.87.

N O T E   It's Revit time! No longer will you see "dumb" placeholder information in a tag. When you create your construction documents and put these views on sheets, Revit will automatically fill out tags with the correct information. To take it one step further, you can tell Revit not to print these annotations if the views they represent aren't on a sheet.

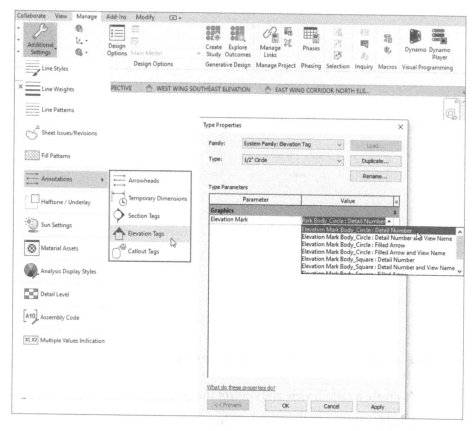

FIGURE 3.86 Modifying the properties for the elevation markers

The ability to add elevations is a must. As you can see, physically adding an elevation is simple. It does, however, take practice to manipulate elevations to look the way you want.

Are You Experienced?

Now you can...

✓ create levels and constrain walls to stretch or shrink if the level's elevation information changes in any way

✓ cut wall sections and building sections through the model

✓ create detail views, allowing you to add plan sections through a wall or a building section

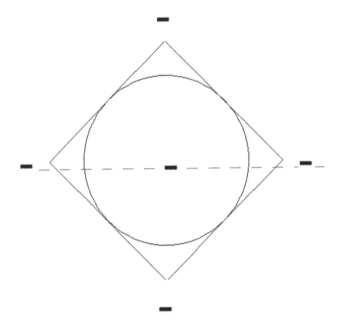

FIGURE 3.87 The revised, less obtrusive elevation markers

✓ create a callout view and control the crop region

✓ add a camera to the model, giving the user a nice perspective of a certain area

✓ create interior and exterior elevations within the model

CHAPTER 4

Working with the Autodesk Revit Tools

You can get only so far when allowing a computer application to place architectural components into a model. At some point, the application needs to be flexible enough to enable users to employ their own sets of drafting and modifying tools, thus providing architects and designers with the freedom to create their own architecture and construction procedures. The Autodesk® Revit® program does provide the basic modify and edit commands, which are quite common in other drafting applications such as Autodesk® AutoCAD® software and MicroStation, but Revit does this with a little more flair and some differences in procedure as compared to a 2D drafting application.

This chapter covers the following topics:

▶ **The basic edit commands**

▶ **The Array command**

▶ **The Mirror command**

▶ **The Align tool**

▶ **The Split Element command**

▶ **The Trim command**

▶ **The Offset command**

▶ **Copy/Paste**

▶ **Creating the plans**

The Basic Edit Commands

In this chapter, you'll learn how to use the geometry you've already placed in the model to build an actual working plan. As you manipulate the plan, all of the other views you made in Chapter 3, "Creating Views," will reflect those changes. You'll start with the edit commands.

 N O T E   As with the previous chapters, it's important that you become comfortable with the material in this chapter. If you're still not comfortable with the first few chapters, I recommend reviewing them now. You may pick up something you missed the first time around and have a "lightbulb" moment.

You aren't going to get very far in Revit without knowing the edit commands. Up to this point, we have been avoiding the edit commands with a few exceptions. There will be some overlap in some of the chapters, because many aspects of Revit span multiple topics.

The basic commands covered in this section are Move, Copy, and Rotate. Then, in the following sections, you'll move on to Array, Mirror, Align, Split Element, Offset, Copy/Paste, and Trim. Each command is as important as the next at this stage of the game. Some are obvious, whereas others can take some practice to master.

The first command, Move, is one you'll recognize from previous chapters. Move is probably the most heavily used command in Revit.

The Move Command

The Move command is generally used to create a copy of an item while deleting the original item.

Begin by finding the model you're using to follow along. If you haven't completed the previous chapter's procedures, open the file called NER-4.rvt found at the book's website, www.wiley.com/go/revit2024ner. Go to the Chapter 4 folder to find the file.

To use the Move command, perform the following steps:

1. Go to Level 1 under the Floor Plans category in the Project Browser.

2. Zoom in on the west wing.

3. Select the south wall of the bump out at the south side of the west wing, as shown in Figure 4.1.

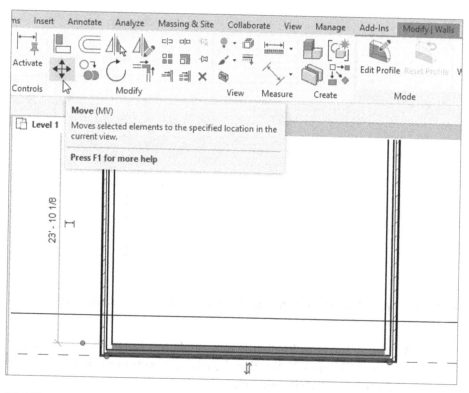

FIGURE 4.1 Select the wall to be moved. The Move button now appears on the Ribbon.

4. On the Modify | Walls tab is the Move button (see Figure 4.1); click it.

5. Now that the Move command is running, you see some choices on the Options bar:

Constrain   If you select Constrain, you can move only at 0, 90, 180, or 270 degrees.

Disjoin   If you select Disjoin, then when you move the wall, any walls that are joined to it won't be affected by the move. The wall will lose its join.

6. To start moving the item, you must first pick a base point for the command. Pick a point somewhere toward the middle of the wall, as shown in Figure 4.2.

7. After you pick this point, move your cursor straight up. You see a blue dimension. At this point, you have two choices: you can eye-ball the increment, or you can type the increment you want (see Figure 4.2).

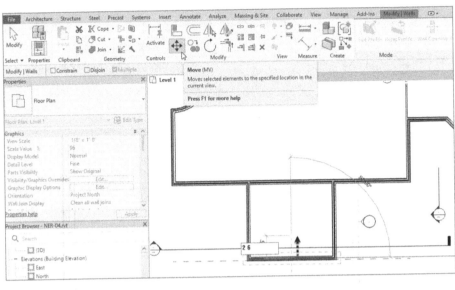

FIGURE 4.2 Choices on the Options bar. The first point has been picked, and the wall is being moved up.

You may be thinking, "But I used to type my commands!" Well, you still can in Revit. If you type **MV**, Revit launches the Move command.

8. Type in the value 2'–6" (750 mm), and press Enter. The wall moves 2'–6" (750 mm). Notice that the adjacent walls move with it. In Revit, there is no stretch command.

TIP   Revit will accept a few different values for feet and fractional inches. For example, instead of typing **2'–6"** (which Revit will accept), you can type **2 6**. Just make sure you have a space between the 2 and the 6. Revit will accept that value. If there are fractional increments, you can type **2 6 1/2"**, and Revit will accept the value. Or you can type **2'–6 1/2"**. (Metric users can just smile here.)

Now that Move is officially in the history books, it's time to move on to Move's close cousin: the Copy command.

The Copy Command

When you need to make duplicates of an item, Copy is your go-to player. The Copy command works like the Move command, except that it leaves the initial item intact. You can also create multiple copies if necessary.

To start using the Copy command, do the following:

1. Make sure you're still in Floor Plan Level 1.

2. Zoom and pan so you're focused on the east wing, as shown in Figure 4.3.

3. Select the right corridor wall (see Figure 4.3).

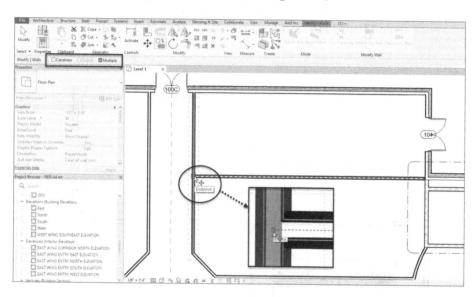

FIGURE 4.3 Creating a copy of the corridor wall

4. Click the Copy command on the Modify | Walls tab.

5. On the Options bar, check the Constrain toggle and uncheck Multiple.

6. Zoom in on the wall close to the midpoint of the selected wall and the intersection of the horizontal wall that divides this portion of the building (see Figure 4.3).

7. If you hover your cursor in the center of the wall (not near the actual finish faces, but the core of the wall), you'll see a blue dotted center-line indicating that you've found the center of the wall. (If you're having difficulty picking the item, change the detail level to Coarse.)

Also, if you move your cursor to the right a little, you can position it so that it picks up the horizontal wall's centerline. After you pick up the horizontal wall's centerline, the centerline for the vertical wall will disappear. This is fine.

When you see that you're snapped to the endpoint of the horizontal wall, pick the point (see Figure 4.4).

8. Move to the right until you pick up the midpoint of the horizontal wall. When you do, pick that point. If the midpoint doesn't appear, type 22′–3″ (6675 mm) or type **SM** for Snap Mid.

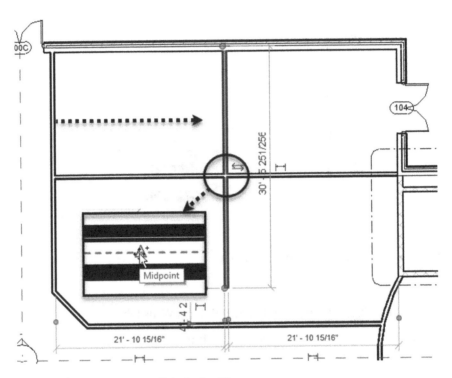

FIGURE 4.4 The two walls in the East Wing

9. Save the model.

The next step is to rotate an item. Although the Rotate command is a simple concept, Revit does have unique processes involved in this command.

The Rotate Command

The Rotate command enables you to change the polar orientation of an item or a set of items. This command may take a little practice to understand. The good thing, however, is that once you have experience with the Rotate command, you'll be better at other commands that share a similar process.

To use the Rotate command, do the following:

1. Open the Level 1 floor plan.

2. Zoom in on the radial portion of the west wing, as shown in Figure 4.5.

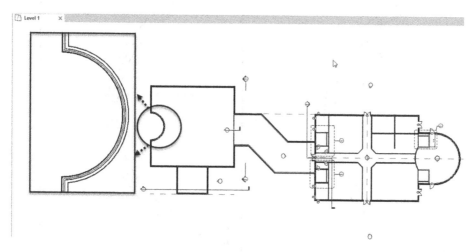

FIGURE 4.5 **The radial portion of the west wing**

3. You're going to add a new reference plane and rotate it by 45°. To do so, click Ref Plane in the Work Plane panel in the Architecture tab (see Figure 4.6).

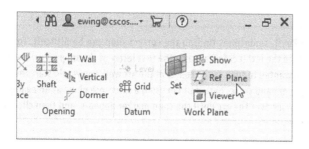

FIGURE 4.6 **Creating a reference plane**

4. In the Draw panel, click the Line button (it should be "the current choice" by default).

5. For the first point, pick the center point of the radial wall, as shown in Figure 4.7. If you are having trouble picking the center point, right-click and choose Snap Overrides. Then, choose Centers.

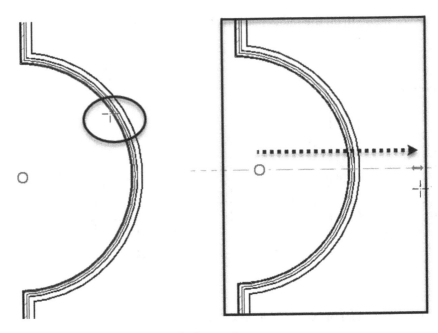

FIGURE 4.7 Adding a horizontal reference plane

6. For the second point, pick a point horizontally to the right, outside the radial wall (again, see Figure 4.7).

7. Press Esc twice, or click Modify.

TIP In Revit, sometimes finding the correct snap can be difficult. To overcome this, you can type the letter **S** followed by the first letter of the snap you wish to use. For example, if you wanted to snap to the center of the arc wall, you would start the Ref Plane command (any command works here, but I'm using a reference plane as an example), type **SC**, place the cursor over the arc until the snap marker appears, and then click. This will snap to the center.

WARNING Before you rotate, be careful. Figure 4.7 shows the second point extended past the radial wall, and that is where you generally want it. However, watch out for your snaps. When you pick the second point, be sure to zoom in on the area, ensuring that you aren't inadvertently snapping to the wrong wall.

Now that you've added the reference plane, you can rotate it into place. (Yes, you could have just drawn it at a 45° angle, but you're practicing the Rotate command here.) Follow these steps:

1. Select the reference plane you just drew.

2. On the Modify | Reference Planes tab, click the Rotate button, as shown in Figure 4.8.

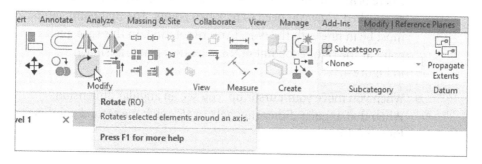

F I G U R E 4 . 8 The Rotate command is active for the specific item you've selected.

3. After you start the Rotate command, look back at the reference plane. Notice the blue dot in the middle of your line. Revit always calculates the center of an object (or group of objects) for the rotate point (see Figure 4.9).

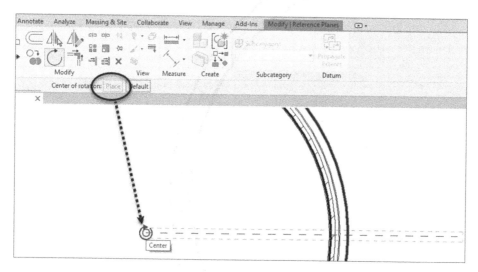

F I G U R E 4 . 9 Relocate the origin point for the rotation.

4. On the Options bar, click the Place button for Center of rotation, and select the end point of the reference plane. A temporary rotate icon appears, indicating that you can now move the blue dot (see Figure 4.9).

You can start the Rotate command by typing **RO**, selecting the item(s) to rotate, and then pressing the spacebar or Enter to place the rotation icon.

5. With the rotate origin in the correct location, it's rotate time! If you swivel your cursor around the reference plane, a line forms from the rotate origin to your cursor. This indicates that the origin is established. Now you need to pick two points. The first point you pick must be in line with the object you're rotating. In this case, pick a point at the right endpoint of the reference plane, as shown in Figure 4.10.

6. When you move your cursor up, you see an angular dimension. When that angular dimension gets to 45°, pick the second point (see Figure 4.10).

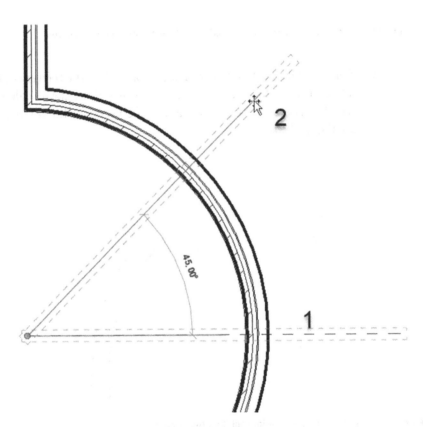

FIGURE 4.10 To rotate an item, you must specify two points.

7. Press Esc.

As you're well aware, you'll use the Rotate command quite frequently. Now that you have some experience with the Rotate command and know how Revit wants you to move the pivot point, the next command—Array—will be easy for you to grasp.

ROTATE OPTIONS

While you're in the Rotate command, don't forget that you have options. The most popular option is to create a copy of the item you're rotating, as shown here:

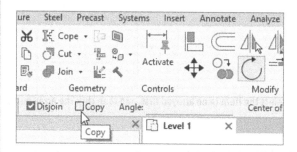

Another popular option is to specify an angle. This can be difficult, because the correct angle may be the opposite of what you think, resulting in your having to undo the command and then redo the rotation with a negative (–) value.

The Array Command

When you need to create multiple duplicates of an item or a group of items, the Array command is the logical choice. The Array command in Revit functions in a fashion similar to the Rotate command. The similarities of the Array command also extend to the Array command in AutoCAD. You have two basic choices:

- ▶ *Radial*, which enables you to array an item around a circle or an arc
- ▶ *Linear*, which enables you to array an item in a straight line or at an angle

Let's look at the radial array first.

Radial Array

A *radial array* is based on a radius. If you need items to be arrayed in a circular manner, the radial array is your best choice. Again, after you start the Array command, don't ignore the Options bar. It will guide you through most of the command.

To start using a radial array, follow these steps:

1. Select the 45° reference plane.

2. On the Modify | Reference Planes tab, click the Array button, as shown in Figure 4.11.

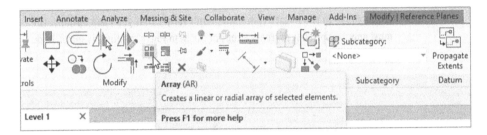

FIGURE 4.11 Select the item to be arrayed first, and then click the Array button on the Modify | Reference Planes tab.

3. With the Array command active, some choices become available on the Options bar, as shown in Figure 4.12. For this procedure, click the Radial button.

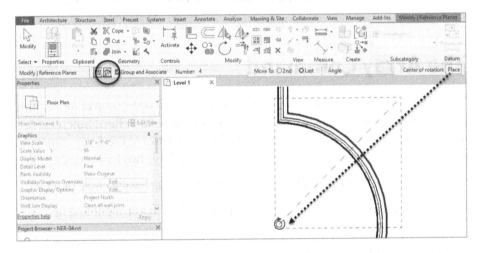

FIGURE 4.12 Setting the options for the Radial array and selecting the center point

4. Select the Group And Associate check box.

5. Set Number to 4.

6. Click the Move To: Last button.

7. With the options set, focus your attention on the object being arrayed. Notice the familiar rotate icon.

8. On the Options bar, click the Place button. It's located next to the Origin label, as shown in Figure 4.12.

I Don't Want to Move Anything!

The Move To: Last and the Move To: Second choices are somewhat misleading. You aren't actually "moving" anything. If you choose Move To: Last, for example, Revit places an additional item in the last place you pick, keeping the first item intact. Revit then divides the space between the two items evenly based on the number of items you specify in the options. If you specify four items, Revit still has two items left to divide.

If you choose Move To: Second, Revit places an additional item at the second point picked (just as with Move To: Last), but this time Revit adds additional items beyond the second item. The overall distance is calculated by the distance between the first two items.

9. Click the center/endpoint of the reference plane (see Figure 4.13).

10. With the pivot point in place, specify two points for the array. The first point will be a point along the angle of the item being arrayed. The second point will be a point along the angle on which you want to end.

11. Pick the endpoint of the reference plane you're arraying.

12. Move your cursor down until you see 90°. Then pick the second point (see Figure 4.13).

13. Pick (left-click) off into another part of the view. This establishes the array. You should have four reference planes at this point, similar to Figure 4.14.

14. Pick (left-click) one of the reference planes. You see a large, dashed box surrounding the reference plane and a temporary arc dimension with a blue number 4 at the quadrant. It may be obscured by the arc, as it is in Figure 4.14, but it's there nonetheless.

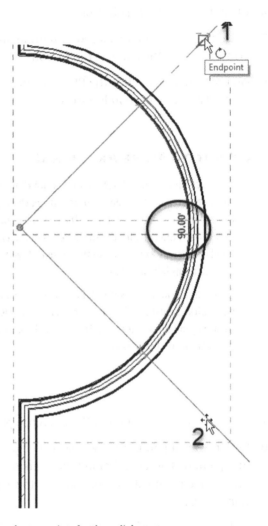

FIGURE 4.13   Specifying the two points for the radial array

15. Click the number 4. Zoom into the radial wall if you can't see it.

16. Change the count to 5. Press Enter, or click outside the array count field to set the change.

Getting the hang of radial arrays may take a few projects. The next array type, the linear array, follows the same concept as the radial array, but it's more straightforward. Yes, pun intended.

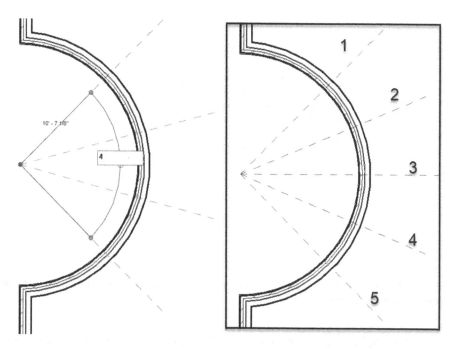

FIGURE 4.14 After the array is created, select one of the arrayed members. Notice that you can change the count.

Linear Array

You may wish to create an array along a line, and you can do this in Revit. When you create a *linear array*, you enjoy the same flexibility that you have with a radial array.

The objective of this procedure is to create an array of windows along the north and south walls, on the west side of the building's west wing. To do this, you'll first need to establish two strong reference planes.

To learn how to use the Linear array command, follow along:

1. Zoom in on the northwest section of the west wing, as shown in Figure 4.15.

2. You'll need to use reference planes to establish the ends of your window array. Go to the Ref Plane command on the Work Plane panel of the Architecture tab.

3. On the Draw panel, keep the Line icon active and add an offset of 1′–6″ (450 mm) on the Options bar (Imperial users, remember that you can just type **1 6**) on the Options bar.

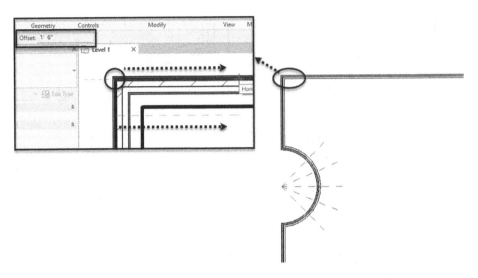

FIGURE 4.15 Creating the first reference plane; remember to hit the spacebar to flip the ref plane into the correct orientation.

4. Select the upper-left corner of the intersection of the walls as shown in Figure 4.15.

5. Move your cursor to the right. Notice the reference plane is above the wall. We want it below the wall.

6. Hit the spacebar. That will flip the reference plane down.

7. Pick a spot 2 or 3 feet to the right. That will add your reference plane.

8. Hit Esc once.

9. Zoom in on the intersection of the vertical wall and the radial wall, as shown in Figure 4.16.

10. Pick the outside corner.

11. Hit the spacebar.

12. Move your cursor to the right about 2 or 3 feet and pick a spot. Your two reference planes should resemble Figure 4.17.

13. Press Esc a few times.

If you're drawing the reference plane and it keeps going above the wall (as opposed to below the wall), you can tap the spacebar as you're drawing. Doing so flips the side of the wall on which the plane is being drawn.

▶

Now you need to add a window based on the bottom reference plane. This window will then be arrayed up the wall to meet the northern reference plane. Here are the steps:

1. On the Architecture tab, click the Window button.

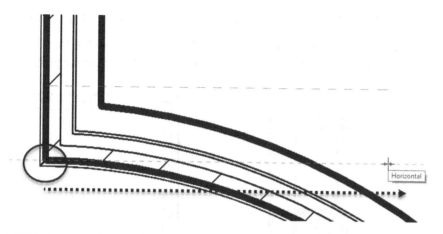

FIGURE 4.16 Creating the second reference plane; remember to hit the spacebar to flip the ref plane into the correct orientation.

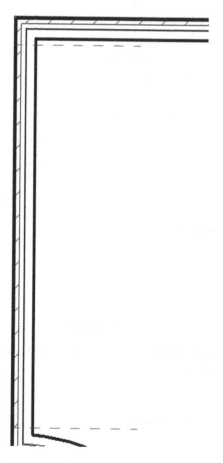

FIGURE 4.17 The two reference planes are established.

2. Change Element Type to Fixed: 24″ × 72″ (610 mm × 1829 mm).

3. Place the window approximately where it's shown in Figure 4.18. You have to move the window in alignment with the reference plane.

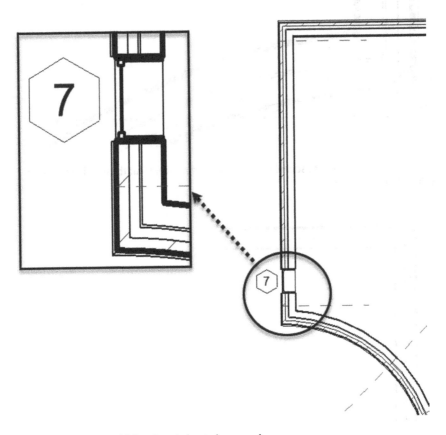

FIGURE 4.18 Adding the window to be arrayed

4. Press the Esc key.

5. Select the window.

6. On the Modify | Windows tab, click the Move button.

7. Move the window from the bottom, outside corner down to the reference plane, as shown in Figure 4.19.

8. Press Esc.

9. Zoom out until you can see the entire wall.

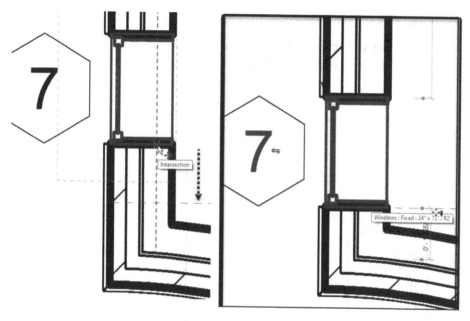

FIGURE 4.19 Moving the window into position

10. Select the window you just inserted into the wall.

11. On the Modify | Windows tab, click the Array button.

12. On the Options bar, select Linear, as shown in Figure 4.20.

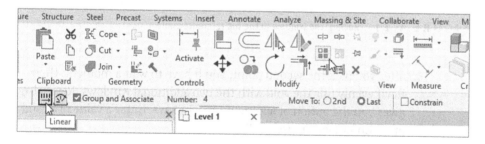

FIGURE 4.20 Choosing the linear array options

13. Select the Group and Associate check box (if it isn't already selected).

14. For Number, enter 4.

15. Select Move To: Last.

16. Pick the top endpoint of the window.

17. Move your cursor up the wall, and pick a point perpendicular to the top reference plane, as shown in Figure 4.21.

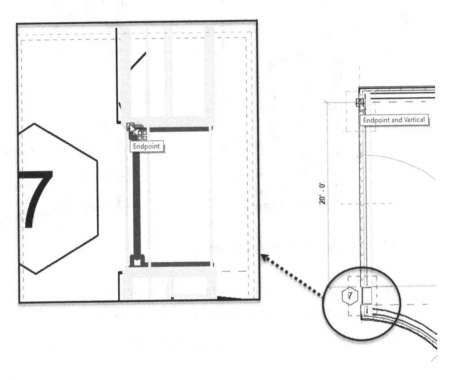

FIGURE 4.21 "Moving" the window to the top reference plane

18. After you pick the second point, you'll have to wait a moment; then Revit evenly fills the void with the two additional windows. Revit also gives you the option of adding more windows. Enter a value of 5, and press Enter (see Figure 4.22).

 N O T E   After your items are grouped and arrayed, you can still move the end item. Not only can you move the end item in the direction of the array, but you can move it laterally to the array, causing a step in the array.

With the array completed, it's time to duplicate your efforts on the other side of the radial portion of this wall. As in CAD, at this point you have a few choices. You can repeat the Array command, copy the items, or mirror the items.

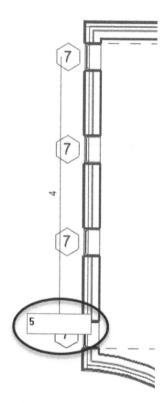

FIGURE 4.22 Changing the number of items in the array. You can always come back to the arrayed group and change this value at any time.

The Mirror Command

The Mirror command works exactly as expected: it makes a copy of an object or a group of objects in the opposite orientation of the first item(s). The crucial point to remember is that you'll need to specify a mirror *plane*.

Although you simply couldn't avoid using this command in previous chapters, we need to address and explore the Mirror command officially. The most useful aspect of the Mirror command is that if reference planes already exist in the model, you can pick these planes to perform the mirror, as opposed to sketching a new plane around which to mirror.

The objective of the following example is to mirror the windows to the south side of the west wall:

1. Zoom in on the windows you arrayed in the previous exercise.

2. Hold down the Ctrl key and individually select all of the windows and tags as shown in Figure 4.23.

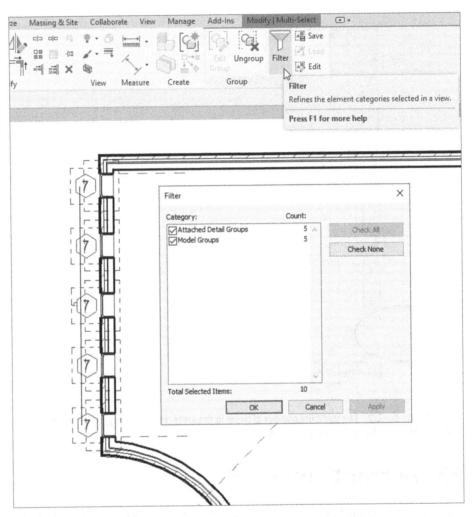

FIGURE 4.23 Selecting the items to be mirrored. Make sure you don't select the wall in which the windows reside.

3. Click the Filter button as shown in Figure 4.23 to ensure you didn't overselect.

   TIP   Oops! You selected the wall. That's OK. You don't need to press Esc and start your selection over. Simply hold down the Shift key and select the wall. It will become deselected.

4. On the Modify tab, click the Mirror - Pick Axis button, as shown in Figure 4.24.

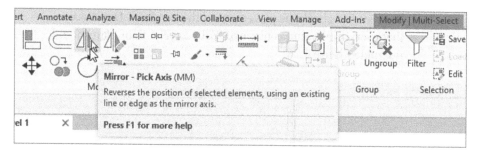

FIGURE 4.24 The Mirror buttons appear when you select an item.

5. Position your cursor over the center reference plane that is part of the Radial array. When you pause, a tooltip indicates that you're about to select the reference plane. When you see this tooltip, select the reference plane, as shown in Figure 4.25.

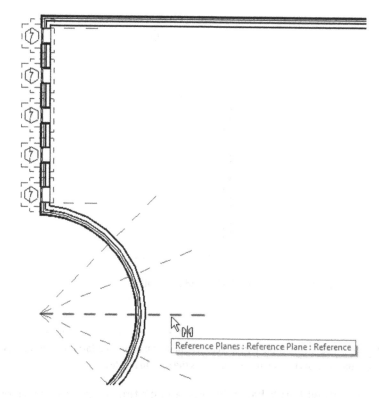

FIGURE 4.25 The line you're going to pick is the reference plane shown here.

6. Zoom out to check the placement of the windows. Don't assume that everything went as planned. Your Level 1 floor plan should resemble Figure 4.26.

FIGURE 4.26 The finished west wall

When you pick the reference plane, Revit mirrors the entire group of windows. Make sure you are selecting the tags during this operation as well!

NOTE   If the mirror went wrong or you aren't comfortable with the results, use the Undo button and try again. Now is the time to practice!

The two straight walls have windows, and it's time to array some windows within the radial portion. The problem is, when you insert a window along a radius, you can't snap it to the intersection of the reference plane and the wall. This is where the Align tool becomes critical.

The Align Tool

You'll find yourself in situations where two items need to be aligned with each other. The Align command is a great tool for accomplishing this task. It's one of the most useful tools in Revit, and you'll use it extensively. Overuse of this command isn't possible! Because Align is a tool, you don't have to select an item first for this function to become available. You can select Align at any time.

To practice using the Align tool, follow along:

1. Zoom in on the radial portion of the west wall, as shown in Figure 4.27.

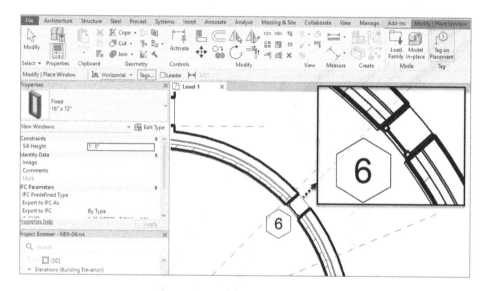

FIGURE 4.27   Place the window approximately in the area shown here.

2. On the Architecture tab, click the Window button.

3. In the Type Selector, choose Fixed: 16″ × 72″ (406 mm × 1829 mm).

4. Place the window in the radial wall in a location similar to that shown in Figure 4.27. Don't attempt to eyeball the center of the window with the reference plane. As a matter of fact, purposely misalign the window.

5. On the Modify tab, click the Align button, as shown in Figure 4.28.

6. The Align tool needs you to select two items. First, select the item you want to *align to*; pick the reference plane as shown in Figure 4.29.

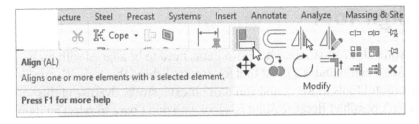

FIGURE 4.28   Click the Align button on the Modify | Place Window tab.

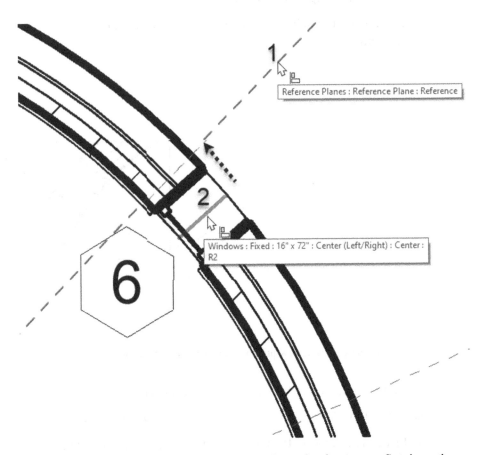

FIGURE 4.29   Choosing the items for alignment. Remember that you must first choose the item you want to align to.

7. Now you need to pick a point on the window: the centerline of the window. By looking at the window, you won't see this line. Hover your cursor over the middle of the window, and a centerline becomes highlighted. When you see this centerline, pick the window.

The window moves into alignment with the reference plane, as shown in Figure 4.30.

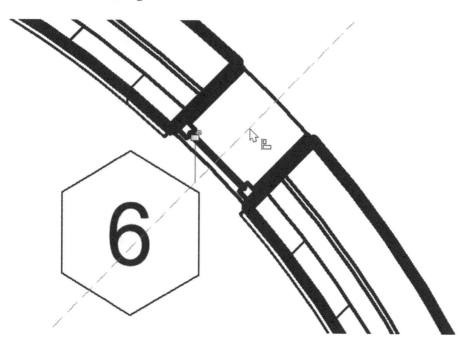

FIGURE 4.30 The window is now in alignment with the reference plane.

8. Press Esc, and then select the window.

9. Pick the Array button on the Modify | Windows tab.

10. Create a radial array of the windows with a count of five (total). You remember how, right? The only thing I want you to do differently is to uncheck Group And Associate on the Options bar. See Figure 4.31.

 NOTE Adding reference planes and working in a controlled environment is typical of Revit. You establish a reference plane, add a component, and then execute a command such as Array, Copy, or Move. Although it may seem like quite a few steps, you're now accurately and deliberately placing items in your model. The accuracy you apply here will propagate itself throughout the project in terms of elevations, sections, and drawing sheets.

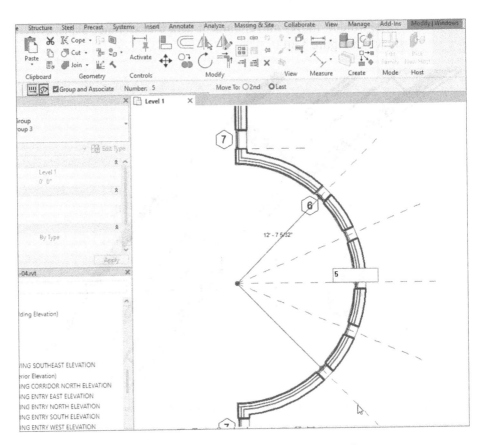

FIGURE 4.31 The window is now in alignment with the reference plane.

Let's practice more with the Align tool. It's one of the most important modify tools in the Revit arsenal, and I don't want to understate its usefulness. Follow along with these steps:

1. Zoom into the end of the corridor in the east wing of the building, as shown in Figure 4.32.

2. On the Architecture tab, click the Door button.

3. On the Mode panel, click Load Family.

4. Browse to the Doors directory, then to Commercial.

5. Select Door-Passage-Double-Flush.rfa.

6. In the Specify Types dialog, select 72″× 84″ (1829 mm × 2133 mm).

7. Place the Double-Passage-Double-Flush: 72″ × 84″ (1829 mm × 2133 mm) door in the radial corridor wall, as shown in Figure 4.33.

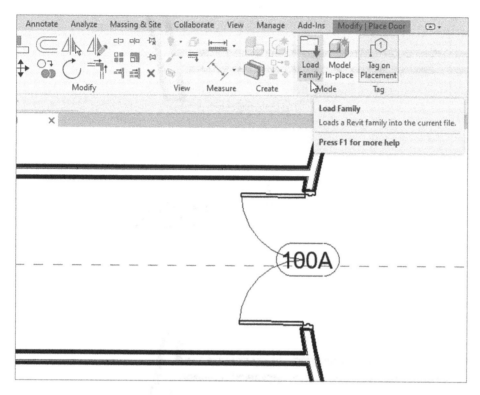

FIGURE 4.32 Adding a double door to the east wing corridor

As when you placed the window along the reference plane in the preceding procedure, don't try to eyeball the correct alignment; you want to misalign the door on purpose.

8. Renumber the door 100A.

9. On the Modify panel, click the Align button (or type **AL**).

10. Pick the horizontal reference plane.

11. Pick the centerline of the door.

The Split Element Command

The Split Element command is the equivalent of the Break command in AutoCAD. You can use the Split Element command on walls and when you edit an element in Sketch Mode.

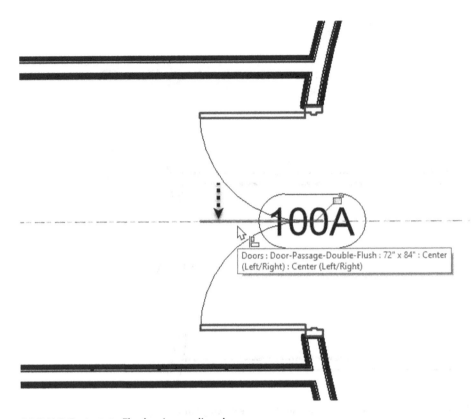

Doors : Door-Passage-Double-Flush : 72" x 84" : Center
(Left/Right) : Center (Left/Right)

F I G U R E 4 . 3 3 **The door is now aligned.**

The objective of this procedure is to cut a notch out of a wall by using the Edit Profile function:

1. In the Project Browser, open the Sections (Building Section) called West Wing South Wall Section, as shown in Figure 4.34.

2. Select the wall beyond, as shown in Figure 4.35.

3. On the Modify | Walls tab, click the Edit Profile button (see Figure 4.35).

   After you select the Edit Profile option, you're put into Sketch Mode. You know you're in Sketch Mode because your Ribbon now has a Mode panel with Finish Edit Mode and Cancel Edit Mode options that you must select to return to the full model. Also, the wall you've selected now consists of four magenta sketch lines, and the rest of the model is shaded into the background.

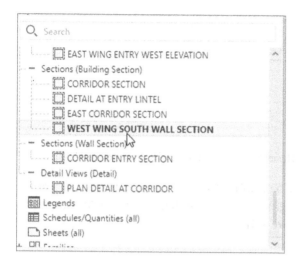

FIGURE 4.34 Open the section called West Wing South Wall Section.

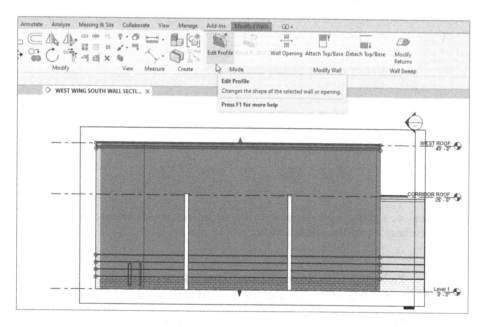

FIGURE 4.35 Select the wall beyond, and click the Edit Profile button on the Modify | Walls tab.

4. On the Modify | Walls ➤ Edit Profile tab, click the Split Element button, as shown in Figure 4.36.

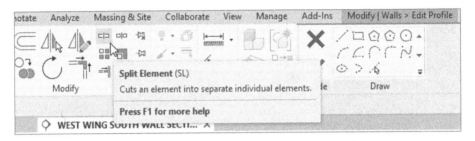

FIGURE 4.36 Select the Split Element button on the Modify | Walls ➤ Edit Profile tab.

5. Look at your Options bar. Notice that you can specify that you want to delete the inner segment. Select the Delete Inner Segment check box, as shown in Figure 4.37.

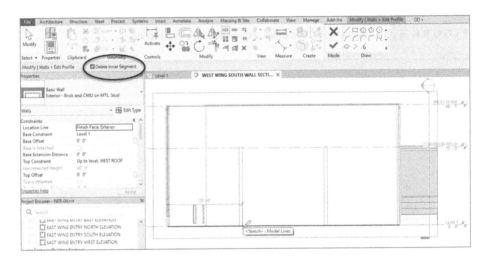

FIGURE 4.37 To remove a segment of a line, you must use the Split Element command and select Delete Inner Segment from the Options bar.

6. Pick the intersection of the bottom magenta sketch line and the inside face of the left wall for the first split point (see Figure 4.38).

7. Pick the intersection of the bottom magenta sketch line and the inside face of the right wall (see Figure 4.38).

YOU CAN ALSO ADD A GAP

There is a second split option. The Split With Gap function enables you to split an item and choose the size of the gap segment.

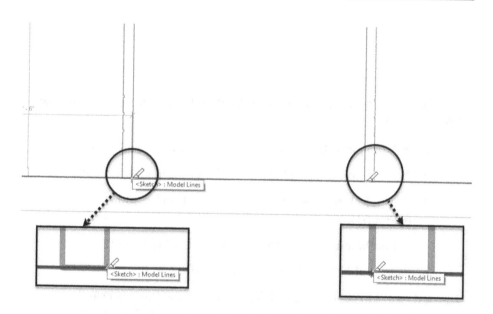

FIGURE 4.38 Splitting the bottom line

After you pick these points, the magenta sketch line is segmented. Now you need to add more lines to the sketch. To do this, leave the Split Element command and follow along by using the sketch tools on the Draw panel:

1. On the Draw panel of the Modify | Walls ➤ Edit Profile tab, click the Pick Lines icon, as shown in Figure 4.39.

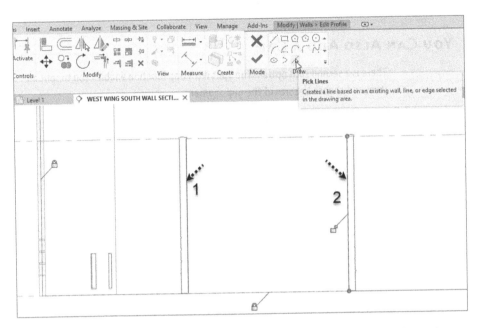

FIGURE 4.39 Tracing the walls to form a notch. This is done by selecting the Pick Lines icon and picking the walls.

2. Pick the inside face of the left wall (item 1 in Figure 4.39).

3. Pick the inside face of the right wall (item 2 in Figure 4.39).

4. Now, select the Line button in the Draw panel as shown in Figure 4.40.

5. In the Options toolbar, set the offset to 1′-0″ (300 mm).

6. Pick point #1 to point #2 in Figure 4.40

The next step is to get the magenta lines to form a continuous loop. This means there can be no gaps or overlapping lines. Each line starts exactly where the last line ends:

1. Press Esc.

2. Select the vertical magenta line on the wall to the left.

3. Zoom in to the top; notice there is a small blue grip on the end of the line.

4. Pick that grip and drag it down so that it meets the horizontal line.

5. Repeat the procedure for the right side. See Figure 4.41.

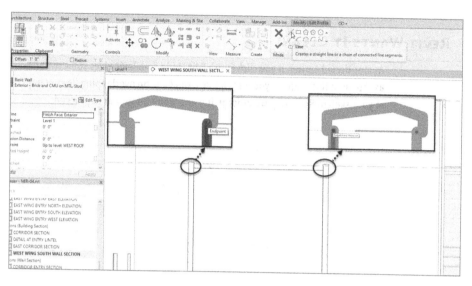

FIGURE 4.40 Drawing the top line with a 1′-0″ (300 mm) offset

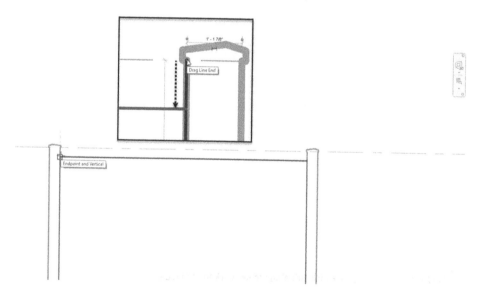

FIGURE 4.41 Modifying the sketch lines by stretching the grips to form a continuous loop

6. Click the Green Checkmark (Finish Edit Mode) as shown in Figure 4.42.

7. Go to a 3D view to check out your model, as shown in Figure 4.43. You can either click the Default 3D View button on the Quick Access toolbar or pick the {3D} view from the Project Browser.

REVIT WANTS IT CLEAN!

As mentioned earlier, if you click Finish Edit Mode and Revit gives you a warning, as shown in this graphic, you *must* be sure you have no overlapping lines or gaps in your sketch. Revit is quite unforgiving and won't allow you to proceed.

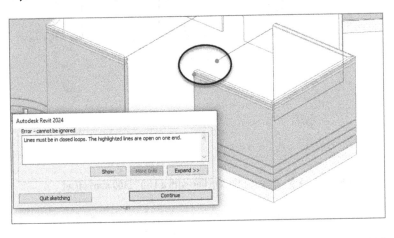

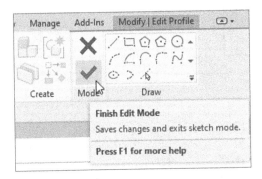

FIGURE 4.42   Click Finish Edit Mode to get back to the model.

The next set of procedures focuses on basic cleanup using the Trim command. Although you can accomplish a lot with this single command, you must get used to a certain Revit method.

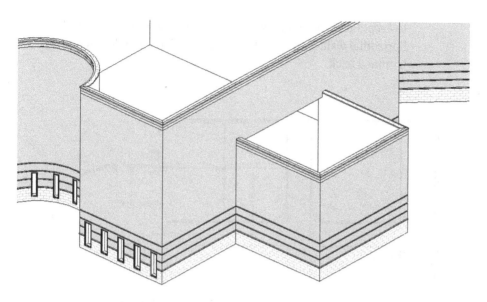

FIGURE 4.43 The building in 3D up to this point

The Trim/Extend Command

Anytime you need to cut or extend an item, you'll use the Trim command. In any design-based application, you won't get very far without this command. You can use the Trim command on walls and in sketch mode, similar to how you would use the Split Element command. As mentioned earlier, however, you need to understand specific procedures to be comfortable using this command.

To use the Trim command, follow along:

1. Go to Level 1 under the Floor Plans category in the Project Browser.

2. Zoom in on the east wing. Select the two walls as shown in Figure 4.44 and mirror them (Mirror Pick Axis).

3. On the Modify tab, click the Trim/Extend Single Element button, as shown in Figure 4.45.

4. Zoom in on the area, as shown in Figure 4.46.

5. To trim the vertical wall back to the horizontal wall, you must first pick the wall that you want to trim *to* (the cutting element). In this case, select the south face of the horizontal wall (see Figure 4.46).

6. Now you must pick a point along the vertical wall. The trick here is that you must pick a point on the side of the wall that you want

to *keep*. Pick a point along the vertical wall above (north of) the horizontal wall, as shown in Figure 4.47. After you do, the wall is trimmed back.

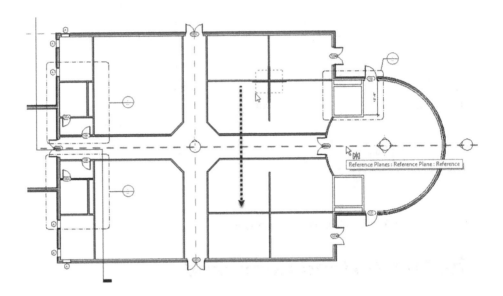

FIGURE 4.44   Mirror these two walls.

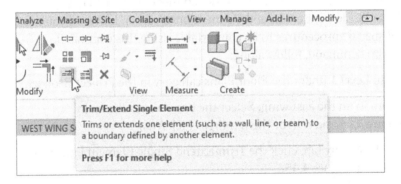

FIGURE 4.45   Click the Trim/Extend Single Element button on the Modify tab.

7. Press Esc to terminate the command.

You may not always want to trim an item. Often, you need to elongate an item to reach a destination point. In the drafting world, this procedure is better known as *extend*. The process for using the Extend feature is similar to the process for the Trim command. First, however, you must select the wall to which you want to extend an object and then select the object to be extended:

1. Zoom in on the south part of the east wing.

2. On the Modify tab, click the Trim/Extend Single Element button.

3. Pick the south corridor wall. This is the wall to which you want to extend.

4. Pick the vertical wall that doesn't quite intersect. Press Esc, and your walls should now look like Figure 4.48.

5. Save the model.

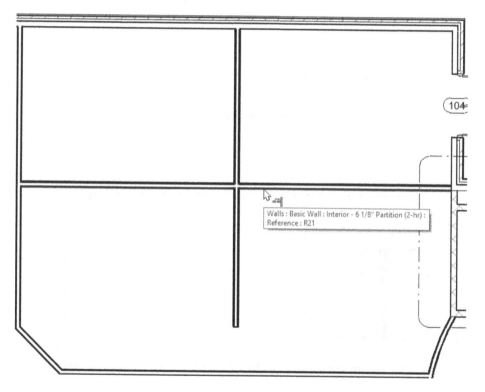

Walls : Basic Wall : Interior - 6 1/8" Partition (2-hr) :
Reference : R21

FIGURE 4.46 Zoom into this area to start trimming the walls.

There is one more command to examine that is used in the day-to-day modification of a Revit model. Most of the commands you've used to place items in the model have had the Offset command built into the options of a specific procedure. The next section focuses on offsetting items by using the stand-alone Revit Offset command.

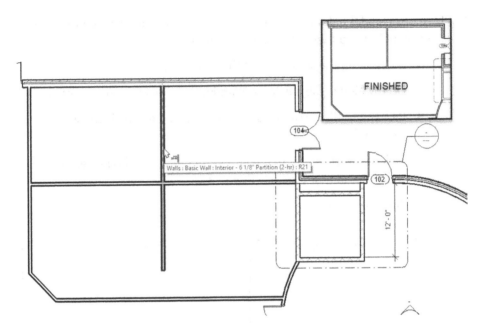

FIGURE 4.47 Pick a point along the wall you want to keep.

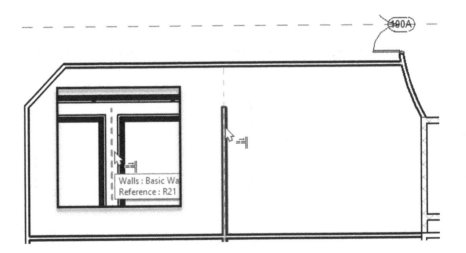

FIGURE 4.48 Extending some interior partitions

The Offset Command

The Offset command enables you to create a copy of a linear item at a specified distance. As mentioned earlier, the need to offset an item crops up much less often in Revit than in a conventional drafting application. This is because in Revit most commands provide offset functionality as an option. Sometimes, however, you need the good-old Offset command.

To get used to using the Offset command, follow these steps:

1. Zoom in on the west part of the east wing. This is the area where the restrooms are located (see Figure 4.49). The objective is to offset the vertical wall that is to the right of the restrooms to the middle of the open space.

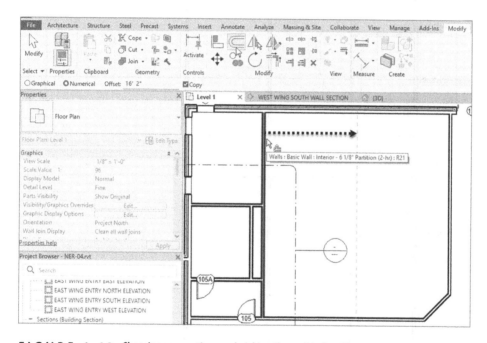

FIGURE 4.49 Choosing your options and picking the wall to be offset

2. On the Modify panel of the Modify tab, click the Offset button, as shown in Figure 4.49.

3. On the Options bar, click the Numerical button.

4. Enter 16'–2" (4850 mm) in the Offset field.

5. Make sure Copy is selected.

6. Hover your cursor over the wall to the right of the lavatory, as shown in Figure 4.49. A dashed alignment line appears to the right of the wall.

7. Pick the wall. The new wall should be in the middle of the large room.

8. Repeat the process for the walls south of the corridor. Your interior should resemble Figure 4.50.

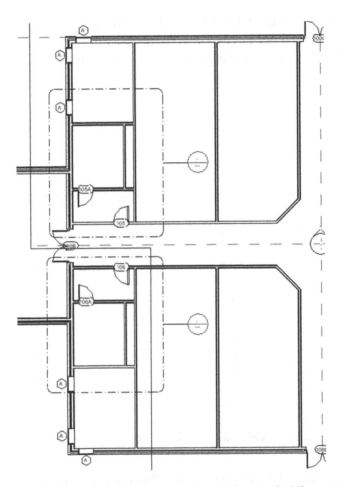

FIGURE 4.50 Completing the floor plan by using the Offset command will be a common procedure.

WARNING Be sure your math is correct. After you offset an item, use the Measure command. I've mentioned this before, and I will mention it repeatedly throughout this book! You'll be glad you measured now rather than later.

This concludes our discussion of Offset. Because this floor plan consists of items you want to repeat on other floors, you can now explore how to do this by using the Copy/Paste command from Windows.

Copy/Paste

Yes, this is the actual Microsoft Windows Copy/Paste function. In Revit, you'll use this feature quite a bit. There is no better way to complete a space or a layout on one level and then use that layout on another level than by copying the geometry.

To practice using the Copy/Paste function, you'll select the two lavatories on Level 1, copy them to the Windows Clipboard, and paste them to the remaining floors:

1. Zoom into the east wing of the building.

2. Select the walls, door, and windows that define both bathrooms. Also select the corridor walls and the radial corridor wall at the east end of the building. Be sure to select the internal doors as well. These selections are shown in Figure 4.51.

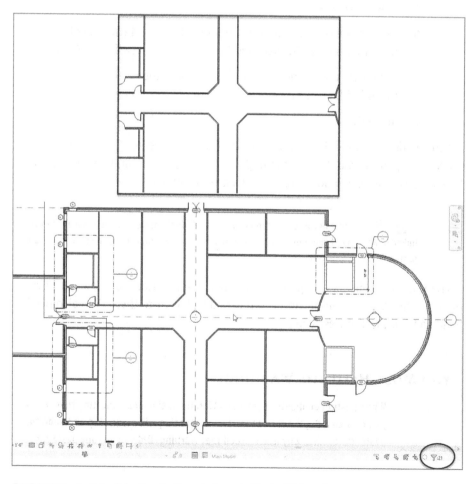

FIGURE 4.51 Selecting the items to be copied to the Clipboard

3. Choose Copy To Clipboard from the Clipboard panel of the Modify |
Multi-Select tab (or press Ctrl+C). See Figure 4.52.

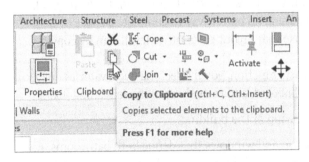

FIGURE 4.52 Good ol' fashioned Copy To Clipboard

4. Go to a 3D view.

5. On the Clipboard panel of the Modify tab, expand the Paste tool and
then click Aligned To Selected Levels, as shown in Figure 4.53.

6. In the next dialog, hold down the Shift key and select Levels 2
through 5 (see Figure 4.53).

7. Click OK.

Your model should look like Figure 4.54. If it doesn't, go back and try the
procedure again. If you did get it wrong, you can right-click and choose Select
Previous. That way, you don't have to pick around all over again.

Remember, when you're
selecting multiple
items, you need to press
and hold the Ctrl key
to add to the selection
set. If you inadvertently
select too much, press
the Shift key to deselect
the items.

NOTE   Just because you copied and pasted identical items doesn't mean they're
linked in any way. If you move, edit, or delete any of the original walls, the new walls you
pasted won't be affected.

The last section in this chapter focuses on actual practice. You now have five
floors in the east wing alone, and you must add a layout to them. You also need
to add a layout to the west wing.

You Must Heed the Warning!

While pasting elements, if you see a Warning dialog box indicating that you've
just created a duplicate and that double counting will occur, stop and undo the
paste. Determine why Revit issued that warning. Did you already paste these

elements to this level? Sometimes the tops of the walls are above the higher level. You can check this as well.

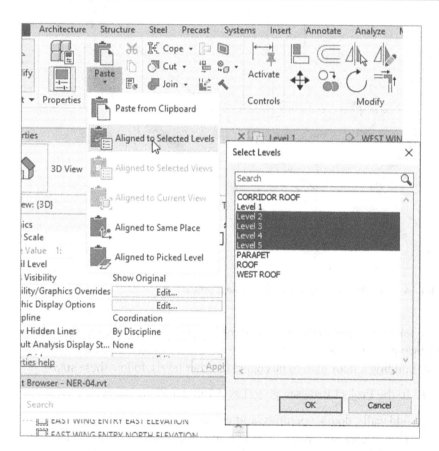

FIGURE 4.53 The Select Levels dialog enables you to choose the levels to which you're pasting the information.

Creating the Plans

Now that you've added walls, doors, and windows, you can begin to combine this experience with your knowledge of the basic Revit editing commands. In the previous section, you *started* to lay out your floor plans.

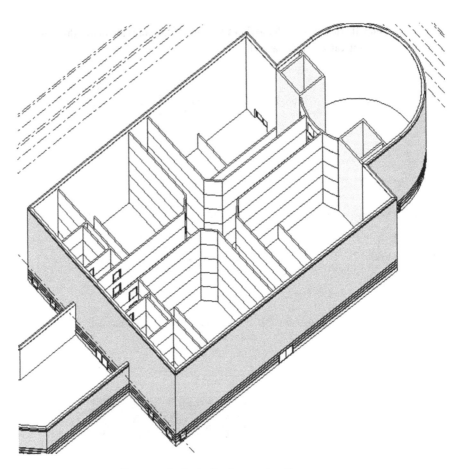

FIGURE 4.54 The east wing is starting to come together.

You can follow along with the book's examples up to floor 3. You can then create your own plans for floors 4 and 5.

To start building a floor plan to be copied to other levels, follow these steps:

1. In the Project Browser, go to Level 1 under Floor Plans.

2. Add walls, doors, openings, and windows to resemble Figure 4.55. These doors and windows can be any type you like. If your model varies slightly from the example in the book, don't be concerned.

3. In the Project Browser, go to Floor Plan Level 2.

4. Press Esc to clear any selection.

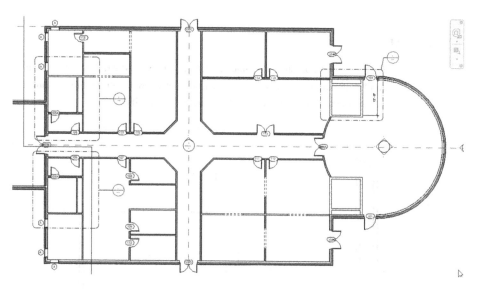

FIGURE 4.55 The first-floor layout for the east wing

5. In the Properties dialog, set Underlay to None, as shown in Figure 4.56. (Underlay is simply the floor below. You can set your underlay to any floor you'd like.)

6. Set Detail Level to Fine.

7. Create a floor plan layout similar to Figure 4.56. Make all of the dimensions as even and as round as possible. Use all the commands and functions you've learned up to this point.

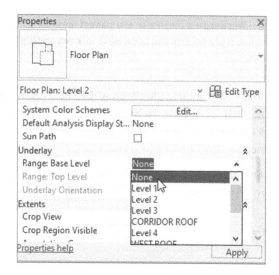

FIGURE 4.56 Switch Underlay from Level 1 to None.

Oh Snap!

Revit has finally added a snap mid between points. Start the wall command, and right-click. Chose Snap Overrides and chose Snap Mid Between 2 Points as shown below. You can model the wall without any reference lines.

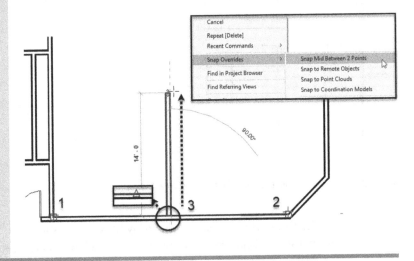

8. Select the windows on Level 2, go to a 3D view, and, using Copy and Paste ➢ Aligned To Selected Levels, align them all the way to Level 5. This way, you know your windows are aligned, and you can follow this procedure in your room layout for each floor (see Figure 4.57).

 WARNING   When you use Copy/Paste, you may get the same duplicate value warning mentioned earlier. If you do, stop and undo. Make sure you aren't pasting windows over other windows.

9. Go to Level 3, and create a floor plan similar to Figure 4.59. You can do this by using Paste ➢ Aligned To Selected Levels from Level 1. The floor plans are identical, other than the wall configuration in the northwest corner.

10. Go to Level 4, and create your own floor plan. The book will give no example. You're on your own!

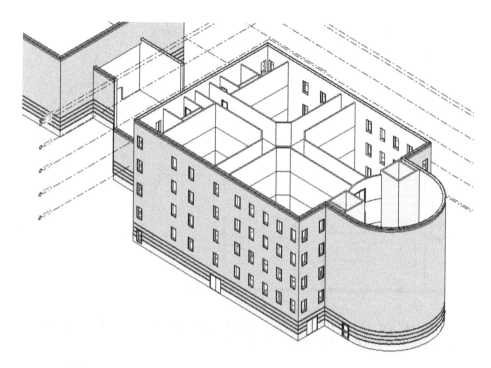

F I G U R E 4 . 5 7   The layout for Level 2. Try to make the dimensions as even as possible, consistent with what is shown here.

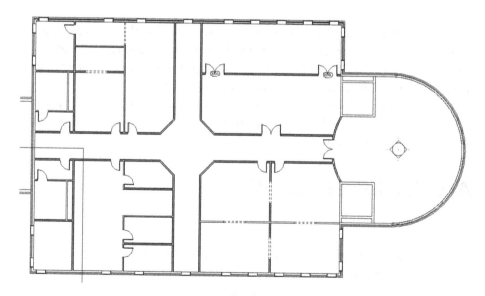

F I G U R E 4 . 5 8   Using Copy/Paste, align the windows to the higher floors. This will influence your floor layout for each level.

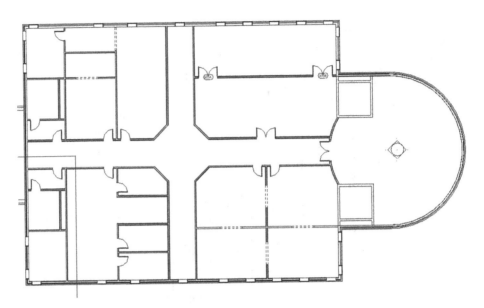

FIGURE 4.59 Level 3: This floor plan was mostly copied from Level 1, with the exception of the east side where the walls conflicted with the windows.

11. Create one more floor plan for Level 5. Again, design your own layout. Be as creative as you wish.

12. Save the model.

If you got through that last procedure and you're happy with the results, you're well on your way to being efficient in Revit. This is because you just created a floor plan on your own. These last few steps were provided to prove that Revit can be quite intuitive when approached with a little experience.

If you aren't comfortable with your results in this section, that's OK. I had an uncomfortable feeling the first time I did this as well. Take a deep breath, and go back through the steps where you think you got lost.

Are You Experienced?

Now you can. . .

✓ use common editing commands to alter the appearance of your model

✓ use reference planes to establish good, accurate methods of layout

✓ array items and change the count, length, and radius if needed

✓ align items and keep them constrained

✓ use locks to constrain the alignment of one element to another

✓ split items to remove a segment or to turn one item into two

✓ use the Copy and Paste ➤ Aligned To Selected Levels commands to create multiple floors that are similar in layout

CHAPTER 5

Dimensioning and Annotating

This chapter focuses on giving you the ability to dimension and annotate a model. After the novelty of having a really cool model in 3D wears off, you need to buckle down and produce some bid documents. This is where the Autodesk® Revit® program must prove its functionality. You should ask yourself, "Can Revit produce drawings consistent with what is acceptable according to national standards and—more importantly—my company's standards? And, if so, how do I get to this point?" These are the questions that owners and managers will be asking you. If you're an owner or a manager, then you should be asking yourself these questions.

This chapter covers the following topics:

▶ **Selecting and applying dimensioning**

▶ **Using dimensions as a layout tool**

▶ **Placing text and annotations**

Dimensioning

The answers to the questions I listed begin with dimensioning and annotations. This is where you can begin to make Revit your own. Also, in this chapter, you'll find that dimensions take on an entirely new role in the design process.

I think you'll like dimensioning in Revit. It's almost fun—*almost*. Before you start, however, let's get one thing out of the way: You can't alter a dimension to display an increment that isn't true. Hooray! As you go through this chapter, you'll quickly learn that when you place a dimension, it becomes not only an annotation but a layout tool as well.

The Dimension command has six separate types: Aligned, Linear, Angular, Radial, Arc Length, and Diameter. Each is important in adding dimensions to a model, and each is covered separately in this section.

Let's get going. To begin, open the file in which you've been following along. If you didn't complete the example in Chapter 4, "Working with the Autodesk Revit Tools," go to the book's website at www.wiley.com/go/revit2024ner. From there you can browse to Chapter 5 and find the file called NER-05.rvt.

Aligned Dimensions

The most popular of all the Revit dimensions is the Aligned option. You'll use this type of dimension 75 percent of the time.

An aligned dimension in Revit enables you to place a dimension along an object at any angle. The resulting dimension aligns with the object being dimensioned. A linear dimension, in contrast, adds a dimension only at 0°, 90°, 180°, or 270°, regardless of the item's angle.

To add an aligned dimension, perform these steps:

1. Go to the Level 1 floor plan.

2. Zoom in on the east wing of the building.

3. On the Annotate tab, click the Aligned button, as shown in Figure 5.1.

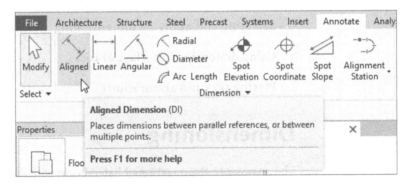

FIGURE 5.1   Starting the Aligned Dimension command from the Annotate tab

4. On the Options bar are two drop-down menus with some choices, as shown in Figure 5.2. Make sure Wall Faces is selected.

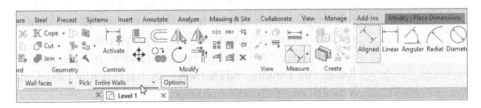

FIGURE 5.2   The Options bar for the Dimension command. Notice the Options button.

5. The next menu lets you pick individual references or entire walls. Select Entire Walls.

6. At the far right on the Options bar is an Options button, which allows you to make further choices when selecting the entire wall. Click the Options button.

7. In the Auto Dimension Options dialog box, select Intersecting Walls (see Figure 5.3). Don't select any other item. Click OK.

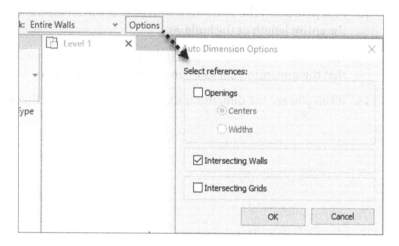

FIGURE 5.3 The Auto Dimension Options dialog box

8. Zoom in on the north wall, as shown in Figure 5.4.

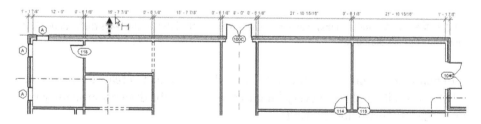

FIGURE 5.4 By choosing the Intersecting Walls option, you can add an entire string of dimensions in one click.

9. Pick (left-click) the north exterior wall. Notice that the dimensions are completely filled out.

10. Pick a point (to place the dimension) approximately 8′ (2400 mm) above the north wall (see Figure 5.4).

11. In true Revit form, you're still in the command unless you tell Revit you don't want to be. In this case, click the Options button on the Options bar (the same one you clicked before).

12. Deselect the Intersecting Walls option in the Auto Dimension Options dialog box, and click OK.

13. Pick (left-click) the same wall. You now have a dimension traveling the entire length of the building.

14. Move your cursor above the first dimension string you added. Notice that the dimension clicks when it gets directly above the first string.

15. When you see the dimension snap, pick that point (see Figure 5.5).

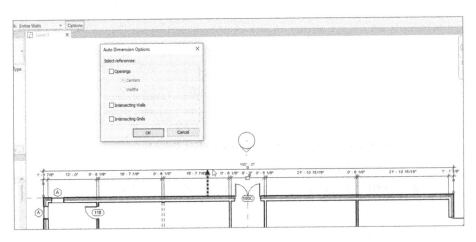

FIGURE 5.5 Adding a major dimension by turning off the Intersecting Walls choice in the Auto Dimension Options dialog box

In many cases, you'll need the ability to pick two points to create a dimension. What a world it would be if everything were as easy as the dimension string you just added. Unfortunately, it isn't.

Creating Aligned Dimensions by Picking Points

Nine times out of ten, you'll be picking two points to create a dimension. This is usually quite simple in Revit—until you get into a situation where the walls are at an angle other than 90°. In a moment, you'll explore that issue, but for now, let's add some straight dimensions:

 N O T E Before you get started, note that this procedure isn't intuitive. If it does come easily to you, great! If not, don't get discouraged. Keep trying.

1. Zoom in on the northeast portion of the east wing, as shown in Figure 5.6.

2. On the Annotate tab, click the Aligned button if it isn't selected already.

3. On the Options bar, select Wall Faces.

4. Next, on the Options bar, choose Individual References from the Pick menu., and do the following:

   a. Pick the outside face of the north wall marked 1 in Figure 5.6.

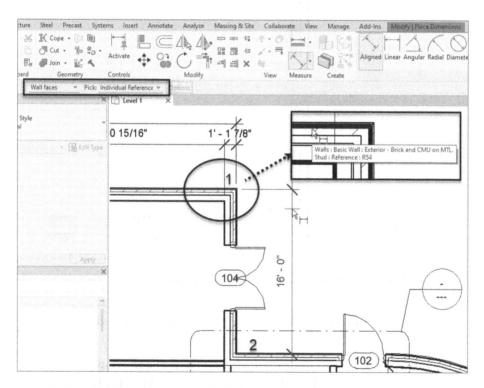

F I G U R E 5 . 6 Placing the dimension by picking two objects

    b. Pick the horizontal wall that ties into the radial wall, marked 2 in Figure 5.6.

    c. Place the dimension about 8′ (2400 mm) to the right of the vertical wall, as shown in Figure 5.6.

5. With the Aligned Dimension command still running, do the following:

    a. Pick the outside face of the northern wall.

    b. Pick the centerline of the door, as shown in Figure 5.7, but don't press Esc or terminate the command.

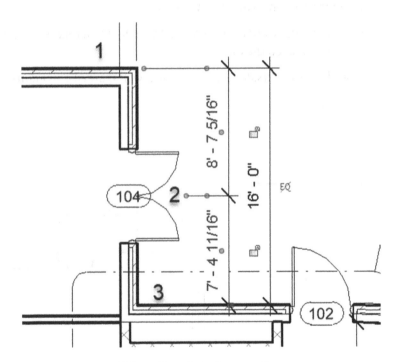

FIGURE 5.7 Adding a dimension string manually

    c. Pick the horizontal wall that ties into the radial wall, marked 3 in Figure 5.7.

    d. Pick a point inside (to the left of) the first dimension (see Figure 5.7). This places the dimension string and finalizes the session.

WARNING   When you add a string of dimensions, you must not stop and then resume the dimension string in the middle of the command. As you'll see in a moment, when you add dimensions in a continuous line, you can do a lot in terms of making adjustments to the objects you're dimensioning.

The actual dimension values are blue. You also see a blue EQ icon with a slash through it (see Figure 5.7).

6. Click the blue EQ button, as shown in Figure 5.8. If the door was not exactly centered, this will force the door to move to an equal distance between the two walls. Notice also that the dimension string is actually one object. This is important.

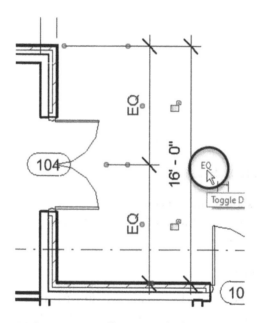

FIGURE 5.8 You can use the dimension string to move the door by clicking the EQ button.

7. Press Esc twice, or click Modify.

Sometimes you may want to display the dimensions rather than the EQ that Revit shows as a default. To do so, follow along:

1. Select the dimension.

2. Right-click.

3. Choose EQ Display (this deselects the option), as shown in Figure 5.9.

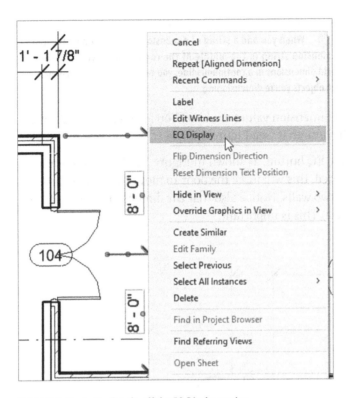

FIGURE 5.9 Toggle off the EQ Display option.

The dimensions will now show an increment.

Pretty cool. I should address one last item involving aligned dimensions: How do you dimension along an angle?

Dimensioning an Angle

Another way to tell Revit how to display dimensions is to select the dimension and then look at the properties. Here you'll be given additional choices.

No, not an *angel*, an angle. Adding this type of aligned dimension isn't the easiest thing to do in Revit. As a matter of fact, it is woefully inadequate. This is why I'm addressing the process as a separate item in this book. Here are the steps:

1. Zoom in on the 45° corridor area (the portion of the east building where the corridors meet).

2. On the Annotate tab, click the Detail Line button, as shown in Figure 5.10.

3. For the first point, pick the intersection 1, as shown in Figure 5.11.

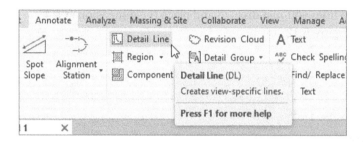

FIGURE 5.10 Clicking the Detail Line button

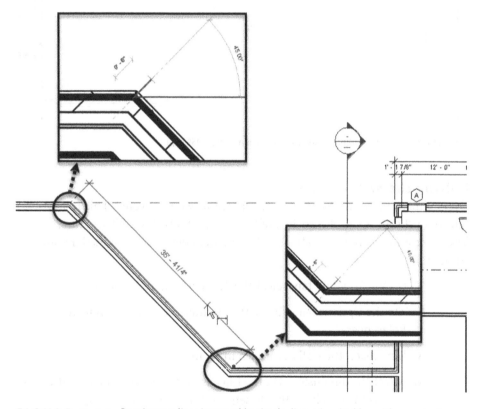

FIGURE 5.11 Drawing two lines just to add a simple dimension. I told you it's annoying!

4. Draw a short line at a 45° angle about 4″ or 5″ (102 mm or 127 mm), as shown in Figure 5.11.

5. Repeat the procedure on intersection 2.

6. Select the Aligned Dimension button

7. Pick the two lines you just drew in and place the dimension at a 45° angle. See Figure 5.12.

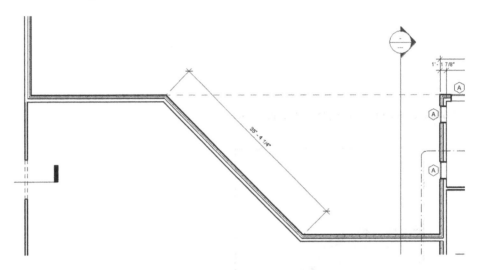

FIGURE 5.12 Adding an aligned dimension along a 45° wall

Editing the Witness Line

Every dimension in Revit has its own grip points when selected. This is similar to most CAD applications. Two of these grips control the witness line. The *witness line* is the line "attached" to the item being dimensioned. Follow these steps:

1. On the Annotate tab, select the Aligned Dimension button

2. On the Options bar, choose Wall Centerline and Pick Individual References

3. Dimension the walls as shown in Figure 5.13.

4. Select the dimension. On the top part of the dimension, pick the blue grip in the middle of the dimension line (See Figure 5.13)

5. While pressing the pick button, drag it to the inside face of the wall.

6. Once your pointer is over the inside face of the wall, hit the Tab key (Just tap it, don't hole the tab key down).

Trust me—this is worth practicing now before you get into a live situation. If you've already run into this, you know exactly what I mean.

Let's look at one more procedure for tweaking an aligned dimension: overriding a dimension's precision.

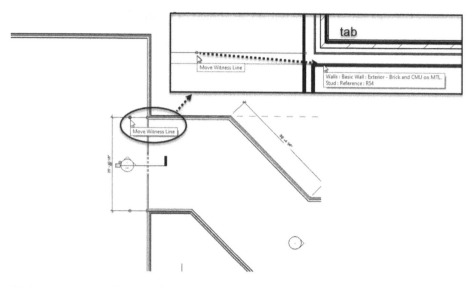

FIGURE 5.13 Dragging the witness line's grip

Overriding the Precision

When you dimension a wall at an angle such as this, the dimension usually comes out at an uneven increment. In most cases, you don't want to override every dimension's precision just to make this one, lone dimension read properly. In this situation, you want to turn to the dimension's Type Properties:

1. Select the angled dimension along the 45° corridor.

2. In the Properties dialog, click the Edit Type button, as shown in Figure 5.14.

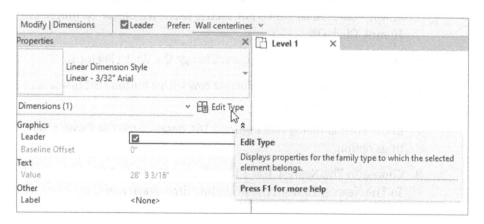

FIGURE 5.14 Clicking the Edit Type button to begin creating a new dimension style

3. Click the Duplicate button, as shown in Figure 5.15.

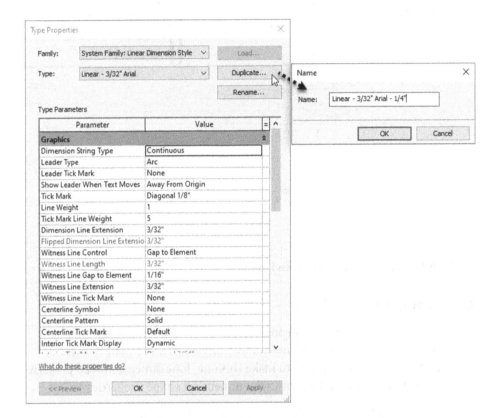

FIGURE 5.15 Select the button in the Text category to access the dimension's precision.

4. In the Name dialog that opens, name the new dimension style **Linear - 3/32″ Arial - 1/4″**. For metric users, it's **Linear - 2 mm Arial - 10 mm**. Click OK.

5. Scroll down to the Text category. Change the Width Factor to .8

6. Near the bottom is a Units Format row with a button that displays a sample increment. Click it.

7. In the Format dialog (see Figure 5.16), deselect the Use Project Settings option.

8. Choose To The Nearest 1/4″ (If you're working in millimeters, chose To The Nearest 10 from the Rounding drop-down menu.)

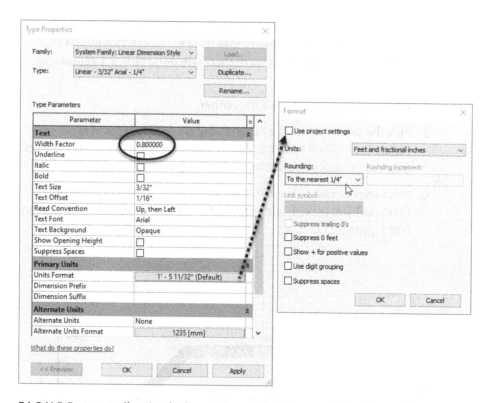

FIGURE 5.16 Changing the dimension's precision. Note some of the other available choices.

9. Click OK twice. Note the new value on the dimension at the angled wall.

Although aligned dimensions will bear the brunt of your dimensioning, there are plenty of other dimension types for you to use.

Linear Dimensions

Linear dimensions are used less frequently than most of the other dimensions. Unlike Autodesk® AutoCAD® software, in which linear dimensions are the go-to dimensions, they're on the bench for most of the game in Revit. The best use for a linear dimension is to put a straight dimension across nonlinear (angled) geometry, as follows:

1. Zoom back in on the corridor area.

2. On the Annotate tab, click the Linear button. Notice that you can't select the entire wall. That option has been taken away. Instead, Revit requires you to pick a point.

3. Move your cursor over the inside corner at the bottom intersection of the corridor. Make sure you're exactly over the exterior intersection of the brick. You'll know you're there when the blue dot appears, as shown in Figure 5.17.

4. When you see the dot, pick the corner.

5. Pick the same spot on the other end of the wall, as shown in Figure 5.17. When you pick the second corner, the dimension follows your cursor in a straight direction.

6. Move your cursor to the left, approximately 8' (2400 mm) past the first point you picked, and pick the third point to place the dimension (see Figure 5.17).

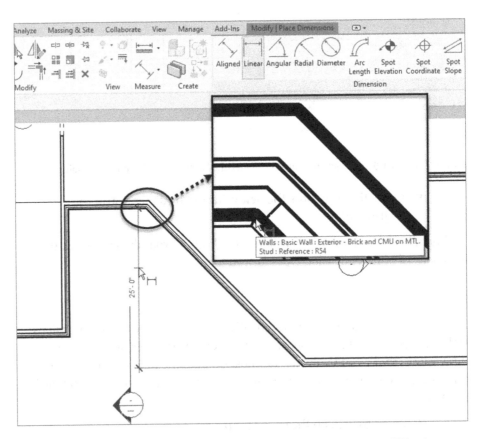

FIGURE 5.17 Select the finished exterior corner of the brick. You'll see a small blue dot appear, indicating that you can pick the start of the dimension.

Aligned and linear dimensions are the two dimension styles that pertain to straight dimensioning. The next three dimension procedures add dimensions to angled and radial geometry.

Angular Dimensions

Angular dimensioning comes close to needing no introduction at all, but I'll introduce it anyway. Angular dimensions are used to calculate and record the angle between two items. These two items are usually walls. You'll add an angular dimension to your lovely corridor walls in the following steps:

1. Zoom back in on the corridor if you aren't there already.

2. On the Dimension panel, click the Angular button, as shown in Figure 5.18. In the Options panel, choose Wall Faces.

3. For the first wall, pick the finished, outside face of the angled corridor wall, which is marked 1 in Figure 5.18.

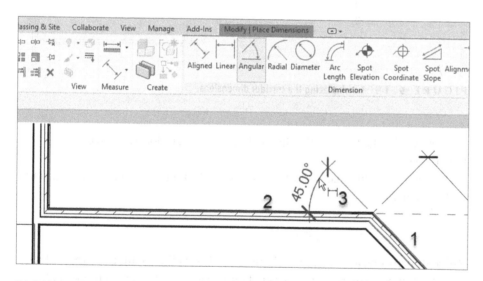

FIGURE 5.18 Placing an angular dimension involves picking two walls and then a point to place the dimension.

4. Pick the finished, outside face of the north corridor wall, marked 2 in Figure 5.18.

5. Move your cursor to the left about 8′ (2400 mm), and place the dimension marked 3 in Figure 5.18.

6. Press Esc.

7. Add the rest of the dimensions, as shown in Figure 5.19. This completes the dimensioning of the corridor area.

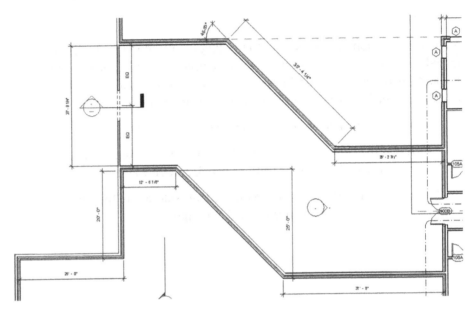

FIGURE 5.19 Finish placing the corridor dimensions.

If you would like to place the dimensions in different locations, feel free to do so.

The next set of dimensions pertains to radial geometry. You can finally get out of this corridor!

Radial Dimensions

Keep in mind that you can add an angular dimension to physically change the angle of the items being dimensioned. Use caution, however, and be sure the correct items are being moved when you alter the angle.

Radial dimensions are used to, well, measure the radius of an item. You're lucky that Revit knows you're adding a radial dimension to a building component. This means the many different choices provided by a CAD application are taken away, leaving just the basics.

The following procedure will lead you through adding a radial dimension:

1. Zoom in on the east radial entry in the east wing.

2. On the Annotate tab, click the Radial button. On the Options panel, choose Wall faces.

3. Pick the outside face of the radial wall, as shown in Figure 5.20.

4. Place the radial dimension somewhere that makes sense. If your model looks like Figure 5.20, you may proceed. If it doesn't, go back and try again.

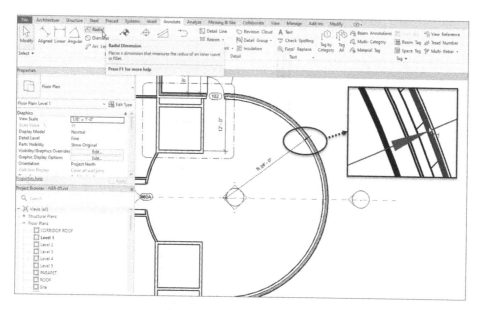

FIGURE 5.20 Adding a radial dimension is about as straightforward as it gets.

5. Pan all the way to the west radial end of the west wing, as shown in Figure 5.21.

6. On the Dimension panel, click the Diameter button, as shown in Figure 5.21.

7. Dimension to the finished outside face of the brick, and place your dimension in a location similar to that shown in Figure 5.21.

WARNING All too often, you can easily dimension from the wrong reference point. This book uses a wall with a concrete ledge below the brick in order to emphasize that you need to be very deliberate in how and where you choose your references for dimensions. Don't be afraid to zoom in and out as you add dimensions.

If you're careful in how you add a radial dimension, you'll find this process quite simple. The next type of dimension, however, can be a little tricky.

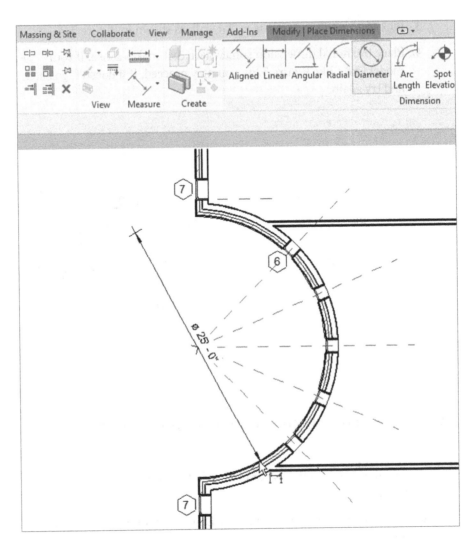

FIGURE 5.21 Adding a diameter dimension

Arc Length Dimensions

I have found the arc length dimension extremely useful in locating items such as windows along an arc. That is, in fact, what you need to do in the west wing of the building.

The following procedure will lead you through adding an arc length dimension:

1. Zoom in on the west radial entry of the west wing, as shown in Figure 5.22.

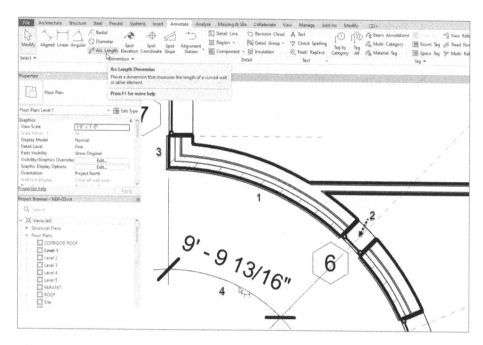

FIGURE 5.22 Placing an arc length dimension involves four separate picks.

2. On the Annotate tab, click the Arc Length button, as shown at upper left in Figure 5.22.

3. Pick the finish face exterior face of the brick on the radial wall marked 1 in Figure 5.22.

4. Pick the centerline of the uppermost window in the radial wall, marked 2. The NO sign won't change, but you'll be able to pick the window centerline.

5. Pick a point along the exterior face of brick that runs along the vertical intersecting wall, marked 3 in Figure 5.22.

6. Pick a point at which to place the dimension, marked 4.

Let's try it again. This time the dimension will be taken from the first window (the one you just dimensioned) to the second window. The process is exactly the same:

1. On the Annotate tab, click the Arc Length button if you aren't still in the command.

2. Pick the exterior face of the brick along the radial wall.

3. Pick the first window's centerline again.

4. Pick the second window's centerline.

5. Pick a point to place the dimension (see Figure 5.23).

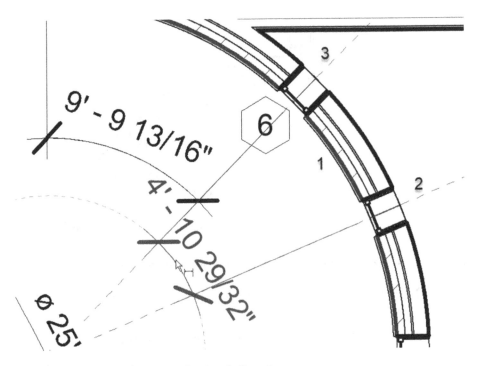

FIGURE 5.23 Adding a second arc length dimension

Now that you have experience adding dimensions to record the placement of items, it's time to see how you can physically use dimensions as a layout tool.

Using Dimensions as a Layout Tool

When it comes to dimensions, using them as a layout tool is my favorite topic. "OK, fine," you may say. "I can do that in CAD." Well, not quite. You see, in Revit you can't alter a dimension to reflect an increment that isn't accurate. You can, however, select the item you're dimensioning and then type a new number in the dimension. At that point, the item you're dimensioning will move. The result will be an accurate dimension.

The first task you need to explore is how to constrain a string of dimensions equally. You were exposed to this task earlier in the chapter, but now let's really dig in and gain some tangible experience using this tool.

For this procedure, you'll add some more walls to the west wing and then constrain them by using the EQ dimension function:

1. In the Project Browser, go to the Level 1 floor plan (not a ceiling plan!).

2. Zoom into the west wing of the building.

3. Draw two interior-partition (2-hr) corridor walls, as shown in Figure 5.24.

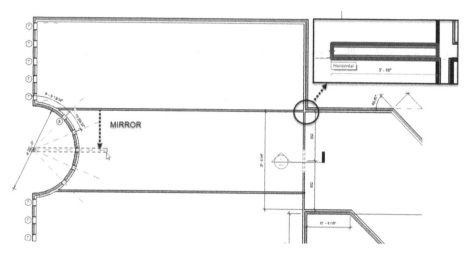

FIGURE 5.24 Adding two corridor walls

4. Draw five more walls, as shown in Figure 5.25. They don't have to be an equal distance from one another.

WALLS KIND OF STICKY?

If you don't intend to draw continuous lines, check out the Options bar and uncheck the Chain button. This allows you to draw separate walls with just two clicks.

5. On the Annotate tab, click the Aligned button (see Figure 5.26).

6. On the Options bar, be sure Justification is set to Center of Core.

7. Zoom in on the left exterior wall, as shown in Figure 5.27. When you see the dotted line, pick it.

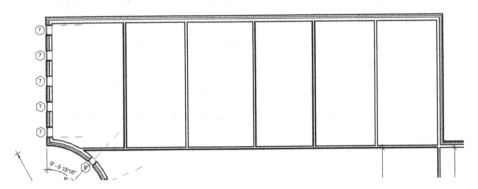

FIGURE 5.25 Place these walls as quickly as possible, and don't worry about their spacing.

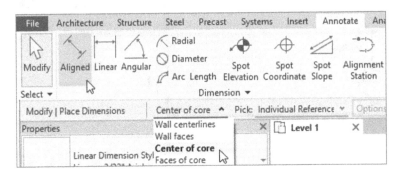

FIGURE 5.26 Changing the options for the dimension

8. Pick the point shown in Figure 5.27.

9. Move your cursor to the right until you pass over the first interior wall. Notice that the core centerline of the interior is highlighted, as shown in Figure 5.28. When you see this, pick the wall.

 WARNING   Just as when you equally constrained the door in the previous procedure, you need to keep the Dimension command running. If you press Esc, undo the last dimension and start over.

10. After you pick the first interior partition, move to the right and pick the center of the next wall.

11. Repeat the procedure until you get to the last wall (see Figure 5.29).

12. Pick the same Center of Core that you did on the first wall.

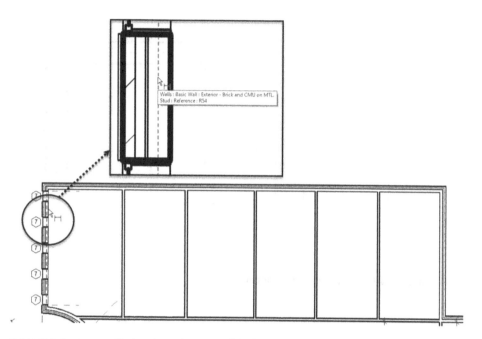

FIGURE 5.27 Placing the anchor point of the first dimension

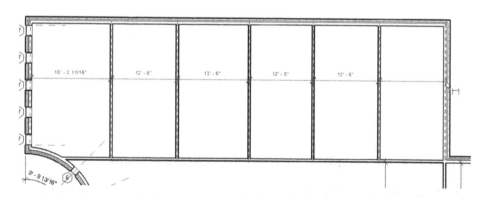

FIGURE 5.28 Adding a string of dimensions to the interior walls

13. Move your cursor up the view. The entire dimension string follows.

14. Placing a dimension in Revit is a little awkward, but you'll get the hang of it. You need to pick a point away from the last dimension in the string, as shown in Figure 5.30, almost as if you're trying to pick another item that isn't there. When you do this, the dimension will be in place.

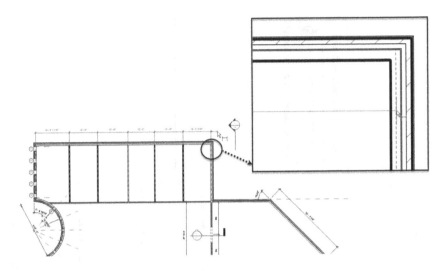

FIGURE 5.29 Adding the continuous dimension

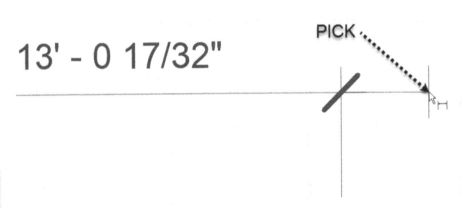

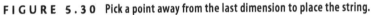

FIGURE 5.30 Pick a point away from the last dimension to place the string.

If you placed the
dimension string and
then escaped out of the
command, that's fine.
You can simply select
the string of dimen-
sions again, and you'll
be back in business.

With the dimension string in place, let's move these walls so they're equidis-
tant from one another. After you placed the dimension string, the familiar blue
icons appeared. You can use them as follows:

1. Find the EQ icon in the middle of the dimension string, and pick it.
The slash through it is now gone and the walls have moved, as shown
in Figure 5.31.

2. Press Esc twice to release the selection and exit the Aligned
Dimension command.

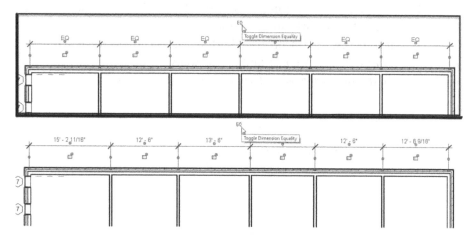

FIGURE 5.31 Before and after the EQ icon is selected

Because these walls are constrained always to be equal, if one wall is moved, these five interior partitions will always maintain an equal relationship to one another—that is, as long as this dimension string is still associated with the walls.

In Revit, you can choose to keep the walls constrained or to use the dimension only as a tool to move the walls around.

Constraining the Model

Choices you make early in the design process, such as constraining a model, can either greatly benefit or greatly undermine the project's flow. As you gain more experience using Revit, you'll start hearing the term *overconstrained*. This is a term for a model that has been constrained in so many places that any movement of the model forces multiple warnings and, in many cases, errors that can't be ignored.

Given that, how you choose to constrain your model is up to you. You'll learn how to constrain (and, of course, *un*constrain) your model in this section, but deciding when and where to constrain your model will vary from project to project.

Unconstraining the Walls

The string of equal dimensions you now have in place has created a constraint with these walls. To unconstrain them, follow along:

1. Select the dimension string.

2. Press the Delete key on your keyboard.

3. Revit gives you a warning, as shown in Figure 5.32. You must choose whether to unconstrain the elements.

If you click the Unconstrain button, the EQ dimension will disappear as well as any constraint on the walls. If you move the exterior wall, the newly spaced walls won't reposition themselves.

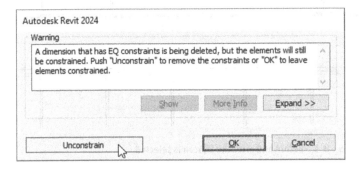

FIGURE 5.32 A Revit warning pertaining to the constraint of the walls

4. Although I always recommend choosing Unconstrain, for this exercise just click OK. You'll learn how to unconstrain these walls via a different method.

5. Select one of the interior walls that were part of the EQ dimension string.

6. The EQ icon appears. Click it to release the constraint set for the walls (see Figure 5.33). You're now free to move around the building. (Note that the EQ icon may be hiding behind a wall in the middle of the array. Zooming out will make the icon larger and easier to pick.)

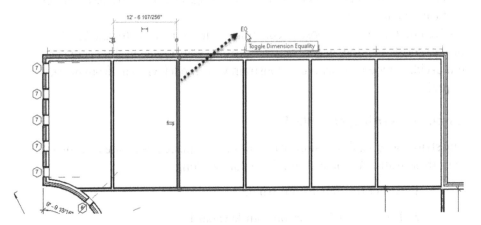

FIGURE 5.33 Unconstraining the walls

N O T E   Sometimes when you select an item that is being constrained, the dimensions are already activated and the Options bar doesn't provide the Activate Dimensions button. If you don't see the Activate Dimensions button on the Options bar for this example, your dimensions have been activated already.

Now that you have experience with dimension equality constraints, it's time to learn about a different type of constraint that involves locking items together at a distance.

Locking a Dimension

At times you may want to always hold a dimension, no matter what else is going on around it. You can do this by physically adding a dimension to an item and then locking that dimension in place. For example, if you want to lock the middle space to a specific dimension, you simply add a dimension and lock it down. Sound easy? It is!

1. On the Annotate tab, click the Aligned button.

2. On the Options bar, change the alignment to Wall Faces.

3. Pick the inside faces of the two middle partitions, as shown in the upper-left corner of Figure 5.34.

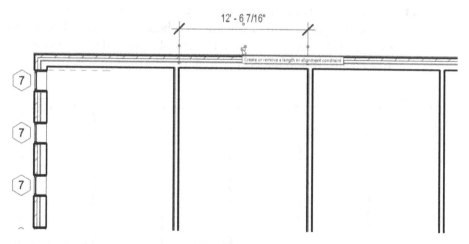

FIGURE 5.34 You can add a dimension and lock the distance between two items.

4. After you place the dimension, a blue padlock icon appears. Pick it. It should change to a locked padlock icon. When it does, press Esc twice or click Modify to terminate the command.

5. Select the left wall that has been dimensioned.

6. Move the wall to the right 2' (600 mm). Notice that the right wall moves as well. If you get a "constraints are not satisfied" message, you need to go back and un-EQ the five walls.

7. Click the Undo button, as shown in Figure 5.35.

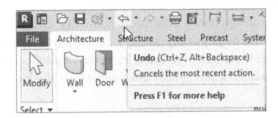

FIGURE 5.35 Click the Undo button.

8. Delete the dimension.

9. When you get the warning, click the Unconstrain button.

10. Save the model.

11. Add doors and windows to the plan, as shown in Figure 5.36. They can be any type of door or window you choose—just try to keep them similar to the ones in Figure 5.36. Also, placement doesn't matter. You'll adjust this in the next procedure.

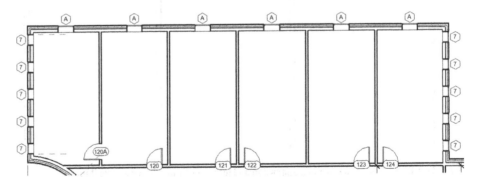

FIGURE 5.36 Adding doors and windows to the floor plan

In the next section, you'll start using dimensions as a tool to move elements around physically. Although this might seem like an exercise in futility, the practice is relevant to what you'll encounter in future projects.

Using Dimensions to Move Objects

As I have mentioned before, you can't type over a dimension and cause the value in that dimension to be inaccurate. Revit does provide tools to get around this. When you add a dimension and select the object being dimensioned, the dimension turns blue. This is a temporary dimension, which can be edited. Consequently, the object being dimensioned will move.

The goal of this procedure is to select an item and modify the temporary dimension, in effect moving the object:

1. Zoom in on the left side of the west wing, as shown in Figure 5.37.

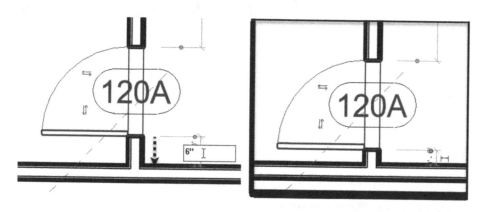

FIGURE 5.37 When you type a different value, the temporary dimension moves the object.

2. Select the door (see Figure 5.37). There is a blue dimension on each side of the door. These are temporary dimensions.

3. Pick the blue text in the lower temporary dimension (see Figure 5.37). The text might be obscured by the wall, but if you hover over it, it will activate, and then you can select it.

4. Type 6″ (150 mm). The door moves.

5. Press the Esc key to release the door.

This procedure used a temporary dimension that appeared when you selected the item. After you edited the dimension, it went away. In the next procedure, you'll add a permanent dimension and do the same thing:

1. On the Annotate tab, select the Aligned Dimension button.

2. On the Options bar, select Wall Faces.

3. Place a dimension between the door and the wall, as shown in Figure 5.38.

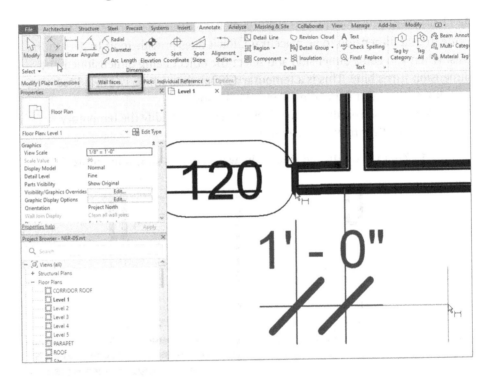

FIGURE 5.38   Placing a dimension

4. Press the Esc key twice.

5. Select the door shown in Figure 5.39. The dimension turns small and blue; it's ready to be modified.

6. When the dimension turns blue, select the text and type 6″ (150 mm) and press Enter. The door adjusts to the 6″ (150 mm) increment.

7. Press the Esc key, or click anywhere in open space to clear the selection.

8. Select the dimension.

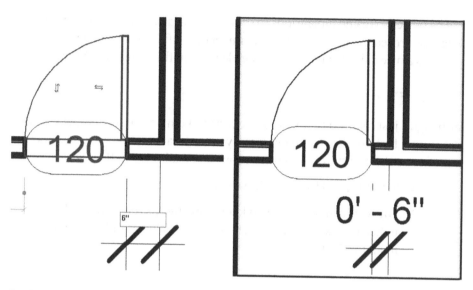

FIGURE 5.39 Making adjustments with the actual dimension

9. There is a blue grip just underneath the text. Pick the grip and move the text out from between the extension lines, as shown in Figure 5.40. Revit places a *leader* (an arrow line extending from the model to your text) in the text.

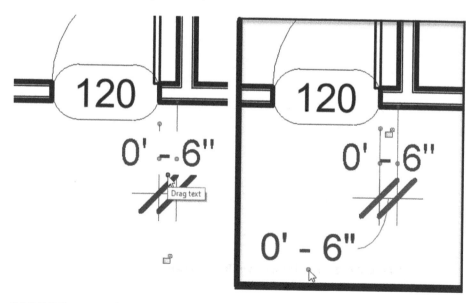

FIGURE 5.40 By grip-editing the text, you can slide it to a cleaner location. Revit automatically places a leader from the text to the dimension line.

The process of using dimensions to move objects takes some getting used to. The next procedure delves into making further modifications to dimensions and provides a nice fail-safe procedure embedded within the Dimension Properties.

Using Dimension Text Overrides

Although I just told you that you can't override a dimension, the following steps get around that problem. In many cases, you may want text or, more commonly, a prefix or a suffix within a dimension. You can do all three in Revit:

1. Select the 6″ (150 mm) dimension.

2. The text turns blue. As you know, blue means this item is editable in Revit. Pick the text. You should see a dialog box like the one in Figure 5.41.

> The fact that Revit displays temporary dimensions lends itself to another common process: the double-check. All you need to do in Revit is select any item, and the temporary dimensions will appear. (If not, remember to click Activate Dimensions on the Options bar.) You can simply look at the dimensions.

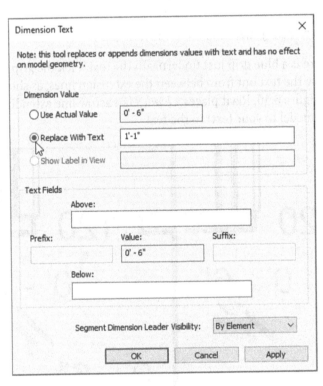

FIGURE 5.41 The Dimension Text dialog box

3. Under Dimension Value, click Replace With Text.

4. Type 1′–1″ (325 mm), and press Enter.

5. You get an Invalid Dimension Value message, as shown in Figure 5.42. Revit won't allow you to do such a foolish thing. Click Close.

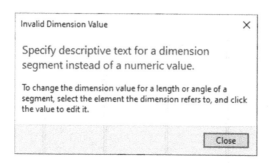

FIGURE 5.42 Any numeric value triggers a warning in Revit. You simply can't type a value over a dimension.

6. In the Dimension Text dialog box, select Use Actual Value.

7. Under Suffix, type **TYP.**, as shown in Figure 5.43.

8. Click OK.

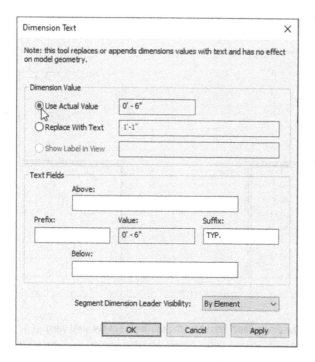

FIGURE 5.43 Under Dimension Value, choose Use Actual Value, and type TYP. as the suffix.

Now, move the rest of the doors along this wall to a 6″ (150 mm) increment from the finished, inside face of the wall to the door opening. Also, dimension the floor plan as shown in Figure 5.44 and Figure 5.45.

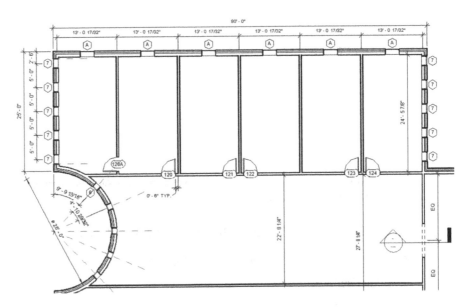

FIGURE 5.44 The dimensional layout for the north part of the west wing

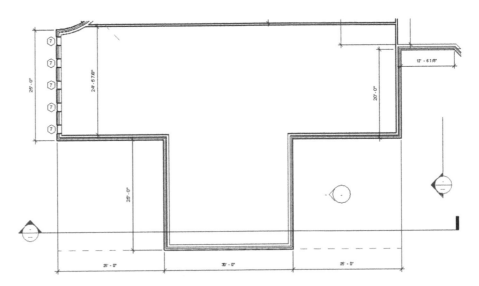

FIGURE 5.45 The dimensional layout for the south part of the west wing

OK, one last thing and then we are done with dimensions. I'm not a big fan of the 0′ in front of a dimension that is under 1′-0″ (305 mm). For example, 0′-6″ (152 mm) is kind of a waste of space. Also, I like to reduce the width factor to .8. To do that, we need to look at the properties of the dimensions. Of course, in the following exercise, steps 1 through 3 can be ignored by metric users.

1. On the Manage tab, click Project Units, as shown in Figure 5.46

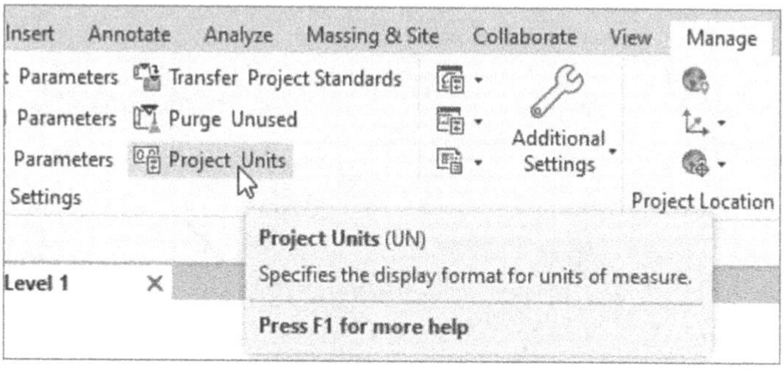

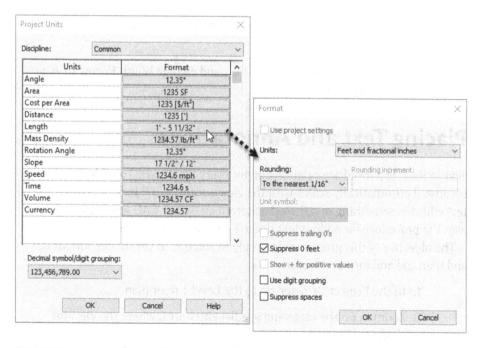

FIGURE 5.46 Clicking Project Units on the Manage tab

2. Next to Length, click the button that says 1′-5 11/32″, as shown in Figure 5.47.

FIGURE 5.47 Changing the rounding and suppressing 0 feet

3. Change the Rounding to 1/16″.

4. Check Suppress 0 feet, and then click OK in both dialogs.

5. Select any aligned dimension and click Edit Type, as shown in Figure 5.48.

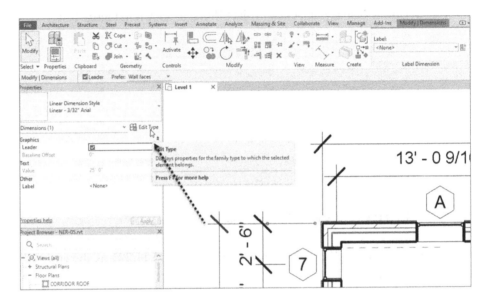

FIGURE 5.48 Click Edit Type to edit the parameters of the aligned dimensions.

6. Scroll down to the Text category, and change Width Factor to .8, as shown in Figure 5.49.

Placing Text and Annotations

Text in Revit is a love/hate relationship for every Revit user. You'll love text because it automatically scales with the view's scale. You'll hate it because the text editor is something of a throwback from an earlier CAD application. Either way, the procedure for adding text doesn't change with your feelings toward it.

The objective of this procedure is simply to add text to the model, format it, and then add and format a leader:

1. In the Project Browser, go to the Level 1 floor plan.

2. Zoom in on the east wing's radial entry area, where the elevator shafts are located.

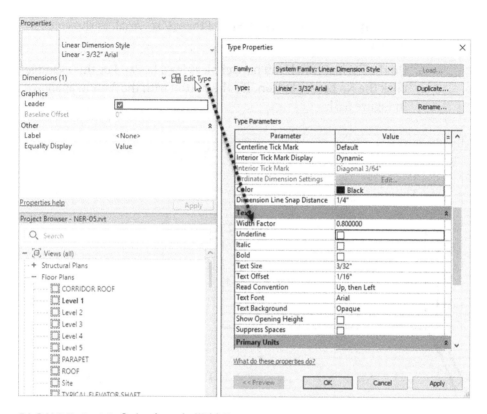

FIGURE 5.49 Paring down the Width Factor

3. On the Text panel of the Annotate tab, click the Text button, as shown in Figure 5.50.

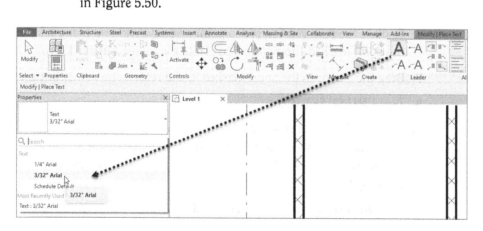

FIGURE 5.50 Click the Text button on the Text panel of the Annotate tab.

4. In the Type Selector, select Text and then 3/32″ Arial, as shown in Figure 5.50.

5. On the Format panel, you have choices for a leader. For this example, click the No Leader button. It's the button with the A on it, as shown in Figure 5.51.

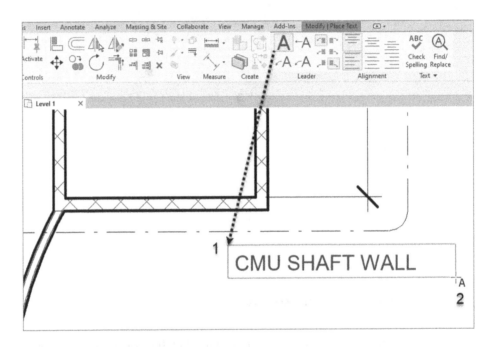

FIGURE 5.51   Placing text

6. To place the text, you can pick a point or drag a window. Left-click at the point marked 1 in Figure 5.51. Hold the mouse button down.

7. Drag the cursor to the point marked 2, and release the mouse button.

8. Type **CMU SHAFT WALL**.

9. Click a point in the view outside the text box. You now have a note in the model, as shown in Figure 5.51. If the window you picked is smaller than the text, the text wraps to fit the size of the window you dragged.

10. Press the Esc key twice, or click Modify.

11. Select the text.

12. On the Format panel, review the choices you have to add a leader to the text.

13. Click the Add Straight Leader button, as shown in Figure 5.52. This option adds a leader to the left end of the text.

14. By clicking the grips and moving the text around, configure the text and the leader to resemble Figure 5.52.

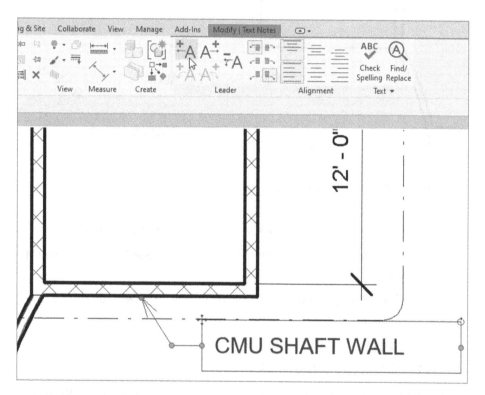

FIGURE 5.52 Placing text

Adding Leader Text

You can add text to a model by placing a leader first and then adding the text within the same command. Although in Revit you can add leaders to all text, you can choose to add text to a model with or without a leader.

The objective of the following steps is to place text with a leader:

1. On the Text panel of the Annotate tab, click the Text button.

2. On the Format panel, click the Two Segments button, as shown in Figure 5.53.

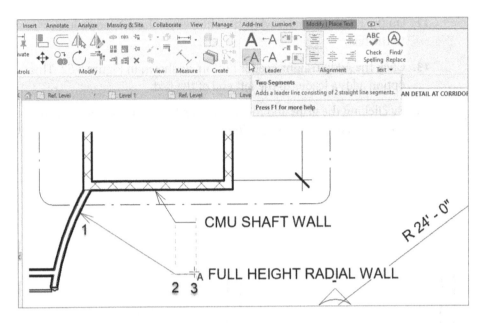

FIGURE 5.53 Adding a piece of leader text

3. Pick a point near the radial wall, marked 1 in Figure 5.53.

4. Move your cursor down and align the second point with the elbow of the text above.

5. Pick a third point in alignment with the end of the leader of the text above, marked 3.

6. Type FULL HEIGHT RADIAL WALL.

7. Click an area outside the text.

Now that you can add text to a model, let's investigate how to modify the text after you add it. You'll begin with the arrowhead on the end of the leader.

Changing the Leader Type

It almost seems as though Revit uses the ugliest leader as a default, forcing you to change it immediately. The large arrowhead you saw in Figure 5.53 isn't the only one Revit provides—had that been the case, Revit might never have gotten off the ground!

To change the arrowhead that Revit uses with a text item, follow this procedure:

1. On the Text panel of the Annotate tab is a small arrow pointing down and to the right, as shown in Figure 5.54. Click it to open the Type Properties.

2. Change the Leader Arrowhead parameter to Arrow Filled 15 Degree, as shown in Figure 5.54.

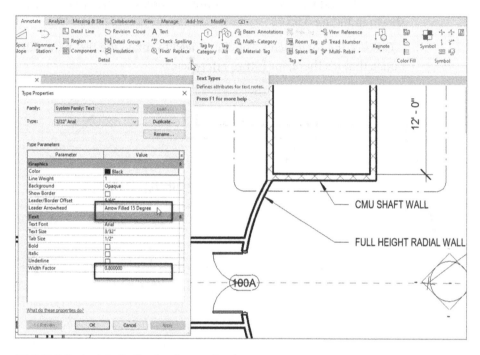

FIGURE 5.54 Configuring the arrowhead

3. Click OK. You've changed a type parameter.

That's a handsome-looking arrowhead, as shown in Figure 5.54. The next item to address is how to modify the placement of text after you add it to the model.

Modifying the Text Placement

With any text item in Revit, you can select the text in your model, and you'll see grips for adjusting text: two grips on the text box, two on the leader, and a rotate icon.

Your next objective is to modify the text placement and to make the necessary adjustments:

1. Select the text you just added to the model.

2. Pick the right blue grip.

3. Stretch the text window to the left until it forces the text to wrap, as shown in Figure 5.55.

    Observe the rotate icon. You don't need to rotate the text here, but notice that it's there, for future reference.

Revit doesn't use an SHX font. As a matter of fact, SHX can't be used at all in Revit. It was invented by Autodesk, but it works only with AutoCAD. Keep this in mind when you're setting up your company's templates. If you're using an SHX font, you'll need to find an alternate font or allow Revit to convert it to Arial. If you don't, this will cause issues in text formatting.

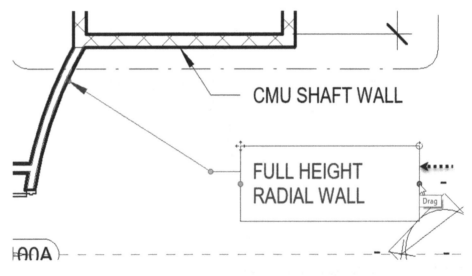

FIGURE 5.55 Wrapping the text

4. Double-click into the Full Height Radial Wall text box.

5. Notice that all of the tabs and panels change to edit the text.

6. Change the text to bold, as shown in Figure 5.56.

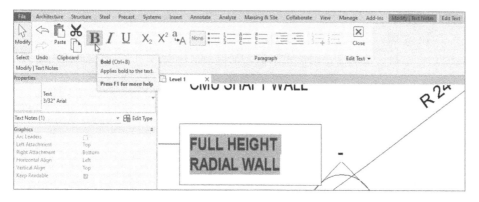

FIGURE 5.56 Bolding the text

Are You Experienced?

Now you can. . .

✓ add a multitude of different types of dimensions to your model simply by altering the options associated with the Dimension command

✓ equally constrain items in a model by adding a string of dimensions and clicking the EQ button

✓ use your dimensions as a layout tool, keeping the items constrained even after the dimension is deleted

✓ add text to a model by starting with either a leader or a paragraph of text

✓ change the text type and arrowhead type for leader text

CHAPTER 6

Floors

It's going to be hard to convince you that floors are easy when an entire chapter is dedicated to this lone aspect of Autodesk® Revit® software. Well, floors *are* easy. I'm devoting an entire chapter to the subject because we need to address a lot of aspects of floors:

▶ Placing a floor slab

▶ Building a floor by layers

▶ Splitting the floor materials

▶ Pitching a floor to a floor drain

▶ Creating shaft openings

Placing a Floor Slab

Adding a floor to a model is quite simple, but in Revit, you're truly modeling the floor. That means you can include the structure and the finish when you create your floor. When you cut a section through the floor, you get an almost perfect representation of your floor system and how it relates to adjacent geometry, such as walls.

Floors, of course, are more than large slabs of concrete. Therefore, in this chapter you'll also be introduced to creating materials, and you'll learn how to pitch these materials to floor drains. You'll examine how to create sloped slabs as well.

The first area you'll explore is how to place a slab into your model. It's as simple as it sounds, but you must follow certain steps, which I'll outline next. As you've learned up to this point, in Revit you do need to add items the way Revit wants you to add them, or you'll probably generate errors—or, worse, inaccuracies in your model.

Creating the Slab

To begin, open the file you've been using to follow along. If you didn't complete Chapter 5, "Dimensioning and Annotating," go to the book's web page at www .wiley.com/go/revit2024ner. From there you can browse to Chapter 6 and find the file called NER-06.rvt.

The objective of the following procedure is to create a floor slab to be placed into the model:

1. In your Project Browser, go to the Level 1 floor plan.

2. Zoom in to the west wing.

3. On the Architecture tab, click the Floor button, as shown in Figure 6.1.

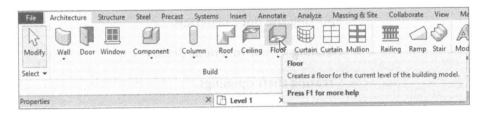

FIGURE 6.1 The Floor button on the Architecture tab

4. In the Properties panel, Floor: Generic 12″ (300 mm) should be current, as shown in Figure 6.2.

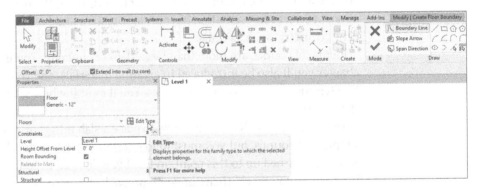

FIGURE 6.2 Clicking the Edit Type button to begin creating a new floor slab type

5. Click the Edit Type button.

You're now accessing the Type Properties. This means any change you make here will affect every slab of this type in the entire model.

 T I P At this point, you should always either create a new floor system or rename the current one. Doing so will avert much confusion down the line when you have a floor called Generic - 12" (Generic 300 mm) and it's actually a 6" (150 mm) concrete slab on grade.

6. Click the Rename button, as shown in Figure 6.3.

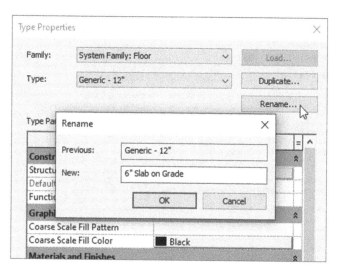

FIGURE 6.3 Renaming the current floor type. You'll never have a Generic 12" (300 mm) floor in your model, so it's a good idea not to keep this floor type around.

7. Call the floor system 6" Slab on Grade (150 mm Slab on Grade); see Figure 6.3.

8. Click OK.

9. In the Structure row, click the Edit button (see Figure 6.4).

The term *layer* may throw you off a bit. Revit uses layer here to describe a component of the floor. This is not to be confused with an Autodesk® AutoCAD® layer.

You're now in the Edit Assembly dialog. This is where you can specify a thickness for your slab. You can add layers of materials here as well.

In the middle of the Edit Assembly dialog is a large spreadsheet-type field that is divided into rows and columns. The rows are defined by a structural component and include a boundary above and below the structure. It's the Structure row you're interested in here:

1. The Structure row is divided into columns. Click in the Material column within the Structure row, as shown in Figure 6.5.

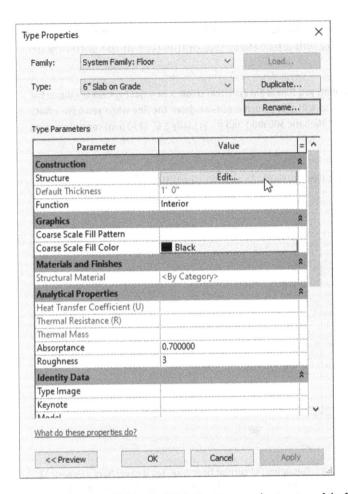

FIGURE 6.4 Clicking the Edit button to access the structure of the floor

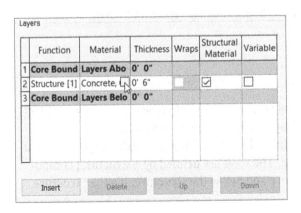

FIGURE 6.5 By clicking in the Material cell within the Structure row, you can access the Material Browser.

2. A small browse button [. . .] appears when you click in the Material cell. This button indicates that you'll be given a menu if you click it. Click the [. . .] button to open the Material Browser.

3. In the search field start typing **concrete** and the list of materials will narrow, as shown in Figure 6.6

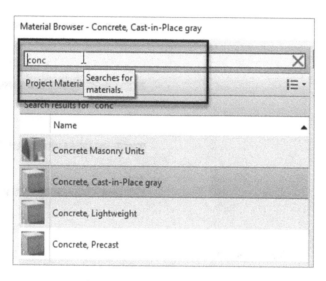

FIGURE 6.6 In search of concrete

4. Select Concrete - Cast-In-Place Gray.

5. Make sure the Graphics tab is current, as shown in Figure 6.7. You can display two different hatches: a sand hatch will be visible for floor plans, and a concrete hatch will be visible for sections (see Figure 6.7). These hatches allow a filling region to designate specific materials graphically.

6. Make sure Concrete - Cast-In-Place Gray is still selected, and click OK.

7. Back in the Edit Assembly dialog, the Thickness column is directly to the right of the Material column. Currently the value in the Structure Row is 1'–0" (300 mm). Click into the cell, and change the value to 6" (150 mm).

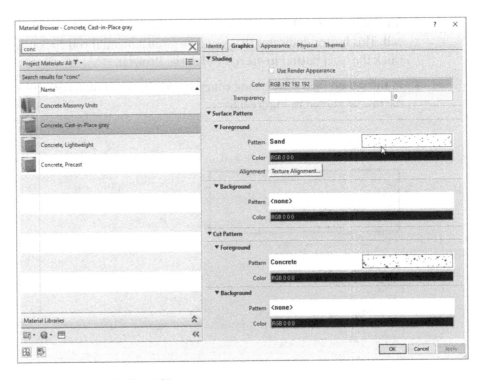

FIGURE 6.7 The Material Browser

 TIP Imperial users, if you just type **6** and press Enter, you'll wind up with a slab 6′–0″ thick. Be sure to add the inch mark (″) after the 6. The value needs to read 0′–6″.

8. Click OK.

9. Click OK again to get back to the model.

Now that the slab type has been created, you can place an instance into the model. Notice that the Modify | Create Floor Boundary tab is in Sketch Mode. You'll now proceed to sketch the slab in place.

Sketching the Slab

You'll have to adjust to the way Revit wants you to proceed with the Create Floor Boundary tab; you're basically limited to the choices provided in this menu. Not to fear; you should have plenty of choices, but you'll still need to get a feel for how Revit works.

Here's what needs to happen: You must draw the perimeter of the slab into the model. This is basically a slab on grade, so you'll pour the concrete to the inside, finished face of the wall. You won't worry about a control joint between the wall and the slab at this point.

Picking Walls

The best way to add a slab is to use the Pick Walls button as much as possible (see Figure 6.8). In doing so, you tell Revit that this edge of slab needs to move if this wall moves. Pick Walls is the default Draw option.

Let's start sketching the slab:

1. In the Modify | Create Floor Boundary tab, click the Pick Walls button, as shown in Figure 6.8, if it isn't already picked.

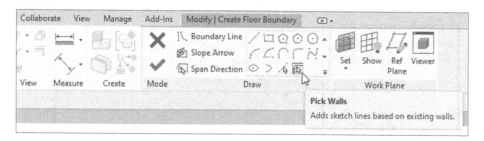

FIGURE 6.8 Picking walls ensures that that edge of your slab will move if the wall moves.

2. With the Pick Walls tool running, hover your mouse over the inside face of the wall.

3. After the wall becomes highlighted and you're sure you're on the inside of the wall, pick it (see Figure 6.9).

4. With the inside face of the wall picked, you need to move on to the next wall. Pick the inside face of the north wall.

    Notice that, as you pick the walls, a magenta *sketch line* appears on the inside face of the walls. This is another indicator telling you whether you're on the correct side of the wall. The first line has two parallel lines, one on each side. These indicate the slab direction for structural decking.

5. Keep picking the walls, as shown in Figure 6.10. You need to have a continuous loop—no gaps and no overlaps.

6. Apply some basic modify commands as well. To clean corners that aren't joined, use the Trim command. For the bottom line where the jog occurs, use the Split Element command. (Make sure the Delete Inner Segment button is selected on the Options bar.)

7. After you've picked the perimeter of the west wing, click Finish Edit Mode on the Modify | Create Floor Boundary tab, as shown

in Figure 6.11. It may be a good idea to check out your model in 3D after making floors just to make sure nothing went wrong. (I constantly have to do that.)

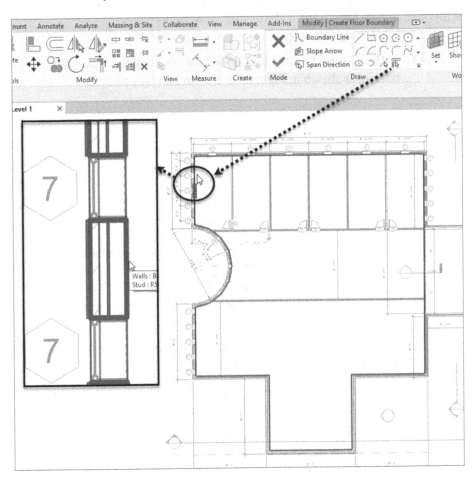

FIGURE 6.9 Picking the inside face of the first wall

WATCH WHAT YOU PICK!

As you pick the walls to place your edge of slab, be careful. If you don't pick the inside face, there is a chance that Revit will try to extend the slab to the core of the wall. Also, make sure the Extend to wall core option is unselected. This will help keep the edge of the slab where you intend it to be. If you zoom into the area that you're picking, an alignment line will appear. Make sure this line is where you want it, as shown in the following image. If it's not, hit Esc and select the line. Click on the double-arrow icon that says Flip.

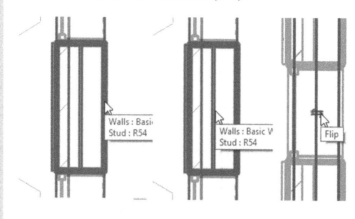

PICKY, PICKY, PICKY!

I'll keep repeating this, but if you get the error message shown here saying that your lines are overlapping, or that they are open on one end. That means your lines are in fact overlapping or not connected. You *must* have a single, closed loop. Click the Show button to zoom in on the offending area.

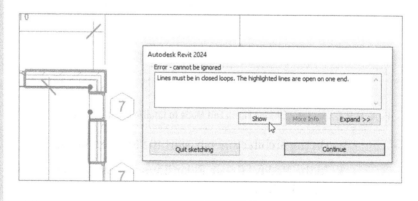

After you finish the floor, you'll have plenty of opportunity to practice adding floors in this model. You need to add a floor to the corridor as well as to the east wing. Follow these steps:

1. Zoom into the corridor, as shown in Figure 6.12.

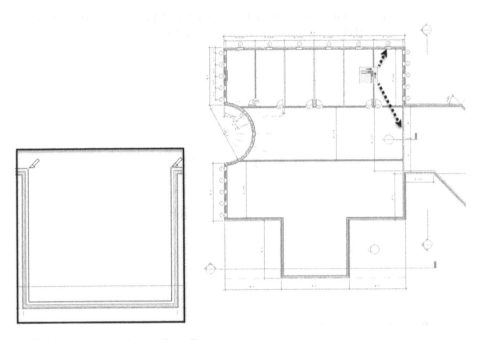

FIGURE 6.10 Selecting the walls

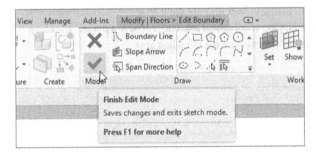

FIGURE 6.11 Clicking Finish Edit Mode to finalize the floor sketch

2. On the Architecture tab, start the Floor command.

3. In the Modify | Create Floor Boundary tab, click the Pick Walls button.

4. Uncheck Extend Into Wall.

5. Pick the walls pointed out in Figure 6.12. Remember to keep the blue line to the inside face (see Figure 6.12).

6. Click the Pick Lines button as shown in Figure 6.13. (Revit might try to pick the wrong side of that wall).

USING FLIP ARROWS

I briefly mentioned it before, but if you accidentally pick the wrong place in the wall, that's OK. Flip arrows appear as you place lines. Realize that a previous line is wrong? Press Esc, and then select the magenta line—a flip arrow will appear. Pick the flip arrow, and the magenta line will flip back to the correct face of the wall, as shown in the following graphic. Also, if other sketch lines are on the wrong face, this one flip will take care of any connected sketch lines.

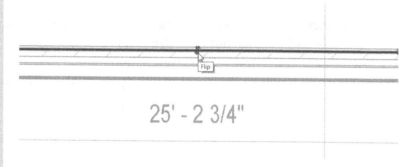

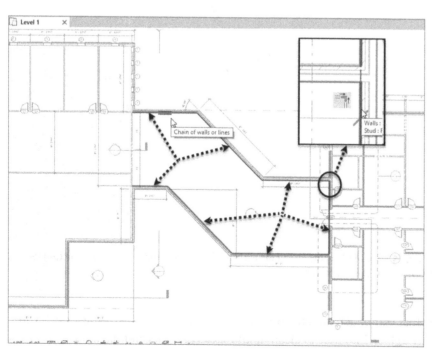

FIGURE 6.12 Picking the north walls of the corridor

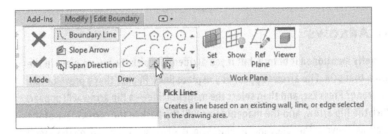

FIGURE 6.13 Sometimes you'll need to click the Pick Lines button to select the edge of the slab. If you have to resort to this, however, the slab edge won't move if the wall does.

7. Pick the face of the interior partition separating the corridor from the east wing, as shown in Figure 6.14.

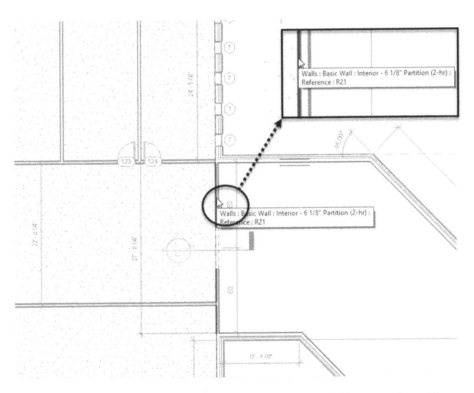

FIGURE 6.14 Picking the face of the partition. The line will probably run past the corridor. That's OK; you'll trim it in a moment.

Now that you understand the process of adding sketch lines to the model, you can start to look into how to clean up the sketch so you can finish.

Using Trim to Clean Up the Sketch

With the lines placed, you need to make sure you don't have any gaps or overlaps. And you do. To fix these gaps and overlaps, you'll use the basic modify commands from Chapter 5.

That partition wall extended the magenta boundary line all the way up and down the entire room. We need to deal with that. We know how! The command you need to use here is Trim:

1. Pick the Trim/Extend To Corner button from the Modify panel, as shown at the top of Figure 6.15. Then click the portions of the two lines you want to keep. This removes the excess from the corner.

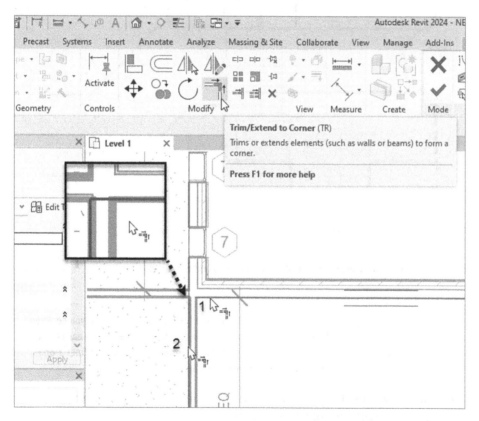

FIGURE 6.15 Pick the magenta lines in the numbered order illustrated in the figure.

2. Repeat this for the south side of that wall.

3. With the corners successfully trimmed, click the green Finish Edit Mode check mark.

When Revit allows you to finish the sketch, your west wing and corridor should have a continuous slab underneath them, as shown in Figure 6.16.

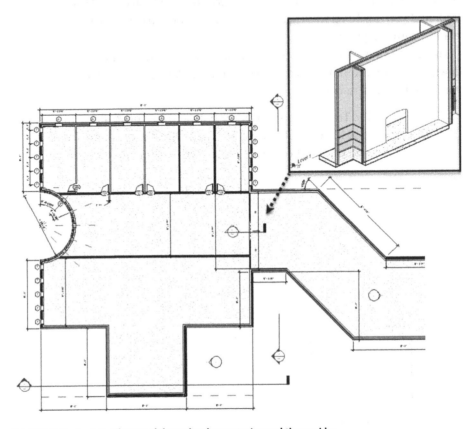

FIGURE 6.16 The two slabs under the west wing and the corridor

TIP I hope you don't get an error stating that lines are overlapping. If you do, keep going with the Trim/Extend to Corner command. You may need to investigate each corner. You may also want to consider whether you've accidentally placed double lines along a wall. This can be easy to do when you're picking walls.

While you create the floor boundary, you can access the basic editing commands such as Trim, Split Element, and Offset that work for sketching.

It's time to add a slab under the east wing. Go ahead and try it on your own. Look at these directions only if you get lost:

1. Zoom in on the east wing.

2. On the Architecture tab, click the Floor button.

3. In the Modify | Create Floor Boundary tab, click the Pick Walls button.

4. Pick the exterior walls of the east wing as shown in Figure 6.17

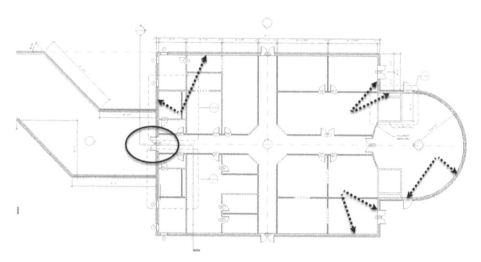

FIGURE 6.17   Adding a slab to the east wing

5. Use the Split, Trim, and Pick Lines commands to extend the slab under the door as shown in Figure 6.18.

6. Click Finish Edit Mode.

Now that you have a nice slab on the first floor, you need to add some more slabs to the rest of the levels. The trick with the slabs on upper levels is that they must extend into the core of the walls. This is where Revit can get sticky. Follow along with the next section, and let's work out this issue together.

Building a Floor by Layers

As mentioned earlier in this chapter, the term *layer* doesn't equate to an AutoCAD layer. It does, however, equate to layers of materials used to design a floor system. When you create a floor system in Revit, you should do it with the mindset of how a floor is actually constructed. You can also specify which material in the floor will stop at an exterior wall and which will pass through to the core.

In the following sections, you'll build on your experience of creating a floor. With the concrete slab in place, you'll start adding materials to create a floor finish.

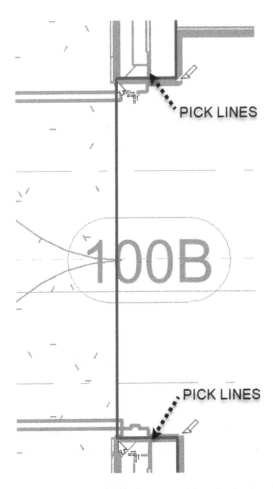

FIGURE 6.18 Extending the slab under the door opening

Adding Materials

Your objective is to create a floor system with a structure and a finish material. You'll also design the floor to interrupt the exterior framing while letting the brick façade pass from grade to parapet. Let's get started:

1. In the Project Browser, go to the Level 2 floor plan. (Remember not to go to the Level 2 ceiling plan.)

2. In the View Control bar (located at the bottom of the view window), be sure the detail level is set to Fine.

3. On the Architecture tab, click the Floor button.

4. In the Properties dialog, click the Edit Type button.

5. Click the Duplicate button.

6. Call the new floor **4″ Concrete with 2″ Terrazzo** (see Figure 6.19). For metric users, it's **102 mm Concrete with 50 mm Terrazzo**.

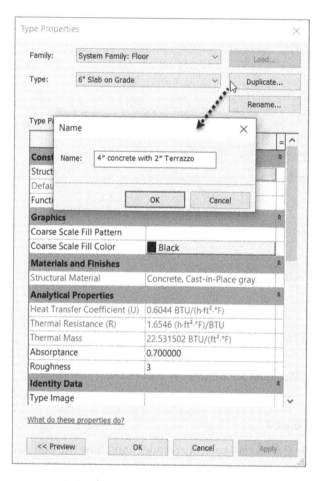

FIGURE 6.19 Duplicating the existing floor

7. Click OK.

8. In the Structure row, click the Edit button, as shown in Figure 6.20.

You're now in the Edit Assembly dialog, as you were in the previous procedure. The objective is to add 2″ (50 mm) Terrazzo flooring to the top of the 4″ (102 mm) concrete.

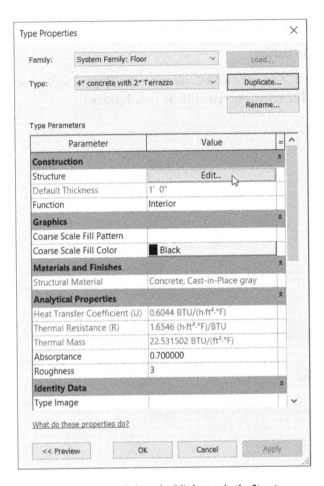

FIGURE 6.20 Clicking the Edit button in the Structure row

Adding a Layer

To add the additional material, you must understand how the Edit Assembly dialog is broken down. Because you want to add a material to the top of the slab, you need to click above the concrete and insert a new layer, as follows:

1. In the Thickness field for Structure [1], change 6″ (152 mm) to 4″ (101.6 mm).

2. In the Layers field are three rows. Each row has a corresponding number. Click the number 1. This is the top row that reads Core Boundary | Layers Above Wrap (see Figure 6.21).

3. Under the Layers field, click the Insert button, as shown in Figure 6.21.

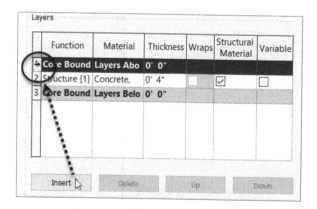

FIGURE 6.21 Inserting a new layer for the terrazzo

4. The new layer is added. The field is now divided into columns. The first column is Function, which is currently set to Structure. This cell is a drop box containing the other available functions. Click the drop-box arrow and select Finish 1 [4] (see Figure 6.22).

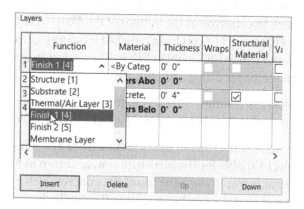

FIGURE 6.22 Choosing a layer function

5. Click in the Material cell for the new Layer 1.

6. Click the [. . .] button.

7. At the bottom of this dialog, you will see a category called Material Libraries. Click the chevron to open the Material Libraries panel as

shown in Figure 6.23. Also notice that you can hover your cursor over the top of the little dialog and stretch it up to see a larger area.

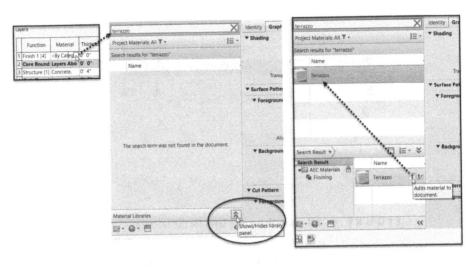

FIGURE 6.23 Selecting a material and adding it to the project

8. In the Material Browser, type **terrazzo** as shown in Figure 6.23. Terrazzo is now actually not in the default library. What you need to do is click the chevron at the bottom of the Material Browser as shown in Figure 6.23 (if you hadn't clicked it before). Once you do that, Terrazzo shows up. Double-click it. Then select it again once it appears in the upper dialog and click OK.

9. In the Thickness column, enter 2″ (50 mm). Imperial users, make sure you're typing 2 inches and not 2 feet (see Figure 6.24).

10. At the far right in the rows in the Layers field are Variable check boxes. Select Variable for the Structure row, as shown in Figure 6.24. This will enable you to slope the top of the concrete slab if need be. Only the layer that is set to be variable will actually slope. Any layer that is on top of this variable layer will be pitched.

11. At the bottom of the Edit Assembly dialog, click the Preview button. A graphic preview of your floor appears in a sectional view (see Figure 6.25).

12. Click OK twice to go back to the model.

Great job. You now have a floor with a finish material on it!

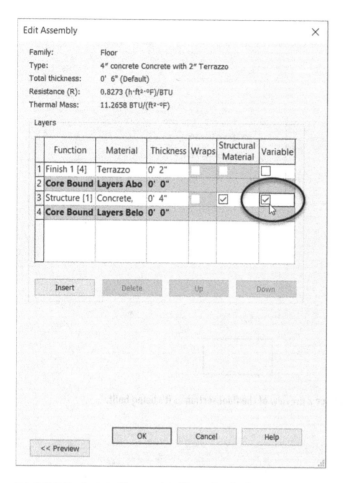

FIGURE 6.24 The completed layers for the floor system

Now you can place your new floor into the model. Remember that you're on the second floor. When you place the slab, you want it to extend directly into the wall core. To do so, follow along:

1. Click the Pick Walls button on the Draw panel. You'll pick every exterior wall in the east wing except the radial wall.

2. Start picking walls, as shown in Figure 6.26. Do *not* pick the radial wall at the east entry.

3. On the Draw panel, click the Line button.

4. Draw a line from the endpoint of the magenta line at the north wall of the east entry (see 1 in Figure 6.27) to the endpoint of the magenta line in the south wall (see 2 in Figure 6.27).

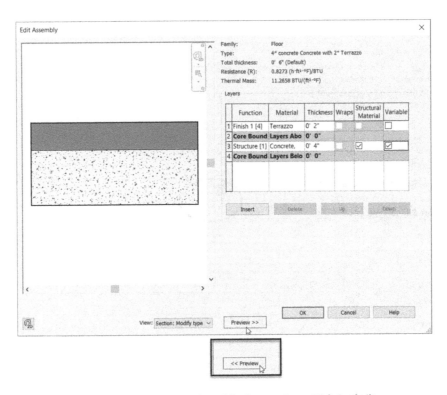

FIGURE 6.25   You can see a preview of the floor section as it's being built.

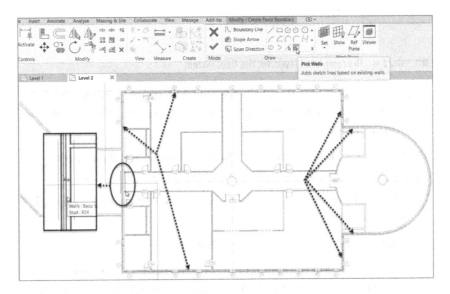

FIGURE 6.26   Picking the core centerline of the exterior walls, except the radial east wall

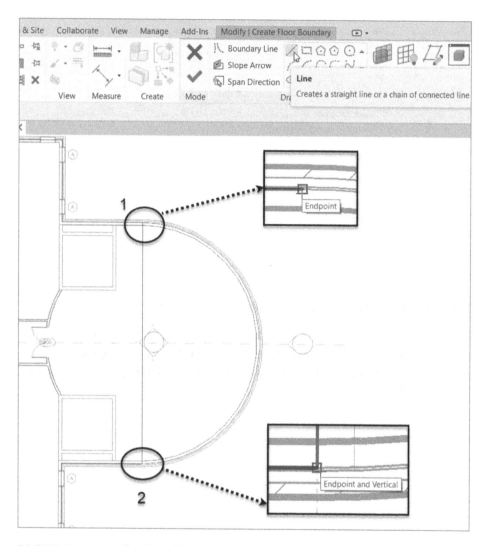

FIGURE 6.27 Sketching a line for the east portion of the entry slab

5. On the Modify | Create Floor Boundary tab, click Finish Edit Mode.

6. Revit begins asking you questions. First it asks whether you want to attach the walls that go up to Level 2 to the bottom of the floor. You *do* want to do this; this cuts the interior walls down to meet the bottom of the floor. Any change in the floor's thickness will alter the tops of the wall. Click Attach, as shown in Figure 6.28.

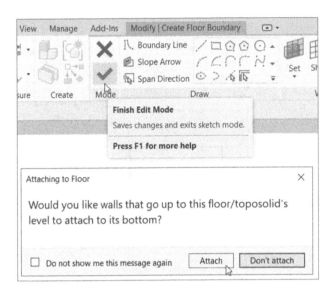

FIGURE 6.28 Click Yes to attach the walls to the floor's bottom.

7. The next message pertains to the exterior walls. Revit asks whether you would like to cut the section out of the walls where the slab is intersecting. In this case, you do, so click Yes in the message box, as shown in Figure 6.29.

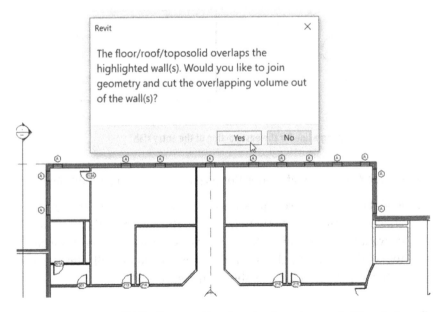

FIGURE 6.29 Click Yes if you want to cut overlapping volumes out of the exterior walls.

N O T E As these messages come up, Revit usually does a good job of highlighting the relevant items in the model. Get into the habit of looking past the messages to see what items in the model are being highlighted.

With the second floor in place, you can now add it to the floors above. To do so, you can use the Copy/Paste Aligned feature you used in Chapter 4, "Creating Views." Try to do this on your own. If you don't remember how or if you skipped Chapter 4, follow these steps:

1. Select the floor in Level 2 if it isn't still selected. (It's easiest to select the floor at the east edge. You can also make sure there isn't a red X on the Select Elements by Face button as shown in Figure 6.30.)

2. On the Modify | Floors tab, click the Copy to Clipboard button on the Clipboard panel, as shown in Figure 6.30.

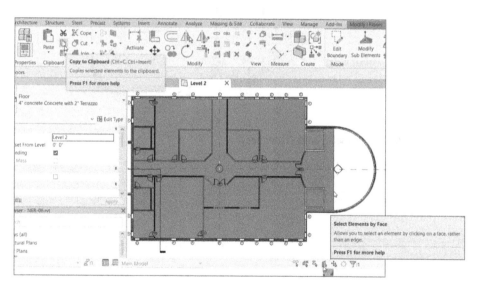

FIGURE 6.30 Clicking the Copy to Clipboard button

A good indication that you've successfully copied the floor to the Clipboard is that the Paste icon directly to the right of the Copy icon becomes activated.

3. Go to the default 3D view, as shown in Figure 6.31.

4. From the Paste flyout on the Clipboard panel of the Modify tab, click Aligned to Selected Levels, as shown in Figure 6.32.

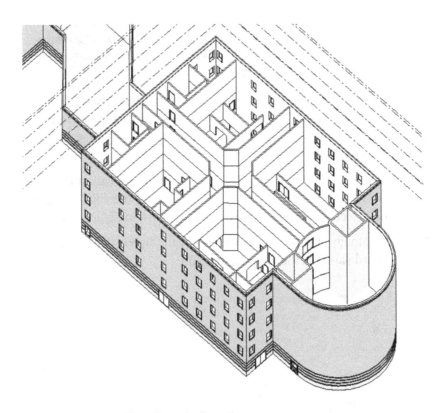

F I G U R E   6 . 3 1   The walls on the floors above

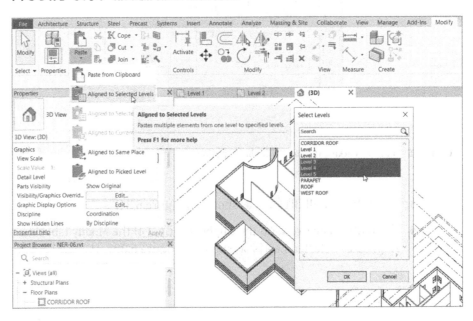

F I G U R E   6 . 3 2   Selecting the levels where you want the slab to be copied

5. The Select Levels dialog appears, where you'll choose the levels to which you want to paste your floor. Choose Levels 3, 4, and 5 (see Figure 6.32; hold down Ctrl to select more than one level).

6. Click OK. The floors are pasted to the specified levels, as shown in Figure 6.33.

Notice that the fifth-level floor isn't joined to any of the walls. This is because when you pasted the floor to this level, Revit didn't prompt you to cut the overlapping geometry from the exterior walls. To fix this, follow these steps:

1. After the floors have been pasted, select the fifth-level floor, as shown in Figure 6.34.

2. On the Modify | Floors tab, click the Edit Boundary button, as shown in Figure 6.34.

3. On the Mode panel of the Modify | Floors ➤ Edit Boundary tab, click Finish Edit Mode.

4. Click Attach to attach the walls that go up to this floor's bottom.

5. Click Yes to cut the overlapping volume out of the walls. Figure 6.34 shows that the walls are now being cut by the slab.

6. Repeat steps 1 through 5 for floors 4 and 3.

7. Save the model.

Note that if Selected Levels isn't available, Selected Views will be. This is because you selected an annotation such as a window tag or a door tag. You can pick Selected Views to achieve the same results.

Not too bad. You have a full building with floors placed. Now you'll drill into these floors (literally) and see how you can make them perform to your specifications.

Your next task is to create different floor materials for a few specific areas such as the restrooms. You'll then pitch the restroom floors to floor drains.

Pitching a Floor to a Floor Drain

Sure, it's the responsibility of the plumbing engineer to specify what floor drains to use, but it's generally the responsibility of the architect to specify where they'd like the floor drain. That being said, let's move on to creating a pitched floor area in the restrooms. Because you have five floors with which to work, let's go to the first floor and start pitching some slabs!

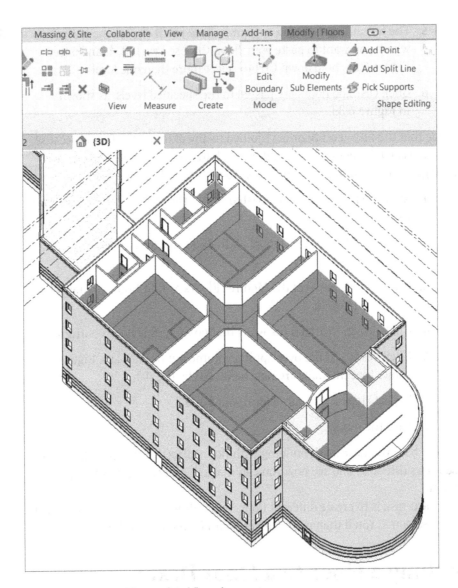

FIGURE 6.33 The completed floor placement

The objective of this procedure is to chop out the lavatory area, add a new floor, and add points in the surface of the slab in order to pitch to a drain:

1. In the Project Browser, double-click the Level 1 floor plan. (Make sure you aren't in the Level 1 ceiling plan.)

2. Zoom in on the lavatory areas, as shown in Figure 6.35, and select the floor.

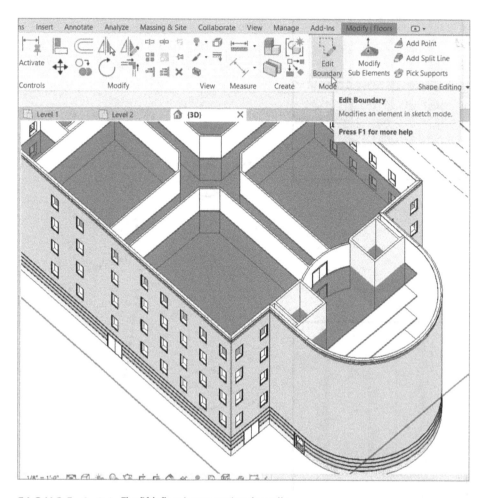

F I G U R E 6 . 3 4 The fifth floor is now cutting the walls.

3. Click Edit Boundary.

4. Trim out the area as shown in Figure 6.35. Remember to use the Split command. Then click Finish Edit Mode.

5. Select the existing slab and right-click. (Remember, you can change the choice by selecting elements by face, as shown (circled) in Figure 6.36.

6. Select Create Similar.

7. In the Properties dialog, click Edit Type.

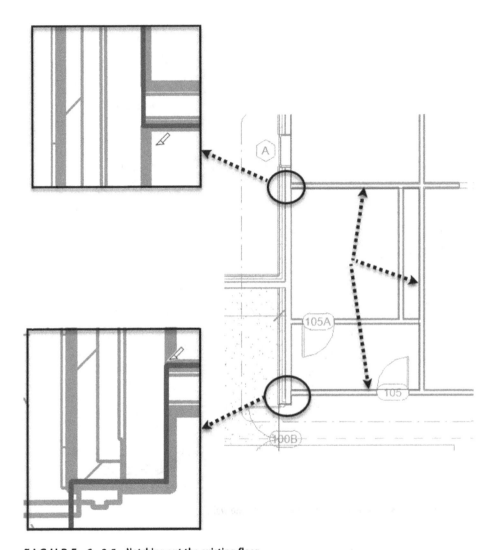

FIGURE 6.35   Notching out the existing floor

8. Click Duplicate.

9. Call the new floor 4" Lavatory With Tiles. See Figure 6.37.

10. Click Edit in the Structure row.

11. Change the thickness of the concrete to 4" (102 mm).

12. Add a new layer above the core boundary and set Function to Substrate. See Figure 6.38.

FIGURE 6.36 Right-click and select Create Similar.

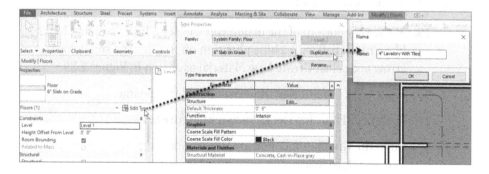

FIGURE 6.37 Creating a floor system specifically for the lavatories

13. For the Substrate material, click into the cell where it says <By Category>.

14. Click the browse icon [. . .].

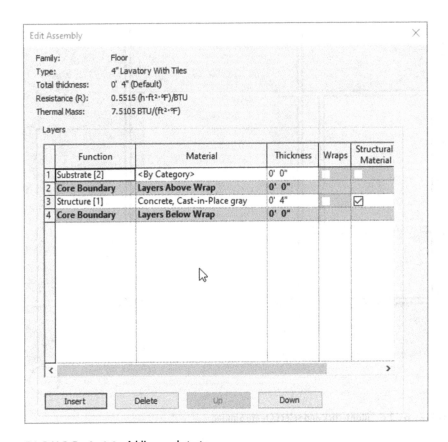

FIGURE 6.38 Adding a substrate

15. At the very bottom of the dialog you will see a little icon that looks like a metal ball with a blue plus sign on it. Click the small down arrow and select Create New Material as shown in Figure 6.39.

16. Right-click Default New Material and select Rename.

17. Rename it **Floor Leveler** as shown in Figure 6.40.

18. Go to the Graphics tab. For the foreground cut pattern, click <none> in the Pattern field.

19. Select Sand-Dense. See Figure 6.40.

20. Click OK twice.

21. Change the Thickness to **1-1/2″ (38mm)**.

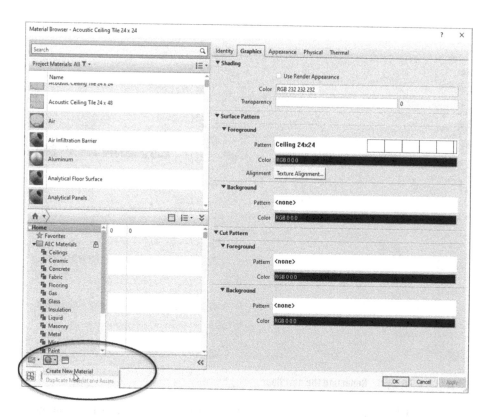

FIGURE 6.39 Creating a new material

22. Select the check box in the Variable column. We want this layer to be able to slope to our floor drain. See Figure 6.41.

23. Click on the number 1 on the row that we just added.

24. Click the Insert button.

25. Set the function to Finish 1 [4].

26. Browse to add a material as we did just moments ago.

27. Type the word **Tile** in the search bar.

28. Select Tile, Porcelain, 4in (or any tile you want for that matter).

29. Click OK.

30. Change Thickness to 1/2″(13mm).

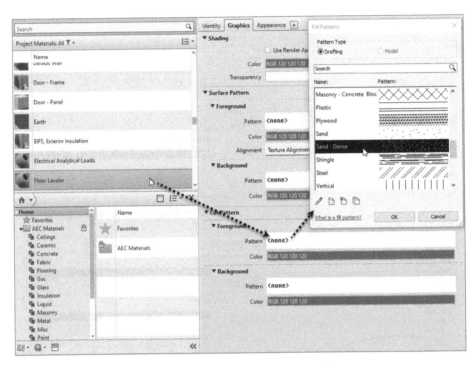

FIGURE 6.40 Renaming the new floor

31. Click the Preview button at the bottom of the Edit Assembly dialog to view the floor. (See Figure 6.42).

32. Click OK.

33. Click OK again.

Now let's place the little floor we just created. The reason we're breaking this floor up is so that we can create an honest assembly when it comes time to cut sections and do material takeoffs.

1. On the Draw panel, click the Pick Walls button.

2. Pick the outside face of the lavatory walls, as shown in Figure 6.43.

3. Trim up the corners as we've been doing all along.

4. When you are done, click the green check mark as shown in Figure 6.44

NOTE Sometimes if you pick a wall and the floors slightly overlap, Revit will give you a warning. In this instance you can just click the X and close the dialog. You can also select the floor and review the warnings as shown in this figure.

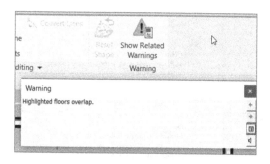

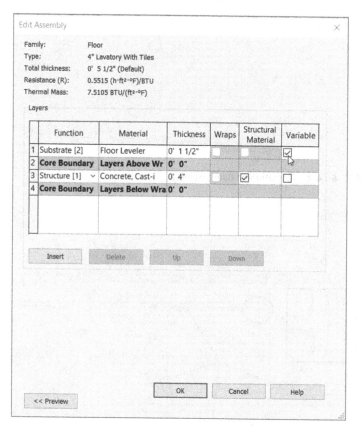

FIGURE 6.41 Changing the thickness and setting the variable constraint

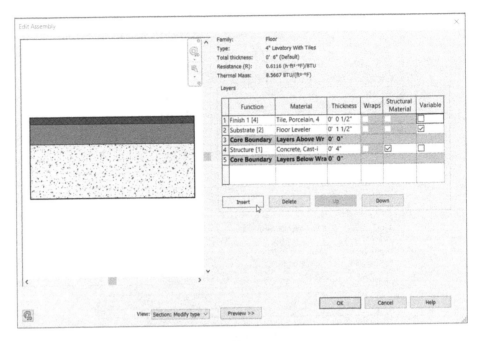

FIGURE 6.42 The bathroom floor assembly

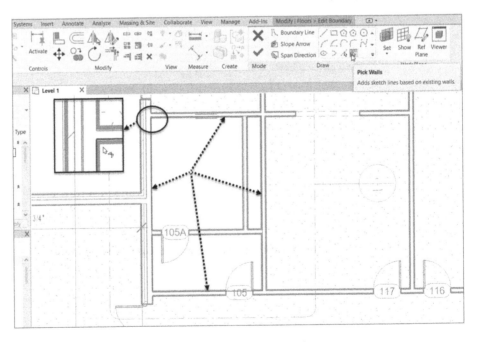

FIGURE 6.43 Adding a new floor is becoming pretty easy!

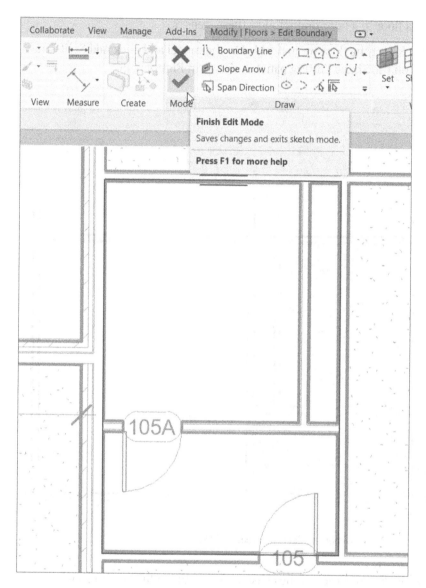

FIGURE 6.44 Click Finish Edit Mode when you are done.

Using the Shape Editing tools

With the floor in place and a floor leveler material set to Variable, we can now start to pitch the floor to a specified location. This tool can be tedious, but with some practice, you'll become an expert.

To pitch a floor to a floor drain, follow these steps:

1. Select the floor we just added to the model and click Add Split Line on the Shape Editing panel as shown in Figure 6.45.

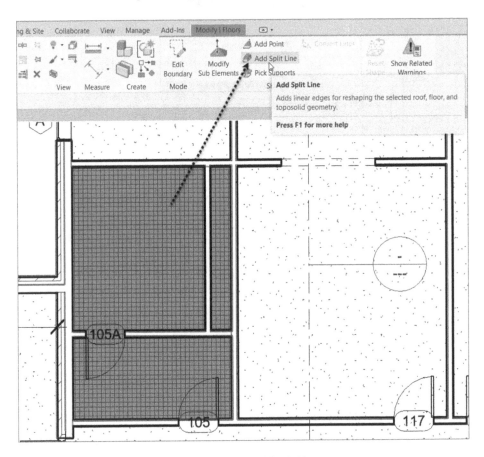

FIGURE 6.45 Selecting the floor and clicking Add Split Line

2. Pick two points on the chase wall, creating a line as shown in Figure 6.46.

3. Pick two more points, creating a line along the bottom wall as shown in Figure 6.46.

4. Hit Esc a couple times to clear the selection.

5. To add a point that will eventually slope the floor, select the floor again.

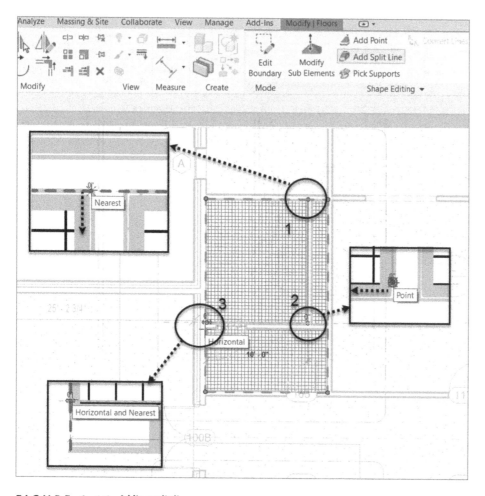

FIGURE 6.46 Adding split lines

6. On the Shape Editing panel, select the Add Point button as shown in Figure 6.47.

7. On the Add Point panel, make sure the Along Surface button is checked, Elevation Base is Current Level, and Offset From Surface is –1″ (–25 mm) as shown in Figure 6.48 (Imperial users, negative 1").

8. Move your cursor into the drawing area and right-click.

9. Select Snap Overrides.

10. Select Snap Mid Between 2 Points as shown in Figure 6.49.

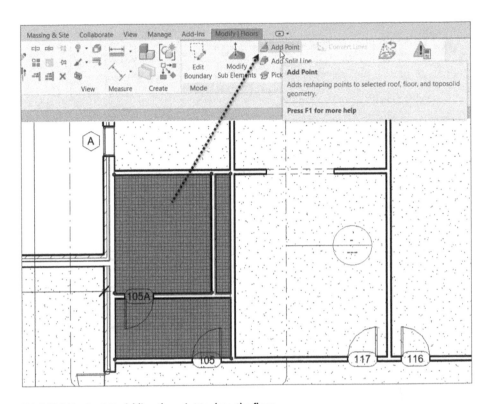

FIGURE 6.47 Adding the point to slope the floor

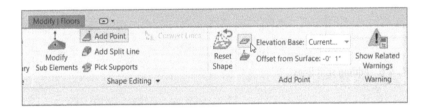

FIGURE 6.48 Setting the slope values

11. Pick the two points shown in Figure 4.50. This will pitch the variable layer.

    See Figure 6.51; does your floor look like this? If not, go back and see where you went wrong.

12. Repeat the steps to add a pitch to the lavatory south of the corridor.

13. Save the model (see Figure 6.52).

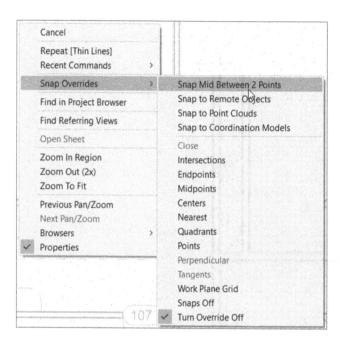

FIGURE 6.49 Snap Mid Between 2 Points

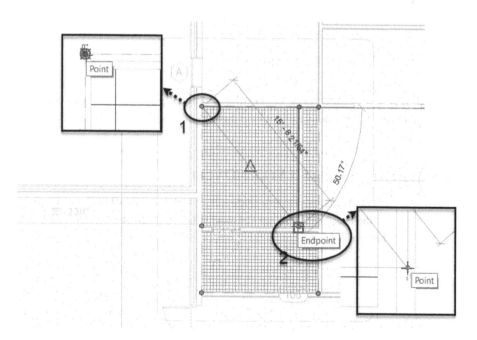

FIGURE 6.50 Pick these points to place the low point in the middle of the room.

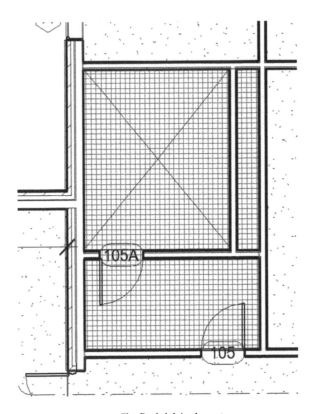

FIGURE 6.51 The final slab in the restroom

Now that you have experience in creating and placing floors, as well as pitching a floor in a specific area, let's look at one more item: shaft openings.

CAN I ERASE THIS AND START OVER?

Often, you may need to clear shape edits of the entire slab and start over. You can do this by selecting the floor and clicking the Reset Shape button on the Options bar, as shown here.

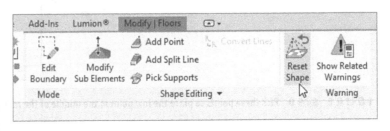

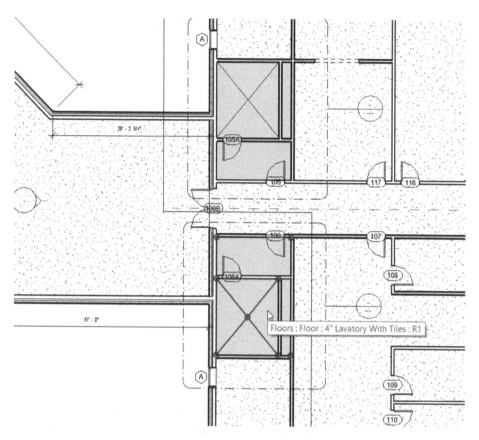

FIGURE 6.52 Both lavatories are pitched and ready to have fixtures added.

Creating Shaft Openings

To create a shaft opening, you just create a void through your model. This void, however, can conform to walls that are set in the model. The elevator shaft walls, for instance, will define the outside edge of your shaft opening. You may notice that the floors you added to the model are indiscriminately running uninterrupted, straight through the shafts. You need to void the floor. Also, the good thing about creating a shaft opening is that if you create another floor, the shaft will be cut out automatically.

First, you need to create two more levels. You need a subterranean level (T.O. Footing) and a penthouse level, through which you'll extend the elevator shaft. Follow these steps:

1. In the Project Browser, go to the South elevation.

2. On the Datum panel of the Architecture tab, click the Level button.

3. On the Draw panel, click the Pick Lines button, and set an offset of 10′–0″ (3000 mm), as shown in Figure 6.53.

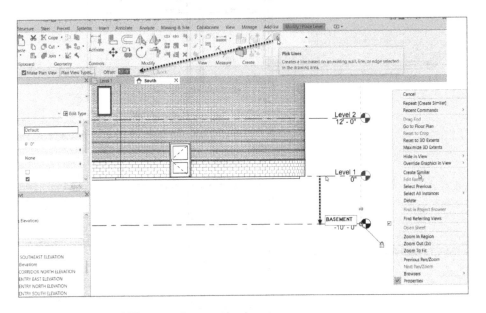

FIGURE 6.53   Adding a new basement level

4. Hover your cursor over Level 1. Make sure the alignment line is below Level 1. When you see the alignment line, pick Level 1. You now have a new level at –10′–0″ (–3000 mm).

5. Click the Modify button on the Select panel to terminate the command.

6. Pick the level that is set to –10′–0″ (–3000 mm), and rename it BASEMENT (see Figure 6.53).

7. Click Yes when Revit prompts you to rename corresponding views.

The next step is to select the CMU elevator shaft walls and modify their properties so the bottoms are extended down to the top of the footing:

1. Go to a 3D view.

2. Select all of the east entry elevator CMU walls. Remember to press and hold the Ctrl key as you select the walls.

3. In the Properties dialog, in the Constraints category, set Base Constraint to BASEMENT, as shown in Figure 6.54.

4. Click Apply.

To select all of the CMU walls, you can select one, right-click, and then click Select All Instances ➢ In Entire Project. Be careful, though; if there are other objects of the same type in the model, they will become selected as well.

▶

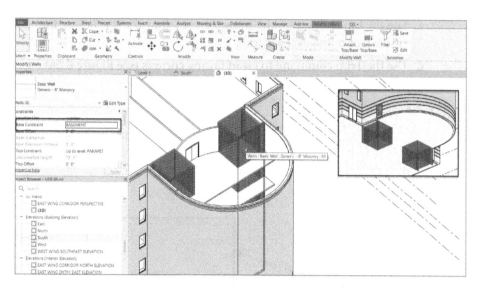

FIGURE 6.54 In the Properties dialog, change Base Constraint to BASEMENT.

With the bottom established at the correct level, it's time to add the shaft:

1. Go to the Level 1 floor plan. (Note that it doesn't matter which floor you're in when you place a shaft opening.)

2. On the Architecture tab, click the Shaft button in the Opening panel, as shown in Figure 6.55.

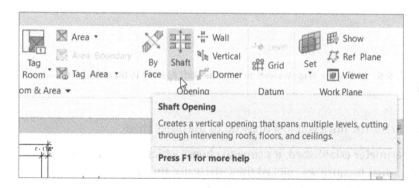

FIGURE 6.55 Clicking the Shaft button on the Architecture tab

3. On the Draw panel of the Modify tab, click Pick Walls.

4. Pick the walls shown in Figure 6.56. Notice that you can have more than one shaft opening in the same command.

5. Use the Line button on the Draw panel to draw the line across the inside face of the exterior wall.

6. Use the Trim command to clean up any corners (see Figure 6.56).

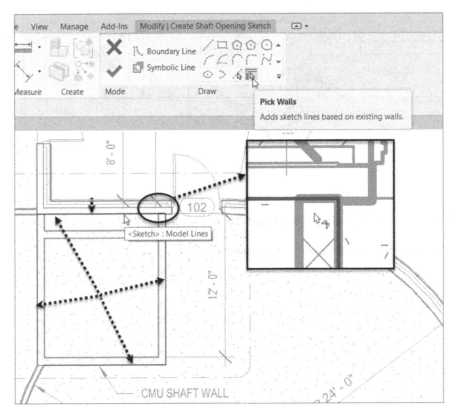

FIGURE 6.56 Adding the magenta lines to form the shaft opening to the outside of the CMU walls

7. Mirror the lines you just drew up to the other shaft.

With the perimeter established, it's time to choose which floors this opening will extend to. Just because you picked the CMU walls, this doesn't mean a base and a top height have been established. Follow these steps:

1. In the Properties dialog, make sure Shaft Openings is selected, as shown in Figure 6.57.

2. In the Properties dialog, set Base Constraint to BASEMENT.

3. Set Top Constraint to Up To Level: Roof.

4. Set Top Offset to –1'–0" (–300 mm); this keeps the roof from having two giant square holes in it.

5. Click Apply. Figure 6.57 shows the settings.

FIGURE 6.57 Setting the properties of the shaft opening

6. On the Modify | Create Shaft Opening Sketch tab, click the Symbolic Line button. This will allow you to sketch an opening graphic into the shaft.

7. Change the Line Style to <Hidden Lines> and draw an X in both openings, as shown in Figure 6.58.

8. Click Finish Edit Mode.

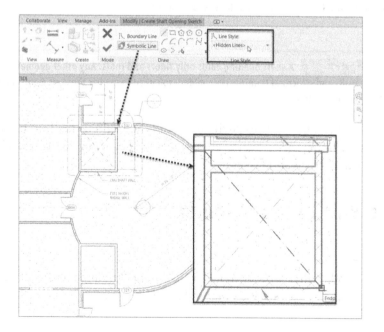

FIGURE 6.58 You can add any "drafting" symbolic lines you deem necessary.

The floor is now voided from the openings. Go to a 3D view, and look down the shafts. They're wide open, as shown in Figure 6.59. The symbolic lines you drew will appear in the floor plans only.

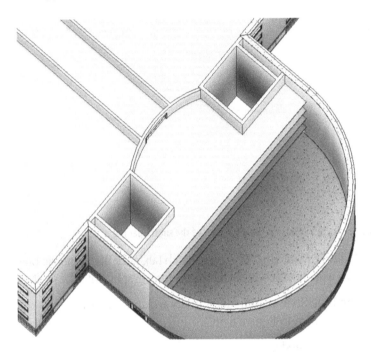

FIGURE 6.59 The completed shafts as seen in 3D

N O T E A shaft opening voids only floors and roofs. Any other geometry, such as walls and structural framing, isn't voided. You need to modify these elements on a piece-by-piece basis.

Now that you know how to pitch floors, you can begin using Revit for its unique capabilities. Also, you're better prepared to move on to the next chapter, which focuses on creating roofs.

Are You Experienced?

Now you can. . .

✓ add a floor to your model by using the building's footprint as a guide and by picking the walls and drawing lines

✓ add additional floors to higher levels by using the Copy/Paste Aligned method of quickly repeating the geometry up through the building

✓ add a specific, alternate material to different parts of the floor by using the Split Face command in conjunction with the paint materials function

✓ split a floor into segments and add additional points to set a negative elevation for pitching to floor drains

✓ create a shaft opening that will cut out any new floor slab

✓ use symbolic lines within a shaft opening to indicate the opening

You're 100% these options while placing a tool by footprint because you're looking at the roof in its plan, which limits your ability to place a tool with true uniformity. Later in the book, you'll learn how to do this, but for now it's a start with placing a flat roof by footprint.

Roofs

Roofs come in all shapes and sizes. Given the nature of roofs, there is a lot to think about when you place a roof onto your building. If it's a flat roof, pitch is definitely a consideration. Drainage to roof drains or scuppers is another concern. But how about pitched roofs? Now you're in an entirely new realm of options, pitches, slopes, and everything else you can throw at a roof design. Also, there are always dormers that no pitched roof can live without! Do the dormers align with the eaves, or are they set back from the building?

This chapter covers the following topics:

▶ **Placing roofs by footprint**

▶ **Creating a sloping roof**

▶ **Creating roofs by extrusion**

▶ **Adding a roof dormer**

Placing Roofs by Footprint

This book can't address every situation you'll encounter with a roof system, but it will expose you to the tools needed to tackle these situations yourself. The techniques you'll employ in this chapter start with the concept of adding a roof to the model by using the actual floor-plan footprint. As with floors, you'll also build the roof's composition for use in schedules, quantities, and material takeoffs.

The command you'll probably use most often when working with roofs is the one to place a roof by footprint. Essentially, you'll create a roof by using the outline of the building in the plan view. There are three roof types you'll place by using a footprint:

▶ A flat roof (OK, no roof is actually flat, but you get the point)

▶ A gable roof, which has two sides that are sloped and ends that are left open

▶ A hip roof, which has all sides sloped

You have only these options while placing a roof by footprint because you're looking at the roof in the plan, which limits your ability to place a roof with non-uniform geometry. Later in the book, you'll explore doing just that, but for now let's start with placing a flat roof by using the footprint of the east wing.

Flat Roofs by Footprint

To begin, open the file you've been using to follow along. If you didn't complete Chapter 6, "Floors," go to the book's web page at www.wiley.com/go/revit2024ner. From there, you can browse to Chapter 7 and find the file called NER-07.rvt.

The objective of this procedure is to create a flat roof by outlining the building's geometry in the plan. Follow along:

1. In the Project Browser, double-click the Roof view in the Floor Plans section (be careful not to click Roof in the Ceiling Plans section).

2. Zoom into the east wing.

3. Select all of the CMU walls.

4. Set the Top Constraint to Up To Level: Roof. See Figure 7.1.

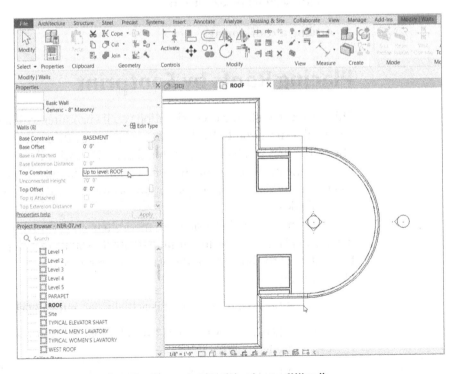

FIGURE 7.1 Lowering the constraints of the elevator CMU walls

5. On the Architecture tab, click Roof ➤ Roof By Footprint, as shown in Figure 7.2.

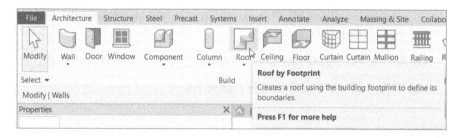

F I G U R E 7 . 2   Clicking Roof by Footprint on the Architecture tab of the Design bar

6. On the Modify | Create Roof Footprint tab, be sure the Pick Walls button on the Draw panel is selected, as shown at the right in Figure 7.3.

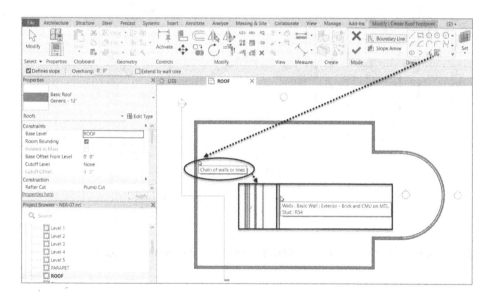

F I G U R E 7 . 3   Adding a sketch line to the perimeter of the building by picking walls

7. On the Options bar, deselect Defines Slope.

8. On the Options bar, make sure Overhang is set to 0'–0" (0 mm).

9. Deselect Extend to Wall Core (if it's selected).

10. Hover your pointer over the leftmost vertical wall. When it becomes highlighted, press the Tab key on your keyboard. All the perimeter walls highlight (see Figure 7.3). When they do, pick (left-click) anywhere along the wall. This places a magenta sketch line at the perimeter of the building.

11. On the Modify | Create Roof Footprint tab, click Finish Edit Mode.

12. Go to a 3D view, as shown in Figure 7.4.

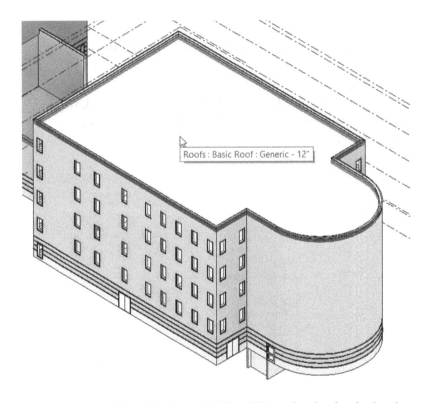

FIGURE 7.4 The roof has been added. You still have a lot of work to do, though.

With the roof added, step 1 is out of the way. Now you need to create a roof system. You'll do this the same way you created your floor system in Chapter 6.

Creating a Flat Roof System

Although you can use this system for a pitched roof, the steps for a flat roof system differ slightly. In the Autodesk® Revit® software, there are two ways to look at a roofing system. One way is to create it by using all the typical roof materials and a large space for the structural framing. In this book, I don't recommend that approach. Creating a roof by using only the roofing components is necessary, but adding the structure will lead to conflicts when the actual structural model is linked with the architectural model. Also, it's hard for the architect to guess what the depth of the structural framing will be. In Revit, you want each component to be as literal and as true to the model as possible. The second way to look at a roofing system, as you're about to explore, is to build the roof in a literal sense—that is, to create the roof as it would sit on the structural framing by the structural engineer.

The objective of this procedure is to create a roof system by adding layers of materials. Follow these steps:

1. Select the roof. (If you're having trouble selecting the roof, make sure the Select Elements By Face button is checked in the lower-right corner of the drawing area.)

2. In the Properties dialog, click Edit Type.

3. Click Duplicate.

4. Call the new roof system **Pitched Insulated Roof (100 mm Pitched Insulted Roof)**.

5. Click OK.

6. Click the Edit button in the Structure row.

7. Change the material of Structure 1 to Concrete, Lightweight. (You do this by clicking in the cell and then clicking the [. . .] button. You can then select the material from the menu.) After the material is selected, click OK.

8. Change the structure Thickness to 4″ (100 mm), as shown in Figure 7.5.

9. Insert a new layer above the core boundary. (You do this by clicking the number on the left side of the Layers Above Wrap row and clicking the Insert button below the Layers section, as shown in Figure 7.6.)

10. Change the function of the new layer to Thermal/Air Layer [3].

11. Click in the Material cell.

12. Click the [. . .] button to open the Material Browser.

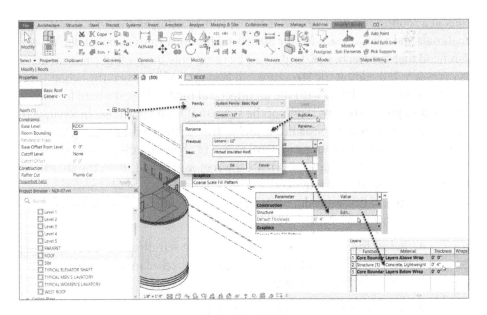

FIGURE 7.5   Changing the material and adding a layer

13. Select Rigid Insulation for the material.

14. Click OK.

15. Change Thickness to 4″ (200 mm).

16. Click the Variable button. When you modify the roof, this insulation layer will warp, enabling you to specify roof drain locations.

17. Insert a new layer above Thermal/Air Layer.

18. Give it a Function of Finish 1 [4].

19. Select Roofing - EPDM Membrane for the material.

20. Click OK.

21. Change Thickness to 1/8″ (3 mm), as shown in Figure 7.6.

22. Click OK.

23. Click OK again to get back to the model.

24. Press Esc or click in open space to clear the roof selection.

Phew! That was a long procedure. It was worth it, though. You'll be using this process a lot in Revit.

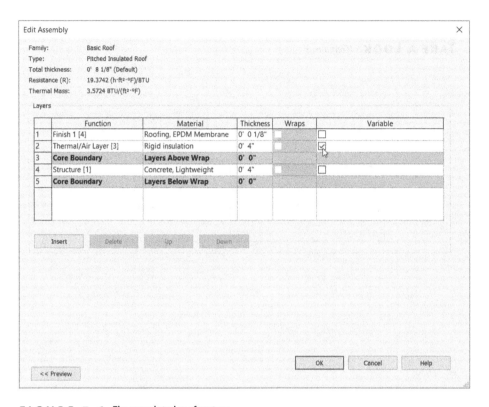

FIGURE 7.6 The completed roof system

For the next procedure, you'll add some roof drain locations and then taper the insulation to drain to those locations.

TAKE A LOOK

It's always a good idea to keep the preview window open when you modify the roof system. If you look toward the bottom of the Edit Assembly dialog, you'll see a Preview button, as shown in the following illustration. Click it, and you can see the roof as it's being constructed.

(Continues)

TAKE A LOOK *(Continued)*

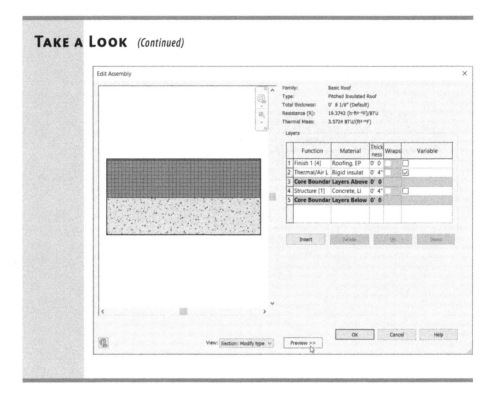

Tapering a Flat Roof and Adding Drains

If you went through the floor procedure in Chapter 6, you'll see that the process for tapering a roof is similar to the process for pitching a floor. You may have also noticed that creating a roof system is identical to creating a floor system.

To taper the roof insulation, you must first divide the roof into peaks and valleys and then specify the drain locations based on the centering of these locations. Follow along:

1. In the Project Browser, make sure you're in the Roof floor plan.

2. On the Architecture tab, click the Ref Plane button on the Work Plane panel as shown in Figure 7.7.

3. On the Draw panel click Pick Lines, and change the offset to 2'–0' (610 mm).

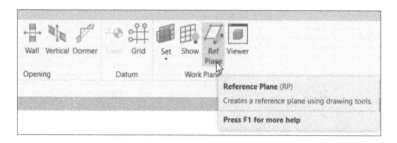

FIGURE 7.7 Selecting the Ref Plane button

4. Use the perimeter walls as shown in Figure 7.8 to offset the reference planes into the roof.

5. Change the offset to 6′–0′ (1829 mm).

6. Offset the middle reference plane 6′–0′ (1829 mm) above and below. See Figure 7.8.

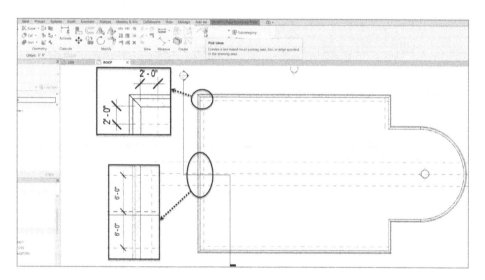

FIGURE 7.8 Adding the reference planes around the perimeter and the middle of the roof

7. Change the offset to 25′–0′ (7620 mm).

8. Use the west wall and the east wall to get the reference planes, as shown in Figure 7.9.

9. Select the roof.

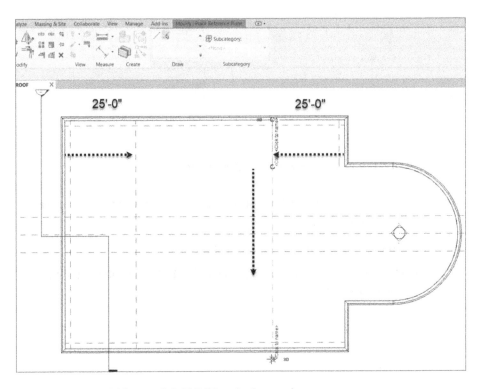

FIGURE 7.9   Adding two 25'–0' (7620 mm) reference planes

 TIP   As mentioned, it is much easier to select surfaces by turning on the Select Elements By Face option.

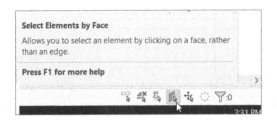

10. On the Shape Editing panel, click the Add Split Line button as shown in Figure 7.10

11. Add the split lines as shown in Figure 7.11. You should have six split lines.

12. Press Esc. It appears as if the split lines disappear, but we will get them back in the next procedure.

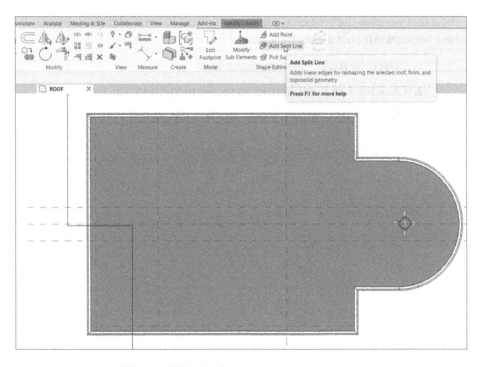

FIGURE 7.10   Click the Add Split Line button.

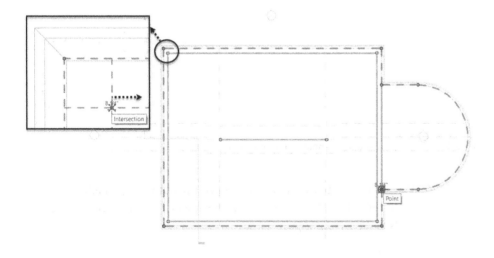

FIGURE 7.11   Splitting up the main roof

Now that we have the roof nicely split up, it's time to start adding the points where we want our roof drains to be placed.

1. Select the roof.

2. Click the Add Point button, as shown in Figure 7.12.

3. Pick the midpoint of the split line (see Figure 7.12).

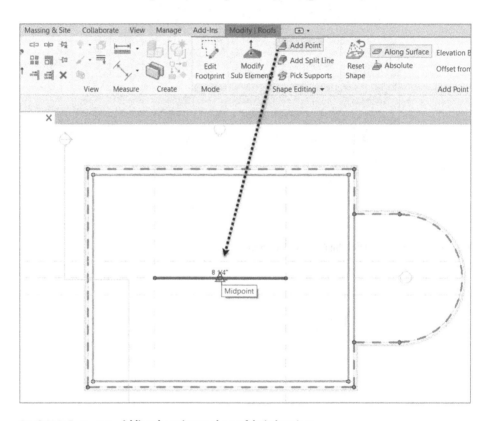

FIGURE 7.12 Adding the points to the roof drain locations

4. Place six more points above and below the point we just added on the 6'–0' reference planes and also above and below the points on the ends, as shown in Figure 7.13.

5. Hit Esc.

With all these points and split lines in our roof, it's time to start manipulating these objects to drive the slope of our roof.

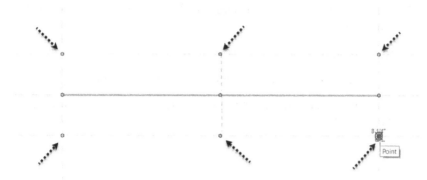

FIGURE 7.13   Adding six more points. This will become our cricket.

1. Select the roof.

2. Click the Modify Sub Elements button, as shown in Figure 7.14.

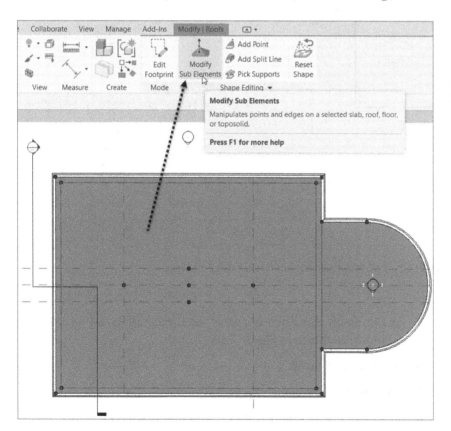

FIGURE 7.14   Editing the sub elements

3. In the Modify Sub Elements panel, make sure Elevation Base is set to Current Level.

4. Zoom in on the upper-left corner of the roof.

5. Click the small blue grip and you will see the elevation of that point.

6. Hold the Ctrl key and select the rest of the blue grips as shown in Figure 7.15.

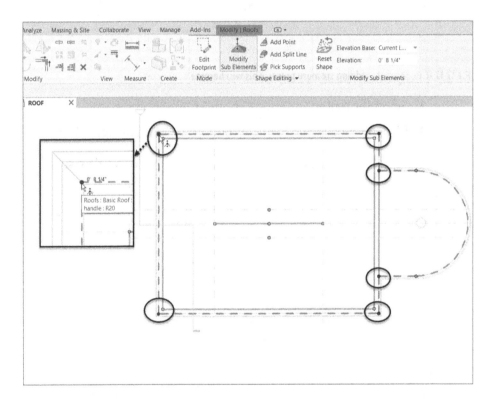

FIGURE 7.15 Selecting the points for our beveled roof edge

7. On the Modify Sub Elements panel, set the elevation to 1'–8 1/4" (514 mm) as shown in Figure 7.16.

8. Select the roof again.

9. Click Modify Sub Elements.

10. Select the four interior points as shown in Figure 7.17.

11. Set the elevation to 1'–0 1/4".

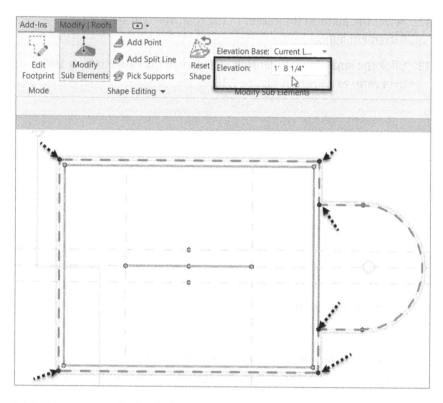

F I G U R E   7 . 1 6   Setting the height

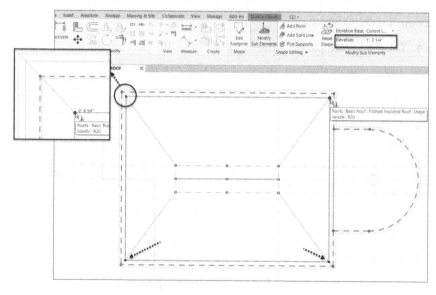

F I G U R E   7 . 1 7   The roof is shaping up! Notice we're starting to get slope lines.

12. Select the point in the center of the roof. You will see a 8 1/2" increment appear

13. Click the small blue dimension and change the value to 1'–8 1/4" (514 mm) as shown in Figure 7.18.

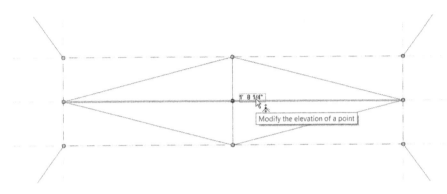

FIGURE 7.18 Changing the dimension value

14. Delete the reference planes we added. This will keep the model less confusing to others. Keep the reference plane in the middle of the building.

To further investigate how this roof works and to illustrate the benefits of using this approach rather than drafting the lines, let's cut a section through the roof and see how the detail looks:

1. On the Create panel of the View tab, click the Section button.

2. Add a section through the roof, as shown in Figure 7.19.

3. Hit Esc and click on the section bubble.

4. In the Type Selector, make sure the type of the section is a building section.

5. Double-click the section head (or find the section called Section 1 in the Project Browser).

6. Change the View Name option (under Identity Data) to Roof Taper Section.

7. Change the View Scale to 3/4" = 1'–0" (1:20 mm).

8. Change Detail Level to Fine as shown in Figure 7.20.

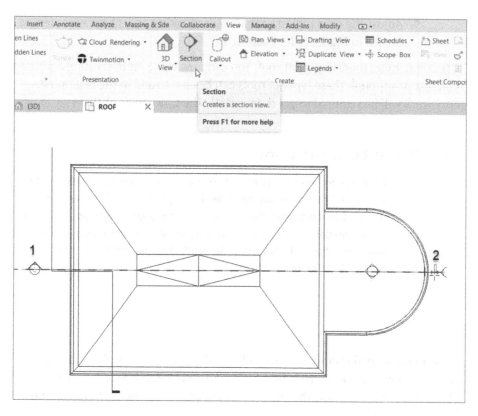

FIGURE 7.19 Adding a section through the roof at this point

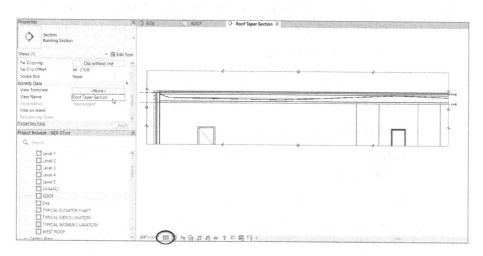

FIGURE 7.20 Changing the properties of the section and previewing the tapered roof

9. Adjust the crop region so that you're looking only at the roof area, as shown in Figure 7.20. Zoom to fit.

This concludes modeling a flat roof. You can now move on to creating a pitched roof. Again, although these types of roofs can be easy to add in the beginning, more work will be required to get them exactly the way you want them.

THE PROOF IS IN THE ROOF!

This is a perfect example of why the Revit approach to design documentation is the way to go. Although the sloping of the slab may have seemed tedious, in reality it didn't take much longer than it would have if you had drafted those lines in a CAD application. But now, to produce a section all you need to do is to cut one. Also, if you change the location or the depth of the roof pitch, your lines in the plan will be accurate, as will your section.

Pitched Roofs by Footprint

You'll add a pitched roof in a manner identical to the way you added the flat roof. The only real difference is that each magenta sketch line will need more attention before you finish the sketch. But after tapering the roof's insulation, this will be a cakewalk.

You'll place the pitched roof over the corridor. The problem with the corridor is that you used a wall system with a parapet cap. This isn't the best wall system to receive a pitched roof. First, you'll change to a simpler wall system, as follows:

1. Go to a 3D view of the model.

2. Select the six corridor walls, as shown in Figure 7.21.

3. In the Properties dialog, click the Edit Type button.

4. Click the Duplicate button.

5. Call the new wall system **Exterior - Brick and CMU on MTL. Stud (No Parapet)**.

6. In the Structure row, click the Edit button.

7. In the Edit Assembly dialog, make sure the Preview button is clicked on and the view is set to Section: Modify Type as shown at the bottom of Figure 7.22.

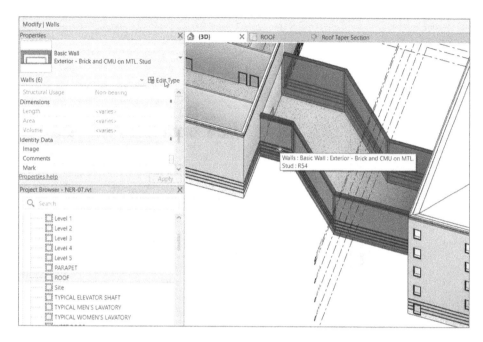

FIGURE 7.21 Select the six walls to be modified.

8. Click the Sweeps button (see Figure 7.22).

9. In the Wall Sweeps dialog box, you see three sweeps. The top sweep is the parapet cap. Select sweep 1 (Parapet Cap), and click the Delete button, as shown in Figure 7.23.

10. Click OK three times.

Your corridor walls should look exactly the same, but they're now void of the concrete parapet cap.

 N O T E Although you have pretty good experience with walls up to this point, Chapter 15, "Advanced Wall Topics," is dedicated to the advanced concepts and creation of wall systems.

Remember, your preview must be in Section: Modify Type for all the buttons to be active.

It's time to add the roof to the corridor. Because the walls your roof will bear on are now correct, the rest will be a snap! Here are the steps:

1. Go to the Corridor Roof floor plan.

2. In the Properties dialog, in the Underlay category, set Range: Base Level to Level 1, as shown in Figure 7.24.

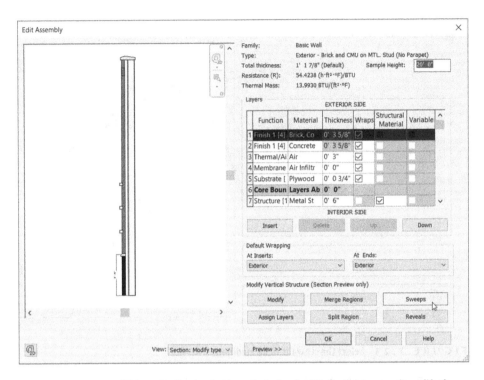

FIGURE 7.22 Without the Preview button selected and set to Section, you can't modify the parapet sweep.

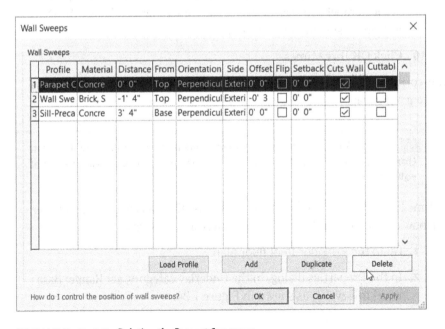

FIGURE 7.23 Deleting the Parapet Cap sweep

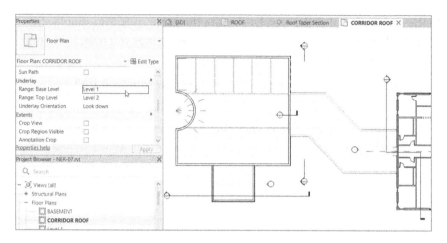

FIGURE 7.24 Setting the underlay

3. On the Architecture tab, choose Roof ➤ Roof by Footprint.

4. On the Draw panel, make sure the Pick Walls button is selected.

5. On the Options bar, make sure the Defines Slope button is selected.

6. Type **1'** (300 mm) in the Overhang field.

7. Pick the six walls that compose the corridor, as shown in Figure 7.25.

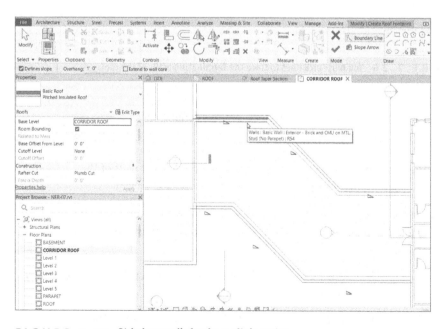

FIGURE 7.25 Pick these walls for the roof's footprint.

With the easy walls out of the way, let's create the gable ends. You should still be in Pick Walls mode. This is OK, but there are a few things you need to change on the Options bar. Follow these steps:

1. Click the Boundary Line button on the Draw panel if it isn't still active.

2. On the Draw panel again, click the Pick Lines icon, as shown in Figure 7.26.

As you pick the walls, notice that you now have an overhang. This overhang obviously needs to extend to the outside of the walls. Just be aware of this as you pick the walls, and watch your alignment lines as you proceed.

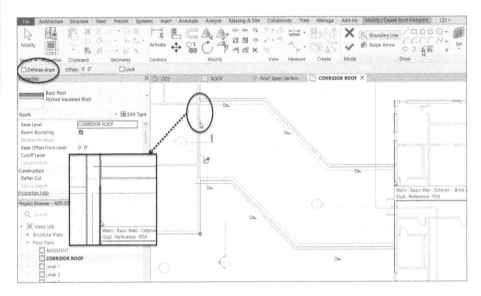

FIGURE 7.26   You must pick lines to trace the terminating walls of the roof.

3. On the Options bar, deselect Defines Slope.

4. For the offset, enter 0.

5. Pick the east wall of the west wing and the west wall of the east wing (see Figure 7.26).

It's cleanup time! Of course, the magenta lines are overlapping at the long walls. This is OK—you're an expert at the Trim command by now, especially in Sketch mode:

1. On the Modify | Create Roof Footprint tab, select the Trim/Extend to Corner command.

2. Trim the intersections that overlap. There are four of them (see Figure 7.27).

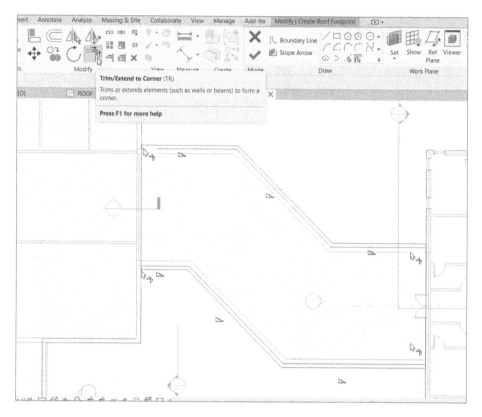

FIGURE 7.27 Using the Trim command in conjunction with the roof sketch

3. On the Mode panel, click Finish Edit Mode, and go to a 3D view.

One ugly roof, huh? Welcome to the world of pitched roofs in Revit. You'll get the roof you want—you just need to add two roofs here. You'll understand this process, but it's going to involve patience and trial and error!

To fix this roof, you simply have to make two separate roofs and join them together. This is a common procedure for the more complicated roof systems in Revit. Here are the steps:

1. If you aren't in Corridor Roof, go there now, and select the roof.

2. On the Modify | Roofs tab, click the Edit Footprint button, as shown in Figure 7.28.

3. Delete every line other than the three shown in Figure 7.29.

4. On the Draw panel, click the Line button.

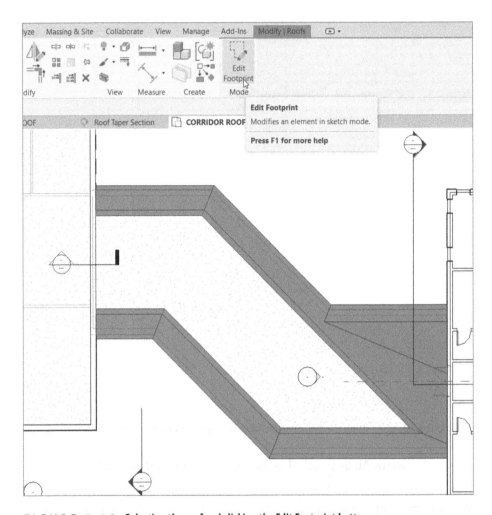

FIGURE 7.28 Selecting the roof and clicking the Edit Footprint button

5. Draw a diagonal line between the endpoints of the two lines, as shown in Figure 7.30. Make sure the Defines Slope button isn't selected.

6. On the Modify | Roofs ➤ Edit Footprint tab, click Finish Edit Mode. The roof displays. It still looks funny, but you'll take care of that soon by altering the view range to make the view deep enough to display the ridge of the new roof.

7. Start the Roof ➤ Roof by Footprint command again on the Architecture tab. You can also select the roof and click Create Similar on the Modify | Roofs tab that is currently active.

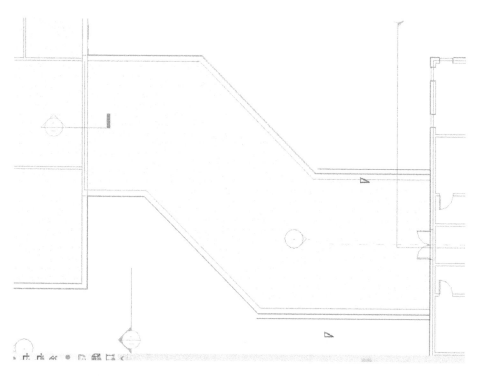

FIGURE 7.29 Keep these three lines.

8. On your own, sketch the roof shown in Figure 7.31. Make sure the lines along the walls are defining a slope. The lines that represent the ends of the roof don't slope.

9. To add the line that matches the roof to the right, make sure the Boundary Line button is selected on the Draw panel and that Pick Lines is selected as well. Now simply pick the roof to the right, and the line appears.

10. Review Figure 7.31 to see if your sketch matches. You should have six lines total, and the right and the left ends should not have a slope.

11. On the Modify | Create Roof Footprint tab, click Finish Edit Mode.

12. Select both roofs.

13. In the Type Selector, click the drop-down and put these roofs on Wood Rafter 8" - Asphalt Shingle – Insulated, as shown in Figure 7.32.

14. Go to a 3D view. Does your roof look like Figure 7.33?

If you accidentally add a line with (or without) a slope, that's fine. You can change it. First, press Esc (to clear the command), and then select the line that needs to be changed. On the Options bar, you can select (or deselect) Defines Slope.

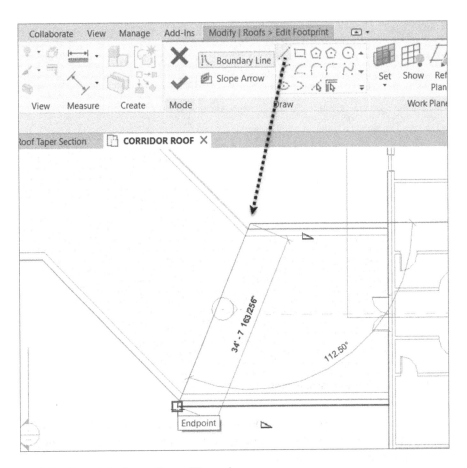

FIGURE 7.30 Draw a diagonal line as shown.

Viewing a Sloped Roof in the Plan

Back in the corridor roof plan, you're having a view problem: the roof is show-ing up only to the cut plane for that level. The standard American Institute of Architects (AIA) plan view dictates that the cut plane for walls or any vertical element is sectioned at 4′–0″ (1219 mm). In this case, we need to change that.

1. Go to the Corridor Roof floor plan.

2. On the View Control toolbar, select Crop View and Crop Region Visible, as shown in Figure 7.34.

3. Select the crop region that surrounds your floor plan by clicking the blue grips. Drag the crop region to show only the corridor roof (see Figure 7.35).

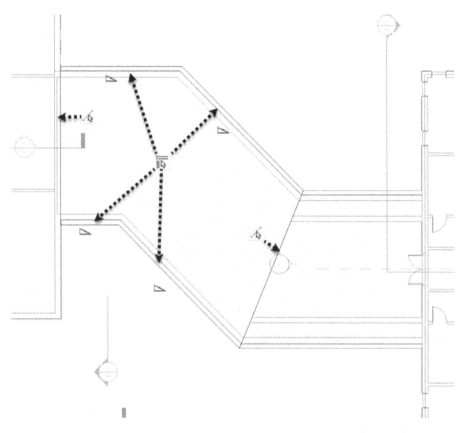

F I G U R E 7 . 3 1 The new outline of the second roof

4. Press Esc a couple times, and in the Properties dialog, change Range: Base Level to None, as shown in Figure 7.36.

5. Scroll down a bit more until you get to View Range. Once you see View Range, click the Edit button.

6. Under Primary Range, set Top to Unlimited.

7. For Cut Plane, set Offset to 50'–0" (15240 mm).

8. Keep Bottom and View Depth | Level the same, as shown in Figure 7.36, and click OK.

There is one more kind of roof to add. It will be a flat roof that has a slope in a single direction. Although you can do this by simply creating a roof with one edge specified as a pitch, at times you'll want a roof sloped at an odd direction that can't be handled by angling a roof edge.

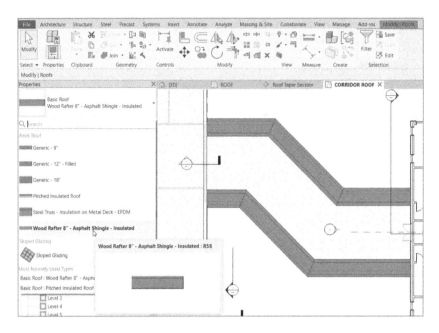

FIGURE 7.32 Changing the roof type

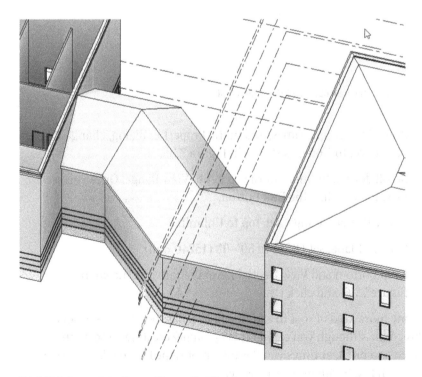

FIGURE 7.33 The corridor roof in 3D

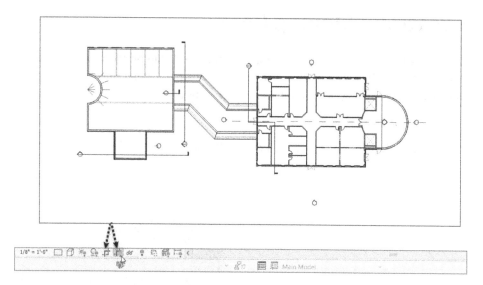

FIGURE 7.34 Turning on the crop region

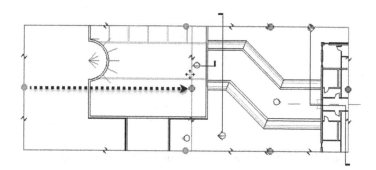

FIGURE 7.35 Dragging the crop region to cut out any unnecessary geometry

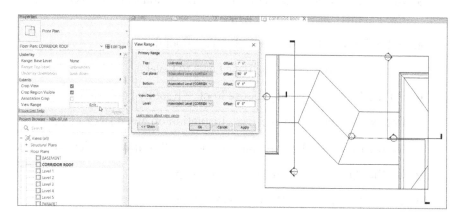

FIGURE 7.36 Changing the view range

Creating a Sloping Roof

To begin the process of creating a sloping roof, you'll cap off the west wing of your building. The exterior walls used for the perimeter need to be altered. You're already a pro at this, so let's start right there:

1. Go to a 3D view.

2. Select the west wing exterior walls (see Figure 7.37).

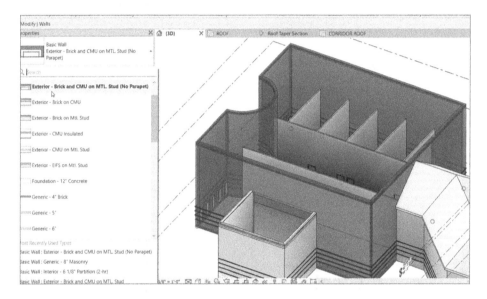

FIGURE 7.37 Changing the walls to Exterior - Brick and CMU on MTL. Stud (No Parapet)

3. In the Type Selector, select Exterior - Brick and CMU on MTL. Stud (No Parapet), as shown in Figure 7.37.

4. In the Project Browser, go to the West Roof floor plan.

5. In the properties set Range Base Level to Level 3.

6. On the Architecture tab, choose Roof ➤ Roof By Footprint.

7. Change the roof to Steel Truss - Insulation on Metal Deck - EPDM.

8. On the Draw panel, verify that the Pick Walls button is selected.

9. On the Options bar, deselect Defines Slope.

10. Type 1' (300 mm) for the Overhang value.

11. Move your cursor over a wall. Make sure the overhang alignment line is facing outside the walls to the exterior.

12. Press the Tab key. All the walls are selected.

13. Pick the wall. The magenta lines are completely drawn in. Your sketch should look like Figure 7.38.

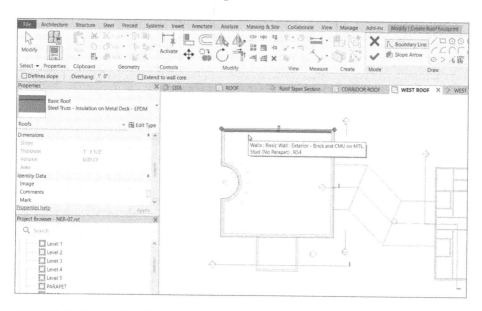

FIGURE 7.38 The perimeter of the roof is set.

Now it's time to set the slope. The objective here is to slope the roof starting at the northeast corner (as the low point) and ending at the southwest corner (the high point). You do this by adding a slope arrow, as follows:

1. On the Draw panel, click the Slope Arrow button, as shown in Figure 7.39.

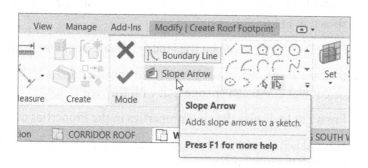

FIGURE 7.39 Clicking the Slope Arrow button on the Draw panel

2. Pick the corner at the upper right and then the corner at the lower left, as shown in Figure 7.40.

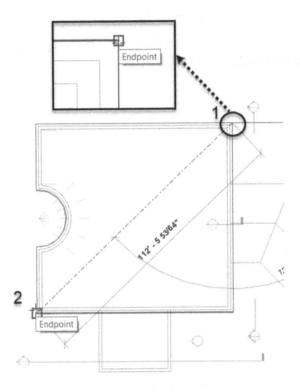

FIGURE 7.40 Adding the slope arrow

3. Press Esc.

4. Select the slope arrow you just added to the model.

5. In the Properties dialog, under Constraints, change Specify to Slope.

6. Under Dimensions, change Slope to 2" / 12" (50 / 1000 mm), as shown in Figure 7.41.

7. Click Finish Edit Mode on the Modify | Create Roof Footprint tab.

Again, you have a view range issue. You can see only the corner of the roof that sits below the cut plane. You can change that with the view range:

1. Press Esc to display the view properties in the Properties dialog.

2. Scroll down the list until you arrive at the View Range row. When you do, click the Edit button.

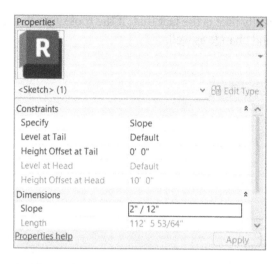

FIGURE 7.41 Changing the Slope Arrow properties

3. Click the Show button in the bottom-left corner, exposing the graph that explains View Range.

4. In the View Range dialog, under Primary Range, set Top to Unlimited.

5. Set Cut Plane | Offset to 40′ 0″ (12000 mm), as shown in Figure 7.42.

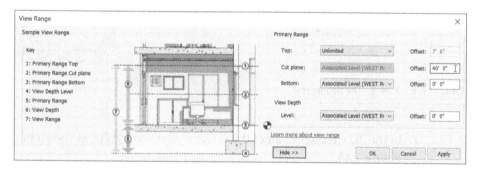

FIGURE 7.42 Setting the view range

6. Click OK. You can see the entire roof.

7. Go to a 3D view. You now have a cool, sloping roof, as shown in Figure 7.43.

As you can see, there is a massive gap between the roof and the walls. Revit has a plan for that. What's nice is, we can tell Revit to attach the tops of the walls to the sloped roof. What's really nice is the fact that, if the roof slope changes, the walls will stay attached and change as well.

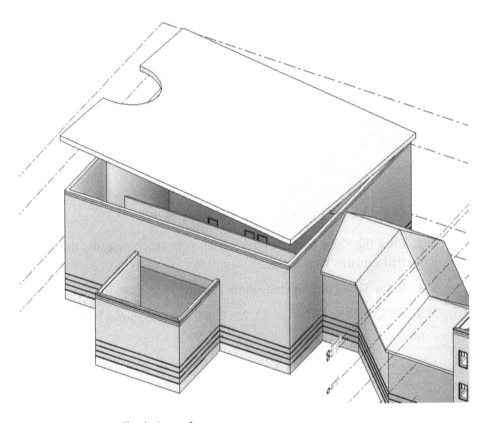

FIGURE 7.43 The sloping roof

1. In the 3D view, select all of the exterior west wing walls, as shown in Figure 7.44.

2. On the Modify | Walls tab, select Attach Top/Base.

3. Pick Top from the Options bar (it's all the way to the left).

4. Pick the sloping roof (see Figure 7.44, and 7.45 for the finished wall).

The next item to tackle will be creating a roof by extrusion. This is where you can design a custom roof.

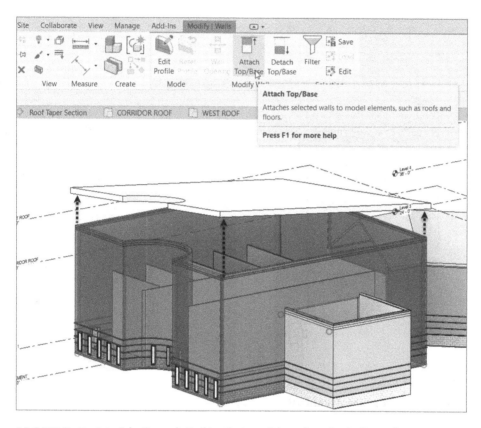

FIGURE 7.44 Selecting and attaching the tops of the walls to the sloping roof

Creating Roofs by Extrusion

Creating a roof by extrusion is almost always done in an elevation or a section view. The concept is to create unique geometry that can't be accomplished by simply using a footprint in a plan. A barrel vault or an eyebrow dormer comes to mind, but there are literally thousands of combinations that will influence how your roofs will be designed.

To get started, the last roof left to be placed is the south jog in the west wing of the model. This is the perfect area for a funky roof!

The first thing to do is to change the three walls defining the jog to the Exterior - Brick and CMU On MTL. Stud (No Parapet) wall type:

1. Go to a 3D view.

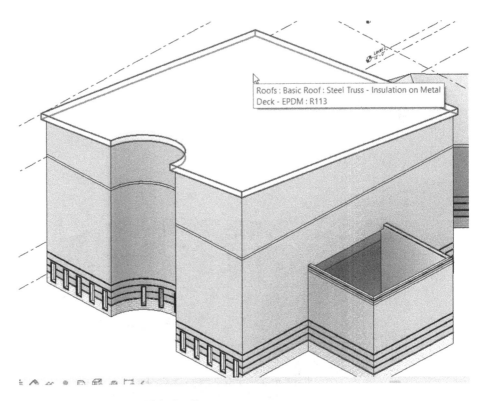

Roofs : Basic Roof : Steel Truss - Insulation on Metal Deck - EPDM : R113

FIGURE 7.45 **The attached walls**

2. Select the three walls that compose the jog in the south wall (see Figure 7.46).

3. In the Properties dialog, switch these walls to Exterior - Brick and CMU on MTL. Stud (No Parapet), as shown in Figure 7.46.

4. Go to the Level 1 floor plan.

5. On the View tab, click the Elevation button.

6. In the Properties dialog, be sure that the elevation is a Building elevation (you're given the choice in the drop-down menu at the top of the Type Selector).

7. Place the elevation as shown in Figure 7.47.

8. Select the elevation you just created. (Remember, you need to select the triangular target part of the elevation, not the circle.)

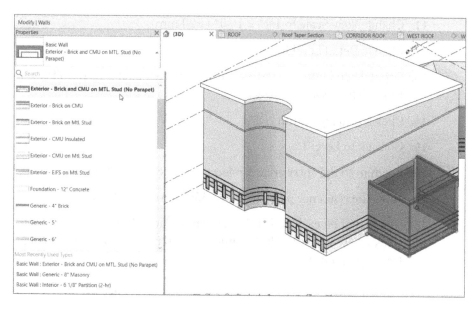

FIGURE 7.46 Changing the wall types as you have been doing all along

After you place the elevation, you'll have no idea where the view is extended to. Is it to the end of the building? You just don't know. If you pick the elevation arrow (the part of the elevation marker), you can then grip-edit the elevation to see what you need.

9. Pick the view extents (the blue grips at the ends of the elevation), and drag them in so that you can see only the west wing.

10. Make sure you pull the view depth window back to see the wall beyond (see Figure 7.47).

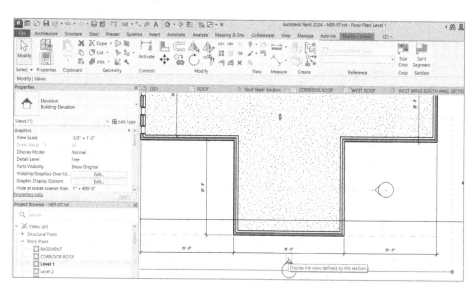

FIGURE 7.47 Adjusting the view

11. Change View Scale to 1/2″ = 1′–0″ (1:20 mm).

12. Change Detail Level to Fine.

13. Scroll down in the properties and change View Name to SOUTH ELEVATION ENTRY.

14. Click the Apply button.

15. Go back to Level 1.

16. Zoom in to the entry area. A reference plane is still there; select it.

17. Move the reference plane to 1′–6″ (450 mm) below the wall.

18. Notice that on each end of the reference plane, it says Click To Name. Click where it says Click To Name, and call it **South Entry Overhang** (see Figure 7.48).

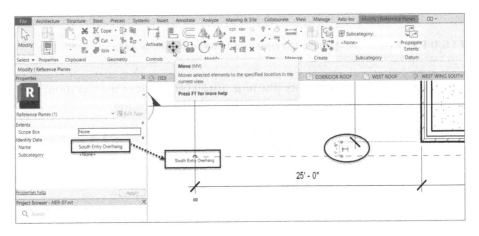

FIGURE 7.48 Modifying a reference plane

19. Open the South Entry Elevation. (You can either double-click on the elevation in plan or find South Entry Elevation in the Project Browser.)

The importance of the reference plane that you just adjusted becomes obvious at this point. You needed to establish a clear starting point for the roof you're about to add. Because the roof will be added in an elevation, Revit doesn't know where to start the extrusion. This reference plane will serve as the starting point. Naming reference planes is the way you can use them when they aren't visible in the view. Continue with these steps:

1. On the Architecture tab, choose Roof ➤ Roof by Extrusion, as shown in Figure 7.49.

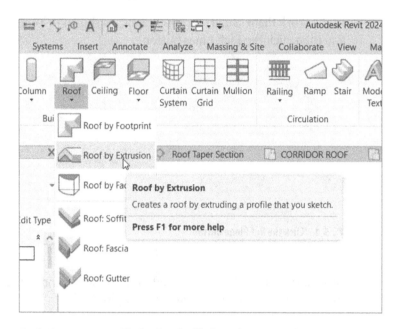

FIGURE 7.49 The Roof ➤ Roof by Extrusion command

2. When you start the command, Revit asks you to specify a reference plane. Select Reference Plane: South Entry Overhang from the Name drop-down list, as shown in Figure 7.50.

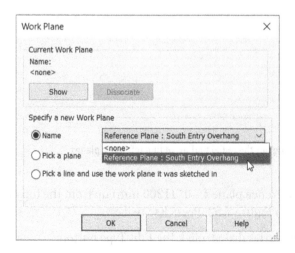

FIGURE 7.50 Selecting the South Entry Overhang reference plane

3. Click OK.

4. In the next dialog, change the Level setting to Level 3, and click OK.

5. In the Work Plane panel, click Ref Plane, as shown in Figure 7.51, and then click the Pick Lines button.

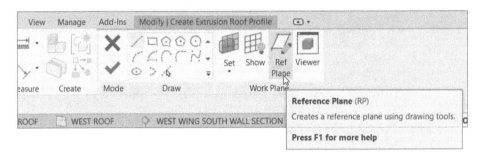

FIGURE 7.51   **Click the Ref Plane button.**

6. Offset a reference plane 3′–0″ (900 mm) to the left and to the right of the exterior walls, marked 1 and 2 in Figure 7.52.

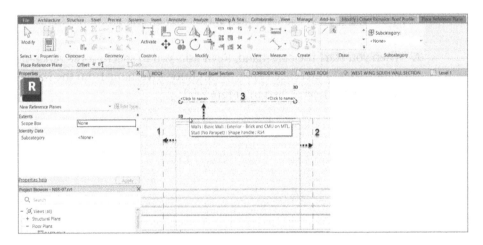

FIGURE 7.52   **Laying out the radial roof by adding reference planes**

7. Offset a reference plane 4′–0″ (1200 mm) up from the top of the wall, marked 3 in Figure 7.52. Press Esc twice.

8. In the Properties dialog, click the Edit Type button.

9. Click Duplicate.

10. Change the name to **Canopy Roof**.

11. Click the Edit button in the Structure row.

12. In the Edit Assembly dialog box, select Row 5 (Structure, Steel Bar Joist Layer) and click Delete. Once Deleted, your dialog should look like Figure 7.53.

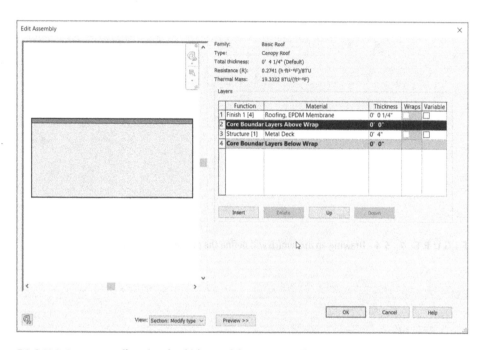

FIGURE 7.53 Changing the thickness of the canopy roof by removing the rigid insulation

13. Change Structure [1] to 4" (102 mm).

14. Click on Row 2 and delete it (it's the rigid insulation).

15. Click OK twice to get back to the model.

It's time to put the actual roof into the model. So far, you've been using great discipline in terms of setting reference planes and creating a separate roof for this canopy. Try to make this a habit! Follow along:

1. On the Draw panel of the Modify | Create Extrusion Roof Profile tab, click the Start-End-Radius Arc button, as shown in Figure 7.54.

2. Draw an arc from the points shown in Figure 7.54.

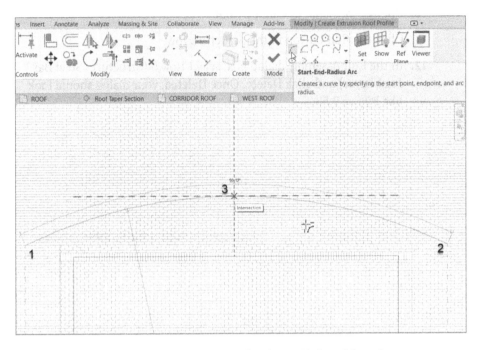

FIGURE 7.54   Drawing an arc, which will define the outside face of the roof

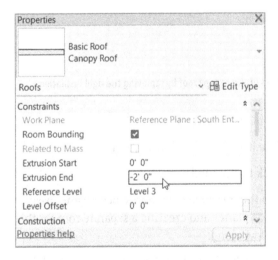

FIGURE 7.55   Setting Extrusion End

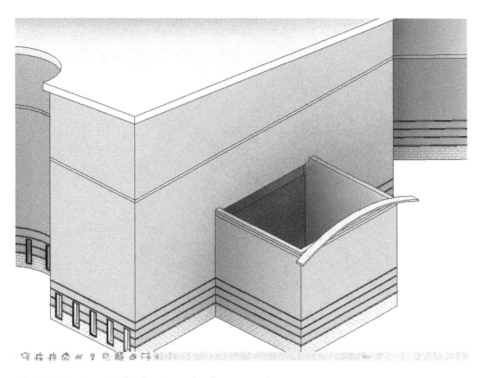

FIGURE 7.56 The almost completed canopy roof

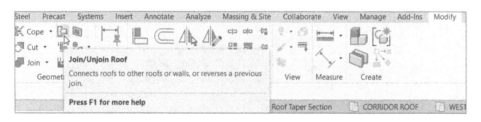

FIGURE 7.57 Join Roofs

TIP When you're adding a roof by extrusion, you need to draw only one line. The thickness is defined in the roof you're using. After you click Finish Edit Mode, the 4″ (100 mm) thickness will be added to the bottom.

3. In the Properties dialog, set Extrusion End to -2′–0″ (-600 mm), as shown in Figure 7.55.

4. Click the green Finish Edit Mode check mark.

5. Go to a 3D view. Your roof should look like Figure 7.56.

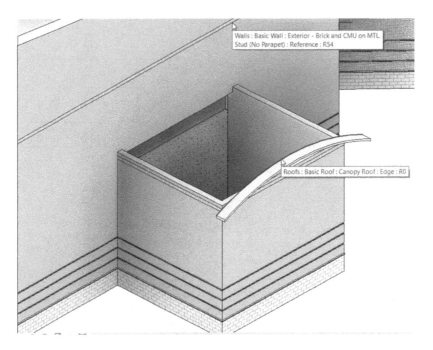

Walls : Basic Wall : Exterior - Brick and CMU on MTL. Stud (No Parapet) : Reference : R54

Roofs : Basic Roof : Canopy Roof : Edge : R0

F I G U R E 7 . 5 8 Picking the roof and the wall to join the two together

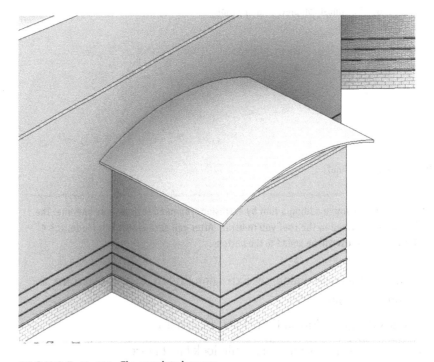

F I G U R E 7 . 5 9 The completed canopy

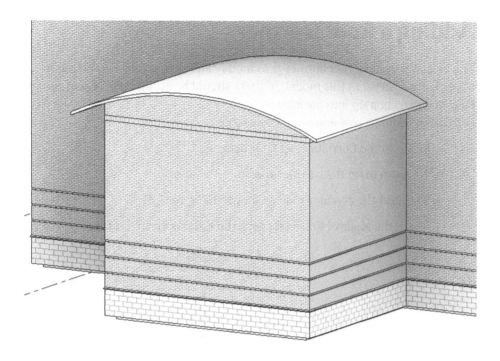

FIGURE 7.60 The walls are now attached to the roof.

There is just one thing left to do, and it's pretty obvious: you need to attach the roof to the wall. This can be done in one command:

1. On the Modify tab, click the Join/Unjoin Roof button, as shown in Figure 7.57.

2. Pick the top, back arc on the canopy roof, as shown in Figure 7.58.

3. Pick the wall into which the roof needs to terminate (see Figure 7.58).

    Your roof should look like Figure 7.58.
    The roof is now joined to the wall, as shown in Figure 7.59.

4. Select all three walls under the canopy.

5. On the Modify | Walls tab, click the Attach Top/Base button.

6. Select the canopy roof. Your walls are now attached to the roof. (See Figure 7.60)

All of the conventional roofing systems have been added. Let's move on and add some dormers. This process will require the use of a collection of the tools with which you've gained experience up to this point.

Picking the wall is easier said than done, mostly because it's hard to tell whether you're picking the correct wall. Simply hover your mouse over the wall until the entire face becomes highlighted. When you see this, pick the wall. The roof will then extend to the wall.

Adding a Roof Dormer

The best way to add a roof dormer is to modify an existing roof. You certainly have plenty of those in this model, so there should be no shortage of roof surfaces you can chop up into dormers.

To begin adding a roof dormer, follow along:

1. Go to the Corridor Roof floor plan.

2. Zoom in on the corridor roof.

3. Select the corridor roof, as shown in Figure 7.61.

4. On the Modify | Roofs tab, click the Edit Footprint button.

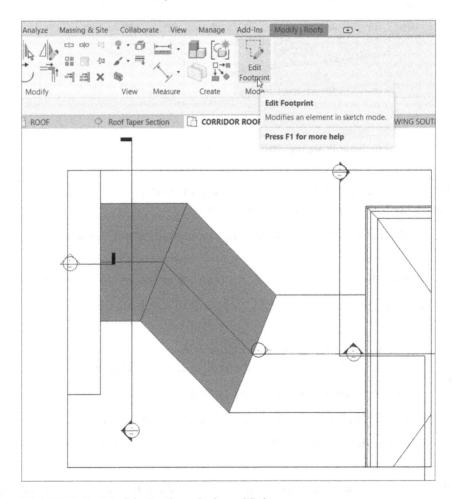

F I G U R E   7 . 6 1   Selecting the roof to be modified

You're now in the Sketch mode for this roof.

The procedure to modify the roof is reminiscent of climbing up on an actual roof and adding a dormer:

1. On the Modify | Roofs ➤ Edit Footprint tab, select the Split Element button, as shown in Figure 7.62.

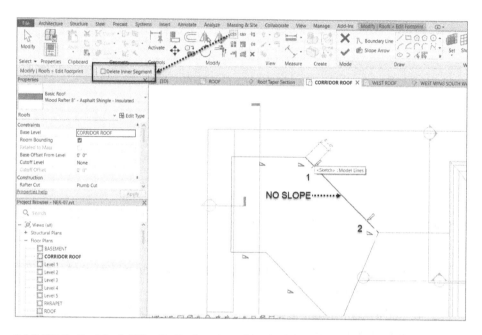

FIGURE 7.62 Splitting the line into three pieces (make sure you deselect Delete Inner Segment)

2. On the Options bar, deselect Delete Inner Segment.

3. Pick two points on the roof edge (see Figure 7.62).
   The two points are an even 4′ (1200 mm) in from each edge.

4. Press Esc twice.

5. Select the middle line.

6. On the Options bar, deselect Defines Slope.

With the length of the dormer established, you need to indicate to Revit that you want it to be a gable-end dormer. You do this by adding slope arrows:

1. On the Draw panel, click the Slope Arrow button.

2. For the first point of the slope arrow, click the endpoint of the first point you split (marked 1 in Figure 7.63).

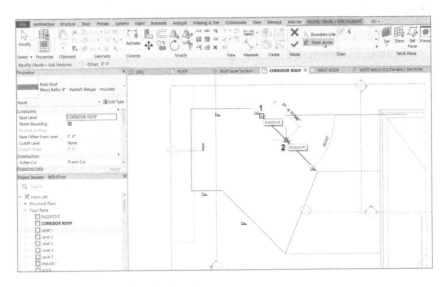

FIGURE 7.63 Adding the first slope arrow

3. For the second point of the slope arrow, pick the midpoint of the same line (see Figure 7.63).

4. Add a second slope arrow coming from the opposite side of the ridge line, as shown in Figure 7.64.

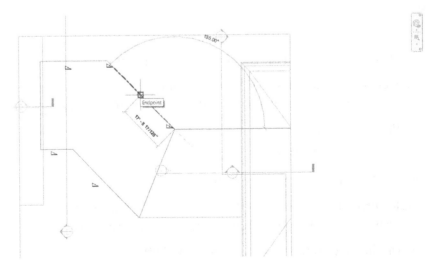

FIGURE 7.64 Adding a second slope arrow

5. Press Esc twice.

6. Select both slope arrows. (Be careful to select only the slope arrows, not the line of the roof underneath.)

7. In the Properties dialog, under Constraints, change Specify to Slope.

8. Under Dimensions, change the slope to 6″ / 12″ (152 / 304 mm) (see Figure 7.65).

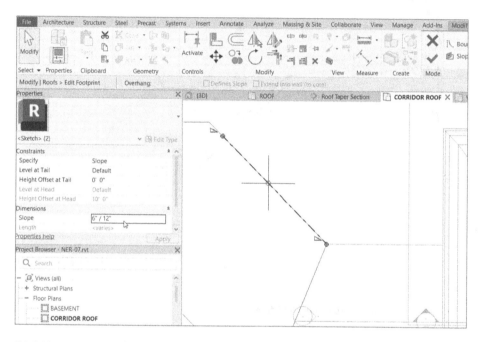

FIGURE 7.65 Changing the values of the slope arrows

9. Click Finish Edit Mode.

10. Go to a 3D view to check out the dormer. It should look identical to Figure 7.66.

11. Notice the gap between the wall and the roof. Select the wall, and click the Attach Top/Base button, as shown in Figure 7.67.

12. Select the roof, and you are done!

Adding roof dormers takes some practice to become efficient. If you don't feel confident that you can add a roof dormer on your own, either go back through the procedure or find another place in the building to add a second dormer.

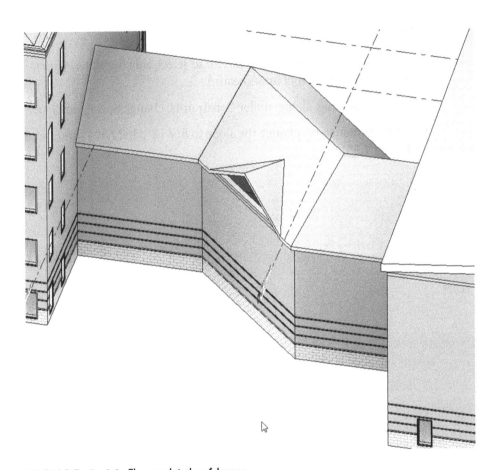

FIGURE 7.66 The completed roof dormer

Are You Experienced?

Now you can. . .

✓ place different types of roofs, including flat roofs, pitched roofs, and unconventional sloping roofs, using the footprint of your building

✓ analyze tricky areas and make multiple roofs if needed instead of relying on a single roof to flex and conform to the situation at hand

✓ edit wall joins to allow walls to attach to roofs after they're created

✓ design different roof systems based on their functionality

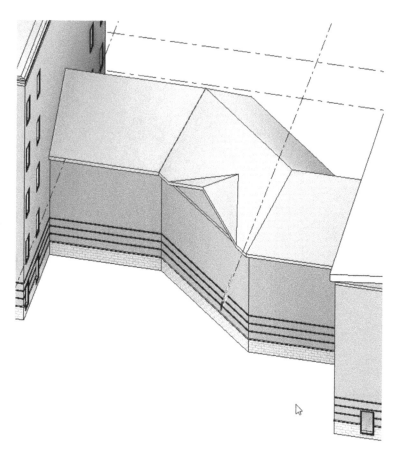

FIGURE 7.67 The completed wall attached to the dormer

✓ create a tapered roof plan using a variable material in the roof system

✓ create a roof by extrusion by setting work planes and using them to lay out a custom roof

✓ create a roof dormer by editing an existing roof and adding slope arrows to indicate a gable end

CHAPTER 8

Structural Items

Well, we can't avoid the topic of structure forever. Because you need
to consider your structure from pretty much the beginning of the project,
I had better add it to the first half of the book before we get too carried
away! As an addition, please note the tried-and-true workflow is that the
structure is contained in a separate model that is linked into the architectural model. However, many times you as the architect are going to lay
out grids as well as add columns and some framing to get a basis of design.
This chapter will cover the latter.

This chapter covers the following topics:

▶ **Adding structural grids**

▶ **Adding structural columns**

▶ **Using structural framing**

▶ **Understanding foundation systems**

▶ **Adding structural footings**

▶ **Using structural views**

Adding Structural Grids

Since we started modeling our building for this book using the architectural
template, you will quickly discover that most structural items aren't loaded
into our model. This is normal, as I eluded to in the opening paragraph of
this chapter that the typical workflow is to link different models. There are a
few reasons for this. One, the structural engineer cannot stand you touching
their framing. Another reason is what we are faced with now. A structural
template will be loaded with structural elements and not many architectural elements.

This chapter explores the structural world by presenting the basic functions
of structural architecture. The first item you'll tackle is usually the first item
in the model: structural grids. Although you add structural grids line by line,

you'll soon discover that these grids are just as smart as the rest of the Autodesk® Revit® software. The starting point for all things structural is most certainly the grid. In Revit, you'll quickly find that placing a structural grid into a model isn't a complicated task. Grids are essentially placed one line at a time. Those lines you place, however, have intelligence. For example, if you place a vertical grid line called A and then place a horizontal grid line called 1 that intersects with A, you'll have a grid location. If you place a column at that intersection, the column will assume a new property called Location. That location is—you guessed it—A-1.

Let's get started. To begin, open the file you've been using to follow along. If you didn't complete the previous chapter, go to www.wiley.com/go/revit 2024ner, browse to the Chapter 8 folder, and find the file called NER-08.rvt.

Placing a Grid

Placing a grid means drawing grid lines one by one. You can copy grids to speed up placement and array them if the spacing is regular. This task sounds tedious, but it's a welcome change from other applications that force you to create an entire rectangular grid, which you have to keep picking at until it resembles your layout. Grids are like snowflakes: no two are the same.

To place a grid, follow these steps:

1. In the Project Browser, go to the Level 1 floor plan. (Make sure you aren't in the Level 1 ceiling plan.)

2. On the Datum panel of the Structure tab, click the Grid button, as shown in Figure 8.1.

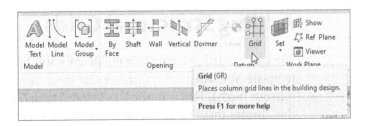

FIGURE 8.1   The Grid button on the Datum panel of the Structure tab

3. Zoom in to the east wing's northwest corner, as shown in Figure 8.2.

4. On the Draw panel of the Modify | Place Grid tab, click the Pick Lines icon, as shown in Figure 8.2.

5. Pick the centerline of the west wall (see Figure 8.2).

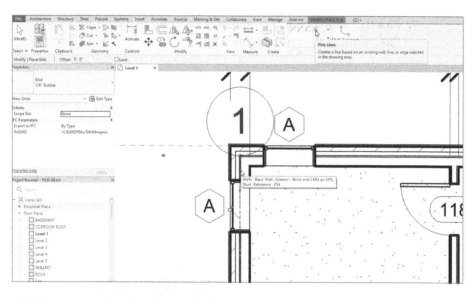

FIGURE 8.2 Your first column grid

6. The grid bubble needs to be moved. Press Esc twice or click Modify (to clear the command), and then select the grid bubble. Notice the round blue grip similar to that in Figure 8.3.

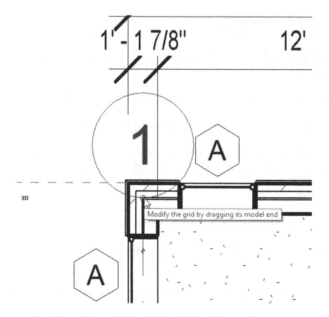

FIGURE 8.3 Examining the column grid grips

7. Pick that round blue grip, and drag the column bubble up about 8′ (203 mm), as shown in Figure 8.4.

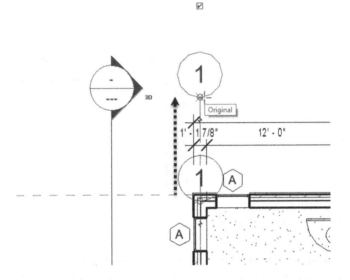

FIGURE 8.4 Dragging the column bubble up

8. Zoom in on the south portion of the same wall.

9. Select the grid. Notice there's the same grip as well as a square blue box.

10. Select the grip and move the grid down about 4′ (102 mm) or so.

11. Click the blue box to turn on the bubble. See Figure 8.5.

Let's start adding more grid lines. This procedure will involve selecting column line 1 and copying it to the right using some walls as placement points.

Notice that a column grid has functionality similar to that of levels, right down to the grips.

1. Select grid 1.

2. Click the copy button, as shown in Figure 8.6.

3. On the Options toolbar, click Constrain and Multiple, as illustrated in Figure 8.6.

4. Select a point on grid 1 approximately where shown in Figure 8.6.

5. Pick a point on the centerline of the wall (see Figure 8.6).

6. Using the same technique in steps 1–5, add grids as shown in Figure 8.7.

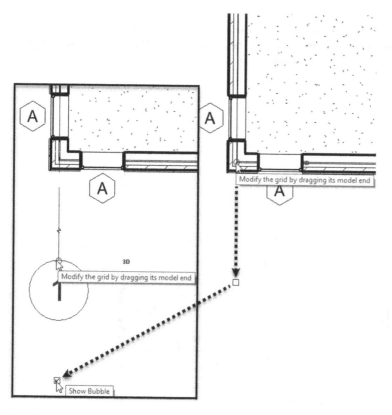

FIGURE 8.5 Adjusting the bottom of grid 1

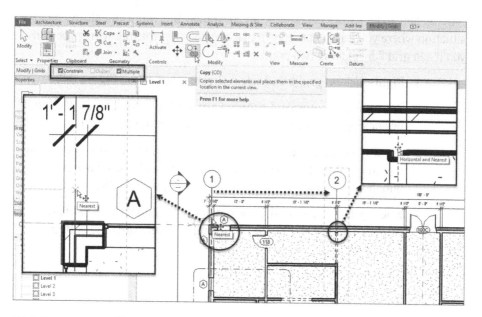

FIGURE 8.6 Adding grid line 2 by using the copy function

TIP Alignment lines, however useful, can be tricky to get to display. The percentage of your zoom has an effect. If you aren't getting the alignment lines, simply zoom back (or in) a small amount, and they will appear.

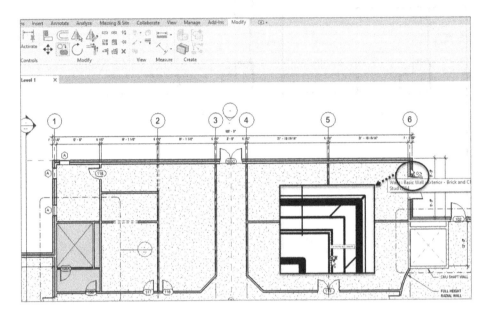

FIGURE 8.7 Adding more grids

Being able to pick lines is certainly an advantage, but you won't always be in a situation where you have geometry in place to do so. In the following procedure, you'll add grid 7 by picking two points:

1. Right-click on grid 6 and select Create Similar (see Figure 8.8).

2. With the grid command running, we want to actually draw this one by clicking two points. Pick the point shown in Figure 8.9.

3. For the second point, move your cursor straight up until you see an alignment line as you come into alignment with the adjacent grid bubbles, and pick the second point (see Figure 8.9). Press Esc twice.

4. Select grid 7 and drag the bottom down to align with the bubble on grid 6 on the south side of the building, and turn the bottom bubble on.

5. Press Esc.

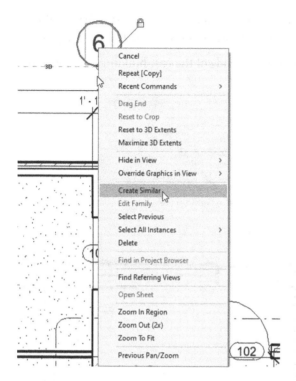

F I G U R E 8 . 8 Right-click on any object for which you'd like to create another instance.

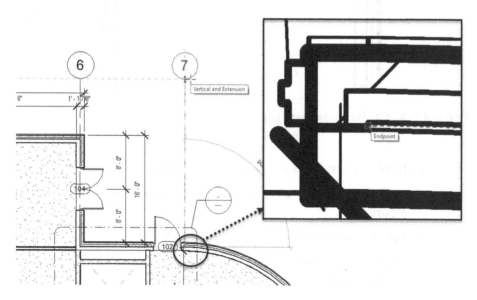

F I G U R E 8 . 9 Draw the new grid by picking two points.

OK, great! Now, let's start adding our horizontal grids. We are going to do this in a fashion that's incredibly similar to how we did the vertical grids.

1. Zoom in to the west side of the east building, as shown in Figure 8.10.

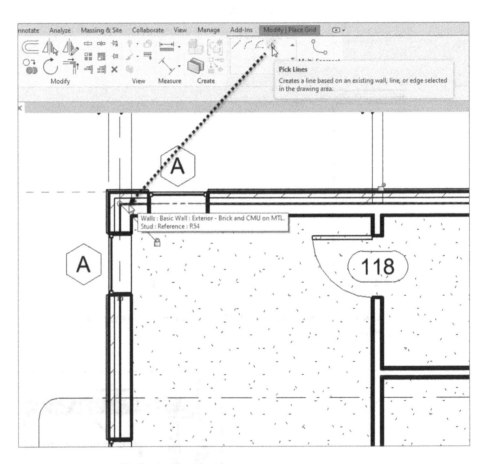

FIGURE 8.10 The first horizontal grid

2. Right-click on grid 1 and select Create Similar.

3. On the Draw panel, select the Pick Lines button, as shown in Figure 8.10.

4. Pick the center of the north horizontal wall.

5. As we have done before, select the grip at the end of the grid line, and drag the line to the left.

6. Click the Show Bubble button to turn on the bubble.

7. Rename the grip to A, as shown in Figure 8.11.

8. Go to the other side of the building and drag the grid to the right to resemble Figure 8.12. Be sure it is stretched out far enough to clear the radial wall because we will be copying this grid down multiple times.

Be careful not to accidentally create another grid on the top of the grid you just placed. If you did, click Undo. Then press Esc a couple of times, hover your mouse over the grid, press Tab once, and select it.

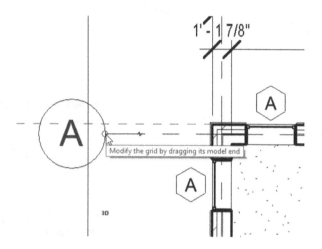

FIGURE 8.11 Edit the grip and rename it to A.

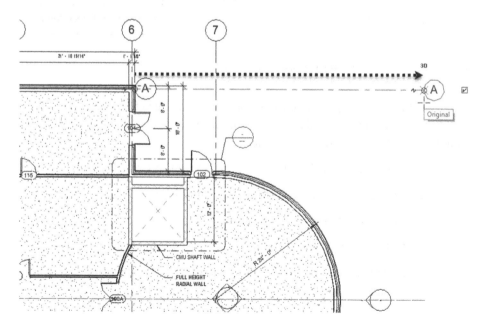

FIGURE 8.12 Completing gridline A

9. OK! Now copy grid A to the center of the walls shown down to grid F. You can do it! See Figure 8.13.

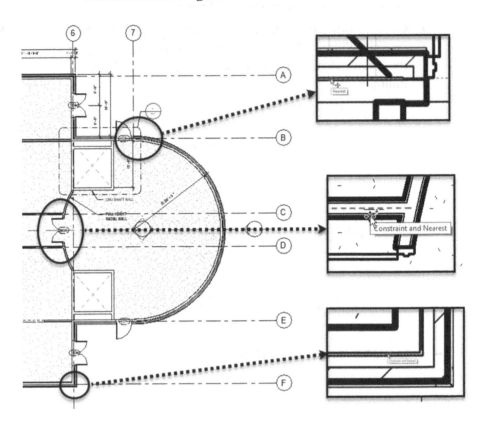

FIGURE 8.13 Completing gridlines A through F

Let's add three more grids and we're done! What we need to do here is add two 45° grid lines as well as a radial grid 6″ (152 mm) inside the face of the radial wall. Let's start with the radial grid line.

1. Find any grid, select it, right-click, and select Create Similar.

2. On the Draw panel, select the Pick Lines button.

3. In the Offset dialog, type 6″ (152 mm).

4. Pick the inside face of the radial wall, as shown in Figure 8.14.

5. Press Esc a couple times, select grid G, and drag the grips as shown in Figure 8.15. Turn on the bubble on both sides.

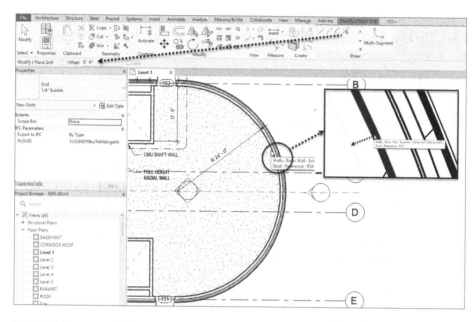

FIGURE 8.14   Adding a radial grid G

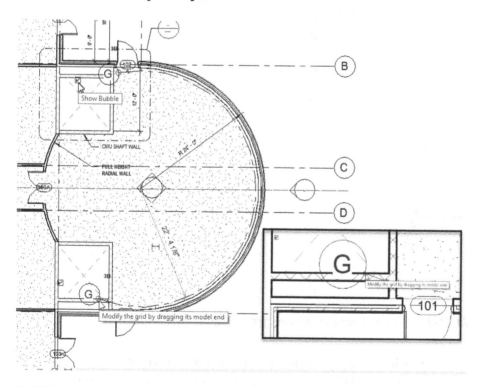

FIGURE 8.15   Completing radial grid G

You need to add two more grids at 45° angles. This will be as easy as drawing lines. The objective here is to manipulate the grids to read the appropriate numbering:

1. On the Architecture tab, click the Grid button if it's not selected already.

2. Pick the center of the radial wall.

 TIP If you can't find the center of the radial wall, simply type **SC** (snap center) and then hover your mouse over the radial wall. When the center snap appears, pick that point.

3. Draw the line at a 45° angle until you're beyond the radial wall, as shown in Figure 8.16 and Figure 8.17.

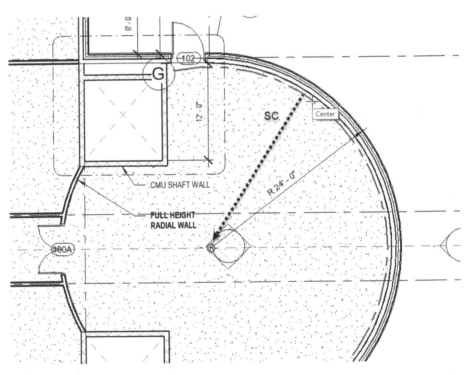

FIGURE 8.16 Hover over grid G and type SC (Snap Center) to find the center.

4. Click in the bubble for the angled grid, and rename the grid line B.1. You can do this while placing grids. Click outside the grid number field to enter the change.

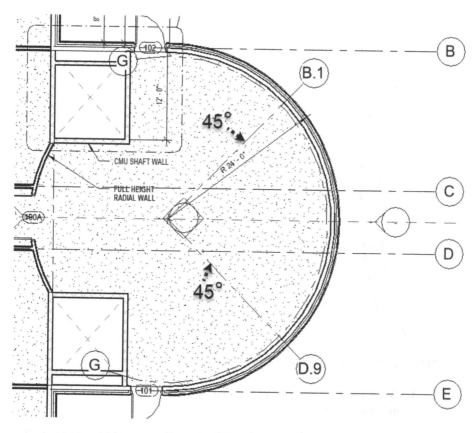

FIGURE 8.17 Grids B.1 and D.9 at 45° angles

5. Draw another grid line at a 45° angle in the opposite direction.

6. Rename it to read **D.9** (see Figure 8.17).

NOTE In many instances, you'll encounter elevation markers and other annotation items that get in the way. You can move these items, but be careful. After you move an item, open the referring view to make sure you didn't disturb anything.

Adding Elbows

As with levels, you can add a break in the line of the grid, allowing you to make adjustments as if the grid were an arm with an elbow. Follow along:

1. Select grid C.

2. Several blue grips appear. Pick the one that appears as a break line, as shown in Figure 8.18.

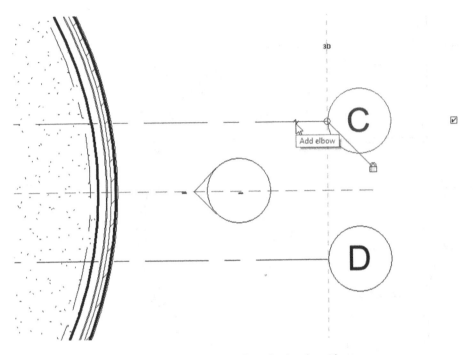

FIGURE 8.18 Clicking the Add Elbow grip after selecting the grid

3. Picking this break line adds an elbow to your grid line, as shown in Figure 8.19.

4. Adjust both C and D to look a little cleaner, as shown in Figure 8.20.

 N O T E Notice that the bubble was broken, and it was moved up and out of the way. This won't always happen. In most cases, the grid will move in the wrong direction. You can then select the blue grips and move the bubble in the direction you intended.

Adding Structural Columns

The hard part is over. Determining where to put the columns is more difficult than physically placing them in the model. But of course there are rules to follow, as well as rules you need to bend in order to accomplish the results you want to see.

This next series of procedures includes adding structural components to the model and placing framing systems in areas where you as the architect would like to see exposed framing.

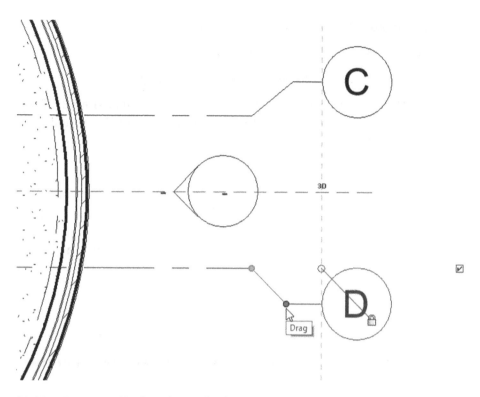

FIGURE 8.19 The cleaned-up grid bubbles

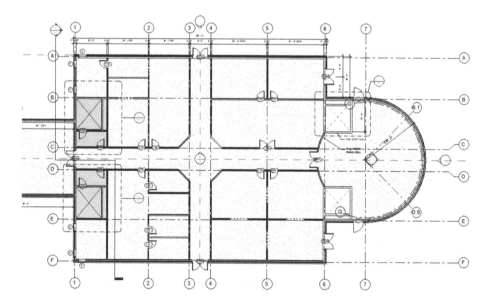

FIGURE 8.20 The finished grids

To add columns to the model, follow this procedure:

1. In the Project Browser, go to the Level 1 floor plan.

2. Zoom into the radial entry area in the east wing.

3. On the Structure tab, choose Column, as shown in Figure 8.21. This tool is also on the Architecture tab under Column ≻ Structural Column.

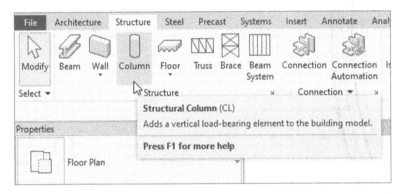

FIGURE 8.21 Column ≻ Structural Column on the Structure tab of the Ribbon

4. Click the Load Family button, as shown in Figure 8.22.

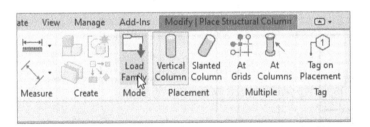

FIGURE 8.22 You can click the Load Family button to add additional columns to your project.

5. Browse to English Imperial ≻ US ≻ Structural Columns ≻ Steel (or Metric ≻ Structural ≻ Columns ≻ Steel).

6. In the Steel folder, browse to HSS-Hollow Structural Section-Column.rfa (or M_HSS-Hollow Structural Column.rfa).

7. Double-click HSS-Hollow Structural Section-Column.rfa (or M_HSS-Hollow Structural Column.rfa). A dialog opens, enabling you to select the type, as shown in Figure 8.23.

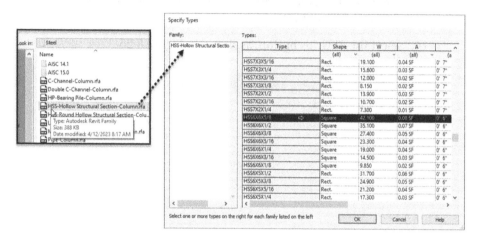

FIGURE 8.23 Select **HSS-Hollow Structural Section-Column.rfa**, and choose the HSS6×6×5/8 (HSS152.4×152.4×12.7) type.

8. Select the HSS6×6×5/8 (HSS152.4×152.4×12.7) column.

9. Click OK.

10. On the Options bar, make sure Height is set to Roof, as shown in Figure 8.24.

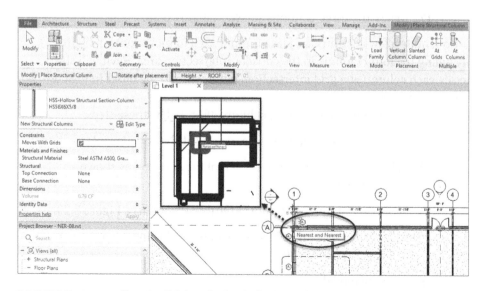

FIGURE 8.24 Changing Height to Roof and selecting grid intersection A-1

11. Place the column at grid intersection A-1.

12. Press Esc twice.

13. Choose Column on the Structural tab. Once you do, make sure Height is still set to Roof.

14. Select the At Grids button, as shown in Figure 8.25.

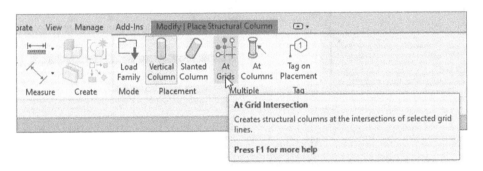

FIGURE 8.25 Select At Grids.

15. Create a pick box (by picking and dragging your cursor) by picking a point at point 1 for the first point and a point at point 2 for the second point (see Figure 8.26).

16. Click the green Finish Edit Mode button, as shown in Figure 8.27.

17. Delete the three columns shown in Figure 8.28.

Now, quite a few columns are placed. You'll need to move some of them, including the four columns in the corridor intersection area. Revit will still locate each column at a grid intersection, but it will add the offset in the column's properties.

To move the columns and create a column offset, follow these steps:

1. Zoom into the middle of the east wing at the corridor intersection.

2. Select the two columns at the left of the corridor, as shown in Figure 8.29.

3. Move the columns 4′–6″ (1372 mm) to the left (see Figure 8.29).

4. Repeat the same procedure (only to the right) for the other two columns (see Figure 8.30).

5. Save the model.

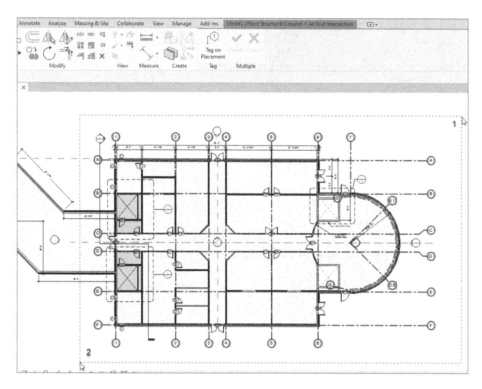

FIGURE 8.26 Picking a box around all of the grids

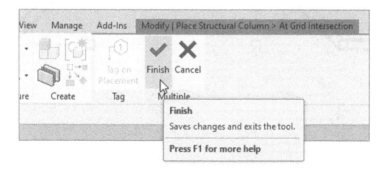

FIGURE 8.27 Click the green Finish Edit Mode button.

That's enough on columns for now. It's time to move on to adding some structural framing. You'll add framing primarily in the canopy areas surrounding the east entry of the east wing.

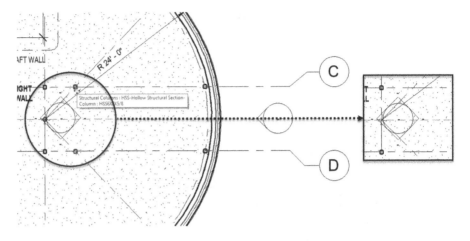

FIGURE 8.28 Cleaning up any errant columns

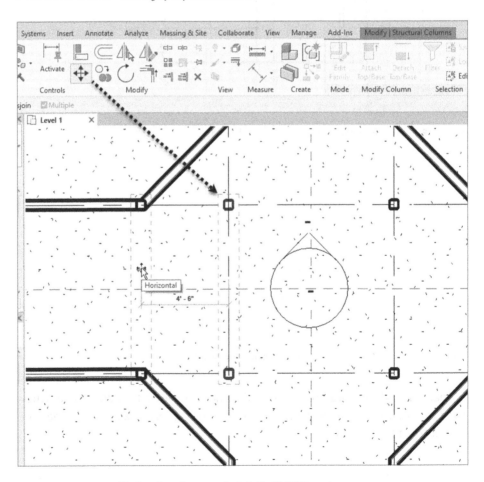

FIGURE 8.29 Moving the columns to the left 4′–6″ (1200 mm)

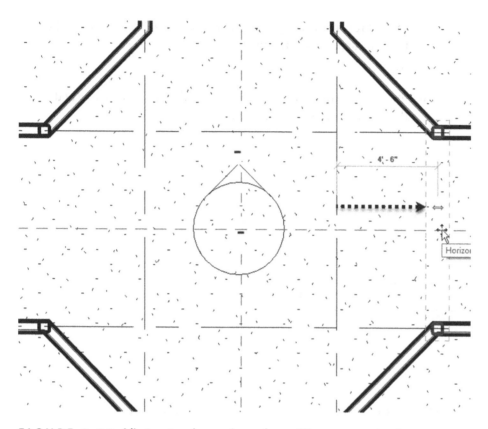

FIGURE 8.30 Adjustments such as moving a column will be necessary quite often.

Using Structural Framing

Although you won't create much structural framing in Revit Architecture, you'll need to add framing in a few areas. Canopies with light structural framing are certainly one area that could call for the architect to wander over to the structural side of the fence.

To begin adding structural framing, follow along:

1. In the Project Browser, go to the Level 2 floor plan.

2. Zoom into the radial entry area.

3. Select columns A-7 and F-7 (these are the columns outside the building).

4. In the Properties dialog, set Top Level to Level 2. (This makes the columns disappear for a moment.)

5. Press Esc.

6. In the Properties dialog, scroll down to the View Range row and click the Edit button (see Figure 8.31).

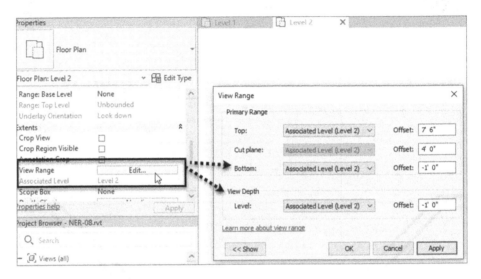

FIGURE 8.31   Setting the view range so you can see below the level

7. In the dialog that opens, in the Primary Range section, set Bottom Offset to –1′–0″(–300 mm).

8. For View Depth, set Level Offset to –1′–0″ (–300 mm), as shown in Figure 8.31.

WARNING   Be careful! Remember that when you make an adjustment to the view range, you're changing the view range for the entire view. Be sure you aren't inadvertently causing items on other floors to appear in the rest of the current view.

9. Click OK. You can now see the column.

Next, you'll place the structural framing. Make sure you're zoomed into the northeast corner of the east wing. Here are the steps:

1. On the Structure panel of the Structure tab, click the Beam button, as shown in Figure 8.32.

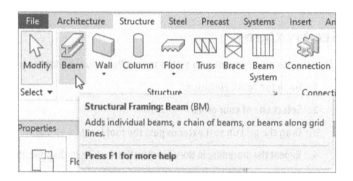

FIGURE 8.32 The Beam button on the Structure panel of the Structure tab

2. Click the Load Family button.

3. Browse to Structural Framing ➤ Steel.

4. Select HSS-Hollow Structural Section.rfa (or M_HSS-Hollow Structural Column.rfa). Click Open.

5. In the Specify Types dialog, select HSS6×6×5/8 (HSS152.4×152.4×12.7), and click OK.

6. Pick the first point at column A-6, which is buried in the corner of the wall.

7. Pick the second point at exterior column A-7, as shown in Figure 8.33.

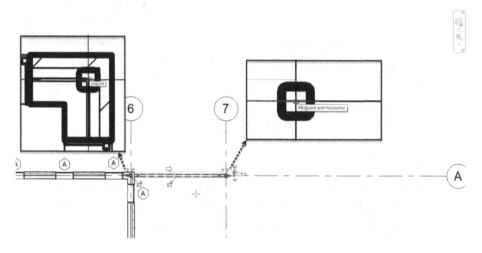

FIGURE 8.33 Adding the beam requires picking two columns.

> ## I CAN'T SEE MY GRIDS!
>
> If your grids aren't showing up on the second floor, do the following:
>
>   1. Go to the south elevation.
>   2. Select one of your grids.
>   3. Drag the grid up so it extends past the roof level.
>   4. Repeat the procedure in the west elevation looking in the opposite direction.

8. With the Beam command still running, pick the exterior column (A-7) and then column B-7, as shown in Figure 8.34.

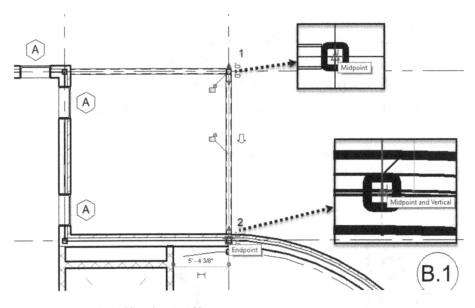

FIGURE 8.34 Adding the second beam

9. Press Esc.

10. Draw a beam 6″ (150 mm) off the finish face of the wall, starting at the top beam and ending on column line B, as shown in Figure 8.35. (This beam will later be supported by the framing within the building.)

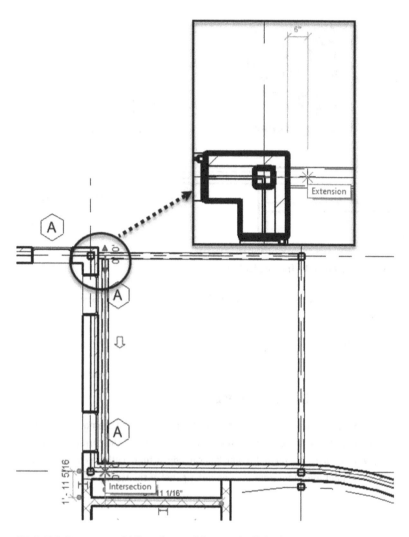

FIGURE 8.35 Adding a beam 6″ (150 mm) off the face of the wall to column line 2

 NOTE Revit may think you're bearing a beam on a nonbearing wall. If you're asked to make this wall bearing, click Make Wall Bearing.

11. In the View Control bar, change Visual Style to Wireframeso the view looks like Figure 8.36. This allows you to see the beam within the wall you're about to draw.

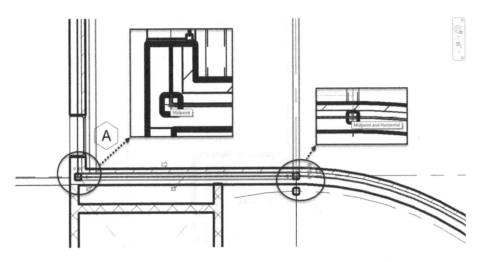

FIGURE 8.36 Completing the framing for the canopy

12. Draw another beam from left to right, inside the wall, as shown in Figure 8.36.

13. Save the model.

Why Is It Cutting Back the Beams?

Well, that's an inherent function of Revit. If you draw your framing to and from beam centerlines, Revit will keep the connection points in the correct locations but will trim back the beam for you. You can adjust these cutbacks by using the Beam/Column Joins tool from the Geometry panel of the Modify tab.

Now let's add some filler beams. In Revit Architecture, you can add a beam system that is controlled by a specified spacing. After the system is in place, you can control the properties for the duration of the project.

Adding a Beam System

Although adding beam systems in Revit is much more crucial for structure, it's useful for architecture as well. Having the ability to space a framing system equally can be quite advantageous.

To create a beam system, follow along with this procedure:

1. On the Structure panel of the Structure tab, click the Beam System button, as shown in Figure 8.37.

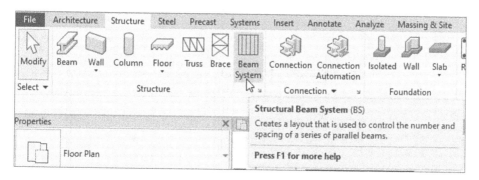

FIGURE 8.37 The Beam System button

2. Make sure the Automatic Beam System button is picked, as shown in Figure 8.38.

FIGURE 8.38 Setting the maximum spacing and the tag style on the Options bar

3. Click the Tag On Placement button (see Figure 8.38).

4. On the Options bar, make sure HSS6×6×5/8 (HSS152.4×152.4×12.7) is the Beam Type selection.

5. Change Layout Rule to Maximum Spacing, as shown in Figure 8.38. Set the distance field to 4'–0" (1200 mm).

6. Change Tag Style to Framing.

N O T E The support you pick first determines the direction in which the beams will run. Notice the double lines in the horizontal beam? They indicate the direction of the beam system. If you want to change this direction, click the Beam Direction button on the Draw panel.

7. Hover your cursor over the top, horizontal beam, as shown in Figure 8.39. Notice the green dashed lines; this is where your beams will be placed.

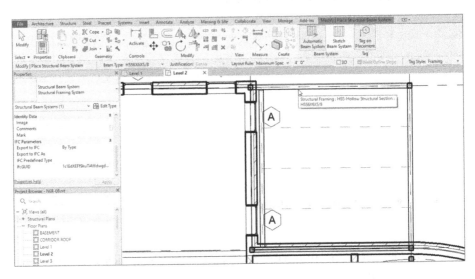

FIGURE 8.39 Getting ready to place the framing system

8. When you see the green lines, pick the top beam, and your framing is placed (see Figure 8.40).

 NOTE That's the ugliest tag in the universe. We will address annotations and drafting standards in Chapter 19.

9. Press Esc a couple times, and pick a box around the framing you just added. Don't worry if you over-selected some stuff.

10. Click the Filter button, as shown in Figure 8.41.

11. Click Check None.

12. Select only the items checked in Figure 8.41.

13. Click OK.

14. Click the Mirror Pick Axis button, as shown in Figure 8.42 (or type MM, which is the keyboard shortcut for Mirror-Pick Axis).

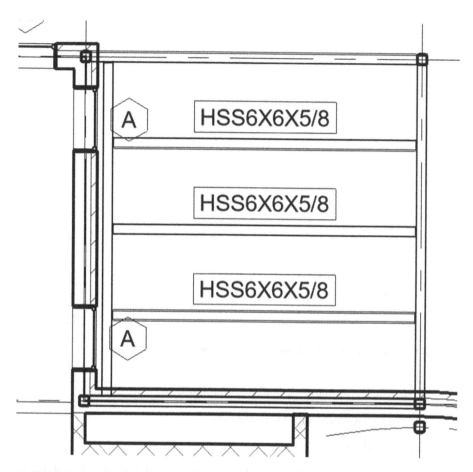

FIGURE 8.40 The framing of the canopy

15. Pick the center reference plane as shown in Figure 8.42, and your
    framing is now mirrored.

By using the Beam System command, you can easily and quickly add multiple
occurrences of framing members. In some cases, however, you need nonuniform
members on a different plane, such as lateral bracing.

Adding Bracing

It would be nice to add a rod to the top of this canopy at an angle. You can
accomplish this by using the Brace command. To do so, you'll need to load the
rod (considered a family in Revit) into the model.

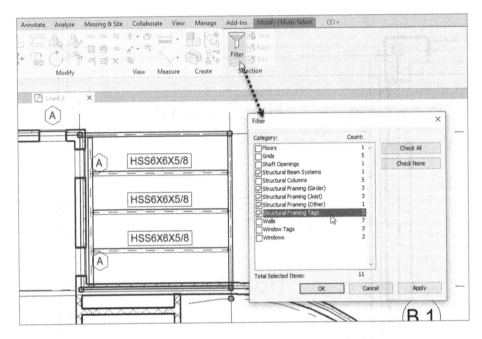

FIGURE 8.41   Selecting the framing you wish to mirror to the south side

To use the Brace command, first add the rod family to your model:

1. Go to the Insert tab on the Ribbon.

2. Click the Load Family button.

3. Browse to Structural Framing ➤ Steel, and open the file Round Bars .rfa (or M_Round Bars.rfa).

4. Select RB 1 1/2 (RB 38).

5. Go to the North elevation in the Project Browser. Notice that grid lines 1–7 are visible in this view—very useful!

6. In the Properties panel for the North elevation, change Detail Level to Fine

7. Zoom in on the east canopy.

8. On the Structure panel of the Structure tab, click the Brace button, as shown in Figure 8.43.

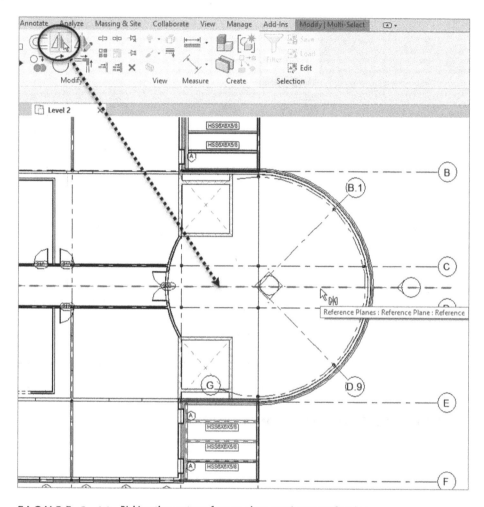

F I G U R E 8 . 4 2 Picking the center reference plane to mirror your framing

9. Revit displays a dialog asking you to specify a work plane. In the Name drop-down list, select Grid : A, as shown in Figure 8.44, and then click OK.

10. Verify that Round Bar: 1–1/2″ (M_Round Bar 38) is the current framing member in the Type Selector.

11. Draw a diagonal bar, as shown in Figure 8.45. (I'll let you eyeball this one, or you can make the top offset a specific increment.)

12. Go to the Level 2 floor plan.

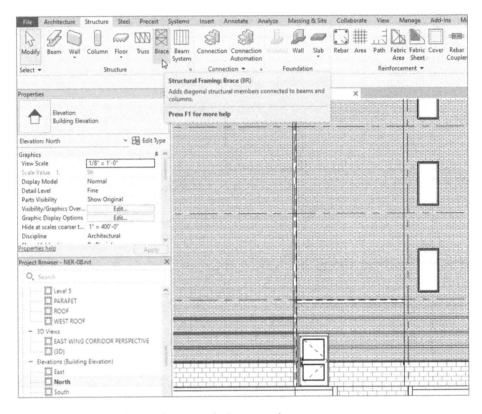

FIGURE 8.43   The Brace button on the Structure tab

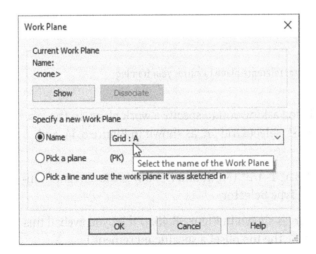

FIGURE 8.44   Selecting Grid : A

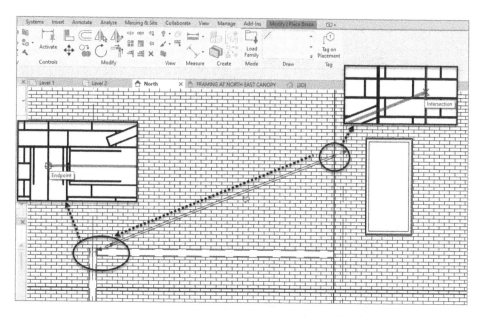

FIGURE 8.45 Adding the rod at an angle

13. On the View tab, click the Elevation drop-down arrow and select Framing Elevation, as shown in Figure 8.46.

14. Hover your mouse over grid line 7. Notice once you come to within range with your cursor, the elevation marker shows up. This indicates that you are about to add an elevation and that elevation will have its work plane set to grid 7.

15. Once you see the elevation marker appear, pick the grid line (see Figure 8.46). Press Esc.

16. Open the elevation by double-clicking on the target in the elevation marker.

17. Rename the elevation **FRAMING AT NORTH EAST CANOPY**.

18. Change Detail Level to Fine and Visual Style to Shaded.

19. On the Structure panel of the Structure tab, click the Brace button.

20. Draw a diagonal rod between the points shown in Figure 8.47, and press Esc.

21. Compare Figure 8.48 to your rods.

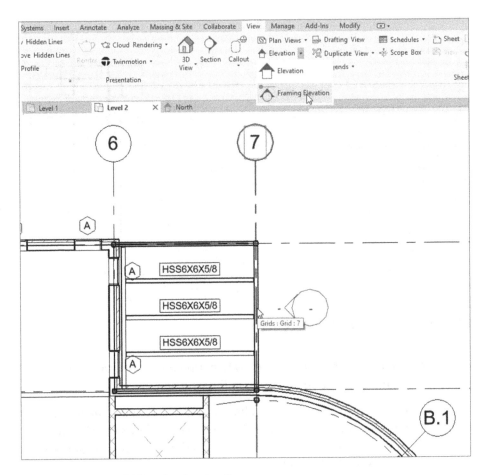

FIGURE 8.46   Adding a framing elevation

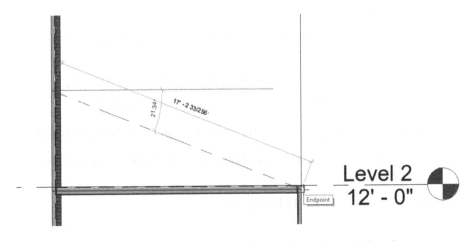

FIGURE 8.47   Finding the points along the column and beam to attach the rod

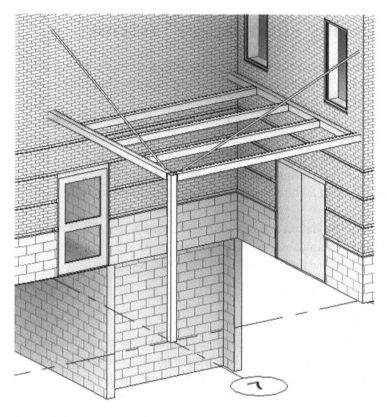

FIGURE 8.48 Isometric of the bracing

22. Mirror the rods to the other canopy. You can open the East elevation to do so.

 N O T E If you receive a warning about a circular reference chain, click Unjoin Elements.

23. Save the model.

That pretty much covers it for framing. The next section will bring you underground into the foundation. Although the structural engineer usually specifies the foundation system, architects must have access to foundation tools to place concrete foundation walls as well as to strip and isolate footings and piers. The next sections addresses these topics.

Understanding Foundation Systems

The first question that arises while addressing structural foundations is, "What if the architect places a foundation in the model and then the structural engineer places one in their model?"

What will happen is the structural engineer will use a method called Copy/ Monitor, whereby the engineer takes the architect's foundation and makes it their own. The engineer is then free to alter the foundation.

This section focuses on creating foundation walls. Although adding this type of wall is similar to adding architectural walls, there are a few things you need to be aware of.

For now, let's add a foundation and deal with coordination later. The task before you is to create a foundation wall constructed of 18″ (450 mm) of solid concrete. To proceed, follow these steps:

1. Go to the Level 1 floor plan.

2. Select one of your grids.

3. On the View Control toolbar, click the button with the sunglasses, as shown in Figure 8.49. This is the Temporary Hide/Isolate function. This allows us to get items out of the way temporarily as we perform tasks that could be hampered by having these elements visible.

4. Select Hide Category (see Figure 8.49).

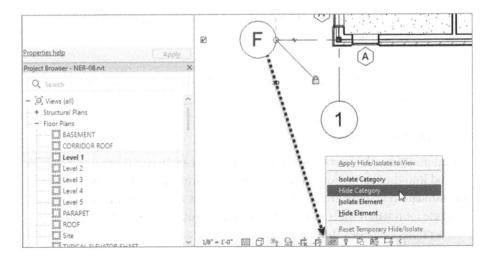

FIGURE 8.49 Using the Temporary Hide/Isolate tool

5. Click the Wall ➤ Wall: Structural button on the Structure tab.

6. In the Type Selector, in the Properties dialog select Foundation - 12″ Concrete (Foundation – 305 mm Concrete), as shown in Figure 8.50.

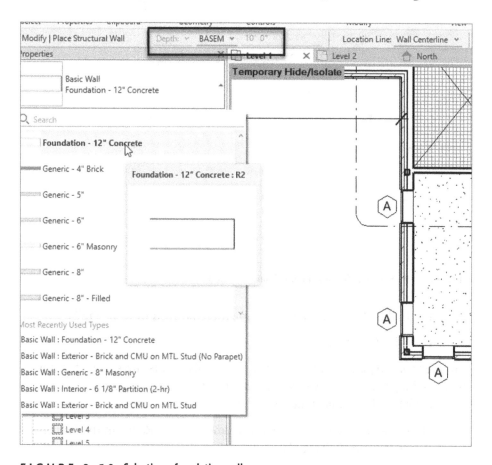

FIGURE 8.50 Selecting a foundation wall

7. Click the Edit Type button.

8. Click the Duplicate button.

9. Name the new wall Foundation - 18″ Concrete (450 mm Concrete), as shown in Figure 8.51.

10. Click the Edit button in the Structure row.

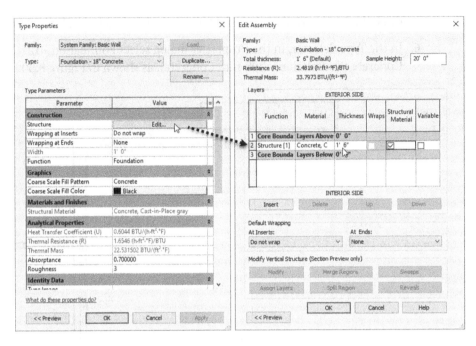

FIGURE 8.51   Building a structural foundation wall

11. In the Structure[1] row, change the Thickness to 1'–6" [457 mm].

12. Click OK twice.

You're about to place a wall under this level. This view is currently set to not show anything below this level, forcing you to alter the view range.

To modify the view range, follow these steps:

1. Press Esc twice, and then scroll down to View Range in the Properties dialog and click the Edit button.

2. For Primary Range, set Bottom Offset to –1'–0" (–300 mm).

3. For View Depth, set Level Offset to -1'–0" (-300 mm).

4. Click OK.

5. Start the Structural Wall command again.

6. On the Draw panel, click the Pick Lines icon.

7. Foundation walls are placed top down, so Depth rather than Height appears on the Options bar. Make sure Depth is set to Basement and Justification is set to Wall Centerline.

8. Pick the centerline of all of the exterior walls, as shown
in Figure 8.52.

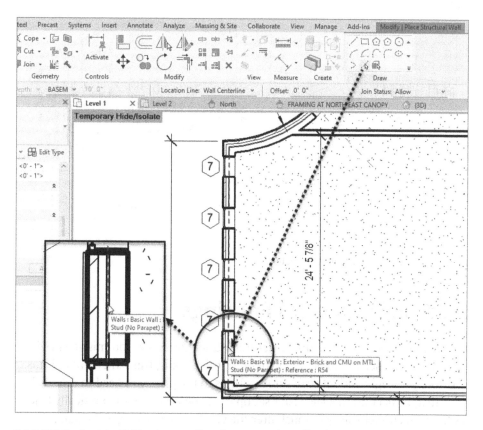

FIGURE 8.52 Picking the centerline of every exterior wall in the model. This includes the
corridor and both wings.

9. Pick every exterior wall in all three sections of the model.

Your 3D model should look like Figure 8.53. Get into the habit of viewing the
model in 3D—especially when you can't see exactly where the walls are being
placed in the plan.

Now that the foundation walls are in place, let's think about what these walls
are bearing on. Revit Architecture has tools to add footings to the bottom of
the walls.

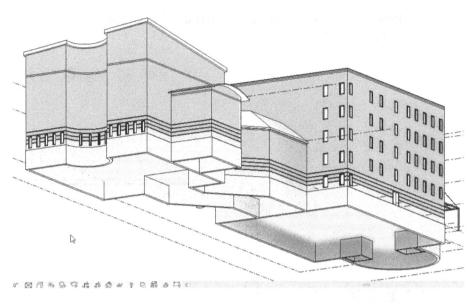

FIGURE 8.53 The foundation walls

Adding Structural Footings

If you're going as far as placing structural foundation walls, you might as well continue and place footings under them, right? Luckily, this isn't a difficult task.

Before you begin adding structural footings to the plan, you need to acknowledge that, by default, this view isn't set up to see objects that are physically below its level. To correct this, you must alter the view range of this specific plan. Follow these steps:

In the View Range dialog, there is a ≪Show button at the bottom of the dialog that allows you to see a graphic representation of how View Range behaves. The figure below has it shown so the icon switched to Hide while expanded.

▶

1. In the Project Browser, go to the BASEMENT plan.

2. In the Properties dialog, go to the View Range row and click Edit.

3. Set Primary Range Bottom to Unlimited.

4. Set View Depth Level to Unlimited, as shown in Figure 8.54.

5. Click OK.

6. On the Foundation panel of the Structure tab, click the Wall button, as shown in Figure 8.55.

At the top of the Properties dialog, it says Bearing Footing - 36″ × 12″ (900 mm × 300 mm). This is a little big for your purposes, so let's make a new footing:

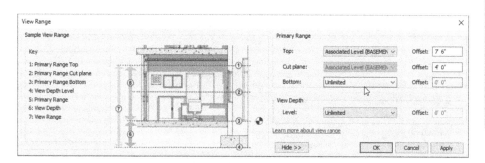

FIGURE 8.54 Again with the view range!

It is misleading that this icon is labeled as wall. This just indicates that a continuous foundation of this type only can reside underneath a wall; therefore, it is called a wall foundation in Revit.

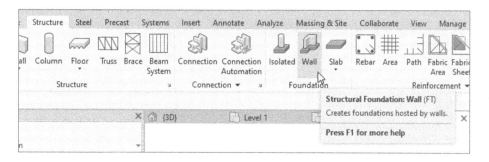

FIGURE 8.55 Adding a wall foundation

1. In the Properties dialog, click the Edit Type button.

2. Click Duplicate.

3. Call the new footing element **Bearing Footing - 30″ × 12″ (Bearing Footing - 750 mm × 300 mm).**

4. Click OK.

5. Change the Width setting to 2′–6″ (750 mm), as shown in Figure 8.56.

6. Click OK again to get back to the model.

7. Start picking walls. This footing will be centered under each wall you pick. Ignore the elevator shaft walls.

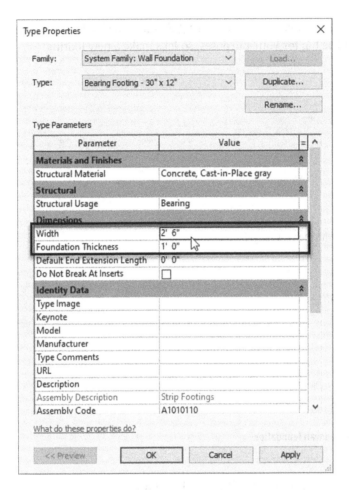

FIGURE 8.56 Changing the width

    8. When you've finished picking the walls, go to a 3D view to make sure all the foundations are covered, as shown in Figure 8.57.

When all the footings are in place, you can see that you need to focus on the elevator shafts. Because an entire foundation mat is required under the elevators, you can use a structural slab.

Structural Slabs

Structural slabs are basically thick floors. The one you're about to use is a solid concrete floor 12″ (300 mm) thick. Of course, Revit doesn't have something this thick built in the library, so you'll take this opportunity to make one. Here are the steps:

    1. Go to the BASEMENT floor plan.

> If you hover your cursor over a wall and press the Tab key, Revit selects all connecting walls, allowing you to add the bearing footing literally in two clicks.

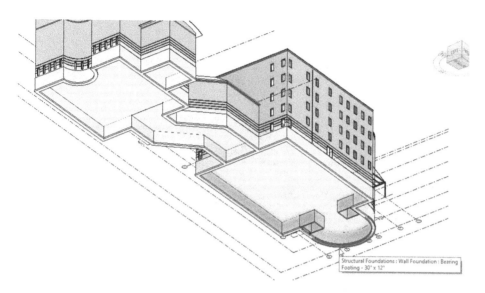

FIGURE 8.57 Doing a 3D investigation to see whether the footings are all in place

2. Zoom into the elevator area.

3. On the Foundation panel of the Structure tab, choose Slab ➤ Structural Foundation: Slab, as shown in Figure 8.58.

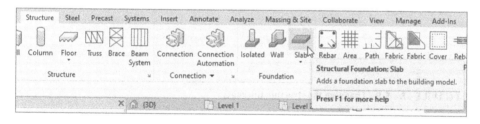

FIGURE 8.58 Choosing Structural Foundation: Slab

4. In the Properties panel, click Edit Type.

5. Click Duplicate.

6. Call the new slab **12″ Elevator Slab (300 mm Elevator Slab)**.

7. Click OK.

8. Click the Edit button in the Structure row.

9. In the Layers field, change Thickness to 1′–0″ (300 mm), as shown in Figure 8.59.

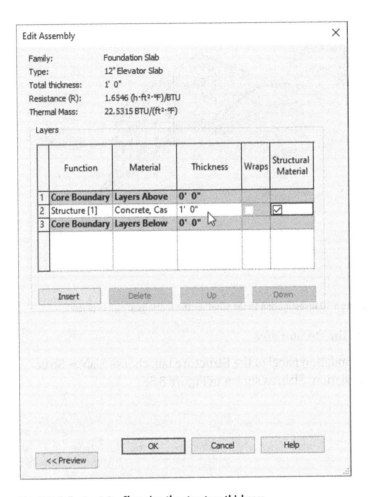

FIGURE 8.59 Changing the structure thickness

10. Click OK twice to get back to the model.

11. On the Draw panel, verify that the Pick Walls button is selected.

12. On the Options bar, set Offset to 6" (152 mm).

13. Pick the three elevator shaft walls, as shown in Figure 8.60.

14. Set Offset back to 0.

15. Select the Pick Lines button. Verify that the offset is 0.

16. Pick the inside of the exterior foundation wall.

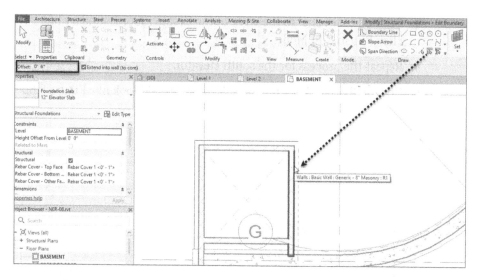

FIGURE 8.60 When picking the elevator shaft walls, be sure to include the 6″ (152 mm) offset.

Now that the perimeter is set, it's time to trim the edges to make sure you have a continuous, closed loop:

1. On the Modify panel, click the Trim/Extend To Corner button.

2. Trim any overlapping corners, as shown in Figure 8.61.

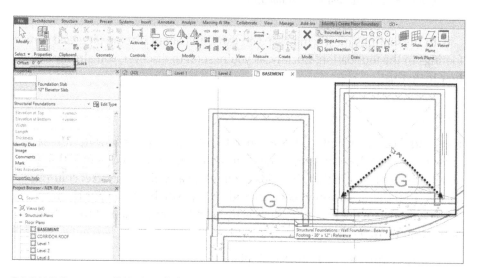

FIGURE 8.61 Trimming all the corners

3. On the Floor panel to the right of the Create Floor Boundary tab, click Finish Edit Mode.

4. Repeat the process for the south elevator.

5. Go to a 3D view. Your finished elevators should look like Figure 8.62

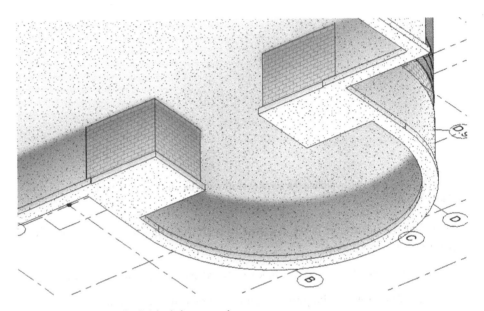

FIGURE 8.62 The finished elevator pads

With the footings mostly in place, you can think about placing piers and spread footings in the foundation. Luckily, as you're soon to discover, you already know how to do this.

Piers and Spread Footings

Piers and pilasters, simply put, are concrete columns. This is how Revit sees these items, and the following is the easiest placement method. A nice thing about this technique is that the grids are in place as well as the steel columns that bear on them. The only real trick is deciding which plan to put them in.

The objective of the next procedure is to add pilasters to support the columns bearing on them. Follow these steps:

1. Return to the BASEMENT plan.

2. On the Structure panel of the Structure tab, click the Column button.

3. On the Modify/Place Structural Column tab, click the Load Family button, as shown at the top of Figure 8.63.

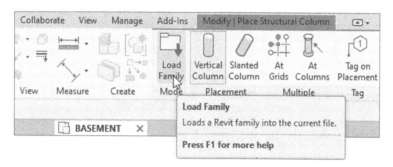

FIGURE 8.63 Starting to place piers

4. Browse to Structural Columns ➤ Concrete.

5. Pick the file called Concrete-Rectangular-Column.rfa (M_Concrete-Rectangular-Column.rfa).

6. Click Open.

7. In the Type Selector, select the 12 × 18 (305 × 457 mm) column. Verify that Height is set to Level 1.

8. Click Edit Type.

9. Click Duplicate.

10. Rename it to 30 × 30 (762 × 762), as shown in Figure 8.64.

11. Change the dimensions b and h to 2′–6″ [762 mm].

12. Click OK.

13. Click at Grids, as shown in Figure 8.65.

14. Pick a box around all of the grids, as shown in Figure 8.66.

15. Click the Finish button (the green check mark).

16. Go to Level 1.

17. Click the Temporary Hide/Isolate button and choose Reset Temporary Hide/Isolate, as shown in Figure 8.67.

18. Move the piers under the columns in the corridor 4′–6″ (1219 mm) that you moved earlier.

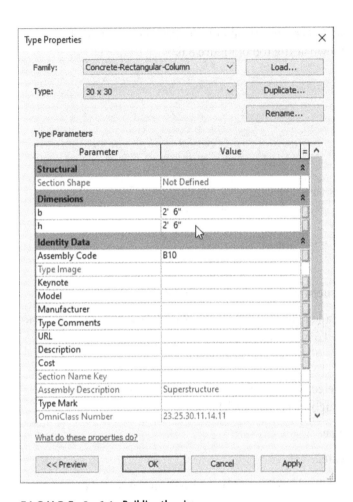

FIGURE 8.64 Building the pier

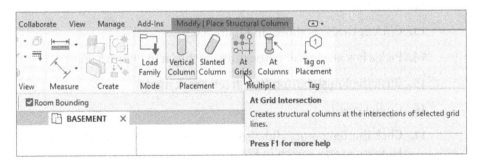

FIGURE 8.65 At Grids—what a time-saver!

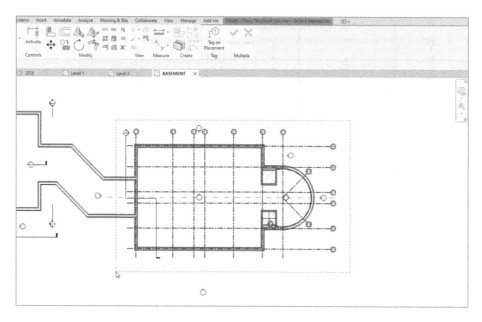

FIGURE 8.66   Selecting the grids to place your columns

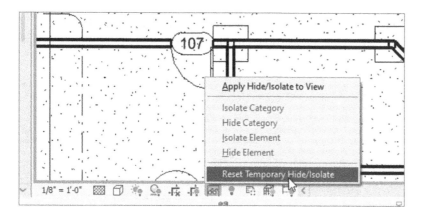

FIGURE 8.67   Choosing Reset Temporary Hide/Isolate

19. Delete the extra piers in the radial entry area where there are no columns. See Figure 8.68.

Now you'll add the spread (Isolated) footings under the piers. This process is almost identical to the previous one:

1. Go back to the BASEMENT floor plan.

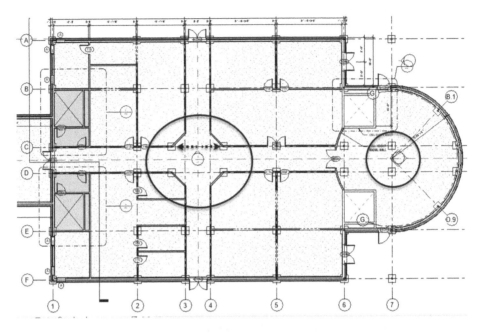

FIGURE 8.68 Making the necessary adjustments

    2. On the Foundation panel of the Structure tab, select the Isolated Foundation button as shown in Figure 8.69

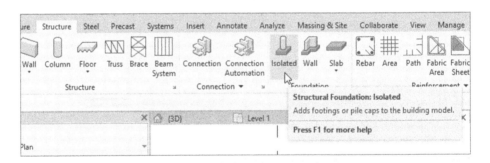

FIGURE 8.69 Adding an isolated footing

    3. No structural foundations are loaded into the project, so click Yes.

    4. Browse to Structural Foundations.

    5. Select the file called `Footing-Rectangular.rfa` (`M_Footing-Rectangular.rfa`).

6. Click Open.

7. In the Properties dialog, click the Edit Type button.

8. Click Duplicate.

9. Call the new footing 42″ × 42″ × 12″ (1067 mm × 1067 mm × 300 mm).

10. Click OK.

11. Change Width to 42″ (900 mm).

12. Change Length to 42″ (900 mm).

13. Change Thickness to 12″ (300 mm).

14. Click OK.

15. Add these footings to each pier. The at Columns option on the Multiple panel works like At Grids and will speed up your work.

Your foundation plan should resemble Figure 8.70.

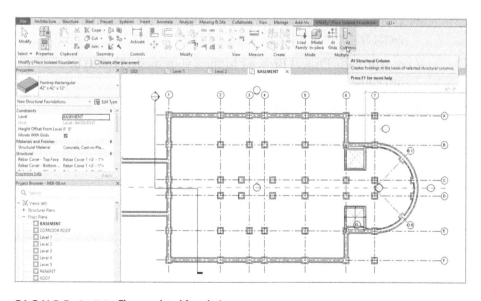

F I G U R E 8 . 7 0 The completed foundation

With the basic foundation design complete, we can either share this with the structural engineer or keep working on it in this model. Either way, you have learned the bulk of how a foundation is designed in Revit.

Are You Experienced?

Now you can. . .

✓ place a structural grid in your model by using the architectural walls as a reference

✓ add additional grids at a radius or by sketch where needed

✓ add columns to the grid lines

✓ add columns at an offset, keeping the relationship to the grid inter-section intact

✓ add structural beams to the model

✓ add structural beam systems, which can follow centering rules or equal-distance spacing

✓ use the Brace command to create brace framing to be used for both architectural appointments and structural bracing

✓ create entire foundation systems complete with foundation walls, piers, and spread footings

✓ organize the Project Browser to show your model broken into disciplines

✓ change a view's discipline to Structural

CHAPTER 9

Ceilings and Interiors

Now that the exterior shell is up and the rooms are basically laid out, it's time to start considering the interiors. As it stands, you have a bunch of rooms with the same wall finish, the same floor finish, and no ceilings to speak of. The restrooms don't have any fixtures, and the other rooms are going to be useless without furniture.

Another issue is that you don't have any separate views such as furniture plans or finish plans. This chapter dives into all these items—and then some!

▶ **Creating ceilings**

▶ **Creating ceiling openings and soffits**

▶ **Adding interior design**

▶ **Adding alternate floor materials**

Creating Ceilings

Placing a ceiling is quite easy; the hard part is finding the view in which to do it. As you've probably noticed, the Project Browser is divided into categories. The categories for plans are Floor Plans and Ceiling Plans. Whereas floor plans show the views standing at that level looking down, ceiling plans show the view standing at that level looking up. In the Autodesk® Revit® Architecture platform, you're looking at a true reflected ceiling plan.

To begin, open the file you've been using to follow along. If you didn't complete Chapter 8, "Structural Items," go to the book's web page at www.wiley.com/go/revit2024ner. From there, you can browse to the Chapter 9 folder and find the file called NER-09.rvt. Then, continue with these steps:

1. Go to the Level 1 ceiling plan, as shown in Figure 9.1 (remember, this is a ceiling plan, not a floor plan).

2. On the Architecture tab, click the Ceiling button, as shown in Figure 9.2.

FIGURE 9.1   The Ceiling Plans category

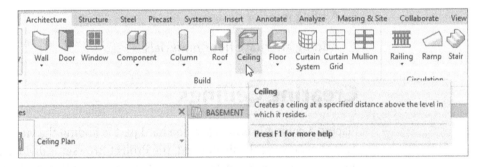

FIGURE 9.2   The Ceiling button on the Architecture tab

3. With the Ceiling command active, choose 2′ × 4′ ACT System (600 mm × 1200 mm Grid) from the Type Selector, as shown in Figure 9.3.

4. Hover your mouse over the room shown in Figure 9.4. Notice that the perimeter is outlined in red. This indicates that the ceiling has found at least four walls you can use as a layout.

5. When you see the red outline, pick a point in the middle of the room. Your ceiling should now look like Figure 9.5.

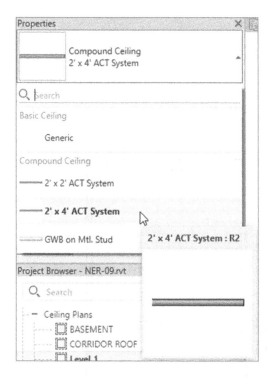

FIGURE 9.3 The available ceiling types listed in the Type Selector

6. Have at it! Add a ceiling to every room in the east wing except the bathrooms, the east radial entry, and, of course, the elevator shafts, as shown in Figure 9.6.

7. With the Ceiling command still running, select Compound Ceiling : GWB On Mtl. Stud from the Type Selector.

8. Pick the bathrooms (not the chases).

9. Press Esc.

N O T E If you notice that some of the grids are running in the wrong direction, don't worry. You'll change that in a moment.

That was just too easy! Too good to be true, right? All right, it was. You always have to make adjustments to this type of item. You probably noticed that you had no control over the direction in which the grids were running. Also, you have no clue as to the height of these ceilings. Let's start modifying the ceilings.

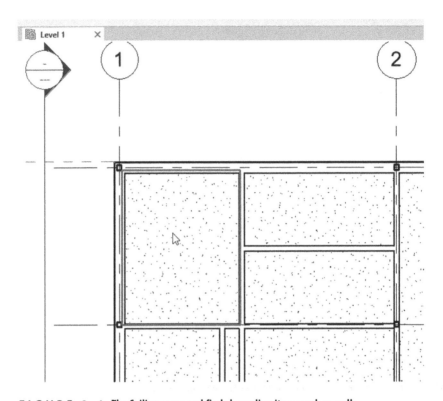

FIGURE 9.4 The Ceiling command finds bounding items such as walls.

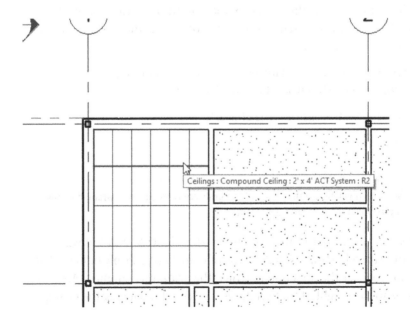

Ceilings : Compound Ceiling : 2' x 4' ACT System : R2

FIGURE 9.5 Placing the 2 × 4 tiled ceiling

TRANSFERRING PROJECT STANDARDS

At times, you won't have the system families you need to carry out the task at hand. Ceiling types seem to be the number-one system family to be inadvertently deleted from a model before being used. If you find that you don't have the ceiling types shown earlier, do the following:

1. Click the Application icon and choose New ➢ Project.

2. In the New Project dialog, click OK to start a new project using the default template.

3. On the View tab, click Switch Windows in the Windows panel, and select Reflected Ceiling Plan from the flyout to get back to the No Experience Required project.

4. On the Manage tab, click Transfer Project Standards in the Settings panel, as shown in the following graphic.

5. In the Select Items to Copy dialog (see the following graphic), click the Check None button.

6. Click Ceiling Types.

7. Click OK.

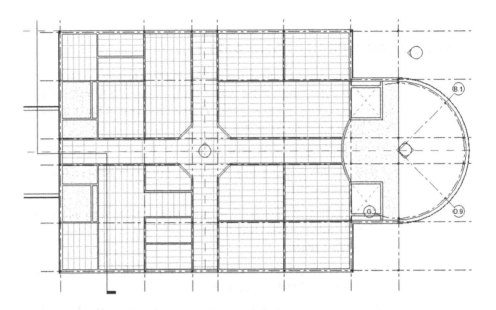

FIGURE 9.6   Adding 2 × 4 ACT ceilings to the specified rooms

Modifying Ceiling Grids

To be honest, a ceiling consists of nothing more than a basic hatch pattern applied to a material. Actually, everything in Revit is a basic hatch pattern applied to a material. That sure does make it easy to understand!

The one unique thing about hatch patterns in Revit is that you can modify them onscreen. That means you can move and rotate a hatch pattern. That also means you can move and rotate a grid pattern. Let's give it a shot:

1. Press Esc or Modify to cancel the command you're in.

2. Pick a ceiling grid line, as shown in Figure 9.7. (Make sure you're zoomed in close enough to make the Rotate command active.)

3. On the Modify | Ceilings tab, click the Rotate button (see Figure 9.7).

4. Rotate the grid 45° by using the two-pick method, as shown in Figure 9.8.

Your ceiling should now look like Figure 9.8.

Now that the ceiling is in, let's look at the ceiling's properties before you go too far. As a matter of fact, it's a good idea to investigate the ceiling's properties before you place it in the model.

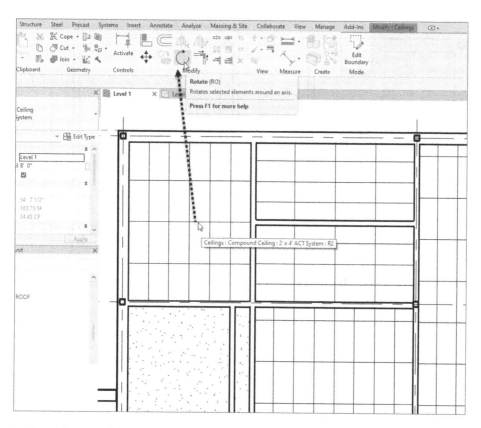

FIGURE 9.7 Select one of the grids, and click the Rotate button.

Setting Ceiling Element Properties

As I mentioned earlier, ceilings are set up in a fashion similar to floors. So it stands to reason that you'll see many similar properties.

Before you get started, let's make some modifications to the west wing. The objective of this procedure is to add a hard ceiling with metal framing, gypsum, and a 3/4″ (18 mm) cherry finish. To do so, however, you need to modify some of the walls:

1. Go to a 3D view of the model.

2. Select the sloped roof that covers the west wing, as shown in Figure 9.9.

3. Right-click.

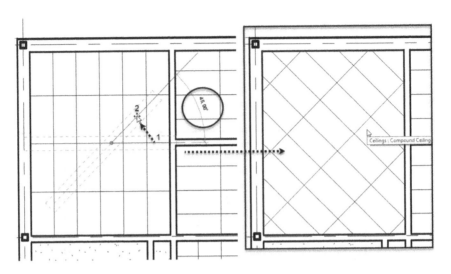

FIGURE 9.8 The rotate process

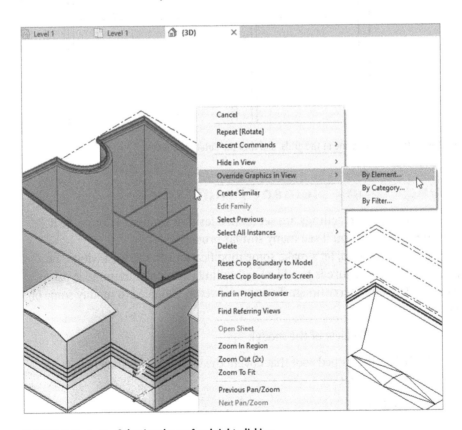

FIGURE 9.9 Selecting the roof and right-clicking

4. Select Override Graphics In View ➤ By Element (see Figure 9.9).

SELECTING ELEMENTS BY FACE

If you are having issues selecting the roof, look down in the lower-right corner of the Revit window. There you will see a row of icons. Look for the one that says Select Elements By Face. Be sure there is no red x in the icon. With Select Elements By Face activated (no red x, as you can see in the following graphic), you can now hover your mouse over the roof anywhere and select it.

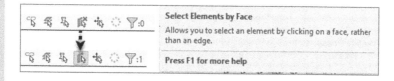

5. In the View Specific Element Graphics dialog, select the small down-pointing arrow in the Surface Transparency row, and slide Transparency to 50 percent. See Figure 9.10.

6. Click OK. The roof is now transparent by 50 percent.

THIS THING IS HAUNTED!

You can set an object to be ghosted—that is, semitransparent—on the fly with the Transparent option. This helps especially with roofs and floors.

You made the roof transparent because some of the walls have to be attached to the roof. It's much easier to attach the walls in a 3D view. But to do so, you need to see the walls on which you'll be working:

1. Select the wall shown in Figure 9.11.

2. On the Modify | Walls tab, click the Attach Top/Base button.

3. Pick the roof.

Your wall should look like Figure 9.11.

Rotating a ceiling grid is a good example of the hatch functionality in Revit. You can rotate and move hatch patterns whether they're ceilings, brick, or any other pattern you need to manipulate.

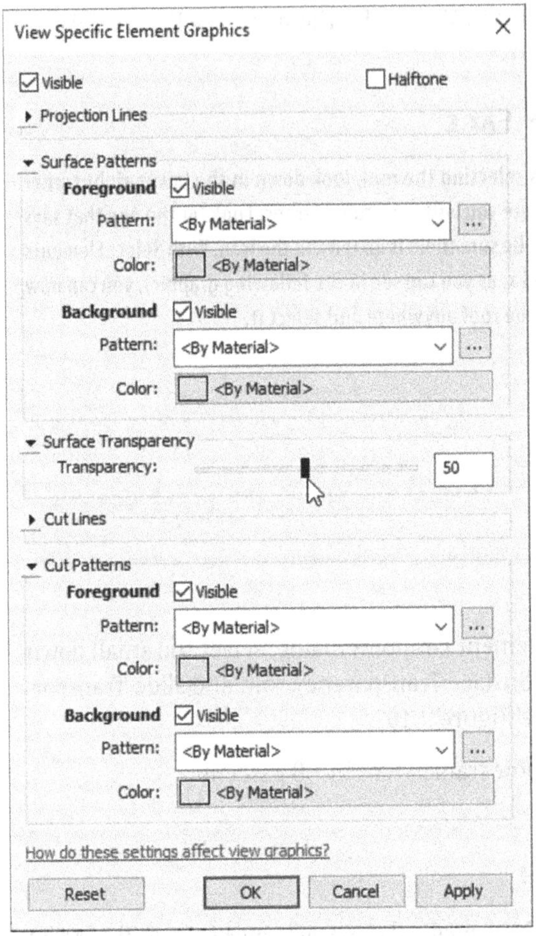

View Specific Element Graphics	×

☑ Visible   ☐ Halftone

▸ Projection Lines

▾ Surface Patterns

Foreground ☑ Visible

    Pattern: `<By Material>` ▾ `...`

    Color: ☐ `<By Material>`

Background ☑ Visible

    Pattern: `<By Material>` ▾ `...`

    Color: ☐ `<By Material>`

▾ Surface Transparency

    Transparency: ▮————— `50`

▸ Cut Lines

▾ Cut Patterns

Foreground ☑ Visible

    Pattern: `<By Material>` ▾ `...`

    Color: ☐ `<By Material>`

Background ☑ Visible

    Pattern: `<By Material>` ▾ `...`

    Color: ☐ `<By Material>`

How do these settings affect view graphics?

Reset	OK	Cancel	Apply

FIGURE 9.10 The View Specific Element Graphics dialog

The next step is to constrain the partition walls in this area to Level 3. The ceilings you'll add to these rooms will be much higher than those in the rest of the building. Follow these steps:

1. While still in a 3D view, select the partitions shown in Figure 9.12.

2. In the Properties dialog box, set the Top constraint to Up To Level: Level 3.

    The walls are now constrained to Level 3.

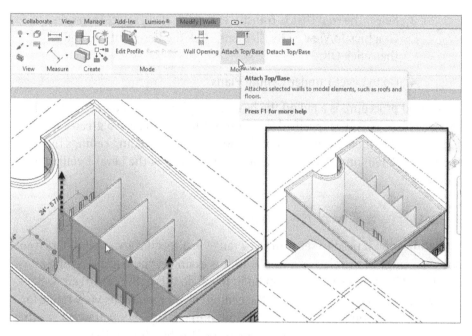

FIGURE 9.11 Attaching the wall to the roof

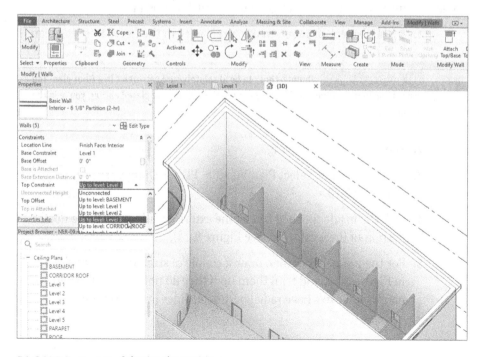

FIGURE 9.12 Selecting the partitions

3. Select the roof that is transparent, right-click, select Override Graphics In View ➤ By Element, click the Reset button, and then click OK.

4. Go to Level 1 under Ceiling Plans.

The next procedure is a tad off the beaten path, but it fits squarely within this process. Because you've specified the walls in this area to be of a greater height than the rest of the walls in the model, you're obviously adding ceilings higher than 8'–0" (2400 mm). This poses a problem in terms of the Level 1 ceiling plan view range.

Creating a Plan Region

Sometimes you'll need to set your view range in a specific area that differs from the view range in the plan as a whole. In this example, you'll add a ceiling at 14'–6" (4350 mm) above the finish floor. If you do this with the current view range settings, Revit won't display the ceiling. If you modify the view range for the entire view, you'll see the 14'–6" (4350 mm) ceilings, but you won't see the regular 8'–0" (2400 mm) ceilings in the rest of the building in that view.

In the following procedure, you'll create a region that has a different view range as compared to the view range in the Level 1 ceiling plan:

1. In the Project Browser, make sure you're in the Level 1 ceiling plan.

 WARNING Double-check to be absolutely sure you aren't in a floor plan. You want to be in the ceiling plan! If you don't see the ceilings you placed earlier, you're in the wrong view.

2. Zoom into the west wing.

3. On the View tab, select Plan Views ➤ Plan Region, as shown in Figure 9.13.

4. Pick the inside finished face of the exterior walls around the north portion of the west wing (see Figure 9.14).

5. For the lower-left corner, draw a couple of straight lines, as shown in Figure 9.14, and trim them up if they do not intersect. (Unfortunately, you can't have radial perimeter lines in a plan region.)

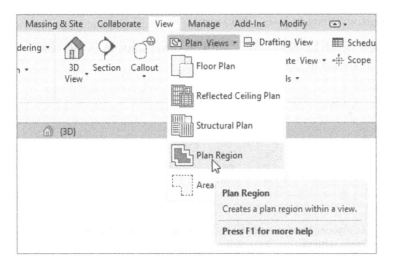

FIGURE 9.13 The Plan Region function on the View tab

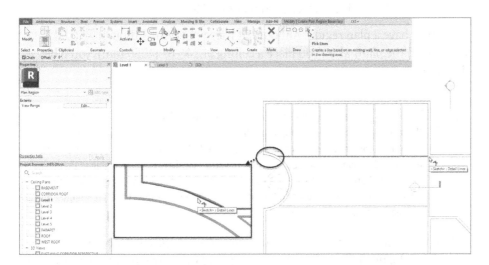

FIGURE 9.14 Defining the limits of the plan region by drawing a rectangle around a specific area

Notice that the View tab has now switched to the Modify | Create Plan Region Boundary tab. You have to define the view range for this region:

1. In the Properties dialog, click the Edit button in the View Range row.

2. In the View Range dialog, set Top to Level 3.

3. Set Cut Plane Offset to 14′–6″ (4350 mm).

4. Set Bottom Offset to **7′–6″** (2250 mm).

5. Set View Depth Level to Level 2 with an Offset value of **16′–0″** (4800 mm), as shown in Figure 9.15.

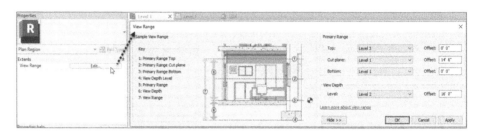

FIGURE 9.15 Configuring the view range for the crop region. Click the Show button to get an illustration of the View Range settings.

6. Click OK.

7. In the Mode panel, click Finish Edit Mode.

You now have a plan region. Although it may not seem as though you did anything in the plan, when you place a ceiling at 14′–6″ (4350 mm), you'll be able to see it.

 NOTE The dotted line you see represents the border of the plan region. Although these borders can get annoying (especially if you collect several plan regions), I recommend that you keep them turned on. It's helpful to know where a plan region is in the model, and it's more important for others to know that there is a plan region in that area. Also, these borders won't plot. In this view it's hard to see because it is overlapping our walls, but if you hover your mouse over the walls you can select the plan region and change the view range.

With the plan region in place, you can now place a ceiling at a higher distance from the finish floor. Because you're going to the trouble of placing a high ceiling, you might as well make the ceiling something special.

Creating a Custom Ceiling

So what do you do if your ceiling isn't an acoustical tile ceiling or a gypsum system? This is Revit! You make a new one.

As mentioned earlier, creating a ceiling is similar to creating a floor or a roof. The Properties dialogs are exactly the same. This procedure guides you through the process of creating a custom ceiling:

1. Be sure that you're in the Level 1 ceiling plan, and zoom in on the northwest room.

2. On the Architecture tab, click the Ceiling button.

3. In the Type Selector, select GWB on Mtl. Stud. To the right and below the picture of the ceiling is the Edit Type button. Click it.

4. Click Duplicate.

5. Name the new ceiling **Wood Veneer on Metal framing**, and then click OK.

6. In the Structure row, click the Edit button, as shown in Figure 9.16.

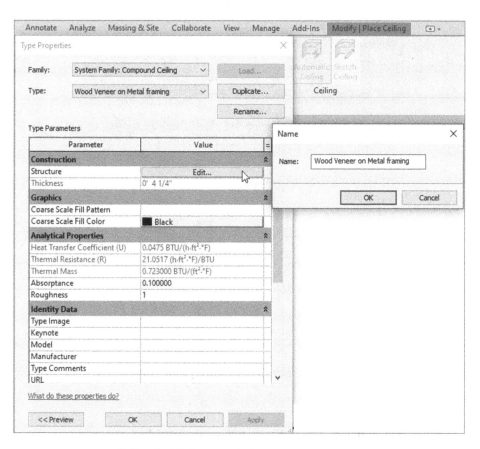

FIGURE 9.16 Clicking the Edit button in the Structure row to gain access to the ceiling's structural composition

7. In the Layers field, as shown in Figure 9.17, click row 4. This is the Finish 2 [5] Gypsum Wall Board row. The entire row should be highlighted in black when you have it selected properly.

8. Just below the Layers field is the Insert button. Click it.

9. Click the Down button to move the new row to the bottom.

10. Change the function from Structure to Finish 2 [5].

11. Click in the Material cell, and click the [. . .] button (see Figure 9.17).

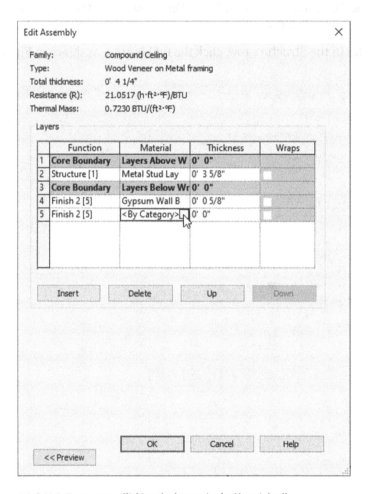

F I G U R E   9 . 1 7   Clicking the button in the Material cell

12. In the top of the Material Browser dialog, type **cherry**, as shown
     in Figure 9.18.

13. At the bottom of the dialog you will see a chevron icon. Click it. That
     will display the Library Panel as shown in Figure 9.18.

Select the darker colored Cherry material and click the Adds Material To Document button.

14. Since there is a material called Cherry there already, click Replace.

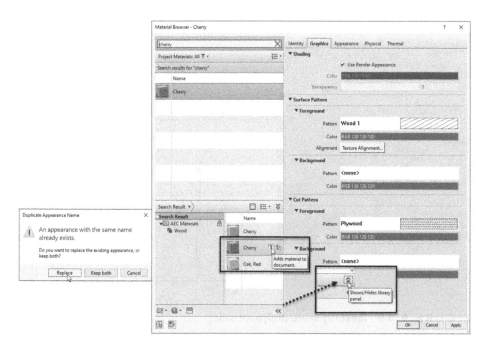

FIGURE 9.18 Selecting and configuring the material for the ceiling

15. In the Material Editor dialog to the right, click the field next to Pattern in the Surface Pattern category. The field contains the word <none>.

16. A new dialog opens. Scroll down until you see the Wood 1 pattern, and select it. Click OK.

17. Below the Surface Pattern category, expand the Cut Pattern category. Change the Pattern field to Plywood. Click OK. (See Figure 9.18.)

18. In the Shading category, click the Use Render Appearance box (see Figure 9.18).

19. In the Material Browser, click OK.

20. Change the Layer 5 thickness to 1/2″ (13 mm).

21. Click OK twice.

22. In the Properties dialog, change Height Offset from Level to 14′–6″ (4350 mm), as shown in Figure 9.19.

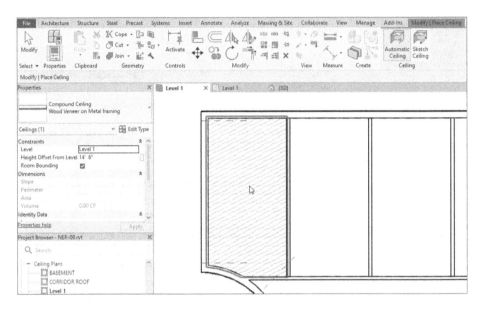

FIGURE 9.19 The cherry-veneered plywood ceiling

23. Place the ceiling in the room shown in Figure 9.19.

 NOTE Don't get discouraged if your final result isn't the same as shown in the figure. You took 21 steps to get to this wonderful cherry ceiling; any one of those steps could have gone wrong. Going back through the steps and retracing your path is something you may be doing quite often until you get used to the program. But remember, you're now set up for plans, sections, and even 3D views and renderings by completing one small task!

For the adjacent rooms, add the same ceiling. You can keep the same height. You can follow along with these steps, but I encourage you to try to put in the ceilings from memory:

1. In the Project Browser, be sure you're in the Level 1 ceiling plan.

2. On the Architecture tab, click the Ceiling button.

3. In the Change Element Type menu on the Element panel, find the ceiling called Compound Ceiling : Wood Veneer On Metal Framing. (It will probably be the current selection.)

4. In the Properties panel, set the height above the floor to **14′–6″** (4350 mm).

5. Pick the rooms shown in Figure 9.20. When you've finished, press Esc a couple of times or click Modify to clear the command.

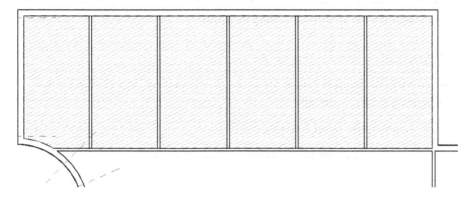

FIGURE 9.20 The north row of rooms will receive cherry ceilings.

Now that you have experience placing ceilings and creating custom ceiling systems, it's time to start adding features. The first items that come to mind are lighting fixtures, but you need to go back even further and figure out how to "cut holes" in the ceilings and add soffits.

ADDING A CEILING IN EMPTY SPACE

Note that you can add a ceiling to a model even if there are no walls defining an enclosed space. To do this, start the Ceiling command in the typical manner by clicking the Ceiling button on the Architecture tab. When the Ceiling command starts, click the Sketch Ceiling button on the Ceiling tab, as shown in the following graphic. This will enable you to simply draft the ceiling boundaries.

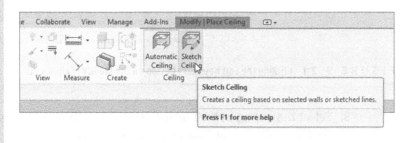

Creating Ceiling Openings and Soffits

Unless you're in a residential dwelling, a prison, or a subway, you can look up and notice that a ceiling is merely serving as a host for electrical, mechanical, and architectural components. Very seldom will you find a ceiling that doesn't require a modification in some capacity. The following sections deal with this issue, starting with creating a ceiling opening.

Creating a Ceiling Opening

The objective of the next procedure is to cut an opening into a ceiling, into which you'll drop a soffit later:

1. Open the Level 1 ceiling plan.

2. Zoom into the wood ceilings in the west wing, as shown in Figure 9.21.

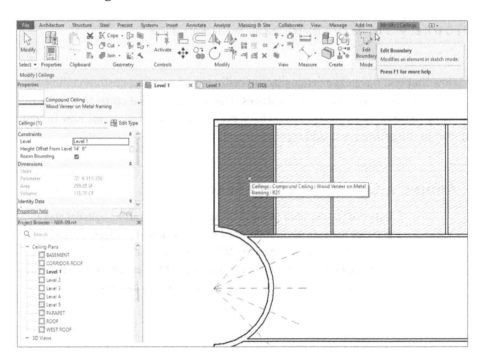

FIGURE 9.21 Clicking the Edit Boundary button on the Modify | Ceilings tab

3. Select the ceiling in the northwest corner of the building, and click the Edit Boundary button, as shown in Figure 9.21.

T I P Ceilings can be difficult to select. If you hover your cursor over the perimeter of the ceiling, you'll see it highlight. If the wall or some other overlapping geometry highlights instead, tap the Tab key on your keyboard to filter through until you find the ceiling. When the ceiling highlights, pick it.

4. On the Draw panel, click the Circle button as shown in Figure 9.22.

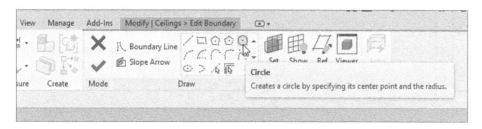

F I G U R E 9 . 2 2 Clicking the Circle button on the Draw panel and snapping mid between two points

5. Right-click into a blank portion of the drawing area.

6. Go to Snap Overrides and then to Snap Mid Between 2 Points.

7. Pick points 1 and 2 as shown in Figure 9.23.

8. Draw a 4′–0″ (1200 mm) radius circle at the intersection of the reference planes (see Figure 9.23).

9. On the Mode panel, click Finish Edit Mode.

10. Verify that your ceiling looks like Figure 9.24.

With the cutout in place, you need to think about closing this feature with a soffit and, perhaps, another ceiling.

Creating a Soffit

Soffits are nothing more than walls with a base offset. This makes sense if you think about it. If your floor level moves, you certainly want the distance from the finish floor to the bottom of the soffit to remain consistent. This one is going to be easy! Here are the steps:

1. On the Architecture tab, click the Wall button.

2. In the Type Selector, select Basic Wall : Interior – 3′ 1/8″ Partition (1-hr) (79 mm), as shown in Figure 9.25.

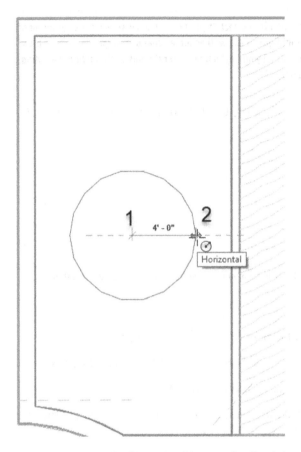

FIGURE 9.23   Sketching a 4'–0" (1200 mm) radius circle

3. In the Properties dialog, set Base Offset to 14'–0" (4200 mm), as shown in Figure 9.26.

4. Set Top Constraint to Up To Level: Level 3 (see Figure 9.26).

You're now ready to place the soffit. You'll add it to the radial hole in the ceiling. If you had nothing to guide you, you would need to draw the wall physically by using the *Arc Sketch* function. In this case, you can simply pick the radial portion of the ceiling opening:

1. With the Wall command still running, click the Pick Lines icon on the Draw panel.

2. Mouse over the radial ceiling opening. A blue alignment line appears. Make sure it's to the inside of the opening, and then press the Tab key twice.

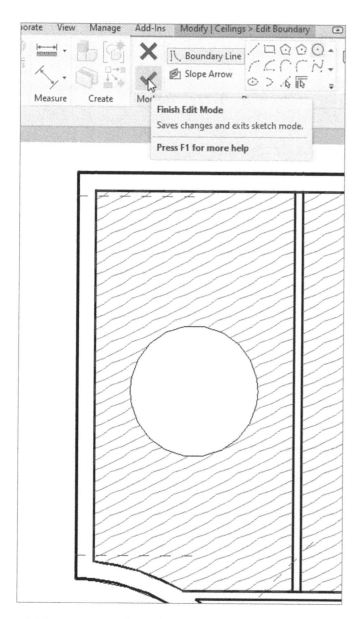

FIGURE 9.24 There's a hole in my ceiling!

3. The entire circle is selected, and the blue alignment line is facing the inside of the hole (see Figure 9.27). When you see this, pick a point to the inside of the hole.

4. Press Esc twice, or click Modify.

Your soffit is complete.

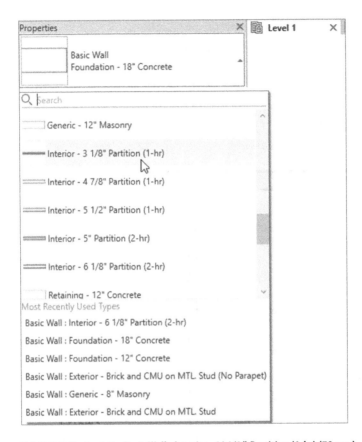

FIGURE 9.25   Basic Wall : Interior - 3' 1/8" Partition (1-hr) (79 mm)

Properties ┃ ×

Basic Wall
Interior - 3 1/8" Partition (1-hr)

New Walls   ∨   Edit Type

Constraints		↕ ↕
Location Line	Finish Face: Interior	
Base Constraint	Level 1	
Base Offset	14' 0"	
Base is Attached	☐	
Base Extension Distance	0' 0"	
Top Constraint	Up to level: Level 3	
Unconnected Height	8' 0"	
Top Offset	-2' 0"	
Top is Attached	☐	

Properties help   Apply

FIGURE 9.26   Setting Top Constraint and Base Offset

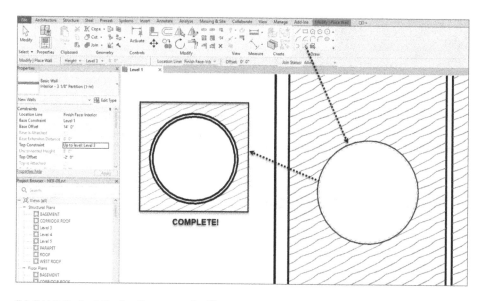

FIGURE 9.27 Creating one cool soffit

Next you'll add a secondary ceiling to the inside of the soffit. This procedure is carried out exactly as it was when you added a ceiling to the entire room:

1. In the Project Browser, go to the Level 1 ceiling plan, and zoom in on the ceiling with the soffit if you aren't there already.

2. On the Architecture tab, click the Ceiling button.

3. Select Compound Ceiling : Wood Veneer On Metal Framing (if it isn't the current selection).

4. Click the Edit Type button.

5. Click Duplicate.

6. Call the new ceiling **Mahogany Veneer on Metal Framing**, and then click OK.

7. Click the Edit button in the Structure row.

8. Click the Preview button at the bottom of the dialog to display a preview of the ceiling.

9. Click in the bottom layer's (5) Material column, and click the [. . .] button to change the material that is now Cherry, as shown in Figure 9.28.

Revit will allow you to add the wall only as a 180° arc. You'll need to pick each side of the circle to accomplish a full 360° soffit.

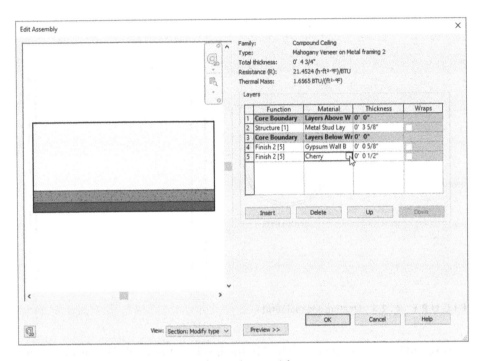

FIGURE 9.28 Click the button to change the material.

10. In the Material Browser, type **mahogany** in the search box, as shown in Figure 9.29.

11. Select the darker mahogany from the Library Panel and add it to the document.

12. At the bottom of the dialog, take the extra step and click the Create New Material button, as shown in Figure 9.29.

13. Right-click and rename Default New Material to **Mahogany**, as shown in Figure 9.30.

14. Change Surface Pattern | Foreground | Pattern to **Wood 2**. (See Figure 9.30.)

15. Change Cut Pattern | Foreground | Pattern to **Plywood**. (See Figure 9.30.)

16. Click OK.

17. Click OK two more times.

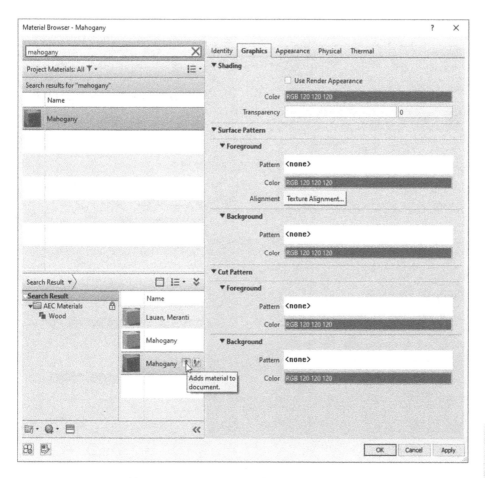

FIGURE 9.29 Adding a new material to the project

18. In the Properties dialog, change Height Offset from Level to 14′–1″ (4225 mm).

19. Place the ceiling inside the soffit. Press Esc, or click Modify.

You need to adjust your plan region. To see the lower ceiling, you have to set it so that the cut plane is either below or equal to 14′–1″ (4225 mm):

1. Pick the dotted rectangle surrounding the rooms. This is the plan region.

2. On the Modify | Plan Region tab, click the View Range button.

3. Change the Offset value for the cut plane to 14′–1″ (4225 mm).

4. Click OK.

You won't be able to see the ceiling at the lower elevation, so stop picking in the middle of the circle! As a matter of fact, if you picked inside the circle more than once, undo back to the point before you started picking in the circle—you probably have several overlapping ceilings.

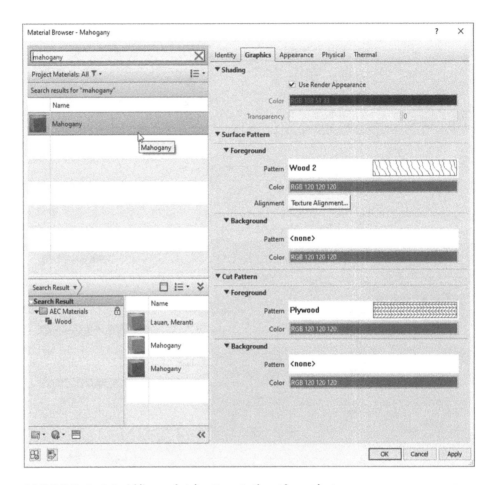

FIGURE 9.30 Adding our hatch patterns to the surface and cut

Your ceiling plan should look like Figure 9.31.

NEVER ASSUME ANYTHING!

They say you should never assume anything, and in this case "they" are right! Let's add a section through this entire row of rooms to gain a perspective on what is going on here:

1. On the View tab, click the Section button.

2. Cut a horizontal section through the entire side of the building, as shown in this image:

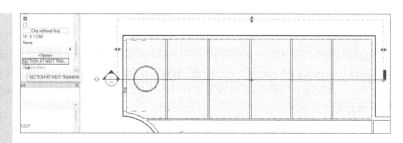

3. Select the section if it isn't still selected.

4. In the Properties dialog, change Detail Level to Fine.

5. Change the name to **SECTION AT WEST TRAINING**. (Yes, these are eventually going to be training rooms.)

6. Open the new section. You now have a clear perspective of what is going on with this area.

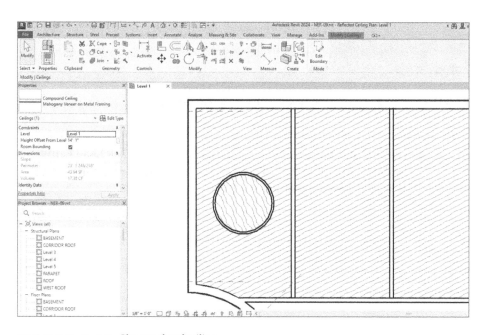

FIGURE 9.31 The completed ceiling

You're getting there with this ceiling, that's for sure! The only task left is to add some light fixtures.

Adding Light Fixtures to Ceilings

Adding lighting fixtures to a Revit Architecture model isn't a difficult task, but you must follow a few guidelines to achieve success in installing lighting. For example, you must work with the Ribbon to find a face in which to insert the component:

1. Go to the Level 1 ceiling plan where you've been adding the wood ceilings.

2. On the Architecture tab, click the Component button, as shown in Figure 9.32.

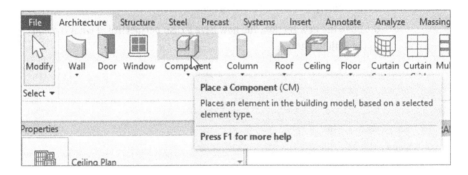

FIGURE 9.32   Click the Component button on the Architecture tab.

3. On the Mode panel of Modify | Place Component, click Load Family as shown in Figure 9.33. Then browse to Lighting ➤ Architectural ➤ Internal ➤ Pendant Light – Disk.

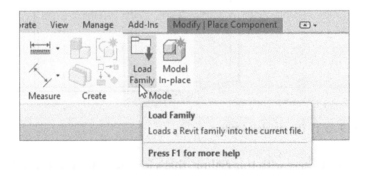

FIGURE 9.33   The Load Family button

4. Open the file Pendant Light - Disk.rfa (M_Pendant Light - Disk.rfa).

5. Place the light approximately in the center of the radial mahogany soffit, as shown in Figure 9.34. (you'll have to move it in a second).

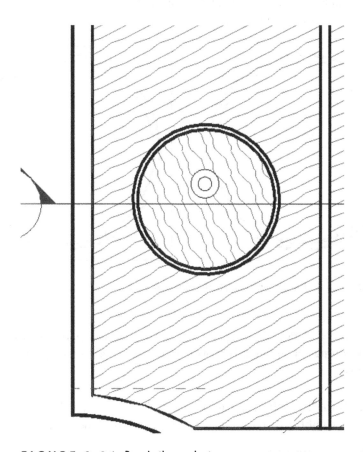

FIGURE 9.34 Drop in the pendant.

6. Press Esc twice.

7. Select the fixture.

8. Click the Move button.

9. Type SC (for Snap Center).

10. Pick a point in the center of the fixture.

11. Uncheck Constrain on the Options toolbar.

12. Type SC again.

13. Hover your cursor over one of the inside radial walls. A center snap appears. Pick the radial wall. Your fixture should snap to the center of the soffit (see Figure 9.35).

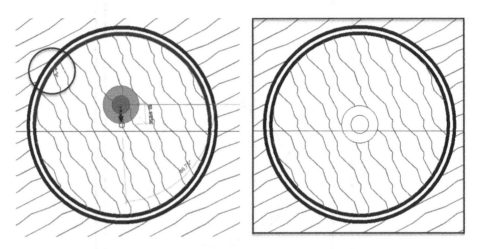

FIGURE 9.35 Moving the fixture to the correct location

N O T E There are no snaps when you're trying to place most components. You'll have to place the fixture and then move it into position. Needless to say, this is an extra step.

14. Open the section called SECTION AT WEST TRAINING. Notice that the light fixture is in the exact location you expect it to be.

15. Select the fixture.

16. Click the Copy button on the Modify Lighting Fixtures tab.

17. On the Options bar, be sure the Multiple button is selected.

18. Copy the fixture 2'–6" (762 mm) to the right and 2'–6" (762 mm) to the left (see Figure 9.36).

The main point of having you open a section to copy the fixture is to illustrate that you're now in a full modeling environment. When you switch back to the plan, you'll see that the fixtures have been placed. In later chapters, you'll learn that the act of simply placing fixtures in the model will also add line items to schedules.

YIKES, THIS ISN'T TO OUR STANDARDS!

Yes, the default line thicknesses are hideous. For now, you can click the Thin Lines icon to scale back the thickness of the lines, as shown here:

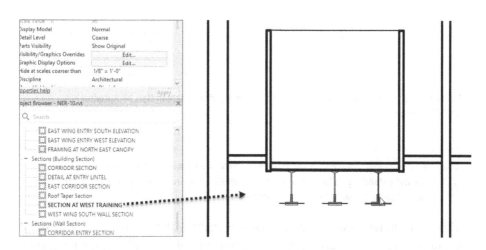

FIGURE 9.36 Copying the fixture in the section

Now let's make some more fixtures:

1. In the Project Browser, go to the Level 1 ceiling plan.

2. Zoom in on the radial soffit. You see the two new fixtures.

3. Select the right and left fixtures.

4. Click the Rotate command on the Modify | Lighting Fixtures tab.

5. On the Options bar, make sure Copy is selected.

6. Rotate the fixtures 90° to create a total of five fixtures, as shown in Figure 9.37.

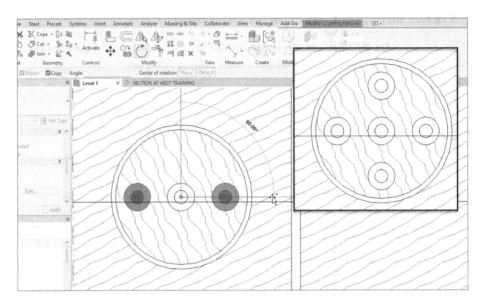

FIGURE 9.37 You're now copying and rotating as if you were in flat, 2D Autodesk® AutoCAD® software.

N O T E Notice that the fixtures overlap the gypsum soffit. This is because you're actually standing on Level 1 looking up. Revit Architecture has finally taken the confusion out of the reflected ceiling-plan mystery.

Now that you have experience dealing with ceilings, let's start working on some interior design. Ceilings are a part of this, but what about wall treatments, trims, and architectural millwork? These items will be covered in the next section.

Adding Interior Design

Congratulations! You've arrived at possibly the most difficult subject when it comes to 3D modeling. Why is that? Well, for starters, this is the area where nothing is easy in terms of shape, configuration, and, for some projects, the sheer amount of millwork and detail. For example, suppose you want a crown molding at the ceiling where it intersects the walls. And suppose you need the same crown at the radial soffit. Of course, the floors and walls aren't the same material, and you need to add furniture as well.

I can go on and on listing the complications you'll face here, so let's just jump in. The first part of the process is adding plumbing fixtures and furniture.

Adding Plumbing Fixtures and Furniture

To begin, you'll have to knock out the less glamorous, but all too important, task of adding bathroom fixtures:

1. In the Project Browser, go to the Level 1 floor plan (floor plan, not ceiling plan).

2. Zoom in on the lavatory area, and turn off the thin lines mode, as shown in Figure 9.38.

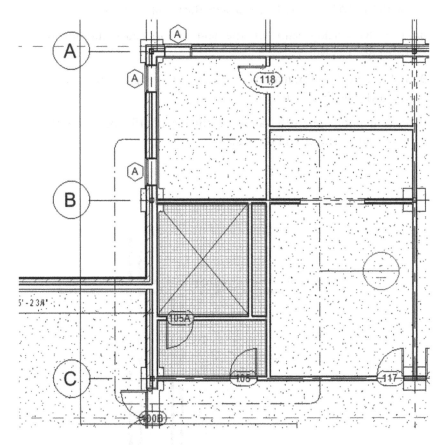

FIGURE 9.38 The lavatory area

3. As you can see, there is a callout of this area. Double-click the callout bubble to open the view called Typical Men's Lavatory.

N O T E Now that you're more experienced with Revit, you can see the benefit of having named this view something understandable at this stage in the game.

4. With the Typical Men's Lavatory view opened, you can start adding fixtures. On the Insert tab, click the Load Family button.

5. In the Imperial Library (or Metric) directory, browse to the Plumbing/Architectural/Fixtures/Water Closets/ folder.

6. Select the file called Toilet-Commercial-Wall-3D.rfa (M_Toilet-Commercial-Wall-3D.rfa), and click Open.

7. Go to the Architecture tab, and click the Component button.

8. If you see a dialog asking whether you want to load a plumbing fixture tag, click No.

9. In the Type Selector, make sure the 15″ Seat Height (380 mm Seat Height) toilet is selected.

10. Place it along the north wall approximately 6″ (150 mm) from the west wall, as shown in Figure 9.39.

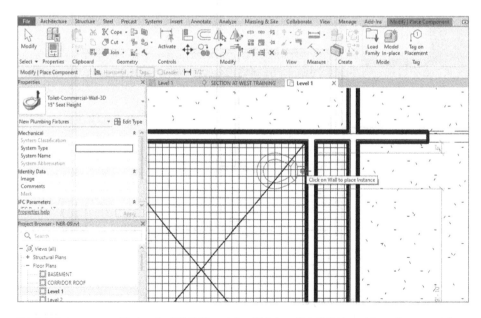

F I G U R E   9 . 3 9 Placing the 15″ (380 mm) Seat Height toilet 6″ (150 mm) from the west wall, along the north wall

Because you're not designing a military barracks from the 1960s, you need some stalls. Unfortunately, Revit doesn't provide any stalls out of the box, but this book you bought does! To add toilet stalls to the model, go to the book's web page at www.wiley.com/go/revit2020ner. From there, you can browse to the Chapter 9 folder and find these files:

▶ Toilet Stall-Accessible-Front-3D.rfa

▶ Toilet Stall-Accessible-Side-3D.rfa

▶ Toilet Stall-Braced-3D.rfa

▶ Grab Bar.rfa

▶ Double Sink - Round.rfa

Download the files to the location where you keep all your Revit families. Then, follow along with the procedure:

1. On the Insert tab, click Load Family.

2. Browse to the location where the new families are kept and select the new files; then click Open. They're loaded into your project.

3. On the Architecture tab, click the Place a Component button.

4. Select Toilet-Stall-Accessible-Front-3D 60″ × 60″ Clear.

5. Pick the corner of the bathroom, as shown in Figure 9.40.

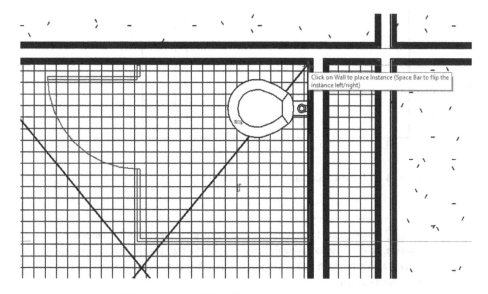

FIGURE 9.40 Placing the accessible stall

The next step is to copy the toilet and add another stall. It would be nice if the family just fit, but this isn't a perfect world!

1. Copy the toilet down (south) 5′–0″ (1524 mm).

2. On the Architecture tab, click the Place A Component button.

3. Select Toilet Stall – Braced – 3D 29″ × 60″ Clear.

4. Place the stall in the model (see Figure 9.41).

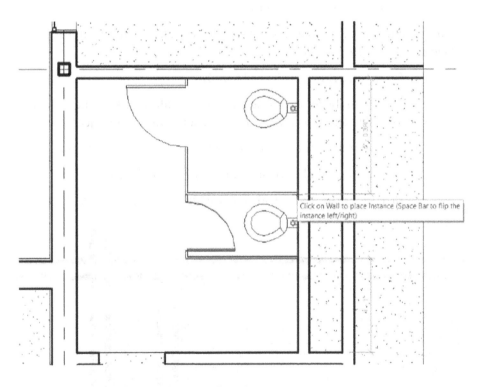

Click on Wall to place Instance (Space Bar to flip the instance left/right)

FIGURE 9.41 The two toilets and stalls in place

With the toilets and the stalls in place, you need to add a grab bar to the accessible stall. Again, Revit doesn't provide this content. You need to either make this component or use the one that you downloaded with the bathroom stalls included with this book.

To add a grab bar, follow these steps:

1. Zoom in on the accessible stall, as shown in Figure 9.42.

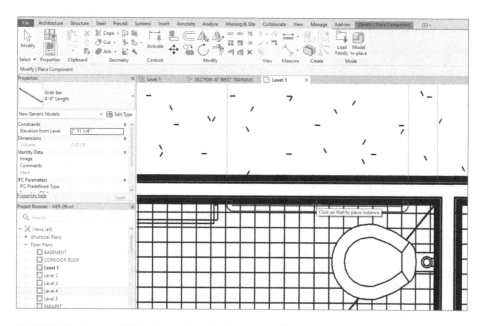

F I G U R E 9 . 4 2 Adding the grab bar family to the wall

2. Click the Place A Component button.

3. Select Grab Bar 4'–0" (1200 mm) Length.

4. Place the grab bar along the wall (see Figure 9.42).

THE SEARCH IS ON!

You may start to notice that your project browser is getting busy. Revit now has a much improved-upon search function. When you click the Type Selector looking for the grab bar, simply type **grab** into the search bar and it jumps to that item, as shown here.

(Continues)

THE SEARCH IS ON! *(Continued)*

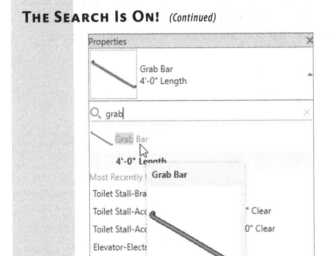

NOTE Remember, although it kind of feels like you're just sticking blocks into your model, these are all 3D parametric parts. This grab bar, for all you know, is 6'–0" above the ground or sitting on the floor. To adjust this, you don't have to cut a section or go to a 3D view. You can simply select the grab bar and, in the Properties dialog, set Elevation to 2'–0".

Because you're in the men's room, you need to add some urinals. You can fit two before you start getting too close to the sink area and the guy standing next to you:

1. On the Insert tab, click the Load Family button.

2. Browse to Plumbing➤ Architectural ➤ Fixtures ➤ Urinals.

3. Select the file called Urinal-Wall-3D.rfa (M_Urinal-Wall-3D.rfa).

4. Click Open.

5. Click the Component button, and place a urinal 2'–6" (762 mm) from the south wall, as shown in Figure 9.43.

What a relief to get those urinals in! The next step is to install a sink with two stations in the bathroom. To do this, you can use the double sink you loaded from the book's website:

1. On the Architecture tab, click the Place A Component button if it isn't still running.

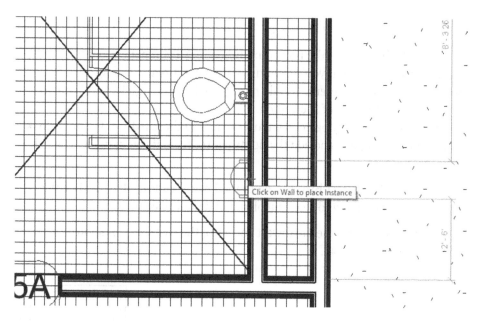

FIGURE 9.43 Adding the urinal to the men's room

2. In the Type Selector, find the family called Sink Vanity - Round 19″ × 19″ (Sink Vanity - Round 483 × 483 mm).

3. Place 12″ from the corner, as shown in Figure 9.44.

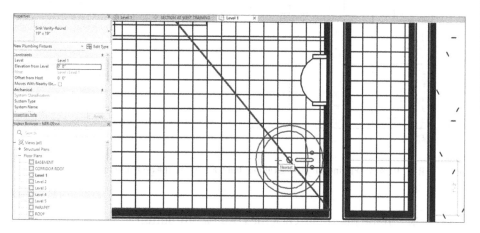

FIGURE 9.44 Placing the sink

Of course, the sink comes in at the wrong rotation. By now you know that you can tap the spacebar three times to orient the sink in the correct direction.

With the first-floor bathrooms done, let's move to some of the actual rooms and offices to furnish them. The first thing you need to do is add lighting to the ceilings.

Adding Parabolic Troffers

As you're starting to see, the procedure for adding a component doesn't change based on the component you're adding. This is great news. Adding a troffer, however, is slightly different. You do need to be in a ceiling plan, and you do need to specify the face of the ceiling.

At this point, you may be good enough at adding these fixtures to simply look at the following figures and add the lights yourself. Or, if you desire a little help, follow these steps:

1. In the Project Browser, go to the Level 1 ceiling plan. (Notice that you're going to a ceiling plan, not a floor plan.)

2. Zoom in on the northwest corner of the east wing, as shown in Figure 9.45.

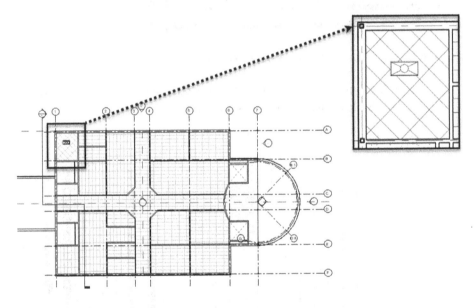

FIGURE 9.45 Placing a light in a ceiling. You'll align it to the grid in a moment.

3. On the Insert tab, click the Load Family button.

4. Browse to Lighting ➤ Architectural ➤ Internal.

5. Select the file called Troffer Light - 2 × 4 Parabolic.rfa (M_Troffer Light Parabolic Rectangular.rfa).

6. Click Open.

7. On the Architecture tab, click the Component button; then place the fixture in your ceiling (see Figure 9.45).

8. Click the Align button on the Modify tab, as shown in Figure 9.46.

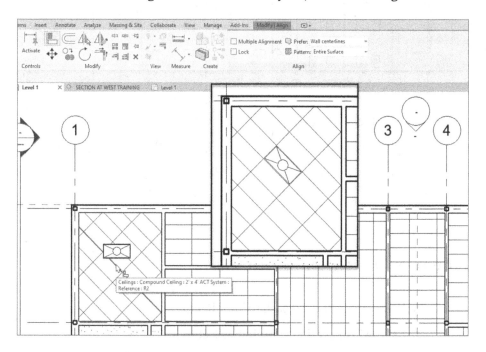

FIGURE 9.46   Aligning the fixture to the grid

9. Align the light fixture to the grid in both directions (see Figure 9.46).

10. Add lights to the rest of the rooms in the east wing, as shown in Figure 9.47. It's quickest to place a single light horizontally and one vertically, align them to the grids, and then make multiple copies.

11. In the Properties dialog, click the View Range button.

12. Set the cut plane to 4'–0" (1200 mm). This way, we can see all of the doors.

Next, you need to illuminate the corridors. This can be done by adding a set of wall-mounted sconces, as follows:

1. Browse to the Level 1 floor plan.

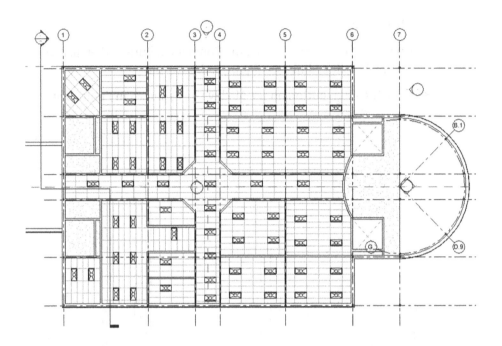

FIGURE 9.47 Adding lights to the rest of the ceilings

2. In the properties, go back to View Range.

3. Set the Primary Range Bottom Offset to 0

4. Set the View Depth Level Offset to 0.

5. Move the door that clashes with the column 6'–0" to the left..

6. Mirror the double door (as well as the tag) along column grid line 5 so you have two double doors going into that room as shown in Figure 9.48.

7. On the Insert tab, click Load Family.

8. Browse to the Lighting/Architectural/Internal folder.

9. Select the file called Sconce Light - Uplight.rfa. (M_Sconce Light - Uplight.rfa).

10. Click the Component button and add the sconce to the corridor wall, as shown in Figure 9.48.

11. Add sconces to the walls of the hallways as appropriate, as shown in Figure 9.49.

Yes, the door numbering got out of sequence. This will always happen. Feel free to organize the door numbers how you feel they should be labeled.

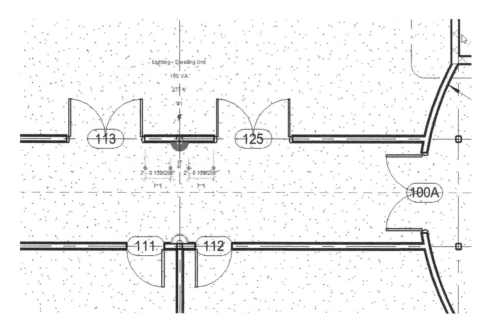

FIGURE 9.48 Adding a sconce

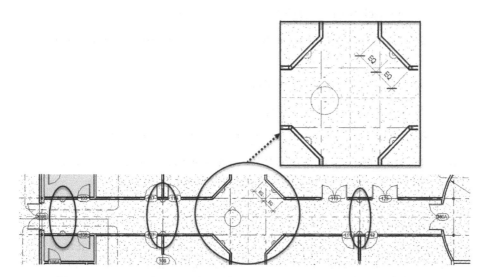

FIGURE 9.49 Copying the sconce to the other hallway walls

12. In the Project Browser, double-click the 3D view called East Wing Corridor Perspective. This gives you a good idea of how the up-lighting influences the corridor (see Figure 9.50).

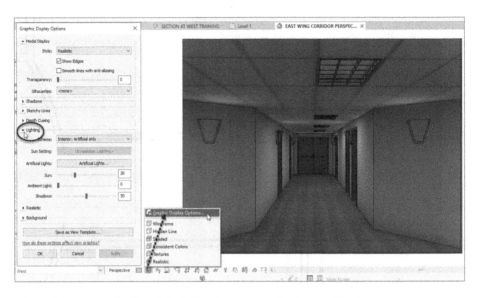

FIGURE 9.50 Looking at the hallway in a semi-rendered perspective view

13. Type VG (for Visibility Graphics).

14. Uncheck Structural Columns. Click Okay.

15. On the View Control toolbar, click the Visual Style button as shown in Figure 9.50.

16. Go to Graphic Display Options.

17. Expand the Lighting category.

18. For the Scheme, chose Interior: Artificial only. Click Okay.

Well, that corridor is looking great! It's time now to begin looking into the offices and also to see whether you can complete a kitchen area.

Adding Casework and Furniture

Adding casework and furniture is the easiest part of this chapter—that is, if you like the casework and furniture that comes right out of the Revit box. Something tells me this isn't going to be adequate. For this chapter, you'll be using the out-of-the box items.

To add some office furniture, follow along:

1. Select the Level 1 floor plan.

2. Zoom into the northeast corner office, as shown in Figure 9.51.

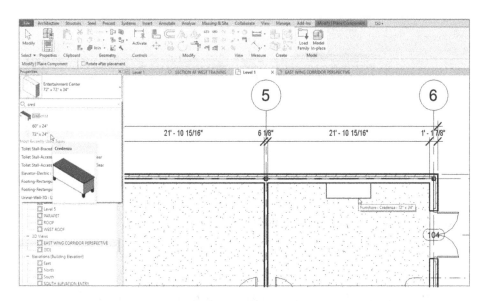

FIGURE 9.51 Zooming in to the northeast corner office

3. On the Insert tab, click the Load Family button.

4. Browse to the Casework/Base Cabinets folder, and select the following item:

   ▶ Base Cabinet-4 Drawers.rfa (M_ Base Cabinet-4 Drawers.rfa)

5. Browse to the Furniture/Seating folder, and open the following:

   ▶ Chair-Executive.rfa (M_Chair-Executive.rfa)

6. Browse to the Furniture/Storage folder, and open the following:

   ▶ Credenza.rfa (M_Credenza.rfa)

   ▶ Entertainment Center.rfa (M_Entertainment Center.rfa)

   ▶ Shelving.rfa (M_Shelving.rfa)

7. Click the Component button on the Architecture tab; then, in the Type Selector, select Credenza 72″ × 24″ (1830 × 610 mm). (Remember, you can use the search function.)

8. Place the credenza desk into the room, as shown near the top of Figure 9.52.

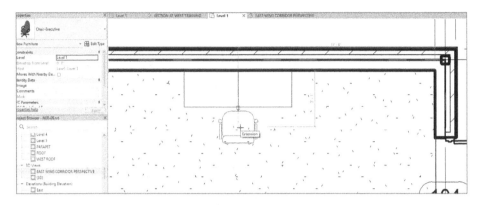

FIGURE 9.52 **Adding furniture to the office**

9. On the Architecture tab, click the Place A Component button if the command isn't still running.

10. From the Type Selector, select Chair-Executive, and place it in front of the credenza, as shown in Figure 9.52.

11. In the Type Selector, select the Entertainment Center 96" × 84" × 30" (2743 × 2134 × 762 mm) and place it in the corner (see Figure 9.53).

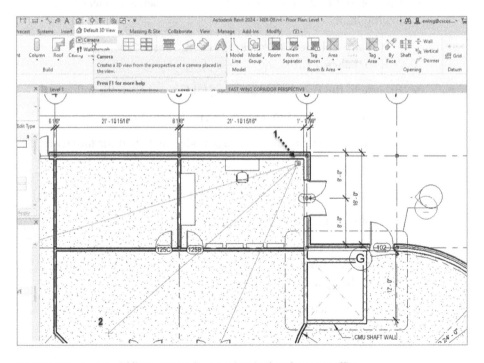

FIGURE 9.53 **Adding a camera (perspective view) to the corner office**

12. Place four 36″ (915 mm) shelving units across the south wall, as shown near the bottom of Figure 9.53.

At this point, it's a good idea to take a perspective shot of this office to see if the space is developing the way you were envisioning. Although you may never put this perspective view onto a construction document, it's still a great idea to see what is going on:

1. On the View tab, select 3D View ➤ Camera.

2. Pick a point in the northeast corner.

3. Pick a second point beyond the southwest corner. The new view opens. You'll probably want to stretch the crop boundaries.

4. In the Project Browser, right-click the new 3D view, and call it PER-SPECTIVE OF CORNER OFFICE.

5. See Figure 9.54 to get an idea of how to stretch the window to show more of the perspective. (Change the Visual style to Realistic, and set the lighting to Interior: Sun and Artificial to make it look like Figure 9.54.)

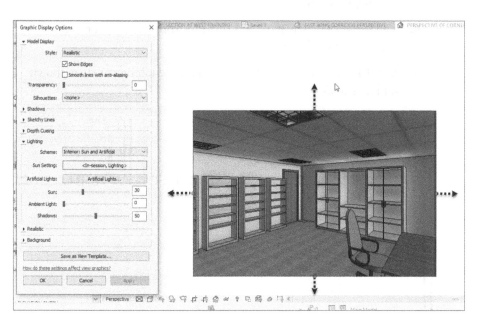

F I G U R E 9 . 5 4   The perspective of the corner office. If your entertainment unit is backward, you'll have to go back to the plan to rotate it.

It's time for a kitchen! This is such a nice office that there seems to be a need for a break area right outside. You wouldn't want your esteemed executive to have to walk very far for a cup of coffee or a snack.

To get started, you'll load some countertops and cabinets:

1. On the Insert tab, click the Load Family button.

2. Browse to the Casework folder.

3. Load the following families. You'll have to choose from the appropriate folders in the Casework directory:

   ▶ Base Cabinet-2 Bin.rfa

   ▶ Base Cabinet-Double Door & 2 Drawer.rfa

   ▶ Base Cabinet-Double Door Sink Unit.rfa

   ▶ Base Cabinet-Filler.rfa

   ▶ Base Cabinet-Single Door & Drawer.rfa

   ▶ Counter Top-L Shaped w Sink Hole 2.rfa

   ▶ Upper Cabinet-Double Door-Wall.rfa

4. Load the file Corner Base Filler.rfa from the Chapter 9 directory on the book's website.

5. Open the Level 1 floor plan. Zoom in on the kitchen area, as shown in Figure 9.55.

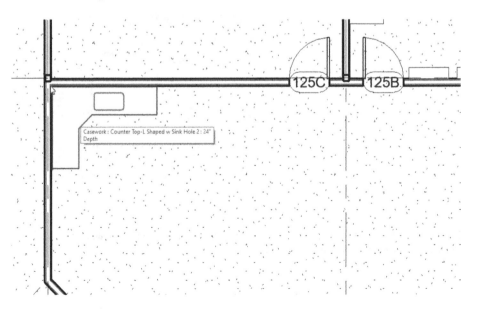

FIGURE 9.55 Adding the countertop

6. Add the countertop (see Figure 9.55).

7. Press Esc twice.

8. Select the countertop.

9. Select the stretch arrows, and stretch the leg of the counter to the end of the wall, as shown in Figure 9.56.

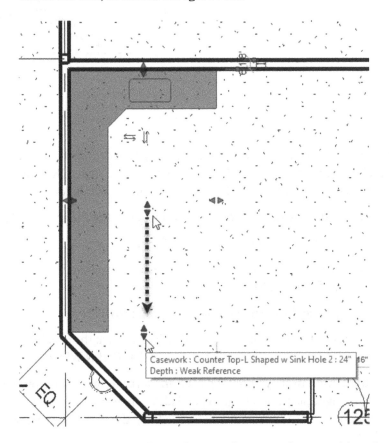

Casework : Counter Top-L Shaped w Sink Hole 2 : 24"   6"
Depth : Weak Reference

FIGURE 9.56 Lengthening the counter leg to meet the corner of the wall

10. Add the Base Cabinet-Double Door Sink Unit 30" (900 mm) under the sink hole in the north leg of the counter.

11. Align the base unit under the sink.

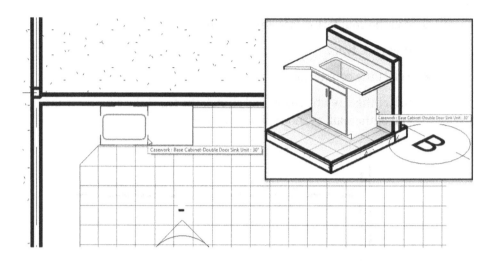

You now have a counter and a sink base. The problem is that you have no idea how high these items are or what they really look like. That's OK—this is Revit. You just need to create two elevations for these items, as follows:

Lots of times it's hard to get the cabinet exactly where you want it. I usually place it and then align it as shown below.

1. On the Create panel on the View tab, click the Elevation button.

2. Add an interior elevation looking north.

3. Select the elevation marker, and turn on the elevation looking west (see Figure 9.57).

4. Rename the north elevation **KITCHEN NORTH**.

5. With the elevation marker still selected, click the check box to the west, and rename the west elevation **KITCHEN WEST**.

With the elevations in, you can flip back and forth to make sure you're putting items in the right places and to get a good idea of how your cabinet run looks.

The remainder of the procedure involves adding the rest of the cabinets. Let's do it!

1. On the Architecture tab, click the Component button.

2. From the Type Selector, select Base Cabinet - Single Door & Drawer 24″ (600 mm).

3. Place the base cabinet to the right of the sink cabinet.

4. Press Esc twice, or click Modify; then open the Kitchen North elevation. Does your elevation look like Figure 9.58?

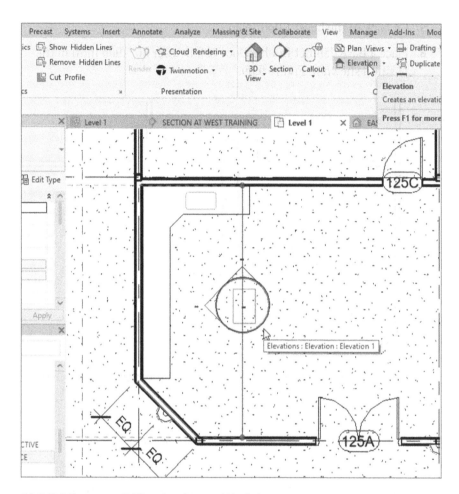

FIGURE 9.57 Adding elevations to aid in design

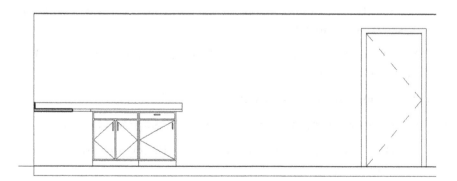

FIGURE 9.58 The elevation of the cabinet run

5. Go back to the Level 1 floor plan.

6. Place a Base Cabinet Double Door & 2 Drawer 36″ (900 mm) in the position shown in Figure 9.59.

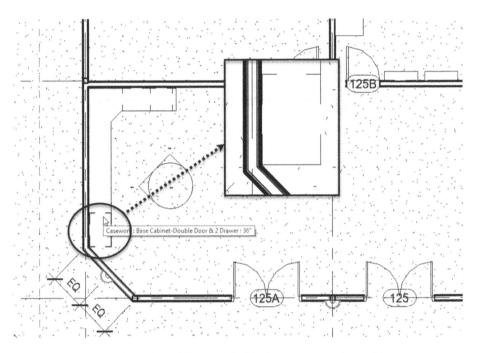

Casewor : Base Cabinet-Double Door & 2 Drawer : 36″

125B

125A

125

FIGURE 9.59　Placing the 36″ (900 mm) double-door, two-drawer base cabinet

7. Press Esc twice, or click Modify; then select the Kitchen West elevation.

8. Move the base cabinet so there is a 1″ (25 mm) counter overhang, as shown in Figure 9.60.

9. Copy the base cabinet to the right three times (four total cabinets), as shown in Figure 9.61.

The bases are done! Let's add some wall cabinets to the kitchen.

1. On the Architecture tab, click the Place A Component button.

2. In the Type Selector, select Upper Cabinet-Double-Door-Wall 36″ (900 mm).

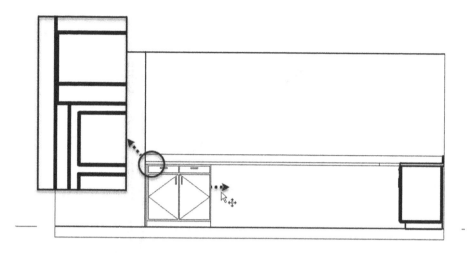

FIGURE 9.60 The 1" (25 mm) overhang on the end

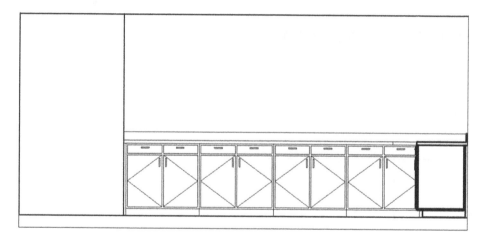

FIGURE 9.61 The base cabinet run

3. Place the wall cabinet in the model, as shown in Figure 9.62. (Don't worry too much about aligning it to the cabinet below. You'll align it in elevation.)

4. Open the Kitchen West elevation.

5. Click the Align button on the Modify tab.

6. Align the wall cabinet to the base cabinet, as shown in Figure 9.63.

7. Copy the wall cabinet to the right three times (for four total cabinets).

8. Save the model.

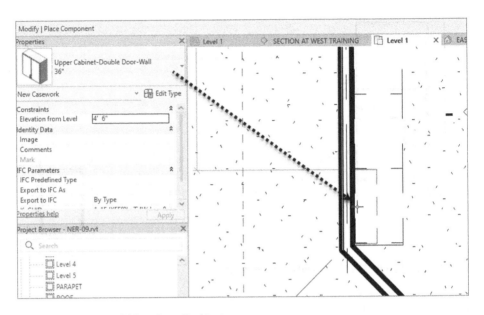

FIGURE 9.62 Adding the wall cabinet

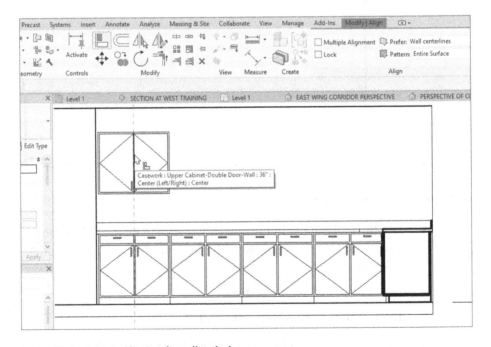

FIGURE 9.63 Aligning the wall to the base

Your cabinets should look like Figure 9.64.

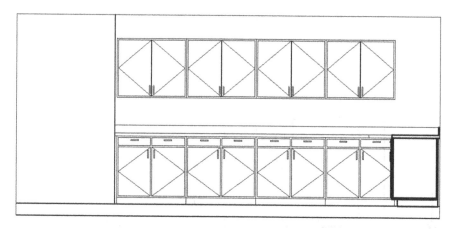

FIGURE 9.64 The finished west wall of the kitchen

Now that the kitchen is in place, it would be nice to add a tile floor only to that area. You can accomplish this without having to add extra floors to the model. You can simply split the face of the floor that is already there and add an additional material.

Adding Additional Floor Materials

Since the kitchen area is a potential wet zone, we want to have another tile flooring system that has a floor leveler built in. Oh hey, we have something very similar!

Cutting and Adding the Floor

You have a floor area targeted for a new material, and the following procedure guides you through the steps:

1. Open the Level 1 floor plan, and select the floor, as shown in Figure 9.65.

2. Select the entire floor. This may require making sure Select Elements By Face is not turned off (see Figure 9.65).

3. Click the Edit Boundary button as shown in Figure 9.66.

4. In the Options bar, make sure the offset is set to 0. With Pick Walls selected, pick the interior walls of our kitchen.

5. With the Draw Line selected, draw a line on the column line.

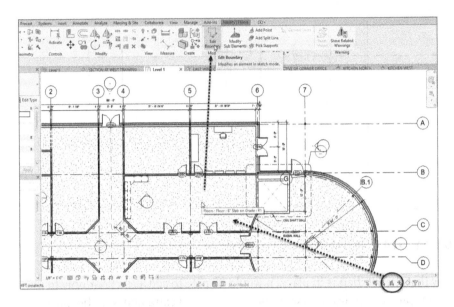

FIGURE 9.65 Selecting the floor for modification

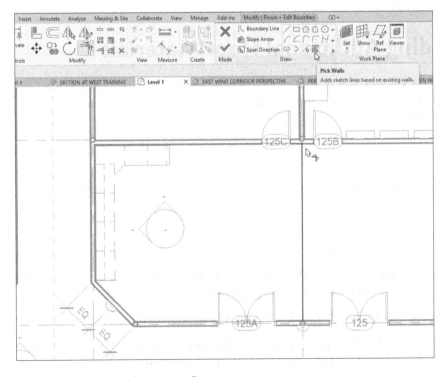

FIGURE 9.66 Hacking up your floor

6. Trim up any overlapping corners.

7. On the Modify | Edit Boundary tab, click Finish Edit Mode.

8. Click Don't Attach for the next dialog.

 N O T E Remember, you can't have any overlapping lines or gaps while adding your magenta sketch lines.

We now have a gaping hole in our floor. The objective now is to fill in that hole with another floor.

Creating a Tile Material

There is one tile material in this model, but it would be beneficial to create a new one with 12″ (300 mm) square tiles. This procedure takes the place of using hatching in a conventional drafting situation.

Follow these steps to create a new material:

1. On the Manage tab, click the Materials button, as shown in Figure 9.67.

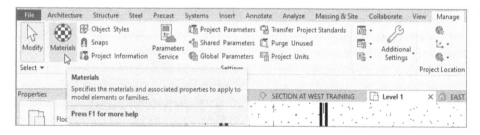

FIGURE 9.67 Clicking the Materials button on the Manage tab

2. In the Material Browser, click Create New Material at the bottom of the dialog as shown in Figure 9.68.

3. Right-click on the new material and rename it **Tile Floor - Terra Cotta**.

4. In the Appearance tab, click where it says (no image selected).

BUT MY DIRECTORY IS BLANK!

Unfortunately, these material mappings are a little shaky, If you wind up in some random blank directory, you need to browse to C:/Program Files/Common Files/Autodesk Shared/Materials/Textures/1/Mats.

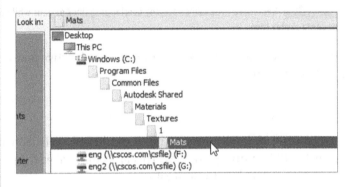

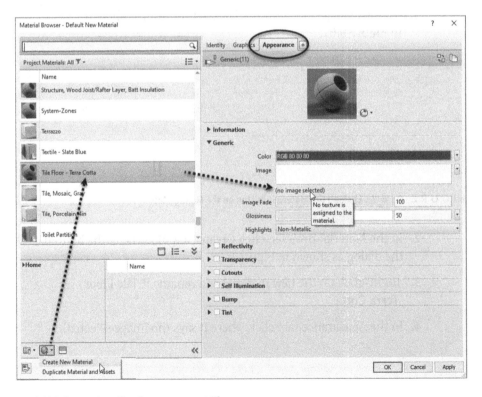

FIGURE 9.68 Creating some sweet tile

5. In the Select File dialog, find an empty area and right-click.

6. Go to View and then to Large Icons as shown in Figure 9.69.

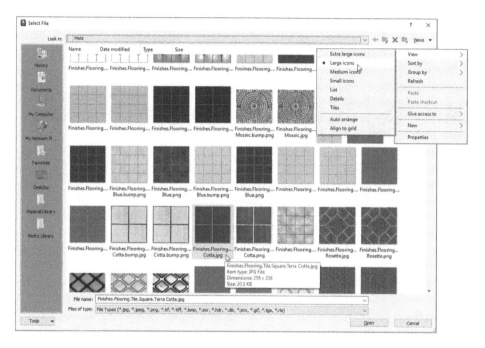

FIGURE 9.69 Finding an image for our material

7. Browse to find the file `Finishes.Flooring.Tile.Square.Terra Cotta.jpg`.

8. Click the Bump check box on as shown in Figure 9.70.

9. Find the file named `Finishes.Flooring.Tile.Square.Terra Cotta.bump.png`.

10. Click into the Graphics tab.

11. For the Surface Pattern Foreground, click the <none> next to Pattern, as shown in Figure 9.71.

12. In the Fill Patterns dialog, check the Model radio button.

13. Select 12″ (305 mm) Tile.

14. Click OK.

The difference between Drafting and Model is the fact that a Drafting hatch pattern will change density with the view scale. A Model pattern will stay dimensionally accurate.

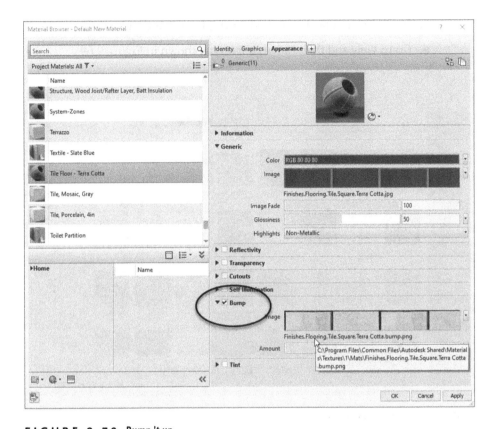

FIGURE 9.70 Bump it up.

15. Change the Cut Pattern Foreground pattern to Diagonal Crosshatch-Small.

16. Click Apply and then OK.

The new material is locked, loaded, and ready to use. We just need to duplicate an existing floor.

1. On the Architecture tab, click the Floor button.

2. Make sure Floor 4″ Lavatory With Tiles is the current selection.

3. Click Edit Type.

4. Click Duplicate.

5. Call it **Terra Cotta Kitchen Floor**.

6. Click Edit on the Structure row.

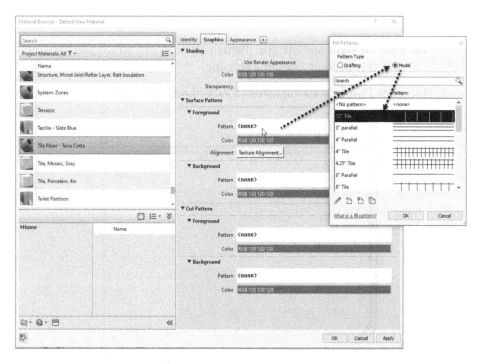

FIGURE 9.71 Adding a Model 12" (305mm) hatch pattern

7. On the Finish 1 [4] row, click into the Material cell.

8. Browse to the Tile Floor - Terra Cotta material you created. See Figure 9.72.

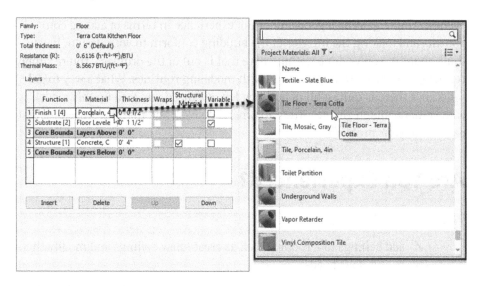

FIGURE 9.72 Adding our tile to the floor

9. Click OK until you are back to the view.

10. Pick the walls and the line. Trim up the corners, which you have most certainly become awesome at doing.

11. Click Finish. Your view should look like Figure 9.73.

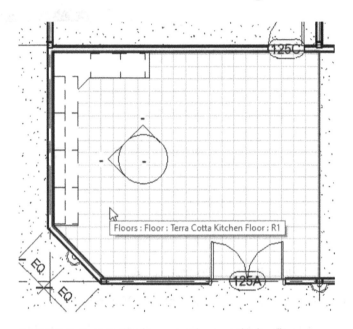

FIGURE 9.73 Finishing up our fancy new kitchen floor

Phew! You're gaining a good amount of experience in terms of adding components and making the interior of the building conform to your design. If you think about it, you've done nothing here that is out of the ordinary. You're simply replacing everyday drafting routines with modeling routines. What a way to go!

Because there is quite a bit of building left, go ahead and load up this model with components. If you get stuck anywhere, go back and find the procedure that pertains to your problem.

Are You Experienced?

Now you can. . .

✓ add ceilings to a room as well as create new ceilings and modify them to suit your needs

✓ transfer ceilings from other projects by using the Transfer Project Standards function

✓ add soffits to your model by using a typical wall and offsetting the base

✓ create a plan region so you can see elements at different elevations
without disturbing the rest of the view

✓ add components such as bathroom fixtures, office furniture, and
lighting to your model

✓ create subregions in which to specify alternate flooring, thus allowing you to avoid hatching

Stairs, Ramps, and Railings

A whole chapter just for stairs, ramps, and railings? You bet! If you think about it, there could be hundreds of combinations of stair and railing systems. As a matter of fact, you very seldom see two sets of stairs that are exactly the same. Kind of like snowflakes, aren't they? OK, they're nothing like snowflakes! But you get the point.

This chapter covers the following topics:

▶ **Creating stairs by using the Rise/Run function**

▶ **Creating a winding staircase**

▶ **Creating a custom railing system**

▶ **Creating custom stairs**

▶ **Adding ramps**

Creating Stairs by Using the Rise/Run Function

To begin, this chapter will address the makings of a staircase—from commercial stairs to those with a more residential feel, with wood members, balusters, and spindles. During this procedure, you'll see how the Autodesk® Revit® software brings stairs together. After you create a common staircase, you'll move on to winding stairs, custom railings, and, of course, ramps.

 NOTE Throughout this book, you'll have the opportunity to download custom families from the book's website.

In this section, you'll focus on creating a staircase by using the traditional Rise/Run method. Then I'll discuss modifying the boundary of the stairs, which allows you to create a more unusual shape than that provided out of the box.

To begin, open the file you've been using to follow along. If you didn't complete Chapter 9, "Ceilings and Interiors," go to the book's web page at www.wiley.com/go/2024revit2024ner. From there you can browse to the Chapter 10 folder and find the file called NER-10.rvt.

The objective of the following procedure is to create a staircase using the Rise/Run method:

1. In the Project Browser, go to the Level 2 floor plan.

2. Zoom in on the radial entry in the east wing, as shown in Figure 10.1.

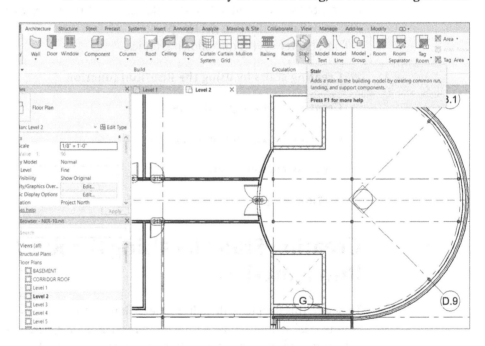

FIGURE 10.1   Click the Stair button on the Circulation panel of the Architecture tab.

3. On the View Control bar, change Visual Style to Hidden Line.

4. On the Circulation panel of the Architecture tab, click the Stair button (see Figure 10.1).

   You're put into Sketch mode for the stairs you're about to design, as shown in Figure 10.2.

FIGURE 10.2 The Modify | Create Stair tab, Sketch mode

5. On the Components panel of the Modify | Create Stair tab, make sure the Run button is checked.

6. On the Options toolbar, set the Location Line to Exterior Support: Left.

7. Set the offset to -6″ (-152 mm).

8. Set Actual Run Width to 4′-0″ (1219.2 mm) (see Figure 10.2).

9. In the Properties dialog, change Base Level to Level 1.

10. Change Top Level to Level 2 (see Figure 10.3).

 NOTE By setting the base to Level 1 and the top to Level 2, you give Revit the dimensions it needs to calculate the rise of the stairs. Later we will create a multilevel staircase out of the very one we are creating now.

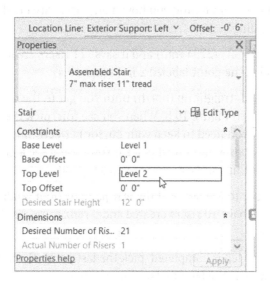

FIGURE 10.3 Changing the element properties of the stairs

Now it's time to physically model the stairs. What we need to do is start picking points and Revit will start guiding us. This specific staircase will have two sections and a landing at the halfway point. To start adding the stairs, follow these steps:

1. Pick point 1 in Figure 10.4. It is the center of the column.

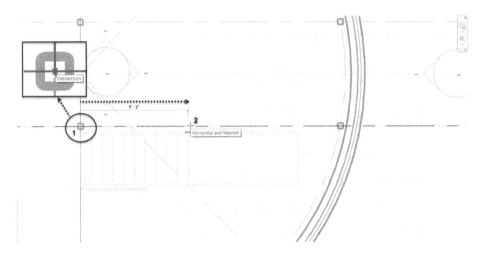

FIGURE 10.4 Adding the first run

2. Once the point is picked, move your cursor to the right. Notice that you get a temporary dimension at the top of the stair run and a display at the bottom telling you how many risers are created and how many remain.

3. Once you get to 9'-2" (2794 mm) and it says "11 risers created, 10 remaining," pick the point labeled 2 in Figure 10.4.

4. Move your cursor straight up (north) until you get to the grid intersection labeled 3 in Figure 10.5. When you see this, pick the third point. Note that you need to keep your cursor perfectly aligned with the edge of the stair run you just placed. You should see a green dotted alignment line indicating that you are good.

5. Move your cursor to the left—all the way past the floor landing. Revit reports that you have 10 risers created and 0 remaining, as shown in Figure 10.6.

6. When the second leg is completed, pick the last point. Revit draws both runs as well as the landing (see Figure 10.6).

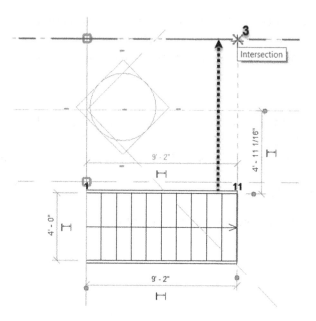

FIGURE 10.5 Move your cursor straight up.

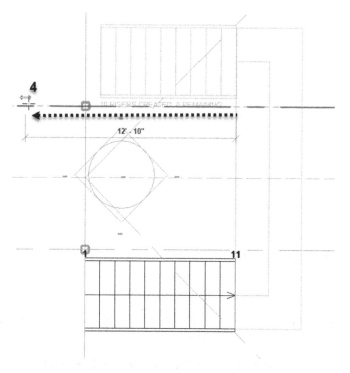

FIGURE 10.6 Move your cursor to the left. It's good to go way past the actual run. Revit will add only the necessary risers.

With the basic layout completed, it's time to examine the perimeter of the stairs. If you're looking for any architectural design outside of the basic box that you get when you place a staircase, you'll want to edit the boundary.

Modifying Boundaries

With the main stairs in place and laid out, you can now start modifying the profile. Given that this is a five-tiered, multilevel staircase, the boundary will be somewhat limited—but not to the point that you can't make something pop out of your design.

To modify the boundary, follow along:

1. Select the landing, as shown in Figure 10.7.

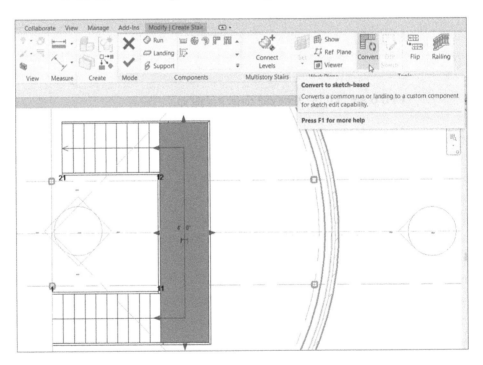

FIGURE 10.7 The Convert button

2. Click the Convert button (see Figure 10.7).

3. When you see the warning that you may be doing irreversible damage, click Close to dismiss it.

4. With the landing still selected, click the Edit Sketch button, as shown in Figure 10.8.

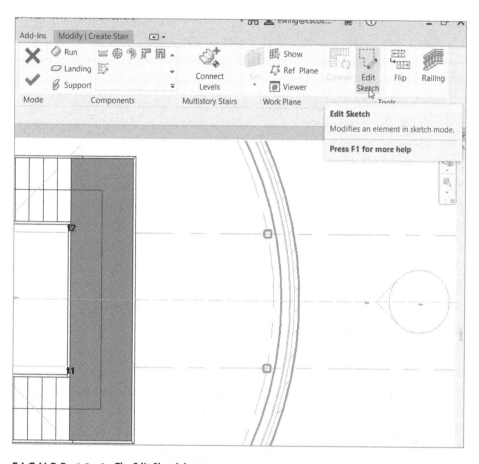

FIGURE 10.8 The Edit Sketch button

5. On the Draw panel, click the Pick Lines button, as shown in Figure 10.9.

6. Set the Offset to 6′–0″ (1829 mm).

7. Pick grid line G. Make sure the temporary alignment line is going into the building as shown in Figure 10.9.

8. Pick grid line G and the radial outside of the landing will be ready to trim up.

9. Trim the corners so your landing looks like Figure 10.10.

With the radius drawn in, it's important to pause at this point. What you have here is an extra line. Similar to when you're sketching a floor, if you have any overlapping line segments or gaps, Revit won't let you continue. Also, if you have any extra lines, Revit won't let you continue.

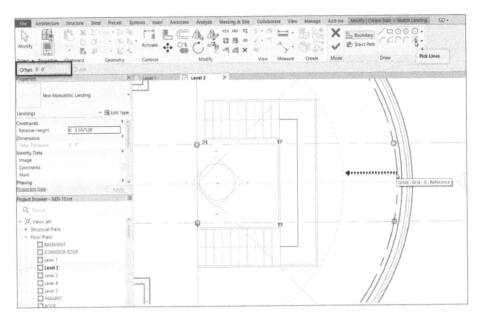

FIGURE 10.9 Offset grid line G.

Let's clean up the stairs:

1. Click Modify or press the Esc key twice, and then select the straight green line at the outside of the landing.

2. Press the Delete key on your keyboard. The line is removed. Your stairs should look exactly like Figure 10.10.

3. Click the Finish Edit Mode button, as shown in Figure 10.11.

Now you can select the railing system to use. Out of the box, Revit provides only four choices. You'll select one of those for this staircase, but you'll add to the list later in this chapter.

Revit provides a small number of railing systems as defaults. You can choose one of these five railings to apply to the staircase during the Sketch mode of the stairs.

Follow this procedure to apply a railing to the stairs:

1. On the Modify | Create Stair tab in Sketch mode, click the Railing button, as shown in Figure 10.12.

2. In the Railing dialog, from the drop-down select Handrail - Pipe, as shown in Figure 10.12.

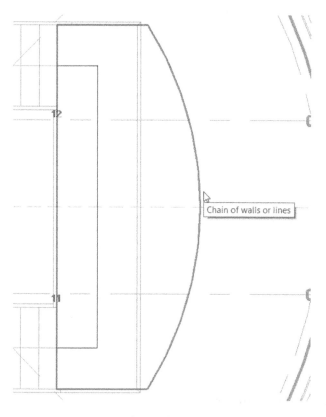

FIGURE 10.10 The completed boundary

3. Under Position, keep the Treads radio button selected (see Figure 10.12). Doing so hosts the railing to the treads.

4. Click OK. With the railings in place, you're on your way to completing this staircase. As a matter of fact, round one is finished.

5. To complete the stairs, click Finish Edit Mode on the Modify | Create Stair tab.

6. You'll get a warning that the rail is not continuous. That's OK. We'll drill into railings later. Click the red X as shown in Figure 10.13

7. Go to Level 2, if you're not already there. Your stairs should look like Figure 10.14.

Uh-oh! We have a serious ankle breaker where the DN (Down) text is. There's a gap between the stairs and the floor. Luckily, we have a simple solution to fix this. We're going to move the entire staircase to the left.

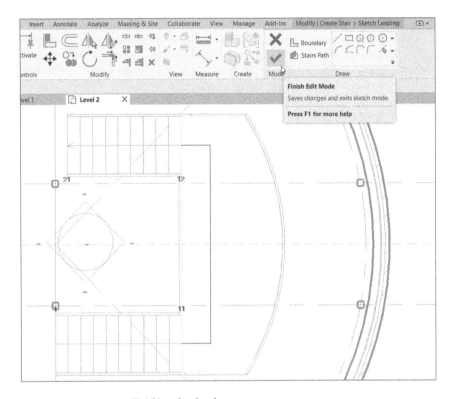

FIGURE 10.11   Finishing the sketch

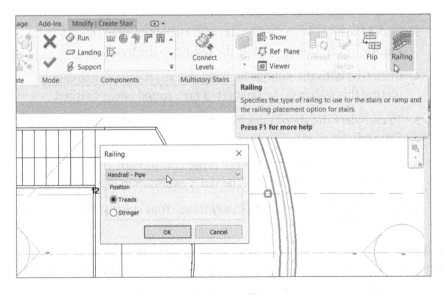

FIGURE 10.12   Adding a more handsome railing

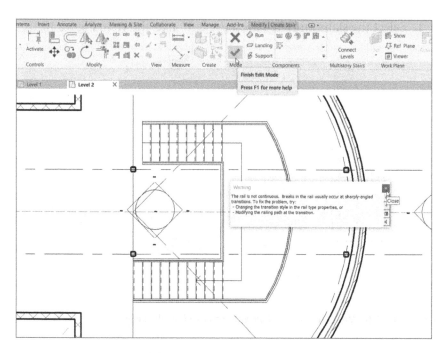

FIGURE 10.13 Finishing the placement of our stairs

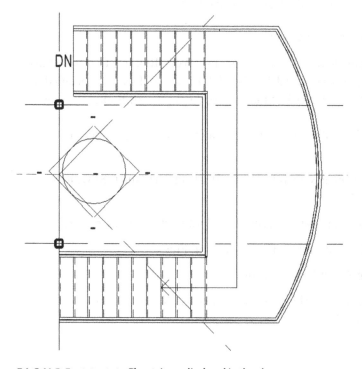

FIGURE 10.14 The stairs as displayed in the plan

1. Select the stairs and click the move button as shown in Figure 10.15.

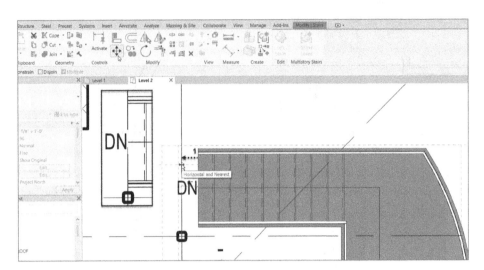

FIGURE 10.15 Move the stairs to align with the face of the floor edge.

2. Pick the point labeled 1 as shown in Figure 10.15.

3. Move the stairs to the face of the landing.

Creating Multi-Level Stairs

This process has changed over the years for sure. We both know that this staircase needs to go higher than Level 1 to Level 2. However, if we had specified in the properties we wanted Level 1 to Level 5, we'd have a continuous stairway to heaven.

To create a multi-level staircase using the stairs we already configured, follow along:

1. Cut a section as shown in Figure 10.16 and rename it **SECTION AT STAIRS**.

2. Press Esc, and open the section by double-clicking the bubble.

3. Select the stair on Level 2, as shown in Figure 10.17.

4. Click the Select Levels button.

5. Hold down the Ctrl key and select Levels 3,4, and 5. (See Figure 10.17).

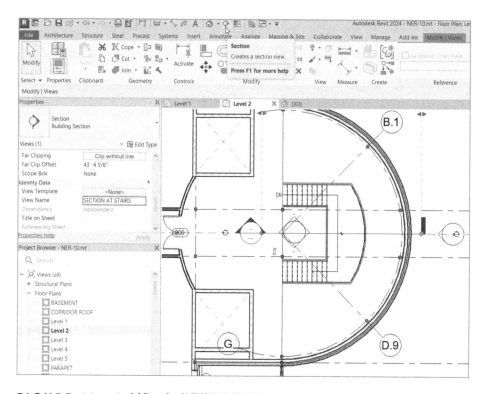

F I G U R E 1 0 . 1 6 Adding the SECTION AT STAIRS section

6. Click the green Finish Edit Mode button. Your stairs should look like Figure 10.18.

7. Hover your cursor over the stairs that are on Levels 3–5. Notice the box that appears indicating that the stairs are connected.

8. When you see that box, pick the stairs.

9. Click the Selection Box button, as shown in Figure 10.19.
   You now have a 3D view that is cropped to your stairs.

10. Select the wireframe box that is cropping your view, as shown in Figure 10.20.

11. Rename the {3D} view in the Project Browser to **ENTRY STAIRS**.

12. Select the grip at the top of the box and stretch the box up so that you can see the roof (see Figure 10.20).

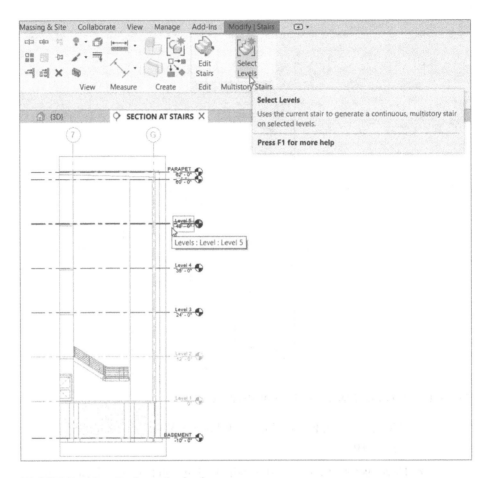

FIGURE 10.17 Connecting levels

13. Click the Default 3D view icon on the Quick Access toolbar. This will regenerate the {3D} view.

Configuring Railings

Here's a problem: the railing just stops dead at the bottom of the stringer. This may have been acceptable practice around the time, say, when the wheel was still on the drawing board. You need some kind of railing extension. To accomplish this, follow along with the next procedure.

1. Go to Level 2.

2. Zoom into the bottom run of the stairs (near the UP text).

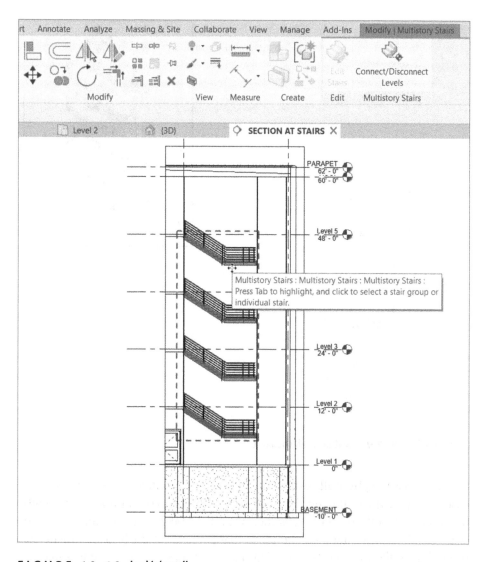

FIGURE 10.18 Lookin' good!

3. On the Architecture tab, click the Reference Plane button, as shown in Figure 10.21.

4. On the Draw panel, click the Pick Lines button.

5. Offset a reference plane 1'-6" (457 mm) to the left of the bottom riser (see Figure 10.22).

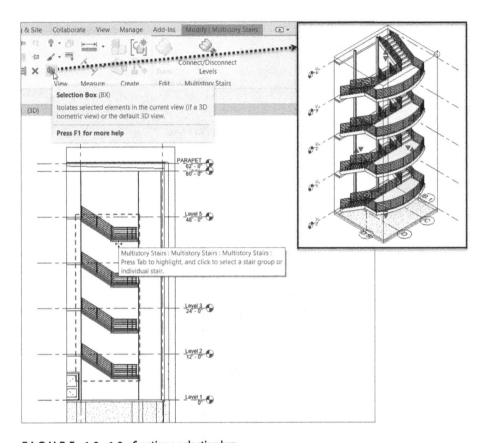

FIGURE 10.19 Creating a selection box

Now we have to physically extend the railing. The problem is, we don't know exactly how far the railing needs to extend past the first riser at the specific angle of the stairs. By offsetting the reference plane 1'-6" (457 mm), we can be assured that the railing will extend far enough at that angle to hit the 3'-0" railing height before it goes flat to meet the floor. This procedure has actually been modified several times over the years. It's actually pretty easy!

1. In the level 2 floor plan, select the bottom railing, as shown in Figure 10.23. Make sure you aren't selecting the stairs.

2. Click Edit Path, as shown in Figure 10.23.

3. On the Options panel, click the Preview button.

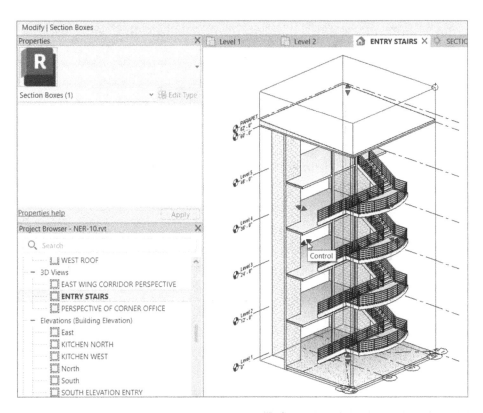

FIGURE 10.20 Renaming {3D} and stretching the box

4. Select the grip at the end of the magenta line representing the rail-ing, and drag it to the left until it meets the reference plane you placed previously. (See Figure 10.24.)

5. Click the green Finish Edit Mode check mark.

6. Go to the ENTRY STAIRS 3D view.

7. Select the section box, and drag the left grip further to the left and to the right so you can see your railing. (See Figure 10.25.)

8. Repeat the procedure with the middle railing, as shown in Figure 10.26.

Further Modifying the Railings

It's time to actually make sure nobody falls over the ledge. The thing is, we don't need what we are about to do be reflected down on Level 1. Therefore, we will now be adding new railings to our model.

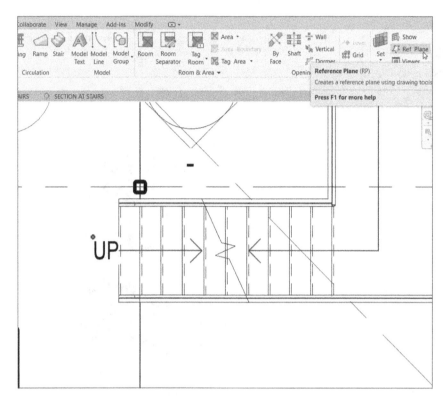

FIGURE 10.21 Click the Ref Plane button.

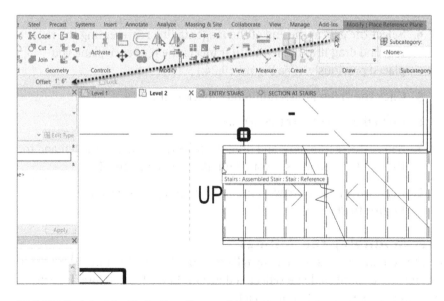

FIGURE 10.22 Placing the reference plane

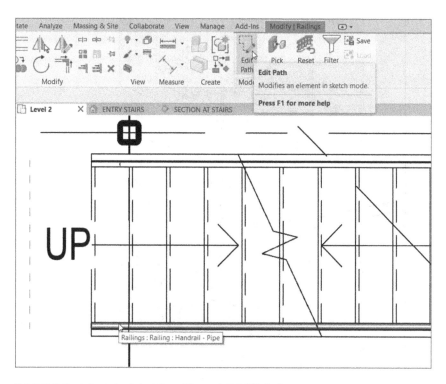

F I G U R E   1 0 . 2 3   Select the railing and click Edit Path.

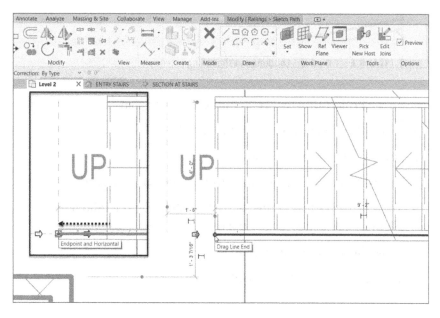

F I G U R E   1 0 . 2 4   Drag the railing to the left.

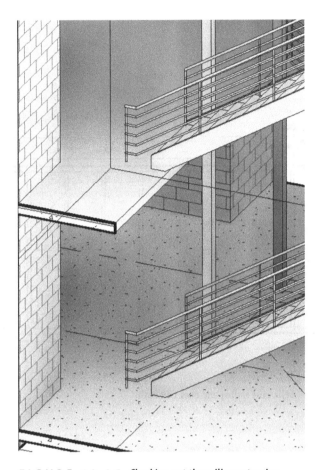

FIGURE 10.25 Checking out the railing extension

1. In the Project Browser, go to the Level 2 floor plan.

2. Select the railing shown in Figure 10.27.

3. Right-click and select Create Similar.

4. On the Draw panel, make sure the Line button is checked.

5. Draw a line starting at the endpoint as shown in the callout in Figure 10.28 to the left 6″ (152 mm).

6. Draw the line straight down 6″ (152 mm).

7. Draw the line back to the right 12″ (305 mm).

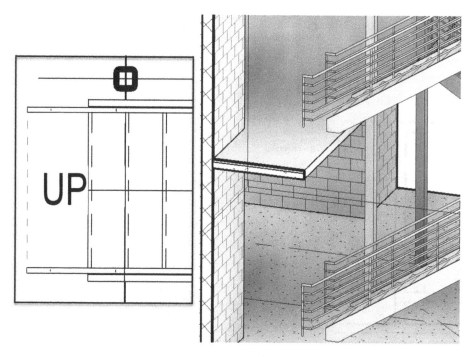

FIGURE 10.26 Both railings extended

8. Draw the line all the way down to intersect with the south wall to the left 1′–0″ (305 mm). See Figure 10.28.

9. On the Draw panel, click the Fillet Arc button.

10. Click the Radius button on the Options toolbar, as shown in Figure 10.29, and add a 2″ (102 mm) radius.

11. Click points 1 and 2, as shown in Figure 10.29.

12. Repeat this for the other two corners.

13. Click Finish Edit Mode.

14. While still in Level 2, select the railing we just added.

15. Select the Mirror Pick Axis button as shown in Figure 10.30.

16. Pick the centerline of the bottom stair as shown in Figure 10.30.

17. Select the new railing and click Edit Path.

18. Mirror only the 6″ and 12″ extensions using the center reference plane of the entire building as shown in Figure 10.30.

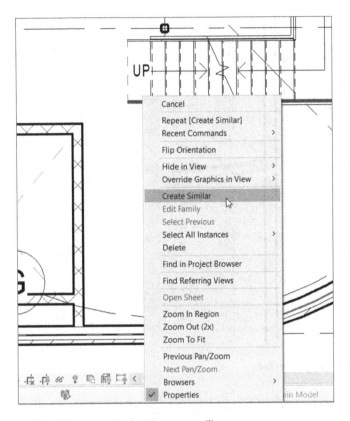

FIGURE 10.27 Creating a new railing

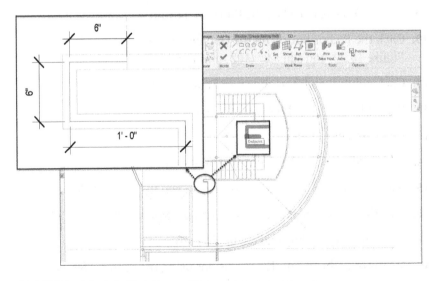

FIGURE 10.28 Modeling a railing

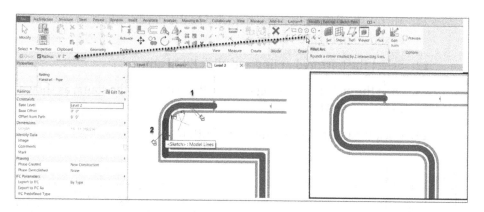

FIGURE 10.29 Modeling a railing

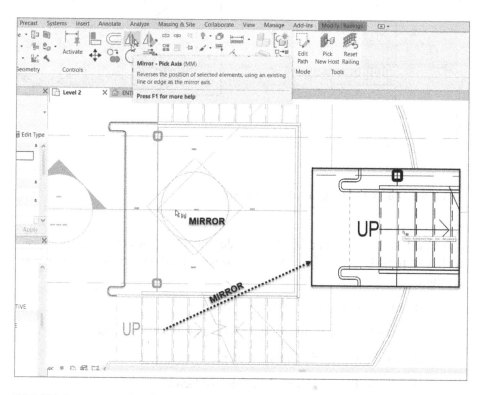

FIGURE 10.30 Completing the middle railing

19. Extend the railing line to meet the railing on the upper stairs.

20. Click the green Finish Edit Mode check mark.

21. Mirror the first railing you modeled to the upper railing on the stairs, as shown in Figure 10.31.

22. Select the mirrored railing and click Edit Path.

23. Drag the end of the railing to meet the railing on the stairs, as shown in Figure 10.31.

24. Click the green Finish Edit Mode button.

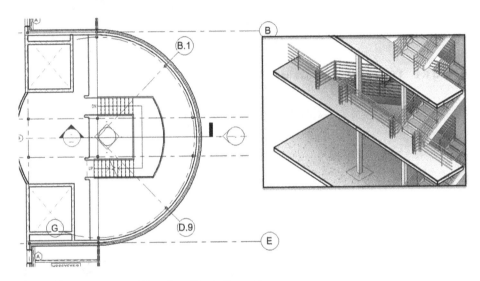

FIGURE 10.31 Adding the railing to the north

The next step is to copy and paste the independent railings to the floors above. We'll have to make some adjustments to the pasted railings on Level 5 when we get there.

1. Go to the 3D view ENTRY STAIRS.

2. Select the three independent railings you just modeled.

3. Click the Copy To Clipboard icon.

4. Choose Paste ➤ Aligned To Selected Levels.

5. Choose Levels 3–5, as shown in Figure 10.32.

6. Go to Level 5.

7. Delete the bottom railing.

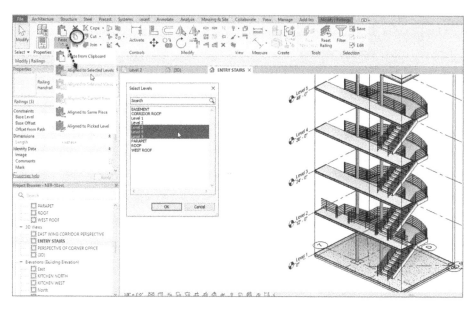

FIGURE 10.32 Using Paste ➤ Aligned To Selected Levels

8. Select the middle railing and click Edit Path as shown in Figure 10.33.

9. Stretch the railing down to the wall, as shown in Figure 10.33.

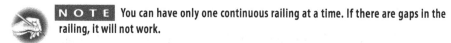

NOTE You can have only one continuous railing at a time. If there are gaps in the railing, it will not work.

Phew! You have built a set of stairs. The good thing is that it's one sweet staircase. The bad thing is that you used all the default layouts and materials. Next, we will get into some more complicated shapes and styles.

Creating a Winding Staircase

Before you get started, you should know that you'll create this staircase by using the separate stair components. You can try to make a winding staircase by using the Run function, similar to the one you used earlier. But in many cases (especially when you run into an existing staircase in either a renovation project or an addition), you may need to draft the stairs and then model over the top of the drafting lines. What? Drafting in Revit? Of course. How else can you expect to get anything done?

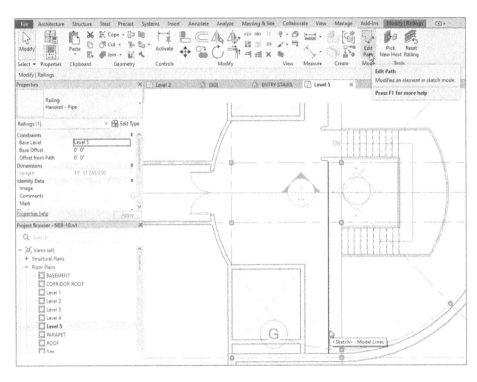

F I G U R E   1 0 . 3 3   Stretching the railing within the Edit Path mode

The first thing you'll need to do is make modifications to the floor in a specific area to create a landing. Follow along:

1. In the Project Browser, go to the Level 2 floor plan.

2. Zoom in on the area between the corridor and the east wing, as shown in Figure 10.34.

3. Select the Level 2 floor in the east wing (by floor, I mean select the actual floor we added to Level 2).

4. Click the Edit Boundary button on the Mode panel of the Modify | Floors tab.

5. Sketch a landing that is 8'–0" (2400 mm) long and 8'–0" (2439 mm) wide. Center it on the reference plane, as shown in Figure 10.34.

6. Click Finish Edit Mode on the Mode panel. If you're asked if you want to attach the walls to the bottom of the floor, click Attach.

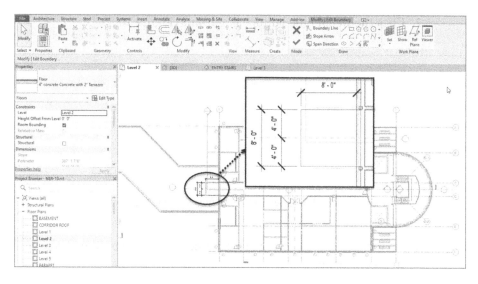

FIGURE 10.34 Creating a landing. You'll add a door in a moment.

With the landing in place, you can now copy a door up to this level. To do this, you'll go to the first floor and copy the door that resides there. You can do this on your own, or you can follow along with these steps:

1. In the Project Browser, go to the Level 1 floor plan.

2. Select door 100B.

3. Copy the door to the clipboard (click Copy To Clipboard on the Clipboard panel).

4. Choose Paste ➢ Aligned To Selected Levels.

5. Select Level 2, and click OK.

6. In the Project Browser, go back to Level 2. The door and the landing are in place.

7. Select the door and press the spacebar twice. This will flip the door into the hallway. We don't want to go knocking someone off our landing!

Next you'll create a winding set of stairs. The first task is to lay out the shape in the plan using simple drafting lines. The second task is to model over the lines you added by using various stair tools as follows:

1. Select the Annotate tab.

2. Click the Detail Line button, as shown in Figure 10.35.

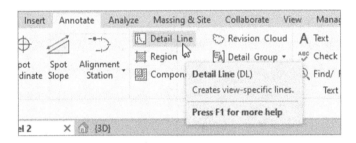

FIGURE 10.35 Select Detail Line from the Annotate tab.

3. On the Draw panel, click the Start-End-Radius Arc button, as shown in Figure 10.36.

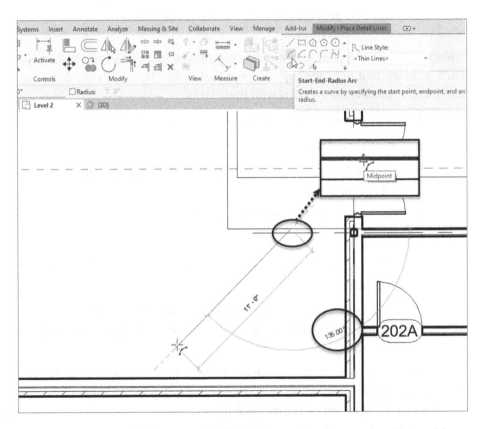

FIGURE 10.36 With the Start-End-Radius Arc button selected, start at the midpoint of the landing and then go southwest at an angle of 135° and a distance of 11′–0″ (3300 mm).

4. For the first point of the arc, pick the midpoint of the landing (see Figure 10.36).

5. Move your cursor down, at 135° from the first point you just picked.

6. Extend your cursor 11'–0" (3300 mm), as shown in Figure 10.36, and then click to set the second point.

7. To form the arc, move your cursor to the right until the radius snaps into place. When it does, pick the point as shown in Figure 10.37.

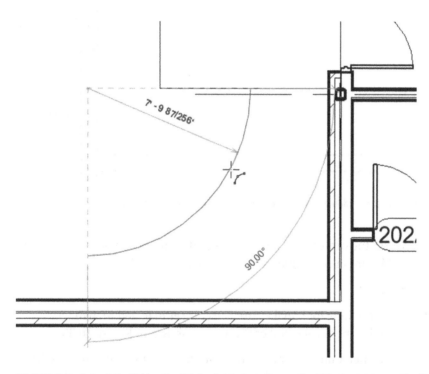

FIGURE 10.37 Picking the third point to form the arc. It will be tangent upon the first two points you picked.

8. Press Esc.

9. On the Draw panel, click the Pick Lines icon.

10. On the Options bar, add an increment of 1'–6" (457 mm) to the Offset field (see Figure 10.38).

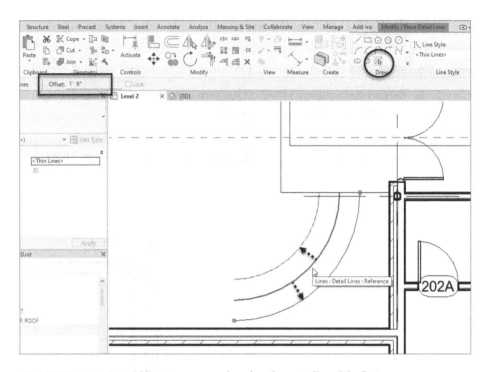

FIGURE 10.38 Adding two more arcs based on the centerline of the first

11. Offset the center arc to the right and then to the left, forming a 3′–0″ (914 mm) overall winder, as shown in Figure 10.38.

12. Press Esc.

13. Click the Line tool, make sure Offset is set to 0, and then draw a straight line at each end of the arcs, as shown in Figure 10.39.

OK, take a breather. Compare the examples in the book to what you have. Are you close? If not, go back and investigate.

NOTE Get used to this drafting thing; it's still very much a part of BIM, regardless of whether people say you can't draft in Revit!

The next step is to make an array of the straight lines you just added. These lines will wind up being the guidelines for your risers:

1. Press Esc, and then select the line you just drew at the landing and the endpoints of the arcs, as shown in Figure 10.40.

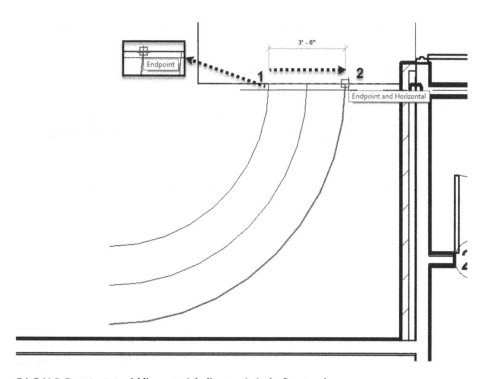

FIGURE 10.39 Adding a straight line to mimic the first tread

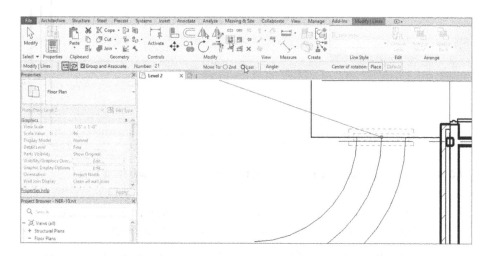

FIGURE 10.40 Choosing the array options

2. On the Modify tab, click the array button, as shown in Figure 10.40.

3. Select Radial.

4. For Number, type 21 (this will be the number of risers required to go from Level 1 to Level 2).

5. Make sure Move To: Last is selected (see Figure 10.40).

 N O T E Combining the number 21 with the Move To: 2nd function is telling Revit that you want 21 lines that are spaced using the distance between the first and second line.

6. Click the Place button next to the Center Of Rotation option, shown in Figure 10.41.

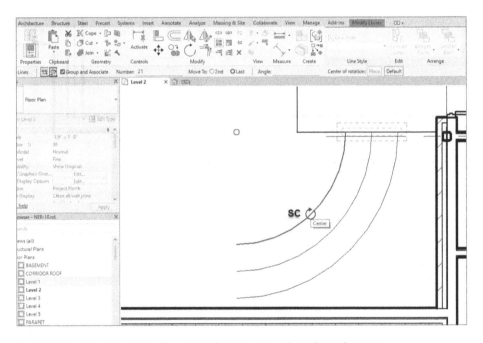

FIGURE 10.41 Moving the center of rotation somewhere that makes sense

7. Type SC (for snap center) and hover your pointer over the smaller arc. Once you see the center snap icon appear, pick the smaller arc.

8. For the first point of the array, pick a point on the endpoint of the center line you drew (point 1, as illustrated in Figure 10.42).

9. For the second point, click the endpoint of the center arc (point 2 in Figure 10.42).You will create 21 lines all pivoting around your center point.

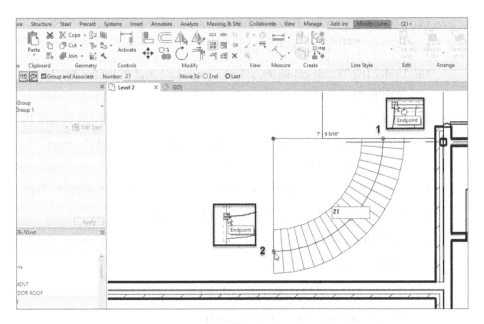

FIGURE 10.42 The linework when complete

Now you can begin modeling the stairs. This procedure is nothing more than tracing the lines you've already added to the model. To do this, you'll use the available tools that you haven't touched in the previous staircase. (You can look ahead to Figure 10.43 for reference.) Follow along:

1. On the Architecture tab, click the Stairs button.

2. In the Properties dialog, change Base Level to Level 1.

3. Change Top Level to Level 2.

4. Click Edit Type.

5. Click Duplicate.

6. Call the stairs **Corridor Entry Stairs**.

7. Click OK.

8. In the Construction category, click the cell to the right of Run Type. It contains the text 2″ (50 mm) Tread 1″ (25 mm) Nosing 1/4″ (6 mm) Riser. When you click in the cell, you see a [. . .] button. Click it.

9. At the top of the dialog, click Duplicate.

10. For the name, call it Cherry Treads.

11. Choose Cherry for Tread Material.

12. For Riser Material, do the same.

13. Under the Treads category, select Front, Left And Right for the Apply Nosing Profile row.

14. Click OK.

15. Scroll down to the Supports category, and change Right Support from Stringer (Closed) to Carriage (Open).

16. Click Carriage - 2″ Width (50 mm) to the right of Right Support Type.

17. Click the small [. . .] button to the right of the cell.

18. Click Duplicate.

19. Call it Mahogany Stringer.

20. Change Material to Mahogany. Click OK.

21. Change Left Support to Carriage (Open).

22. Make sure the Left Support Type is set to Mahogany Stringer. Your Properties dialog should look like the one shown in Figure 10.43.

23. Click OK to get back to the model.

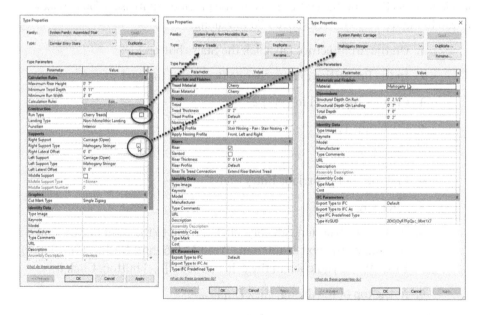

FIGURE 10.43 Customizing the stairs

It's time to add the stairs to the model. To do this, you'll first sketch the boundary:

1. On the Modify | Create Stairs tab in Sketch mode, click the Create Sketch button, as shown in Figure 10.44.

FIGURE 10.44 Click the Create Sketch button.

2. Make sure the Boundary icon is current. On the Draw panel, click the Pick Lines icon.

3. Pick the two arcs defining the outside of the stairs. Notice the green arcs. This indicates that this is your boundary.

  N O T E Notice that when you commence adding the boundary, Revit gives you the number of risers created and the number of risers remaining. I am not sure why it appears quarter toned so that you can barely see it.

4. On the Draw panel, click the Riser button.

5. On the Draw panel, click the Pick Lines icon.

6. Pick all of the lines you arrayed. This includes the bottom and the top lines (see Figure 10.45).

  N O T E When you try to pick the line that overlaps the landing, you must first hover over the line, press Tab, and then select the line.

7. Click the Stair Path button.

8. Click the Pick Lines button.

9. Pick the centerline of the staircase.

10. Click Finish Edit Mode on the Mode panel.

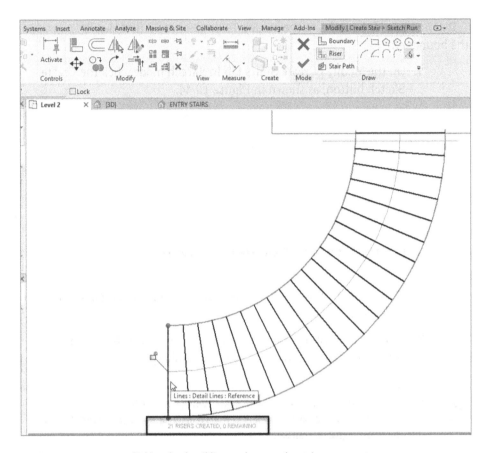

FIGURE 10.45 Picking the detail lines to lay over the stair components

11. Click the Railing button.

12. Change the railing to Handrail - Pipe, make sure the position is set to Treads, and click OK.

13. Click the Finish Sketch button (the green check mark).

With the stairs roughed in, you need to get a better look at them. If you use the default 3D view, you need to turn off way too many items to see your stairs. Let's add a perspective view, just to see what's going on here!

If you're confident about adding your own perspective view, go ahead and put one in and name it **EAST ENTRY FROM CORRIDOR**. If not, follow along with these steps:

1. In the Project Browser, go to the Level 1 floor plan.

2. On the View tab, click the 3D View ➢ Camera button.

3. Pick the first point shown in Figure 10.46.

4. Pick the second point shown in Figure 10.46.

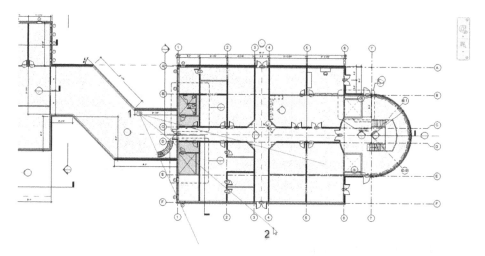

FIGURE 10.46 Adding the perspective view

5. In the Project Browser, find the new perspective view, and rename it **EAST ENTRY FROM CORRIDOR**.

6. Adjust the crop region so you can see the stairs and the landing.

7. Set Detail Level to Fine.

8. Check out the view (see Figure 10.47).

The next series of steps involves mirroring the stairs to the other side of the landing. Then, of course, you need to add a landing railing so that people don't just walk out the door and off the ledge:

1. Go to the Level 2 floor plan in the Project Browser.

2. Select the stairs, as shown in Figure 10.48. You might have to move your cursor over the stairs so you don't accidently select one of the drafting lines.

NOTE To select only the stairs and the railings, you can pick a window around the entire set of lines, groups, railings, and stairs. From there, you can click the Filter button on the Ribbon, and select only Stairs and Railings.

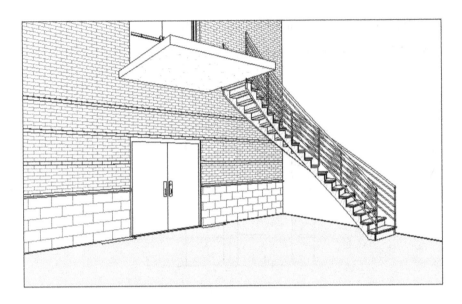

FIGURE 10.47 Looking nice

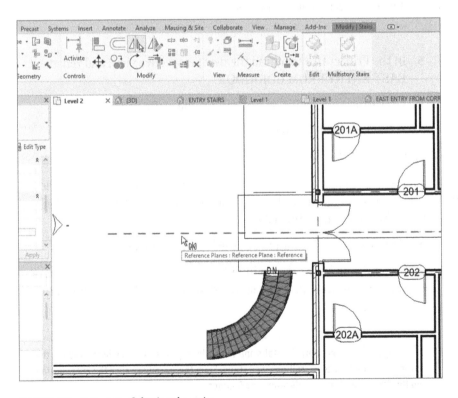

FIGURE 10.48 Selecting the stairs

3. On the Modify | Multi-Select tab, click the Mirror ➤ Pick Mirror Axis button, as shown in Figure 10.49.

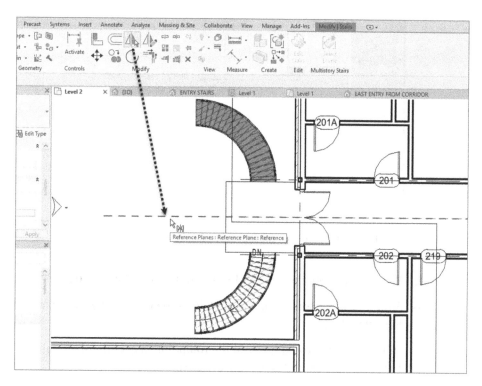

FIGURE 10.49 The mirrored stairs

4. Pick the center reference plane. (I told you this thing would come in handy.)

Your stairs are now mirrored to the other side of the landing (see Figure 10.49).

Let's tie in the railings. If you're feeling up to the challenge, try it on your own by using the railing Handrail - Pipe. If not, just follow along with these steps:

1. On the Architecture tab, click the Railing button.

2. In the Type Selector, change the type to Handrail - Pipe, as shown in Figure 10.50.

3. On the Draw panel, click the Pick Lines icon.

4. Set Offset to 4″ (100 mm).

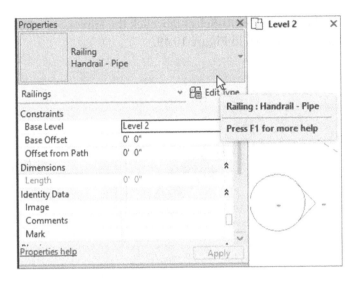

F I G U R E   1 0 . 5 0   Setting the landing handrail type

5. Pick the landing lines to offset in the railing (see Figure 10.51).

6. After the offsets are complete, click the Line icon on the Draw panel. Set Offset to 0.

7. Draw the lines extending from the midpoint snap of the stair railing to the landing railing (see Figure 10.52).

8. Trim the corners so your railings look like Figure 10.53.

9. On the Mode panel, click Finish Edit Mode.

10. You may have to flip the railing by selecting it and then clicking the Flip arrow.

11. Add two more railings between the stairs and the brick wall. Your stairs should look like Figure 10.54.

Remember, you must create only one railing at a time. If you try to do more than one continuous line, Revit won't let you proceed. Try creating one short railing and mirroring it.

Great! You're getting there. Now you'll see how a staircase and the accompanying railings come together. For example, it sure would be nice to have a railing with spindles or, better yet, panels added to it. Also, a nice half-round bullnose would improve your staircase. The next section will focus on this concept.

Stair and Railing Families

Similar to the model as a whole, stairs and railings comprise separate families that come together to form the overall unit. Although stairs and railings are considered a system family (a family that resides only in the model), they still rely heavily on hosted families to create the entire element.

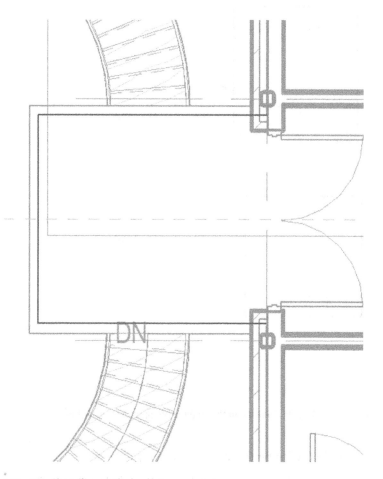

FIGURE 10.51 The railing on the landing

The next procedure will involve loading separate families into the model and then using them in a new set of stairs and railings that you'll create in the west wing:

1. In the Project Browser, go to the Level 3 floor plan and change Detail Level to Fine.

2. Zoom in on the west wing.

3. On the Architecture tab, click the Floor button.

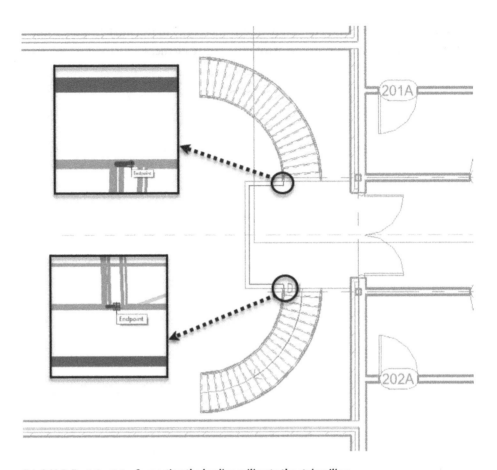

FIGURE 10.52 Connecting the landing railing to the stair railing

4. In the Properties dialog, click the Edit Type button.

5. Select the 4″ (152 mm) Concrete with 2″ (50 mm) Terrazzo floor system from the Type drop-down list, as shown in Figure 10.55.

6. Click OK.

7. On the Draw panel, click the Pick Walls button.

8. Pick the walls, and make sure the lines are set to the core centerline, as shown in Figure 10.55.

9. When picking the south wall, select the Pick Lines button on the Draw panel, and set Offset to 5′–0″ (1500 mm) in the Options bar.

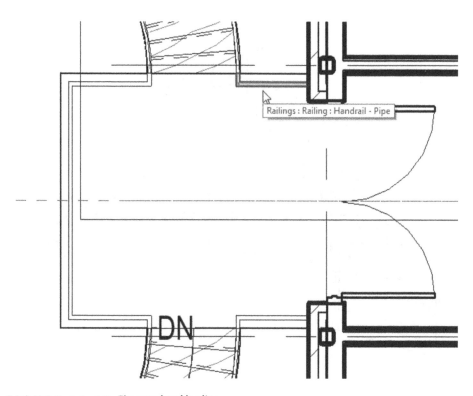

FIGURE 10.53 The completed landing

TIP Again, make sure you have no gaps or overlapping lines. Use the Trim/Extend Single Element command to clean up the lines to look like the figure.

10. Once the sketch lines are in place, trim the corners and click Finish Edit Mode on the Mode panel.

11. Revit asks if you want to attach the walls that go up to this floor's bottom. Click Don't Attach.

12. Revit asks if you want to cut the overlapping volume out of the walls. Click Yes.

Your floor is now in place. The next item you'll tackle is creating a completely custom railing system.

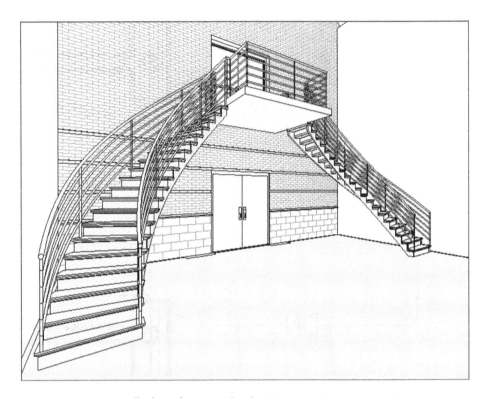

FIGURE 10.54 Check out the perspective view.

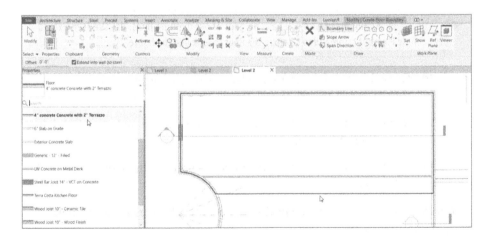

FIGURE 10.55 You must add a floor at the Level 3 floor plan for the stairs to have a landing.

Creating a Custom Railing System

Next, you'll load the components that make up your stairs. Although Revit makes an attempt to supply you with some families, in this case you'll download the families included with this book by going to the book's web page at www .wiley.com/go/revit2024ner. From there, browse to the Chapter 10 folder and find the following files:

- ► 6210 (2-5_8).rfa
- ► landing.rfa
- ► post.rfa
- ► raised panels.rfa
- ► spindle.rfa
- ► stair nosing.rfa

To get started, you need to load the families into your model so that they're available when it comes time to assemble your new railing. If you remember how to do this, go ahead and load all the families that you just downloaded from the web page. If you need some assistance, follow these steps:

1. On the Insert tab, click Load Family.

2. Find the files that you downloaded from the web page.

3. Select all of them, and click Open to load them.

4. Save the model.

The next step is to create a new railing and add some of these items to it:

1. In the Project Browser, find the Families category and expand it, as shown in Figure 10.56.

2. Find the Railing category and expand it.

3. Find Handrail - Rectangular, and double-click it (see Figure 10.56).

4. Click Duplicate.

5. Call the new railing **Wood Railing with Spindles**.

6. Click OK.

7. Click OK again.

FIGURE 10.56   The railing family called Handrail - Rectangular

8. In the Project Browser, under the Families category, scroll down until you see Top Rail Type, as shown in Figure 10.57.

9. Double-click the Circular - 1 1/2″ (38 mm) Top Rail Type.

10. Click Duplicate.

11. Change the name to 6210, and click OK (this is the AWI number for this specific style of railing).

12. Change Profile to 6210 (2-5_8) : 2 5/8″ (67 mm).

13. Change Transitions to Gooseneck.

14. Change Material to Cherry, as shown in Figure 10.57.

15. Click OK.

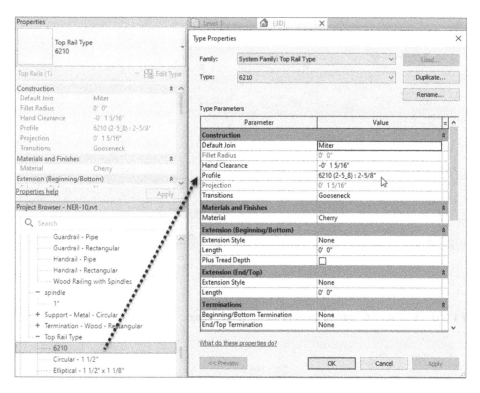

FIGURE 10.57 Changing the rail. Note that you can add as many rails as you wish. Here, you're adding only one.

16. Under the Families category in the Project Browser, double-click Wood Railing with Spindles, located in the Railing category.

17. Scroll down to the Top Rail category.

18. Click the browse [. . .] button in the Type row (it currently has Rectangular – 2″ × 2″ [51 mm] selected).

19. In the Type category, change the type to 6210 (see Figure 10.58).

20. Click OK.

21. Click the Edit button in the Baluster Placement row.

22. In the Main Pattern area, change Baluster Family to Spindle: 1″ (25 mm) (see Figure 10.59).

23. Just below the Main Pattern area is the Use Baluster Per Tread On Stairs option. Select it, as shown in Figure 10.59.

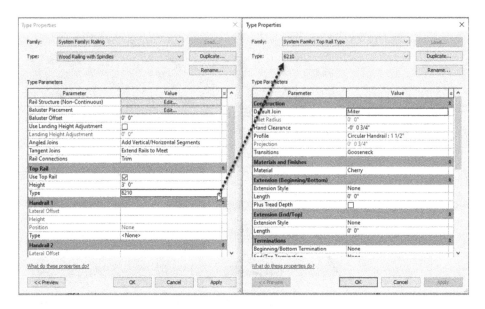

FIGURE 10.58 Adding the 6210 top rail to the railing

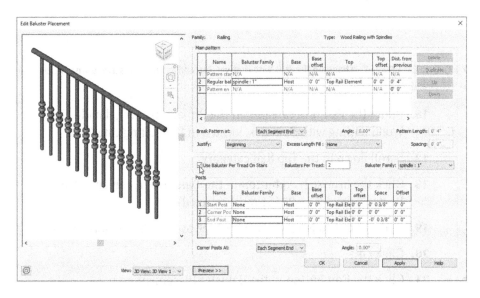

FIGURE 10.59 Adding the spindle to the Main Pattern area and specifying two balusters per tread and no actual posts

24. To the right is the Balusters Per Tread field. Specify two balusters per tread (see Figure 10.59).

25. Change Baluster Family to Spindle: 1″ (25 mm), as shown in Figure 10.59.

26. In the bottommost field is the Posts category. Change each of the three posts to None in the Baluster Family column. Your spindles are all you need (see Figure 10.59).

27. Click OK.

28. Click the ≪ Preview button at the bottom left of the dialog. This will give you a picture of the railing up to this point.

29. Click OK again to exit the dialog.

You may or may not have noticed that you didn't get the opportunity to change the baluster's material as you did with the railing. This action must be done in the family itself, as follows:

1. In the Project Browser, the Spindle category is just below Railing, as shown in Figure 10.60. Expand Spindle to expose the 1″ (25 mm) family.

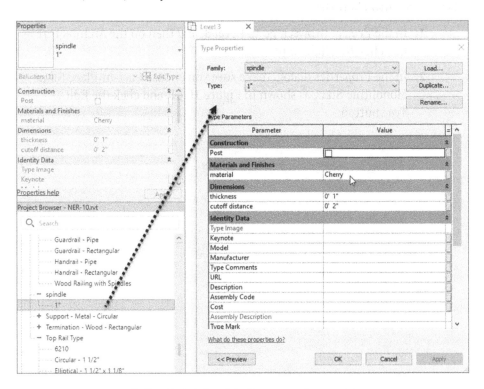

FIGURE 10.60 Finding the Spindle 1″ family to access the material

2. Double-click the 1″ (25 mm) family to open its Type Properties dialog.

3. Find the Material row, click into the <By Category> field, and click the [. . .] button.

4. Change Material to Cherry.

5. Click OK twice.

This completes the railing setup. Once you add it to the stairs, however, some tweaking will be required. The next step is to customize the stairs themselves.

Creating Custom Stairs

This is the third staircase you've created in the same chapter, so you've certainly gained some experience regarding the placement of stairs and railings into the Revit model. You're also becoming familiar with the stair and railings dialogs. This last procedure will tie all of that together.

Let's create that staircase:

1. In the Project Browser, go to Level 3, and then on the Architecture tab, click the Stairs button.

2. In the Properties dialog, make sure you choose Cast-In-Place Stair Monolithic Stair, as shown in Figure 10.61, and click the Edit Type button.

F I G U R E   1 0 . 6 1   Configuring the stairs. As you can see, you have quite a few options.

3. Click Duplicate.

4. Call the new staircase **Custom Bullnose Stairs.**

5. Click OK.

6. Under Construction, next to Run Type, click where it says 3/4 Nosing and click the browse button as shown in Figure 10.62.

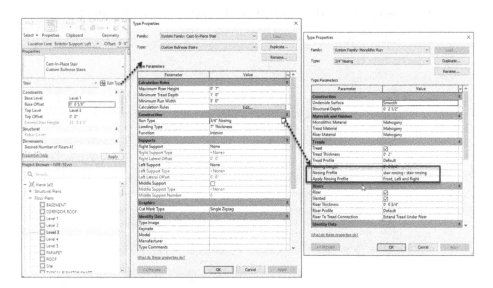

FIGURE 10.62 Configuring all aspects of our stairs

7. Under Treads, change the Nosing Profile to **stair nosing** : stair nosing.

8. Apply the nosing profile to Front, Left And Right.

9. Select the Riser check box.

10. Change the riser thickness to 3/4″ (19 mm).

11. For Riser To Tread Connection, choose Extend Tread Under Riser.

12. Change Monolithic Material to Mahogany.

13. Under Treads, make sure Treads is selected.

14. Change Tread Material to Mahogany.

15. Change Riser Material to Mahogany.

16. Click OK.

17. Click the 7" (178 mm) Thickness cell next to Landing Type, and click the [. . .] button to the right.

18. Click Duplicate.

19. Call the new landing 1'–0" (300 mm) **Mahogany Landing**.

20. Change Monolithic Thickness to 1'–0" (300 mm).

21. Change Monolithic Material to Mahogany. See Figure 10.63.

22. Click OK twice.

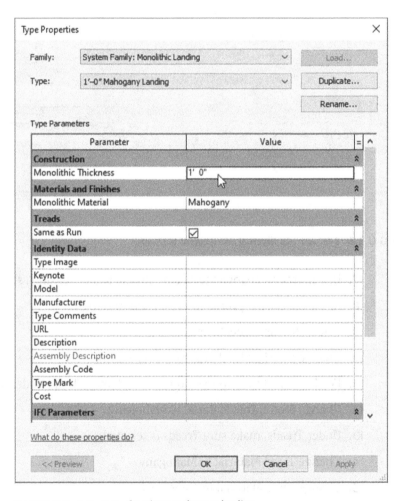

FIGURE 10.63 Creating a mahogany landing

It's time to configure some of the layout properties. These will allow you to calculate the rise/run count as well as some basic offsets you'll need:

1. In the Properties dialog, set Base Level to Level 1.

2. Set Base Offset to 6 5/8″ (152 mm), as shown in Figure 10.64.

3. Set Top Level to Level 3. (Yes, this is going to be one long staircase!)

The next step is to place this monster into the model. Given the fact it is spanning 24′ (7315 mm), you'll need multiple landings to give your visitors a breather as they travel up the stairs. This layout will require a little more care in the initial planning stage:

1. On the Work Plane panel, click the Ref Plane button.

2. Click the Pick Lines button, and then create a layout, as shown in Figure 10.64 starting with the north and east walls. (It will make sense, I promise)!

3. Click the Railing button.

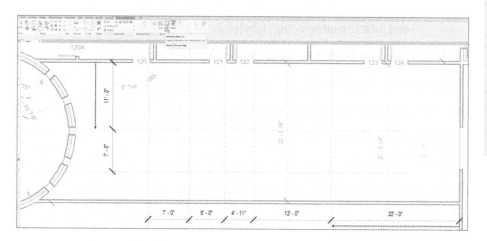

FIGURE 10.64   Using dimensions to lay out the centerlines of the stairs.

> The nice thing about using reference planes while in Sketch mode is that they will disappear once you finish the sketch. If you need to go back and edit the stairs, the reference planes will appear again!

4. Change the railing type to Wood Railing With Spindles, and make sure Position is set to Treads. Click OK.

5. On the Modify | Create Stairs tab in Sketch mode, click the Run button.

6. For the Location Line, select Run: Center.

7. Draw your stairs as shown in Figure 10.65 up to point 6. (Pick the points in the figure as sequenced.)

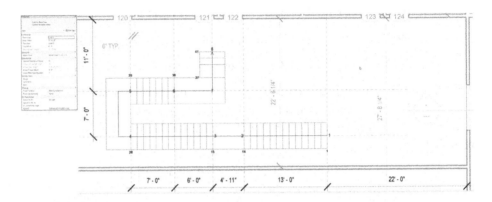

FIGURE 10.65 Picking the intersections of the reference planes to determine where the stairs will go

8. For the next point, align your cursor with the upper stair stringer and pick the intersection labeled 7.

9. Now pick point 8 (see Figure 10.66).

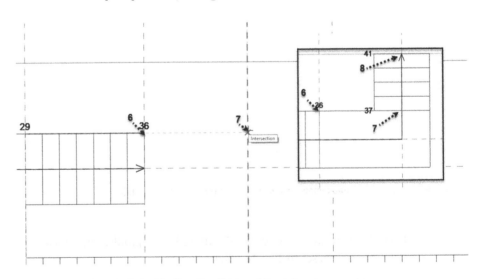

FIGURE 10.66 Point 7 is aligned to the top of the stairs.

10. Click Finish Sketch. Your stairs should look like Figure 10.65.

11. Go to a 3D view to check out the stairs. (Remember, you can select the stairs and click the Section Box button on the View panel.) Your stairs should resemble Figure 10.67.

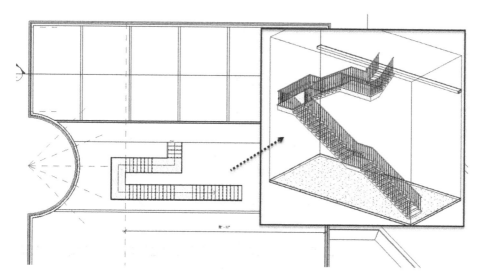

F I G U R E   1 0 . 6 7   The finished stairs

The next step (pun intended) is to add a landing to the bottom of the stairs. This requires creating a family. Be sure you have downloaded the families included with this chapter.

Adding a Custom Landing

You left the 6 5/8″ (152 mm) offset for the bottom tread because you need to introduce your own version of how that bottom tread should look. If you haven't already loaded the family, go to www.wiley.com/go/revit2024ner. From there, browse to the Chapter 10 folder and find the Landing.rfa and Post.rfa files. After you've loaded the families, proceed with these steps:

1. In the Project Browser, go to the Level 1 floor plan.

2. On the Architecture tab, click the Component button.

3. In the Type Selector, find and select the Landing family.

4. As you are inserting the family, press the spacebar three times to rotate the landing into the correct orientation.

5. Place the landing under the last tread at the point shown in Figure 10.68.

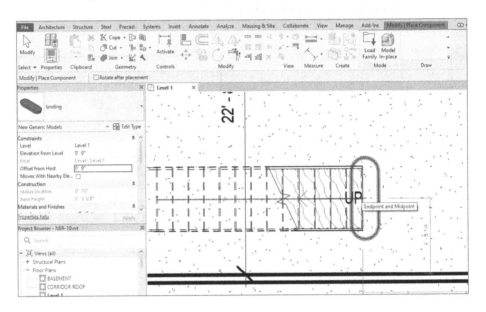

FIGURE 10.68 Placing the landing

6. Press Esc twice.

7. Select the landing.

8. In the Properties dialog, change Tread Material to Cherry.

9. Change Base Material to Mahogany, and click OK.

10. Scroll down and change the Length to 6'–0" (1829 mm). See Figure 10.69.

The next task is to add a post.

Adding a Gooseneck

In this style of railing system, it would be nice to have a gooseneck to catch the railing as it slopes downward and spiral it into the post. Of course, Revit doesn't have families for this built in, but this book does! If you didn't download the post family earlier in this chapter, go to the book's web page, browse to the Chapter 10 folder, and find the Post_up.rfa file. After you download it and load it into the model, follow these steps:

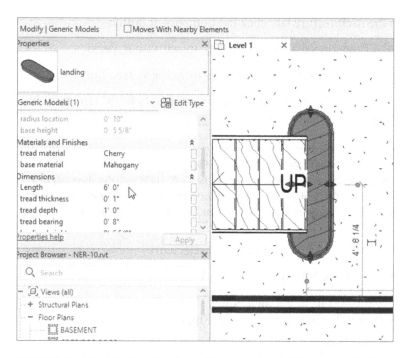

FIGURE 10.69 Changing the landing material and width to match the theme of the staircase

1. In the Project Browser, go to the Level 1 floor plan, and zoom in on the landing area, as shown in Figure 10.70.

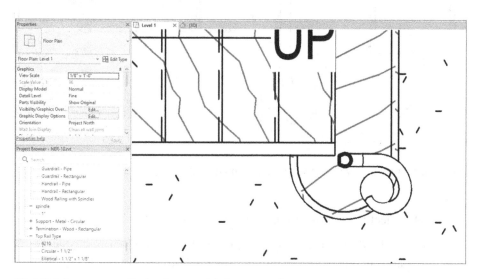

FIGURE 10.70 Placing the post with the gooseneck

2. On the Architecture tab, click the Component button.

3. In the Properties dialog, select Post_up: with Gooseneck.

4. Place it on the landing slightly away from the stair railing.

5. Select the post, and change Offset From Host to **6 5/8"** (152 mm) in the Properties dialog.

 N O T E If the end of the post seems to be clipped in the plan, you need to adjust the view range in the Properties dialog. Right now, the 4'–0" (1200 mm) clip plane may be a tad too low. To fix this, find the View Range row in the Properties dialog and click the Edit button. In the View Range dialog, adjust Cut Plane Offset to **4'–6"** (**1250** mm).

6. Select the post again (if it's not still selected).

7. Click the Move button.

8. Move the post from the midpoint of the post's end to the midpoint of the stair railing's end, as shown in Figure 10.71.

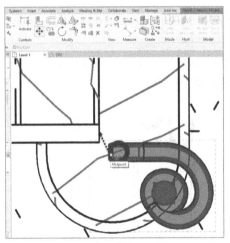
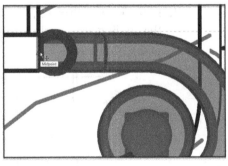

FIGURE 10.71 Moving the post to align with the stair railing

9. Select the post again (if it's not selected already).

10. In the Properties dialog, go to the Materials And Finishes category, and change materials for both the rail and the post to Cherry.

11. Mirror the post to the other railing.

In 3D, your landing should now look like Figure 10.72.

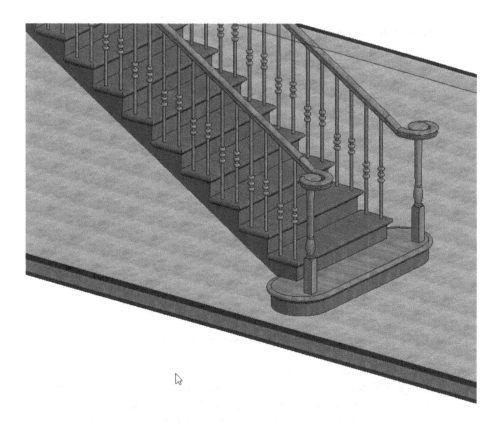

FIGURE 10.72 The completed landing

Adding a Railing to the Landing

Let's add the railing to the Level 3 balcony. Compared to that landing you just did, this is going to be a snap! If you feel as though you have the experience required to add your own landing railing, go ahead and take a shot at it. If not, follow these steps:

1. In the Project Browser, go to Level 3.

2. Zoom in on the stairs.

3. Right-click one of the railings on the stairs, and click Create Similar.

4. Sketch a railing that is 6″ (152 mm) in from the face of the landing, as shown in Figure 10.73.

5. On the Railing panel, click Finish Edit Mode.

6. Repeat the procedure on the other end (see Figure 10.73).

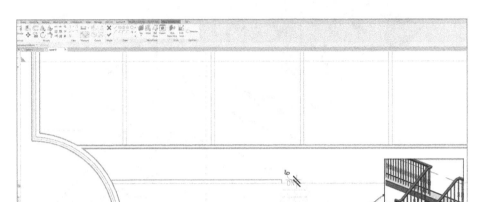

FIGURE 10.73 Adding the railing. This process is becoming old hat!

 NOTE To repeat the procedure on the other end, either you can mirror the railing you just put in and then edit it to reach the far end of the landing, or you can start the Railing command and do it again. I recommend mirroring the railing, selecting the new railing, and then selecting Edit Path from the Modify | Railings tab. You can then grip-edit the right end to meet the wall. This assures you that the railing will be aligned with the railing on the stair.

OK, so we just looked at three different ways to model stairs. Up to this point we have dealt with railings, but we have not considered how we can make custom adjustments to the top rail. The objective of this next series of steps is to add a bottom extension to the railing in our entry area.

1. Go to Level 1 and zoom in on where the corridor and the East part of the building connect at the winding stairs.

2. Add a section at approximately where it is shown in Figure 10.74.

3. Rename the section to RAILING EXTENSION.

4. Double-click the section bubble to open the view.

5. Hover over the top rail on the railing going down the stairs.

6. Press Tab until only the top rail is highlighted. Once it is, select it.

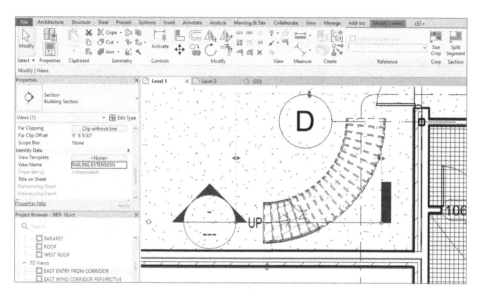

FIGURE 10.74 Cutting a section to access the rail system better.

7. Click the Edit Rail icon, as illustrated in Figure 10.75.

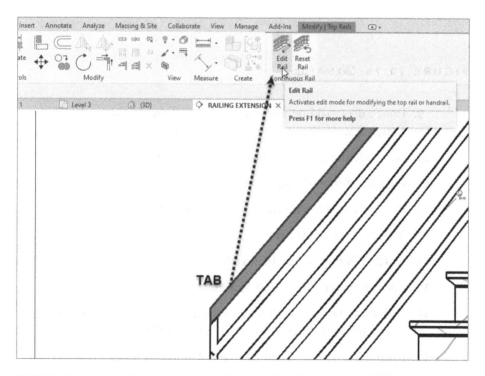

FIGURE 10.75 You can edit the top rail independent of the rest of the railing system.

8. Zoom into the bottom of the rail and click the Edit Path button, as shown in Figure 10.76.

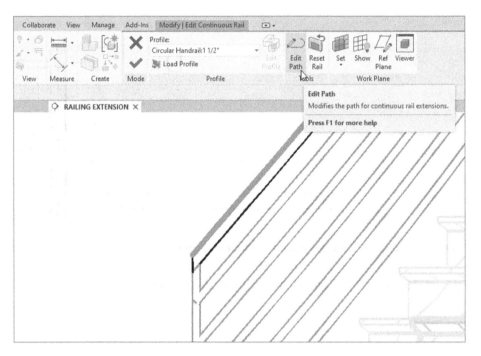

FIGURE 10.76 Click Edit Path.

9. Draw a diagonal line 1'-0" (305 mm), as shown in Figure 10.77. Notice that it will align with the slope of the railing.

10. Complete the rail extension as shown in Figure 10.77.

11. Click the Edit Rail Joins icon.

12. Pick the upper intersection, as shown in Figure 10.78

13. Select Fillet from the menu.

14. Add 3" (76 mm) to the Radius field.

15. Click the green Finish Edit Mode icon.

16. Go back to Level 1 and flip the section so that it is looking at the railing on the other side, as shown in Figure 10.79.

17. Open the section and edit the top rail following steps 9–14. You can do it!

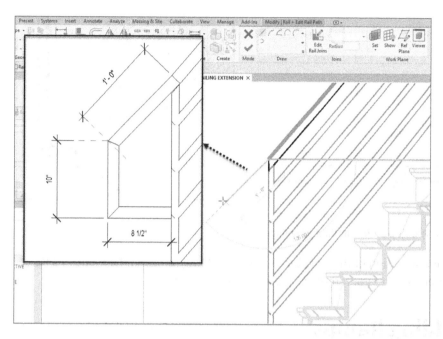

F I G U R E 1 0 . 7 7 Adding a custom rail extension

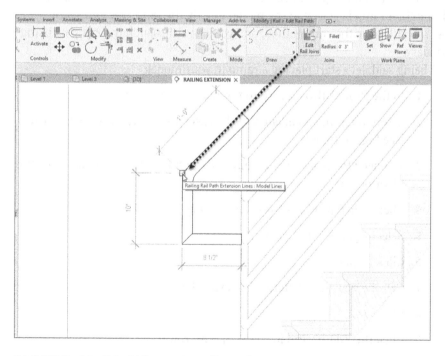

F I G U R E 1 0 . 7 8 Adding a custom rail extension

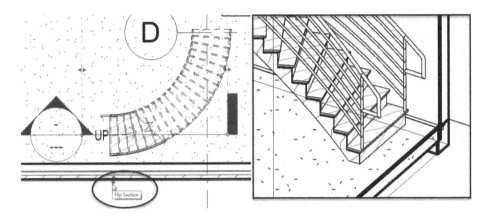

FIGURE 10.79 The finished railings

The last section of this chapter focuses on adding ramps to the model. As far as Revit procedures go, ramps are the kid sister to stairs.

Adding Ramps

When you think of a ramp in Revit, think of a one-tread, one-rise staircase at a 1/12 pitch. A ramp is placed in the model exactly the same way as a set of stairs. You still have the run method, and you can still sketch the ramp by using a boundary.

That being said, let's start placing a ramp in your model:

1. In the Project Browser, go to the Level 1 floor plan.

2. Zoom in on the radial entry of the east wing at grid intersection F-7 (see Figure 10.80).

3. You need to create a flat landing, so, on the Architecture tab, click the Floor button.

4. Click Edit Type in the Properties dialog.

5. Select Generic - 12″ (305 mm) Filled.

6. Click Duplicate.

7. Call the new floor **Exterior Concrete Slab**.

8. Click OK.

9. Click the Edit button in the Structure row.

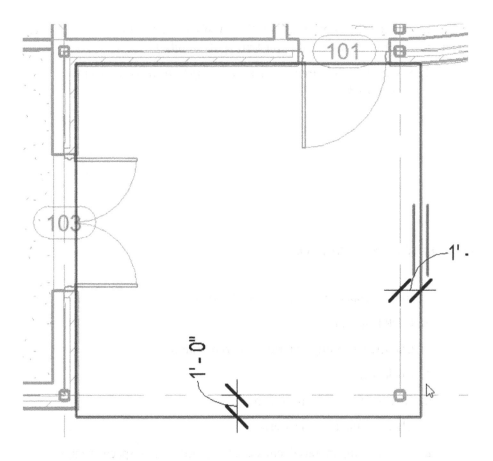

FIGURE 10.80 Sketching the slab perimeter

10. Change Structure [1] Material to Concrete - Cast-In-Place gray.

11. Change Thickness to 6″ (150 mm).

12. Click OK twice to get back to the model.

13. Using the Pick Lines tool, Place the concrete at the points shown in Figure 10.80.

WARNING Make sure you're using Pick Lines mode and are picking the outside face of brick. That extra line represents the water table above this floor's level.

14. When the slab is in place, click the Finish Edit Mode button.

15. Click Don't Attach if you get a prompt asking if you want to attach the walls to the bottom of the floor.

Now you can add the ramp. You'll set the ramp's properties for the top to Level 1, and the bottom will also be at Level 1 but with an offset:

1. On the Architecture tab, click the Ramp button, as shown in Figure 10.81.

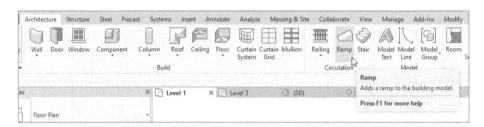

FIGURE 10.81 The Ramp button

2. In the Properties dialog, click Edit Type.

3. Click Duplicate.

4. Call the new ramp **Exterior Concrete Ramp**.

5. Click OK.

6. Give it a **6″ (150 mm)** thickness.

7. Change Function to Exterior.

8. For the ramp material, click the [. . .] button, and specify Concrete - Cast-In-Place Gray, as shown in Figure 10.82.

9. Notice that Maximum Incline Length is set to the ADA standard of 30′–0″ (10000 mm).

10. In the Other category, notice that Ramp Max Slope is set to 1/12.

11. Click OK.

12. In the Properties dialog, set Base Level to Level 1.

13. Set Base Offset to -2′–6″ (-750 mm), as shown in Figure 10.83.

14. Set Top Level to Level 1.

15. Set Width to 5′–0″ (1500 mm) (see Figure 10.83).

16. On the Draw panel, click the Run button.

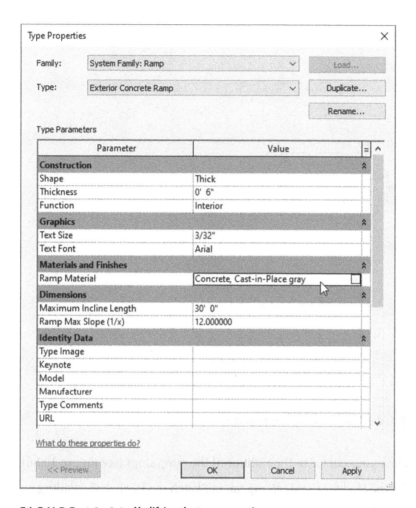

FIGURE 10.82 Modifying the type properties

17. In the model, click the first point for the ramp, similar to the point shown in Figure 10.84. (You have to place the point near the midpoint. Revit does not allow you to snap while in Sketch mode for some annoying reason.)

18. Move your cursor down the view (south) 15′–0″ (4500 mm), as shown in Figure 10.84. (You'll see the temporary dimension.)

19. Pick a point about 6′–0″ (1800 mm) below the end of the ramp, in alignment with the right boundary, as shown in Figure 10.85.

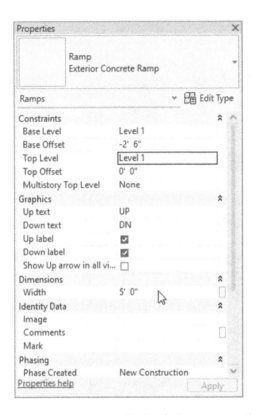

FIGURE 10.83 Setting the instance properties

20. Move your cursor to the right until the ramp stops (see Figure 10.86).

21. On the Modify | Create Ramp tab in Sketch mode, click the Railing Type button.

22. Select Handrail - Pipe in the Railing Type dialog that opens.

23. Click OK.

24. Click Finish Edit Mode.

25. Select the entire ramp (including the railing).

26. Move the ramp so that the midpoint of the top of the ramp meets the midpoint of the landing slab.

It's best if you keep moving your cursor past the end of the ramp. This ensures that the entire ramp has been put in place.

You may notice immediately that the ramp is sloping in the wrong direction. Also, you need to tie the railings into the slab. If you would like to pick around and see how to do these things on your own, go right ahead. Otherwise, follow along:

1. Select the ramp.

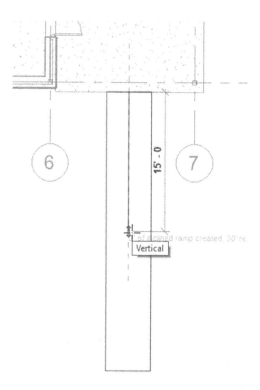

FIGURE 10.84 Pick the first point on the landing, and then move your cursor down 15'–0" (4500 mm).

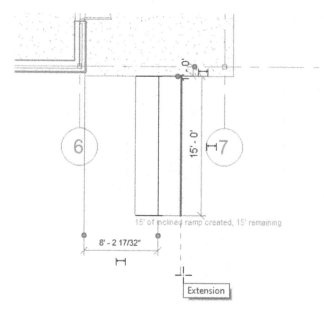

FIGURE 10.85 Pick a point to start the second leg of the ramp and to create the landing.

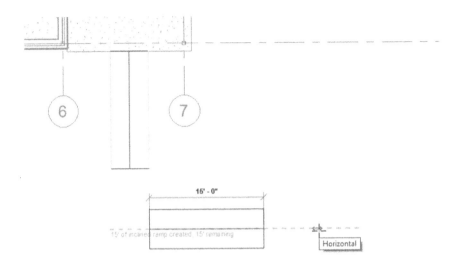

FIGURE 10.86 Pick the last point on the ramp.

2. Pick the small blue arrow—this flips the direction of the ramp.

3. On the Architecture tab, click the Railing button.

4. In the Properties dialog, click Edit Type, change the type to Handrail - Pipe, and click OK.

5. Draw a railing 6″ (152 mm) in from the slab edge, as shown in Figure 10.87.

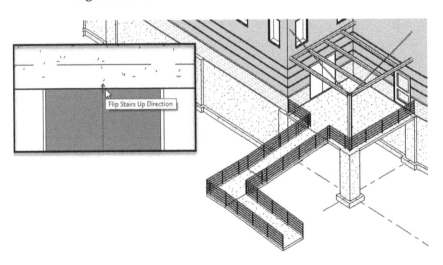

FIGURE 10.87 Adding the railing just as you've been doing this entire chapter

6. Mirror the slab, the ramp, and the railing to the other side of the building, as shown in Figure 10.88. If it gives you a warning that floors overlap, you can ignore it. They really do not.

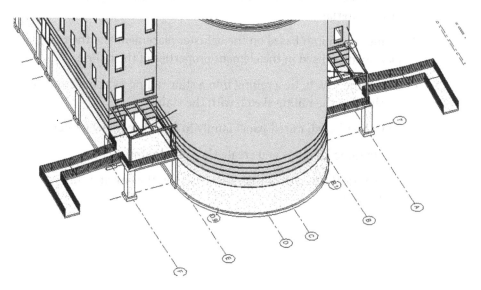

FIGURE 10.88 The two ramps

7. Save the model.

Creating ramps is necessary in almost every project. Some will be easier than others, and at times, they may try your patience. Keep at it, and before long you'll have the experience you need to feel confident in creating ramps.

Are You Experienced?

Now you can. . .

✓ create stairs with the conventional method by using the Run command to generate the height and length you need

✓ create stairs by first laying out the geometry by placing linework in the model and then tracing over the lines with the stair components

✓ determine the difference between the boundary and the riser when you need to sketch the stair profile

✓ load necessary components used to customize stairs and railings such as railing types, spindles, posts, and landings

✓ use separate components and access them in the Project Browser to place materials

✓ configure railings based on the baluster placement and the railing placement as used in the element properties of the railing

✓ determine how to tie a railing into a stair railing by using offsets and by aligning the railing sketch with the stairs

✓ add a line-based, raised-panel family to complete millwork items

✓ create ramp landings and create the actual ramp

✓ determine the length of the ramp based on the rise and run of the slope

CHAPTER 11

Detailing

Simply put, if detailing doesn't work, then you'll use the Autodesk®
Revit® software only as a schematic design application. It's imperative
that you can detail efficiently in Revit. When firms fail in their attempt to
use Revit, in many cases it's because of detailing. In fact, many who have
bought this book may jump straight to this chapter. And why is that? It's
because many people (including me) buy into the concept of really cool 3D
perspectives and one-button modeling.

This chapter covers the following topics:

▶ **Working with line weights**

▶ **Drafting on top of the detail**

▶ **Adding notes**

▶ **Creating blank drafting views**

Working with Line Weights

When you understand Revit, you find out immediately that the real hurdle
in getting it to work lies in the detailing. Sure, you can cut sections and
create callouts, but how do you add that fine level of detailing needed to produce a set of documents that you're willing to stamp and sign? This chapter
addresses the issues surrounding detailing.

Line weights in Revit work two ways. First there are global line weights.
This is what we are going to adjust in the next series of steps. What I mean
by global line weights is the project-wide default line weights when you start
a Revit project. These line weights are object-based. For example, if you
add a door to your model, that door's jamb, panel, and even door swing will
have line weights associated with them consistently throughout the project.
Second, there are view-specific line weights. We call these Visibility Graphics
Overrides. This allows us to change (override) the display of any object on a
view-by-view basis and even on an object-by-object basis. Luckily, we don't
need layers to do this. We will examine Visibility Graphics Overrides thor-
oughly in the next chapter.

To begin, we will examine global line weights, so open the file you've been using to follow along, or go to the book's web page at www.wiley.com/go/revit2024ner. From there, you can browse to the Chapter 11 folder and find the file called NER-11.rvt.

The objective of this procedure is to format some line weights and to see where and how they're displayed by Revit:

1. In the Project Browser, go to Floor Plan Level 1.

2. Make sure the Thin Lines button is not active, as shown in Figure 11.1.

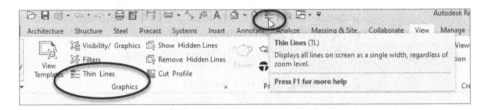

FIGURE 11.1 Turning off Thin Lines makes it so you can see all of your line weights exactly how they will print.

3. Zoom in on the east area of the east building. This is where the radial entry is and the stairs we added in the previous chapter. I'd like to format the line weights of the stairs, the callouts, and the text leaders.

4. On the Manage tab, click the Object Styles button. Figure 11.2 shows the Object Styles dialog.

   Notice this dialog is broken down into tabs across the top. Since there are so many categories in Revit, this makes it easy to find what you are looking for. As we start adding links, file sharing, and design options to Revit, you will start seeing more tabs. For now, we will focus on these four tabs. These categories are embedded into Revit and cannot be changed or added to. Notice the current tab is the Model Objects tab. This covers all the 3D objects in your model.

5. Scroll down to the Stairs category. Notice you can expand that category to "drill" into the overall stairs category. These subcategories will allow us to view the line weights of every aspect of the stairs.

PROJECTION AND CUT

In Revit, we control the line weights two ways. One is "projection" (shown in plan or elevation) and one is "cut" (if we are looking at a view where the objects are being cut, such as in a section).

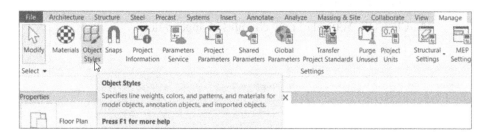

FIGURE 11.2 Finding the Object Styles dialog

> **6.** Change the Projection line weight for Stairs to 3, as shown in Figure 11.3.

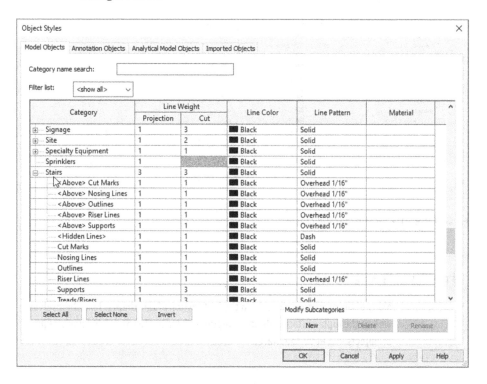

FIGURE 11.3 Finding the Stairs category and changing the Projection line weight to 3

7. Find Floors, and change Cut Line Weight to 4.

8. Find Walls, and change Cut Line Weight to 4.

9. Go to the Annotation Objects tab.

10. Change Callout Boundary to 5.

11. Expand Callout Boundary and change Callout Leader Line to 2. See Figure 11.4.

12. Click OK. Your plan now changes in appearance.

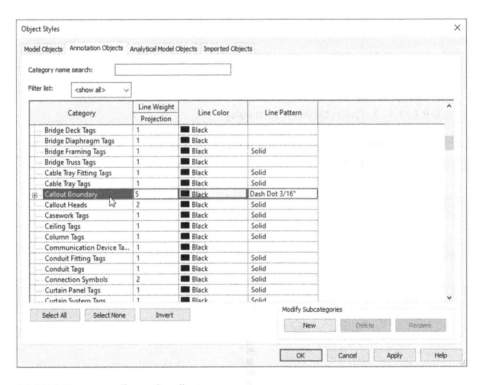

FIGURE 11.4   Change the callout.

IT'S TEMPLATE TIME!

Many of the procedures covered in the first section of this chapter lend themselves well to the topic of standards and templates. You need to change the line weights of objects in a Revit template.

Drafting on Top of the Detail

As mentioned before, Revit provides a good number of 2D details that you can insert at any time. When Revit doesn't have the component you need, you can always create one. It isn't that hard to do.

In this section, you'll physically create a detail. The procedures you'll apply consist of adding detail components, linework, and filled regions and doing some good old-fashioned drafting!

Using Predefined Detail Components

The first procedure focuses on inserting predefined detail components. The great thing about this is that you'll do nothing you haven't done repeatedly throughout this book—it's just a matter of finding the right button to get started:

1. Open the section called Roof Taper Section.

2. Go to the Annotate tab, and in the Detail panel, click Component ➤ Detail Component, as shown in Figure 11.5.

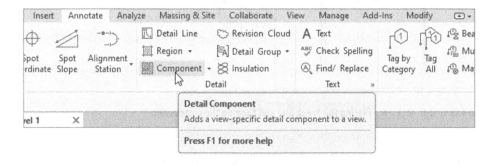

FIGURE 11.5 The Annotate tab

3. Click Load Family.

4. Browse to the Detail Items directory. (It's located in the US directory.)

5. Open the Div 01-General folder.

6. Click the file called Break Line.rfa.

7. Click Open.

8. In the Type Selector of the Properties dialog, be sure Break Line is selected, as shown in Figure 11.6.

9. Press the spacebar twice. (This flips the break line into the correct orientation.)

10. Pick a point like the one shown in Figure 11.6.

11. If some of the wall is peaking through the bottom, click on the break line and drag the bottom grip to the edge of the crop region.

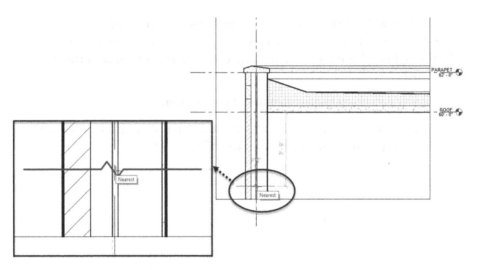

FIGURE 11.6 Placing the break line and flipping the component

The next step is simply to start drafting. As mentioned earlier, you're going to get only so far with 3D modeling before you must take matters into your own hands and draft. You can approach this in Revit by taking the parts of the detail you want to keep and hiding the rest. After you hide portions of the detail, it's time to begin adding your own ingredients, such as detail components and lines.

THIS FLIPPIN' BREAK LINE IS BACKWARD!

If you forgot to flip the break line as you were inserting it and it's masking the wrong region, that's OK. Press Esc, and then select the break line. Now you can press the spacebar twice to flip the break line, as shown in the following image:

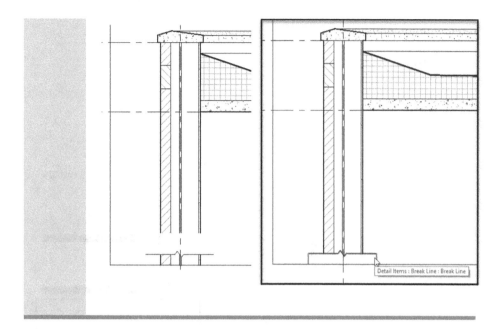

Detail Items : Break Line : Break Line

Materials

Materials play an important part of Revit. We think of materials as a tool for rendering. Although this is true, it's not the full use of materials in Revit. Materials allow us to specify hatch patterns when we cut sections. By making a few material edits, we can gain control over how the out-of-the-box sections look! Let's see how we can edit materials to behave correctly in Revit.

1. On the Manage tab, click the Materials button, as shown in Figure 11.7.

2. Type **Brick** in the search panel.

3. Select Brick, Common.

4. For Cut Pattern, Foreground, click into where it says Diagonal Up and change it to <None> after the word Pattern. Change the background pattern to Diagonal Up.

5. Click OK.

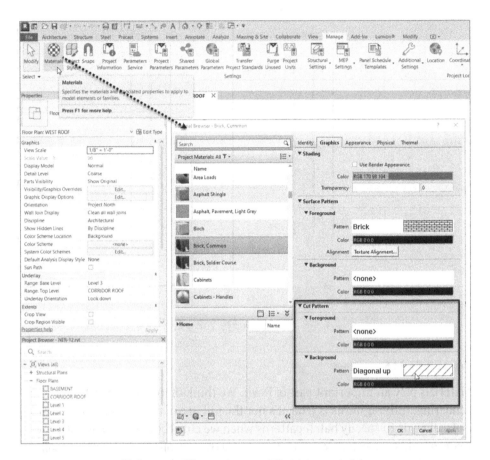

FIGURE 11.7 We have two different places to add hatch to a material

6. In the Roof Taper Section properties, click Visibility/Graphics Overrides, as shown in Figure 11.8.

7. Find and select Walls.

8. For Cut Patterns, click the Override button.

9. Deselect Background Visible for Pattern Overrides. The reason we want to do this is because we want to draft over the bricks without having that annoying hatch in our way (see Figure 11.8).

10. Click OK.

It's Just This View!

When you go to Visibility Graphics Overrides, notice that the top of the dialog says Visibility Graphics Overrides for view: ROOF TAPER SECTION. That means any override you perform modifies *only* that view. The rest of the model, and every other view, does not change.

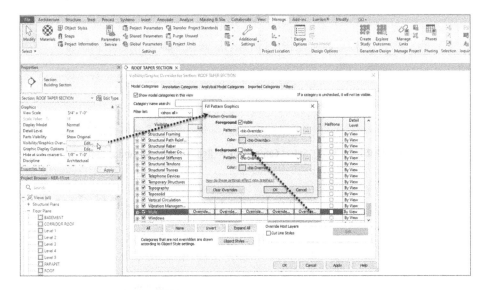

FIGURE 11.8 Choosing which hatch to show

Repeating Details

Revit has a technique that allows you to add a detail component as a group. You do this by basically drawing a line; Revit then adds the detail in an array based on the points you pick.

To learn how to add a repeating detail, follow this procedure:

1. In the Detail panel of the Annotate tab, select Component ➤ Repeating Detail Component, as shown in Figure 11.9.

2. In the Properties dialog, choose Repeating Detail: Brick from the Type Selector.

3. Pick the point labeled 1 in Figure 11.10.

4. After you pick the first point, move your cursor down the view.

5. Pick the endpoint 8″ (203 mm) down, as shown in Figure 11.10, so that three copies of the brick section are placed.

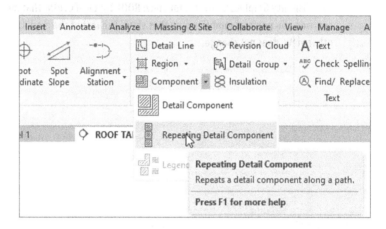

FIGURE 11.9 Select Component ➤ Repeating Detail Component.

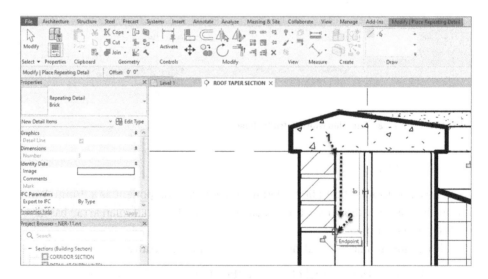

FIGURE 11.10 The first repeating detail

Let's keep going with the repeating detail. The problem you're facing is that you need to deal with the soldier course in the exterior wall. You can add that in a moment. Right now, complete the brick down past the break line.

If you feel as though you're getting the hang of adding the repeating brick detail, go ahead and add the second repeating detail. If you would like some instruction, follow along:

1. Click the Component ➤ Repeating Detail Component button in the Detail panel of the Annotate tab.

2. Pick point 1, as shown in Figure 11.11.

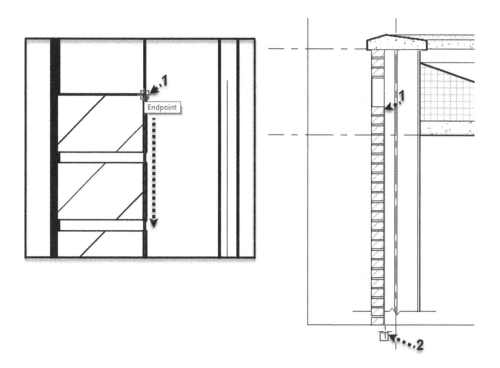

FIGURE 11.11 Picking two points

3. Press the spacebar.

4. Pull the cursor straight down, and pick point 2 (see Figure 11.11). Make sure you pick the second point well past the break line or the brick will stop short.

5. Press Esc twice. Look at Figure 11.12. Does your detail look the same?

6. If the repeating detail is obscuring the break line, select the break line.

Remember, you can add a second repeating brick detail by right-clicking the first one you added and selecting Create Similar.

7. In the Arrange panel, click the Bring To Front button, as shown in Figure 11.12. The repeating detail is now behind the break line.

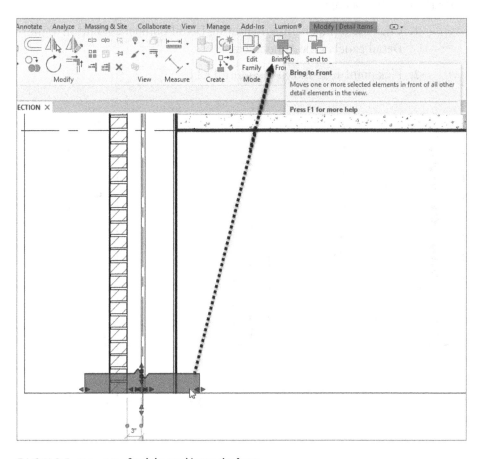

FIGURE 11.12 Send the masking to the front

The next step is to add the soldier course. You'll do this the same way you added the break line. In this respect, Revit offers a good library broken down into the Construction Specifications Institute (CSI) format.

To add the soldier course, follow along:

1. In the Detail panel of the Annotate tab, click the Component ➤ Detail Component button.

2. In the Type Selector in the Properties dialog, select Brick Standard: Soldier & Plan.

3. Press the spacebar until it's flipped as shown in Figure 11.13, and place the new detail component into the model as shown.

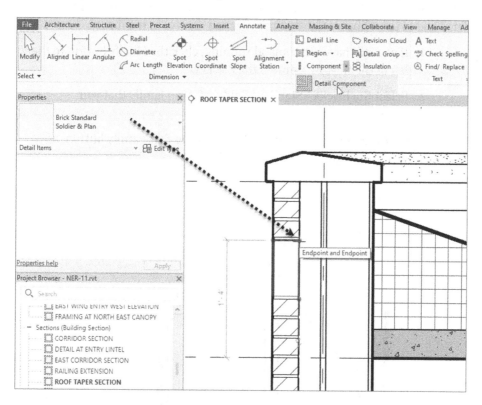

FIGURE 11.13 Placing the new detail component

 TIP If you haven't noticed, when you click the Component ➤ Repeating Detail Component button, you always go to the Families/Detail Items directory in the Project Browser. This may go without saying, but it took a few months for me to understand this simple concept.

Well, the soldier course is in place, but that fat line weight is horrendous. It would be nice if everything that came out of the Revit box looked nice and met your specifications—but alas, that isn't the case. Let's modify this component to make it presentable.

Modifying a Detail Component

Right about now is when every CAD/BIM manager around the globe raises an eyebrow—for good reason. Revit allows you to modify a component by actually opening the file! But don't worry; you have to issue a Save As command to save the detail.

The objectives of the following procedure are to create a texture on the brick detail and to use a line weight that the user can control in the model:

1. If you still have a command running, click the Modify button to the left of the Ribbon, or press the Esc key.

2. Select the Bricks - Standard Soldier & Plan family that you just placed.

3. On the Modify | Detail Items tab, click the Edit Family button, as shown in Figure 11.14.

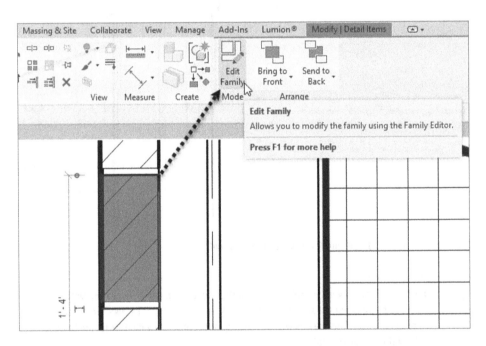

FIGURE 11.14 Open the family for editing after selecting the detail component.

4. The next dialog may ask you if you want to open this file to edit it. Click Yes if you get that message.

The detail component family is now open. It's time to operate, Doctor. The next set of procedures will focus on modifying the linework of the brick and adding what is called a *filled region*.

Modifying Filled Regions

A *filled region* is similar to a masking region in that you apply both in the same manner. A filled region, however, contains a hatch pattern that is visible when the region is completed. This is how you hatch in Revit. It takes the place of the conventional hatch command found in Autodesk AutoCAD® and MicroStation.

The goal of the next procedure is to modify the filled region that makes up the brick. You'll also use the region's outline to define the perimeter and the texture of the brick itself:

1. Click the blue File tab, and select Save As ➤ Family.

2. Call the new family **Brick - Soldier**.

3. Click the Family Types button, as shown in Figure 11.15.

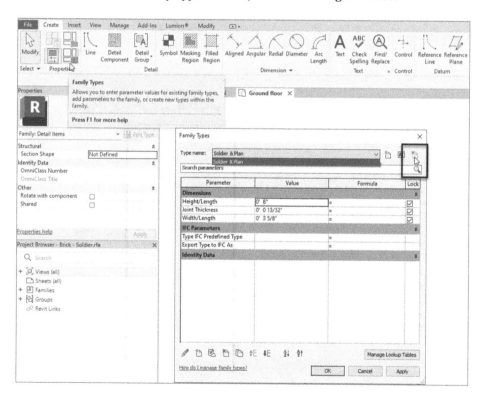

FIGURE 11.15 Cleaning out the extra types

4. In the Type Name menu, click the drop-down and delete the other types other than Soldier & Plan by clicking the Delete button at the right in the dialog.

5. Click OK.

6. Select the line that is hovering over the top of the brick, and mirror it to the bottom using the Mirror - Draw Axis command (DM) so that you have a line above and a line below the brick, as shown in Figure 11.16.

7. Select one of the heavy lines that form the outline of the brick (see Figure 11.16). Revit indicates that this is a filled region, as revealed in the tooltip that appears when you hover your pointer over one of the boundaries.

8. In the Mode panel of the Modify | Detail Items tab, click the Edit Boundary button (see Figure 11.16).

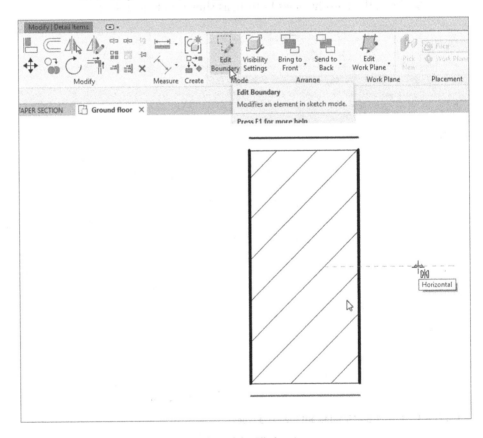

FIGURE 11.16 Editing the boundary of the filled region

9. Delete the two thick, vertical lines.

10. In the Draw panel, select the Line button, as shown in Figure 11.17.

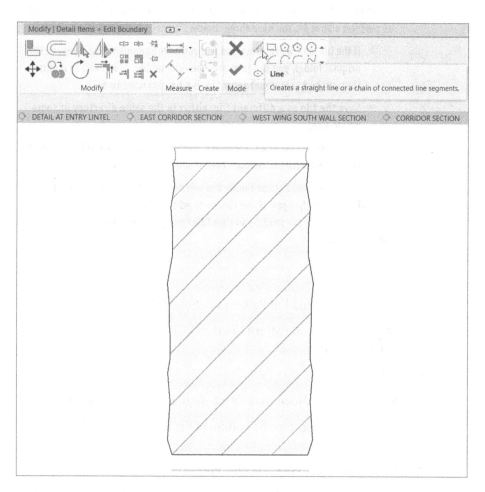

FIGURE 11.17 Adding a texture to the brick family

11. In the Line Style panel that appears, select Detail Items.

12. Draw a series of jagged lines on the right and left of the brick, as shown in Figure 11.17.

13. After you finish sketching the texture, click Edit Type.

WHERE SHOULD YOU SAVE THIS?

When you click the Save icon, Revit doesn't save over the original file. You're forced to perform a Save As. You have three choices:

▶ If the file isn't write-protected and you have administrative access to the original folder, you can save over the original file. (Do I need to mention that you had better make sure this is what you want to do?)

▶ Save the file as a different file, either in the same directory or some-where else.

▶ Don't save the file at all, and load it into your project. Revit will still update the project with the changes even if you don't save the family file.

You can even close out of the family file and not save any changes. Your model will still hold the changes. If you choose to edit the file at a later date, you can select the family in the model and click Edit Family. Revit will open a copy of the modified family.

14. Change Background Fill Pattern to <Solid Fill>.

15. Change Background Pattern Color to RGB 223-223-223, as shown in Figure 11.18.

16. Click OK.

17. Click Finish Edit Mode. Your brick should resemble Figure 11.19.

Next, you'll add a mortar joint to the bottom of the brick. You simply add drafting lines:

1. On the Create tab, click the Line button.

2. In the Draw panel, click the Start-End-Radius Arc button.

3. Draw two arcs to the left and right of the top of the brick, as shown in Figure 11.20.

4. Click Save.

5. Click Load Into Project And Close, as shown in Figure 11.20.

6. Make sure you have the Roof Taper Section open (Revit may have thrown you into another view).

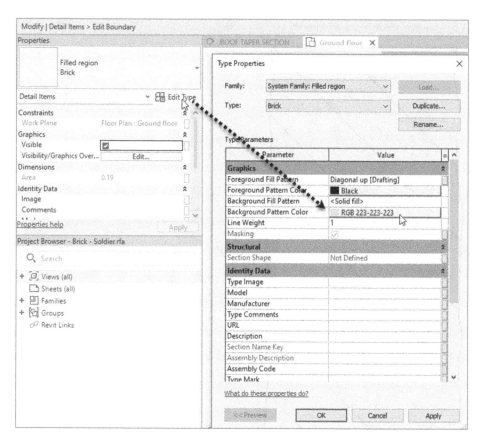

FIGURE 11.18 Changing the filled region

 N O T E By putting all the lines on the Detail Items line type, you tell Revit that you don't want to specify a line weight here. Rather, Revit should let you specify the line weight by changing the Detail Items in the Object Properties dialog after you load the detail back into the model.

7. Pick a spot and place the new soldier.

8. Select the smooth, boring, existing soldier.

9. In the Type Selector, change it to Brick - Soldier: Soldier & Plan.

10. Delete the extra brick. Your wall should look like Figure 11.21.

11. Save the model.

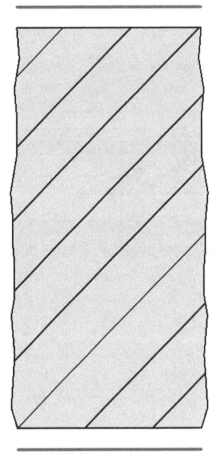

FIGURE 11.19 The finished soldier

The next group of procedures focuses on editing the bricks used in the repeating detail. You certainly want the same face texture, and it would be nice if there was a mortar joint between them.

Before you modify the bricks, let's explore how a repeating detail is created. The objective of the next procedure is to discover how a repeating detail works and how you can create a new one:

1. Make sure you're in the detail called Roof Taper Section.

2. Select one of the repeating details, as shown in Figure 11.22.

3. In the Properties dialog, click Edit Type, as shown at the upper left in Figure 11.22.

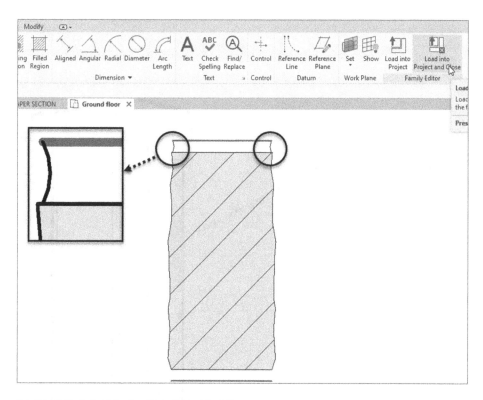

FIGURE 11.20 Load Into Project And Close

4. Click into the detail Value list. Every detail component listed in your model is available. The detail component being used here is Brick Standard: Running Section. This is the profile family we want to pretty up.

TAB, TAB, TAB!

It is sometimes difficult to select items once they become overlapped by another object. To select the running brick repeating detail, you may have to hover over the element and press Tab multiple times until you can grab it.

You can change the spacing and the patterns of how the repeating detail will perform.

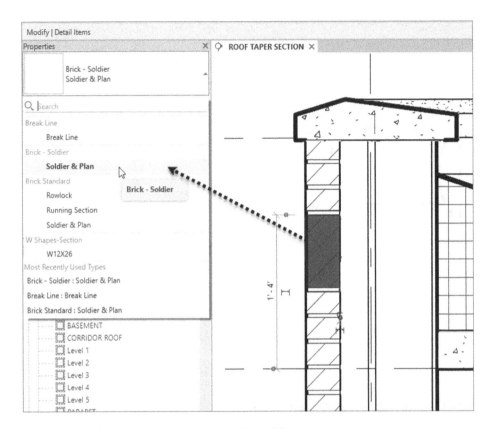

FIGURE 11.21 The new soldier brick in the model

   5. Click Cancel.

The next objective is to modify the specific detail component that the repeating detail is using. To do so, you must add an instance of the detail component (in this case, Brick Standard: Running Section) and then edit the family. After you load it back into the model, the repeating detail will be up-to-date.

If you would like to give it a shot and do it on your own, go ahead. If you would rather have some guidance, follow along:

   1. In the Detail panel of the Annotate tab, click the Component ≻ Detail Component button.

   2. In the Type Selector in the Properties dialog, pick the Brick Standard: Running Section detail component. (Remember, this was the component that you discovered the repeating detail was using.)

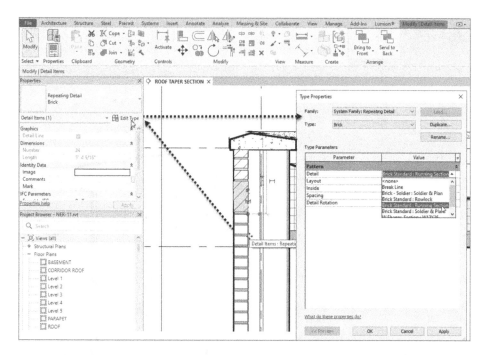

FIGURE 11.22 Click the Edit Type button after selecting one of the brick repeating details.

3. Place the detail component off to the side of the wall, as shown in Figure 11.23.

4. Press Esc twice, or click Modify.

5. Select the Brick Standard: Running Section that you just inserted.

6. In the Mode panel, click the Edit Family button.

7. Select the filled region.

8. In the Mode panel, click Edit Boundary.

9. Delete the right and left thick lines.

10. In the Draw panel, click the Line button.

11. In the Type Selector in the Properties dialog, click Detail Items.

12. Draw the jagged lines on both sides, as shown in Figure 11.24.

13. Click Finish Edit Mode on the Mode panel.

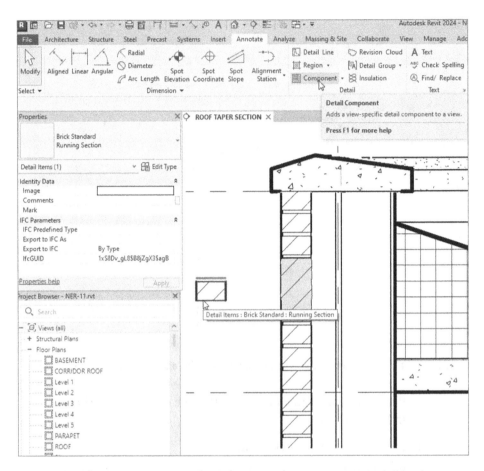

FIGURE 11.23 Place the Brick Standard: Running Section detail component off to the side. You'll delete this occurrence of the component later.

14. On the Create tab, click the Line button.

15. In the Draw panel, click the Start-End-Radius Arc button.

16. In the Subcategory panel, be sure Detail Items is chosen from the Type Selector list.

17. Draw an arc on both sides of the brick (see Figure 11.24).

18. When you're finished, save the new brick as **Brick Standard**. You can also find this brick on the book's web page in the Chapter 11 folder. It's called Brick Standard.rfa.

19. In the Family Editor panel, click Load Into Project And Close.

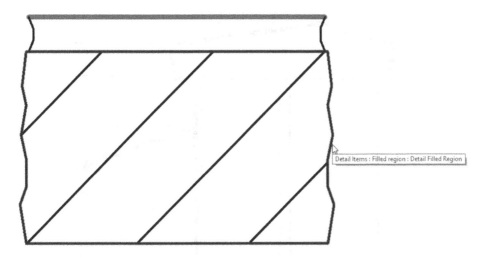

Detail Items : Filled region : Detail Filled Region

FIGURE 11.24 Draw the textured face while you're in Edit mode for the filled region. Draw the arcs for the mortar joint using lines.

20. You will get a "Family Already Exists" dialog. Select Overwrite the existing version.

21. Delete the stray detail component you placed. (You were using it only for access to the family.)

Compare your detail to the detail in Figure 11.25.

Notice the heavy lines on the outside and the inside of the brick façade. These are part of the wall in the model. The bad thing is, they are in the way. The good thing is, we can make them disappear in this view by simply using the Linework tool. Let's do that now.

1. On the Modify tab, click the Linework button, as shown in Figure 11.26.

2. In the Line Style menu, select <Invisible Lines> (see Figure 11.27).

3. Now start selecting the lines to be invisible in this view, as shown in Figure 11.27. You will have to select the lines multiple times to remove them completely.

Next, you'll anchor this façade back to the wall. You need to add two things: a structural relief angle above the soldier course and a brick tieback to a lower course. Follow along:

1. On the Annotate tab, click the Component ➤ Detail Component button.

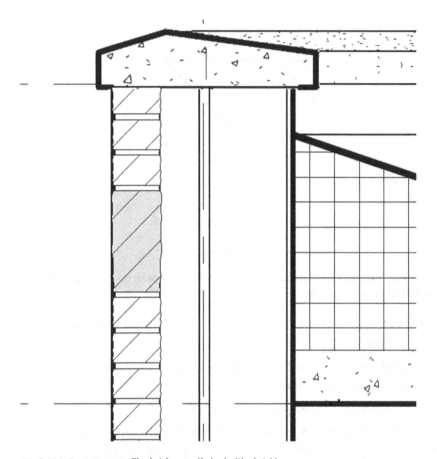

F I G U R E 1 1 . 2 5   The brick actually looks like brick!

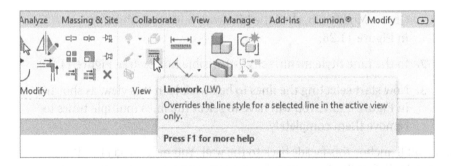

F I G U R E 1 1 . 2 6   We can override the display of the lines in the model with the Linework tool.

2. In the Mode panel, click the Load Family button.

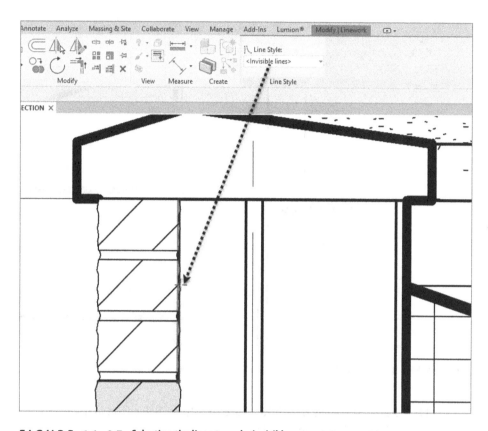

FIGURE 11.27 Selecting the lines to make invisible

3. Open the Detail items folder.

4. Select Div 05-Metals.

5. Select 051200-Structural Steel Framing.

6. Double-click the file AISC Angle Shapes-Section.rfa.

7. In the Type list, select L6×4×5/16 (152×102×8).

8. Click OK. You'll have to use the spacebar and flip controls to rotate and flip the instance. You may need to place the instance in order to use the flip controls.

9. Place it into the model, as shown in Figure 11.28.

10. Press Esc twice, or click Modify.

    Of course, the line weight is basically a blob, so let's take a look at object styles.

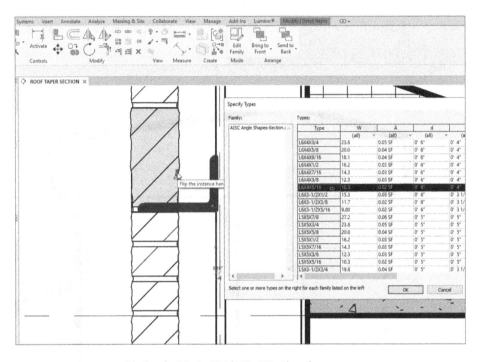

FIGURE 11.28 Placing the L6×4×5/16 (152×102×8) angle

11. I think the heavy detail items are too thick. Select the Manage tab, and then click Object Styles.

12. Expand Detail Items and change Heavy Lines to 3, as shown in Figure 11.29.

The next step is to find a fastener to anchor the angle back to the wall's substrate. Since this is a metal stud wall, we will need to add some lag screws that fasten into wood blocking that will be installed between the metal studs.

1. On the Annotate tab, click the Component button.

2. Click Load Family.

3. Browse to Detail Items - Div 06-Wood And Plastic - 060500-Common Work Results For Wood Plastics And Composites - 060523-Fastenings - Lag Screws-Side.rfa.

4. Insert two lag screws into the angle, as shown in Figure 11.30.

5. Press Esc twice.

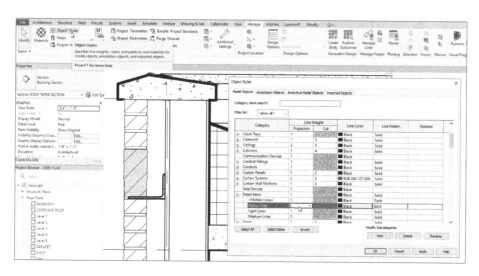

FIGURE 11.29 The angle in place and looking like an angle

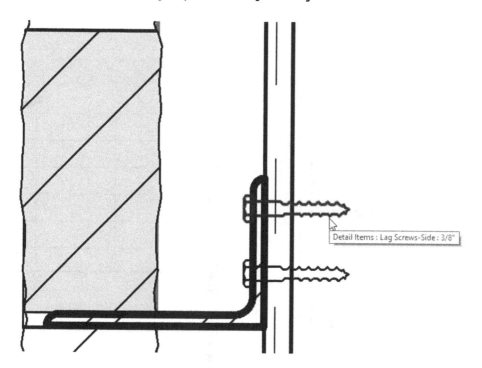

FIGURE 11.30 Inserting the lag bolt

Now you'll add a corrugated wall tie to the brick below the soldier course. Because the brick is a pretty good distance away from the wall, you first need to add some wood blocking to the model:

1. On the Insert tab, click the Load Family button.

2. Go to the Detail Items folder.

3. Select Div 06-Wood And Plastic.

4. Select 061100-Wood Framing.

5. Click the file Nominal Cut Lumber-Section.rfa.

6. Select the 2×6 (51×152) type, and click OK.

7. Select the Annotate tab, click the Component ➤ Detail Component button, and place the 2×6 (51×152) into the wall, as shown in Figure 11.31. Also, place one behind the lag screws.

8. Select the blocking the lag screws are anchored into and click the Send to Back button. See Figure 11.31.

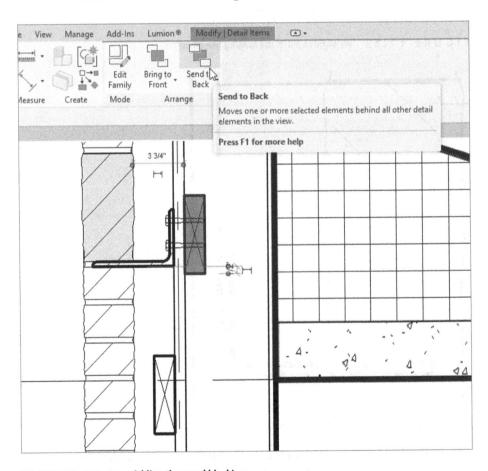

FIGURE 11.31 Adding the wood blocking

The next step is to add the corrugated wall tie. You'll do this in the same manner, except that it's located in a different directory:

1. On the Insert tab, click the Load Family button.

2. Go to the Detail Items folder.

3. Select Div 04-Masonry.

4. Select 040500-Common Work Results For Masonry.

5. Select 040519-Masonry Anchorage And Reinforcing.

6. Select the file called Corrugated Wall Tie-Section.rfa.

7. Use the Detail Component button to place the wall tie into your model, as shown in Figure 11.32.

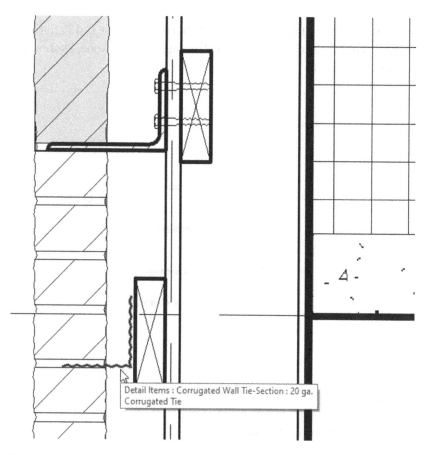

Detail Items : Corrugated Wall Tie-Section : 20 ga. Corrugated Tie

FIGURE 11.32 Placing the corrugated wall tie

When you're drafting over a true section of your model, it's always good to try to use as much of the graphical information from the actual model as possible. For example, the 3/4″ (16 mm) void you see the bolt going through is actually 3/4″ (16 mm) plywood sheathing. For some reason, the default plywood material has its cut pattern set to None. Let's fix this:

1. Select the wall.

2. Click Edit Type.

3. Click the Edit button in the Structure row.

4. Click into the Material column in row 5. It's the substrate row, and the material is –Plywood, Sheathing.

5. When you click –Plywood, Sheathing, you see a tiny [. . .] button. Click it.

6. On the Graphics tab, click into the Pattern field in the Cut Pattern Background category, and change the pattern to Plywood, as shown in Figure 11.33.

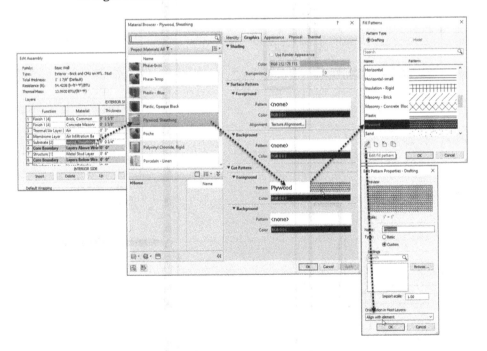

FIGURE 11.33 Show us your plywood!

7. Double-click the plywood pattern (see Figure 11.33 for the location of the cursor).

8. Click the Edit button (it looks like a little pencil).

9. Select the Align With Element drop-down for the Orientation In Host Layers: field.

10. Click OK five times to get back to the model. Your wall should look like Figure 11.34.

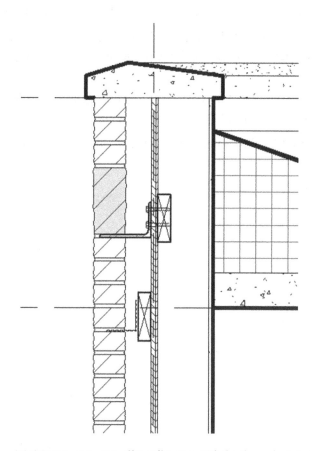

FIGURE 11.34 The wall section with the plywood substrate

 N O T E It's a great idea to plot this detail right now. Although Revit does a nice job of letting you see the contrasting line weights on the screen, it may be a different story at the plotter. Do yourself a favor, and make sure this is the line weight you want.

So what makes a Medium Line medium and a Thin Line thin? This is a part of Revit over which you need to have full control. After all, your biggest challenge will be getting your plotted sheets to match your old CAD-plotted sheets. Specifying line weights is crucial.

Specifying Drafting Line Weights

In CAD, you wouldn't dare draw even a single line if you didn't know the proper layer on which it was being drafted, right? Why should Revit be any different?

The objective of the next procedure is to investigate where the line weights are stored and how they relate to the lines you're drawing:

1. On the Manage tab, choose Additional Settings ➤ Line Styles.

2. In the Line Styles dialog, expand the Lines category by clicking the plus sign next to Lines. Some of the line styles were generated in AutoCAD.

3. Click into the Wide Lines category, and change the value from 5 to 4, as shown in Figure 11.35.

4. Click OK. Wide Lines in all project views will now show the new line weight.

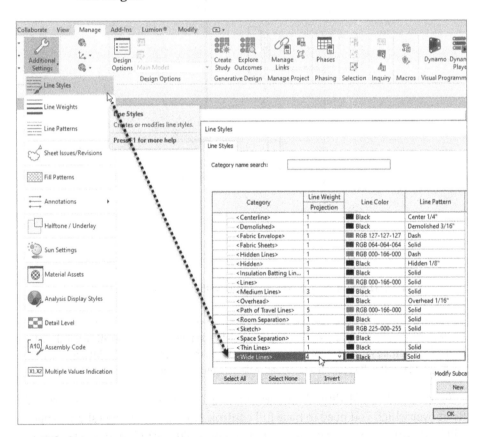

FIGURE 11.35 Changing Wide Lines from 5 to 4

The next item to tackle is the fact that this detail looks naked without any text or dimensions added to it. Although you've applied both of these items in past chapters, you need to use them because they're relevant to detailing.

WHAT DO 5 AND 4 REPRESENT?

In Revit, line weights are sorted from thinnest to heaviest. You can add additional line weights, but I recommend that you stick to the 16 available. To see where these settings are stored, choose Additional Settings ➤ Line Weights. In the Line Weights dialog, the numbers 1 through 16 are listed. These numbers represent what you see in the Line Styles dialog. Also notice that the thicker line weights degrade in thickness as the scale is reduced (see the following graphic):

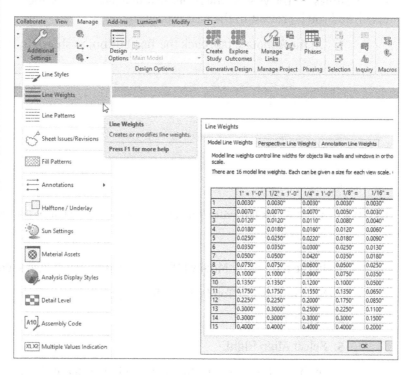

Adding Notes

In Revit, adding notes to a section can take on a whole different meaning than in CAD.

Or, if you wish, adding notes to a detail can be exactly as it was back in CAD. Sometimes, sticking to the tried-and-true method isn't such a bad thing.

The goal of the next set of procedures is to add notes by simply leadering in some text.

Adding Textual Notations

We're duplicating efforts with text to drive home the fact that Revit lets you add text regardless of the view or the scale. Text in a plan is the same as text in a detail, and you'll prove it in the next procedure:

1. On the Annotate tab, click the Text button, as shown in Figure 11.36.

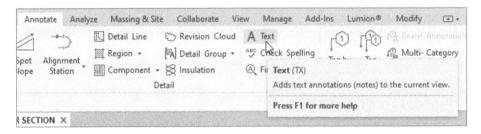

FIGURE 11.36 The Text button in the Annotate tab is also found on the Quick Access toolbar.

2. In the temporary Modify | Place Text panel, select Two segments.

3. Select Leader at Top Left and Top Right.

4. Select Top Align.

5. Select Align Right.

6. In the section, pick the first point of the leader at the top of the brick tie detail (shown in Figure 11.37).

7. Pick the second point above and to the left of the first point (shown in Figure 11.37).

8. Pick the third point for the second segment (as shown in Figure 11.37).

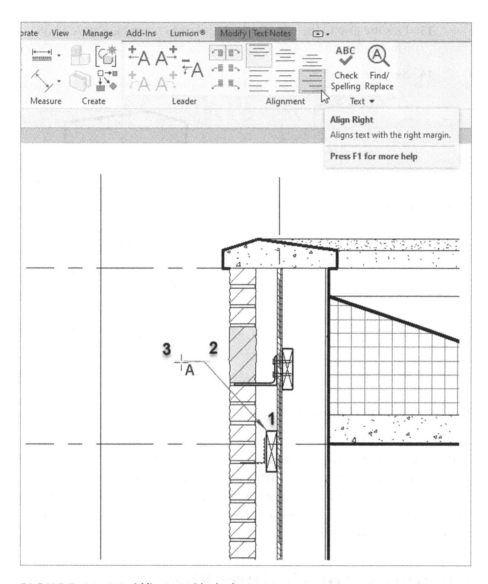

FIGURE 11.37 Adding text with a leader

9. Type the note CORRUGATED BRICK TIE ON 2X6 BLOCKING.

10. Click off the text into another part of the model, and your text justifies to the leader.

11. Press Esc twice.

12. Select the text.

13. Pick the grip to the left, and drag the box to resemble Figure 11.38. The text wraps.

14. Save the model.

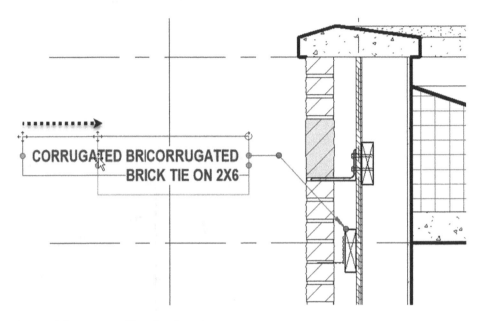

FIGURE 11.38 Wrapping the text

These steps are the most common procedure for adding detail to a model. In other words, take what you can from the model, and then add linework and detail components to the view. However, eventually you'll find yourself in a situation where you would rather draft your detail from scratch. You can do this as well, as you'll see in the next section.

Creating Blank Drafting Views

Over the years, Revit has been labeled as a "poor drafting application." I concede that AutoCAD is a better drafting program. And if all you do is 2D linework, perhaps stick with AutoCAD. But you're learning Revit, so let's see how Revit can be a very good drafting application when given the chance. The only challenge is to figure out where to start!

The objective of the next procedure is to create a blank view and then simply learn how to draw lines:

1. On the View tab, click the Drafting View button, as shown in Figure 11.39.

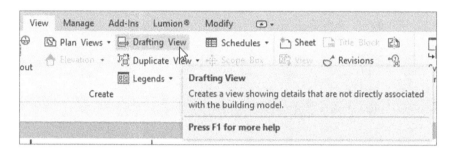

FIGURE 11.39 Click the Drafting View button on the View tab.

2. In the New Drafting View dialog, name the new view **TYPICAL WALL TERMINATION**.

3. Change the scale to 3/4″ = 1′–0″ (1:20 for metric users). See Figure 11.40.

4. Click OK.

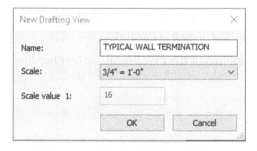

FIGURE 11.40 Changing the view name and scale

You're now in a completely blank canvas. Anything you draw here is truly drafting, and it isn't tied back to the model at all.

The objective of the next procedure is to start adding lines and more detail components. The item you'll draft is a detail showing a flexible top track of a metal-stud partition:

1. On the Annotate tab, click the Detail Line button.

2. In the Properties dialog, click Medium Lines.

3. Draw a horizontal line about 4′–7″ (1375 mm) long, as shown in Figure 11.41.

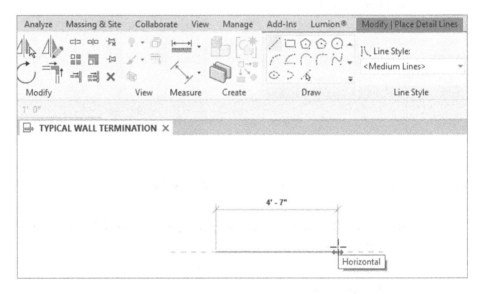

FIGURE 11.41 Drawing a detail line approximately 4′–7″ (1375 mm)

4. With the Detail Line command still running, change the Offset setting in the Options bar to 8″ (200 mm).

5. Using the two endpoints of the first line, draw another line below.

GET DOWN THERE

Remember, if your line is above the first line you drew, press the spacebar to flip the line down below the first.

6. In the Draw panel, click the Pick Lines icon.

7. Again, on the Options bar, change Offset to 1 1/2″ (38 mm).

8. Offset the bottom line down 1 1/2″ (38 mm). Your detail should look like Figure 11.42.

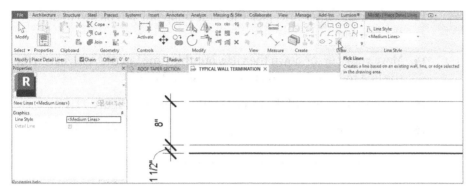

FIGURE 11.42   Using Pick Lines and adding an offset of 1 1/2" (38 mm)

9. With the Detail Line command still running, click the Line button and set the Offset value to 3" (75 mm).

10. On the Options bar, make sure the Chain option is deselected.

11. For the first point of the line, pick the midpoint of the bottom line, as shown in Figure 11.43.

12. For the second point of the line, pick a point about 1'–9" (525 mm), straight down, as shown in Figure 11.43. (This draws a line offset 3" [75 mm] to the right from the center of the line above.)

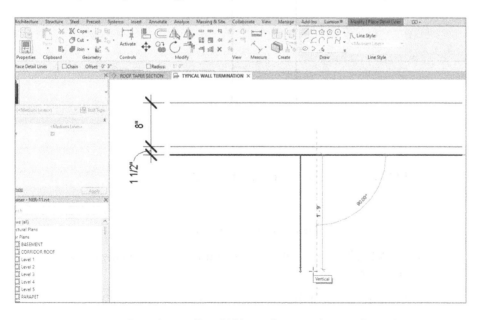

FIGURE 11.43   By setting an offset of 3" (75 mm), you can draw two lines using a common centerline.

13. To draw the other line, pick the same midpoint you picked to draw the first line.

14. Move your cursor down the view, but this time tap the spacebar to flip the line to the other direction (see Figure 11.44).

15. Draw another line of the same length (again, see Figure 11.44).

16. Click Modify.

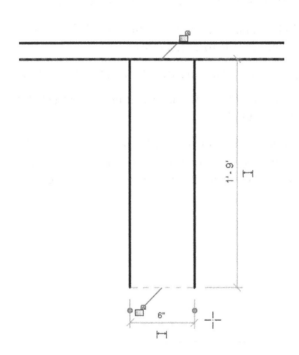

FIGURE 11.44 The detail up to this point

17. Compare your lines with the lines in Figure 11.44.

18. Click the Trim/Extend To Corner button on the Modify tab, as shown in Figure 11.45.

19. Trim the edges of the top of the wall (see Figure 11.45).

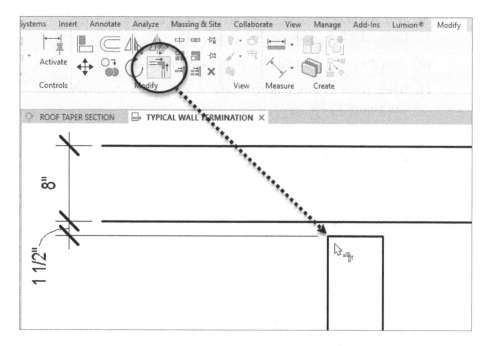

FIGURE 11.45 Trimming the corners

The next step is to add the track to the bottom of the floor. You'll do this by creating three wide lines. The trick is to do a good amount of offsetting. If you want to explore and try the procedure on your own, look ahead to Figure 11.46 and try to match it dimensionally. Remember, you're using wide lines for the track.

If you would rather have guidelines, follow these steps:

1. On the Annotate tab, click the Detail Line button.

2. In the Properties dialog, click Wide Lines.

3. In the Draw panel, click the Pick Lines button.

4. On the Options bar, set Offset to 3/8″ (9 mm).

5. Offset the bottom of the floor down 3/8″ (9 mm).

6. With the Detail Line command still running, make sure the Offset is still set to 3/8″ (9 mm).

7. Offset the left and the right lines, as shown in Figure 11.46.

8. Offset the bottom of the "floor" down 3″ (75 mm).

9. Trim the bottoms of the thick vertical lines to the 3″ (75 mm) horizontal line, as shown in Figure 11.46.

10. Trim the top horizontal line to the new vertical lines.

11. Delete the 3″ (75 mm) horizontal line. Your detail should now look like Figure 11.46.

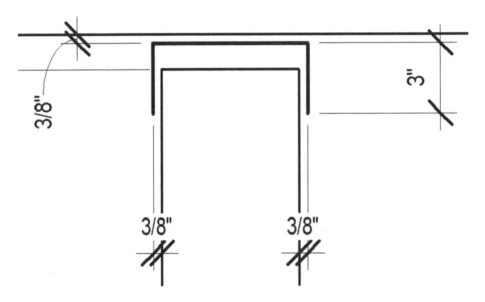

FIGURE 11.46 The top track is now in place.

It's time to add the gypsum to both sides of the wall. By using the same method as you did before, you'll use thin lines to denote two layers of 5/8″ (15 mm) gypsum on both sides of the stud. If you're ready to complete this task on your own, go ahead. (Remember, you're adding two layers of 5/8″ [15 mm] gypsum to both sides of the wall, and you're using thin lines to denote this.)

If you would rather have some guidelines with which to practice, let's step through the procedure:

1. On the Annotate tab, click the Detail Line button.

2. Select Thin Lines in the Properties dialog.

3. In the Draw panel, click the Pick Lines icon, as shown in Figure 11.47.

4. Type 5/8″ (15 mm) in the Offset field.

5. Offset two lines inward from the right and two lines inward from the left (see Figure 11.47).

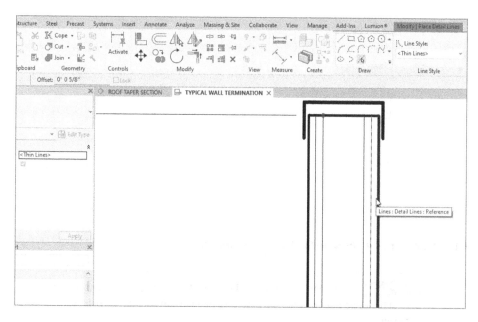

FIGURE 11.47 Adding the lines for the gypsum

Look at this: the steps are getting shorter. You used only the Detail Line command but have successfully offset every line you needed without leaving the command that you were running at the time. Who says you can't draft in Revit?

The next procedure involves adding a filled region to the "floor." Although you don't want to be too specific about what you're calling out, you still need some contrasting hatch.

1. On the Annotate tab, click the Region ➤ Filled Region button.

2. In the Line Style panel, select <Invisible Lines>, as shown in Figure 11.48. On the Options bar, pick Chain.

Or, if you would like to venture out on your own, try to duplicate Figure 11.49. You'll need to add a filled region using diagonal lines. If you would rather follow the procedure, let's get started:

1. Draw a boundary (see Figure 11.48), and press Esc.

2. In the Properties dialog, click the Edit Type button.

3. Click Duplicate.

4. Call the new region ROOF.

5. Change Fill Pattern to Diagonal Up-Small [Drafting].

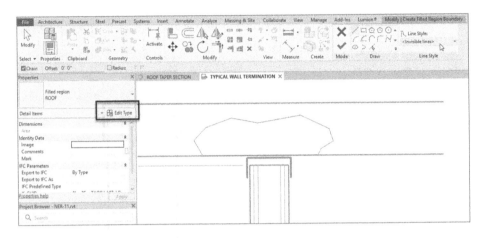

FIGURE 11.48 Draw the filled region with invisible lines.

> **NOTE** Remember to change the Fill pattern by clicking the [. . .] button after you click in the Value cell. You can then browse to find the pattern that you're looking for in the menu.

6. Click OK.

7. Click Finish Edit Mode in the Mode panel. Your pattern should look like Figure 11.49. (Remember, the loop must be completely closed, with no gaps or overlaps.)

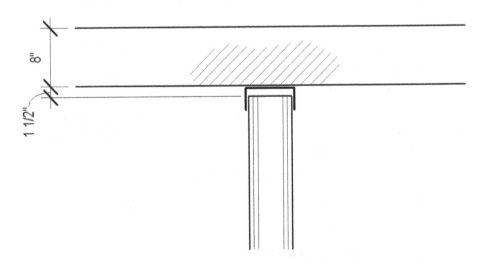

FIGURE 11.49 The detail with the hatching included

This detail is looking good—so good that it would be nice to never have to draw it again. Let's proceed with creating a special group that you can drag onto another view.

Creating a Detail Group

Groups can be extremely advantageous to the drafting process. Although I mentioned earlier that details and drafting views aren't linked to the model, you can still provide some global control within the details themselves by creating a group. This will give you further control over every instance of this specific detail in the entire model.

The objective of the following procedure is to create a new group and add it to another view:

1. Select the filled region, the top track and the "gypsum wall."

2. On the Modify | Multi-Select tab in the Create panel, click the Create Group button, as shown in Figure 11.50.

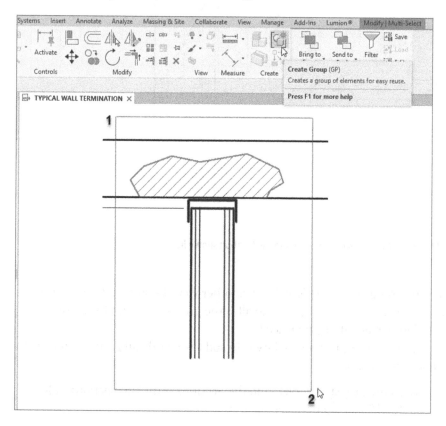

FIGURE 11.50 The Create Group button in the Create panel

3. In the Create Detail Group dialog, call the new group **Typical Slip Track**. Click OK.

4. The group has been created. You see an icon similar to the UCS icon in AutoCAD; this is your origin. Pick the middle grip, and drag it to the left corner of the track (where it meets the floor), as shown in Figure 11.51.

5. Save the model.

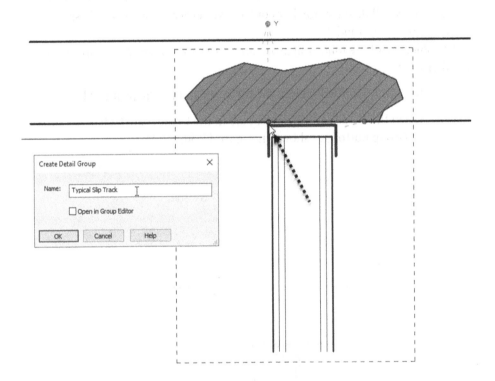

FIGURE 11.51 Move the origin to the location shown here.

With the group created, let's add it to another view. Because not every view shows exactly the same thing, you can alter the group's instance to conform to the detail into which it's being placed.

The objective of this next procedure is to add the new detail group physically to the Roof Taper Section:

1. In the Project Browser, find the Sections (Building Section) called Roof Taper Section, and open it.

2. On the Annotate tab, click Detail Group ➤ Place Detail Group, as shown in Figure 11.52.

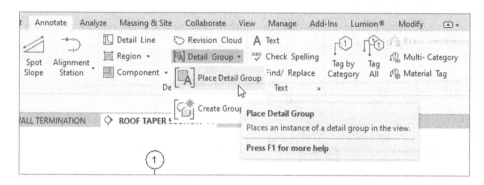

F I G U R E   1 1 . 5 2   Choose Place Detail Group.

3. Move your cursor over the underside of the roof. You get a snap; this is the origin point of the detail.

4. Pick a point along the bottom of the roof, similar to what is shown in Figure 11.53.

5. When the group is placed, press Esc.

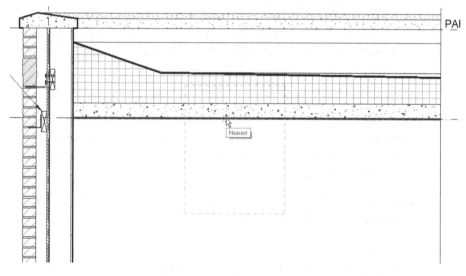

F I G U R E   1 1 . 5 3   Picking a point along the bottom of the roof to place the group

The next step is to remove some of the extraneous hatch and lines. You can do this within a group, but you must be careful not to edit the group in a way that affects all other instances:

1. Hover your cursor over the bottom line of the filled region, as shown in Figure 11.54.

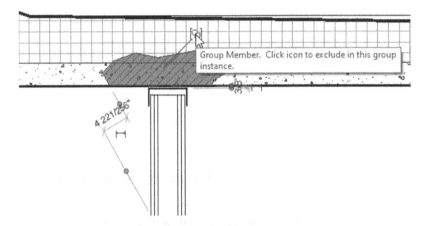

FIGURE 11.54 Excluding an element from the group

2. Press the Tab key. This allows you to select the filled region.

3. Pick the region (see Figure 11.54).

4. A small, blue group icon appears. When you hover your cursor over it, it says that you can exclude this member from the group. This is what you want to do, so click the button.

5. Save the model. Your detail should now look like Figure 11.55.

Now you'll open the original group and make modifications to it to see how each insertion of a group is influenced. This is where the advantage of using groups in a model comes into play. When the modifications are completed, the other groups will be updated:

1. In the Project Browser, find the Typical Wall Termination view under Drafting Views (Detail), and open it.

2. Select the group.

3. On the Modify | Detail Groups tab, click Edit Group.

4. In the Detail panel of the Annotate tab, click the Insulation button, as shown in Figure 11.56.

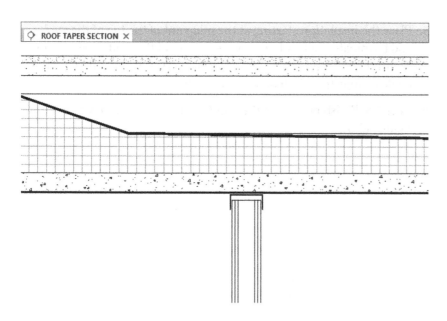

FIGURE 11.55 The slip track without the filled region

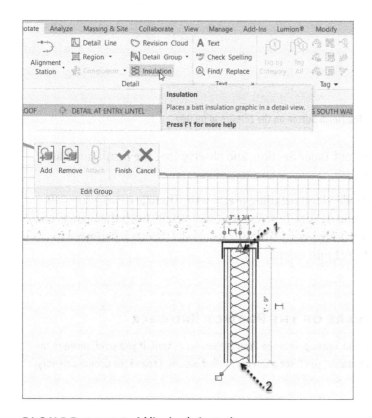

FIGURE 11.56 Adding insulation to the group

5. Place the insulation starting at the midpoint of the top of the stud, and terminate the insulation at the bottom of the stud, as shown in Figure 11.56. You're lucky the width fits perfectly. If it didn't, you could change the width on the Options bar.

6. Click the Finish button on the Edit Group toolbar, as shown in Figure 11.57.

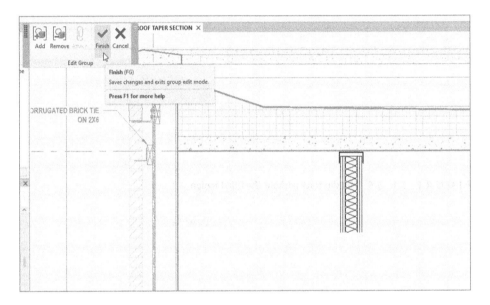

F I G U R E 1 1 . 5 7 The Finish button on the Edit Group toolbar

7. Open the Roof Taper Section, and observe that the insulation has been added.

You're starting to understand detailing pretty well. There are two issues left to discuss. First, it would be nice to reference these details from the plan, even knowing that they aren't physically tied into the model. Second, you need to know how to import CAD into a detail.

ALWAYS BE AWARE OF THE PROJECT BROWSER

You can add a group from the Project Browser as well. If you scroll down in the Project Browser, you'll see a category called Groups. Expand the Groups category, and locate the Detail category. Expand this, and find the Typical Slip Track group, as shown in the following graphic. All you need to do is click this group and drag it into the model.

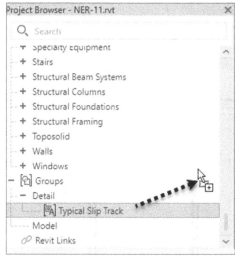

Adding a Section to Another View

You already know how to add a section marker in a plan. What you may not know is how to tell Revit that you would rather specify the reference.

In this procedure, you'll go to the Level 1 ceiling plan and add a section pointing to your drafting view:

1. In the Project Browser, open the Level 1 floor plan.

2. Zoom in on the area of the east wing shown in Figure 11.58.

3. On the View tab, click the Section button. Pick Detail in the Type Selector.

4. Before you place the section, click the Reference Other View button on the Options bar.

5. In the menu to the right of the Reference Other View label, expand the drop-down and select Drafting View: TYPICAL WALL TERMINATION.

6. Place the section into the model (see Figure 11.58).

7. Press Esc.

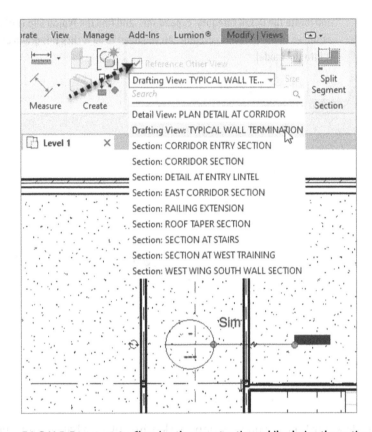

FIGURE 11.58 Choosing the correct options while placing the section

8. Double-click the section marker that you placed in the model. Doing so opens your drafting view.

9. Save the model.

WARNING Be careful! In AutoCAD and MicroStation, you got used to doing this type of referencing daily. In Revit, your coworkers may not be accustomed to this hatchet-job, inaccurate style. Be deliberate when you add sections referring to other views, and try not to do it too often.

Creating a drafting view is behind you. Now it's time to look at our old friend CAD. (Some may say that the new meaning of the acronym is Ctrl+Alt+Delete.) Regardless of the existing sentiment toward CAD, it did get us this far. And we still need it—more so in the drafting capacity. Yes, you can import CAD files into a detail.

Importing AutoCAD Files into a Drafting View

I'll go out on a limb and venture to guess that you have a handful of CAD details that you use on a daily basis. The question always is, "What do I do with this pile of details I spent years and thousands of dollars to create?" Well, you can still use them.

The objective of the next procedure is to create a new drafting view and import an AutoCAD detail. If you would like, you can attempt to import your own detail, or you can use the file provided. Just go to the book's web page at www.wiley .com/go/revit2024ner. Browse to the Chapter 11 folder, and find the base cabinet.dwg file. You can then place it on your system for later retrieval.

Follow along:

1. In the View tab, click the Drafting View button.

2. In the next dialog, name the new view **TYPICAL BASE CABINET.**

3. Set Scale to 1 1/2″ = 1′–0″, and then click OK.

4. On the Insert tab, click the Import CAD button.

5. Browse to the location where you placed your CAD file.

6. Select the file, but don't click Open yet.

7. At the bottom of the Import dialog, set Colors to Black And White.

8. Set Layers/Levels: to Visible.

9. Set Import Units to Auto-Detect.

10. Set Positioning to Auto - Center To Center.

11. Click Open.

12. Type **ZA**. The detail should now be in full view.

13. Select the detail.

14. On the Modify | Base cabinet.dwg tab, click Explode ➤ Full Explode.

15. Select one of the filled regions.

16. In the Properties dialog, click Edit Type.

17. Change Fill Pattern to Sand - Dense, and select the Drafting radio button.

18. Click OK.

19. Click OK one more time to get back to the model.

20. Make sure your cabinet is hatched properly.

21. Save the model.

USE THE BUILDER BUTTON!

To change the pattern to Sand, make sure you click the [. . .] button next to the area that says Fill Pattern, as shown in this graphic. From there, you can choose the hatch pattern.

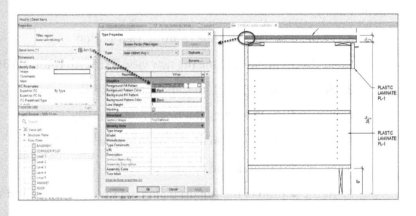

Up to this point, you've been using detail lines for your drafting. The one issue is that detail lines are visible only in the specific view in which you're working. Suppose you wanted linework to show up both in plan/elevation and in a 3D view. In this situation, you should use the actual Lines tool.

Adding 2D and 3D Lines to the Model

Just because you're drafting, that doesn't mean you can't create lines in all views, such as in a 3D view in a 3D function. Revit has a tool that is simply called *Lines*, and you use it to project lines into multiple views. You apply the Lines tool just as you would a detail line—only it behaves the same as a Revit 3D family in that you can see it in every view (unless you turn it off).

In this procedure, you'll add detail lines to the west sloping roof. They're nothing fancy, but you'll quickly get the idea of how to use this feature:

1. In the Project Browser, find the West Roof floor plan and open it.

2. On the Architecture tab, click the Set button in the Work Plane panel, as shown in Figure 11.59

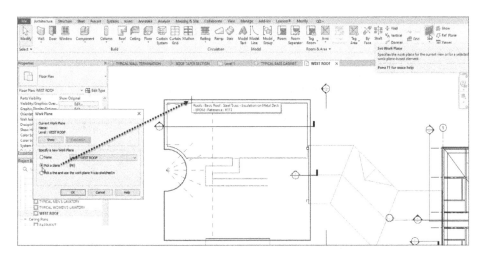

FIGURE 11.59 The Set button in the Work Plane panel of the Architecture tab

3. In the Work Plane dialog, select the Pick a Plane radio button.

4. Click OK.

5. Pick the roof, as shown in Figure 11.59

6. In the Model panel of the Architecture tab, click the Model Line button.

7. In the Line Style menu, select Medium Lines, as shown in Figure 11.60

8. In the Draw panel, click the Start-End-Radius Arc button, as shown in Figure 11.60.

9. Draw an arc from the two endpoints shown in Figure 11.60. Make the radius 80′–0″ (24000 mm). Simply enter the numbers on the keyboard and press Enter, and they will fill in the radius field. Click Modify.

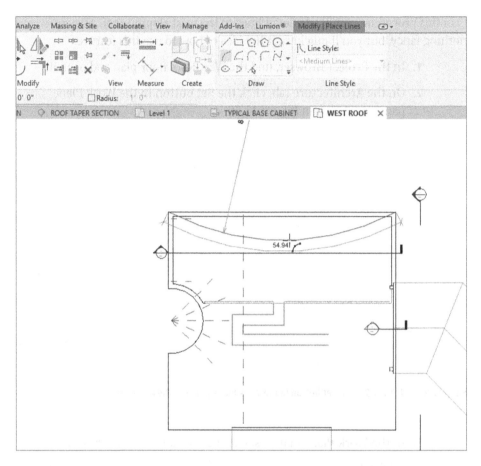

F I G U R E   1 1 . 6 0   Drawing an 80'–0" (24 m) radius arc

10. Go to an exterior 3D view. You can still see the arc.

11. Save the model.

It's a good idea to keep this feature in mind. This drafting tool will become useful when it comes to sketching in 3D. You'll encounter many situations in which you'll use this little nugget.

Are You Experienced?

Now you can. . .

✓ modify and add line weights to be used in both the 3D and 2D environments

✓ add linework in a drafting view as well as a 2D and a 3D view

✓ create both masking regions and filled regions to provide hatching to a model

✓ mask an area so that you can draft over it

✓ add detail components to the model and create repeating details

✓ modify detail families to suit your needs

✓ create a group to be used in multiple drafting views, change the group, and update each copy in each view

✓ create a new drafting view to draft from scratch and import a CAD file into a drafting view

CHAPTER 12

Creating Specific Views and Match Lines

As you can see, the Autodesk® Revit® platform is all about the views. In fact, by using Revit, not only are you replacing the application you use for drafting, but you're also replacing your existing file storage system (to some degree). This is largely because you're now using one model, and you're using views of that model for your project navigation.

This chapter covers the following topics:

▶ **Duplicating views**

▶ **Creating dependent views**

▶ **Adding match lines**

▶ **Using view templates**

Duplicating Views

I wanted to dedicate an entire chapter to project navigation. Although you've steadily gained experience in this area, we can expand on it much more to round out your Revit expertise.

The first item we'll tackle in this chapter is the process of duplicating a view to create another. Although it's a straightforward procedure, a lot is riding on the hope that you proceed with this function correctly. As you're about to find out, this command isn't a simple copy-and-paste operation.

Revit will change how you organize a project. You'll no longer open a file and save it as another file so that you can make changes without affecting the original. As you know, Revit is all-inclusive in terms of files. There is only one. From that one file, there are views that reside in the Project Browser.

Of course, I'm not telling you anything you haven't learned already. If you've gone through the book from page 1, you've gained experience in creating views (especially in Chapter 3, "Creating Views"). If you're jumping to this chapter, you most certainly have had some exposure to view creation. This topic is broken into two chapters to help you gain a more in-depth understanding of how you can manipulate and organize views.

Now let's duplicate some views! To begin, open the file you've been using to follow along. If you didn't complete the previous chapter, go to the book's web page at www.wiley.com/go/revit2024ner. From there, you can browse to the Chapter 12 folder and find the file called NER-12.rvt.

The objective of the following procedure is to create a furniture plan of Level 1 and then turn off the furniture on the original Level 1. Follow along:

1. In the Project Browser, find the Level 1 floor plan, and right-click.

2. Select Duplicate View ➢ Duplicate With Detailing, as shown in Figure 12.1.

The difference between choosing Duplicate with Detailing and Duplicate is that Duplicate With Detailing also copies all the tags and annotations you have in the original view. Duplicate copies only the geometry.

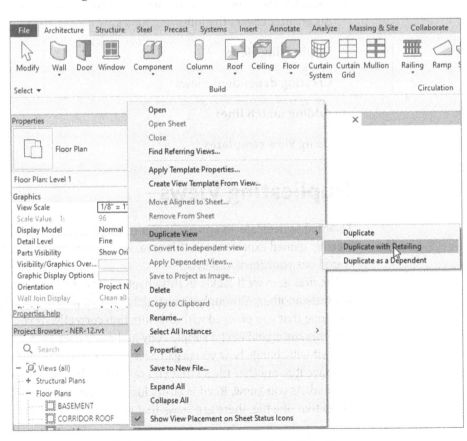

FIGURE 12.1 Right-clicking the Level 1 floor plan in the Project Browser

3. You now have a view called Level 1 Copy 1. Right-click it in the Project Browser.

4. Rename it **Level 1 Furniture Plan**.

5. Make sure you're in the Level 1 floor plan, not the new furniture plan. In the Level 1 view window, type **VG**. Doing so brings up the Visibility/Graphics Overrides window. Or you can click the Visibility/Graphics Overrides in the Properties dialog,.

6. In the Visibility column, deselect Casework, Furniture, and Furniture Systems. See Figure 12.2.

7. Click OK.

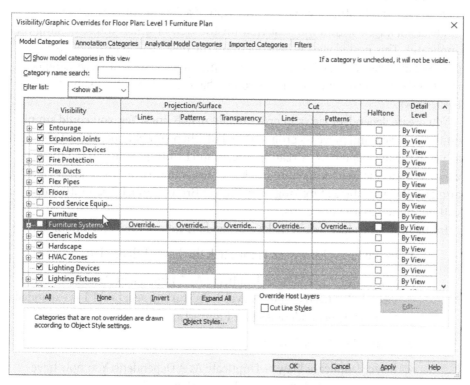

FIGURE 12.2 Turning off some items with Visibility Graphics

Now, anytime you add furniture or casework, it will appear only in the furniture plan. You don't need to deal with layer or display configuration.

N O T E   Remember, this is just a view of the model. It is like a pile of pictures. When we turn objects on and off or when we override graphics in this view, it is *only* for this view. No other view in the model will be affected.

The ability to create a copy of a view and then modify its visibility graphics to display certain items is a critical function in Revit. Another similar task is also available: creating coordinated match-line divisions in a model by creating dependent views.

Creating Dependent Views

You create a dependent view in much the same way you duplicate a view. In fact, you *are* duplicating a view. The function of a dependent view is to nest a duplicate of a view within the host view (or the view of which you're making the duplicate). This nested view is dependent on the host view in terms of visibility graphics and view properties. You can have multiple dependent views categorized under the host view. This gives you global control over the visibility of these views.

You create dependent views in order to add match lines. Yes, you could simply duplicate a view and move its crop region, but when you have dependent views, as you'll see in Chapter 13, "Creating Sheets and Printing," you can tag those views in a specific way for Revit to track the sheets they're on. Dependent views also give the advantage of making your Project Browser much less cluttered, without unnecessary floor plans.

In the next procedure, you'll make a dependent view of the Level 1 floor plan:

1. In the Project Browser, right-click the Level 1 floor plan.

2. Select Duplicate View ➢ Duplicate As A Dependent. You now have a view that is nested under Level 1. As you can see, Level 1 is expanded to show its dependencies (see Figure 12.3).

3. Right-click Level 1 again.

4. Select Duplicate View ➢ Duplicate As A Dependent. You now have two views nested under Level 1 (see Figure 12.4).

5. Right-click Dependent (2) on the Level 1 dependent view.

6. Rename it **Level 1 East**.

7. Rename the other dependent view **Level 1 West** (see Figure 12.4).

FIGURE 12.3 Creating a dependent view

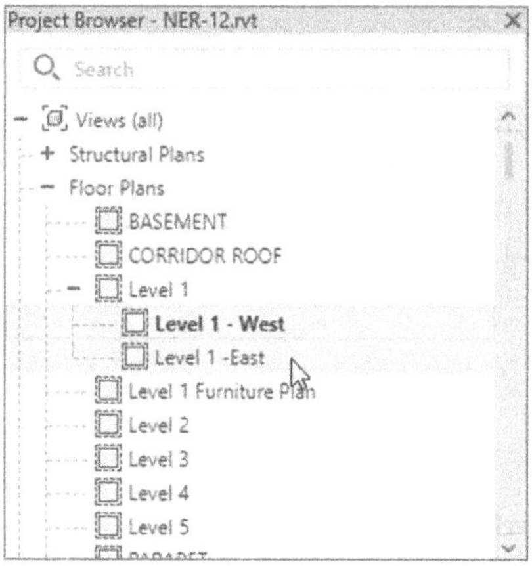

Project Browser - NER-12.rvt   ✕

🔍 Search

− 🗗 Views (all)
  + Structural Plans
  − Floor Plans
    ▢ BASEMENT
    ▢ CORRIDOR ROOF
    − ▢ Level 1
      ▢ **Level 1 - West**
      ▢ Level 1 - East
    ▢ Level 1 Furniture Plan
    ▢ Level 2
    ▢ Level 3
    ▢ Level 4
    ▢ Level 5
    ▢ PARAPET

FIGURE 12.4 The two dependent views

Now that the views are duplicated and nested in the host view, it's time to divide the Level 1 floor plan. You'll do this by adjusting the crop region.

Adjusting the Crop Regions

Every view in Revit has a crop region. Crop regions play an important role when your plan is too large to fit on a sheet. All you need to do at this point is to slide the east and west crop regions to display the appropriate parts of the plan based on the name of the views:

1. Open the Level 1 West dependent view.

2. Select the crop region, as shown in Figure 12.5.

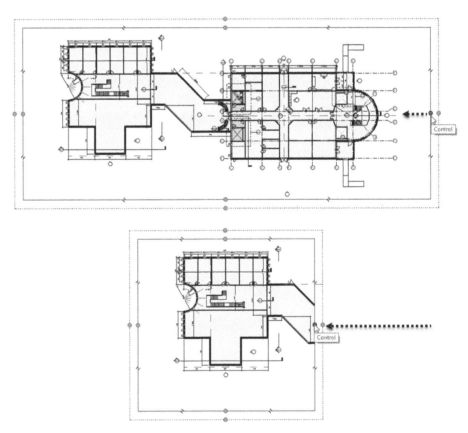

FIGURE 12.5 Dragging the crop region in the Level 1 West view

3. Drag the right side of the crop region to the position shown in Figure 12.5. by selecting the blue grip.

4. Open the Level 1 East view.

5. Select the crop region.

6. Drag the left side of the region to the right, as shown in Figure 12.6.

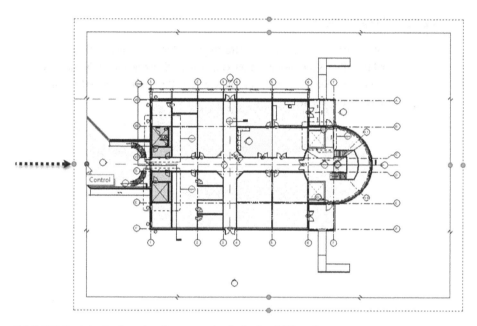

FIGURE 12.6 Dragging the crop region in the Level 1 East view

7. Select the crop region again, if it isn't selected already, and right-click.

8. Choose Go to Primary View to open the Level 1 floor plan.

9. In the Level 1 floor plan, turn on the crop region by clicking the Show Crop Region button on the View Control toolbar, as shown in Figure 12.7.

FIGURE 12.7 Turning on the crop region from the View Control toolbar

You can see the area where you need to draw the match line. The crop region should overlap in the corridor. If not, drag the crop regions so they match Figure 12.8.

STRETCH THAT VIEW

You'll notice that there are two stretch grips. One is for the actual crop region, and the other is for the annotation crop region. We'll cover what the annotation crop region means in a moment. For now, pick the stretch grip to the inside, as shown in this image:

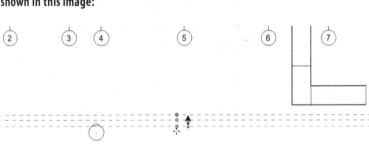

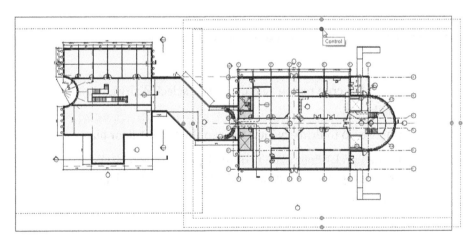

FIGURE 12.8   Adjusting the crop regions to overlap in the corridor

 NOTE   If you want to turn a dependent view back into an independent view, you can right-click the dependent view and select Convert to Independent View. Doing so breaks the link to the host view.

Unfortunately, if you have a match-line situation in your project, you must follow this procedure with each floor plan separately. For multifloor projects, doing so can become time consuming. Alternatively, you can right-click a view that has dependencies and select Apply Dependent Views. From there, you can select the views to which the dependent views will be added.

As you can see, adjusting the crop region is how you specify which part of the plan will appear on your sheet. This poses one issue: if you have text that you would like to lie outside the crop region—that is, if a leadered note is pointing to an item within the cropped boundary—you may not see the note. To fix this, you can adjust the annotation crop region.

Adjusting the Annotation Crop Region

Because the crop region cuts off the model at a specified perimeter, what is to become of text that needs to lie outside this boundary? This is where the annotation crop region comes in handy. You'll always have the situation where leadered text must be outside the geometry it's labeling. You can make adjustments to ensure that this can happen.

Let's adjust an annotation crop region to clean up a plan. Follow along:

1. In the Project Browser, open the Level 1 West dependent view.

2. Select the crop region, as shown in Figure 12.9. Notice the two perimeters; one is a solid-line type, and the other is a dashed-line type.

N O T E The Annotation Crop feature is available in any view. This example uses a plan, but you can use the same procedure in a section or an elevation as well.

Now that you understand how to add crop regions and display them appropriately, let's add the match line.

THE SECOND LINE

If you don't see the second line, follow these steps:

1. In the Properties dialog, scroll down to the Extents area.

2. Make sure the Annotation Crop option is selected, as shown here:

(Continues)

THE SECOND LINE *(Continued)*

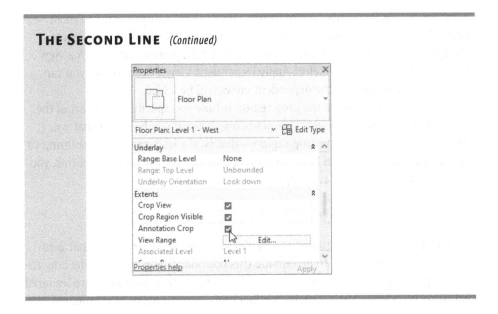

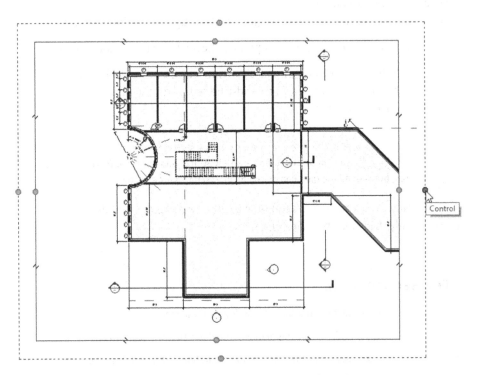

FIGURE 12.9 Selecting the plan's crop region. Notice the additional region on a dashed-line type—this is the annotation crop region.

Adding Match Lines

In CAD, adding a match line is nothing more than the simple practice of drawing a line. The same is true in Revit, except that in Revit, you draw that line in Sketch mode, and you can propagate it to other views. Also, in Revit, after you place the line, it registers as having two sides of a model. In the next chapter, when you drag your views onto sheets, Revit will know where each side of the model is located in terms of being placed on a sheet.

The objective of the next procedure is to place a match line into the model. Follow these steps:

1. Open the Level 1 floor plan.

2. In the Sheet Composition panel of the View tab, click the Matchline button, as shown in Figure 12.10.

FIGURE 12.10 The Matchline button on the View tab

3. In the Properties dialog, make sure the Top and Bottom constraints are set to Unlimited.

4. In the Draw panel, click the Line button.

5. Draw the match line as shown in Figure 12.11.

6. Click the green Finish Edit Mode check mark icon in the Mode panel.

Your match line appears as a bold, dashed line. Because the physical appearance of a match line never seems to be the same from firm to firm, you can adjust the line's appearance.

Match-Line Appearance

A match line isn't an actual line by definition; it's a 3D object. Therefore, you can control its appearance by using the Object Styles dialog.

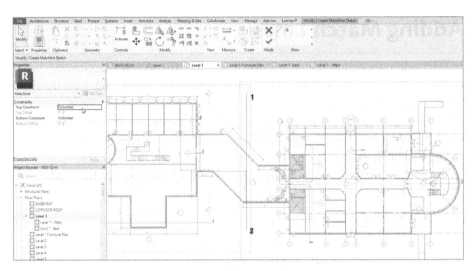

FIGURE 12.11 Placing the Matchline

The next procedure focuses on changing the appearance of the match line:

1. On the Manage tab, click the Object Styles button.

2. Click the Annotation Objects tab, as shown in Figure 12.12.

3. Scroll down to the Matchline category.

4. Click into Line Pattern (the Dash cell).

5. You see a menu arrow. Click it, and select Dash Dot 3/8″ (10 mm) (see Figure 12.12).

6. Click OK. Your match line is now a different line type.

With the match line in place and the plan split into two halves, let's add an annotation to label the match line. For the match-line annotation, you'll place a piece of text that says MATCHLINE. But when you're referencing each side of the plan, you'll need to add view references.

Adding View References to a Match Line

After the plan is split and the match line is in place, you can tag each side of the match line. When you drag the view onto a drawing sheet, the tag will be filled out with the correct page name. It's important to note, however, that although this process is automatic, it isn't *fully* automatic. You do need to specify the correct view name as you're placing the tag.

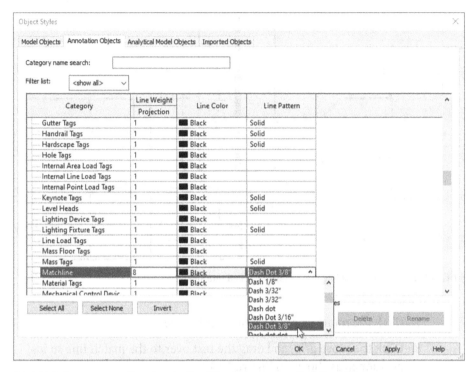

FIGURE 12.12 Changing the Matchline line pattern to Dash Dot 3/8"

In this procedure, you'll place a piece of text that says MATCHLINE along the match line and add a view reference to each side of the match line. Follow along:

1. In the Project Browser, open the Level 1 floor plan view.

2. On the Annotate tab, click the Text button.

 NOTE Unfortunately, when you're placing text, you can't rotate the text until after you've added it. In this procedure, place the note, rotate it, and then move it into position.

3. On the Modify | Place Text tab are leader options. Click the No Leader button (the letter A), as shown in Figure 12.13.

4. Pick a window near the match line for the text.

5. Type the word **MATCHLINE**, click off the text, and press Esc twice (see Figure 12.13).

6. Select the text (if it isn't selected already).

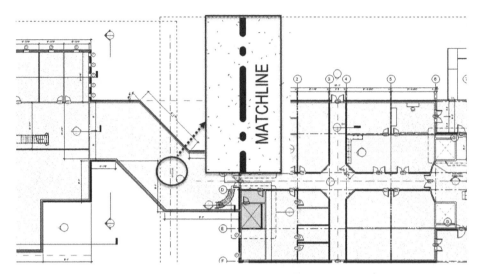

FIGURE 12.13 Adding some simple text and rotating it

7. Click the rotate grip, and rotate the text 90°.

8. Click the move grip, and drag the text over to the match line so it's positioned as shown in Figure 12.13.

9. In the Sheet Composition panel of the View tab, click the View Reference button, as shown in Figure 12.14.

FIGURE 12.14 Clicking View Reference

10. In the View Reference panel is a Target View list. Make sure Floor Plan: Level 1 West is current (see Figure 12.15).

11. Pick a point to the left of the match line (again, see Figure 12.15).

12. With the View Reference command still running, change Target View to Floor Plan: Level 1 East.

13. Place a view reference to the right of the match line.

14. Press Esc. You have two view references, and you're ready to add these views to a drawing sheet in the next chapter. Once you do this, the tags will become populated with the sheets on which you placed the views.

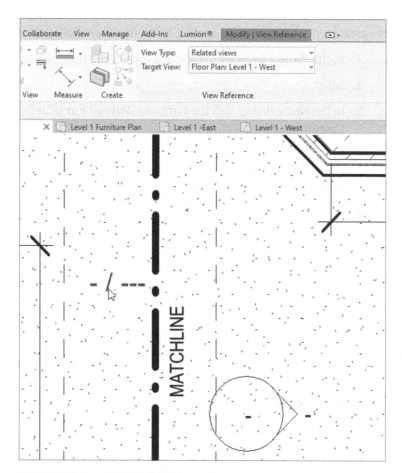

FIGURE 12.15 Placing a view reference

One last item to discuss before we close this chapter is how to create and use settings from a single view, after you determine that you want to repeat the view settings.

Using View Templates

When you created the furniture plan in the beginning of the chapter, you manipulated the data in the Visibility/Graphics Overrides options to hide furniture in a specific plan. It would be nice to build settings like these into a template so you could simply apply that template to a view the next time the situation arose.

Let's create a view template and apply it to another view. Follow these steps:

1. In the Project Browser, right-click the Level 1 floor plan.

2. Select Create View Template From View.

3. In the Name dialog, call the template **Without Furniture or Casework**, and then click OK.

4. In the View Templates dialog, Revit allows you to further control the view properties and visibility graphics. Because you don't need to make any other adjustments, click OK.

5. Right-click the Level 2 floor plan.

6. Select Apply Template Properties.

7. In the Apply View Template dialog, select the Without Furniture or Casework template, as shown in Figure 12.16.

8. Click OK.

As you can see, using view templates will help you immensely with maintaining company-wide standards. Use templates as often as possible.

> ▶
> You can also select multiple items and apply the same template to many plans, if you desire.

Are You Experienced?

Now you can. . .

✓ create duplicates of views and tell the difference between duplicating with detailing and simply duplicating a view

✓ create dependent views, allowing separate views to be nested under one host view

✓ add match lines and view reference tags

✓ create and use view templates

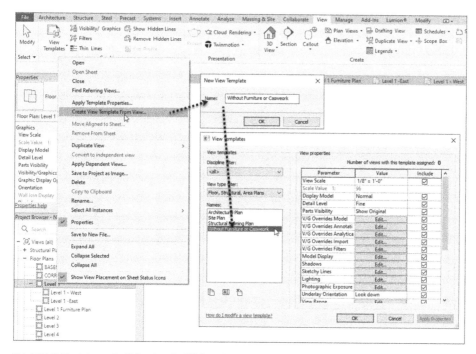

FIGURE 12.16 Selecting the Without Furniture or Casework template

CHAPTER 13

Creating Sheets and Printing

Your deliverable product is a set of construction documents and specifications, so it stands to reason that the application you use to produce these construction documents is at its strongest in this area. Unfortunately, when you see marketing campaigns related to Autodesk® Revit® software, all they show are huge skyscrapers and realistic renderings. And, of course, you see the slide of the architect handing a model to the contractor and then the contractor handing it to the owner. Don't get me wrong—all that stuff is good, but one of the most powerful features of Revit is its ability to create and organize drawing sheets. You wouldn't think this is the standout feature—but when it's 4:30 in the afternoon and the job is going out the door at 5:00, you'll never go back to a drafting application after you've used Revit at the eleventh hour.

This chapter covers the following topics:

▶ **Creating and populating sheets**

▶ **Modifying a viewport**

▶ **Adding revisions to a sheet**

▶ **Addressing project information**

▶ **Generating a cover sheet**

▶ **Printing from Revit**

Creating and Populating Sheets

The first part of this chapter will focus on creating a sheet and demonstrating how to populate it with views. Now it's time to drill into the ins and outs of sheet creation.

The objective of the following procedure is to create a new sheet. To get started, open the file you've been using to follow along. If you missed the previous chapter, go to the book's web page at www.wiley.com/go/revit2024ner. From there, you can browse to the Chapter 13 folder and find the file called NER-13.rvt. Follow along:

1. In the Project Browser, scroll down until you see the Sheets category, as shown in Figure 13.1.

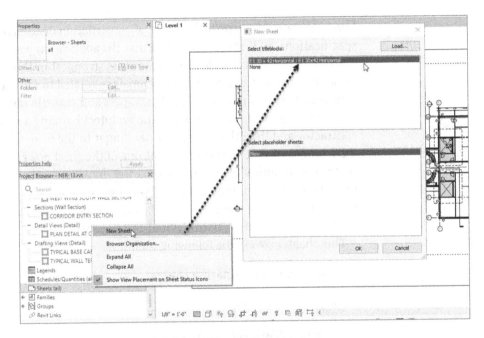

FIGURE 13.1   Right-click Sheets (All) and select a new sheet.

2. Right-click Sheets (All) and select New Sheet (see Figure 13.1).

3. In the Select Titleblocks area of the New Sheet dialog, select the E1 30 × 42 Horizontal title block. (It's probably the only one available.)

4. Click OK.

 NOTE You're using a standard Autodesk-supplied title block. Later in this chapter, you'll learn how to make custom title blocks. Also, your new sheet may be numbered differently from the example in the book. This is OK; you'll change the numbering in a moment.

Congratulations! You now have a blank sheet. Next, you'll add views to it by using the click-and-drag method:

1. On the View tab, click Guide Grid, as shown in Figure 13.2.

2. In the Guide Grid Name dialog, call the guide **Grid 30×42 (750×1050)**, and click OK.

3. Select the guide grid and drag it into place by using the blue grips (see Figure 13.2).

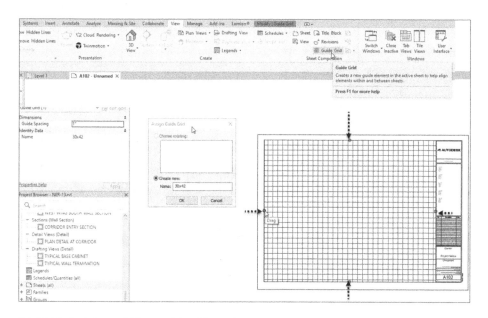

FIGURE 13.2 Adding a guide grid to a sheet

 NOTE You don't have to add a guide grid. It is also annoying that it won't snap to anything. The guide grid keeps your plans in the same spot from sheet to sheet, however, which can be a good idea.

4. In the Project Browser, find the dependent view called Level 1- West, as shown in Figure 13.3.

5. Pick the view and hold down the left mouse button.

6. Drag the view onto the sheet (see Figure 13.3).

7. When the view is centered in the sheet, let go of the pick button. The view follows your cursor. Try to align the lower-left corner of the viewport with a guide grid, and then click. Doing so places the view onto the sheet.

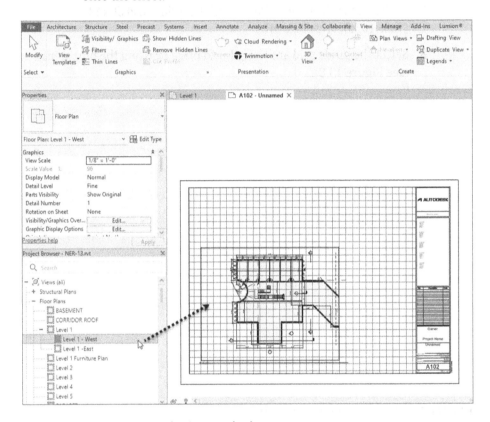

FIGURE 13.3 Dragging the view onto the sheet

This is how you populate a sheet using Revit—quite the departure from CAD. One nice detail is that the title is filled out, and another is that the scale will never be incorrect. The next step is to begin renumbering sheets so that you can create a logical order.

Sheet Organization

If you've been following along with the book, you already have a sheet numbered A101. It would be nice if you could give this sheet a new number and start your sequence over. Revit lets you do just that.

The goals of the next procedure are to change the sheet numbering and to add more sheets, allowing Revit to number the sheets sequentially as they're created. Follow these steps:

1. In the Project Browser, find the sheet you just made, and right-click.

2. Select Rename, as shown in Figure 13.4.

3. Change the sheet number to **A101** (if it is not that already) and change the sheet name to **WEST WING LEVEL 1**.

4. Click OK.

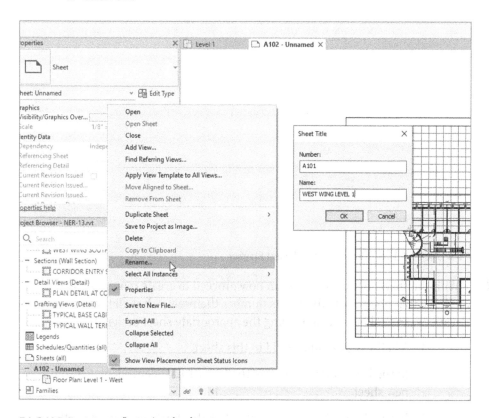

F I G U R E 1 3 . 4 Renaming the sheet

5. Right-click Sheets (All) and create a new sheet.

6. Make sure the number is **A102**.

Your Project Browser should now resemble Figure 13.5.

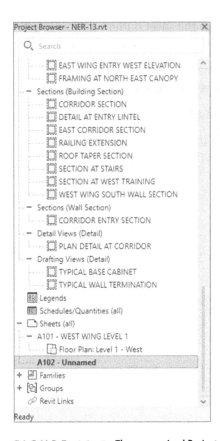

FIGURE 13.5 The reorganized Project Browser

You may notice a plus sign (+) next to A101. If you expand the tree by clicking the +, you can see the views that are included on this view. This can prove to be immensely useful, because you can't add a view to another sheet (or the same sheet, for that matter) if it's already included in a sheet.

With the sheets organized, you can now proceed to create more. As you do, you'll see that not only do the sheets number themselves, but all the sections, elevations, and callouts begin reading the appropriate sheet designations:

1. Add the 30x42 Guide Grid to this sheet.

2. In the Project Browser, drag the Level 1 East dependent view onto the new sheet.

3. In the Project Browser, double-click the A101 sheet, opening the view. Notice that the view reference next to the match line is filled out with the appropriate designation.

4. Double-click A102 to open the view again.

In the Project Browser, sheet A102 is still unnamed. The next procedure describes a different way to rename and renumber a sheet:

1. With sheet A102 open, zoom into the right side of the view, as shown in Figure 13.6.

2. Select the title block. A few items turn blue. If you remember, any item that turns blue can be modified.

3. Click into the text that says Project Name, and type **NO EXPERI-ENCE REQUIRED.**

4. Click into the text that says Unnamed, and type **EAST WING LEVEL1**

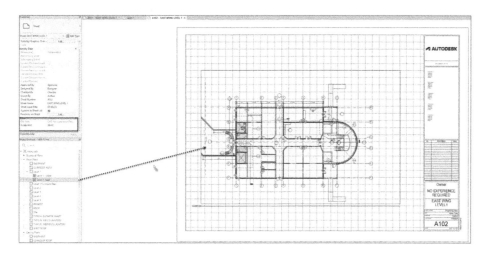

FIGURE 13.6 Dragging the dependent view onto the sheet

5. Create another sheet using the 30 × 42 Horizontal title block.

6. Number it A201.

7. Name it **ENLARGED PLANS.**

8. Add the 30 × 42 grid guide.

NOTE Sometimes a view will not properly crop a section. For example, the view TYPICAL WOMAN'S LAVATORY may have a section marker way outside of the view. Simply right-click on the section, and select Hide In View ➤ Category. See the following image.

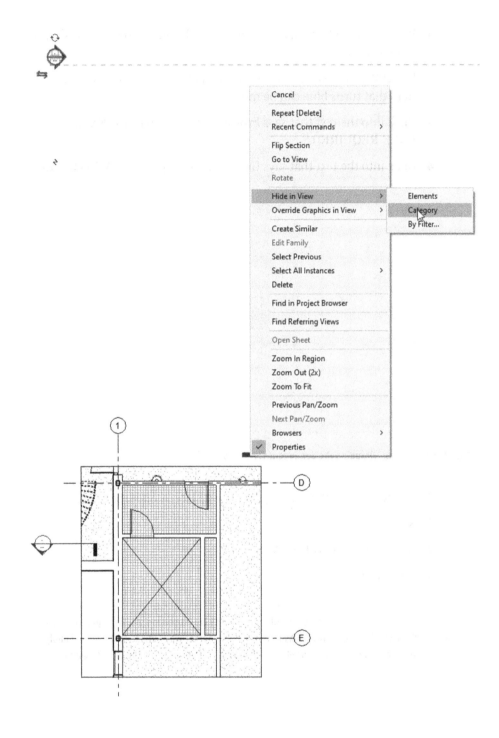

9. Drag the following views onto the sheet:

> **TIP** New to Revit 2024. You can select multiple views and drag them onto a sheet all in one shot just by holding down Shift and selecting the views you want.

- ▶ Typical Elevator Shaft
- ▶ Typical Men's Lavatory
- ▶ Typical Women's Lavatory

10. Views are randomly placed onto a sheet, as shown in Figure 13.7. They may or may not be in the exact position as shown, but we'll fix that in a moment.

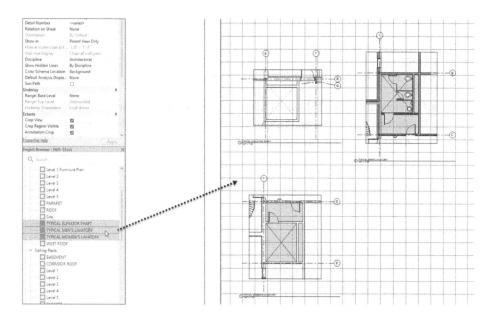

FIGURE 13.7 Dragging multiple views onto a sheet.

The next step is to move the views into position. Revit has a really cool way of lining up views. It will either track the building into alignment or it will track the view title. Let's align the views into a horizontal row at the bottom of the sheet.

11. Select the TYPICAL MENS LAVATORY view and click and drag it so that its view title tracks into alignment with the TYPICAL WOMEN'S LAVATORY view as shown in Figure 13.8.

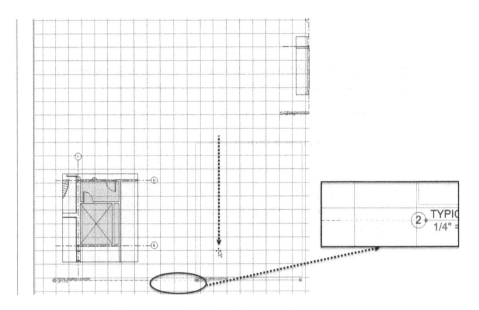

FIGURE 13.8 Aligning views while tracking the view title.

12. Select the TYPICAL ELEVATOR SHAFT view. This time, drag it so it aligns with the actual modeled elements of the TYPICAL MEN'S LAVATORY as shown in Figure 13.9.

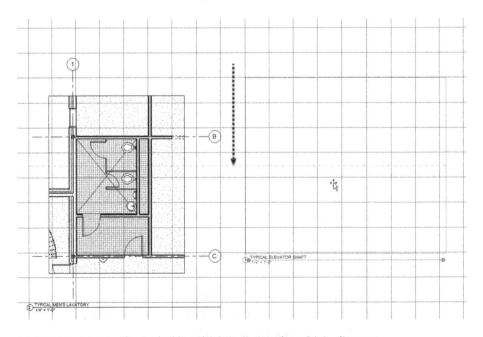

FIGURE 13.9 Aligning building elements. Notice column B is in alignment.

N O T E The title block is filled out. The page number and the sheet name are filled out because you edited those names when you made the sheet, but the project name will appear on every new sheet that you create.

Now that the first floor plans and typical enlarged plans are placed on a sheet, let's move on to adding the details you've created.

If you feel as though you have enough experience creating a sheet and adding views, go ahead and proceed on your own. Your new sheet will be numbered A301 and will be called BUILDING SECTIONS, and you'll add the views EAST CORRIDOR SECTION, WEST CORRIDOR SECTION, SECTION AT WEST TRAINING, and WEST WING SOUTH WALL SECTION. Your sheet should look like Figure 13.10.

If you'd like some assistance in putting the section sheet together, follow along with this procedure:

1. In the Project Browser, right-click the Sheets category.

2. Select New Sheet.

3. Select the E1 30 × 42 Horizontal title block and click OK.

4. In the Project Browser, right-click the new sheet and select Rename.

5. Give the new sheet the number **A301** and the name **BUILDING SECTIONS**.

6. In the Properties dialog, add the 30 × 42 grid guide.

7. In the Project Browser, find the Sections (Building Sections) category.

8. Drag the section called EAST CORRIDOR SECTION onto the lower-left corner of the sheet.

9. Drag the section called SECTION AT WEST TRAINING onto the sheet to the right of EAST CORRIDOR SECTION.

10. Drag the section called WEST CORRIDOR SECTION onto the sheet and place it in the upper-left corner. Be sure you align it directly above EAST CORRIDOR SECTION.

11. Drag the section called WEST WING SOUTH WALL SECTION to the right of WEST CORRIDOR SECTION and directly above SECTION AT WEST TRINING. The alignment lines allow you to place the section accurately. After you have these four sections in place, your sheet A301 should look like Figure 13.10.

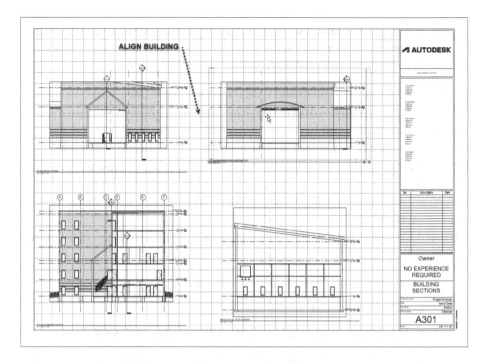

FIGURE 13.10 The sections positioned on sheet A301

You've created a few sheets, and you may want to make some adjustments to the view without leaving the sheet. The next section of this chapter will focus on the properties of a viewport and how to make it *live* on the sheet so you can make modifications.

Modifying a Viewport

Wait a second! Isn't a viewport Autodesk AutoCAD® vernacular? Yes, it is. But a viewport in AutoCAD and a viewport in Revit are two somewhat different things.

In Revit, when you drag a view onto a sheet, a linked copy of that view becomes a viewport. This is what you see on the sheet. Any modification you make to the original view is immediately reflected in the viewport and vice versa. See Figure 13.11 for a graphical representation of the completed sheet when we are done.

In the next procedure, you'll activate a viewport to make modifications on the sheet, and you'll also explore the element properties of the viewport. Follow along:

1. Open sheet A301 (if it isn't open already).

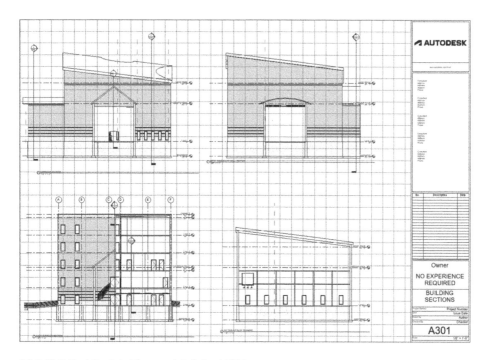

FIGURE 13.11 The completed sheet A301

2. Zoom in on the viewport West Wing South Wall Section, as shown in Figure 13.12.

3. Select the view.

4. Right-click and select Activate View (you can also select the viewport and click the Activate View button on the Viewport panel). See Figure 13.12.

NOTE You can also double-click on the viewport, which allows you to edit the actual view. If you double-click in a space away from the view, Revit will deactivate the viewport, allowing you to go back to editing the sheet.

5. With the view activated, you can work on it just as if you had opened it from the Project Browser. Select the crop region, as shown in Figure 13.13.

6. Stretch the top of the crop region upward so you can see the entire view. See Figure 13.13

7. Stretch the bottom down so you can see the entire foundation.

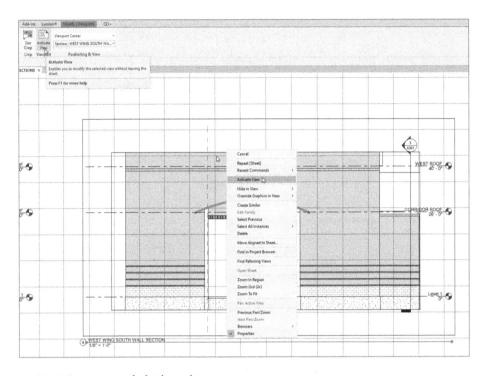

FIGURE 13.12 Activating a view

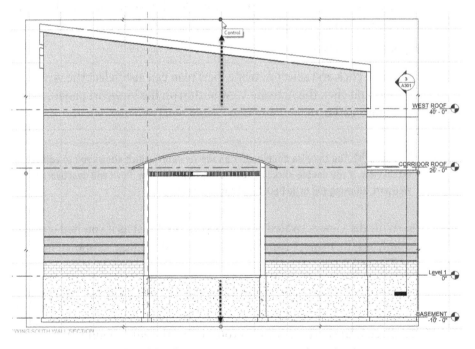

FIGURE 13.13 Stretching the crop region so you can see the entire view

NOTE By activating the view in this manner, you're essentially opening the view. The only difference between physically opening the view in the Project Browser and activating the view on the sheet is that by activating the view, you can see the title block, which helps in terms of layout.

UNSIGHTLY CROP REGIONS BEGONE!

By selecting Hide Crop Region, as shown in this image, you're simply cleaning up the view. As we'll explore in this chapter, you can also keep the crop region on and tell Revit not to print it.

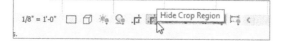

8. On the View Control toolbar, select Hide Crop Region.

9. Right-click and select Deactivate View.

10. Repeat these steps for each view to adjust them how you'd like them to be presented. Use Figure 13.11 at the beginning of this section for guidance.

With the view widened, it's coming close to the actual title. You can move the viewport and the title independently of one another.

1. Select the WEST WING SOUTH WALL SECTION view title, as shown in Figure 13.14.

2. Move it down. As you move the view title, it snaps in alignment to the view title to the left (see Figure 13.14).

3. Repeat this so all of your views and view titles are in alignment.

Now that you have some experience creating sheets and adjusting the views and viewports, you can easily create one more sheet that contains sections.

The following procedure focuses on creating a detail sheet. If you feel as though you can create this sheet on your own, go ahead. The sheet will be number A401, it will be named DETAILS, and the views to be added are CORRIDOR ENTRY SECTION, CALLOUT OF CORRIDOR ENTRY SECTION, ROOF TAPER SECTION, and TYPICAL WALL TERMINATION. Your finished sheet should look like Figure 13.15.

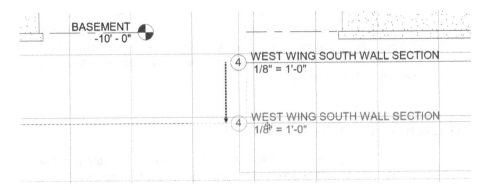

FIGURE 13.14 You can select the view title independently of the actual viewport.

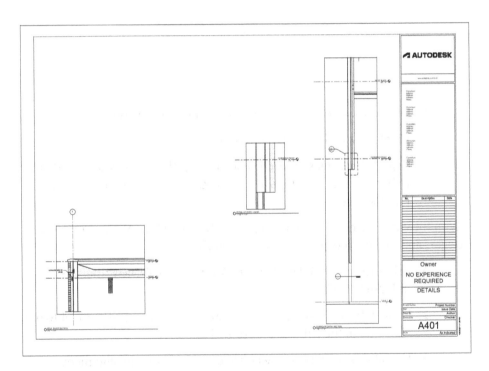

FIGURE 13.15 Building the A401 DETAILS sheet

If you'd rather have some assistance, follow along:

1. In the Sheets category in the Project Browser, right-click the Sheets title.

2. Select New Sheet.

3. Number it **A401**, and name it **DETAILS**.

4. In the Project Browser, drag the Sections (Wall Section) item COR-RIDOR ENTRY SECTION and place it in the sheet all the way to the right.

5. In the Project Browser, drag the Sections (Building Section) item DETAIL AT ENTRY LINTEL onto the sheet to the top left of the previous section.

 T I P If you tried to align the larger scale callout view to the smaller scale parent view, it won't let you. To align items, they need to be the same scale.

6. Drag the section called Roof Taper Section to the bottom left of the first view you added.

7. Zoom in on the view title for the Corridor Entry Section, as shown in Figure 13.16.

8. Select the Corridor Entry Section viewport. Notice the blue grips on the view title.

9. Extend the line by stretching the grip on the right to the right (see Figure 13.16).

10. Save the model.

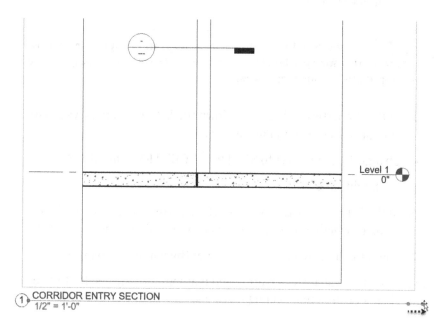

Level 1
0"

① CORRIDOR ENTRY SECTION
1/2" = 1'-0"

FIGURE 13.16 Stretching the view title line to the right using the blue grip

Pan and zoom around to investigate all the reference markers. They're starting to fill themselves out based on the sheets where you placed the referring views.

 N O T E You can place only one instance of a view on a sheet. You also can't place a view on multiple sheets. This is how Revit keeps track of what view is on a page and which page the view is on. The only types of view that you can place on more than one sheet are legends and schedules. If you would like to place a model view on a sheet more than once, you'll need to duplicate the view in the Project Browser.

Now that you know how to manipulate a viewport, it's time to look at the viewport's properties. I think you'll be glad to see how familiar these properties are.

Viewport Properties

Just like anything else in Revit, viewports have associated properties. You can select the viewport and click the Properties button on the Ribbon if the Properties dialog isn't already open.

The objective of the following procedure is to look through the viewport's properties and make some minor modifications. Follow along:

1. Open the view A401 - DETAILS (if it isn't already open).

2. Select the CORRIDOR ENTRY SECTION view (the tall section to the right of the sheet).

 N O T E Notice that the properties for the viewport are exactly the same as those for a typical view. When you change the properties of a viewport, you're actually changing the properties of the corresponding view.

3. In the Properties dialog, scroll down the list until you arrive at Title On Sheet, as shown in Figure 13.17.

4. Change Title On Sheet to **SECTION AT ENTRY CORRIDOR**.

5. Click Edit Type.

6. In the Type Parameters, you can choose which view title you'll be using or whether you want any view title at all. For now, click OK.

7. Zoom in on the detail and notice that the name has changed.

You've pretty much exhausted creating and manipulating sheets. It's time to explore another sheet function: adding revisions.

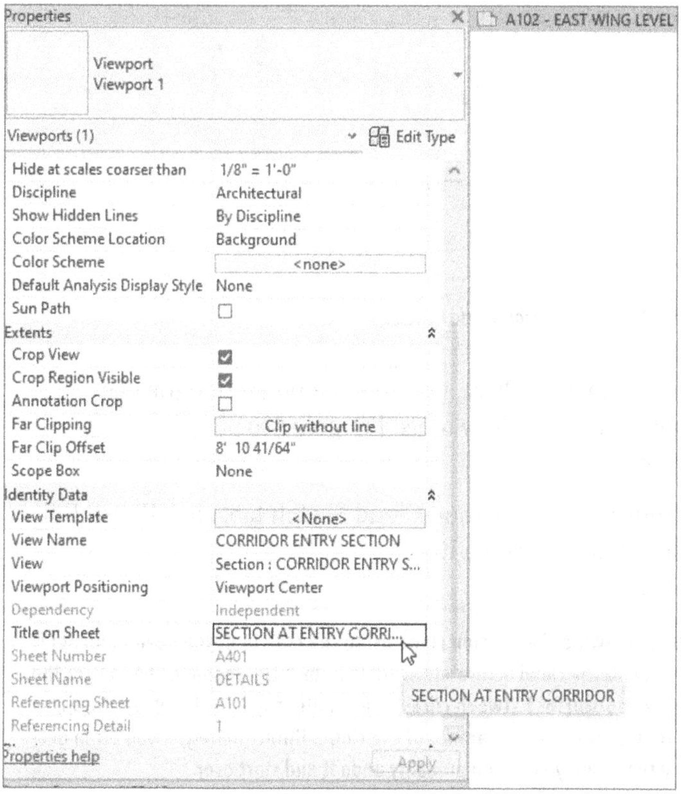

FIGURE 13.17 You can make the title on the sheet different from the view name.

Adding Revisions to a Sheet

An unfortunate reality in producing construction documents is that you must eventually make revisions. In CAD, you normally create a duplicate of the file, save that file into your project directory, and then create the revisions. The only way to keep track of them is to add a revision cloud and change the attribute information in the title block. In Revit, however, you're given a revision schedule and the means to keep track of your revisions.

In the next procedure, you'll add a revision cloud and populate a schedule that is already built into the sheet. Follow these steps:

1. In the Project Browser, open Sheet A101.

2. On the Annotate tab, click the Revision Cloud button, as shown in Figure 13.18. You're now in Sketch mode.

When you select the viewport, the name and detail number turn blue. This means you can change the values right on the sheet.

FIGURE 13.18 Finding the Revision Cloud button

3. Notice the Draw panel. Place a revision cloud around the plan by using any one of the draw tools. I'm going to pick the Rectangle button.

4. On the Modify | Create Revision Cloud Sketch tab, click Finish Edit Mode as shown in Figure 13.19

TIP If you are drawing the revision cloud using the Line tool, you need to model it point by point. To place the cloud accurately, work in a clockwise manner. The shorter the distance you move your cursor between clicks, the smaller the arcs that Revit draws, so you have some control over the appearance of the cloud. Unfortunately, if you err in getting the cloud on the sheet, you should probably undo it and start over.

5. On the Annotate tab, click Tag By Category.

6. Pick the revision cloud.

7. You may get a dialog stating that you don't have a tag loaded for this category. If you see this dialog, click Yes to load one.

8. Select Annotations ➢ Revision Tag.rfa.

9. Pick the revision cloud. It's now tagged (see Figure 13.20).

Zoom closer to the title block. The revision schedule has the first revision added to it. Revit is keeping track of your revisions.

Next, you'll modify the revision scheme so that you can better keep track of the revision schedule. Follow along:

1. On the View tab, click the Sheet Issues/Revisions button in the Sheet Composition panel. The dialog shown in Figure 13.21 opens.

2. In the Sheet Issues/Revisions dialog, change the date to today's date.

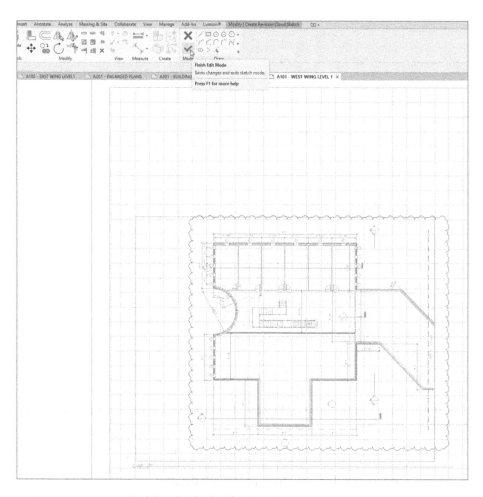

FIGURE 13.19 Modeling the cloud in Sketch mode

3. For the description, type **FIRST FLOOR REVISIONS**.

4. Click the Add button (see Figure 13.21).

5. Give the new revision a date in the future.

6. For the description, enter **REVISED SECTIONS** (again, see Figure 13.21).

7. For Numbering, make sure the Per Project radio button is picked.

8. Click OK.

9. In the Project Browser, open the sheet A301 - BUILDING SECTIONS.

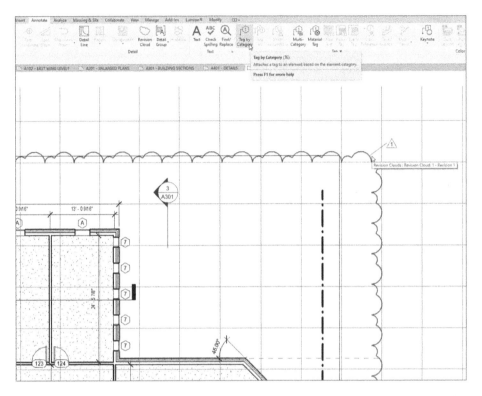

FIGURE 13.20 The revision tag has been added to the cloud. Also, notice that the title block has Revision 1 added to it.

10. On the Annotate tab, click the Revision Cloud button.

11. Place a cloud around the upper-right detail.

12. In the Mode panel, click Finish Edit Mode.

13. Select the cloud you just added.

14. On the Options bar, make sure Seq. 2 - Revised Sections is selected, as shown in Figure 13.22.

15. On the Annotate tab, select Tag By Category.

16. Place the revision tag on the cloud. The schedule in the title block is filled with only the appropriate revision relevant to this sheet.

Now that you have experience with the concept of how sheets and revisions come together, we need to explore one more avenue of populating sheet information. You may have noticed that the title blocks aren't yet complete. The empty fields relate to project information that needs to be included on each sheet. This is where project parameters come in.

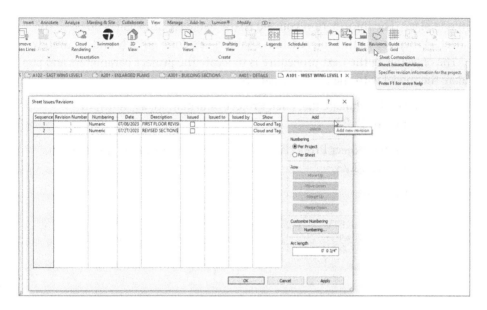

FIGURE 13.21 The Sheet Issues/Revisions dialog

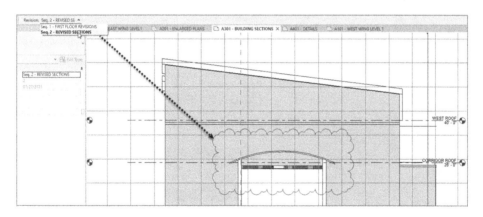

FIGURE 13.22 By selecting the revision cloud, you can specify the sequence from the Options bar.

Addressing Project Information

Because Revit is built on a database, it makes sense that items like Project Name and Project Number are added to the design in a different manner than in CAD. In CAD, you fill out attributes sheet by sheet, or you externally reference a title block with the sheet information. In Revit, you fill out the project information in one place. The information you add to the database propagates down to the sheets. When (or if) this information changes, it's done quickly and accurately.

The objective of the next procedure is to locate the project parameters and populate the model with the job information:

1. On the Manage tab, click Project Information, as shown in Figure 13.23.

2. In the Project Properties dialog, add the information as shown in Figure 13.23.

3. Click OK.

FIGURE 13.23 Filling out the project data

SAVE THAT MODEL!

You may have noticed that a save reminder keeps popping up (as shown here). Revit likes to ask you if you want to save the model *before* you execute a command. This process has greatly reduced the number of crashes when compared to the number in AutoCAD.

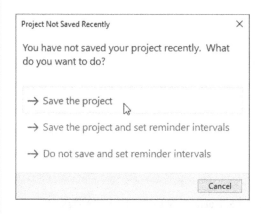

NOTE The NO EXPERIENCE REQUIRED text has already been entered in the Project Name field. This is because you added it to the appropriate field in the title block. Remember, when you're dealing with Revit, and databases in general, it's a two-way flow of information.

4. Open any sheet and examine the title block. All the information should be filled out.

You can now populate the information in a sheet. Before we jump into printing, we need to cover one more item quickly: adding a drawing list.

Generating a Cover Sheet

It goes without saying that this ingenious method of creating and managing sheets wouldn't be quite perfect unless you could generate a sheet list and put it on a cover sheet. Well, this is Revit. Of course you can do this! The best part is that you already have the experience necessary to carry out this procedure.

The objective here is to create a sheet list and add it to a cover sheet. Follow these steps:

1. On the View tab, click Schedules ≻ Sheet List, as shown in Figure 13.24.

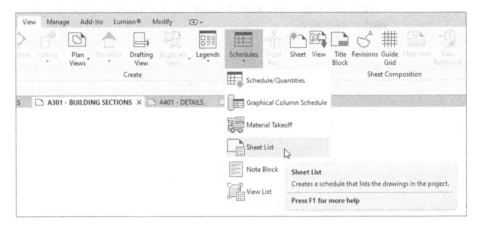

F I G U R E 1 3 . 2 4 Selecting Schedules ≻ Sheet List on the View tab

2. In the Sheet List Properties dialog, add Sheet Number and Sheet Name, as shown in Figure 13.25.

3. Click the Sorting/Grouping tab.

4. Sort by Sheet Number.

5. Select Ascending.

6. Click OK.

Wow! Creating a schedule is so easy, you'll probably be doing this on your lunch break instead of going on LinkedIn.

For now, let's keep this schedule in the Project Browser and create a cover sheet onto which you can drag it. You'll create a new title-block family, add it to the project, and then drag the drawing list onto the cover. Follow these steps:

1. Click the blue File tab, and choose New ≻ Title Block, as shown in Figure 13.26.

2. Select E1 - 42 × 30.rft (1050 × 750).

3. Click Open.

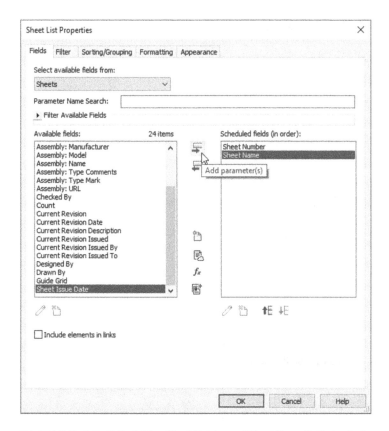

FIGURE 13.25 Adding Sheet Number and Sheet Name (in that order)

4. In the Text panel of the Create tab, click Label, as shown in Figure 13.27.

5. In the Properties dialog, click Edit Type.

6. Click Duplicate.

7. Call the new tag TITLE and click OK.

8. Make sure Text Font is set to Arial.

9. Change Text Size to 1″ (25 mm).

10. Click Bold.

11. Click OK.

12. In the Alignment panel, click the Middle Align and the Align Center buttons.

13. Pick a point in the upper center of the sheet.

FIGURE 13.26 Creating a new title block

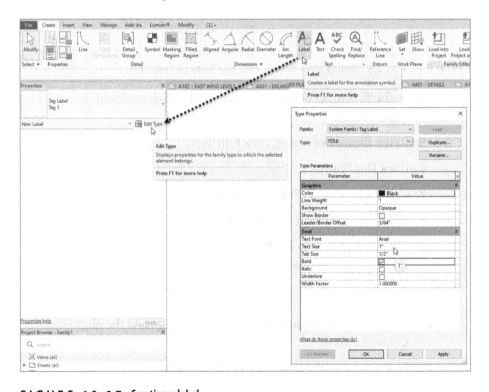

FIGURE 13.27 Creating a label

After you place the tag, you immediately see the Edit Label dialog. This dialog lets you add the label you wish. When you load this cover sheet into the project and add it to a new sheet, the project information will populate automatically.

Next, you'll add the correct tags to the sheet. Follow along:

1. Select Project Name and click the Add Parameter(s) To Label button, as shown in Figure 13.28.

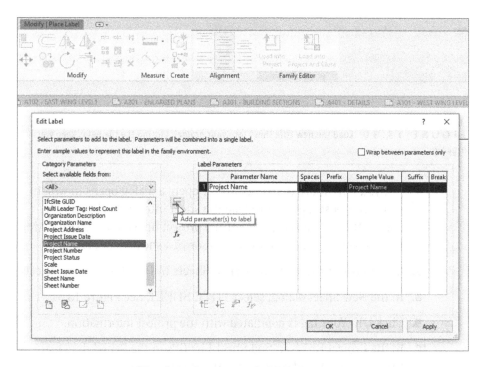

FIGURE 13.28 Adding the project name to the label

2. Click OK.

3. Click the label and widen the grips. You may have to adjust the label so that it's centered in the sheet, as shown in Figure 13.29.

FIGURE 13.29 Adjusting the label so that it's centered in the sheet

4. Click the Application button, and then click Save As ➤ Family.

5. Save the file somewhere that makes sense to you. Call it TITLE SHEET.

6. Click Load Into Project and Close as shown in Figure 13.30.

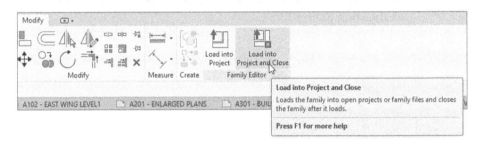

FIGURE 13.30 Load the new title sheet into your project. Closing the file helps keep you organized.

If you have more than one project open, a dialog opens in which you can choose a project to load the sheet into. If this is the case, choose the No Experience Required project on which you're working. If the sheet appears under your cursor in a sheet view, press Esc.

7. In the Project Browser, right-click Sheets (All) and select New Sheet.

8. In the New Sheet dialog, select TITLE SHEET. See Figure 13.31.

9. Click OK. Your tag is populated with the project information.

10. In the Project Browser, find Sheet List (it's in the Schedules/Quantities category), and drag it onto the sheet.

11. Rename the sheet to **A100 COVER SHEET**.

12. Select the schedule and adjust it so that the text is readable. Your title sheet, although not very glorious, should look like Figure 13.32.

In most cases, you don't want the actual cover sheet to be an item in the schedule. You can fix this. While still in the cover sheet, deselect Appears In Sheet List in the Properties dialog, as shown in Figure 13.33.

Perfect! You have a handful of sheets. The beauty is that you don't have to leave the model to see how these sheets are shaping up. In Revit, they're always just a click away.

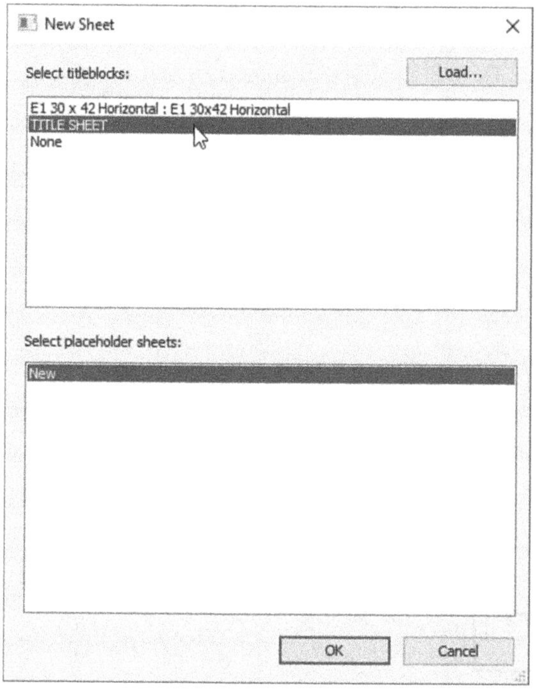

New Sheet

Select titleblocks: Load...

E1 30 x 42 Horizontal : E1 30x42 Horizontal
TITLE SHEET
None

Select placeholder sheets:

New

OK   Cancel

FIGURE 13.31   Adding the new sheet

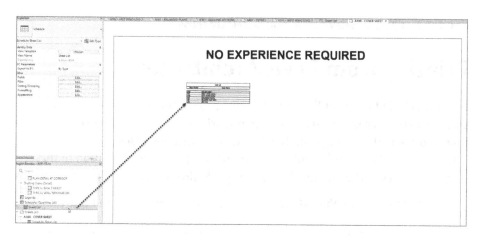

NO EXPERIENCE REQUIRED

FIGURE 13.32   The completed title sheet

You have these sheets, so let's explore how you send them to the plotter. After all, you're producing paper construction documents.

FIGURE 13.33 Deselect the Appears In Sheet List option.

Printing from Revit Architecture

Luckily, printing is one of the easiest things you'll confront in Revit. However, you must consider some dangerous defaults when printing. I will go out on a limb and say that printing from Revit is too easy in some cases.

In this procedure, you'll print a set of drawings. Pay special attention to the warnings—they will steer you clear of danger. Follow along:

1. On the blue File tab, choose Print ➤ Print, as shown in Figure 13.34.

 T I P So, what's cool is that Revit is a Windows-based application. Why is that cool? It's cool because the Ctrl+P key combination works to print from Revit. Try it!

2. For the printer name, select the printer to which you wish to print.

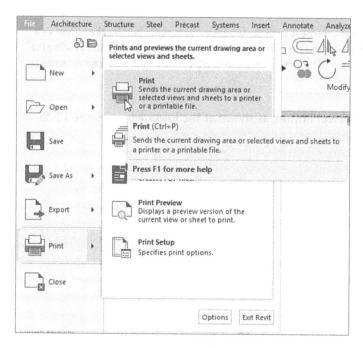

FIGURE 13.34 Finding the option to print

If you're printing to a file, you can choose to combine all files into one or create separate files. Choose to combine into one file. If you aren't printing to a file, ignore this choice.

 NOTE If you want to make PDFs, Revit now has an export to PDF function that's awesome.

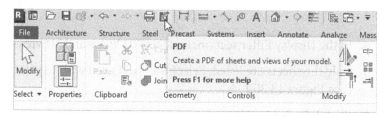

3. For Print Range, you can print the current window, print the visible portion of the current window, or choose Selected Views/Sheets. In this case, choose Selected Views/Sheets.

TIP When you choose to print the current window, you're printing the current view. When you choose to print the visible portion of the current window, you're printing the area into which you're currently zoomed. In Revit, you don't pick a window as you do in CAD.

4. Click the Select button, as shown at the lower left of Figure 13.35.

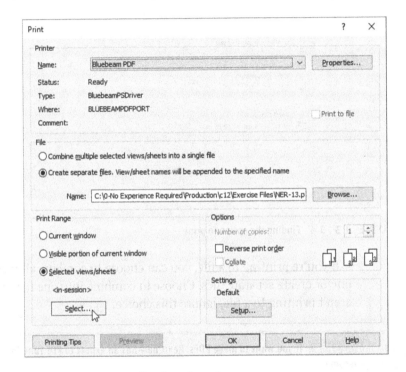

FIGURE 13.35 Choosing print options

5. In the Display Filter section, uncheck 2D Views and 3D Views.

6. Only the sheets are listed. Select the sheets you wish to print. (See Figure 13.36.)

7. Click Edit Print Order.

8. Order the sheets the way you'd like them printed.

9. Click OK or Cancel.

10. Click Select.

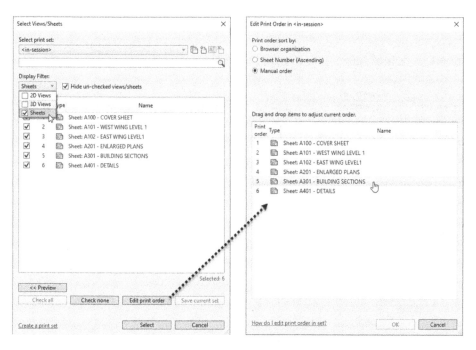

FIGURE 13.36 Adding selected views and print order

11. Revit might ask if you want to save the settings for a future print. Click No.

12. In the lower-left corner in the Settings area, click the Setup button, as shown in Figure 13.37.

T I P Printing from Revit is similar to printing from an AutoCAD paperspace or model-space environment where you can print a specific view or print an entire sheet. The only difference is that you aren't bothered by scale. The sheets and views are printed at the scale specified in Revit.

W A R N I N G Make a habit of clicking the Setup button before you print. You need to verify some crucial settings in the resulting dialog.

13. For Paper, choose the paper size you wish to print.

14. For Paper Placement, choose Center.

15. For Zoom, select Zoom: 100% Of Size.

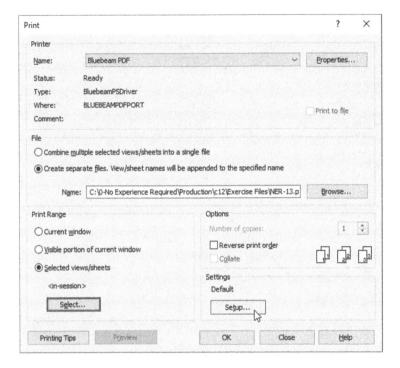

FIGURE 13.37 Clicking the Setup button

 W A R N I N G The Fit To Page radio button should never be selected unless you know you aren't plotting to scale. If you want a reduced set of drawings, you can specify Zoom and then change to a smaller percentage (50% is a half-size set).

16. Under Options, make sure the following are selected, as shown in Figure 13.38:

   ► Hide Ref/Work Planes

   ► Hide Unreferenced View Tags

   ► Hide Scope Boxes

   ► Hide Crop Boundaries

17. For Appearance, under Colors, select Black Lines (see Figure 13.38).

18. Click OK.

19. Click OK again, and your plot is off.

20. Save the file.

F I G U R E 1 3 . 3 8 Specifying your options

There you have it.

The exercises in this chapter don't create a sheet for every single view. If you feel as though you're still lacking experience in creating sheets and printing, go ahead and create more sheets and keep printing away until you're confident about moving on to Chapter 14, "Creating Rooms and Area Plans."

Are You Experienced?

Now you can. . .

      ✓ create sheets by dragging views and creating viewports

      ✓ configure project parameters to populate the sheets

      ✓ create a drawing list for a cover sheet

Creating Rooms and Area Plans

I think this part of Revit is awesome! I can't tell you how many times in the past I had to manually type in text for room names, them use some graphical program to "color" in those rooms. Revit makes this process so much more streamlined!

This chapter covers the following topics:

▶ **Creating rooms**

▶ **Adding a room schedule**

▶ **Adding a color-fill plan**

▶ **Adding room separators**

▶ **Creating an area plan**

Creating Rooms

The first topic we'll tackle is the task of creating a room and adding it to the model. The procedures that follow will focus on finding where to launch the room and areas and the parameters the Autodesk® Revit® Architecture software looks for while placing a room into the floor plan.

Because Revit draws from a database to gather information, the process of creating a room boils down to your adding some notes to an already-built form. When you place the room in the model, Revit automatically tags it. Unlike other drafting applications, however, Revit doesn't rely on the tag for its information. When a room is in the model, it can either contain or not contain a tag. This is a great way to organize the flow of room information.

To get started, open the model on which you've been working. If you skipped the previous chapter, go to the book's web page at www.wiley.com/go/revit2024ner. From there, you can browse to Chapter 14 and find the file called NER-14.rvt.

The objective of the following procedure is to find the Room & Area panel of the Architecture tab and to configure and add some rooms to the model. Follow along:

1. In the Project Browser, find the dependent view called Level 1 East, and open it.

2. On the Architecture tab, click the Room button, as shown in Figure 14.1.

FIGURE 14.1 Click the Room button on the Architecture tab.

3. On the Tag panel, make sure Tag on placement is selected. (See Figure 14.2.)

4. Hover your cursor over the southeast room, as shown in Figure 14.2. An X appears, along with the outline of a room tag.

5. Pick a spot in the middle of the four walls.

6. Press Esc.

You've now added a room to the model. Of course, it's a nondescript room name with a nondescript room number. Let's correct that by changing the room name and number on the screen:

1. Select the room tag that you just added to the model.

NOTE You may be sick of hearing this by now, but I'll say it again: when you select a component in Revit, the items that turn blue are always editable.

2. Click the Room text. The text turns blue. Once it does, click it again.

3. Change the name to SOUTHEAST CORNER OFFICE.

4. Click room number 1.

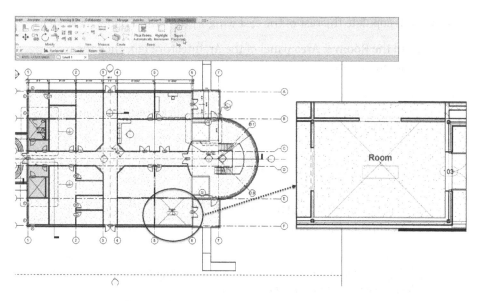

FIGURE 14.2 When you hover your mouse over the intended area of the room, you see an indication that Revit has found the bounding edges.

5. Change the number to **112A** (see Figure 14.3).

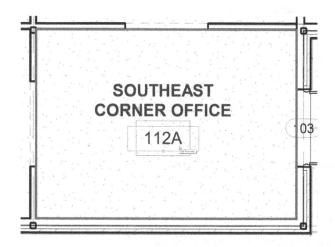

FIGURE 14.3 Changing the room name and number to SOUTHEAST CORNER OFFICE and 112A, respectively

When you modify the fields in a tag in Revit, the best method to finalize the data is to click an area away from the tag. Doing so ensures that you don't inadvertently create an additional line in the tag's value.

Now that you have a room in place and it's named properly, you can start cooking in terms of adding more rooms. This is because Revit will begin to number the rooms sequentially as you place them into the model.

Next you'll populate the rest of the east wing with rooms. Follow these steps:

1. In the Room & Area panel of the Architecture tab, click the Room button.

TIP   If you get the Save reminder, be sure to save the model. In no situation is this ever a bad idea!

2. Place a room in the adjacent area, as shown at the lower left in Figure 14.4.

3. Call the room **SOUTHEAST CONFERENCE** (see Figure 14.4). Renumber the room 111A.

NOTE   Did you notice that the room tag tries to align itself with the adjacent tag? This is a fantastic feature in Revit Architecture.

4. In the Room & Area panel of the Architecture tab, click the Room button again.

5. Place a room in the radial entry area.

6. Rename the room **EAST ENTRY**.

7. Renumber the room 113.

8. Place a room in the south elevator shaft.

9. Rename and renumber it **SOUTHEAST ELEVATOR** and 115.

10. Place a room in the north elevator shaft.

11. Rename and renumber it **NORTHEAST ELEVATOR** and 114.

12. Place a room in the corridor.

13. Call it **EAST WING CORRIDOR**, and number it 100.

14. Just north of SOUTHEAST CONFERENCE and SOUTHEAST CORNER OFFICE, place two rooms, each called **GATHERING**. Number them 112 and 111. See Figure 14.4.

15. Zoom over to the west portion of the east wing, where the lavatories are located.

16. In the north lavatory, add a room named **MEN's**, numbered 105.

17. In the south lavatory, add a room named **WOMEN's**, numbered 106.

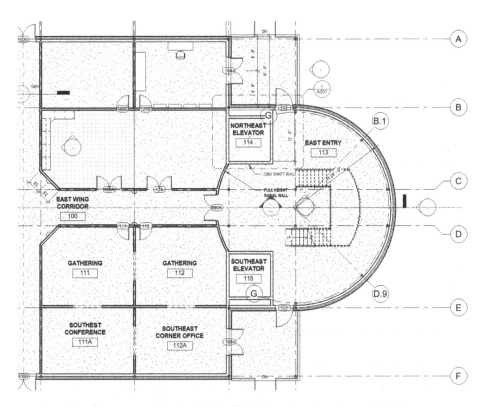

FIGURE 14.4 The first floor layout up to this point

I think you're getting the concept of adding rooms. Although you've added a number of rooms to the east wing, you need to begin adding some plain-old offices. The next procedure will involve adding offices to the rest of the spaces in the east wing of Level 1. From there, you can look at a room's properties and figure out how to alter the room information. Follow along:

1. Make sure you're in the east wing area of the model, on Level 1.

2. In the Room & Area panel of the Architecture tab, click the Room button.

3. Pick the large area to the right of the women's lavatory, as shown in Figure 14.5.

4. Rename the room OFFICE, and change the number to 107 (see Figure 14.5).

N O T E   If the numbering starts to become inconsistent with the examples in the book, that's OK. This will happen from time to time in Revit. You can accept the differences between the book and your model, or you can renumber the rooms to match. Either way, the numbering won't affect the outcome of the procedures.

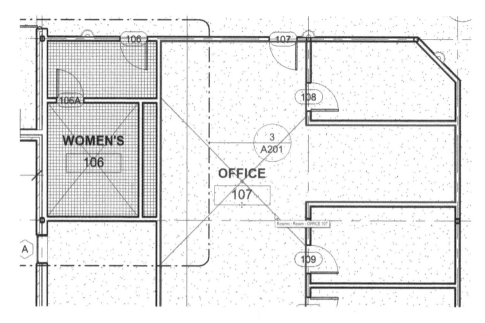

FIGURE 14.5 Renaming the office

5. Click the Room button.

6. Add rooms to the rest of the vacant areas, renaming them all
   OFFICE. (Skip the kitchen area and the room to the right of it, as
   shown in Figure 14.6.)

With all the rooms in (at least in this section of the building), you can begin
examining specific properties to see how you can add functionality and further
populate the database information pertaining to each room.

Configuring Properties

Each room has specific properties associated with it. There are floor finishes and
wall finishes as well as ceiling types and finishes. It would be nice if Revit picked
up this information by "reading" the ceilings, walls, and floors, but it doesn't.
And for good reason—imagine having to create a different wall type for each
paint color and then splitting each partition as it passed through each room. In
Revit, you specify individual room finishes in the properties of the room itself.

In the next procedure, you'll generate additional room information in the properties of a room. Follow these steps:

1. Zoom in on the SOUTHEAST CORNER OFFICE 112A room.

2. Hover your cursor over the room until you see the X, as shown in
   Figure 14.7. You may need to press the Tab key.

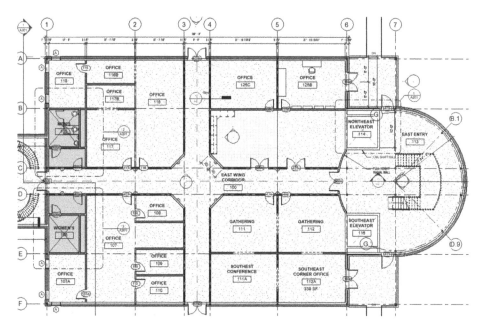

FIGURE 14.6 Add rooms to the remainder of the spaces. (Yes, we still have two that don't have rooms yet.)

TIP Anytime you wish to view the properties of a room, you need to click the actual room, not the room tag. Sometimes, selecting a room can be difficult because the room is invisible until you hover over it. With some practice, this process will soon become second nature. Also, be sure the Select Elements By Face icon has a red X through it, as shown in Figure 14.7.

3. Pick the room, as shown in Figure 14.7.

4. In the Properties dialog, scroll down to the Identity Data group.

5. Add **WD-1** to Base Finish.

6. Add **ACT** to Ceiling Finish.

7. Add **PT** to Wall Finish.

8. Add **VCT** to Floor Finish (see Figure 14.7).

9. Select the SOUTHEAST CONFERENCE room.

10. In the Properties dialog, click into the Base Finish field. Click the arrow for the pull-down menu, and select WD-1, as shown in Figure 14.8.

11. Change the rest of the fields using the previous entries.

12. Save the model.

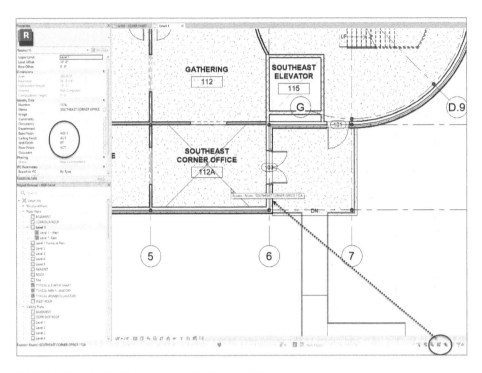

FIGURE 14.7 Adding values to the identity data

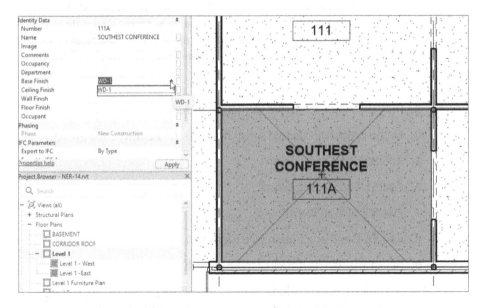

FIGURE 14.8 When a field has been added to the database, it's available for the rest of the rooms.

Changing a room's properties is a simple task. There is, however, one more item to discuss. It pertains to a room that spans multiple floors, such as the east entry.

The objective of the next procedure is to change the height of the east entry room's properties:

1. Zoom in on the east entry area and select the room, as shown in Figure 14.9.

2. In the Properties dialog, change Upper Limit to Roof.

3. Change Limit Offset to 0. Doing so sets the east entry room to extend from Level 1 to the roof.

If you're having trouble selecting the room, remember that you can pick an entire window around the area and use the Filter button in the Filter panel.

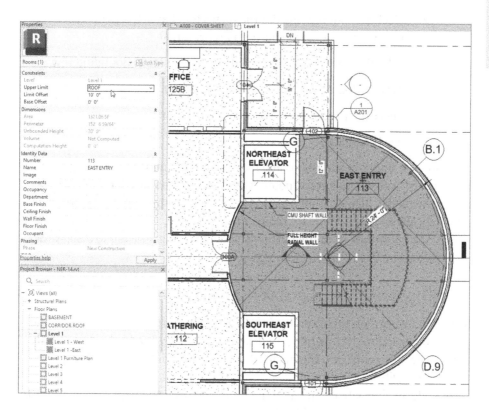

FIGURE 14.9 Selecting the east entry room

Now that you have experience changing the properties of the rooms, it's time to look at the properties of the walls that divide the rooms. You noticed that when you placed the rooms in the lavatories, the rooms didn't fill the small entry areas. You can correct this by changing the walls' room-bounding properties.

Room-Bounding Properties

By default, each wall you add to the Revit model automatically defines a room boundary, and this is what you want 95 percent of the time. In some situations, however, you don't want a wall to separate the room. In such cases, you can modify the instance parameters of the wall to disallow the division of the room.

In this procedure, you'll turn off the room bounding in certain walls. Follow along:

1. In the East Wing floor plan, zoom in on the lavatory area.

2. Select the wall that divides the men's toilet area from the men's lavatory entry area, as shown in Figure 14.10.

3. In the Properties dialog, scroll down to the Room Bounding row.

4. Deselect Room Bounding (see Figure 14.10).

5. Repeat the procedure in the women's lavatory.

6. Save the model.

Having the ability to add rooms and manipulate the information easily in the Revit database gives you a tremendous advantage as you move forward with the rest of the model. Also, that information is relayed into the room's tag, which is automatically added as you place rooms into the model.

This concept brings us to the next topic: how to change the tag to display the information you desire on the drawings.

Placing and Manipulating Room Tags

As mentioned earlier, the room tag is merely a vehicle to relay the room's data to the construction documents. As a default, a room tag is added automatically as you place the room into the model. A default room tag is included, but you aren't stuck with it.

Let's add an alternate room tag to the room and open the tag's Family Editor to investigate the composition of the tag:

1. Zoom in to SOUTHEAST CORNER OFFICE.

2. Select the room tag.

3. In the Type Selector, select Room Tag With Area. The tag displays the area, as shown in Figure 14.11.

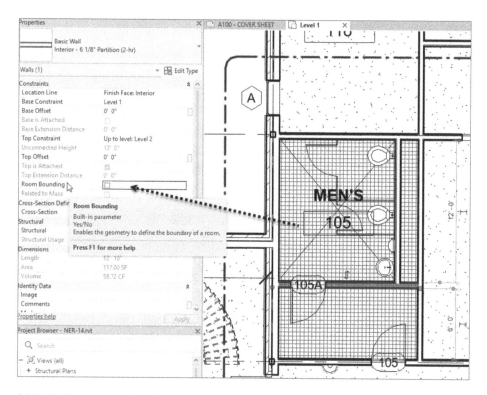

FIGURE 14.10 Selecting the partition within the men's lavatory

That was way too easy! Let's take a closer look at what you just did. A room tag is nothing more than the cover sheet label you created back in Chapter 13, "Creating Sheets and Printing." All you need to do is open the file and place a tag into the family.

To open the tag's Family Editor, follow this procedure:

1. Select the room tag for SOUTHWEST CORNER OFFICE.

2. On the Modify | Room Tags tab, click the Edit Family button.

3. With the family file open, click the Room Name piece of text that is visible. (These pieces of text are actually labels.)

4. On the Modify | Label tab, click the Edit Label button.

5. In the Edit Label dialog, the list to the left displays all the parameters that you can add to the room tag (see Figure 14.12). Don't change anything; click OK.

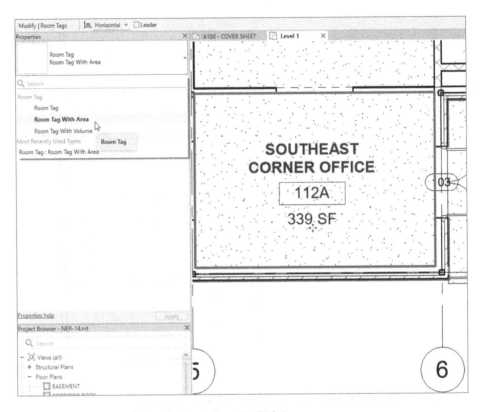

FIGURE 14.11 Change the type to Room Tag With Area.

 WARNING If you're modifying the room tag, do yourself and the rest of your design team a huge favor and inform everyone that you're changing your company's standards! If you're the BIM manager, set the permissions to this network directory accordingly.

6. Close this file without saving any changes.

Now that you know what tag Revit uses when it places a room and how to manipulate that tag, let's tie the tag into something more robust. A tag is just a reflection of the room data. You can add another Revit object that does the same thing: a room schedule.

Adding a Room Schedule

Up to this point in your career, you've been adding room information twice, or sometimes three times. Why? Because you had to fill out the tag in the plan and then fill out the same information in the room schedule. If you were in the unfortunate situation of having an enlarged plan, then you added the information a third time. When you needed to change that information, you had to do so in several places. I'm not saying that Revit will end all your problems, but it sure will make life easier.

The objective of the next procedure is to create a room schedule. You'll then

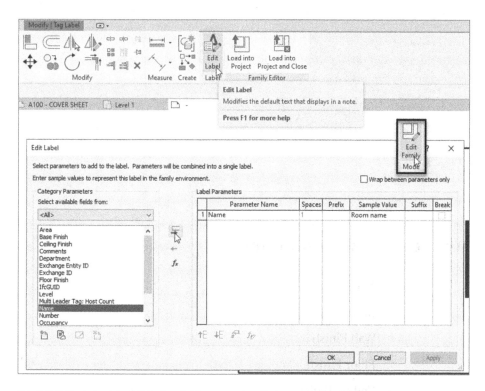

FIGURE 14.12 A list of available parameters that you can add to the room tag

finish filling out the room information from the schedule, thus saving time and increasing accuracy. Follow along:

1. On the View tab, click Schedules, and then click the Schedule/Quantities button.

2. In the New Schedule dialog, select Rooms from the list at the left (see Figure 14.13).

3. Click OK.

4. On the Fields tab of the Schedule Properties dialog that opens, add the following fields in the specified order (see Figure 14.14):

   ▶ Number

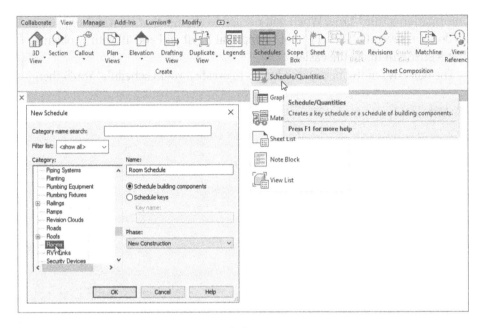

FIGURE 14.13 Selecting Rooms from the list

▶ Name

▶ Base Finish

▶ Wall Finish

▶ Floor Finish

▶ Ceiling Finish

▶ Comments

▶ Level

▶ Area

5. Click the Sorting/Grouping tab.

6. Sort by number.

7. Toward the bottom of the dialog, click Grand Totals, as shown in Figure 14.14.

8. Click the Formatting tab.

9. Click the Area field.

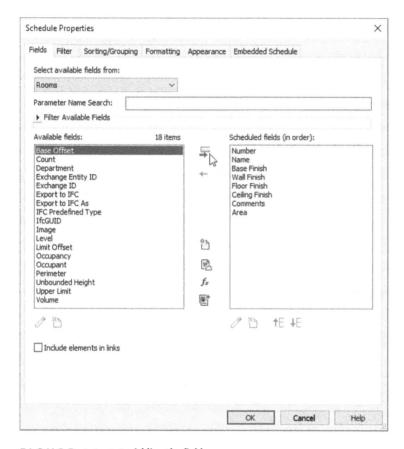

FIGURE 14.14 Adding the fields

10. Select Calculate Totals, as shown in Figure 14.15.

11. Click OK. Your schedule should look similar to Figure 14.15.

12. With the schedule still open, click into the EAST ENTRY Base Finish cell, and type **WD-2**.

13. Click into the Floor Finish cell, and type **TER** (for Terrazzo).

14. Click into the Wall Finish cell, and type **VINYL**.

15. Click into the Ceiling Finish cell, and type a hyphen (-).

16. Click into the EAST WING CORRIDOR Base Finish cell. Click the menu arrow, as shown in Figure 14.16. You have a choice between two base finishes: choose WD-2.

17. Change the other values to VINYL, TER, and ACT (see Figure 14.16).

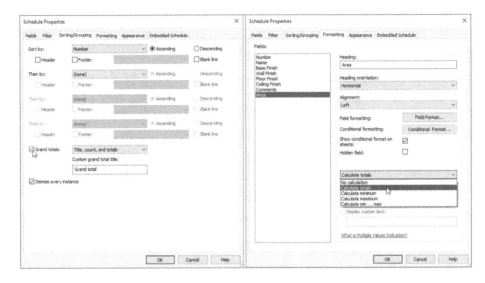

FIGURE 14.15 Making sorting and calculation adjustments

	A	B	C	D	E	F	G	H
	Number	Name	Base Finish	Wall Finish	Floor Finish	Ceiling Finish	Comments	Area
	100	EAST WING CORRIDOR	WD-2	VINYL	TER	ACT		1360 SF
	105	MEN'S						216 SF
	106	WOMEN'S						216 SF
	107	OFFICE						668 SF
	107A	OFFICE						184 SF
	108	OFFICE						121 SF
	109	OFFICE						126 SF
	110	OFFICE						130 SF
	111	GATHERING						393 SF
	111A	SOUTHEAST CONFERENCE	WD-1	PT	VCT	ACT		339 SF
	112	GATHERING						394 SF
	112A	SOUTHEAST CORNER OFFICE	WD-1	PT	VCT	ACT		339 SF
	113	EAST ENTRY	WD-2	VINYL	TER	-		1321 SF
	114	NORTHEAST ELEVATOR						99 SF
	115	SOUTHEAST ELEVATOR						99 SF
	116	OFFICE						528 SF
	116B	OFFICE						116 SF
	117	OFFICE						290 SF
	117B	OFFICE						116 SF
	118	OFFICE						184 SF
	125B	OFFICE						339 SF
	125C	OFFICE						339 SF
	Grand total: 22							7919 SF

Title bar: A100 - COVER SHEET   Level 1   Room Schedule ✕   <Room Schedule>

FIGURE 14.16 Filling out the room schedule

With the rooms in place and a schedule filled out, let's move on to a more colorful aspect of placing rooms in the model: adding a color-fill plan.

TURNING OFF UNWANTED ROOMS

Your model may have an errant room that doesn't belong in the schedule. Because going step by step through a book doesn't give you a true feel for a real-world scenario, I can tell you that you'll wind up with some misplaced rooms. This is OK, because you can turn them off in the schedule. If you click the Not Placed/Not Enclosed menu, you'll see that you can show, hide, or isolate unwanted data. For this example, choose Hide to remove the row (see the following graphic):

Adding a Color-Fill Plan

Another benefit of using the room feature in Revit is that you can add a color-fill plan at any time, and you can create virtually any type of color or pattern scheme you desire. Here's the best part: adding one is so easy, it's almost fun.

In this procedure you'll make a duplicate of the East Wing floor plan and create a color scheme based on room names. Follow these steps:

1. Right-click the Level 1 floor-plan view, and select Duplicate View ➤ Duplicate With Detailing, as shown in Figure 14.17.

2. Right-click the new view and select Rename.

3. Rename the view LEVEL 1 COLOR PLAN.

4. Press Enter.

5. Open the new plan if it isn't open already.

6. On the Analyze tab, click the Color Fill Legend button, as shown in Figure 14.18.

7. Place the color scheme into the model in the upper-right corner of the view (inside the crop region).

8. Change Space Type to Rooms and Color Scheme to Name (see Figure 14.19).

FIGURE 14.17 Duplicating the view

FIGURE 14.18 Clicking the Color Fill Legend button

9. Click OK. You have a nice color plan.

10. Select the color scheme legend.

11. Click the Edit Scheme button on the Modify | Color Fill Legends tab, as shown in Figure 14.20.

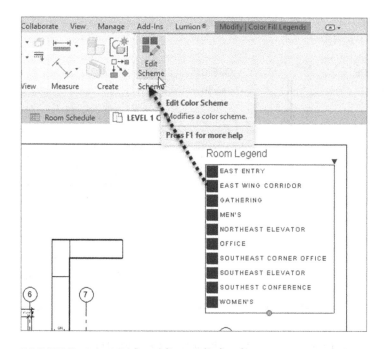

FIGURE 14.19 Specifying the color scheme

FIGURE 14.20 Proceeding to edit the scheme

12. In the Edit Color Scheme dialog that opens, you can alter the color and the fill pattern for each room. After you investigate this area, click OK.

Pretty cool concept! You may notice that the two rooms you skipped are still white. It's time to look at this situation. The problem is, there are no walls dividing the two rooms, but it would be nice to have two separate rooms anyway. To do this, you can add a room separator.

Adding Room Separators

Although it seems like a small issue, adding room separators has been known to confuse people. In Revit, you can physically draw a room without any walls. Or you can draw a line in the sand between two rooms that aren't separated by an actual wall. This is known as adding a *room separator*.

Let's separate the kitchen from the break room by adding a room separator:

1. In the Level 1 floor plan, zoom in on the area shown in Figure 14.21.

2. In the Room & Area panel of the Architecture tab, choose Room Separator, as shown in Figure 14.21.

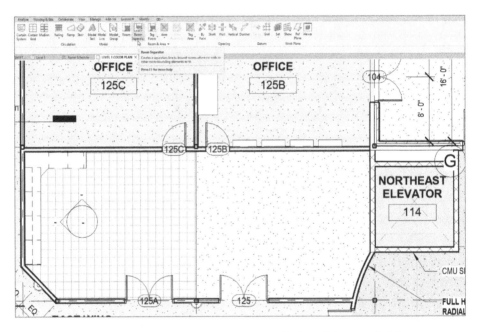

FIGURE 14.21 Click the Room Separator button in the Room & Area panel of the Architecture tab.

3. On the Draw tab, click the Draw Lines icon.

4. Draw a line along the edge of the flooring, as shown in Figure 14.22.

5. Click the Room button.

6. Place a room in the kitchen area and in the break area.

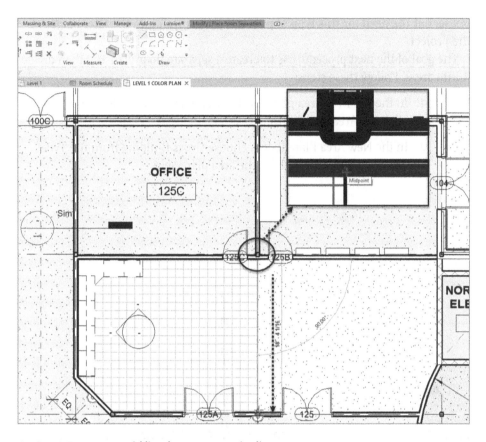

FIGURE 14.22 Adding the room-separation line

7. Change the room to the left to **KITCHEN**.

8. Change the room to the right to **BREAK**.

You're really moving along. You now have a fully coordinated room schedule tied into a room color-fill plan that can be modified by simply changing a room tag. How did you ever live without Revit?

The next item we'll discuss is how to create a gross area plan. The process is similar to, but slightly more involved than, creating a room color plan.

Creating an Area Plan

Almost any job of considerable size will require an area plan at some point in the project's early development. This normally occurs in the programming phase, but the need for this type of plan can persist well into the later stages of the project.

The goal of the next procedure is to create a separate floor plan and then divide it into areas. Follow these steps:

1. In the Room & Area panel of the Architecture tab, select Area and click the Area Plan button, as shown in Figure 14.23.

2. In the New Area Plan dialog, choose Gross Building from the Type list, and choose Level 1 for the area plan views.

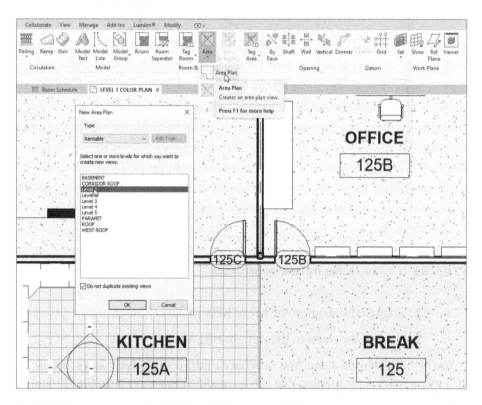

FIGURE 14.23 Clicking the Area Plan button

3. Click OK.

4. Click Yes to create area boundaries automatically. You now have a new floor plan with a blue boundary around the perimeter of the entire building.

5. In the Room & Area panel, click the Area Boundary button, as shown in Figure 14.24.

FIGURE 14.24 Clicking Area Boundary

6. Draw a line, as shown in Figure 14.25, separating the corridor from the east wing.

7. Draw another similar separator between the west wing and the corridor.

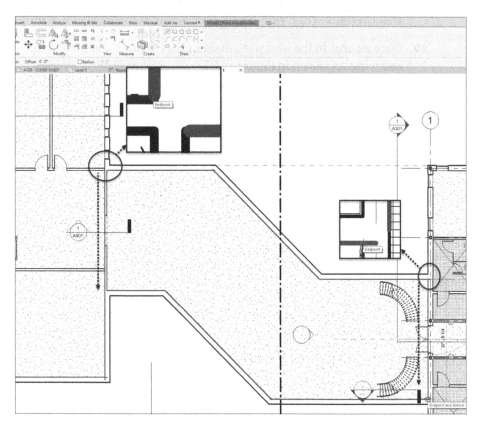

FIGURE 14.25 Separating the areas

N O T E It's weird, but if your lines aren't exactly snapping to the endpoints, it isn't a big deal. Unlike in Sketch mode, Revit is much more forgiving when it comes to creating area separations.

8. In the Room & Area panel, click the Area button, as shown in Figure 14.26.

FIGURE 14.26 The Area button

9. If Revit says a tag isn't loaded, click Yes to load the family. Browse to Annotation ➤ Area Tag.rfa.

10. Place an area in the west wing, then in the corridor, and then in the east wing, as shown in Figure 14.27.

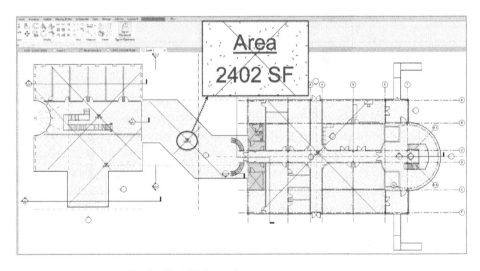

FIGURE 14.27 The plan is divided into three areas.

11. Select the tag in the west wing.

12. Rename it WEST WING.

13. Click the Corridor tag.

14. Rename it **LINK**.

15. Click the East Wing tag.

16. Rename it **EAST WING**.

17. In the Color Fill panel of the Annotate tab, click the Color Fill Legend button.

18. Place the legend in the upper-right corner of the view as shown in Figure 14.28

19. Click OK.

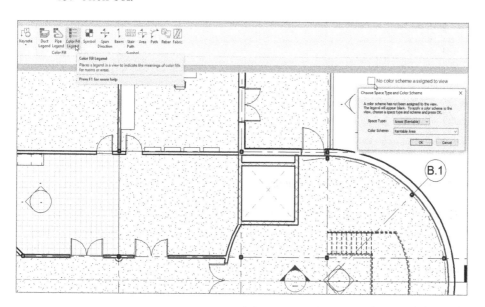

FIGURE 14.28   Adding an area legend

20. Select the color scheme legend.

21. Click the Edit Scheme button on the Modify | Color Fill Legends tab.

22. For Color, change Area Type to Name.

23. Click OK in the warning dialog.

24. Change the title to **AREA LEGEND**.

25. Click OK to return to the model (see Figure 14.29).

26. Save the model.

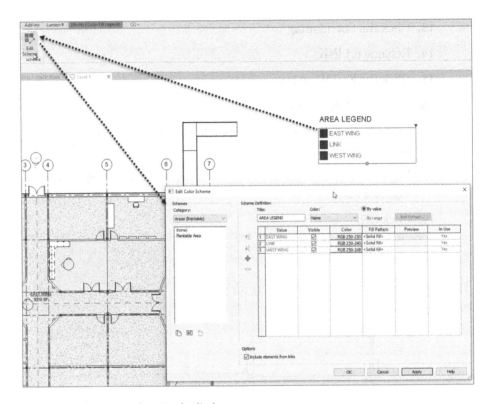

FIGURE 14.29 Changing the display

Great job! You now have experience with creating area plans. If you feel as though you could use some more practice before you begin a real project, there are five more floors in this model that you can work on. You can either work on your own or step back through this chapter's procedures.

Are You Experienced?

Now you can. . .

✓ add rooms to the model

✓ add room separators to the model

✓ create color-scheme plans

✓ create area plans

✓ create room schedules

✓ update the rooms in the model directly from a room schedule

Advanced Wall Topics

More on walls? Really? It seems as though all we do is walls. Well, that's because buildings are composed mainly of walls. As you may have noticed, the exterior walls are compound wall structures with reveals and parapet caps. In the west wing, you have a staircase that is completely unsupported. It would be nice to add a wall to make those stairs less spongy. Given the fact that the west wing is a high-end architectural woodwork area, that wall could use some trims that can be added right to the wall's profile. Also, we haven't touched on a curtain wall of any kind.

This chapter covers the following topics:

▶ **Creating compound walls**

▶ **Adding wall sweeps**

▶ **Creating stacked walls**

▶ **Creating curtain walls**

Creating Compound Walls

The first item to tackle is how to develop a wall with different materials as well as different layers (no, not Autodesk® AutoCAD® layers!). The exterior walls you've been using in this model are a prime example of compound walls. The bottom 3′ (900 mm) of the wall consists of concrete block, and the rest of the wall is brick. When you cut a section through the wall, you can see that the wall has an airspace as well as a metal stud–wall backup.

Usually, these chapters start with a claim that "the following procedure is so easy . . . a child could do it" (or something of that nature). The development of compound walls isn't the easiest thing you'll tackle in the Autodesk® Revit® software. This procedure is somewhat touchy, and doing it well takes practice. In this section, you'll create an interior wall with a wood finish on the bottom, along with different wood materials on the top. You'll also extrude a chair rail along the wall.

WARNING Before we even start. I am constantly telling you to "Press Esc a couple times." Suspend that habit for this chapter. If you press Esc in the middle of creating a compound wall, you will lose a lot of work—in some cases, all of your work.

To get started, open the model you've been using to follow along. If you missed the previous chapter, go to the book's web page at `www.wiley.com/go/revit2024ner`. From there, you can browse to the `Chapter 15` folder and find the `NER-15.rvt` file.

The objective of this procedure is to create a compound wall from a basic wall. Follow along:

1. Open the Level 1 West dependent floor plan view.

2. On the Architecture tab, click the Wall button.

3. In the Type Selector in the Properties dialog, choose Basic Wall: Generic - 6″ (152 mm).

4. In the Properties dialog, click the Edit Type button.

5. Click Duplicate.

6. Call the new wall **West Stairwell Support Wall**, and click OK.

7. Click the Edit button in the Structure row.

8. Click into the Material cell for the Structure row, as shown in Figure 15.1.

9. Click the [. . .] button.

10. In the Material Browser, select Metal Stud Layer, and click OK.

11. Change the thickness to 5′1/2″ (140 mm) (see Figure 15.1).

12. At the bottom of the Edit Assembly dialog, click the Preview button (see Figure 15.2).

13. With the preview open, change View to Section: Modify Type Attributes.

Adding a preview to the Edit Assembly dialog is not only a nice feature; it's also necessary to continue with the editing of the wall. As you'll soon see, you won't have access to certain buttons without the preview being displayed in a sectional view.

▶

It doesn't seem as though you've done much, but you've set the stage to start building your wall. It's time now to return our focus to the Layers field.

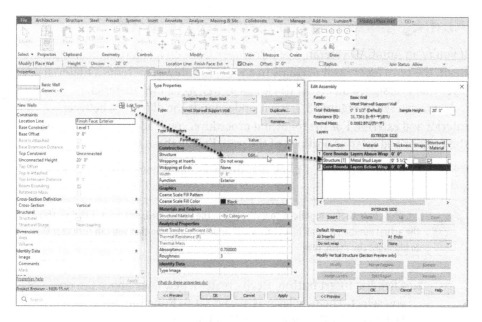

FIGURE 15.1 Changing the structure to a 5′ 1/2″ (140 mm) metal stud layer

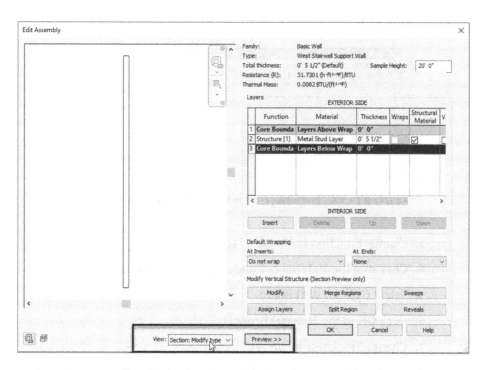

FIGURE 15.2 Changing the view to a section

Adding Layers to the Compound Wall

If you're an AutoCAD veteran, the term *layer* takes on a different meaning. In Revit, the term *layer*, as it pertains to a wall assembly, represents a material layer that is assigned an actual thickness as well as its own material.

As you can see in Figure 15.3, Revit understands the difference between interior and exterior. For the following procedure, you'll add materials to both the exterior and interior portions of the wall. Follow these steps:

1. In the Layers area, click the number 1, as shown in Figure 15.3.

 T I P Note that to highlight an entire row in the Layers area, you must click directly on the actual number. A small black arrow will appear, indicating that you can click that spot to highlight the entire row.

---

2. Click the Insert button. Revit creates a new layer above the one you select. The new layer is always set to Function: Structure [1], Material: <By Category>, and Thickness: 0.

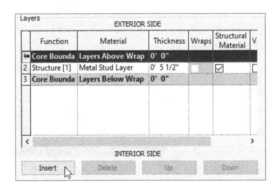

F I G U R E 1 5 . 3   Clicking row 1 to highlight the entire row

3. Change Function to Finish 1 [4].

4. Click into the Material cell and click the [. . .] button.

5. Select Gypsum Wall Board.

6. Click OK in the Material Browser.

7. Change Thickness to 5/8″ (13 mm).

8. Click row 4 (Layers Below Wrap).

9. Click the Insert button.

The preview instantly adds the changes to the wall. This interaction will be of great benefit down the road. Note that you can zoom in on it as shown in Figure 15.4.

10. Click the Down button, as shown in Figure 15.4. It's located below the Layers area all the way to the right. Your new layer becomes 5.

11. Change Function to Finish 1 [4].

12. Click into the Material cell and click the [. . .] button.

13. Find and select Gypsum Wall Board.

14. Click OK in the Material Browser.

15. Change Thickness to 5/8″ (13 mm). Your Layers field should resemble Figure 15.4.

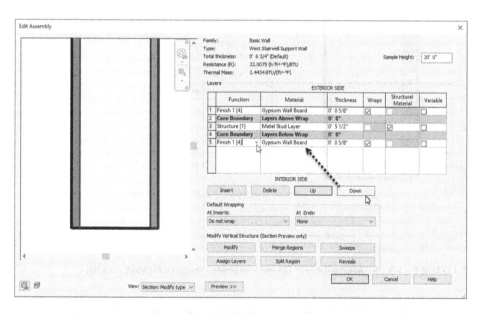

FIGURE 15.4 Adding a 5/8″ gypsum layer to the interior side of the wall

Now that the wall is wrapped with one layer of 5/8″ (15 mm) gypsum on each side, let's start placing the veneered plywood layers on the exterior of the wall.

In the next procedure, you'll add a 1/2″ (13 mm) plywood layer to the exterior of the wall. Follow along:

1. Click 1 Finish 1 [4] (the top layer).

2. Click Insert.

3. Change Function to Finish 2 [5].

4. Change Material to Mahogany (it's the mahogany material that has Plywood for the cut pattern). Click OK.

5. Change the Thickness to 1/2″ (13 mm). Your wall's layers should resemble Figure 15.5.

6. At the bottom of the dialog, click the OK button.

7. Click Apply.

In the preview, you can hold down the wheel button on your mouse and pan around. You can also spin the wheel in and out to zoom in and out of the preview.

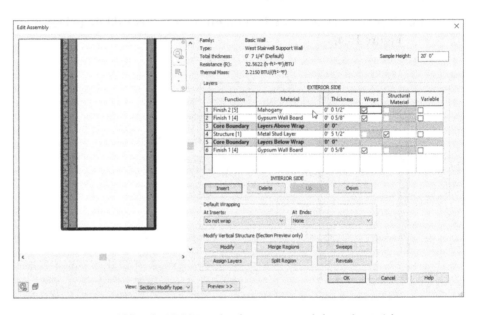

FIGURE 15.5 Adding the 1/2″ (13 mm) mahogany veneered plywood material

WARNING By clicking OK and then Apply, you're basically saving your work. In the Edit Assembly dialog, there is no Save or Apply button as you create the wall. Also, never press Esc—doing so will cancel every change you've made and will almost certainly result in costly repairs to your computer as you rain blows upon it.

Next, let's go back in and split the wall materials in two. It would be nice if you could have cherry at the top and mahogany at the bottom. Revit gives you the ability to do this.

Adding New Materials by Splitting a Region

If you want more than one material along the face of a wall, you can use the Split Region command in the Edit Assembly dialog. The objective of the following procedure is to add a new material and then apply it to the top half of the plywood face:

1. Click the Edit button in the Structure row.

2. Click Layer 1 (the top mahogany layer).

3. Click Insert.

4. Change Function to Finish 2 [5].

5. For Material, select Cherry, and click OK. (Don't give it a thickness. The next procedure takes care of that.)

6. Notice you can pan and zoom in the preview dialog. Zoom in on the bottom of the wall as shown in Figure 15.6.

7. Click the Split Region button, as shown in Figure 15.6.

8. Move your cursor up the plywood face. The cursor turns into a knife. You also see a short, horizontal line within the plywood; this indicates where the region will be cut.

 N O T E Splitting the correct region can be extremely difficult even if you've done this procedure many times. Make sure you zoom into the area, take a deep breath, and try again if you're getting frustrated.

9. When you see 3'–0" (900 mm) in the temporary dimension, pick the point as shown in Figure 15.6. *Do not press Esc when you're finished!* If you place the split in the wrong place, click the Modify button and then select the split line you just created. You can then click the dimension field to edit the location. There is also a direction arrow that specifies whether the split is set from the bottom up (what you just did) or from the bottom down.

You've split the plywood. The only thing left to do is apply a new material to the upper region. You can accomplish this by using the Assign Layers button.

Assigning Material to Different Layers

The Assign Layers command lets you choose where you would like to assign a layer. This is useful in the context of this dialog because you aren't stuck without the ability to move the layers around the wall as necessary. Of course, when you split the wall layer as you just did, notice that the thicknesses of the two wood layers are set to 0 and Variable. Revit needs you to assign an alternate layer at this point.

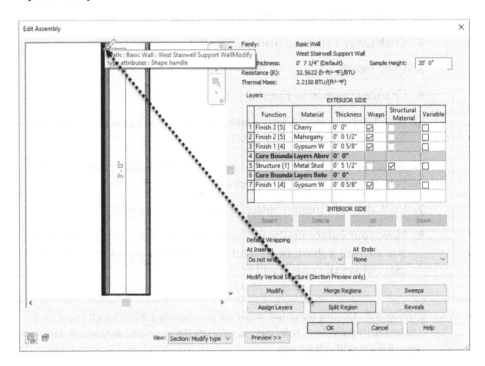

FIGURE 15.6 Cutting the plywood at a specific height

Next, you'll assign the cherry layer to the upper portion of the plywood. Follow along:

1. Pick the Layer 1 row (Cherry), as shown in Figure 15.7.

2. Click the Assign Layers button (see Figure 15.7).

3. Move your cursor over the upper region of the plywood layer, and pick. Cherry is assigned to the upper portion of the wall, and the thicknesses are set to 1/2″ (13 mm). Again, see Figure 15.7.

4. At the bottom of the dialog, click OK.

NOTE   Easy, right? I just need you to do two things if this is not working that easily for you:

▶ Take a breath and keep trying.

▶ Please don't blame me—I didn't invent Revit.

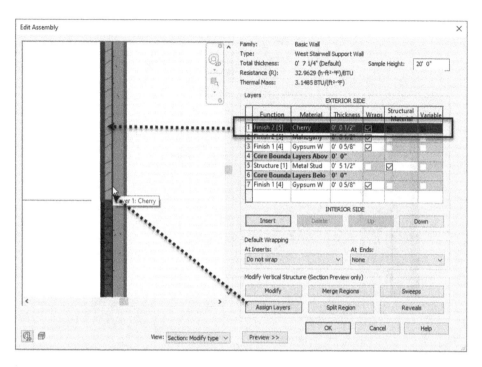

FIGURE 15.7 Assigning the cherry layer to the upper portion of the wall

5. Click Apply.

6. Click the Edit button in the Structure row to get back to the Edit Assembly dialog.

7. Pan to the top of the wall in the display, as shown in Figure 15.8.

8. Click the Modify button.

9. Hover your cursor over the top of the 1/2″ (13 mm) plywood.

10. When the top of the Cherry becomes highlighted, pick the line.

11. Unlock the blue padlock.

12. Click OK.

13. Click OK one more time to get back to the model.

14. Press Esc.

15. Save the model.

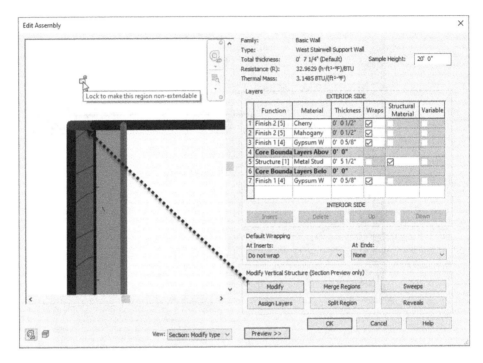

FIGURE 15.8 Unlocking the plywood to enable independent movement after the wall is placed into the model

By unlocking the layer, you can move it up or down depending on what you need. Another good example of the usefulness of this functionality is when you need to slide a brick ledge down past a foundation.

Some people find splitting the regions in the Edit Assembly dialog easy, whereas others consider it more difficult. I found the procedure difficult at first. If you're like me, this technique will require practice until you've done a few more walls. Don't worry—it gets easier as time passes.

Adding an automatic sweep along this wall would be nice. Come to think of it, a wood base and a chair rail would finish this wall perfectly.

Adding Wall Sweeps

The concept of adding a wall sweep is as close to actual construction as you can come without setting up a chop saw. That is because, when you want to add a specific profile to sweep along a wall, you need to go outside the model, find (or create) the profile, and then bring it into the model. This process is similar to ordering trim and installing it.

In the following procedure, you'll load a base and a chair rail trim into the model. You'll then include these items in the wall on which you've been working. Follow along:

1. On the Insert tab, click the Load Family button.

2. Go to the Profiles directory, and then go to Finish Carpentry.

3. Load the files Base 1.rfa and Casing Profile-2.rfa. (Press Ctrl to select both files.)

4. On the Architecture tab, click the Wall button.

5. Make sure the current wall is West Stairwell Support Wall.

6. In the Properties dialog, click Edit Type.

7. Click the Edit button in the Structure row.

8. Click the Sweeps button, as shown in Figure 15.9.

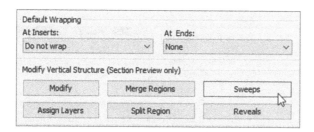

FIGURE 15.9 Adding a sweep to the wall

9. In the Wall Sweeps dialog, click the Add button at the bottom of the dialog, as shown in Figure 15.10.

10. Click the Profile drop-down and select Base 1: 5 1/2" × 5/8" (140 mm × 16 mm).

11. For Material, click where it says <By Category> and then click the browse button [. . .].

12. Find Mahogany, select it, but do not double-click.

13. At the bottom of the Material Browser, click Duplicate Select Material And Assets, as shown in Figure 15.11.

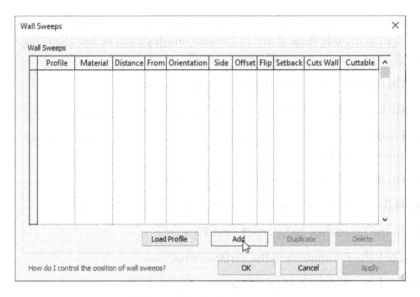

FIGURE 15.10 Adding a profile for the sweep

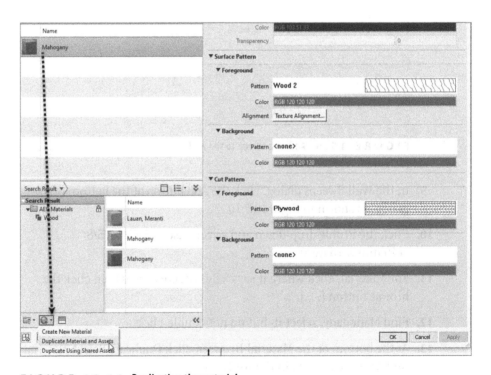

FIGURE 15.11 Duplicating the material

14. Rename the new material to **Mahogany Hardwood** (the other one was veneered plywood—that is why we are doing this).

15. For Cut Pattern: Foreground, select **Wood 1**, as shown in Figure 15.12.

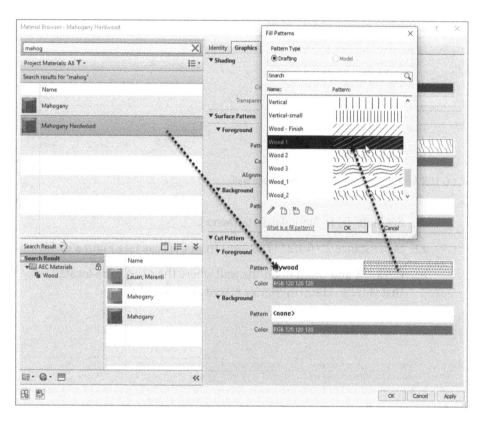

FIGURE 15.12 Adding a solid hatch pattern

16. Click OK.

17. Click OK again.

18. In the Sweeps dialog, make sure your distance is 0′–0″ from base and that it is set to Exterior, as shown in Figure 15.13.

19. Click the Add button again.

20. For the profile, choose Casing Profile-2: 5 1/2″ × 13/16″ (140 mm × 21 mm).

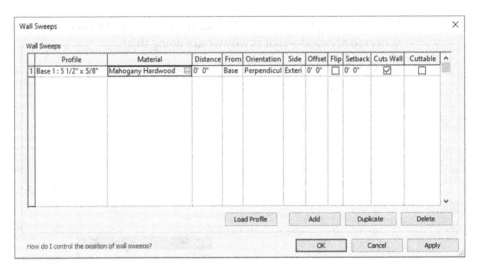

FIGURE 15.13 The base applied to the wall

21. Set Material to Mahogany Hardwood.

22. Set Distance 2′–6 1/2″ (775 mm) from the base (see Figure 15.14).

23. Click OK and zoom in on the wall where the sweeps are located so that you can confirm they're placed as expected.

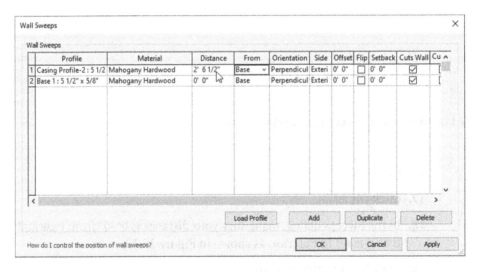

FIGURE 15.14 The chair rail applied to the wall

24. Click OK again.

25. Click OK one more time to get back to the model.

26. In the Project Browser, go to Level 3.

27. Click the Wall button again.

28. In the Properties panel, make sure Base Constraint is set to Level 1 and Base Offset is set to 0'–0".

29. In the Options bar, set Top Constraint to Level 3, as shown in Figure 15.15.

30. Set Location Line to Finish Face: Exterior, and make sure the Chain option is on.

31. Draw the wall by snapping to the inside of the stringers, as shown in Figure 15.15. You want to go in a clockwise direction, so start with the eastern part of the staircase, marked 1 in Figure 15.15.

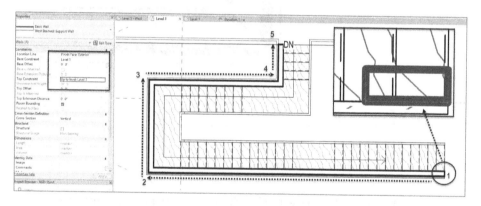

FIGURE 15.15   Placing the wall clockwise in the model

32. In the Geometry panel on the Modify | Place Wall tab, click the Wall Joins button.

33. Using the Wall Joins tool, go to each wall corner and make the join Mitered. See Figure 15.16.

 TIP If you receive a warning stating that a sweep can't be added, ignore it. This warning is sometimes generated when there is a sweep on the face of a wall.

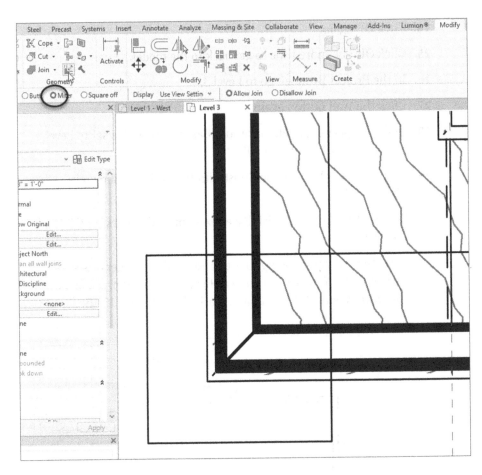

FIGURE 15.16 Creating a mitered wall join

The wall has been added to the model. Because you're placing it underneath a staircase, there will be issues with the wall's profile. This brings us to the next section of this chapter, which guides you through modifying a wall's shape after it has been placed into the model.

Modifying a Wall's Profile in Place

Although we touched on modifying a wall profile back in Chapter 2, "Creating a Model," in this section we'll take this technique to the next level. You can make a wall conform to any odd geometric shape you wish if you follow a few simple rules and procedures.

Let's edit the profile of the new walls to conform to the profile of the stairs. Follow these steps:

1. Go to Level 1.

2. Go over to the west wing as shown in Figure 15.17.

3. Select the wall directly below the stairs.

4. Change the dimension as shown to be 24′–0″ (7315 mm).

5. On the View tab, click the Elevation button.

6. Place an interior elevation, as shown in Figure 15.17. (You may have to place it closer to another wall so it is pointing up and then move it. Remember, you need to select both the view and the elevation target when you move it.)

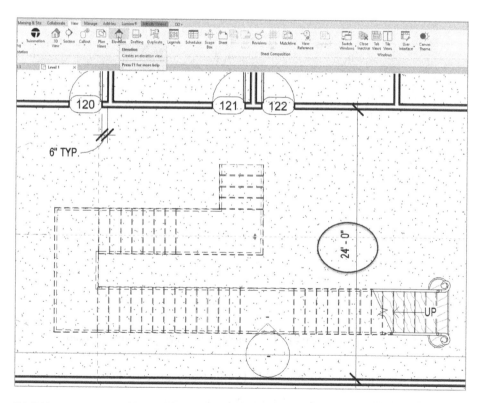

FIGURE 15.17 Placing an interior elevation

N O T E If you ever think an elevation isn't where it is supposed to be, simply click on the target and you will see a blue line indicating where the elevation is starting.

7. Open the elevation.

8. Select the wall, as shown in Figure 15.18.

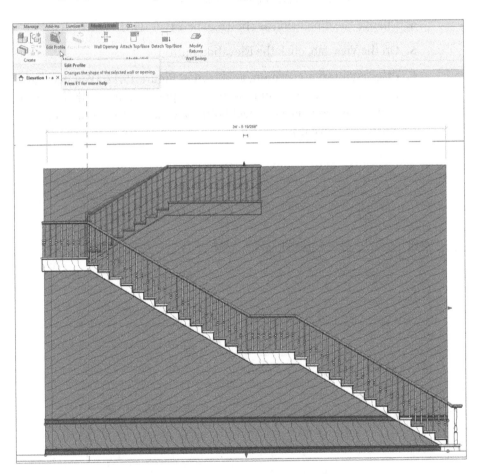

F I G U R E   1 5 . 1 8 Selecting the wall to be modified and clicking the Edit Profile button

9. On the Mode tab, click Edit Profile (see Figure 15.18).

10. In the Draw panel, click the Pick Lines icon.

11. Pick the underside of the stairs. Follow the profile exactly.

12. Delete the existing top magenta line and the existing left magenta line by selecting them and pressing the Delete key. All you should have left is the profile shown in Figure 15.19.

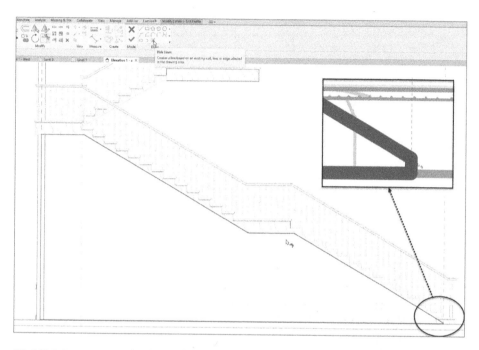

FIGURE 15.19   Cleaning up the lines so that they form a continuous loop

13. Use the Trim/Extend Single Element command to clean up all the corners. Revit won't allow you to continue if you don't. See Figure 5.19.

14. Click Finish Edit Mode. Your wall is trimmed to the underside of the stairs. See Figure 15.20.

NOTE If you get an error as shown in the following image and can't find what they are complaining about, you can click the expand button, drill into the error, and click the Show button.

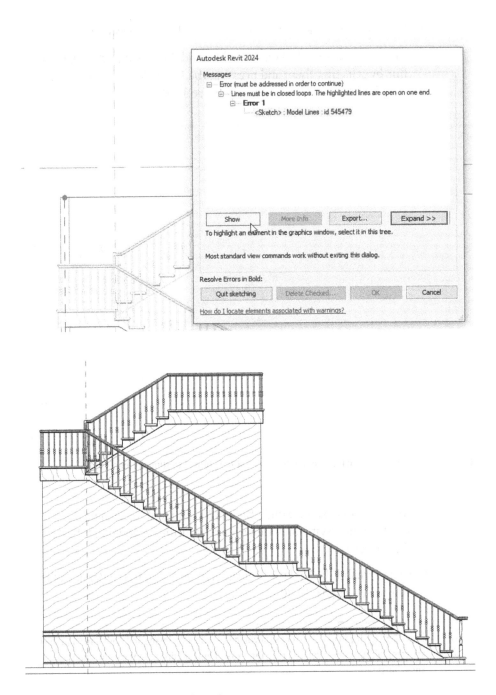

FIGURE 15.20 Looking really good!

15. Repeat the procedure for each wall under the stairs. Remember to add elevations for each. Your finished walls should look like Figure 15.21.

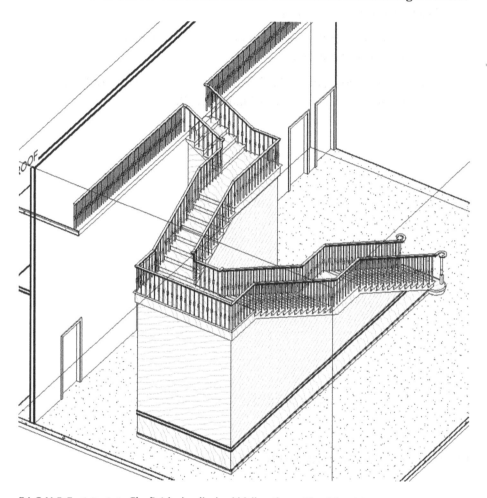

FIGURE 15.21   The finished walls should follow the profile of the stairs.

Now that you can create a compound wall and modify it to fit in an odd place, it's time to learn how to add some sweeps manually.

Manually Adding Host Sweeps

The problem with the wall scenario that you created in the previous procedure is that you have only horizontal wall sweeps. Suppose you need some vertical wall sweeps? This is where host sweeps come into play.

A host sweep is exactly like the sweeps you just added to the wall's properties, but by adding a host sweep, you can add sweeps manually. Next, you'll configure and add a host sweep to the model:

1. Go to the elevation shown in Figure 15.22 (the first one you placed, looking at the stairs).

2. On the Architecture tab, click the down arrow on the Wall button, and select Wall: Sweep (see Figure 15.22).

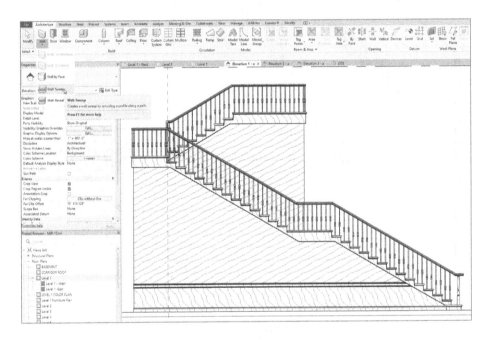

FIGURE 15.22 Choosing the Wall: Sweep command

3. In the Properties dialog, click Edit Type.

4. Click Duplicate.

5. Call the new sweep **Chair Rail Sweep**. Click OK.

6. For the profile, choose Casing Profile-2: 5 1/2″ × 13/16″ (140 mm × 21 mm) from the list.

7. For Material, choose Mahogany Hardwood. See Figure 15.23.

8. Click OK.

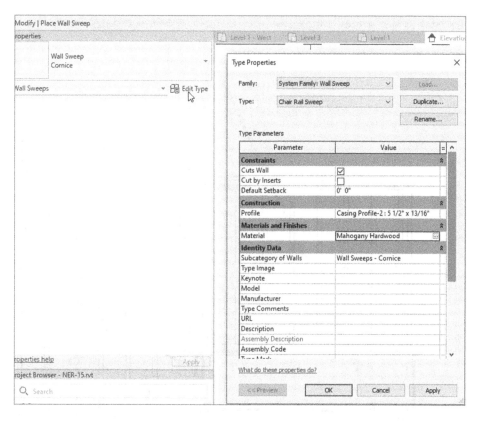

FIGURE 15.23 Configuring the sweep

9. On the Modify | Place Wall Sweep tab, click Vertical in the Placement panel (see Figure 15.24).

10. Make sure your Chair Rail Sweep is current in the Type Selector menu.

11. Pick the place shown in Figure 15.24.

NOTE If you're having trouble placing the sweep on the corner, you need to go to the plan and select Edit Wall Joins from the Tools toolbar. Pick the corner of the walls and select Mitered from the Options bar. If you need further assistance with this procedure, go back to Chapter 2 and read up on creating mitered wall joins.

12. Click the Restart Sweep button (next to the Vertical button in the Placement panel).

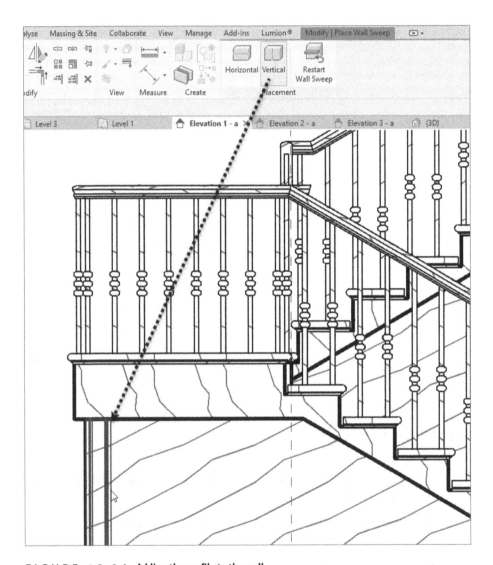

FIGURE 15.24 Adding the profile to the wall

13. After the trim is placed, press Esc. (See Figure 15.25 for the proper placement of the vertical trim.)

14. Select the vertical trim. Notice the grips on the top and the bottom. Pick the bottom grip and drag it up to meet the top chair rail, as shown in Figure 15.26.

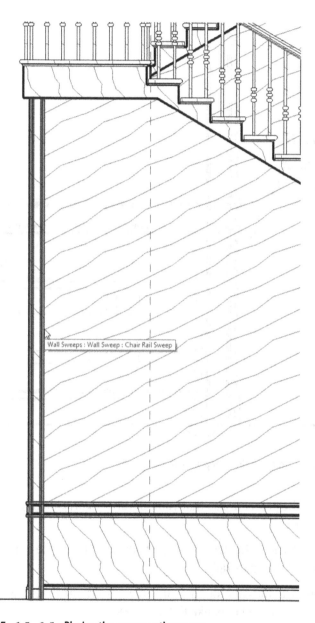

FIGURE 15.25 Placing the sweep on the corner

15. Copy the first sweep about 3′ (900 mm) to the right.

16. When the sweep is in, select it. A temporary dimension appears. Change the dimension to 3′–0″ (900 mm).

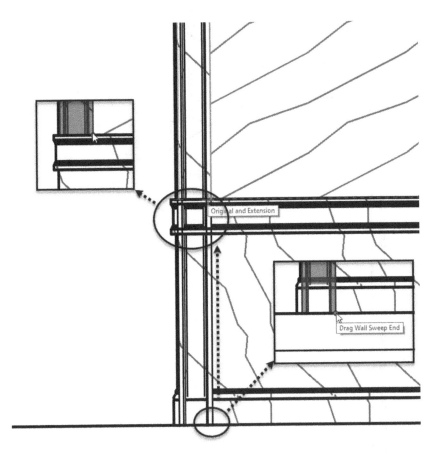

FIGURE 15.26 Dragging the sweep up to the chair rail

17. Repeat the procedure so that your elevation starts looking like Figure 15.27.

18. Now go back to the sweeps you just added and drag the bottoms up to the top of the chair rail.

19. Add vertical rails at around 3'–0" (900 mm) to the other walls as well. Your walls should look like Figure 15.28.

You can now make modifications to a simple wall in any direction. You have experience adding sweeps to the wall's composition, and you can add sweeps free-hand when you need to.

One other type of wall that we should cover before we get to curtain walls is a stacked wall. When you need a compound wall, the outside face must always be in alignment. When you run into this situation, you have to construct an entirely new wall.

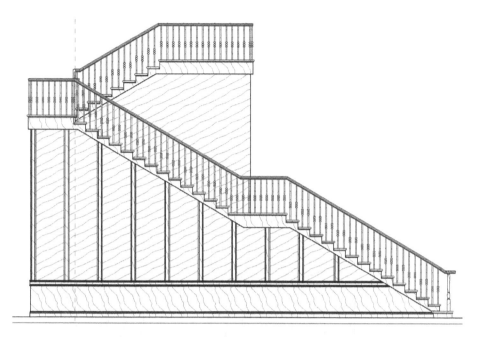

FIGURE 15.27 The finished south wall of the stairs

Creating Stacked Walls

A *stacked wall*, simply put, is a wall created by stacking two premade walls together. You can't have a stacked wall without at least two basic walls that you can join. The good thing about stacked walls is that you can stack as many as you like. I recommend that you use some restraint, though—these walls can use up memory if you get too carried away.

OPEN THIS DOOR ONLY IN CASE OF EMERGENCY!

Although it's true that a stacked wall is basically the only good way to create a wall system with an offset face, stacked walls are notoriously bad in terms of hosting items and joining other walls. In addition, one of the biggest drawbacks of a stacked wall is that it doesn't appear in a wall schedule—only the separate parts that form the wall will show up.

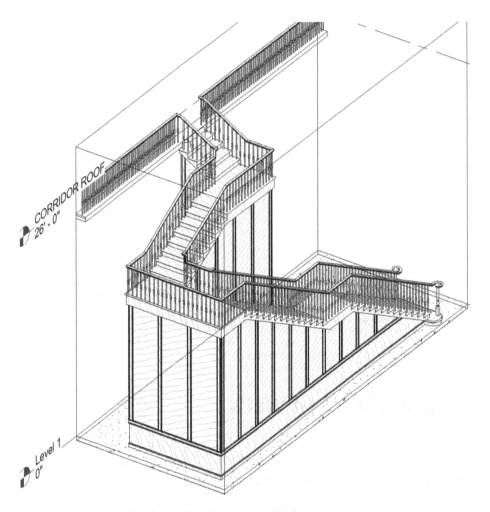

FIGURE 15.28 The final walls with the sweeps added

The objective of the following procedure is to join three basic walls together to create one stacked wall. The result will create an alcove for architectural casework. Follow these steps:

1. Go to Level 1 West and, on the Architecture tab, click the Wall button.

2. In the Type Selector menu in the Properties dialog, select Basic Wall: Interior 6 1/8″ (156 mm) Partition (2-Hr).

3. Click Edit Type.

4. Click Duplicate.

5. Call the wall 18″ (450 mm) **Soffit Wall**, and click OK.

6. Change Wrapping at Inserts and Wrapping At Ends to Interior.

7. Click the Edit button in the Structure row.

8. In the Layers area, click 3 Core Boundary (Layers Above Wrap), and click Insert.

9. Set Function to Thermal/Air Layer [3].

10. Set Material to Air Barrier - Air Infiltration Barrier.

11. Set Thickness to 8 1/4″ (210 mm).

12. Click Insert (to insert another layer above).

13. Set Function to Finish 1 [4].

14. Set Material to Metal Stud Layer.

15. Set Thickness to 3 5/8″ (92 mm) (see Figure 15.29).

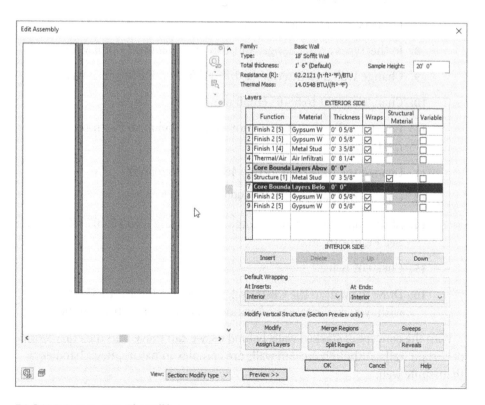

FIGURE 15.29 The wall layers

16. Click OK twice.

17. To the left of the Ribbon, click the Modify button (doing so clears the Wall command).

Let's begin building the stacked wall. Because you have two walls to work with, you can specify them in the Edit Assembly dialog for the stacked wall.

The next procedure joins the 18″ (450 mm) soffit wall with the 6 1/8″ (156 mm) partition wall:

1. On the Architecture tab, click the Wall button if it isn't already running.

2. Scroll down the Type Selector until you arrive at Stacked Wall: Exterior – Brick Over CMU w Metal Stud and select it.

3. Click Edit Type.

4. Click Duplicate.

5. Call the new wall **Recessed Wall** and click OK.

6. Click Edit in the Structure row.

7. For Offset, select Finish Face: Interior.

8. In the Types area, change Wall 1 to **18″ (450 mm)** Soffit Wall.

9. Change Wall 2 to Interior - **6 1/8″ (156** mm) Partition (2-Hr).

10. Change Height to 5′–6″ (1650 mm).

11. Insert a wall below the Interior - **6 1/8″ (156** mm) Partition (2-Hr) wall.

12. Change the third wall to **18″ (450 mm)** Soffit Wall.

13. Change the height to 3′–0″ (900 mm).

14. At the top of the dialog, change Sample Height to 10′–0″ (3000 mm). See Figure 15.30.

15. Click OK twice.

16. Draw the wall in the west wing, as shown in Figure 15.31. (If you wish, you can create an elevation or cut a section through the wall.)

With the concept of stacked walls behind us, we can move into the crazy world of curtain walls. Although curtain walls are complex in nature, Revit handles them quite well.

A good way to establish the overall thickness is to look at the top of the Edit Assembly dialog. There you can see the Total Thickness value.

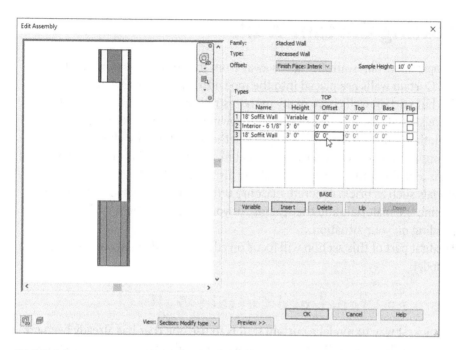

FIGURE 15.30 Creating the stacked wall

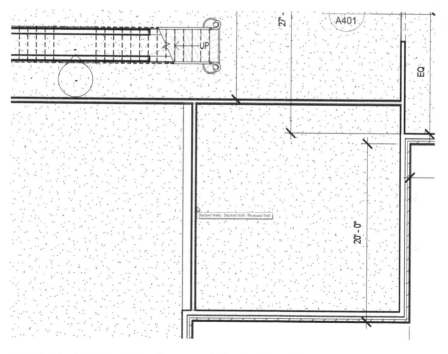

FIGURE 15.31 Adding the new stacked wall to the model

Creating Curtain Walls

The topic of curtain walls brings us away from the conventional mindset of walls. Curtain walls are placed into the model the same way as conventional walls, but curtain walls have many more restrictions and element properties that we should examine before you go throwing one into your model.

With that said, curtain walls also provide the most dramatic effect on your building. As this section will explain in detail, a curtain wall is not only composed of glass and aluminum extrusions but can also be constructed from building materials such as brick, concrete masonry unit (CMU), and wood. You can also predefine the materials and the spacing, or you can create them grid by grid, depending on your situation.

The first part of this section will focus on adding a predefined curtain system to the model.

Adding a Predefined Curtain Wall

The quickest way to model a curtain wall is to use one that has already been created for you. The out-of-the-box curtain walls provided with Revit have enough instance and type parameters available to make the curtain wall conform to your needs for each situation.

In the next procedure, you'll add a predefined curtain-wall system to the radial east entry wall. Follow these steps:

1. In the Project Browser, open the Level 1 East plan view.

2. Zoom in on the east entry.

3. On the Architecture tab, click the Wall button.

4. In the Type Selector, select Curtain Wall: Storefront.

5. Click Edit Type.

6. Click Duplicate.

7. Call the new curtain wall **East Entry** and click OK.

8. You can configure many parameters. Verify that Automatically Embed is selected. For Vertical Grid Pattern, change Spacing to 4′–0″ (1200 mm).

9. Select Adjust For Mullion Size.

10. For Horizontal Grid Pattern, change Layout to Maximum Spacing, and change the spacing to 4'–0" (1200 mm).

11. Click OK.

12. In the Instance Properties dialog, change Base Offset to 3'–7" (1075 mm).

13. Set Top Constraint to Up To Level: Roof.

14. Set Top Offset to -1'–0" (that's minus 1'–0") (-300 mm). See Figure 15.32.

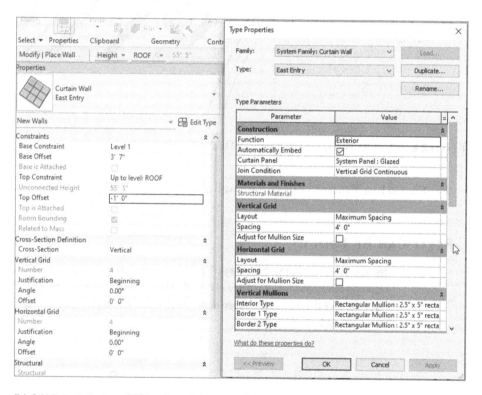

FIGURE 15.32 Picking the radial entry wall to add the curtain wall

15. In the Draw panel, click the Pick Lines icon.

16. Pick the radial entry wall, as shown in Figure 15.33. Make sure you're picking the wall centerline.

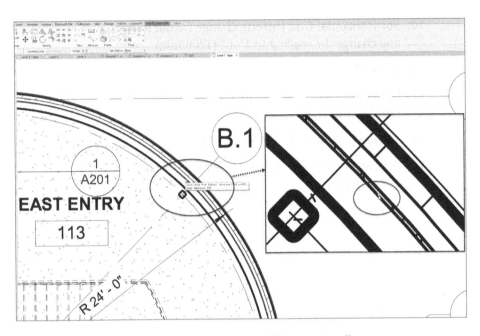

FIGURE 15.33 Picking the radial entry wall to add the curtain wall

17. Go to a 3D view. Your curtain wall should resemble Figure 15.34.

REVIT CAN BE TOUCHY

You may receive a warning that says, "Could not create integral reveal for wall instance. Sweep position is outside of its wall. Please check sweep parameters." If you do, click the red X in the upper-right corner of the warning to dismiss it (as seen in the following graphic):

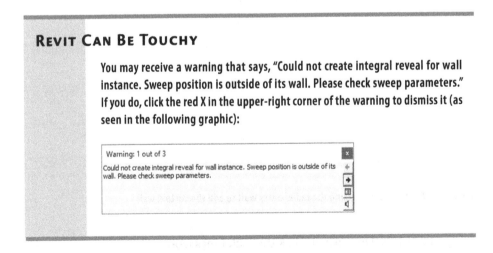

The ability to create an automatic curtain wall such as the radial one in the west entryway is quite an advantage when it comes to modeling a curtain system quickly. However, you won't always be presented with a perfectly square,

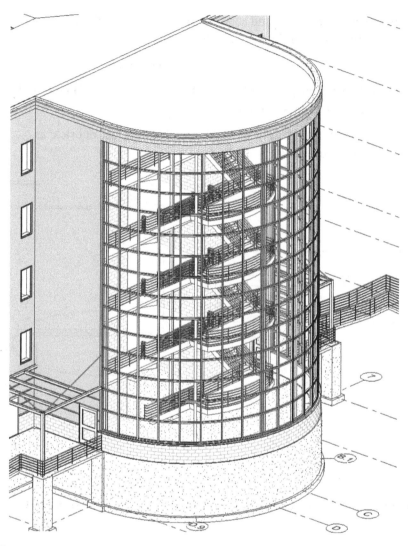

FIGURE 15.34 The curtain wall in 3D

vertical shape. This is where creating a blank curtain wall comes in handy. You can then add grids and mullions at spaces that are at odd intervals.

Adding a Blank Curtain Wall

A blank curtain wall is nothing but a giant chunk of glass. By adding a blank curtain wall, you tell Revit, "Don't bother spacing the panels—I'll do it myself."

Let's create a blank curtain wall and add it to the model. You'll then go to an elevation and edit the profile of the panel. Follow along:

1. In the Project Browser, open the Level 1 West view.

2. In the Work Plane panel of the Architecture tab, click Ref Plane, and then click Pick Lines in the Draw panel.

3. Offset a reference plane 2′–0″ (600 mm) from the face of brick, as shown in Figure 15.35.

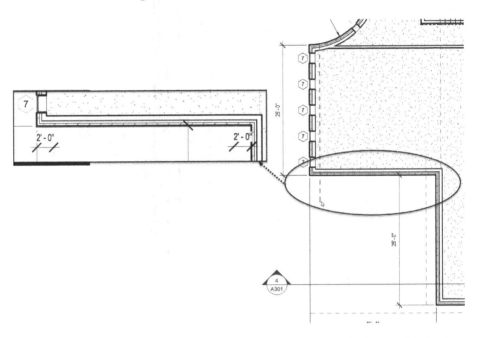

FIGURE 15.35 Offsetting two reference planes 2′–0″ (600 mm) from the face of the brick

4. On the Architecture tab, click the Wall button.

5. In the Type Selector, pick Curtain Wall: Curtain Wall 1 from the list.

6. Click Edit Type.

7. Click Duplicate.

8. Call the new curtain system **South West Entry**, and click OK.

9. Select the Automatically Embed check box.

10. Click OK.

11. For Base Offset, change the value to 0'–0".

12. For Top Constraint, set the value to Up To Level: Level 5.

13. For Top Offset, change the value to 0'–0".

14. Draw the wall at the centerline of the wall between each reference plane, as shown in Figure 15.36. Note that if you draw from right to left, the exterior face of the new wall will be to the inside.

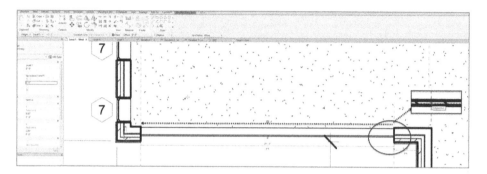

FIGURE 15.36 Drawing the curtain wall at the centerline of the wall between the two reference planes

15. In the Project Browser, open South Entry Elevation.

16. In the South Entry Elevation, change Visual Style to Shaded (so that you can see the glass wall better).

Now that you have drawn the wall and are looking at the elevation, you can begin to alter the profile and add some curtain grids of your own. To edit the curtain profile, follow these steps:

1. Select the curtain wall.

2. On the Modify | Walls tab, click Edit Profile.

3. In the Draw panel, click Pick Lines.

4. Using the Options bar, offset the roof down 2'–0" (600 mm), and trim the edges of the curtain wall to the offset line.

5. Delete the horizontal magenta line that is now floating.

6. Click Finish Edit Mode. Your curtain wall's profile should resemble Figure 15.37.

To select the curtain wall, you have to hover your pointer over an edge. When the curtain wall's perimeter becomes highlighted, select it.

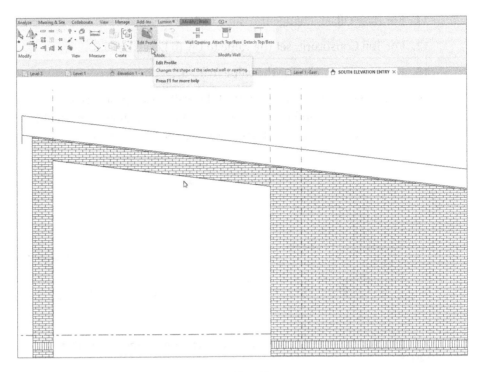

FIGURE 15.37 The complete curtain-wall profile

With the shape of the curtain wall finished, let's create some divisions along the vertical and horizontal plane of the wall. In Revit, these are called *curtain grids*.

Creating Curtain Grids

Because all you have is a single pane of glass, you need to dice it up. In this situation, you can begin dividing the glass panel by using the Curtain Grid command. When you've finished, you can add mullions, doors, and even materials to the panels.

Begin by adding curtain grids to the glass panel:

1. In the Build panel of the Architecture tab, click the Curtain Grid button, as shown in Figure 15.38.

2. On the Modify | Place Curtain Grid tab, click the All Segments button, as shown in Figure 15.38.

3. Move your cursor up the left side of the curtain wall and pick a horizontal point that is 8'–0" (2400 mm) up from the base of the wall (see Figure 15.39).

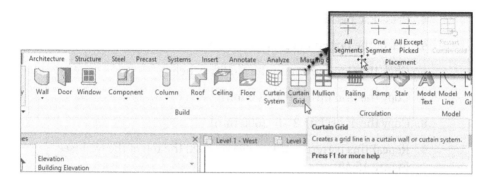

FIGURE 15.38   Click the Curtain Grid button in the Build panel of the Architecture tab.

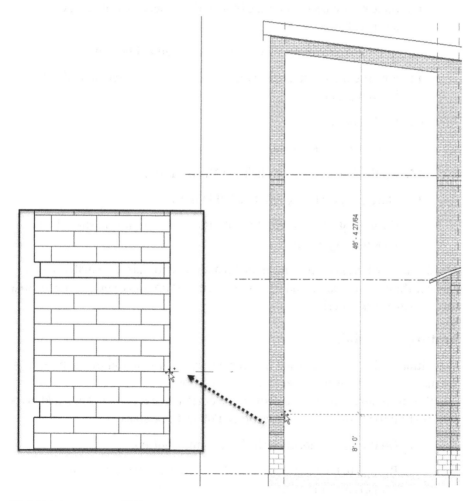

FIGURE 15.39   Picking a point 8′–0″ (2400 mm) up from the base of the wall

4. Press Esc twice.

5. Select the horizontal grid you just added.

6. Click the Copy button in the Modify panel.

7. Copy the grid up 4'–0" (1200 mm).

8. Copy the 4' grid up 2'–0" (600 mm).

9. Repeat this pattern until you've reached the top of the wall (see Figure 15.40).

10. Click the Curtain Grid button.

11. Slide your cursor along the base of the panel (the grid is extended in a vertical direction).

12. In the Placement panel, click the One Segment button.

13. Pick the midpoint of the panel. (You should have segmented only the bottom panel.)

14. Click Modify.

15. Select the vertical grid.

16. On the Modify toolbar, click the Move button.

17. Move the grid to the left 3'–0" (900 mm).

18. Copy the grid to the right 6'–0" (1600 mm). Your wall should now look like Figure 15.41.

With the panel broken up, you can begin adding materials. One material you may not think of is an actual door! Yes, in Revit curtain walls, you add a door to a curtain panel as a material.

Adding Materials

In addition to doors, you can add to a curtain wall any material that is present in the model. You can even add separate wall systems.

In this procedure, you'll add a door to the curtain system. Then you'll add brick belts that fill the 2'–0" (600 mm) sections. Follow these steps:

1. On the Insert tab, click the Load Family button.

2. Browse to Doors and open the Door-Curtain-Wall-Double-Storefront.rfa file.

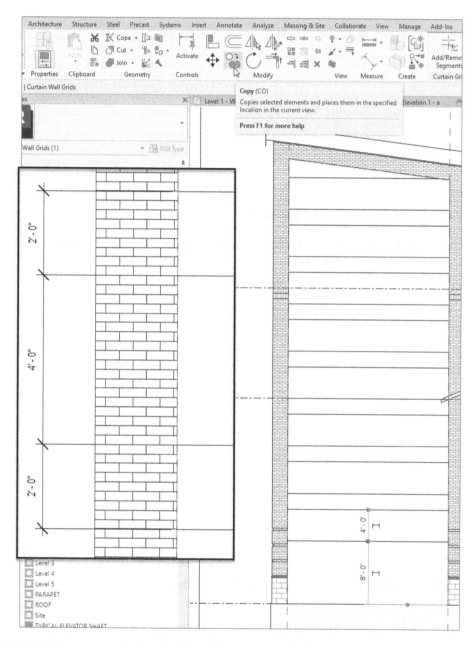

FIGURE 15.40 Copying the grids to form the custom curtain wall

3. Zoom into the 6' × 8' (1800 mm × 2400 mm) panel.

4. Hover your cursor at the top of the panel.

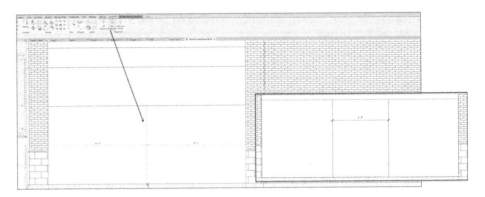

FIGURE 15.41 Chopping up the panel

5. Press the Tab key twice. When the panel is highlighted, pick it (see Figure 15.42).

FIGURE 15.42 Selecting the 6′ × 8′ (1800 mm × 2400 mm) panel

6. In the Type Selector, pick Door-Curtain-Wall-Double-Storefront. A door appears in the panel. See Figure 15.43.

7. Go to a 3D view.

8. Select the 2′–0″ (600 mm) panel above the door by hovering your cursor over the panel and pressing Tab until it becomes highlighted.

9. In the Type Selector, pick Exterior - Brick On Mtl. Stud.

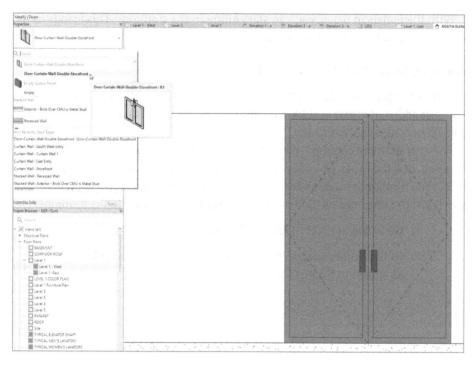

FIGURE 15.43 Adding the door

10. Press Esc.

11. Fill the rest of the 2'–0" (600 mm) bands with the same Generic - 12" (300 mm) Masonry. See Figure 15.44.

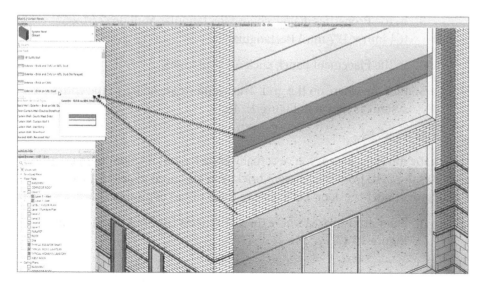

FIGURE 15.44 Adding the brick rows

With the panels in place, you can start filling in the mullions. This brings us to the next step: adding mullions to the grid.

Adding Mullions to the Grid

The next logical step is to create the mullions that will be attached to the grid you just added. Because you have a few areas where there shouldn't be mullions, the job becomes more tedious.

The next example could go one of two ways. One technique adds mullions *piece by piece*, and the other procedure lets you add mullions all at once and then delete the mullions you don't need. This procedure takes the latter approach; you'll add the mullions all at once and then remove the superfluous mullions:

1. Go to the SOUTH ELEVATION ENTRY view.

2. In the Build panel of the Architecture tab, click the Mullion button, as shown in Figure 15.45.

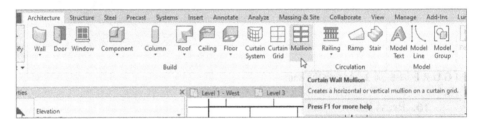

FIGURE 15.45 Click the Mullion button on the Architecture tab.

3. In the Properties dialog, choose Rectangular Mullion: 2.5″ × 5″ (64 mm × 127 mm) Rectangular.

4. In the Placement panel, click All Grid Lines.

5. Pick anywhere on the grid. The mullions are added to the entire system as shown in Figure 15.46.

6. Press Esc.

With the mullions added, you've actually gone too far! An aluminum extrusion separates the CMU from the adjacent brick. You also need to delete the mullion that appears under the door. Let's remove these pieces of mullion:

1. Zoom into an area where the CMU meets the brick, as shown in Figure 15.47.

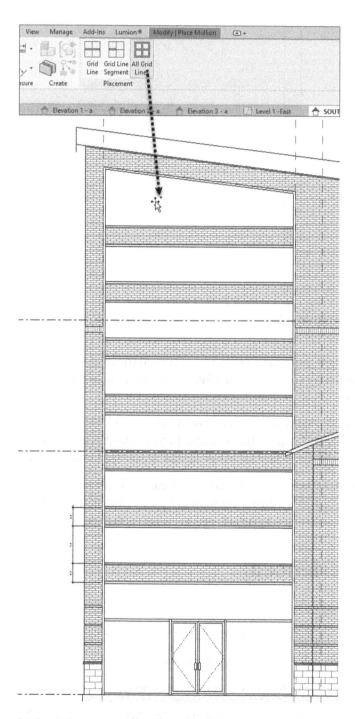

FIGURE 15.46 Place the 2.5″ × 5″ (64 mm × 127 mm) rectangular mullion above the door.

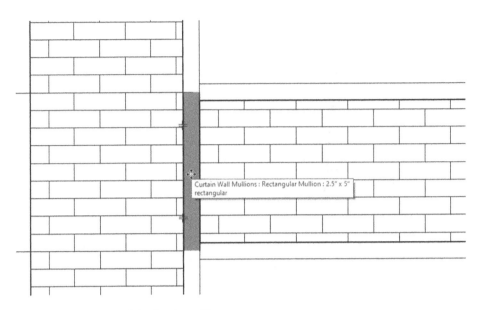

Curtain Wall Mullions : Rectangular Mullion : 2.5" x 5" rectangular

FIGURE 15.47 Selecting the mullion

2. Select the small mullion piece that lies between the brick and the CMU. (You'll have to press the Tab key several times to accomplish this.)

3. You can either modify the join (as shown in Figure 15.47) or press the Delete key and remove the mullion. In this case, delete the mullion. Repeat the procedure for other similar areas. See Figure 15.48.

What have you accomplished? You've embedded a predefined curtain wall into a radial profile, and you've added a curtain system to a giant glass panel by hand. The only thing left to do is to apply a curtain wall to a sloping surface.

Are You Experienced?

Now you can...

✓ create custom compound walls by using the Edit Assembly dialog

✓ create stacked walls by joining compound walls together

✓ create sweeps in a wall's profile and freeform sweeps

✓ create curtain walls by using a predefined wall system and also from a blank panel

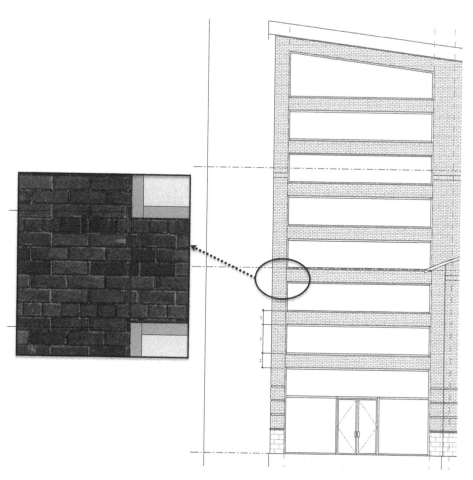

FIGURE 15.48 Cleaning up the mullions

CHAPTER 16

Schedules and Tags

To begin, I want to clarify something specific for the people who have been using Autodesk® AutoCAD® software: you don't need to tag an item in order for it to appear in a schedule in the Autodesk® Revit® platform. You can't just draft a schedule either. But this isn't a bad situation to be in. Say, for example, you have a typical door schedule. Wouldn't it be nice to add a door to the model and have that door automatically show up in the schedule?

This chapter covers the following topics:

▶ **Creating schedules**

▶ **Creating material takeoffs**

▶ **Creating key legends**

▶ **Adding tags**

▶ **Keynoting**

Creating Schedules

Revit allows you to schedule an item instantly based on a database. A door, for example, already has most of the information you need built into it. Didn't it seem funny that when you placed a door in the model, it was automatically tagged with a sequential door number? This is the power of BIM. We're now going beyond 3D into 4D.

Schedules don't stop at doors and windows in Revit. You can schedule almost any item that goes into the model. Along with schedules comes the ability to quantify materials and areas. You can even create a schedule for the sole purpose of changing items in the model. In Revit, it's always a two-way street.

The first topic we'll tackle is creating the most common of the schedules in architecture: the door schedule. When you get this procedure down, you'll be off and running.

The good news is that you have most of the information you need to create a multitude of schedules. The bad news is that Revit-produced schedules may not look like your company's schedules at all. Before we go further, it's important to note that some of you will be able to get a perfect duplication of your company's standard schedules; some of you won't. Those of you who don't will have to get as close as possible to your standards and, at that point, know that sometimes the cost of doing BIM isn't in the pocket but at the plotter.

Given that, let's get started. I think you'll find that creating and using schedules is a wonderful experience. You're about to learn how to save hours upon hours of work, all the while maintaining 100 percent accuracy.

Adding Fields to a Schedule

To begin, open the file on which you've been following along. If you didn't complete the previous chapter, go to the book's web page at www.wiley.com/go/revit2024ner. From there, you can browse to the Chapter 11 folder and find the file called NER-16.rvt. The following procedure focuses on creating a door schedule. Grab a cup of coffee or power drink, and follow along:

1. In the Project Browser, go to the Level 1 floor plan.

2. In the Create panel of the View tab, click the Schedules ➤ Schedule/Quantities button, as shown in Figure 16.1.

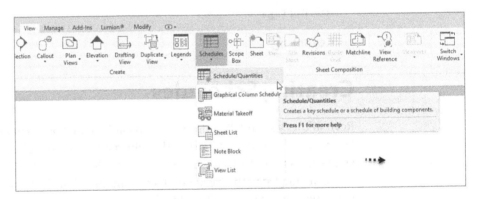

FIGURE 16.1 Click the Schedule/Quantities button on the View tab.

3. The next dialog, shown in Figure 16.2, allows you to choose which item you would like to schedule. Select Doors, and click OK.

4. The next dialog lets you add the fields (parameters) required for your schedule. The first field you'll add is Mark. To do this, select Mark in the Available Fields area to the left, and click the Add button in the middle of the dialog to move the Mark field to the right, as shown in Figure 16.3.

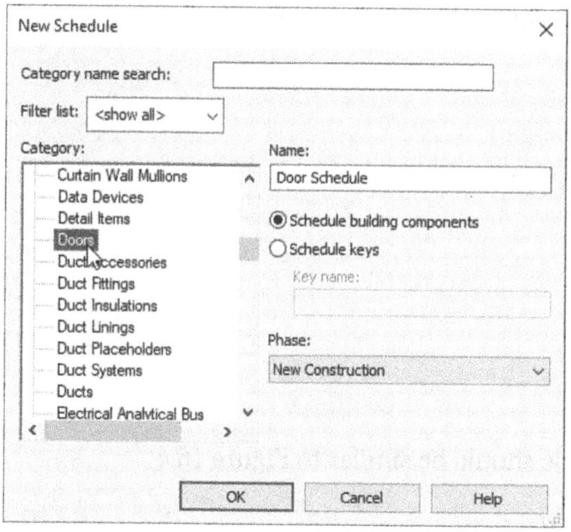

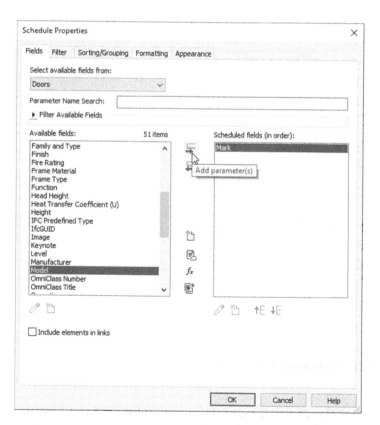

FIGURE 16.2 Select Doors and then click OK.

FIGURE 16.3 Adding the fields to produce a door schedule

5. Add the rest of the following fields using the same method.

▶ Height

▶ Width

▶ Level

▶ Finish

▶ Frame Material

▶ Frame Type

▶ Comments

6. Click OK. Your schedule should be similar to Figure 16.4.

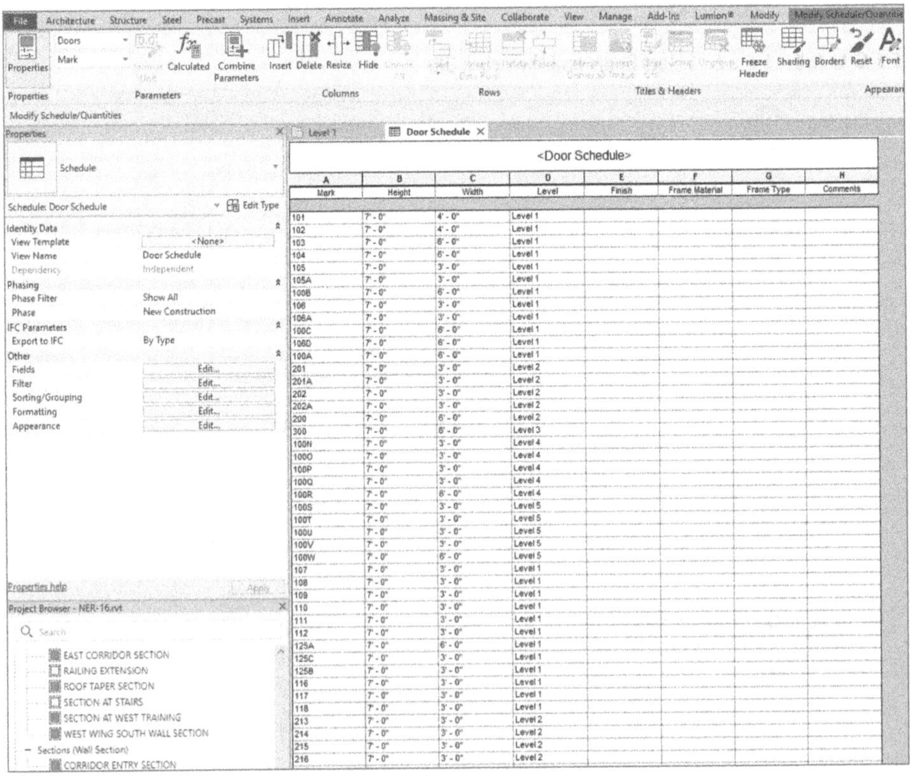

FIGURE 16.4 The door schedule up to this point

The next step is to start organizing your data in your preferred display format. You have a long way to go, but when you're finished, you can use this schedule over and over again.

NOTE A schedule doesn't have to be placed on a drawing sheet. Many times, you'll produce a schedule so that you can manipulate data without having to search for it in the model.

Sorting and Grouping

Because Revit is a database, think of building a schedule as creating a query in a database, because that's exactly what you're doing. By creating a sort, you can begin to see your doors in groups and have a tangible understating of where you are. Let's get started:

1. Because you never use lowercase lettering, click into the header and title rows and change the names to all capital letters, as shown in Figure 16.5.

2. Select the rows that contain the headers from COMMENTS to MARK. Do this by clicking into the COMMENTS cell and dragging your cursor to the left.

3. With the cells highlighted, click the Shading button (see Figure 16.5).

4. Change the shading to the gray basic color as shown in Figure 16.5.

5. In the Properties dialog is a category called Other. Here you can return to the Schedule Properties dialog. Click the Edit button in the Sorting/Grouping row, as shown in Figure 16.6.

6. On the Sorting/Grouping tab of the Schedule Properties dialog, set Sort By to Level.

7. Select the Header option.

8. Select the Footer option.

9. Select Title, Count, And Totals from the Sort By drop-down list (see Figure 16.7).

10. Click OK.

11. Save the model.

The next step is to group the header information the way you would like it. Most schedules include groups such as Frame Material and Frame Type. You'll create similar groupings.

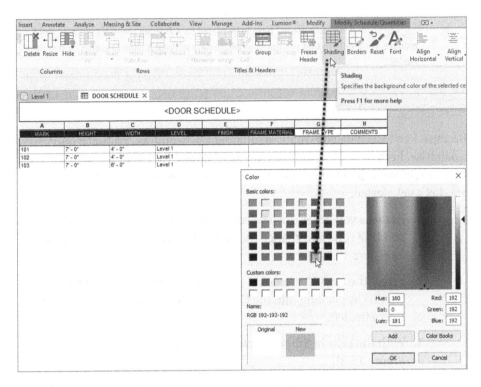

FIGURE 16.5   Edit all the field names and change the shading of the row.

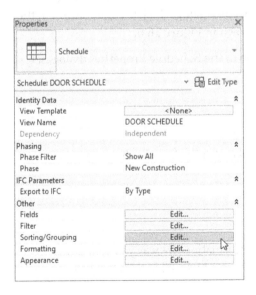

FIGURE 16.6   Click the Edit button in the Sorting/Grouping row.

FIGURE 16.7 Sorting the schedule by level

Controlling Headers

Although this step isn't crucial to producing an accurate, readable schedule, it's important in the attempt to get this Revit-produced schedule to look like the schedule you've been using for years in CAD. The objective of this procedure is to combine the header content into smaller groups under their own header, similar to what you can do in a spreadsheet.

To begin controlling the schedule headers, follow these steps:

1. In the Project Browser, open DOOR SCHEDULE (if you don't already have it open).

   At the top of the schedule are the title (DOOR SCHEDULE) and the headers (which include MARK, HEIGHT, WIDTH, and LEVEL, among others), as shown in Figure 16.8. Focus your attention here.

2. The goal is to combine MARK, HEIGHT, WIDTH, and LEVEL into a group under one header called DOOR INFORMATION. To do this, click the MARK cell, and drag your cursor to the left. You're selecting all four cells.

3. When the cells are selected, click the Group button in the Headers panel.

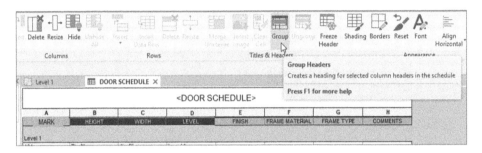

FIGURE 16.8 Click and drag across the four cells to activate the Group button.

 TIP Sometimes, when you're picking the first cell to do this task, you'll accidentally click into the cell. You don't want this. If this keeps happening, click into the LEVEL cell, and then click just below the cell into the gray area. Doing so selects the cell the way you want it. You can now pick the cell and drag your cursor to the left to highlight all the cells.

4. Click into the new cell, and type **DOOR INFORMATION**.

It would be nice if the defaults in Revit were all caps, but they aren't. The next procedure will rename some of the headers, but it won't change any values.

1. Select the cells FRAME MATERIAL and FRAME TYPE, as shown in Figure 16.9.

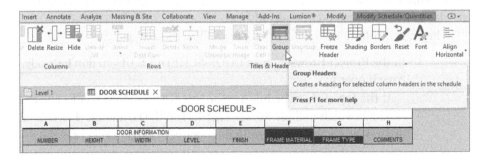

FIGURE 16.9 Adding the new header and changing the descriptions

2. On the Options bar, click Group in the Headers panel.

3. Call the new header **FRAME INFORMATION** (see Figure 16.10).

Level 1		DOOR SCHEDULE ×						
<DOOR SCHEDULE>								
A	B	C	D	E	F	G	H	
		DOOR INFORMATION			FRAME INFORMATION			
NUMBER	HEIGHT	WIDTH	LEVEL	FINISH	FRAME MATERIAL	FRAME TYPE	COMMENTS	

FIGURE 16.10 The groups are complete.

Now it's time to begin filling out some of the blank fields. This is where you can increase productivity by using schedules. Instead of going door by door in the model, you have a list of every door right in front of you!

Modifying Elements in a Schedule

In Revit, data flows in multiple directions. When you created a schedule, the data from the doors flowed into the schedule to populate it. Now you'll ask Revit to collect data that you input into the schedule to flow into the doors.

To learn how to populate the schedule, follow along with the procedure:

1. In the Project Browser, open DOOR SCHEDULE (if it isn't open already).

 NOTE Note that Door Schedule is now DOOR SCHEDULE in the Project Browser. This is because you renamed the title in the schedule—proof that you're dealing with bidirectional information.

2. Click into the FINISH cell for door number 101.

3. Type PT (for paint).

4. Click in the FINISH cell below the one you just changed.

5. Click the menu arrow and notice that PT is in the list. Click PT (see Figure 16.11).

6. Save the model.

Let's see how this affected the actual doors in the model and perhaps find a door that needs to be tagged with a WD (wood) finish:

1. In the Project Browser, open the Level 1 floor plan.

C	D	E	F
DOOR INFORMATION			FRAME INFOR
WIDTH	LEVEL	FINISH	FRAME MATERIAL
4' - 0"	Level 1	PT	
4' - 0"	Level 1		
6' - 0"	Level 1	PT	
6' - 0"	Level 1		
3' - 0"	Level 1		

FIGURE 16.11   When you start filling out the fields in a schedule, the items become available in the list for future use.

2. Zoom in on the door between the corridor and the east wing, as shown in Figure 16.12.

3. Select the door.

4. In the Properties dialog, scroll down to the Materials and Finishes category, and find Finish.

5. Click in the Finish field, and type **WD** (see Figure 16.12).

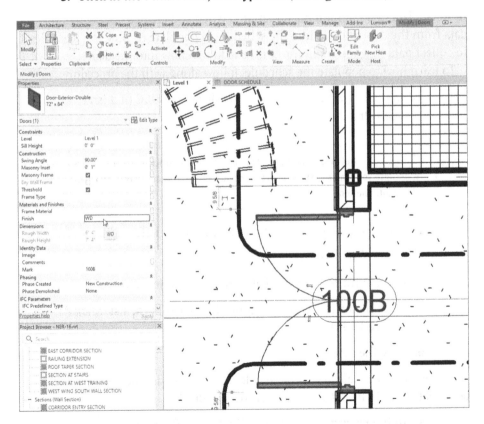

FIGURE 16.12   Changing the property of an element in the model does the same thing as changing the element in the schedule.

6. Click the Apply button at the bottom of the Properties dialog.

7. Open the door schedule. Notice that door 100B has a WD finish.

8. Save the model.

If you click the menu drop-down arrow in the Finish field, you'll see that PT is available. The schedules and the actual doors are linked together.

In the interest of not getting carried away with the mundane process of filling out the entire schedule, note that this process is applicable for every field in this type of schedule. The main takeaway is that you can populate a schedule by either changing the data in the schedule itself or by finding the scheduled component and changing it there, such as a door or window.

 NOTE Also, it's worthwhile to note that if you click any row in the schedule, the Element panel has a Highlight In Model tool that essentially does the same thing as right-clicking.

The next step is to further modify the appearance of the schedule you're working on. You can then begin using this schedule to focus on a specific group of doors and change them based on a filter.

Modifying the Schedule's Appearance

As it stands, not everyone uses the same fonts, headers, and linework around the border of the schedule.

The objective of this procedure is to examine what font this schedule is using, as well as the line weights and spacing applied to the schedule. To learn how to adjust the appearance of a schedule, follow along:

1. In the Project Browser, open DOOR SCHEDULE (if it isn't open already).

2. In the Properties dialog, click the Edit button for Appearance.

3. On the Appearance tab of the Schedule Properties dialog are two categories: Graphics and Text. In the Graphics category, click Outline and select Medium Lines, as shown in Figure 16.13.

4. In the Text category, make sure Show Title and Show Headers are selected (see Figure 16.13).

5. Click Stripe Rows, and select a darker shade as shown in Figure 16.13.

6. Click OK.

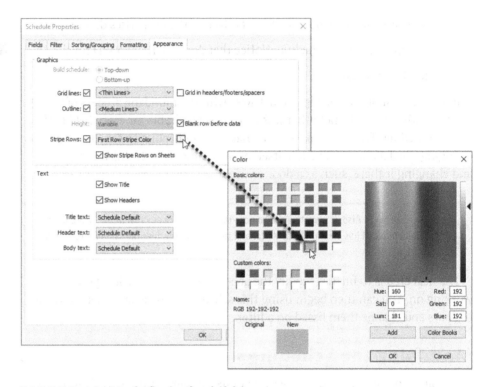

FIGURE 16.13 Configuring the schedule's appearance

Your schedule doesn't change much! You've simply created a situation where the appearance of the schedule won't be apparent until you literally drag it onto a drawing sheet.

Adding a Schedule to a Sheet

With the schedule complete, we can drag it onto a sheet. The cool thing about when we do this is, we have additional functionality in terms of making the schedule more presentable.

1. In the Project Browser, find the Sheets (All) category. Coincidentally, it's located directly below Schedules/Quantities.

2. Right-click Sheets (All).

3. Select New Sheet.

4. Select E1 30 × 42 Horizontal, and click OK.

    You now have a new sheet containing a blank title block.

The next objective is to click and drag the schedule onto the sheet. If the schedule fits, this is literally the easiest thing to do in Revit:

1. In the Project Browser, find DOOR SCHEDULE.

2. Click it, but don't double-click it—pick it and hold down the left mouse button.

3. With the left mouse button pressed, drag the schedule onto the sheet. You can place it anywhere you see fit (see Figure 16.14).

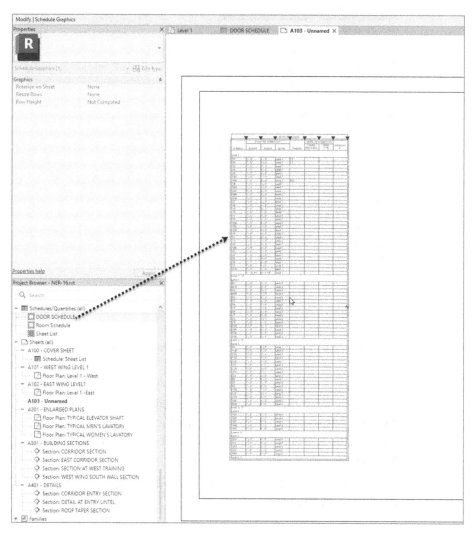

F I G U R E 1 6 . 1 4   Clicking and dragging the schedule onto the sheet

4. When you've moved your cursor to the correct position, release the mouse button. If the bottom hangs over the sheet, that's OK—you'll fix it in a minute.

5. Notice the blue break grip located halfway up the schedule. This is the same type of grip that is used in grids, levels, and sections. Pick it, as shown in Figure 16.15.

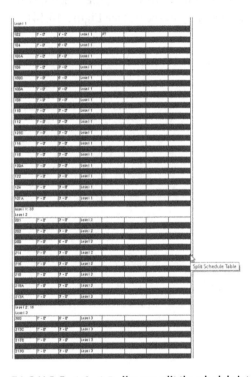

FIGURE 16.15 You can split the schedule into two (or more) sections.

6. With the schedule split in two, you can see that it fits onto the sheet quite nicely. With the schedule still selected, notice the blue grip at the lower left, as shown in Figure 16.16. Pick the grip and drag. You can slide the schedule so that the length of each side adjusts up and down evenly.

7. Zoom in on the top of the schedule, as shown in Figure 16.17, and select the schedule.

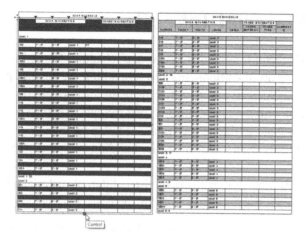

FIGURE 16.16 You can make further adjustments to the schedule by picking the round blue grip.

FIGURE 16.17 Pick the triangle grip to give the COMMENTS field some more room.

8. There are blue triangle-shaped icons at each cell in the title and the header. Pick the one on the COMMENTS column, and drag it to the right. The COMMENTS header is now readable.

You can make two more adjustments to the schedule after you place it onto a sheet. They involve rotating and joining the two columns back together:

1. Select the schedule (if it isn't already selected).

On the Modify | Schedule Graphics tab, there is a Rotation on Sheet menu on the Options bar. You don't need to change the rotation—just note that it's there.

2. Save the model.

Phew! I think you get the picture. If you like, feel free to create a bunch of schedules on your own. Practice does make perfect.

Let's venture now into creating a material takeoff. It would be a shame to have all these computations go unused!

When you have a schedule that's split like this, any adjustment you make to a column is reflected in the other half of the schedule. You don't have to make the same adjustment twice to the COMMENTS column.

Creating Material Takeoffs

Creating a material takeoff is similar to creating a schedule. The only difference is that you're breaking down components and scheduling the smaller pieces. For example, as you know, you can make a schedule of all the doors in the model—you just did that. But with a material takeoff, you can quantify the square footage of door panels or glass in the doors. To take it a step further, you can do material takeoffs of walls, floors, and any other building components you want to quantify.

The objective of this procedure is to create three different material takeoffs: one for the walls, one for the floors, and one for the roofs. Let's get started:

1. On the View tab, click Schedules ➤ Material Takeoff, as shown in Figure 16.18.

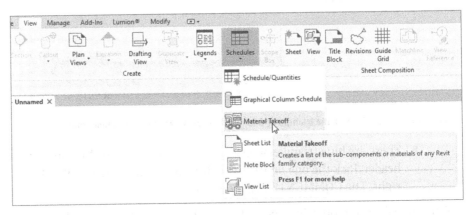

FIGURE 16.18   To add a new material takeoff, you can go to the View tab.

2. In the New Material Takeoff dialog, select Walls.

3. Click OK.

4. In the next dialog, add the following fields (see Figure 16.19):

   ▶ Material: Area

   ▶ Material: Name

   ▶ Count

5. Select the Sorting/Grouping tab.

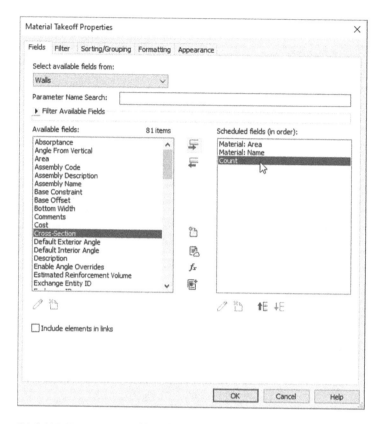

FIGURE 16.19 Adding the materials

6. Sort by Material: Name.

7. Add a footer.

8. Choose Title, Count, and Totals from the menu, as shown in Figure 16.20.

9. Select the Blank Line option.

10. At the bottom of the dialog, select Grand Totals.

11. Choose Title, Count, and Totals from the menu.

12. Select the option Itemize Every Instance (see Figure 16.20).

13. Click OK.

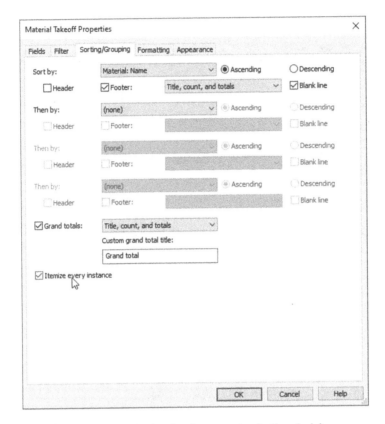

FIGURE 16.20 Configuring the parameters for the schedule

The next step is to begin taking some totals on your own. The first thing you can do is have Revit automatically format a column to produce an independent total; then, you can break out this takeoff and drill in to more specific line-item totals:

1. In the Properties dialog, click the Edit button next to the Formatting row to bring up the Material Takeoff Properties dialog, as shown in Figure 16.21.

2. In the field to the left, select Material: Area (see Figure 16.22).

3. On the right, select Calculate Totals (see Figure 16.22).

4. Click OK.

You now have a total area at the bottom of your takeoff groups, as shown in Figure 16.23.

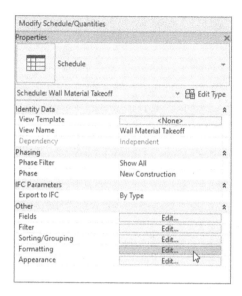

FIGURE 16.21 Going to the Formatting tab

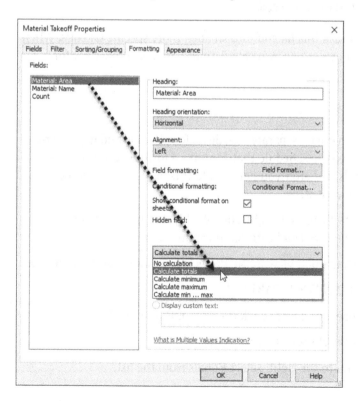

FIGURE 16.22 Specifying we want this field to have a total.

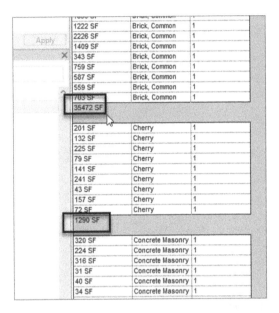

FIGURE 16.23 The total area is calculated.

The next step is to break this takeoff into smaller, more specific takeoffs. When you do this, you can provide your own calculations based on almost any formula you need.

Creating a Calculated Value Field

The objective here is to create separate schedules for plywood and gypsum by adding a new variable to the schedule that contains a formula you create. Yes, it's as hard as it sounds, but after you get used to this procedure, it won't be so bad! Perform the following steps:

1. In the Project Browser, right-click Wall Material Takeoff, and select Duplicate View ➤ Duplicate, as shown in Figure 16.24.

2. Right-click the new view in the Project Browser and select Rename.

3. Rename it **PLYWOOD TAKEOFF**.

4. In the Properties dialog, click the Edit button in the Filter row.

5. For Filter By, choose Material: Name.

6. In the menu to the right, select Equals from the list.

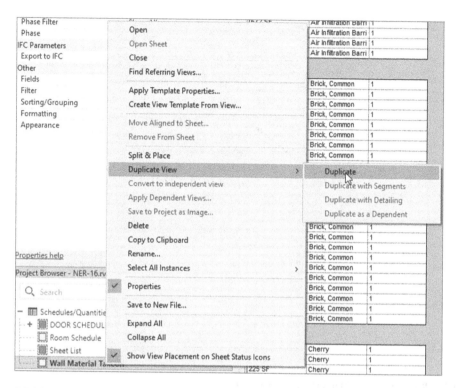

FIGURE 16.24 Duplicating the schedule

7. In the field next to Equals, select Plywood, Sheathing (see Figure 16.25).

8. Click OK.

Your takeoff should look like Figure 16.26.

The next step is to break down the plywood into 4 × 8 sheets. You'll need to add a formula based on the square footage given by Revit divided by 32 square feet to come up with the plywood totals:

1. Open the Plywood Takeoff schedule in the Project Browser (if it isn't already).

2. In the Properties dialog, click the Edit button in the Fields row.

3. On the Fields tab in the Material Takeoff Properties dialog, click the Calculated Value button, as shown in Figure 16.27.

4. For the name, enter **Number of Sheets**.

5. Make sure Discipline is set to Common.

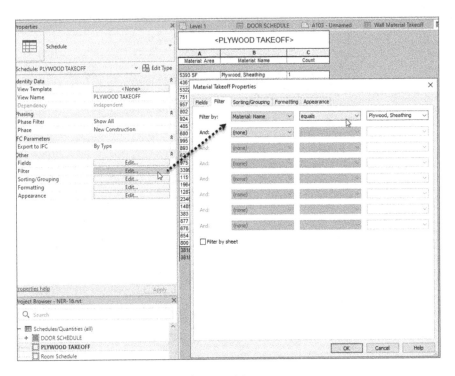

FIGURE 16.25 Filtering based on material

A	B	C
	\<PLYWOOD TAKEOFF\>	
Material: Area	Material: Name	Count
5393 SF	Plywood, Sheathing	1
4361 SF	Plywood, Sheathing	1
5322 SF	Plywood, Sheathing	1
751 SF	Plywood, Sheathing	1
957 SF	Plywood, Sheathing	1
802 SF	Plywood, Sheathing	1
924 SF	Plywood, Sheathing	1
485 SF	Plywood, Sheathing	1
680 SF	Plywood, Sheathing	1
995 SF	Plywood, Sheathing	1
893 SF	Plywood, Sheathing	1
620 SF	Plywood, Sheathing	1
975 SF	Plywood, Sheathing	1
3399 SF	Plywood, Sheathing	1
1151 SF	Plywood, Sheathing	1
1964 SF	Plywood, Sheathing	1
1287 SF	Plywood, Sheathing	1
2346 SF	Plywood, Sheathing	1
1485 SF	Plywood, Sheathing	1
383 SF	Plywood, Sheathing	1
877 SF	Plywood, Sheathing	1
678 SF	Plywood, Sheathing	1
654 SF	Plywood, Sheathing	1
800 SF	Plywood, Sheathing	1
38182 SF		
38182 SF		

FIGURE 16.26 The takeoff is filtered based only on plywood, sheathing.

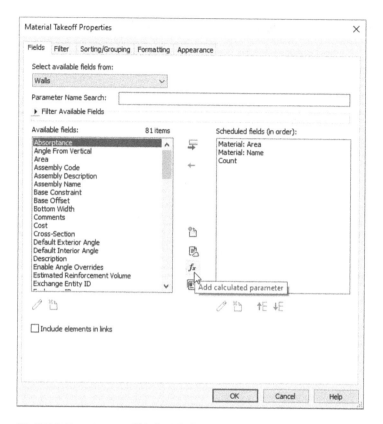

6. Make sure Type is set to Number (see Figure 16.28).

7. Add the following formula: **Material: Area / 32 SF** (metric users type this formula: **Material: Area / 2.88 SF**).

8. Click OK.

You must type the fields being used exactly as they're displayed. For example, the formula: Material: Area must be typed exactly as specified in terms of spacing and capitalization. All formulas in Revit are case sensitive. You can also click the [...] button to add the available fields.

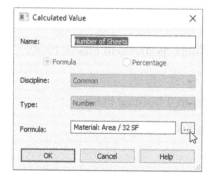

FIGURE 16.28 Changing the calculated values

9. Click the Formatting tab, as shown in Figure 16.29.

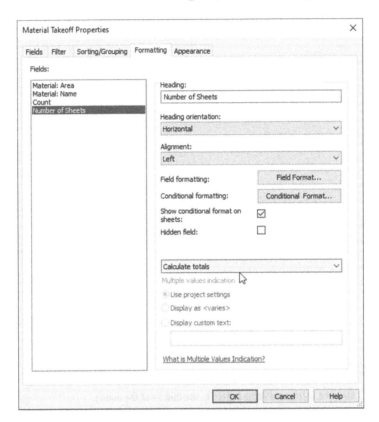

FIGURE 16.29 Selecting the Calculate Totals option

10. In the Field Formatting section, select Calculate Totals (see Figure 16.29).

11. Select the new field called Number of Sheets.

12. Click the Field Format button.

13. Deselect Use Default Settings, as shown in Figure 16.30.

14. Change Units to Fixed.

15. Make sure Rounding is set to 0 Decimal Places.

16. Select Use Digit Grouping (see Figure 16.30).

17. Click OK.

18. Click OK again.

Your material takeoff should resemble Figure 16.31.

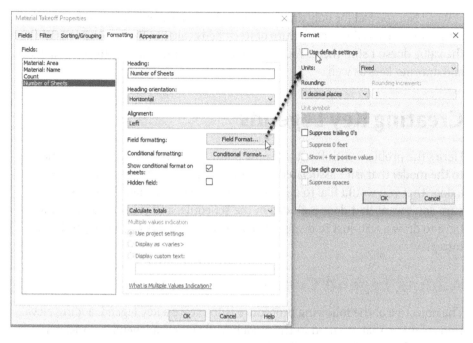

FIGURE 16.30 Overriding the units to allow this field to round

		<PLYWOOD TAKEOFF>	
A	B	C	D
Material: Area	Material: Name	Count	Number of Sheets
5393 SF	Plywood, Sheathing	1	169
4361 SF	Plywood, Sheathing	1	136
5322 SF	Plywood, Sheathing	1	166
751 SF	Plywood, Sheathing	1	23
957 SF	Plywood, Sheathing	1	30
802 SF	Plywood, Sheathing	1	25
924 SF	Plywood, Sheathing	1	29
485 SF	Plywood, Sheathing	1	15
179 SF	Plywood, Sheathing	1	6
204 SF	Plywood, Sheathing	1	6
893 SF	Plywood, Sheathing	1	28
620 SF	Plywood, Sheathing	1	19
975 SF	Plywood, Sheathing	1	30
3399 SF	Plywood, Sheathing	1	106
1151 SF	Plywood, Sheathing	1	36
1964 SF	Plywood, Sheathing	1	61
1287 SF	Plywood, Sheathing	1	40
2346 SF	Plywood, Sheathing	1	73
1485 SF	Plywood, Sheathing	1	46
383 SF	Plywood, Sheathing	1	12
877 SF	Plywood, Sheathing	1	27
678 SF	Plywood, Sheathing	1	21
654 SF	Plywood, Sheathing	1	20
800 SF	Plywood, Sheathing	1	25
36889 SF			1,153
36889 SF			1,153

FIGURE 16.31 The finished plywood material takeoff

Wow! Not too bad for only drawing a bunch of walls. As you can see, using the scheduling/material takeoff feature of Revit adds value to this application. Well, the value doesn't stop there. You can use the same functionality to create legends and drawing keys as well.

Creating Key Legends

Here's the problem with Revit. At some point, you'll need to add a component to the model that isn't associated with anything. Say, for example, you have a door that you would like to elevate on a sheet with the door schedule. You sure don't want that door included in the schedule, and you sure don't want to have to draw a wall just to display it. This is where creating a key legend comes into play.

Adding Legend Components

The objective of the following procedure is to create a key legend, adding elevations of doors that are used in the model. As it stands, a legend can mean any number of things. It can be a list of abbreviations, it can be a comprehensive numbering system keyed off the model itself, or it can be a graphical representation of items that have already been placed into the model for further detailing and coordinating. Another special aspect of legends is that a single legend may need to be duplicated on multiple sheets in a drawing set. You don't know it yet, but this is a problem for Revit. By creating a legend, however, you can get around this issue.

Follow these steps to create a door-type legend:

1. On the View tab, click the Legends ➤ Legend button, as shown in Figure 16.32. You can also right-click Legends in the Project Browser and pick New Legend.

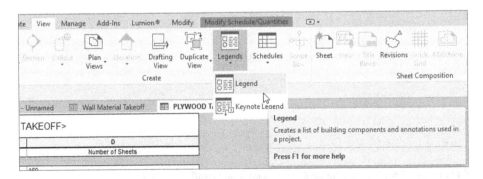

FIGURE 16.32 Click the Legends a Legend button on the View tab.

2. The next dialog wants you to specify a scale. Choose 1/4″ = 1′–0″ (1:50mm). This is fine for now (see Figure 16.33).

3. Call the view **Door Type Legend**.

4. Click OK.

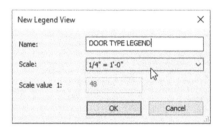

FIGURE 16.33 Choose 1/4″ = 1′–0″ (1:50mm).

Congratulations! You now have a blank view. This is actually a good thing. Think of it as a clean slate where you can draft, add components, and throw together a legend.

OTHER FUNCTIONS HAVE BEEN ACTIVATED

Without knowing it, you've made some tools available that we haven't explored yet. You'll start to learn that Revit knows the type of view you happen to be in at present. Some commands are available in one view, but they may not be in the next. Keep this in mind as you venture through Revit and become frustrated that a command isn't working. You usually just need to switch views.

The next step is to begin adding components. You'll need to go to the Annotate tab for this:

1. Go to the Detail panel of the Annotate tab.

2. Click the Component ➤ Legend Component button, as shown in Figure 16.34.

3. In the Options bar, choose Doors: Door Passage-Single-Flush: 30″ × 80″, as shown in Figure 16.35.

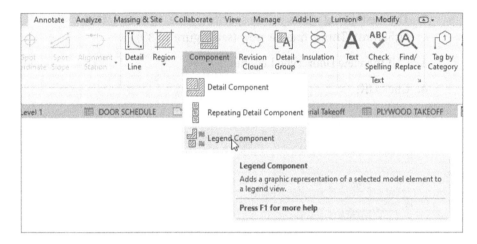

F I G U R E   1 6 . 3 4   Clicking the Legend Component button

4. Change the view to Elevation : Front.

5. Pick a point to place the elevation.

6. With the command still running, you can place another instance. Change the view to Floor Plan. Place another instance of the door just above the elevation. Revit provides a snap line on the left side for alignment.

7. In the Options bar, be sure Host Length is set to 6′–0″ (1800 mm).

The next step is to add some text in an attempt to label the doors. These items can't be labeled, which can be a disadvantage to breaking away from the model. This is basically a dumb sheet. Follow along:

1. In the Text panel, click the Text button.

2. Make sure the text style is Text: 3/32″ Arial and that the leader is set to None.

3. Place some text centered under each door elevation, and label the doors **Type A** (see Figure 16.36).

4. Save the model.

It's nice to have accurate blocks available based on what you've added to your model up to this point. By using the Revit method of building a legend like this, you're removed from the horror of stealing old legends from other jobs. I think we all know what a nightmare this turns into when they aren't accurate. Plus, in

Revit, you have a library of the doors you're using right at your fingertips. They don't have to be managed or updated constantly. They will always be there, and they will always be accurate.

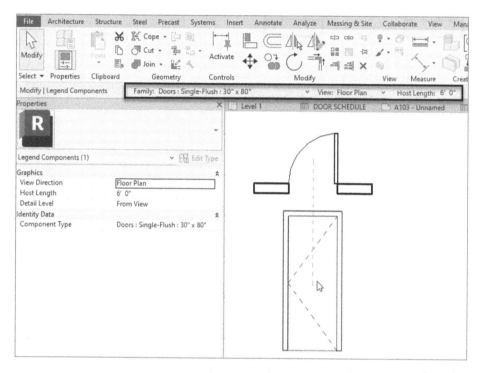

FIGURE 16.35 Changing the options for the legend

Next, you'll create a symbol legend—that is, you need to make a sheet that contains all your typical symbols. This task will be carried out in a similar manner.

Adding Tags

You're nearing the end of the book, and you've probably noticed that some subjects, such as tags, were brushed over in earlier chapters. Tags simply can't be avoided because they come in automatically with many items. But a mystery surrounds them. Where do they come from, how does Revit know what tag to associate with what element, and how the heck do you make Revit tags look like your tags?

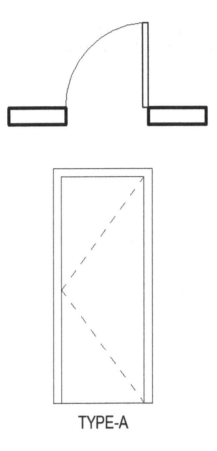

TYPE-A

FIGURE 16.36 Placing text underneath the doors

You can almost see a tag as a "window" looking into the item itself. A tag allows you to pull a parameter out of an item and put that parameter onto the drawing in a physical sense. Given that, tags are how you label things.

To start, let's concentrate on the simple and then move to the more complex. First, you'll learn how to add a tag that wasn't added automatically.

Adding Tags Individually

As you may have noticed, not everything you placed in the model received a tag—especially many of the doors and windows that you copied to different floors. The objective of the following procedures is to add tags to individual objects. The first type of tag will be by category.

Tagging Walls

Tagging walls is almost as automatic as tagging doors and windows. The only difference is that when you tag a wall, the tag might be initially blank.

To learn how to tag a wall, follow along with this procedure:

1. In the Project Browser, go to the Level 2 floor plan if you are not there already.

2. Zoom in on the east wing.

3. Click the Tag by Category button.

4. Make sure the Leader button is checked.

5. Pick the wall indicated in Figure 16.37.

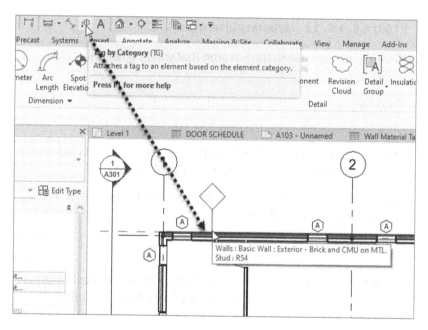

FIGURE 16.37 Picking one of the corridor partitions to tag

6. Press Esc twice.

7. Select the new wall tag (it's blank).

8. Notice the blue items. Click the blue question mark in the tag.

9. Call it **MC-1**, as shown in Figure 16.38.

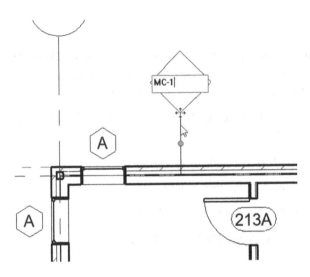

FIGURE 16.38 Adding the wall tag data

10. Click Yes in response to the warning that you're changing a type parameter.

11. Press Esc.

12. Click Tag by Category on the Annotate tab.

13. Pick any other exterior wall in Level 2. This time the tag is automatically placed with the appropriate MC-1 tag filled out.

Suppose you would like to tag a number of the same items in one shot. Revit lets you do this by using the Tag All command.

Using the Tag All Command

The Tag All command is a favorite among Revit users. One of the most common examples of using this command is when you Copy/Paste Aligned multiple items to higher-level floors. You'll almost always miss a few tags, or even all of the tags. This is where Tag All comes into play.

The objective of this next procedure is to find the Tag All feature and tag many items in one shot:

1. In the Project Browser, go to the Level 4 floor plan.

2. Notice that many doors and windows aren't tagged. (If for some reason all the doors and windows are tagged, select the tags, and delete them for this procedure.)

BUT WHERE IS THAT INFORMATION STORED?

When you modify this type of tag, it's generally the type mark that carries the data. To see the location of the type mark, select any one of the interior partitions, and click Edit Type in the Properties dialog. In the Type Parameters, you can scroll down to find Type Mark, as shown in the following image:

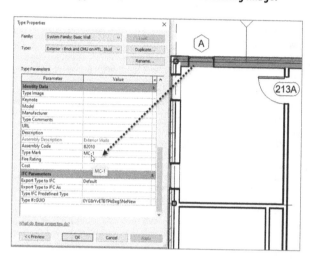

This information is also tied into the schedule. As you're selecting fields to add to the schedule, you're selecting from the same list that Revit used to tag items in the model. This is the definition of BIM: the right information is used in the right places.

3. On the Annotate tab, click the Tag All button, as shown in Figure 16.39.

FIGURE 16.39   The Tag All button on the Annotate tab

4. In the Tag All Not Tagged dialog, click Door Tags.

5. Hold the Ctrl key and select Window Tags. This specifies that every door and window in the view is about to receive a tag.

6. Make sure the All Objects in Current View radio button is selected (see Figure 16.40).

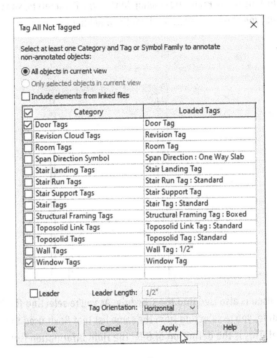

FIGURE 16.40 Selecting door and window tags

7. Click Apply.

8. Click OK.

It almost goes without saying that Tag All is quite a valuable tool. Another valuable tool is the ability to reach into a component and tag a specific material within the component.

Tagging by Material

Tagging by material may be one of the most underused commands in all of Revit. The reason is that most people think of a tag as, well, a tag—a drawn box containing some abbreviations or letters. That's too bad, because you can also use tags as a means to place notes. Tagging an item's material is one way of doing just that.

The objective of the following procedure is to create a material description and then place a tag pursuant to that note:

1. In the Project Browser, go to the Level 1 floor plan.

2. Go to the Manage tab, then to Materials.

3. Find the material Tile Floor - Terra Cotta.

4. Go to the Identity tab.

5. Under Descriptive Information, add the Description **TERRA COTTA**. See Figure 16.41.

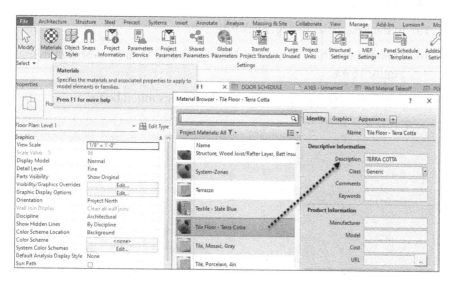

FIGURE 16.41 Adding information to the material

6. Click OK

7. Zoom in on the kitchen area in the east wing.

8. In the Tag panel of the Annotate tab, click the Material Tag button, as shown in Figure 16.42.

FIGURE 16.42 The Material Tag button in the Tag panel

9. You may get the message stating that no material tag family is loaded into the model. If so, click the Yes button to load one.

10. Browse to Annotations ➤ Architectural ➤ Material Tag.rfa.

11. Click Open.

12. Place your cursor over the tile floor. The tag reads "TERRA COTTA." When you see this tag, pick a point on the tile floor, and then place the note to the right, as shown in the figure.

13. Press Esc twice or click Modify.

14. Select the tag.

15. In the Properties dialog, click Edit Type.

16. Change Leader Arrowhead to Arrow Filled 15 Degree, as shown in Figure 16.43.

17. Click OK to reveal the leader. Yes, that looks much better.

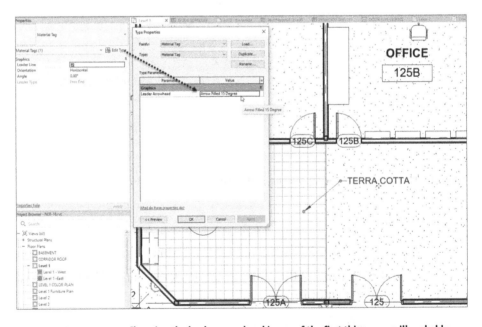

F I G U R E 1 6 . 4 3 Changing the leader arrowhead is one of the first things you will probably have to do.

The next topic we'll explore is where these tags come from and how you can create your own. Notations and symbols are the basis for maintaining graphical standards. If you simply use the examples given to you by Revit, you'll have a set of drawings that look very generic and immediately turn off your design team.

Using Multi-Category Tags

If you think about it, you used a door tag for the doors, a window tag for the windows, and a wall tag for the walls. Jeepers! How many different tags do you need to complete a set of construction documents? Well, in Revit, you can create a multi-category tag. This will be the same tag (aesthetically) that identifies a common property in any element.

Unfortunately, Revit doesn't provide a sample multi-category tag, so you'll have to make one. The objective of the next set of procedures is to create a new multi-category tag and then use it on various furniture items.

As mentioned earlier, you should create any new family by using a template. Doing so will ensure that you're using the correct data, so the family will behave as expected. This is what you're doing right now:

1. Click the blue File tab, and then choose New ➤ Family.

2. In the Annotations folder, locate the file called Multi-Category Tag.rft.

3. Open the Multi-Category Tag.rft template.

4. Because you have started the family by using a template, the Ribbon has changed. In the Create panel, click the Label button.

5. Pick the point at the intersection of the two reference planes.

6. In the Edit Label dialog, add the Family Name and Type Name parameters, as shown in Figure 16.44.

7. In the Family Name row, select the Break check box (see Figure 16.44).

8. Click OK.

9. Click the Application button and select Save As ➤ Family. Place the file somewhere you can find it later.

10. Call the new tag **Multi-Category Tag**.

11. In the Family Editor panel, click Load Into Project.

12. In the NER-16 project (or whatever project name you're in at present), go to the Level 1 Furniture floor plan and zoom in on the northeast office in the east wing.

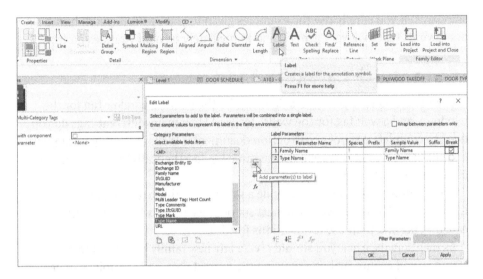

FIGURE 16.44 This time you're adding two parameters. By selecting the Break check box, you tell Revit to stack the parameters.

13. On the Annotate tab, click the Multi-Category button in the Tag panel, as shown in Figure 16.45.

FIGURE 16.45 The Multi-Category button in the Tag panel

14. On the Options bar, select the Leader option, as shown in Figure 16.46.

15. Again, on the Options bar, select Free End (see Figure 16.46).

16. Hover your mouse over the furniture items shown in the room in Figure 16.46. The tag reports the information for any item over which you hover. Pick the entertainment unit to the left of the room, and then pick two points to the right of the unit.

17. Click Modify. Select the tag you just placed into the model.

18. Click the Edit Type button.

19. For Leader Arrowhead, select Arrow Filled 15 Degree.

20. Click OK.

21. Using the grips on the tag, move it out of the way, and adjust the leader so it looks like the one in Figure 16.46.

22. Add another tag to the credenza located on the north wall. Adjust this tag as well (see Figure 16.46).

23. Add one more tag to the shelving on the south wall of the room and adjust the leader so it looks acceptable. Notice that when you select the tag, you can add multiple hosts. (again, see Figure 16.46).

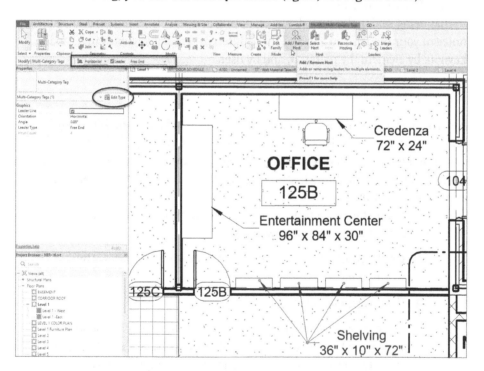

FIGURE 16.46 Adding the multi-category tag to the entertainment unit. Make sure you adjust the tag to show the information unobscured.

Using multi-category tags is a great way to label a model. It's nice because you don't need specific tags for the various elements. These items could have been different types of furniture and casework. As long as they have a family name and a type name, the label tag will work.

Another way to record items in a model is by adding keynoting. This procedure is done in conjunction with a schedule. The last section of this chapter will focus on this procedure.

Keynoting

Keynoting has been used in construction documents dating back to the Pharaohs. OK, maybe not that far back, but you get the point. Revit does a nice job in terms of tracking keynotes. The only issue is that nothing comes pre-keynoted in Revit. That is, a keynote value needs to be assigned to each item. If your company uses keynoting, you'll have to assign a keynote to every item in Revit in your template.

That being said, let's break down keynoting and start learning how to add key-notes to your model. You can add three different types of keynotes to a model: keynote by element, by material, and by user.

Keynoting by Element

Keynoting by element means you select an object and place the keynoted text. This procedure is the same as when you tag an object, except that this time the information you're reporting is actually formatted according to the Construction Specifications Institute (CSI) standard or a standard for your installation location.

Before you get started on this exercise, make sure there is a keynote.txt file to which Revit is pointing. Then follow along:

1. On the Annotate tab, click the small down arrow below the word *Keynote*.

2. Click Keynote Settings.

3. Make sure you're mapped to C:\ProgramData\Autodesk\RVT 2024\ Libraries\US Imperial\RevitKeynotes_Imperial_2024.txt (RevitKeynotes_Metric.txt), as shown in Figure 16.47.

4. Click Okay.

To use the keynoting by element function, follow this procedure:

1. In the Project Browser, go to the Level 1 floor plan.

2. Zoom in on a hallway sconce lighting fixture.

3. In the Tag panel of the Annotate tab, select Keynote ➤ Element Keynote, as shown in Figure 16.48.

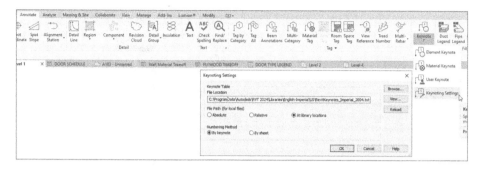

FIGURE 16.47 Mapping the **Keynote.txt** file

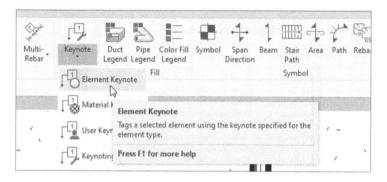

FIGURE 16.48 Select Keynote ➤ Element Keynote.

NOTE If no keynote tag is loaded, click Yes in the subsequent dialog and browse to Annotations ➤ Keynote Tag.rfa.

NOTE At this point, it's up to you to determine which style of keynoting your firm uses. Do you keynote the plans with the CSI number, with the keynote description, or with a combination of the number and the description? Either way, you'll be making a keynote schedule with these items in a list.

4. In the Type Selector, click Keynote Tag ➤ Keynote Text, as shown in Figure 16.49.

5. Pick the wall sconce shown in Figure 16.50.

6. Pick a second point for the leader line.

7. Pick a third point to place the keynote text (see Figure 16.50).

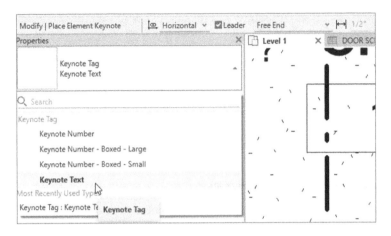

FIGURE 16.49 Choosing Keynote Tag ➤ Keynote Text

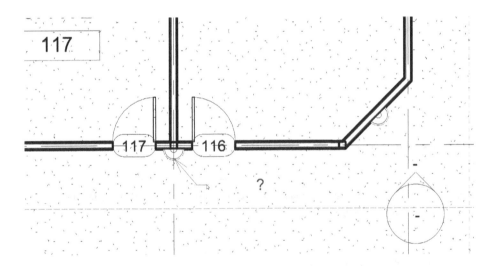

FIGURE 16.50 Placing the keynote with a leader

Because no keynote has been assigned to this family, you can specify one now. Revit lets you specify keynoting information either by assigning the information through the Properties dialog or by placing a keynote tag, after which Revit will prompt you to specify the missing information.

After you pick the third point, Revit displays the Keynotes menu shown in Figure 16.51. Follow these steps to place the keynote value into the sconce family:

1. Scroll to Division 26 Electrical and click the plus sign.

2. Go to the group 26 51 00 Interior Lighting.

3. Go to the group 26 51 00.B2 Wall Mounted Incandescent Fixture, as shown in Figure 16.51.

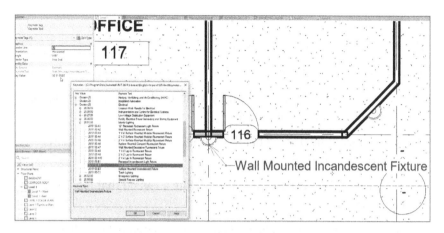

FIGURE 16.51 Selecting the proper keynote value for the sconce

4. Click OK.

5. Drag the text to the right to see the arrow and the note clearly.

6. In the Tag panel of the Annotate tab, select Keynote ➤ Element Keynote again.

7. Go down the corridor and add a keynote to another sconce.

8. Change the tag to Keynote Number – Boxed – Small.

9. Select the keynote and change the type properties for Leader Arrowhead to Arrow Filled 15 Degree. See Figure 16.52. Because we are using keynotes, we can chose between the text or the number.

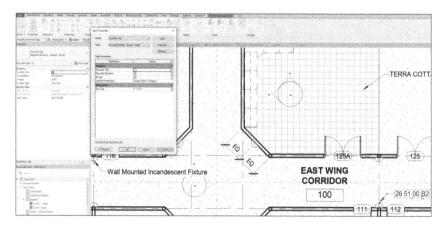

FIGURE 16.52 Adding the keynote number

Are You Experienced?

Now you can. . .

✓ create several different types of schedules

✓ add custom fields to the schedules that calculate values

✓ create material takeoffs that give you up-to-the-second information as you add items to the model

✓ create legends by using a blank view and basically drafting items into the model

✓ import AutoCAD-generated data to create a legend that looks exactly like your CAD

✓ create drawing sheets, add a schedule, and manipulate a schedule to fit on the sheet

✓ add tags to the model in addition to the tags that were automatically added when you placed the components

✓ place tags that reach into a component and display different materials

✓ create custom tags to display any information

CHAPTER 17

Rendering and Presentation

Well, here we are—the chapter you've probably been chomping at the bit to get into, and for good reason. The output that you create from this chapter will make your bosses and, better yet, your clients get behind your presentations. As I always say, none of this software is any good if you can't capture the work to begin with. That being said, in this chapter we'll focus on creating renderings, adding animations, and providing solar studies based on a project's geographical location.

This chapter covers the following topics:

▶ **Creating an interior rendering**

▶ **Creating walkthroughs**

▶ **Creating a solar study**

Creating an Interior Rendering

The first item we need to tackle is how to go about creating an interior rendering with no natural lighting. Trying to address the subject of rendering as a whole would convolute the matter. The thing is, when you create a rendering, lighting obviously plays a major role. Day lighting and artificial lighting are two completely different beasts—one will influence the effect of the other. For example, if you're rendering an exterior scene, there are bound to be windows. If this rendering appears at night or at dusk, the interior lights will be turned on.

The objective of the first section of this chapter is to create a rendering from the interior of a building but to rely on daylighting to illuminate the scene.

To begin, open the file on which you've been following along. If you didn't complete the previous chapter, go to the book's web page at www.wiley .com/go/revit2024ner.

The goal of this procedure is to create a camera view that you can use for your first rendering. You'll then adjust the view controls and look at the sunlight effects. Follow along:

1. In the Project Browser, open the Level 1 floor plan.

2. Zoom in on the corridor area in the middle of the building.

3. Add some curtain walls to the corridors, as shown in Figure 17.1. (Come on, I know you can do it.) These are Level 1 to Level 3 with a –6″ (–150 mm) offset from Level 3. You can use Curtain Wall Storefront. Use Reference Planes to offset the wall 2′–0″ from the ends of the walls. See Figure 17.1 for dimensions.

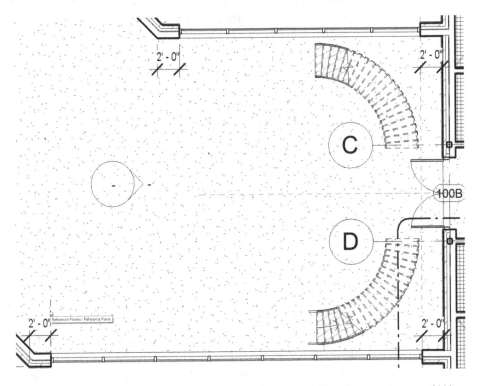

FIGURE 17.1 Add the curtain walls to let the light shine in! (Note that some items are hidden for clarity)

4. On the View tab, select 3D View ➤ Camera, as shown in Figure 17.2.

5. Click the point labeled 1 first, then the point labeled 2, as shown in Figure 17.2.

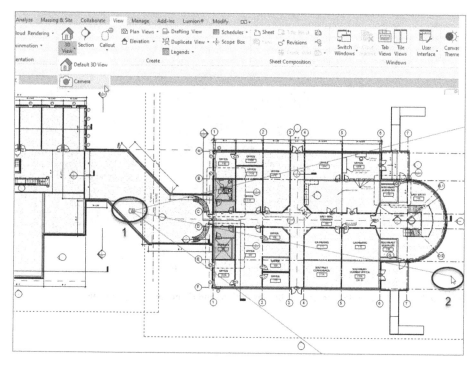

FIGURE 17.2 Adding the perspective view

6. When the view opens, rename it **RENDERING AT CORRIDOR**.

7. Open the RENDERING AT CORRIDOR view (it should open automatically).

8. Select the crop region and widen the view, as shown in Figure 17.3.

9. On the View Control bar, set Detail Level to Fine.

10. Change Visual Style to Realistic.

11. In the Properties dialog, click the Edit button in the Graphic Display Options row (see Figure 17.4).

12. Expand the Shadows panel, and click Cast Shadows and Show Ambient Shadows.

13. In the Lighting section, turn Sun up to 100%. (See Figure 17.4).

14. Click into the Realistic section, and change Exposure to Manual.

15. Set the Exposure value to 13.09

You can also access the Graphic Display Options dialog by clicking the small black arrow in the right corner of the Graphics panel, on the View tab.

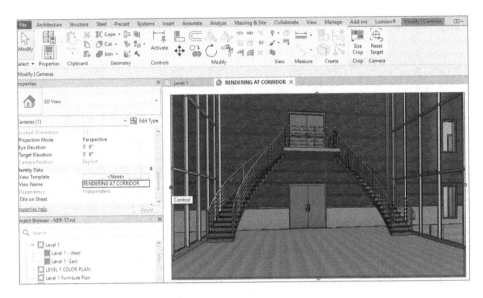

FIGURE 17.3 Selecting Graphic Display Options and changing the crop region

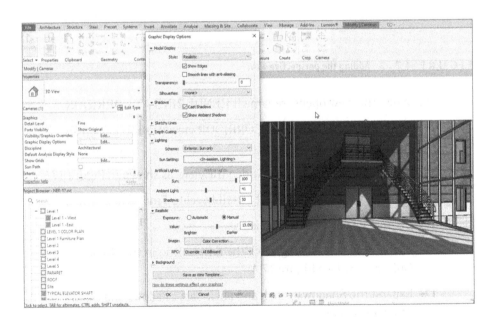

FIGURE 17.4 Brightening up the view

16. Click OK.

17. Click the Show Rendering Dialog button on the View Control bar, as shown in Figure 17.5.

FIGURE 17.5 The Show Render Dialog button

In the Rendering dialog, you'll see quite a few choices. They vary depending on the scene you're trying to capture. The next procedure will move through the Rendering dialog from top to bottom.

At the top of the Rendering dialog is a Render button. This is the last button you'll click—it starts the rendering process. For the rest, follow these steps:

NOTE The Region check box (to the right of the Render button) allows you to pick a window to be rendered. Because the scene in this example is somewhat small, you won't need to select this option. If you were rendering a much larger scene, you would render a region. That way, it wouldn't take hours upon hours to complete the rendering, and the resulting rendered scene would be a smaller size. Also, it is good practice to set the first rendering as a test and crank out a much lower dpi (dots per inch), perhaps 150. Once you've verified that the rendering will work, let 'er rip at a higher dpi, such as 300.

1. For Quality, set Setting to Draft.

2. For Output Settings, set Resolution to Printer and 150 dpi.

3. In the Lighting category, set Scheme to Interior: Sun And Artificial.

4. In the Background category, set Style to Sky: Very Cloudy (see Figure 17.6).

5. Click the Render button. After the scene is rendered, it should be similar to Figure 17.7 in appearance.

6. Click the Adjust Exposure button in the image section.

7. Change the settings to your liking. You may use the settings in Figure 17.7 for reference.

TIP Before you click the Render button, find something else to do for two to three hours—at this resolution, the Autodesk® Revit® software needs about that much time to render this scene. I recommend that you have Revit installed on another machine at your place of business. You don't want to watch the rendering process because it's similar to gazing into a campfire. Plus, if your model is being rendered on another machine, you can get some work done at the same time. If you're trying to avoid work, disregard this statement. Also, you can use Autodesk Cloud Rendering. It will cut your rendering time to minutes.

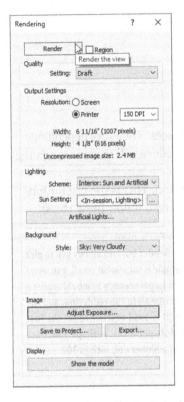

FIGURE 17.6 The Rendering dialog

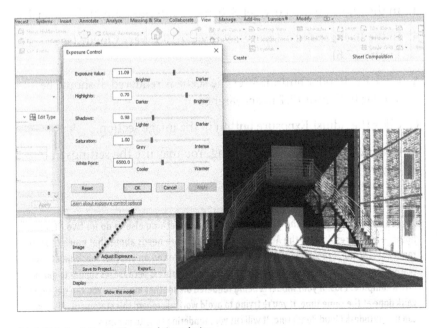

FIGURE 17.7 The 150 dpi rendering

The next procedure will look at how to save the rendering to the model and also how to export the rendering to an image. Follow these steps:

1. In the Rendering dialog, click the Save To Project button, as shown in Figure 17.8.

FIGURE 17.8 Saving the rendering to the project

2. Call the new rendering view **Rendering at Corridor**; then click OK.

3. Click the Export button, and you can save the image as a JPEG or a TIFF.

THAT'S NOT A VERY GOOD IMAGE!

After you create a rendering that you like, export it immediately. That's how you get the best resolution in the external image you create. Also, you don't want a lot of trial renderings clunking around in your project—they will make your Project Browser messy, and your coworkers will start getting annoyed with you. Unless that rendering is going on a sheet, throw it out.

4. Save the file somewhere you can retrieve it. You can choose whichever file format you prefer.

5. At the bottom of the Rendering dialog, in the Display section, click Show The Model. The rendering reverts to the original graphic style.

6. Click the Show The Rendering button. The rendering reappears.

The ability to jump back and forth from the model to the rendering is a nice feature, but it's short-lived. After you close this project, the rendering is no longer available. Don't close this project until you've finished saving the view to the model and exporting it (if you wish to do so).

Creating Lighting Groups

All too often, you render scenes with no real consideration for the lighting that has been added to the model. Because you lean heavily on Revit to produce accurate scenarios to present to clients, you should spend some time thinking through your lighting before you create a rendering.

In this procedure, you'll create a lighting group, then render an entirely indoor scene with no natural light. Follow along:

1. Go to the Level 1 floor plan.

2. Zoom in on the corridor area, as shown in Figure 17.9.

3. Select one of the wall sconces.

4. In the Type Properties dialog, click Edit Type.

5. Scroll down to Light Loss Factor and click the 1 button.

6. In the Light Loss Factor dialog, brighten Temperature Loss/Gain Factor to 1.5. See Figure 17.9.

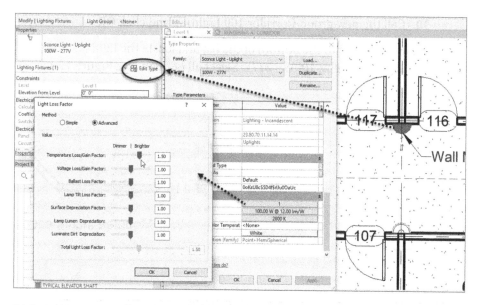

FIGURE 17.9 Adjusting the lighting levels

7. Click OK twice.

8. With the light still selected, on the Options bar, click the Light Group menu, and select Edit/New (see Figure 17.10).

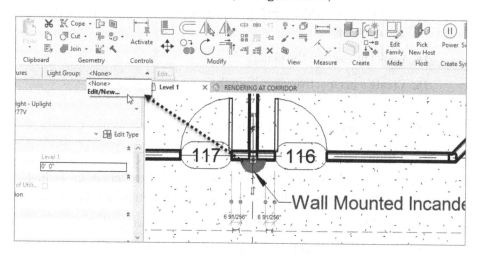

FIGURE 17.10 Creating a new group and adding the proper lights

9. In the Artificial Lights - Level 1 dialog, click the New button in the Group Options area.

10. Call the new group **Corridor 100 Lighting** and click OK.

11. Scroll down to the bottom of the list and locate the lights Sconce Light - Uplight: 100W - 277V. Select all of them (see Figure 17.11).

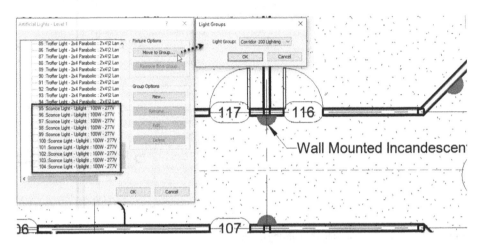

FIGURE 17.11 Moving our sconces to the new group

12. Click the Move To Group button under Fixture Options.

13. Choose the Corridor 100 Lighting group in the Light Groups dialog and click OK.

14. Click OK to close the dialog.

15. Create a perspective view down the corridor, as shown in Figure 17.12.

16. Rename it **CORRIDOR 100 PERSPECTIVE**.

17. Change Visual Style to Realistic.

18. In the Corridor Perspective view, select all the troffers in the ceiling and add them to the lighting group, as shown in Figure 17.13.

19. Type **VG** for Visibility Graphics and turn off Structural Columns.

20. Go to Graphic Display Options, as shown in Figure 17.14.

21. Change the settings, as shown in Figure 17.15.

22. Click OK.

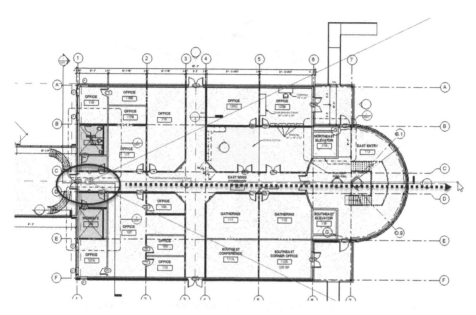

FIGURE 17.12   Creating the perspective view

FIGURE 17.13   Assign the corridor lights to the correct group.

FIGURE 17.14 The graphics display results before actually rendering the scene.

23. On the View tab, click the Render button, as shown in Figure 17.15.

24. Click the Artificial Lights button.

25. Make sure Lighting Corridor is selected.

26. Deselect Ungrouped Lights (see Figure 17.15).

27. Click OK.

28. Click Render.

29. Adjust the exposure to suit your needs. See Figure 17.16.

Creating Walkthroughs

For some reason, you can show a client a beautiful rendering of a space or building that you plan to design for them and still be met with a blasé, half-hearted reaction. But if you show them the same space as though you're walking through it . . . well then, the client perks right up!

Although this part of the chapter isn't crucial to your expertise in Revit, it's certainly worth a glance. Sometimes the special tools you pull out of your belt can win a job or impress your friends on a Saturday night.

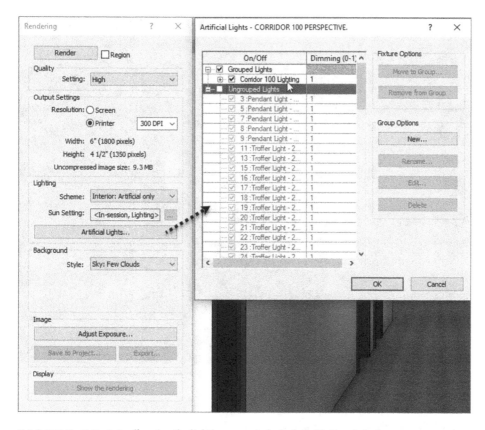

FIGURE 17.15 Choosing the lighting group to be included in the rendering

A *walkthrough* is a series of points you pick in a sequence in a plan view. It's sort of like connecting the dots, but these dots will advance a frame as if you were walking to the points you picked.

The objective of this procedure is to create a walkthrough of the building and to export the walkthrough to an AVI (Audio Video Interleave) file. Follow these steps:

1. Go to the Level 1 floor plan.

2. On the View tab, choose 3D View ➤ Walkthrough, as shown in Figure 17.17.

3. Zoom in on the west entry.

4. Start picking points, as shown in Figure 17.18.

FIGURE 17.16 The corridor rendering

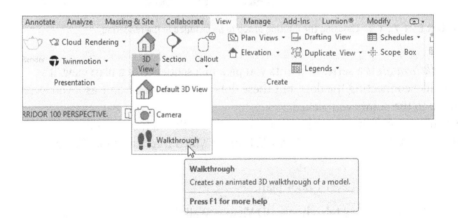

FIGURE 17.17 The Walkthrough command

5. Keep picking points down the hallway, into the corridor, and into the east wing, as shown in Figure 17.18. (I numbered where I picked, but you can pick more or fewer points.)

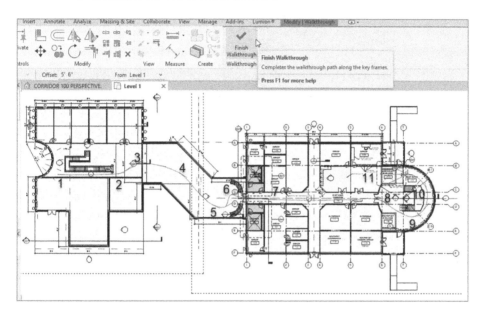

FIGURE 17.18 Picking the points in the floor plan

6. On the Modify | Walkthrough tab of the Ribbon, click the green Finish Walkthrough check mark.

7. On the Modify | Cameras tab of the Ribbon, click the Edit Walk-through button, as shown in Figure 17.19.

WHERE DID MY WALKTHROUGH GO?

If you hit Esc or clicked off of the walkthrough, it'll disappear. To select the walk-through, go into the Project Browser and scroll down to Walkthroughs. Right click on Walkthrough 1 and select Show Camera as illustrated in the following image.

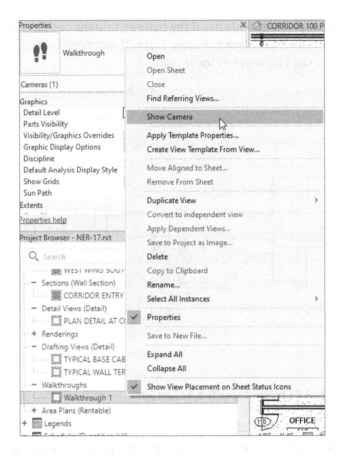

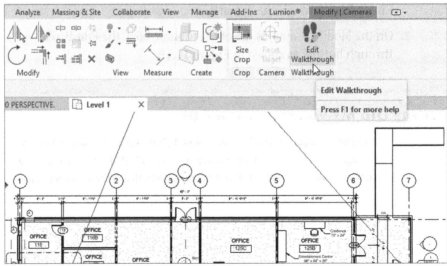

FIGURE 17.19 Selecting Edit Walkthrough

8. Select Open Walkthrough, as shown in Figure 17.20.

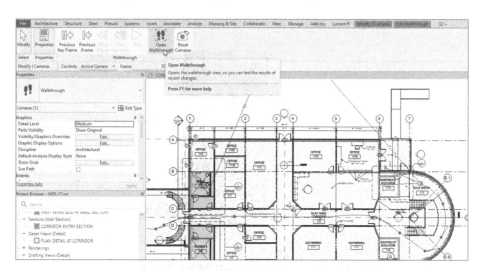

FIGURE 17.20 Selecting Open Walkthrough

9. On the Options bar, change the first frame to 1.

10. On the View Control bar, click Realistic.

11. Select the crop region.

12. On the Modify | Cameras tab, click the Edit Walkthrough button (again).

13. On the Modify | Cameras tab, click the Play button, as shown in Figure 17.21.

14. When the walkthrough is finished, click the button that contains the value 300 (the number of frames) on the Options bar, as shown in Figure 17.22.

15. In the Walkthrough Frames dialog, change the Frames Per Second value to 20. Click OK.

16. Run the walkthrough again. This time it's sped up.

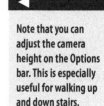

Note that you can adjust the camera height on the Options bar. This is especially useful for walking up and down stairs.

The walkthrough is complete. One thing you will be asked is whether you can give the walkthrough to someone to use for a presentation. Luckily, the answer is yes, and the person presenting doesn't have to be Revit literate or even own the application.

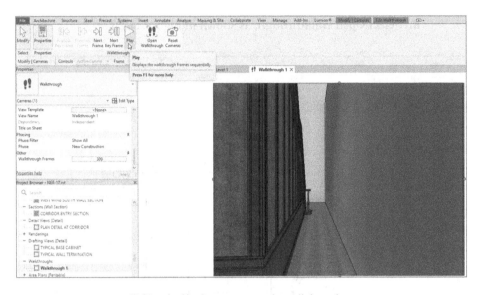

FIGURE 17.21   Clicking the Play button to start the walkthrough

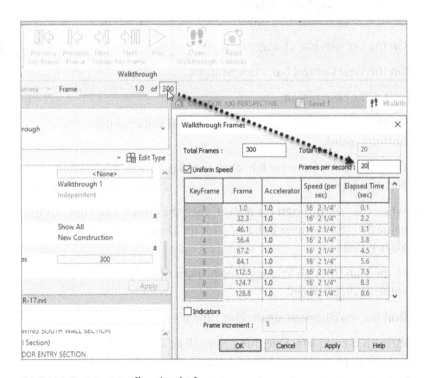

FIGURE 17.22   Changing the frames

Exporting an Animation

Exporting an animation is a great, but slightly hidden, feature. The Export function isn't located on the Ribbon—you'll find it on the File tab, as shown in Figure 17.23. By exporting a walkthrough, you're creating an Audio Video Interleave (AVI) that will translate the native Revit walkthrough. It's quick and almost completely painless.

To create an AVI of the walkthrough, follow these steps:

1. Make sure the walkthrough view is open, and click the blue File tab.

2. Choose Export ➤ Images And Animations ➤ Walkthrough (see Figure 17.23).

FIGURE 17.23 Choosing to export the walkthrough

3. Select the defaults in the next dialog and click OK.

4. Find a location for the file and click Save.

5. Click OK in the Video Compression dialog. (You'll have to wait for Revit to go through the walkthrough as it creates the AVI.)

6. Find the AVI and run it to make sure it works.

 NOTE In case you're wondering, yes, the size of this AVI is over a gigabyte. If necessary, you can attempt to compress the file as you export it, but the quality will probably degrade. Besides, memory is cheap these days.

With the walkthrough complete, there is one more animation we need to look at. It's not as cool as the walkthrough, but it's just as interesting. This animation is called a solar study.

Creating a Solar Study

A *solar study* is a shaded 3D view that provides a time-lapsed visual of how the building will cast shadows over the course of a day or multiple days. Let's create a single-day solar study by specifying the geographical location of your building. Follow along:

1. Go to the view {3D} in the Project Browser.

2. Right-click and choose Duplicate View ➤ Duplicate With Detailing.

3. Rename the new 3D view **ONE DAY SOLAR STUDY**.

4. On the View Control toolbar, click the Shadows On button, as shown in Figure 17.24.

F I G U R E 1 7 . 2 4 Shadows need to be turned on for a Solar Study.

5. To the left of the Shadows button is the Sun Path button. Click it and select Sun Path On.

6. Click the Sun Settings button, as shown in Figure 17.25.

7. In the Sun Settings dialog, click the Single Day radio button, as shown in Figure 17.25.

8. Select Spring Equinox Solar Study in the Presets category.

9. In Settings under Location, click the browse button, which will open the Location And Site dialog.

10. Set Define Location By to Internet Mapping Service.

11. Add the address you'd like. Mine is my office in Syracuse.

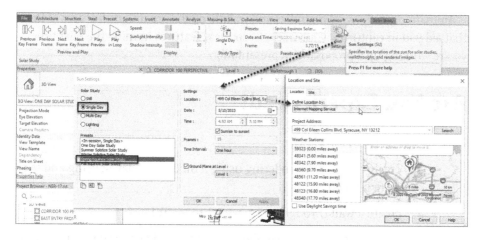

FIGURE 17.25 Setting up the solar study

12. Click OK.

13. Change Date to **5/10/2023**. Select Sunrise To Sunset. Set Ground Plane At Level to Level 1.

14. Set Time Interval to One Hour (see Figure 17.25).

15. Click OK.

16. Click on the Sun Path button again, and choose Solar Study.

17. On the Preview And Play panel, click the Play Preview button, as shown in Figure 17.26.

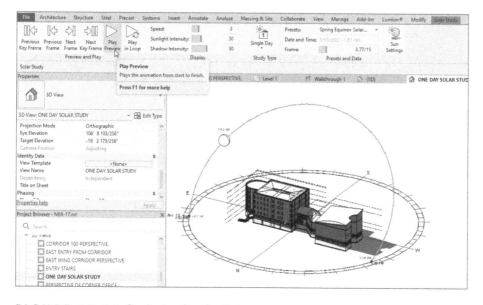

FIGURE 17.26 Previewing the solar study

Animations such as solar studies and walkthroughs are unique features of Revit that aid you in capturing your work. Keep these features in mind the next time you're working up a proposal or a presentation.

Are You Experienced?

Now you can. . .

- ✓ create an interior rendering using a mixture of day lighting and artificial lighting

- ✓ create a walkthrough and export it to an AVI

- ✓ create a solar study that allows you to visualize the shadowing effect of your model

CHAPTER 18

Creating Families

As you're probably becoming acutely aware, having the right content makes or breaks an Autodesk® Revit® Architecture project. I'm sure you're also very aware that, other than the content Autodesk has provided and the content you downloaded from this book's web page, you don't have anywhere near the amount of content you need to start a project! That being said, it's time to buckle down and dig into how Revit works and see how having adjustable, parametric families will turn you into a Revit fan for life.

This chapter covers the following topics:

▶ **Creating a basic family**

▶ **Using a complex family to create an arched door**

▶ **Creating an in-place family**

Creating a Basic Family

The first item we'll tackle is how to create a basic family. We'll start with the creation of a wall sweep and then move on to creating an arched doorway. As you become fluent with these two basic family types, you'll start to be able to create families quite fast.

You have to start somewhere. To be honest, no good family is "basic," but some are easier to create than others. The concept is the same, however.

Essentially, a family has three fundamental components:

Reference Planes   Yes, reference planes drive the family. Look at these as the family's skeleton.

Parametric Dimensioning   When dimensions are added while creating a family, we have the opportunity to make that dimension parametric. For example, we can add a dimension between two reference planes. That dimension can have a parameter called Length. Now the Length parameter can be changed to alter the length of the object.

Geometry   Linework, or 3D massing, is locked to the skeleton. We'll call this the skin. Corny, I know, but it gets the point across.

First you need to figure out where to start. Any family that you want to insert into a Revit model must begin with a template. Choosing the correct template, as you'll soon discover, will make your life much simpler.

The objective of this procedure is to start a new family by choosing a template in Revit. Follow these steps:

1. On the Revit home screen, click the New. . . link in the Families category, or click the Application button and select New ➤ Family.

2. Select Profile-Hosted.rft (Metric Profile-Hosted.rft), and then click Open. See Figure 18.1.

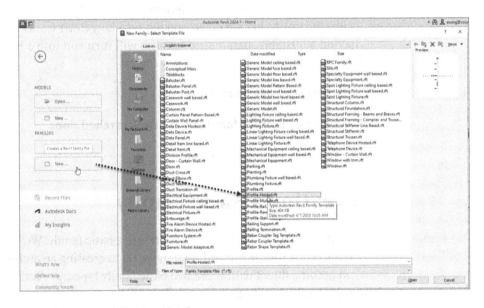

FIGURE 18.1 Starting a Family

As mentioned earlier, you'll notice the reference planes. A good family starts and ends with these. Next, you'll notice some text. Revit adds *advice* in each of its family templates. After you read the advice, you can delete it. You'll do that in a moment, but first let's add reference planes to the family.

Adding Reference Planes to a Family

The one bad thing about creating a family is that you can get away with doing so without using reference planes. This is unfortunate, because a family made with no (or not enough) reference planes will be faulty at best. I've learned that lesson the hard way. Although it may seem redundant to add reference planes, I strongly advise you to use them, and use them often.

In the following procedure, you'll offset some reference planes to create the wall sweep. Follow along:

1. On the Datum panel of the Create tab, click the Reference Plane button as shown in Figure 18.2.

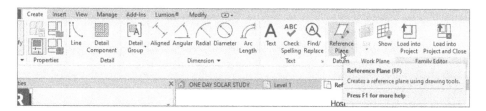

FIGURE 18.2 The Reference Plane button on the Create tab

2. On the Draw panel, click the Pick Lines button.

3. On the Options bar, set Offset to 1'–0" (300 mm).

4. Hover your cursor over the center, vertical reference plane. When the blue reference line appears to the right of the vertical plane (as shown in Figure 18.3), pick the center reference plane. You now have two vertical reference planes spaced 1'–0" (300 mm) apart.

5. With the Reference Plane command still running, pick the horizontal reference plane, and offset it down using the same offset increment of 1'–0" (300 mm). Your family should resemble Figure 18.4.

These two reference planes represent the body of the sweep. Next, let's add two more secondary reference planes for more control over the family:

1. Set Offset to 2" (50 mm).

2. Offset the top horizontal reference plane down.

3. Offset the left vertical reference plane to the right (see Figure 18.5).

With the reference planes in place, you can move on to adding dimensions to them. After you add the dimensions, you'll add parameters to those dimensions to make your family flexible when you add it to the model.

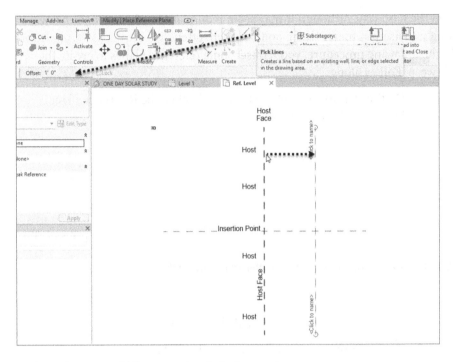

FIGURE 18.3 Adding a second vertical reference plane

FIGURE 18.3 Adding a second vertical reference plane

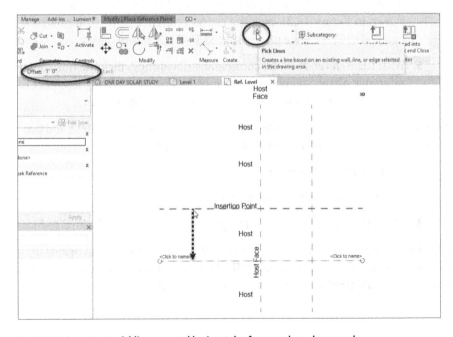

FIGURE 18.4 Adding a second horizontal reference plane downward

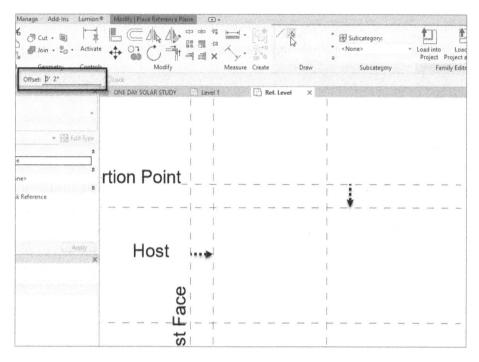

FIGURE 18.5 Offsetting two more reference planes

Adding Dimensions and Parameters to a Family

I like to start adding dimensions after I lay out a few things to keep myself from getting confused, which happens to me often. Also, it's good to keep in mind which reference planes we want as the justification of our family. The two reference planes that were there right when we started the family will be the anchor point (or origin) for our family. They are considered "strong" references. The additional reference planes are considered "weak" references. This is important to remember when we are adding parameters to our family.

The next procedure involves adding dimensions to the reference planes you've already put in place. The procedure after that will add parameters to the dimensions you've added. Follow along:

1. On the Measure panel of the Modify | Place Reference Plane tab, click the Aligned Dimension button as shown in Figure 18.6.

    The next step is to add the first dimension starting from the strong reference to the weak reference. This will dictate which reference plane will actually move when the dimension is altered.

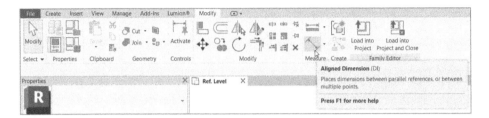

FIGURE 18.6 The Aligned Dimension

2. With the dimension command running, click point 1 first, then point 2 second (strong to weak).

3. With the dimension visible, move your cursor up and pick a third point away from the initial dimension. See Figure 18.7 for the procedure.

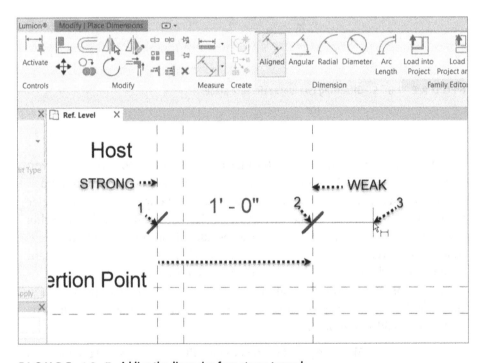

FIGURE 18.7 Adding the dimension from strong to weak

4. Repeat the procedure adding a vertical dimension from strong to weak as shown in Figure 18.8.

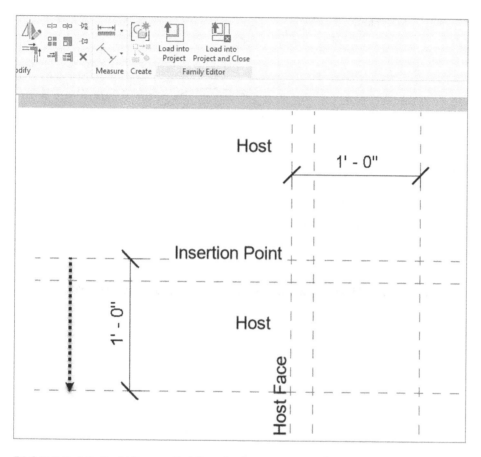

FIGURE 18.8 Adding a vertical dimension from strong to weak

    5. Add dimensions from strong to weak for the 2″ (51 mm) reference planes as shown in Figure 18.9.

The objective of the next procedure is to make these dimensions flexible (parametric). When this family is loaded into a project, whoever is using it can change the size of specific elements based on the parameters you associate with the dimensions.

    1. Select the horizontal 1′-0″ (305 mm) dimension.

    2. On the Label Dimension panel, click the Create Parameter icon as shown in Figure 18.10.

    3. For Name: call it **Length** as shown in Figure 18.11.

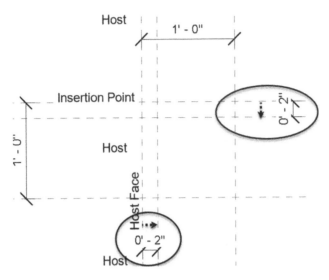

FIGURE 18.9 Adding two more dimensions from (you guessed it) strong to weak

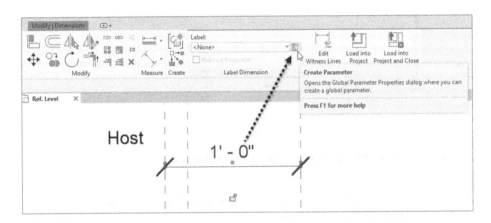

FIGURE 18.10 Assigning a parameter to a dimension

 NOTE When you add a name to the parameter, you're actually adding part of a formula. There is a chance that this name will be part of a mathematical expression. When you name parameters, be deliberate, and give the names some thought. Also, keep in mind that the mathematical expressions built in to the parameters are case sensitive. If you capitalize the first letter of each word, be consistent.

4. Click OK. The parameter is added to the dimension.

5. Select the 1'–0" (305 mm) vertical dimension.

6. Add a parameter called **Height**.

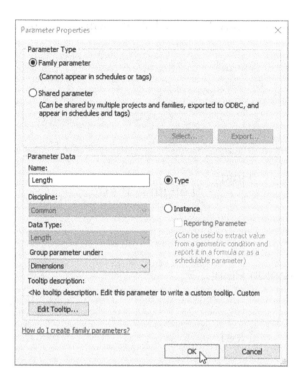

FIGURE 18.11 Assigning a parameter to a dimension

7. Click OK.
8. Select the two 2″ (50 mm) dimensions.

CHOOSING INSTANCE OR TYPE

The decision to use Instance or Type may be the most important decision you make when creating family parameters. As you've noticed, when you're modifying a family in the model (such as a wall, door, or window), you can either make a change to the single instance of the component you've selected or click Type and change the component globally in the model.

When the parameter was created, either Instance or Type was selected. So, when you're creating a parameter, you need to ask yourself, "Do I want the user to modify only one instance of this family by changing this parameter, or do I want the user to change every instance of this family by changing this parameter?"

To complicate matters, if you plan to use this parameter in a mathematical expression, every parameter in that expression must be of the same type. For example, you can't add an instance parameter to a type parameter. Revit won't allow it.

9. Add a parameter called **Reveal** to both of them. See Figure 18.12.

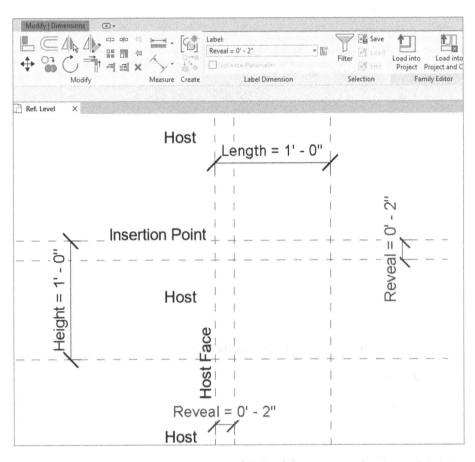

FIGURE 18.12 Becoming fully parametric

The reference planes are in place, and the dimensions are set with the parameters. It's time to go behind the scenes and see how these families operate by examining the family types and adding formulas to the parameters.

The Type Properties Dialog

Within the Family Editor lies a powerful dialog that lets you organize the parameters associated with the family you're creating. The Type Properties dialog also allows you to perform calculations and to add increments in an attempt to test the flex of the family before it's passed into the model.

The objective of the following procedure is to open the Family Types dialog and configure some parameters. Follow along:

1. On the Properties panel, click the Family Types button as shown in Figure 18.13.

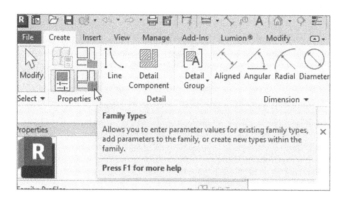

FIGURE 18.13 The Family Types button on the Properties panel

2. In the Family Types dialog, click into the Formula cell in the Height row.

3. Type **Length,** and press the Tab key (see Figure 18.14).

4. In the Reveal cell of the Formula column, type **Length/5** (this is Length *divided* by 5).

5. Click into the Length Value (the area in the Width row that has the 1'–0" [305 mm] increment).

6. Change Length from 1'–0" (305 mm) to 6" (152 mm). The Height value changes too.

7. Click OK. The 1'–0" (305 mm) dimensions are reduced to 6" (152 mm).

8. Click the Family Types button.

9. Change Length back to 1'–0" (305 mm).

10. Click Apply. The dimensions update in the drawing area.

11. Click the New button in the Family Types area as shown in Figure 18.15.

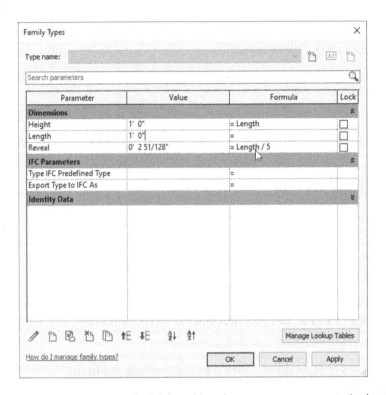

FIGURE 18.14 The Height and Reveal parameters are now constrained to the Width parameter.

12. Call the new type 1′–0″ (305 mm), and click OK (see Figure 18.15).

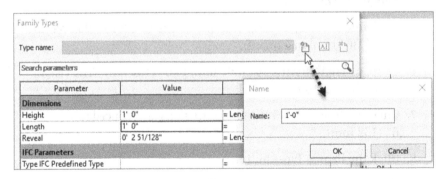

FIGURE 18.15 Creating a new family type

13. Click the New button again.

14. Call the new type 6″ (150 mm × 150 mm), and click OK.

15. Change Length to 6″ (150 mm).

16. Click Apply. The reference planes and dimensions update.

17. Change Type back to 1'–0" (305 mm). By changing it back to 1'–0" similar to Figure 17.15

18. Click OK.

19. Click Save, and save the family somewhere you'll be able to retrieve it later. Name the file `Cove sweep.rfa`.

Now that the reference planes and parameters are in place, you can flex the family to make sure it will work properly when you load it into the project.

IT's TIME TO FLEX YOUR FAMILY

With the family complete, you need to go back to the Type Properties dialog and change the parameters to see where the family will break. This testing is called *flexing* in the Revit world and should be done as often as possible.

The next step is to add the physical lines that form the perimeter of the sweep. Given that this was created using the hosted profile template, the actual family will merely be a 2D profile. The family won't become a 3D object until you pass it into the model and use it as a wall sweep.

In this procedure, you'll draw the perimeter of the cove sweep. Follow these steps:

1. On the Detail panel of the Create tab, click the Line button as shown in Figure 18.16.

2. Draw a line continuously from the points shown in Figure 18.17.

3. On the Draw panel, click the Start-End-Radius Arc button, and draw an arc from the last point (point 5) to point 6. When the two points are snapped in place, move your cursor to the left until the radius snaps into place. Your family should look like Figure 18.18.

Now you can load the family into the model and use it as a wall sweep. This is when you get to enjoy the fruits of your labor. To get started, open the building model on which you've been working. If you missed the previous chapter, go to the book's web page at www.sybex.com/go/revit20152024ner. From there, you can browse to the Chapter 17 folder and find the NER-18.rvt file. Follow along with these steps:

1. Open the Cove Sweep file (if you've closed it).

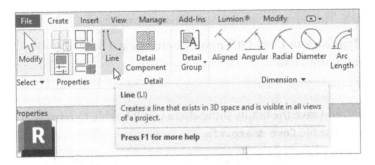

FIGURE 18.16 Starting to draw a line for our profile

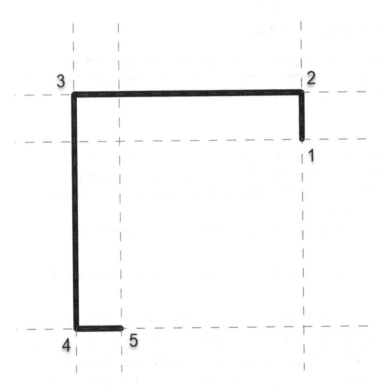

FIGURE 18.17 Drawing the boundary of the profile

2. On the Family Editor panel, click the Load Into Project button as shown in Figure 18.19.

3. In the NER-18 project, select one of the exterior walls in the east wing (Exterior - Brick and CMU on MTL. Stud).

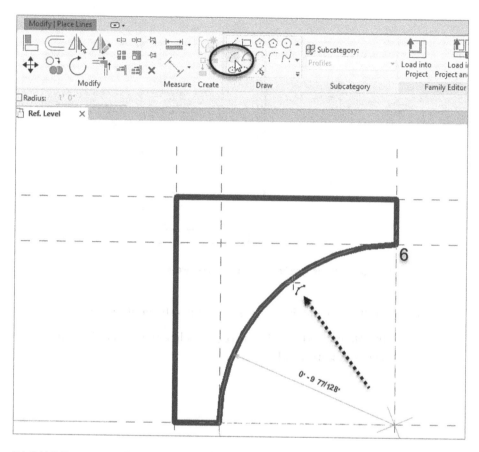

FIGURE 18.18 Drawing the radial portion of the profile

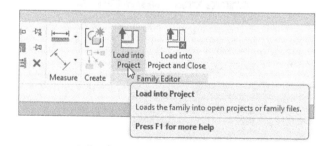

FIGURE 18.19 Load your profile into your project.

4. In the Properties dialog, click Edit Type.

5. Click the Edit button in the Structure row (see Figure 18.20).

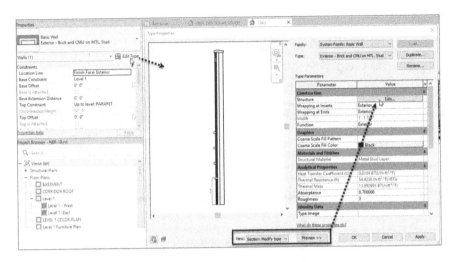

FIGURE 18.20 Open the Type Properties to add the sweep.

6. Make sure the preview is on and that it's showing a section.

7. In the Modify Vertical Structure area, click the Sweeps button as shown in Figure 18.21.

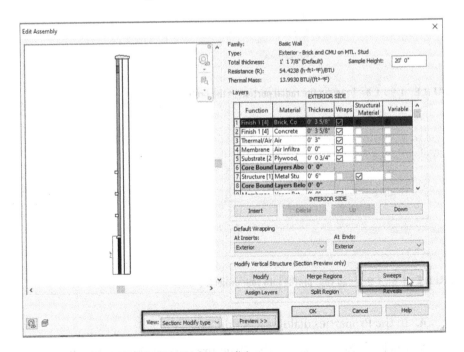

FIGURE 18.21 Going into the Sweeps dialog

8. In the Wall Sweeps dialog, click the Add button.

9. For the Profile, select Cove Sweep: 1'–0" (303 mm) from the list (notice that 6" [152 mm] is available too).

10. For Material, apply Concrete - Precast.

11. Set Distance to –1'–4" (–406 mm).

12. In the From column, make sure the value is Top.

13. In the Side column, make sure the choice is Exterior. See Figure 18.22.

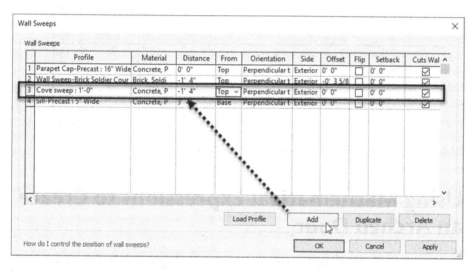

FIGURE 18.22 Adding the cove to our wall system

14. Click OK three times.

15. Click OK yet again.

16. Zoom in on the walls. There should be a sweep as shown in Figure 18.23.

You're getting a taste for what you can do with this powerful tool. And as you can see, you're only scratching the surface of the fun you can have. Now you're ready to try a real family!

The next section of this chapter will be spent on creating an opening with a radial header. Think about the lessons learned with the cove sweep, and let's dig in.

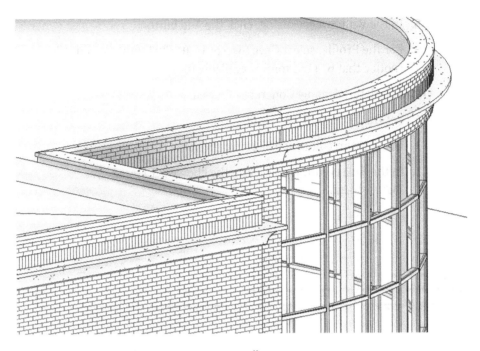

FIGURE 18.23 The new precast concrete wall sweep

Using Mathematical Expressions to Create an Arched Door

The "easy" family is out of the way, and next you'll begin blending the procedures of creating a parametric frame with actual 3D extrusions and sweeps. These 3D extrusions and sweeps will behave exactly like the cove family you just made. When you learn how to create one type of family, the knowledge transfers to the next.

This section of the chapter starts with a blank door template. The idea is that we have a custom door that needs to be flexible enough to add shim spaces, jamb thicknesses, and unique geometry. The first issue, however, is what we consider a rough opening and a finish opening. On the Blue file tab, go to New ➤ Family as shown in Figure 18.24. Then follow these steps:

1. Find the template called Door.rft (Metric Door.rft), and click Open.

2. Quite a bit of work has been done for you. This is great, but you don't need all the items in the template. Select the door jambs as shown in Figure 18.25, and delete them from either side of the door.

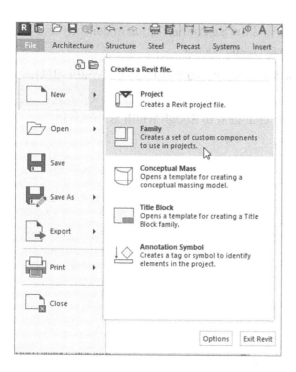

FIGURE 18.24   Creating a new family

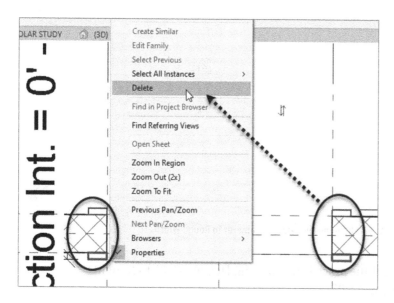

FIGURE 18.25   Deleting the jambs from either side of the door

3. In the Project Browser, find the Exterior elevation under the Elevations (Elevation 1) category, and open it.

4. In this view, you see a dimension called **Width=3′–0″ (Width=914)**. Select it.

5. In the Label drop-down, change it to **Rough Width** as shown in Figure 18.26.

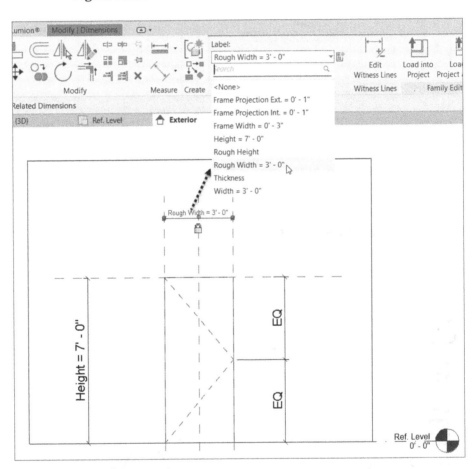

FIGURE 18.26 Changing the Width parameter to Rough Width

6. Repeat the procedure replacing **Height=7′–0″** to **Rough Height=7′–0″**.

7. Click the Family Types button as shown in Figure 18.27.

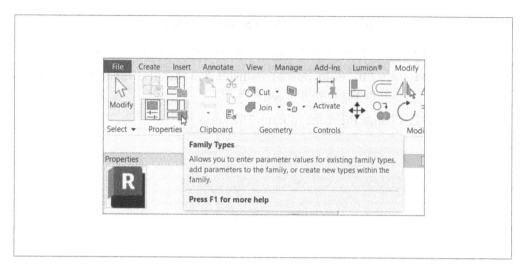

FIGURE 18.27 Let's now edit the family types.

8. Click the New Parameter button as shown in Figure 18.28.

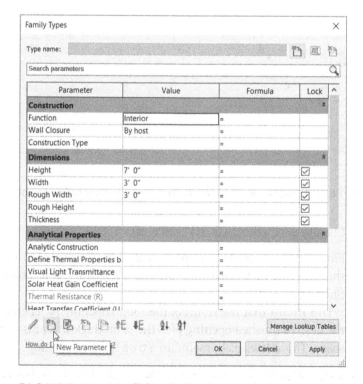

FIGURE 18.28 Clicking the New Parameter button

9. For the Name, call it **Shim Space**, and click OK.

10. In the Value column, give it an increment of **1/2″ (6 mm)**.

11. Select the Shim Space parameter, and click the Duplicate Parameter button as shown in Figure 18.29.

12. Change the name to Jamb Thickness.

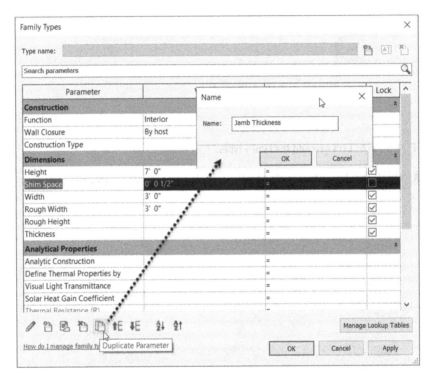

FIGURE 18.29 Duplicating a parameter makes it much easier to build a parametric family.

13. Change the thickness to 3/4″ (20 mm).

14. Find the Rough Width parameter, and in the Formula column, enter the following mathematical expression: **Width + (Jamb Thickness + Shim Space) * 2**.

    This means that the result of the rough opening is dependent on the desired finished opening plus the jamb thickness plus a shim space. This allows us to maintain a true finished opening.

15. Copy and paste the formula into the Rough Height row but remove the *2, and change Width to Height. **Height + (Jamb Thickness + Shim Space)**. (See Figure 18.30.)

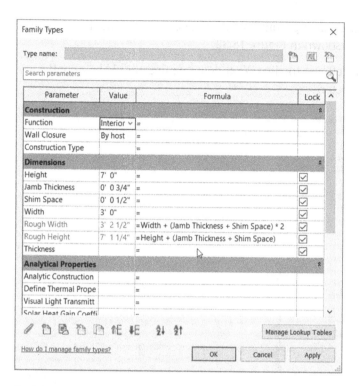

FIGURE 18.30 Making the family flexible so we can adjust just about anything

Now it's time to alter the geometry of the opening. Notice the dimensions are set to the rough openings and we can build into the void with our door jamb. The objective here is to add a radial top to the door.

NOTE The wall that you see is provided by Revit in order for you to design your opening to be flexible with any size wall in the model after you load this family. After the door family is in the project, this wall is removed. It's provided merely for layout.

Follow these steps:

1. Make sure you are in the Exterior elevation.

2. Select the bottom of the door opening as shown in Figure 18.31.

3. On the Options bar, click Transparent in Elevation.

4. Click the Edit Sketch button as shown Figure 18.31.

5. On the Draw panel, select the Start-End-Radius Arc button as shown in Figure 18.32.

6. Draw an arc starting from the top left and ending at the top right of the door as shown in Figure 18.32.

7. Delete the leftover top line. Your door opening should be a continuous perimeter.

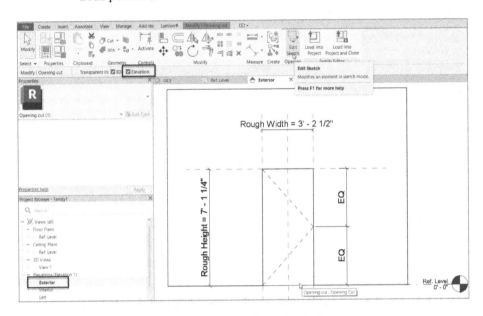

FIGURE 18.31 Selecting the opening and editing the sketch

8. Click the green Finish Edit Mode check mark.

With the opening in place, you can begin testing. Yes, you need to test the width to see if the actual radial top will behave as expected. Taking the time to do this now is an extremely small concession to the pain of deleting half the family later trying to find out what broke:

1. Click the Family Types button on the Properties panel.

2. Change the value for Width to 4′–0″ (1200 mm).

3. Next to Type Name, click the New Type icon, circled in Figure 18.33.

4. Call it 4′–0″ × 7′–0″ (1219 mm × 2134 mm).

5. Click Apply. Notice that your formulas are adjusting to the change. (See Figure 18.33).

6. Verify that the arc behaved as expected. If it didn't, you need to reedit the opening and make sure you're snapped to the correct points.

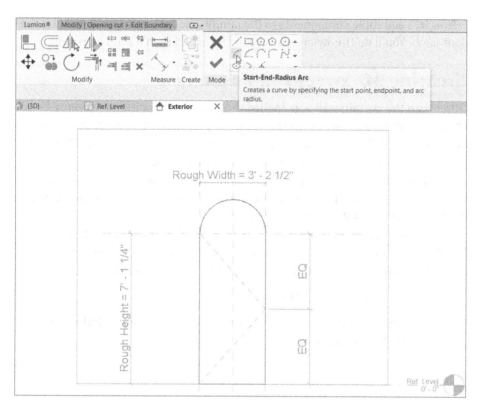

FIGURE 18.32 Adding a radial header

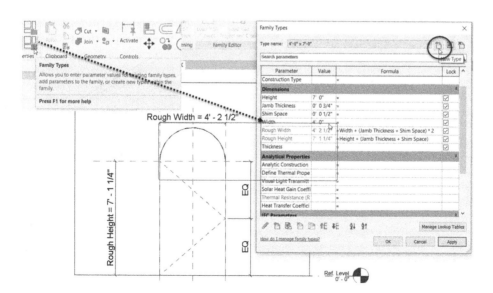

FIGURE 18.33 Flex the model before you give it to someone.

Now let's add some components to the family. The first item you'll tackle is the door jamb. You'll do this by creating a solid form and then a solid extrusion.

Creating 3D Sweeps in a Family

Other than the curtain wall you applied to a face of a mass in the previous chapter, you've been working in this huge 3D program without doing a single 3D operation. Well, that has come to an end. At some point, you'll need to deal with 3D and massing. When it comes to learning families, you can't avoid it.

But 3D in a family is slightly different than any 3D item you may have created in the past. The wonderful thing about creating 3D items in a family is that these items are fully adjustable after they're created.

The objective of the next procedure is to create a door jamb using a sweep. You'll then lock the faces of the sweep to the walls so that the family will adapt to any wall thickness when passed into the model. Follow these steps:

1. Go to the Default 3D view.

2. On the Forms panel of the Create tab, click the Sweep button as shown in Figure 18.34.

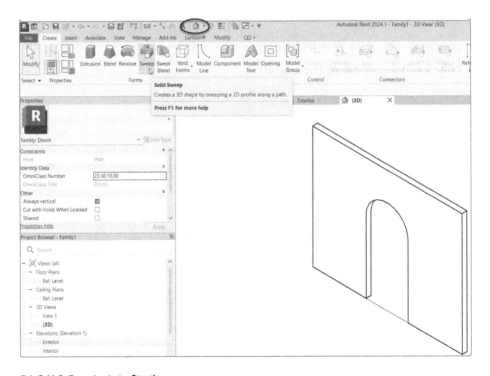

FIGURE 18.34 Starting a sweep

3. On the Work Plane panel, click Pick Path as shown in Figure 18.35. (This allows you to select a 3D element for the path of your sweep.)

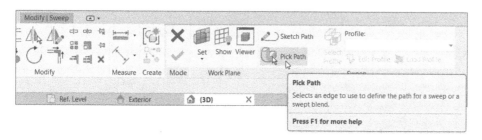

FIGURE 18.35 Pick 3D Edges.

4. Pick the edge of the wall opening starting with the left vertical side of the opening. (You can tell if you picked the right one first by the red dot and the reference planes surrounding it.) See Figure 18.36.

5. Once you are finished with picking the edges, click the green Finish icon. This means you are finished with picking edges and it's time to move on to the profile.

6. In the Project Browser, go to Floor Plans ➤ Ref.

7. Zoom in on the corner of the wall where the red dot is.

8. On the Sweep tab, click Select Profile.

9. Select Edit Profile as shown in Figure 18.37.

10. On the Create tab, find the Reference Plane button and click it. (See Figure 18.38.)

11. On the Options bar, type in 1/2″ (13 mm).

12. Offset the reference plane to the right as shown in Figure 18.39.

13. Change the Offset to 3/4″ (20 mm).

14. Offset the reference plane you just added to the right. You now have two reference planes with a total of **1.25″ (32 mm)** between the wall opening and the right-most reference plane.

The next step is to add our dimensions and then apply the Shim Space and Jamb Thickness parameters. Keep in mind the sequence: strong to weak.

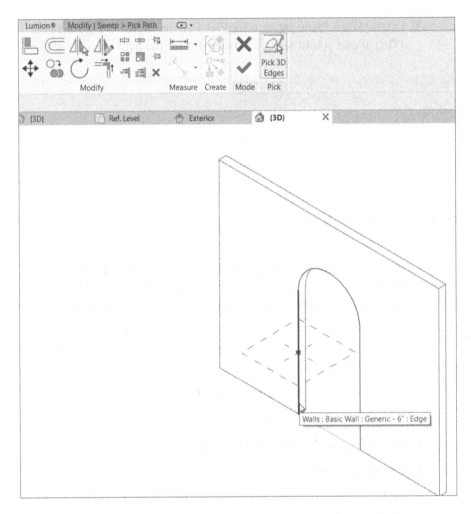

FIGURE 18.36   Pick the edges in order.

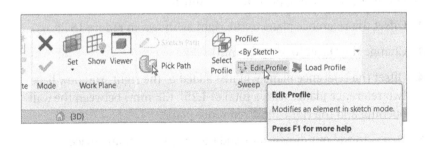

FIGURE 18.37   Moving to the Edit Profile stage

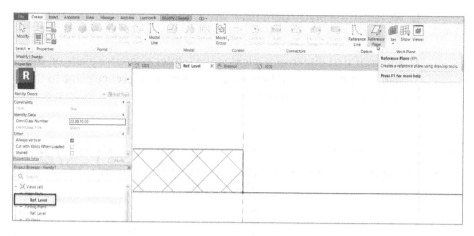

FIGURE 18.38 Adding reference planes for the profile

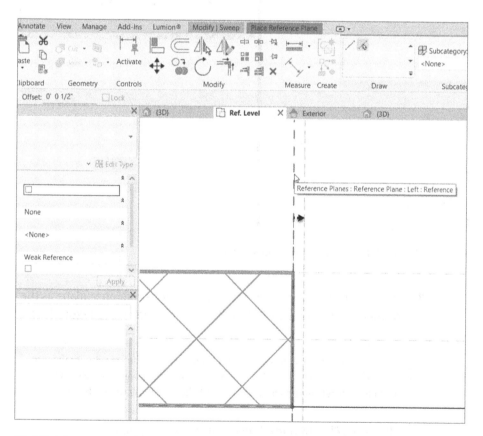

FIGURE 18.39 Adding a new reference plane, which will become the parameter for Shim Space

1. We're getting pretty tight here, so change the view scale to **6″=1′–0″ (1 : 2)**.

2. Add your first dimension, picking the lighter reference plane on the wall opening first and then the 1/2″ (13 mm) reference plane to the right as shown in Figure 18.40.

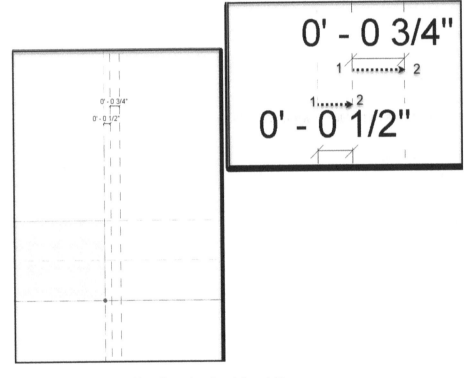

FIGURE 18.40 Adding dimensions from left to right.

3. Add your second dimension using the previous reference plane as the strong reference to the right to the weak reference. See Figure 18.40.

 N O T E   You might have missed this but I had you select the grayed-out reference plane first to place the first dimension. This ties it to the proper origin as it relates to the wall. Don't pick the reference plane associated with the red dot. It's weird, I know.

4. Select the 1/2″ (13 mm) dimension and add the parameter Shim Space.

5. Select the 3/4″ (20 mm) dimension and add the parameter Jamb Thickness. See Figure 18.41.

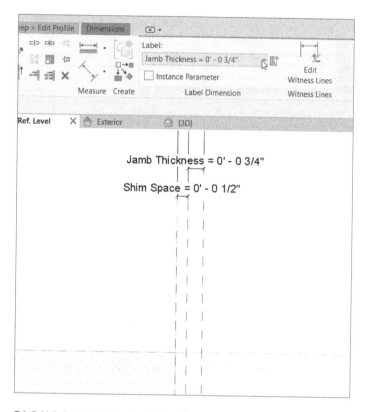

FIGURE 18.41 Associating the parameters.

6. Zoom in on the edge of the opening.

7. On the Draw panel, click the Pick Lines button as shown in Figure 18.42.

8. On the Options bar, make sure the lock toggle is checked.

9. Pick the four reference planes as shown in Figure 18.42.

10. On the Draw Panel, click the Fillet Arc button.

11. On the Options bar, check on the Radius toggle and give it a 1/8″ (3 mm) increment.

12. Pick all four corners to round off the edges as shown in Figure 18.43.

13. Click the green finish check mark.

14. Click the green finish check mark again.

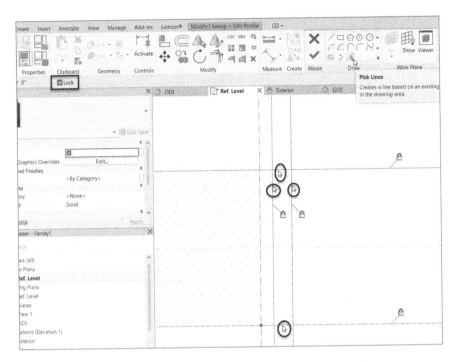

FIGURE 18.42 Picking and locking our profile lines to our reference planes

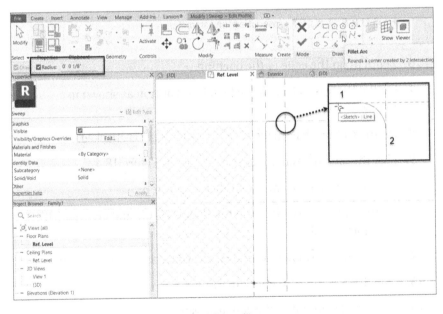

FIGURE 18.43 Easing the edges of the profile

15. Select the new sweep.

16. In the properties, click the drop-down menu next to Subcategory.

17. Set Subcategory to Frame Mullion.

18. For Material, click the little gray button shown in Figure 18.44. It is called Associate Family Parameter.

19. Click the New Parameter button.

20. Call it **Jamb** Material.

21. Hit OK twice. You will notice the material field cannot be edited. This allows the material to be changed in the project.

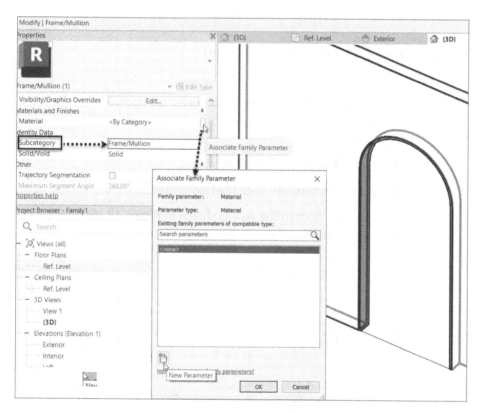

FIGURE 18.44 Change the Subcategory value and associate a parameter to Frame.

22. Click the Save icon.

23. Save the door in a directory where you'll be able to find it.

24. Call it **Arched Door.rfa**.

25. Make sure your project is open.

26. In the Arched Door.rfa file, click Load Into Project as shown in Figure 18.45.

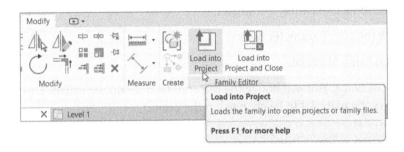

FIGURE 18.45 Loading the family into the project

If you have more than one project or family open, Revit will make you choose a model to load the family into. Be sure to pick your project file.

27. In the model, open the Level 1 view.

28. On the Architecture tab, click the Door button.

29. Insert the new door in the wall as shown in Figure 18.46. (Don't worry too much about placement.)

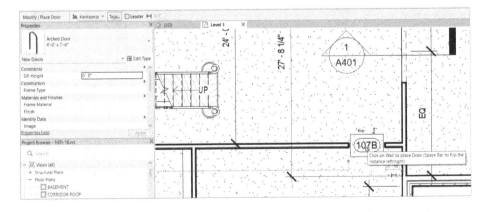

FIGURE 18.46 Adding the family to the project

30. Select the door.

31. In the Properties dialog, click Edit Type, and observe the parameters. Look familiar? You created them! Also notice you have a door type called 4′–0″ × 7′–0″ **(1219 mm × 2134 mm)**. This now can be duplicated to have a different size.

32. Click OK.

33. Select the door and click Edit Family as shown in Figure 18.47.

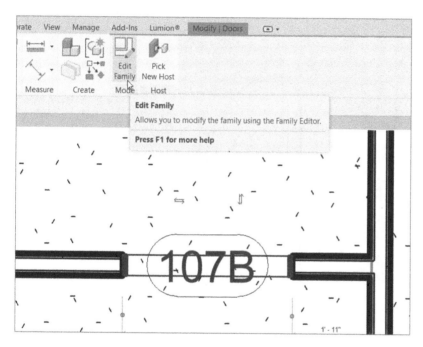

FIGURE 18.47 Select the door and go to Edit Family.

Wow! This thing actually works. Good deal. The next trick is to add some casing to the outside of the frame. To do so, we'll use another sweep.

Creating a Casing Sweep

Going along the same lines (literally) as the previous sweep, you can create a situation where you sketch a path and extrude a profile along that path. The trick is to make sure this sweep can flex along with the door.

The objective of the next procedure is to create the door casing by using a 3D sweep. Follow these steps:

1. Go to a 3D view (if you aren't there already), and position the view so that it looks like Figure 18.48.

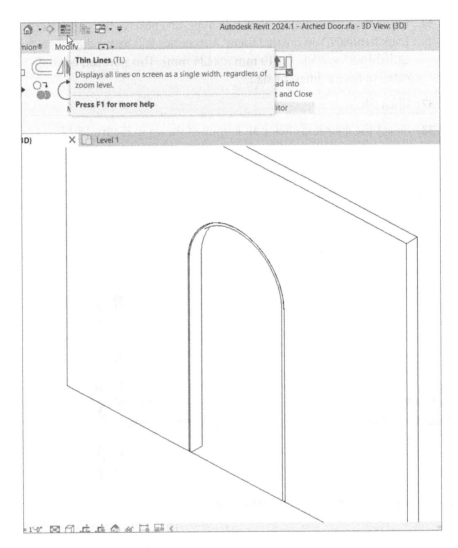

FIGURE 18.48 Orient your view and turn on Thin Lines.

2. On the Quick Access toolbar, click the Thin Lines button as shown in Figure 18.48.

3. On the Create tab, click the Sweep button.

4. On the Sweep panel, click the Pick Path button.

5. Pick the inside corner of the jamb starting with the left side as we did when we created the first sweep (see Figure 18.49).

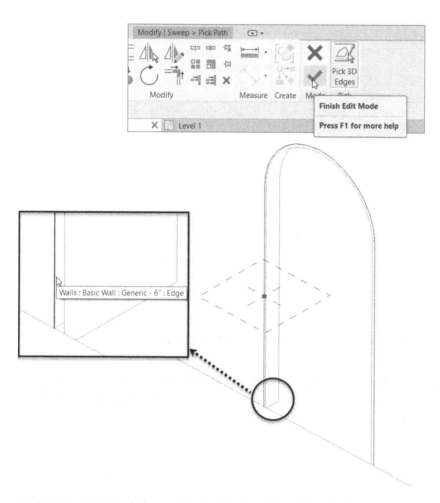

FIGURE 18.49 Pick your path using the edge of the wall opening.

6. Click Finish Edit Mode on the Mode panel.

7. On the Sweep panel, click the Load Profile button.

8. Go to the Profiles ➤ Finish Carpentry folder, and select Casing Profile-2.rfa as shown in Figure 18.50.

9. Click Open.

10. In the menu on the Sweep panel, click the Profile drop-down, and select Casing Profile 2: 5 1/2″ × 13/16″ (the red dot is replaced with the actual profile).

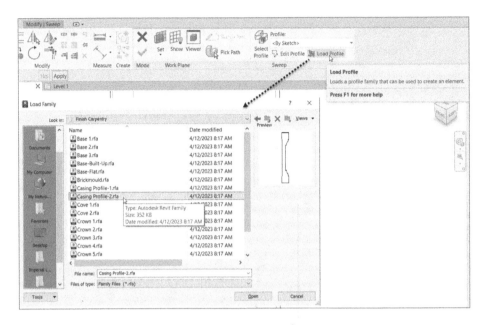

FIGURE 18.50 Loading some casing from the **Profiles** directory

11. On the Options bar, type –0'–4 3/8″ (–111 mm) for the Y offset. The profile is pushed back onto the wall with a 1/8″ (3 mm) reveal. See Figure 18.51.

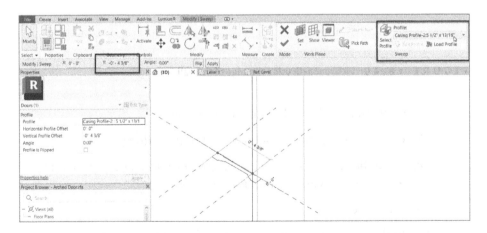

FIGURE 18.51 Adjusting your new sweep

12. Click Finish Edit Mode. Select the new sweep.

13. In the Properties dialog, click the small button to the right of the Material category.

14. Click Add Parameter.

15. Call the parameter **Casing Material**.

16. Group it under Materials And Finishes. (I didn't add an image here; you got this!)

17. Click OK twice.

18. Repeat steps 2 through 11 on the other side of the door. (Don't try to mirror the sweep—it won't work.)

19. Save the family.

20. Load it into the project. Select Overwrite Existing Version.

21. In your model, select the door.

22. In the Properties dialog, click Edit Type.

23. Change the Width value to 3'–0" (900 mm).

24. Select the door and click Edit Type.

25. Change the Casing Material and the Jamb Material to Cherry.

26. Click Okay.

Your door is still working properly and looks better as shown in Figure 18.52.

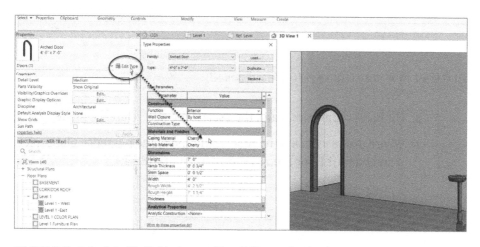

FIGURE 18.52 The finished sweep. If you'd like, go ahead and create a new camera view of this door.

Let's move forward and begin working on adding a stop and a panel to the family. The biggest challenge here will be the plan swing representation, but with a few new items to learn, this won't be a problem.

In the next procedure, you'll add a door, a stop, and some plan symbolic line-work. Follow along:

1. Open the door family.

2. Go to the Ref. Level Floor Plan.

3. Right-click on the reference plane that aligns with the exterior of the wall shown in Figure 18.53, and select Create Similar.

4. Select pick lines and set the offset to 1 3/8″.

5. Offset that reference plane down. See Figure 18.53.

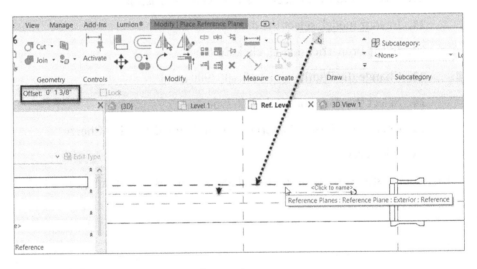

FIGURE 18.53 Creating a new reference plan

6. Hit Esc a couple times and then select the new reference plane.

7. Where it says <Click to name> on the end of the reference plane, pick it and name it Door Stop as shown in Figure 18.54.

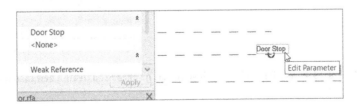

FIGURE 18.54 You can name a reference plane.

8. On the Measure panel, add a dimension from strong to weak (the reference plane on the face of the wall to the Door Stop reference plane).

9. Select the dimension and add a parameter called **Panel Thickness**.

10. Select the Panel Thickness dimension and click the little padlock icon as shown in Figure 18.55. In this case, this is necessary to ensure the dimension moves with the wall.

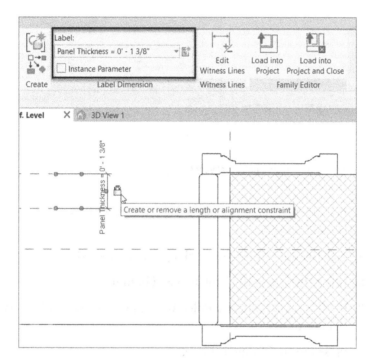

FIGURE 18.55 Constrain the dimension.

11. Zoom out and select the wall.

12. In the Properties dialog, change the size of the wall in the type dropdown to make sure this will work. See Figure 18.56.

Now we can make the choice if we want a separate sweep for the door stop or if we want to modify the existing sweep. Let's modify the existing sweep.

1. Select the door jamb sweep and click Edit Sweep.

2. On the Sweep panel, click Select Profile.

3. On the Sweep panel, click Edit Profile.

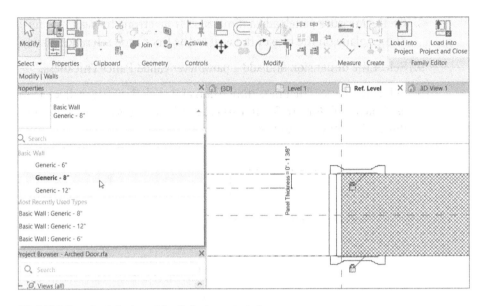

F I G U R E   1 8 . 5 6   A good family is always tested.

4. Pick the new reference plane using the Pick Lines button, making sure it's locked.

5. Pick the wall center line, making sure it's locked.

6. Offset the face of the jamb in 5/8″ (10 mm).

7. Use the Trim, Split, and Fillet Arc commands to clean it up as shown in Figure 18.57.

8. Press Finish Edit mode twice.

Now it's time to add the door panel. This will be done by a simple extrusion. Now that all of our parameters are set, this should be easy.

1. Go to the Exterior elevation.

2. Create a Reference Plane 1/2″ (13 mm) from the Ref. Level up.

3. Dimension it (Ref. Level first, reference plane second).

4. Add a parameter called Undercut.

5. On the Create tab, click the Extrusion button as shown in Figure 18.58.

6. On the Work Plane panel, click the Set Work Plane button.

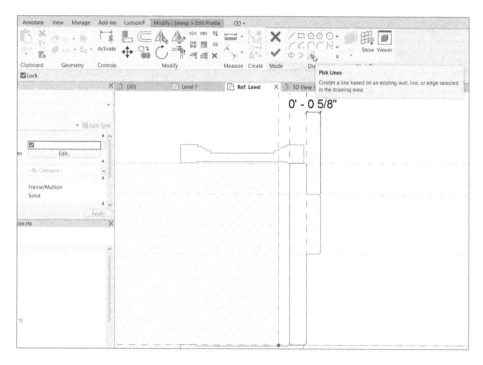

FIGURE 18.57 Adding a stop

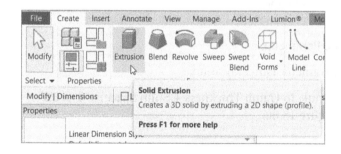

FIGURE 18.58 Starting our extrusion

7. Specify Name and then set the work plane to Reference Plane: Exterior as shown in Figure 18.59.

Notice we don't have any reference planes to the right and left to pick. Plus, we want our door offset 1/8″ (3 mm) from the actual frame. I think it's time for another parameter!

1. Click the Family Types button.

2. Select the Rough Height parameter.

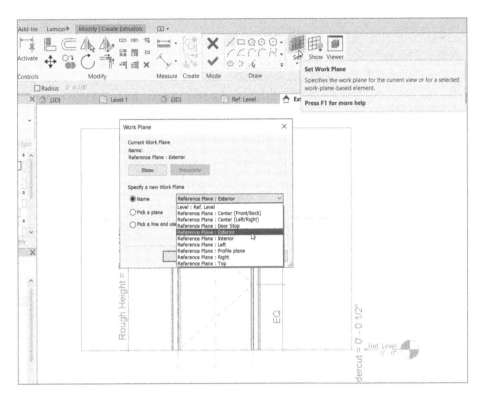

FIGURE 18.59 Setting the work plane

3. Click Duplicate Parameter.

4. Call the new parameter Panel Location.

5. Change the formula to **(Jamb Thickness + Shim Space) + 0' 0 1/8"** (3 mm). See Figure 18.60.

6. Click OK.

7. On the Create tab, click the Reference Plane button.

8. Add two reference planes from the vertical rough opening reference planes. (You can make it 2"; we're going to add the parameter to them so it doesn't matter.)

9. Add dimensions to both (strong to weak).

10. Select the dimensions and add the parameter Panel Location to them.

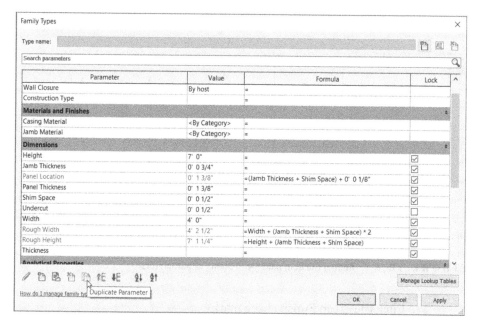

Family Types

Parameter	Value	Formula	Lock
Wall Closure	By host	=	
Construction Type		=	
Materials and Finishes			
Casing Material	<By Category>	=	
Jamb Material	<By Category>	=	
Dimensions			
Height	7' 0"	=	☑
Jamb Thickness	0' 0 3/4"	=	☑
Panel Location	0' 1 3/8"	=(Jamb Thickness + Shim Space) + 0' 0 1/8"	☑
Panel Thickness	0' 1 3/8"	=	☑
Shim Space	0' 0 1/2"	=	☑
Undercut	0' 0 1/2"	=	☐
Width	4' 0"	=	☑
Rough Width	4' 2 1/2"	=Width + (Jamb Thickness + Shim Space) * 2	☑
Rough Height	7' 1 1/4"	=Height + (Jamb Thickness + Shim Space)	☑
Thickness		=	☑
Analytical Properties			

How do I manage family ty | Duplicate Parameter | Manage Lookup Tables

OK   Cancel   Apply

FIGURE 18.60 Adding a new parameter

11. Pick (locked) the two reference planes (remember we are still in the extrusion command).

12. Draw an arc along the Rough Height reference plane from the left to the right.

13. Trim it up.

14. Pick the reference plane for the Undercut.

15. Trim from the bottom up.

16. In the properties, click the Associate Family Parameter button next to Extrusion End.

17. Associate it with the Panel Thickness parameter.

18. Click the same button next to Material.

19. Create a new parameter here called Panel Material (see Figure 18.61).

20. Set the Subcategory to Panel.

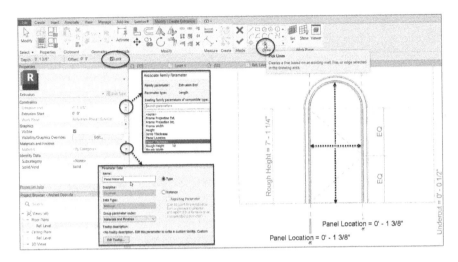

FIGURE 18.61 Adding the door panel with plenty of parameters

21. Click the green Finish check mark.

22. Select the door panel.

23. Click the Visibility Settings button as shown in Figure 18.62.

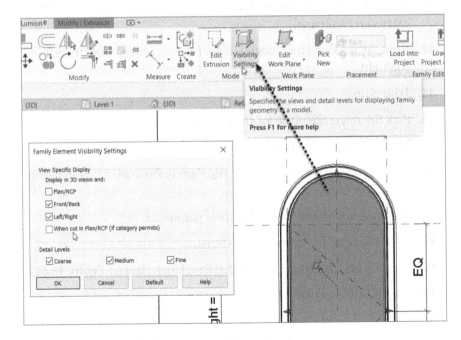

FIGURE 18.62 We don't want to see the panel in plan.

24. Uncheck Plan/RCP.

25. Uncheck When Cut In Plan/RCP (If Category Exists).

The next step is to add the symbolic door swing in plan. Funny enough, we are going to simply use linework.

1. On the Annotate tab, click the Symbolic Line button as shown in Figure 18.63.

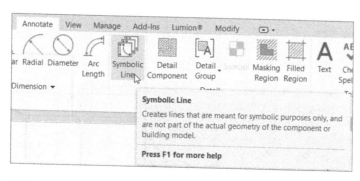

FIGURE 18.63 The Symbolic Line button

2. Change Subcategory to **Panel Swing [projection]**.

3. Draw a line straight up from the right corner of the jamb (on the exterior side of the wall) 3′–11 3/4″ (1200 mm), as shown as point 1-2 in Figure 18.64.

4. Draw another line to the left 1 3/8″ (35 mm) (point 2-3).

5. Draw another line straight down 3′–11 3/4″ (1200 mm) (point 3-4).

6. Draw another line to the right 1 3/8″ (35 mm) (point 4-5). See Figure 18.64.

7. Click the Symbolic Line button again (if it isn't currently running).

8. Draw an arc from the left side of the jamb to the top of the symbolic swing as shown in Figure 18.65. Click Modify.

9. Save the family.

10. Load it into the project. Overwrite the existing version. If it didn't explode, your door is complete!

As you can see, it isn't that difficult to create a family. This topic could be a book within a book. Start experimenting with your own families. If you run into a snag, send me an email at ewing@cscos.com and we can work on it.

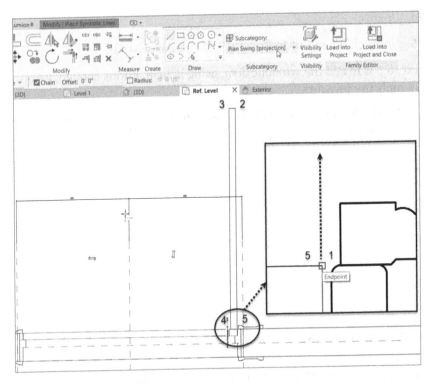

FIGURE 18.64 Sketching the door swing

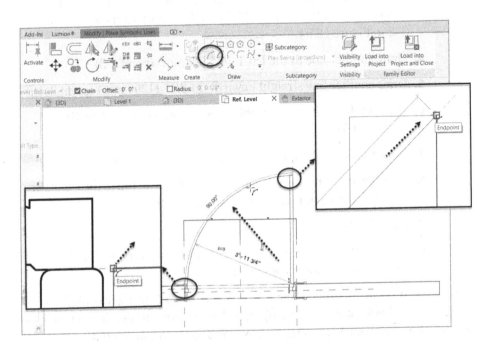

FIGURE 18.65 Drawing the plan swing arc

The next type of family we'll study is one that literally can't be avoided. Eventually, you'll need the surrounding geometry of the model to create the family. This is called an *in-place family*.

Creating an In-Place Family

An in-place family gives you the best of both worlds. When you start the In-Place Family command, your model turns into the Family Editor. You can make a family exactly the same way you just did, except that it's native to the model. Many times, you'll need this flexibility when you have a family that you'll never use again in any other building. This also gives you the flexibility to create custom content that can't be created using the conventional Revit commands.

To create an in-place family, follow along with this procedure:

1. Open the West Elevation. It is actually pointing at the winding stairs in the area between the east and west buildings.

2. On the Architecture tab, click Component ➤ Model In-Place as shown in Figure 18.66.

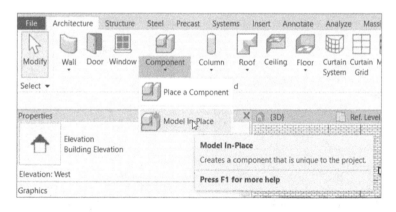

FIGURE 18.66 Starting an in-place family

3. Set Family Category to Walls, and then click OK.

4. Call the new "wall" **Link Wall Panel**.

5. Click OK.

6. Click the Extrusion button.

7. Pick the wall behind the stairs to set as your work plane. (It's important here that you are sure you have selected the wall behind the stairs.)

8. Model any shape you want. This is just going to be a wall accent.

9. Set the material to whatever you want. I chose Concrete Lightweight. See Figure 18.67.

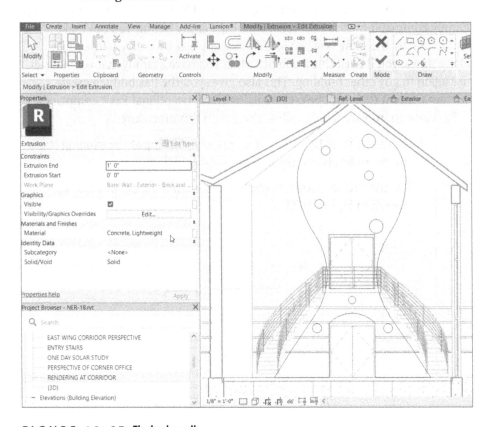

FIGURE 18.67 The kooky wall

10. Click Finish Edit Mode.

11. Go to the view RENDERING AT CORRIDOR.

12. Click the Extrusion button again.

13. Click Set Work Plane.

14. Pick the face of the extrusion.

15. Model some extrusions off the face of the first extrusion.

16. Make the extrusion end 4″.

17. Click Finish Edit Mode.

18. Click Finish Edit Mode again. See Figure 18.68.

FIGURE 18.68 Your new accent wall.

The moral of the story is this: when you have a custom situation in the model that can't be created using the conventional Revit tools, create an in-place family. You should make it as flexible as possible and give the user some choices, such as materials, so that anyone can manipulate the family as if Autodesk provided it.

Are You Experienced?

Now you can. . .

✓ create a cove sweep family

✓ identify the family template you need to use to start a family

✓ create a door family

✓ add symbolic lines to a family

✓ create an in-place family

✓ create sweeps and extrusions

✓ create parameters

CHAPTER 19

Project Management

The first thing that comes to mind when I think project management is phasing. Of all the projects with which I have been involved over the years, I can remember only a handful that didn't involve some kind of existing condition. It would be nice if we could find a giant, flat field on which to construct our buildings, but those projects are few and far between.

This chapter covers the following topics:

▶ **Managing project phasing**

▶ **Examining graphic overrides**

▶ **Creating design options**

Managing Project Phasing

The term *phasing* in the Autodesk® Revit® platform is often taken literally, and it can be confused with construction sequencing. When we talk about phasing in a Revit context, we're talking about adding new construction to an existing building and demolishing the existing structure. Although you can use Revit to track all aspects of construction, the base use and purpose of phasing is dealing with existing conditions.

The first section of this chapter will focus on the setup of your phasing scheme. By default, Revit Architecture provides two phases: Existing and New Construction. As it stands, everything you've placed into your model in the last 18 chapters has been exclusively related to the New Construction phase. You'll now alter that.

I've seen this scenario played out more times than I would have liked. People get Revit, build a model, and then start clicking the Demolish button found on the Phasing panel on the Manage tab. Yes, doing so forces hidden lines, and now you're demolishing walls that were constructed in the same phase in which they're being removed. You can't do that!

With some practice, and by following the procedures in this chapter, you'll be able to swing that hammer all you want. But for now, to get started, go to the book's web page at www.sybex.com/go/revit2024ner. From there, you can browse to the Chapter 19 folder and find the NER-19.rvt file. (If you prefer, you can follow along with your own model as well.)

The objective of the following procedure is to create a Demolition phase and insert it between the Existing phase and the New Construction phase. Follow along:

1. On the Manage tab, click the Phases button on the Phasing panel, as shown in Figure 19.1.

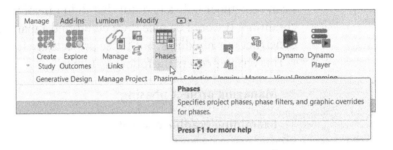

FIGURE 19.1 Clicking the Phases button

2. In the Phasing dialog, click the number 1. This is the control for the Existing phase row.

3. In the Insert section, click the After button, as shown in Figure 19.2.

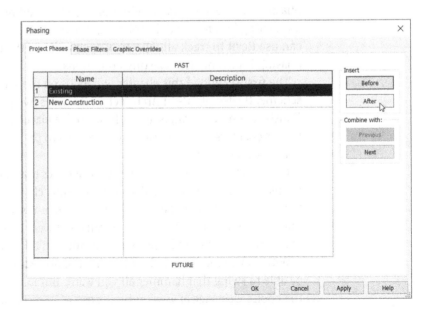

FIGURE 19.2 Starting to add the Demolition phase

4. Rename the phase that is now in the middle to **Demolition**.

5. Click OK.

6. Make sure you're in Level 1. Right-click Level 1 and click Duplicate View ➤ Duplicate, as shown in Figure 19.3.

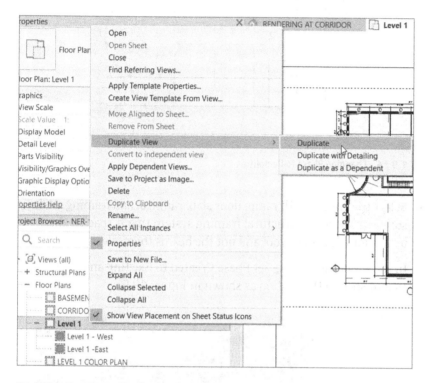

FIGURE 19.3 Duplicating the view

7. Right-click the new view, and rename it **Level 1 Demolition**.

8. Open the Level 1 Demolition plan, if it's not already open.

9. Select every exterior wall in the east building, including the curtain wall and change Phase Created to Existing at the bottom of the Properties dialog.

10. Press Esc. See Figure 19.4.

11. Go to a 3D view.

12. Change Visual Style to Shaded.

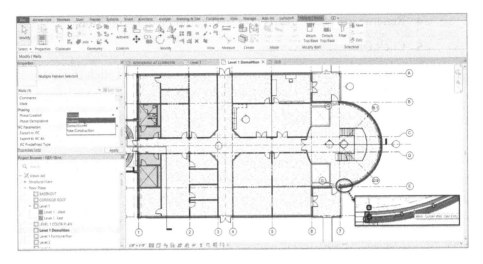

FIGURE 19.4 Changing Phase to Demolition

13. Select the entire south ramp, floor slab, railings, and framing. Make sure you select the structural framing system that is spacing the beams for the canopy roof and not the beams themselves.

14. In the Properties dialog, set Phase Created to Existing and Phase Demolished to Demolition as shown in Figure 19.5.

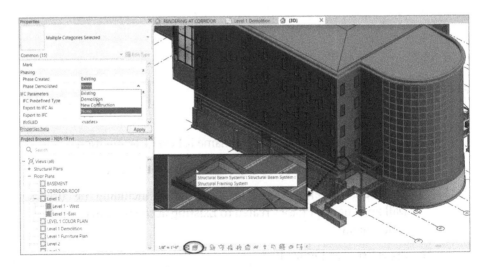

FIGURE 19.5 Changing Phase to Existing and Demolition

WHAT'S ALL THIS RED?

Since you only put the exterior walls on the Existing phase, but not the doors and windows, Revit assumes you are now adding new windows and doors (because they are still on New Construction). Revit automatically demolished that portion of the insert and adds an infill element. Also notice everything you selected and put on Demolition is gone from this view.

15. Go to the Level 1 floor plan (not the demolition). There is no longer a ramp. No sense living in the past. The demolition plan shows the items on a demo line type. Who needs layers, right?

16. Go back to the Level 1 Demolition floor plan.

17. In the Properties dialog for the Level 1 Demolition plan, scroll down to Phasing, and change Phase to Demolition, as shown in Figure 19.6. Change Phase Filter to Show All.

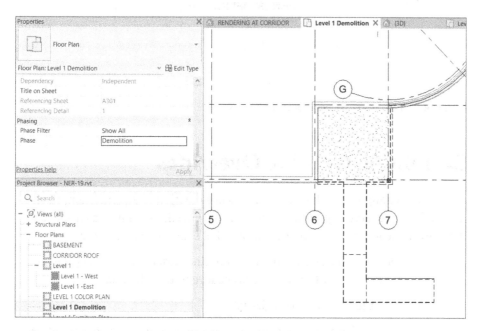

FIGURE 19.6 Seeing the results of demolishing an item

18. Zoom in on the east entry, specifically where the ramp enters the building to the south, as shown in Figure 19.6. Revit automatically changes the line weight to Heavy, and the line type to Demolished.

19. Go back to the Level 1 plan, and select the two doors shown in that area.

20. Set Phase Created to Existing.

21. In the properties, set Phase Demolished to Demolition. Revit removes the doors and infills the openings, as shown in Figure 19.7. (It's understood that the entire building should be existing. This is an example of how Revit behaves during the phasing process.)

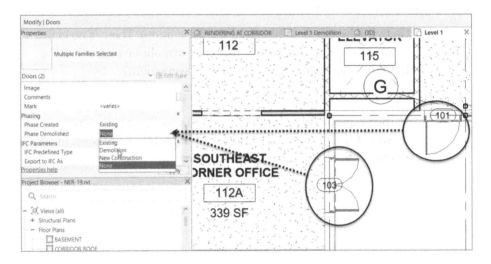

FIGURE 19.7   You no longer need these doors.

Examining Graphic Overrides

After you've changed the phasing of an object's creation and demolition, Revit magically puts everything on the correct display. Well, as magical as it seems, there are some features driving this display. Let's take a look at them:

1. Click the Phases button on the Phasing panel of the Manage tab as you did in step 1 of the first procedure in this chapter.

2. Click the Graphic Overrides tab.

3. In the Existing row, for the Lines column under the Projection/Surface heading, click the button that displays a hidden line, as shown in Figure 19.8.

4. Click the Weight drop-down.

5. Change Weight to 5 (see Figure 19.8).

6. Click OK to exit all dialogs.

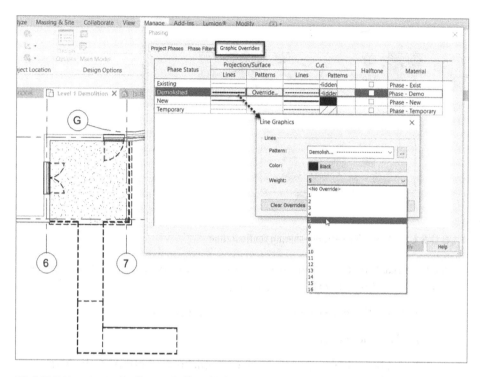

FIGURE 19.8 Beefing up the line weight

Activating and Explaining Worksharing

It's quite ironic that the last chapter of this book contains information that many of you will need to get your first Autodesk® Revit® Architecture project off the ground. That is, how do you work on a project when multiple people need to be in the model? Revit is only one model, right? The end of this chapter will discuss the following topics:

▶ Enabling and utilizing worksharing

▶ Working in the Revit shared environment

In Revit, we can all be in the same model at the same time. In a way. We're not actually in the same model. We are in a model that is tied to what is called a central model. Every time we go to Open, we select the central model and, in the background, Revit places a linked copy to your C:\ drive under My Documents. When you save (or as you will soon learn, Synchronize), you can see what others have saved as well as send your new work to the central model. Now you and your co-workers can all access the same model at the same time. What a productive way to get a job out the door! (See Figure 19.9.)

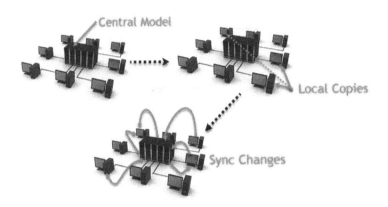

FIGURE 19.9 The basic file-sharing configuration

Okay, so that's the concept of worksharing. It's now time to drill down and see how to activate this network of linked files.

1. Open the NER-19.rvt file (if you're not still in it).

2. Save the model.

3. On the Collaborate tab, click the Collaborate button on the Manage Collaboration panel, as shown in Figure 19.10.

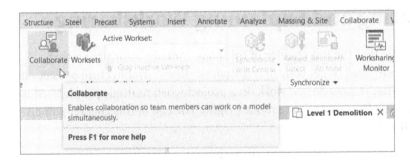

FIGURE 19.10 Clicking the Collaborate button

4. Click Within Your Network. Click OK.

5. Save the model as shown in Figure 19.11.

6. Click Yes.

NOTE Turning on worksets is a one-time activation process. You don't have to do this every time you want to work on the project.

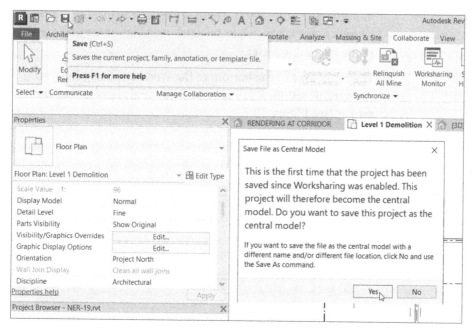

FIGURE 19.11 The Worksharing dialog

1. Click the Worksets button as shown in Figure 19.12.

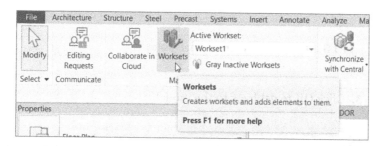

FIGURE 19.12 Find the Worksets button. It is also located at the bottom of the screen drawing area.

2. Your two worksets are presented in a spreadsheet format that says they're both editable and you own them as shown in Figure 19.13. Congratulations. There is plenty to explain here:

   ▶ Active Workset indicates the workset in which any new item will be either drawn or inserted (sort of like the current *layer* in Autodesk® AutoCAD®). There is also a Gray Inactive Workset Graphics check box. When selected, it shades items that aren't in the current workset.

▶ The Show area at the bottom of the Worksets dialog lets you add specific families, project standards, and views to the workset list (see Figure 19.13).

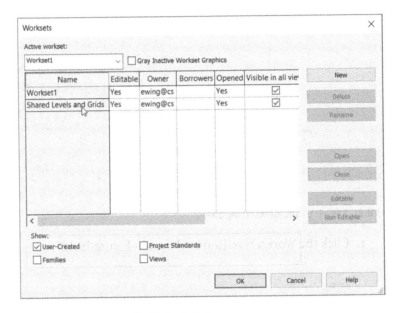

FIGURE 19.13 The Worksets dialog

3. Click OK to get back to the model.

N O T E You can turn on additional items in the Show category. But unless there is a compelling reason to do so, *don't*—especially if this is the first project your team is taking on in Revit. Try to keep your worksets as simple and painless as possible. Just because you *can* assume ultimate control over your users doesn't mean you *have* to.

Now that you've activated the worksets and saved the model, it's time to create the central model. This will always be the next step in the process.

Creating a Central Model

Creating the central model is generally a one-time deal. You create it immediately after you enable your worksets. The individual who creates the central model needs to be your best Revit user. If not, and this procedure is done incorrectly, you'll have struggles for the entire life of the project.

Okay, best Revit user, follow this procedure to learn how to create the central model:

1. Go to the blue File tab, and choose Save As ➤ Project, as shown in Figure 19.14.

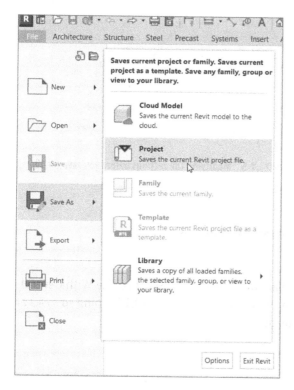

FIGURE 19.14 Saving the project using Save As

2. In the Save As dialog, click the Options button in the lower-right corner.

3. In the File Save Options dialog, change Maximum to 1 (see Figure 19.15).

4. Make sure Make This A Central Model After Save is selected.

NOTE Notice that the Worksharing area isn't active. This is because you're saving the file for the first time after activating worksharing. You have no choice but to make this the central model.

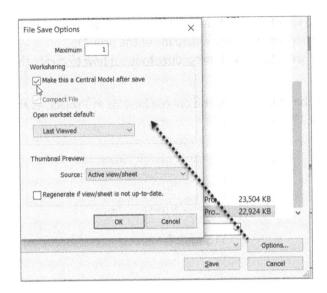

FIGURE 19.15 Modifying the settings before you save the file

5. Click OK.

6. Call the file **NER-CENTRAL.rvt**.

7. Click Save.

8. On the Collaborate tab, choose Synchronize With Central ➤ Synchronize Now, as shown in Figure 19.16. Doing so saves any changes made.

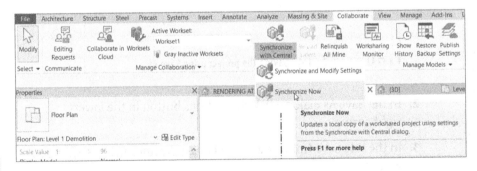

FIGURE 19.16 Choosing Synchronize Now

On the Quick Access toolbar, the Synchronize button is also available. Because this is the central model, the Save icon is inactive.

9. On the Worksets panel in the Collaborate tab, click the Worksets button.

10. Change both worksets by choosing No in the Editable column (see Figure 19.17).

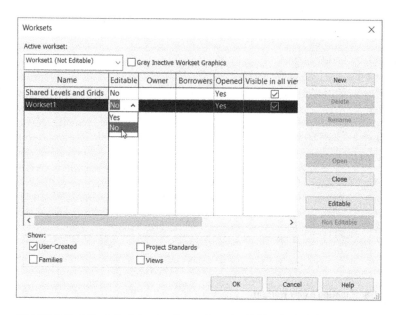

FIGURE 19.17 Releasing the worksets by clicking No for Editable

11. Click OK. (Don't worry—I'll explain what all this means in a moment.)

12. Click the Synchronize Now button.

You made these worksets not editable because, when you're working in the central file, you always want to leave it without editable worksets. That way, users don't have access to these worksets in their local models.

The next task you need to tackle in the creation of a central model is how to make a new workset and move some components onto it. In this procedure, you'll create a Site workset and move the topography and the site components to it. Follow these steps:

1. Click the Worksets button on the Collaborate tab.

2. In the Worksets dialog, click the New button, as shown in Figure 19.18.

3. In the New Workset dialog, call this workset **Structure**, and then click OK.

4. Make sure Structure has Yes in the Editable row.

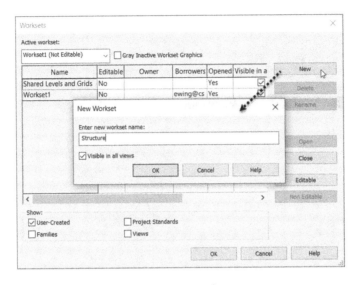

FIGURE 19.18 Creating a new workset

5. Click OK.

6. Click No to make Structure the active workset.

7. Go to the default 3D view.

8. Select the structural framing on the north side as shown in Figure 19.19.

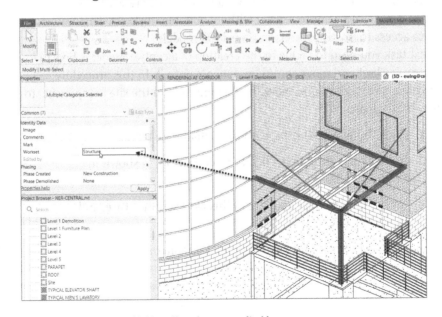

FIGURE 19.19 Making all worksets not editable

9. In the Properties dialog, find the Identity Data category, locate the Workset row, and change the workset to Structure.

10. On the Collaborate tab, click the Synchronize Now button.

11. On the Collaborate tab, click the Worksets button.

12. Make all worksets not editable (see Figure 19.20), and then click OK.

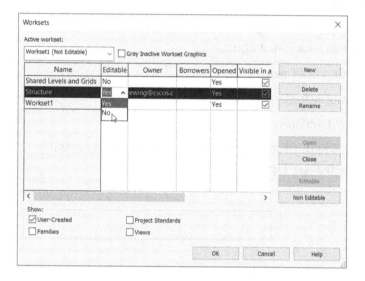

FIGURE 19.20 Making all worksets not editable

13. Click the Synchronize Now button.

N O T E   You make sure all the worksets aren't editable because, in the central model, everything needs to be turned off. Look at the central model as a *hub* that serves as a conduit for passing data as your team collaborates on the project.

Next you'll create your local model. Luckily, you've done all the difficult work. Setting up the central file is the hardest part of the worksharing process, and it's usually done by the BIM manager or at least the BIM lead on the project. The act of creating a local file is as simple as issuing a Save As.

Creating a Local File

With the central model in place, you're ready for the rest of your team to have at it. Although I keep mentioning how easy most of this stuff is, there is one danger to look out for. Please, never open the central model and stay in it, if you don't want to be thrashed by your co-workers. When you're in the process of creating a local model, you select the central model and choose the Create New Local option. If you don't make sure this check box is selected, guess what? You're sitting in the central model. If this occurs, nobody has access to synchronize with the central model. Shame on you.

This section of the chapter will guide you through the process of creating a local model. Follow along:

1. Without completely closing Revit, close out of the central model. You'll never go back into it again.

2. Under Models, click Open.

3. Browse to your NER_CENTRAL file.

4. Select it, but don't open it yet.

5. At the bottom of the dialog is a Create New Local check box. Make sure it's selected (see Figure 19.21).

6. Click Open.

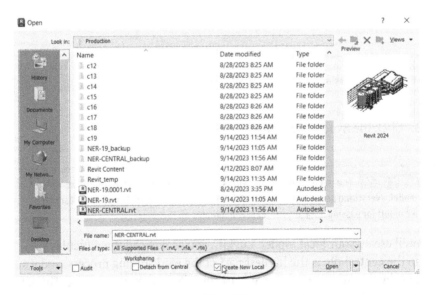

FIGURE 19.21   Creating a new local model

Congratulations! You're the proud owner of a new Revit file that knows your name and everything.

Yes, it knows your name. You see, when you create the local model, it's yours to keep. This file resides in your personal documents folder on your C:\ drive, with your username. Not only does your local model keep a live link back to the central model, but it also knows to whom it belongs. Revit does this for a good reason: this file represents you within the team.

Loading or Not Loading a Workset during Open

I'm making a big deal out of a simple task only because it can speed up your performance—nothing can bog down a Revit model more than a huge site complete with landscaping and maybe an image.

Switching the Opened status to No in a workset forces Revit to not load the workset into your model. If you make an edit that has an influence on the site, don't worry: Revit will take care of that in the central model.

To not load the Structure workset, follow this procedure:

1. If your model is still open, sync and close.

2. Browse to the NER-CENTRAL model and select it.

3. Next to the Open button is a down arrow. Select it and select Specify as shown in Figure 19.22.

4. Click Open.

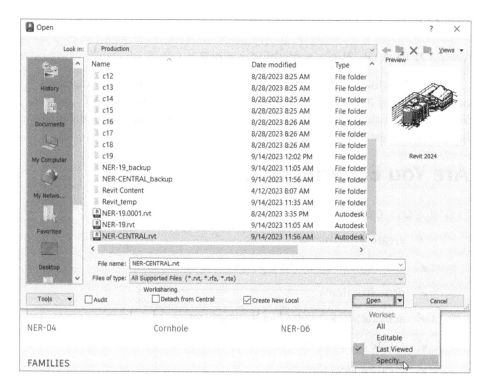

FIGURE 19.22 Specifying only the worksets you want to open

5. Overwrite the existing version.

6. Select Structure and click the Close button as shown in Figure 19.23.

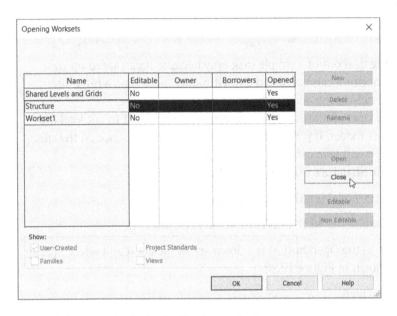

FIGURE 19.23 Closing the Structure workset

7. Click OK. Notice something missing?

Having the ability to turn off large portions of a model can be a tremendous advantage as you move forward in Revit. You need to exercise caution, however. You could easily deceive yourself into thinking that some portions of the model haven't been created yet.

Are You Experienced?

Now you can. . .

✓   create a new phase

✓   add items to an existing phase

✓   demolish items

✓   activate worksharing in a Revit project

✓   create a central file

✓   create a local file

✓   manipulate worksets

INDEX

G

ONLINE TEST BANK

Although this book is not an exam prep Study Guide, we've added a new online practice test for you if you are interested in preparing for the valuable Autodesk Certified Professional in Revit for Architectural Design certification exam. This practice test will be available by January 3, 2024. After that date, register to gain one year of FREE access after activation to the online interactive practice exam—included with your purchase of this book!

Register and Access the Online Test Bank

To register your book and get access to the online test bank, follow these steps:

1. Go to www.wiley.com/go/sybextestprep. You'll see the "How to Register Your Book for Online Access" instructions.

2. Click "here to register" and then select your book from the list.

3. Complete the required registration information, including answering the security verification to prove book ownership. You will be emailed a pin code.

4. Follow the directions in the email or go to www.wiley.com/go/sybextestprep.

5. Find your book on that page and click the "Register or Login" link with it. Then enter the pin code you received and click the "Activate PIN" button.

6. On the Create an Account or Login page, enter your username and password, and click Login or, if you don't have an account already, create a new account.

7. At this point, you should be in the test bank site with your new test bank listed at the top of the page. If you do not see it there, please refresh the page or log out and log back in.